# THE ROUTLEDGE HANDBOOK OF SUSTAINABLE FOOD AND GASTRONOMY

T0330647

The issues surrounding the provision, preparation and development of food products are fundamental to every human being on the planet. Given the scarcity of agricultural land, environmental pollution, climate change and the exponential growth of the world's population where starvation and obesity are both widespread, it is little wonder that exploring the frontiers of food is now a major focus for researchers and practitioners.

This timely Handbook provides a systematic guide to the current state of knowledge on sustainable food. The volume begins by examining the anthropology of food and then discusses various local food initiatives in the form of case studies, examines sustainable food trends and movements and explores current and future food science innovations. It continues with a section on social entrepreneurship in food and gastronomy with a thorough discussion on the concept of sustainable restaurant systems. Finally, it concludes by exploring the ties between food and tourism, discussing the linkages between food security and a sustainable food system. Developed from specifically commissioned original contributions, the *Handbook's* inherent multidisciplinary approach paves the way for deeper understanding of all aspects linked to the evolution of food in society, including insights into local food, food and tourism, organic food, indigenous and traditional food, sustainable restaurant practices, consumption patterns and sourcing.

This book is essential reading for students, researchers and academics interested in the possibilities of sustainable forms of gastronomy and gastronomy's contribution to sustainable development.

The title includes a foreword written by Roberto Flore, head chef at the Nordic Food Lab, Copenhagen, Denmark.

**Philip Sloan** is one of the founding members of the Department of Hospitality Management at the IUBH in Bonn, Germany. He holds a Master's degree in Environmental Management, an MBA and has a long list of peer-reviewed scientific journal articles covering various aspects of sustainability in hospitality to his credit. Philip teaches culinary arts in addition to lecturing on a variety of hospitality subjects.

**Willy Legrand** is a professor at the IUBH School of Business and Management located in Bonn, Germany. Willy holds a Master of Business Administration degree with a specialisation in Corporate Environmental Management and has completed his PhD in Hospitality Management and Marketing. With co-authors Philip Sloan and Joseph S. Chen, Willy published a leading university textbook on sustainable matters in hospitality (*Sustainability in the Hospitality Industry: Principles of Sustainable Operations*, Elsevier).

**Clare Hindley** is a professor in the Language and Communication Department at IUBH School of Business and Management, Bonn, Germany. She gained her PhD in the field of sociolinguistics, focusing on language and social networks. She also holds a BA in English and Classical Civilization and an MA in Applied Linguistics. Her research interests include the world of hospitality and tourism with particular focus on education, culture and sociology.

'*The Routledge Handbook of Sustainable Food and Gastronomy* is an extremely comprehensive and informative overview of a full range of food issues, beautifully updated with the last critical developments in the field. Anyone who wants to start food related projects or research effort could find inspiration here. Global food crisis, the importance of grassroot food movements and the emerging insect gastronomy, just to give a taste.'

*Anne-Mette Hjalager, Professor, Head of Centre, Danish Centre for Rural Research,*
*University of Southern Denmark*

# THE ROUTLEDGE HANDBOOK OF SUSTAINABLE FOOD AND GASTRONOMY

*Edited by Philip Sloan, Willy Legrand and Clare Hindley*

*Preface by Roberto Flore, Nordic Food Lab*

LONDON AND NEW YORK

First published 2015
by Routledge
2 Park Square, Milton Park, Abingdon, Oxon OX14 4RN

and by Routledge
52 Vanderbilt Avenue, New York, NY 10017

First issued in paperback 2020

*Routledge is an imprint of the Taylor & Francis Group, an informa business*

*British Library Cataloguing in Publication Data*
A catalogue record for this book is available from the British Library

*Library of Congress Cataloging in Publication Data*
   The Routledge handbook of sustainable food and gastronomy / edited by Philip Sloan,
   Willy Legrand and Clare Hindley.
      Includes bibliographical references and index.
   1. Food supply—Environmental aspects.   2. Food industry and trade—Environmental aspects.
   3. Gastronomy.   I. Sloan, Philip.   II. Legrand, Willy.   III. Hindley, Clare.
   HD9000.5.R68 2015
   338.1'90286—dc23
                                                                        2014042676

ISBN 13: 978–0–367–66011–6 (pbk)
ISBN 13: 978–0–415–70255–3 (hbk)

Typeset in Bembo
by RefineCatch Limited, Bungay, Suffolk, UK

# CONTENTS

# FOREWORD

Andiamo a mangiare aqualcosa
Let's go eat something!

We say this phrase all the time, but often without considering what we really mean. That indefinite 'something' reveals a lot about our current relationship with food. The overabundance of food choices growing through industrialization and globalization makes us think our needs are met. But actually, this thoughtless feeding has alienated us from what, for most of human history, has been an object of sacredness and deep respect. Food has lost its value, and we are forgetting ours.

How many times in our lives have food or drink been a key part of a gathering, and how many times have they contributed to making it special? How many times in our lives have we booked a table in a restaurant, not only out of a need to quench our thirst and sate our hunger? In these ways, our daily choices develop into a larger system of values, a universe of hospitality, which informs how we nourish ourselves and each other and the earth that sustains us.

The concept of global sustainability started to be developed in the 1970s, largely in response to the overconsumption of natural resources. It took another 20 years, however, for a broader vision of sustainable development to arise in many other areas of society, including those surrounding food. The pioneers of this movement inspired new ways of thinking, introducing progressive ideas such as food sovereignty and the right to healthy food to the public agenda.

The fervour fuelled by these movements, and further taken up by the scientific community and the media, has helped to spread awareness of many vital issues related to our food systems. These affect everyone – building robust local economies, revalorizing the landscape and improving animal welfare, among other things. All of these topics are interconnected, and are unavoidable when we speak of food and sustainability in the world today.

Yet there are examples of solutions to these complex problems all around us. When we look to communities where food and gastronomy and hospitality have value, it becomes clear how food functions as a social glue, holding these communities together and maintaining the delicate balance of ecology, history, economy and culture that is the foundation of true sustainability. Engaging with these diverse communities and their particular qualities and needs is thus of great importance if we want to be able to investigate food in any meaningful way.

As a chef, I notice how the exploration of these interconnections from different perspectives has been changing how many of us interact with the wider food world. More and more of us are directing our focus to our immediate local surroundings, drawing inspiration from our specific place and time. We are discovering and rediscovering our unique and diverse histories, shaping our own gastronomic identities through cooking in the context of our larger environments.

Nevertheless, despite this growing environmental awareness in cooking, the persistence of many other problems such as job insecurity, insufficient salaries, extreme commodification, food waste and the devaluation of living an agricultural life are signs that our current approach to sustainability is fundamentally incomplete. One of the most powerful aspects of this manual is that it makes us confront the paradox of 'unsustainable sustainability', a narrow model that only takes environmental factors into account. This handbook stimulates us to re-envision the role of food and gastronomy in creating a more holistic model of truly sustainable development for humanity and the planet. It offers examples of best practices for how to engage with such diverse realities, and creates part of the necessary foundation for more sustainable gastronomy. The wide-angle approach adopted by the authors and editors provides us with a broad perspective of the different actors involved and these many intricate connections between people, food, and the environment. In short, it is an essential working tool for those who wish to acquire a deeper knowledge of this complex subject.

I am proud to recommend this book in the hope of helping to grow the emerging global gastronomic revolution. This revolution must be supported by knowledgeable people who work in synergy across many different areas of food and its systems, developing new standards and strategies towards a world where the only hunger that persists is that for knowledge.

*Roberto Flore*
*Head Chef at the Nordic Food Lab*
*Copenhagen, Denmark*

# EDITORS' BIOGRAPHY

**Philip Sloan**

Philip Sloan is one of the founding members of the lecturing team that started the Department of Hospitality Management at the IUBH in Bonn, Germany, in September 2000. Philip's earlier career was in the management of London hotels before creating his own small chain of organic restaurants in England and then in Strasbourg, France, where he is now based. He holds a Master's degree in Environmental Management, an MBA and has a long list of peer-reviewed scientific journal articles to his credit. In addition to teaching Sustainable Hospitality Management Studies, he is a passionate environmental entrepreneur and is currently working on various sustainable food projects in addition to running a small organic vineyard with co-writer Willy Legrand on the university campus.

p.sloan@iubh.de

**Willy Legrand**

Willy Legrand is a professor at the IUBH School of Business and Management located in Bonn, Germany. After completing his undergraduate degree in Geography followed by a diploma in Hospitality Management in Canada, Willy held numerous managerial positions in the hospitality industry in Canada and Germany, before accepting a position at the IUBH School of Business and Management in Bonn. Willy holds a Master of Business Administration degree with a specialization in Corporate Environmental Management and has completed his PhD in Hospitality Management and Marketing. In Bonn, he teaches a variety of courses within the Hospitality curriculum, including his specialization in sustainability and environmental management in hospitality as well as facilities management in hospitality. With co-authors Philip Sloan and Joseph S. Chen, Willy published a leading university textbook on sustainable matters in hospitality (*Sustainability in the Hospitality Industry: Principles of Sustainable Operations*, Elsevier). Willy's personal background includes formative years spent working in agriculture in Canada and a family involved in organic cultivation and production in France. As a wine enthusiast and founder of the university's wine club, Willy, together with co-editor Philip Sloan, created an organic vineyard, which functions as an educational tool for Hospitality Management students.

w.legrand@iubh.de

## Clare Hindley

Clare Hindley is a professor in the Language and Communication Department at IUBH School of Business and Management, Bonn. She gained her PhD in the field of Sociolinguistics, focusing on language and social networks. She also holds a BA in English and Classical Civilization and an MA in Applied Linguistics. Her career began by teaching English followed by specialization in the fields of teacher training and business communication. She was the academic manager of a large educational institute in London before moving to Germany. Her career includes international experience in Europe and South America. Prior to working at IUBH, Clare worked as a language consultant in several international companies in the Bonn–Cologne area, as a freelance teacher trainer and as a tutor for Birmingham University distance Master's programme. At IUBH she predominantly lectures in Research Methods and Business Communication. Her career has been diverse in location and focus, but language, culture and communication have remained the guiding lights. Her research interests include the world of hospitality and tourism with particular focus on education, culture and sociology.

c.hindley@iubh.de.

# INTRODUCTION

Throughout the history of human development, food has always had special significance. Those societies and people who did not eat well tended not to prosper and disappeared early in their development. Good food is a critical factor in physical well-being, a major source of pleasure but also worry and stress, a major concern for governments and the single greatest category of expenditures. Hunger, from time immemorial, has always been the source of mankind's energies for the doing of good and bad, the reason for its advance, the origin of its conflicts and the fuel of its labours. The practice of hunting and gathering, the discovery of farming cereals, the science of stock breeding, the consumption of salt, sugar, spices and potatoes from far-off places, have all in turn shaken the known world to its foundations. Civilizations have been built on food, empires have done battle for it, crimes have been committed, laws have been made and knowledge has been exchanged. Now, because of severe heat waves, deplenishing water tables, crops such as maize and sugar beet being diverted from human consumption to produce fuel plus a growing and in places more carnivorous population, food is once again at the top of the political agenda and source of conflict.

Directly and indirectly the food we eat has serious environmental impacts and produces greenhouse gas emissions. The Brazilian savannah is being destroyed faster than the Amazon rainforest because of the soya produced to feed the animals we eat. In Borneo, ancient tropical forests are being felled to provide palm oil for our confectionery and low-fat spreads. Daily reports of rising food prices, not to mention civil unrest arising from food insecurity, have the net result that what we eat matters more than ever before. In the West, a doubling of grain prices means a few extra coppers on the price of a loaf of bread; for a peasant family in Somalia, this increase can mean surviving on a couple of bowls of rice each day or not. Taking personal responsibility for our eating habits and understanding as much as possible about the food we eat is a matter of urgency. The demand for nutritious food, without causing additional resource depletion and damage on our planet, is increasing. Population growth in less developed countries often coincides with more poorly nourished people.

The present food production, supply and consumption system does not generally fit present and future human needs. It is unable to feed everybody correctly and relies on high fossil energy use, chemicals and energy inputs, long-distance transport, low-cost human work and cultural loss. Fortunately researchers are producing innovative strategies that measure and promote sustainable food systems, as well as fully understanding the role of agricultural biodiversity in human health and nutrition. The understanding of sustainable food systems is as relevant to the challenges of under-nutrition as it is to dietary transition and nutrition-related chronic diseases linked closely to overweight and obesity. With a greater emphasis on food systems that embrace the sustainability concept, it is possible that nutritional and livelihood benefits for small farmers, food manufacturers and consumers across the globe will be made.

Since all of us have had an intimate familiarity with food, usually on a daily basis, throughout life, it is perhaps why it makes all of us feel qualified to evaluate and discuss issues that surround it. There are few topics that elicit more emotional responses and on which people have stronger opinions than food. In the West, we are all interested in food and health-related issues and nearly everyone admits having given at least some thought to the healthy balance of their diet, physical activity and the safety of food. Media reports constantly highlight concern over the 'obesity epidemic' and the seemingly contradictory news stories that promote and condemn various nutrients. Food fads come and go, the Western consumer is in a constant quest for the most exotic, tastiest, most beneficial, cheapest and trendiest new product. Counting calories is the currency of purchasing decisions, dietary components (such as whole grains, fibre, sugars, salt and fat) is the language of over-the-counter exchange; weight management, stress reduction and unclogged arteries is the nutritional aim.

It took exploration and colonization – that resulted latterly in pollution and resource depletion – of half of the planet by the other half to create a kind of nutritional standardization to be gradually imposed. In general, the evolution of food has been in the direction of Western customs (white bread made from imported wheat has replaced local starchy food crops in many emerging economies). Dietary adaptations tend to be imposed in the same way as TV soaps and automobiles. Again, the call for reconnecting with traditions, local foodstuffs and real needs can be heard. For our ancestors and indeed for more than a billion people around the world today obtaining sufficient food, and often drinking water, to maintain life was and is a constant battle. For the first time in history, malnutrition and overeating are evident in the same countries and even the same families. The telling of the story of the Western diet has tones of gluttony which the Oxford English Dictionary defines as 'habitual greed or excess in eating'. Gluttony is a mutation: an aberration of a need that ends up by taking over from our desire to simply satiate our appetites. Could it not be that the Western consumer needs to reconnect with their bodies to discover its real needs? Surely, a more reasonable attitude to the food we consume and the food waste we produce would in effect result in a slightly larger bowl of rice for the world's starving?

Despite our obsession with food, Western households appear to be losing the cooking skills their grandmothers held dear. In an age of specialization, preparing food is perceived as time-consuming and requiring years of training. One wonders if the widely heard mantra, 'I just don't have the time to cook', is true. Common culinary wisdom seems to have been relegated to the top drawer of history; those green beans and big red strawberries on the supermarket shelves in February look so normal, it is just so much easier to pop over the road and fetch yet another juicy, fat drenched hamburger. Is preparing a plate of curly kale with grilled sardines and garlic butter that difficult? Would replacing the amount of chicken we put in our curries with tofu or chick peas destroy the taste? The answer is of course no, and being more food independent is good for the planet, the body and the soul. Not only are we wasteful and throw away much of the food we purchase but we have stopped understanding ingredients and now rely on far less variety throughout the year. We are dependent on imports and a lack of understanding of how to cook the very ingredients that would help reduce the negative impacts on our planet.

The history and development of food relates to the human sciences (ethnology, sociology, history, medicine), to environmental analysis (geography, climatology, botany, agronomics) and to the economy. In this book, historians and sociologists show how local culinary traditions appeal to gastronomy tourists and people discovering new identities. Ethnologists examine how eating habits have developed and nutritionists show how diet can affect body and mind. Geographers map the underlying influences on what societies grow and consume, botanists lead us through the world of little-known edible plant species and agronomists explain new ways to grow crops.

Food and drink are, of course, the building blocks of gastronomy, which also has elements of philosophy and art: 'the art and science of delicate eating' as first coined by the French poet Joseph Berchoux in 1801. Historically and etymologically, gastronomy relates to advice and guidance on what to eat and drink where, when, in what manner, in which combinations. Gastronomy can, in some circles, become a kind of religion for many with its own places of worship, its pontiffs such as Escoffier and Brillat-Savarin and its sacred scriptures in the form of multiple cookery blogs and cookery shelves in bookshops. In English-speaking culture the connections between the cordon bleu, Escoffier, gastronomy-cuisine and Frenchness are invariably made. Connections of taste with elitism are as true today as in the early nineteenth century. At this time the restaurant became a setting for the generation of new cultural forms and political engagement. As in the past, restaurateurs and chefs have the power to change opinions and have highly influential roles to play in shaping the gastronomic desires of society to a more sustainable future.

In this book, educators explore the progress restaurants have made in shifting the public desire to more healthy and equitable forms of gastronomy. Food commentators explain how vegetarian and vegan movements echo the culinary habits of our ancestors and how the Slow Food movement can best be described as a return to local food traditions using local ingredients.

Lastly, food scientists and restaurateurs bring to our plates heirloom vegetables and insect gastronomy, and report on progress in the development of new vegetable proteins. The era of a more sustainable gastronomy is upon us.

The editors, October 2014

# ACKNOWLEDGEMENTS

We firstly thank all who contributed to this book with articles, case studies and results from academic research.

We are particularly grateful to those who have continuously shown support in assisting the book project. Thank you especially to:

- Katharina Scharrer for your extraordinary organization skills, professionalism, support and patience;
- Vanessa Menezes for your attention to details and numerous hours proofreading.

We also gratefully acknowledge the help of Yuri Kork and Magda Sylwestrowicz.

We are also thankful to our affiliation, the IUBH School of Business and Management, Bonn, and the many colleagues here and at other universities who share our passion for this industry.

Finally, we are grateful to our families and friends for their support, patience and encouragement.

# CONTRIBUTORS

**Charles Barneby** holds a BS in Hotel and Restaurant Management from the University of New Haven, where he is currently pursuing an MSc in Community Psychology.

**Sean Beer** is an academic with a passionate interest in the interaction between tourism, culture, food, the countryside and the food supply chain. Originally he trained as an agricultural scientist, gaining a BSc in Agriculture from Reading, a DipAgSci from Massey University in New Zealand and a CertEd from Wolverhampton. This academic work has been backed up with considerable practical experience in agriculture, marketing, the food supply chain and the rural economy in general, gained on the family farm and within associated family businesses and the food industry, both local and international. He is currently a senior lecturer in the School of Services Management at Bournemouth University. He has been awarded a Rotary Foundation Scholarship, a Winston Churchill Fellowship and he is a Nuffield Scholar.

**Sonja Beier** graduated from the International University of Applied Sciences, Bonn, with a degree in Hospitality Management. She now lives in Cologne, Germany and is a consultant with Oscar GmbH, Cologne. Sonja.Beier@iubh.de

**Tracy Berno** did her PhD fieldwork in the Cook Islands more than 20 years ago. This was the start of an enduring relationship with the Pacific that has seen her living and working in the Pacific region since, including being head of the Tourism and Hospitality Department at the University of the South Pacific (USP) for many years. As a tourism academic and consultant, Tracy's main area of interest has been the relationship between local agricultural production and the tourism and hospitality industry. With a catering and cooking background, Tracy has always had a strong interest in sustainable cuisine. This grew into a research programme focusing on how the produce and cuisines of the South Pacific could be highlighted as part of tourism, and how these linkages could support integrated rural development and sustainable livelihoods. Tracy has researched and published in this area, as well as contributed to cookery books in New Zealand and the Pacific. Tracy is an associate professor at Lincoln University in New Zealand.

**Thomas Berron** was born in Germany in 1986. He was diagnosed with wheat intolerance in 2001 and completed a farming apprenticeship with one of the most prestigious organic farms in Germany, the Herrmannsdorfer Landwerkstätten (www.herrmannsdorfer.de). 'Tommi' went on to study Retail and Wholesale Management at the European University of Applied Sciences EUFH. This cooperative programme was completed in collaboration with EDEKA (www.edeka.de), Germany's largest food retailer. This hands-on education included an apprenticeship as a merchant in wholesale and foreign trade. With one university and two apprenticeship degrees as well as a total of five years in the food industry, Tommi felt he had a basic understanding of how food went from farm to fork. Fascinated by the community-supported agriculture (CSA) concept, Tommi made his way to Fingal, Australia, to contribute to setting up a CSA on a family farm called Transition Farm (www.transitionfarm.com) for three months, gaining first-hand experience in launching a CSA venture. In June 2012, Tommi returned to Germany where he joined the Kartoffelkombinat and the Sigi Klein Farm where he has been working ever since. Tommi@kartoffelkombinat.de

**Stéphanie Bonsch Buri** holds an MSc in Entrepreneurship and is a scientific collaborator at Ecole hôtelière de Lausanne (EHL). A member of the Food and Beverage Industry Chair, she specializes in quantitative analysis and innovation in the F&B industry. Additionally, Stéphanie is in charge of marketing research for the F&B Chair. Before joining the Chair, she worked in Madagascar in purchasing and operational functions for restaurants.

**Jeffery Bray** is the Waitrose Fellow of Retailing and Senior Lecturer in Retail Consumer Behaviour at Bournemouth University. His recent research has focused on the role of ethical attributes in consumers' purchase decision-making and has involved a large survey of UK consumer attitudes in this regard. Prior to work in academia, Jeffery held a number of management positions within the retail sector and continues to maintain strong links with the industry. Currently his post is supported by Waitrose, where he contributes to the company's innovation team.

**Alice Brombin** is a PhD candidate in Social Sciences at the University of Padua Department of Sociology, Philosophy, Education and Applied Psychology. Currently she is working on research on Italian ecovillages and ecological lifestyles, focusing on food self-sufficiency and the symbolic meanings linked to food practices. She is part of the research study group Food Culture and Society at the University of Padua. She is a visiting scholar at UCSC Anthropologic Department, Santa Cruz, California, and holds a Bachelor degree in History, Faculty of Philosophy and Letters from the University of Padua and a Master's degree in Cultural Anthropology, Ethnology and Ethnolinguistics from the Faculty of Philosophy and Letters, University Ca' Foscari of Venice. alice.brombin@gmail.com

**Amy Burns** gained her doctorate in the School of Biomedical Sciences at Ulster and now is a lecturer in Consumer Studies at the Ulster Business School. She has published in a variety of prestigious peer-reviewed scientific journals, and she published a monograph entitled *Controlling Appetite* in 2009. Amy has considerable experience of working with private companies in Northern Ireland, making use of Invest NI Innovation Vouchers to conduct research that has enabled these companies to make improvements in production, promotion, market estimation and sales. Her particular areas of expertise include nutritional evaluation, new food product development and the sensory evaluation of food and drink products.

**Clare Carruthers** is a lecturer in tourism and marketing in the Department of Hospitality and Tourism Management, University of Ulster. Clare attained her Master's degree in Tourism from the University of Strathclyde in 1998 and has worked in the higher education sector since then, teaching and researching in the areas of tourism and marketing. Clare teaches across a range of modules and levels at both undergraduate and postgraduate level in the areas of festivals and cultural tourism, cultural policy, services marketing and tourism environments. Clare's doctoral thesis compared the development of cultural tourism in four UK cities and developed a comprehensive model of post-industrial urban cultural tourism development in the UK. Her current research interests include tourism destination marketing, sustainable tourism, social enterprises in tourism and the relationship between tourism and gastronomy. She also undertakes research and has published in the area of culture-led regeneration of post-industrial cities, the role of the European City of Culture in urban tourism and urban tourism destination marketing. In addition Clare is engaged with academic enterprise and consultancy work with external agencies involved in tourism development and marketing in Northern Ireland and the Republic of Ireland.

**Elena Cavagnaro** was born in 1963 in Rome (Italy). She holds a Master's degree from the University of Rome 'La Sapienza' and a PhD from the Vrije Universiteit in Amsterdam. In 1997 she joined Stenden University of Applied Sciences (the Netherlands) as lecturer in Business Ethics. In 2004 she became Stenden professor in Service Studies. In this role, she has consulted several organizations in sectors such as hospitality, retail and health care on sustainability strategy and implementation. She is visiting professor at the University of Derby (UK). She has published extensively on sustainability in the service industry. Following her understanding of sustainability as a multidimensional and multilayered concept, her research focuses on issues that run across and connect the social, organizational and individual layer of sustainability. In 2012, Greenleaf published her major work on sustainability, co-authored with George Curiel, under the title *The Three Levels of Sustainability*.

**Chan Weng San** graduated from the Institute for Tourism Studies, Macao, majoring in Tourism Business Management.

**Gaurav Chawla** is currently working as programme leader for BA (Hons) programmes at the Swiss Hotel Management School, Leysin. His hospitality journey started with undergraduate studies at the Institute of Hotel Management, Mumbai. Thereafter, he worked for the Taj group of hotels in Mumbai before moving to Scotland to pursue his Master's in Hospitality Management from Edinburgh Napier University. His research areas include sustainability, CSR and lifelong learning in higher education.

**Christina Ciambriello** is interested in the processes by which plants and animals become foods for human consumption. A primary focus of her work concentrating on food systems, is to build awareness in her local urban environment of how food is grown and produced through physical manifestations – gardens, composting sites, apiaries, etc. – demonstrating these practices. She is a graduate of the Food Studies MA programme at New York University and is a certified master composter for the City of New York.

**Paul Cleave**, a freelance researcher and lecturer, has a background in tourism and hospitality, and has been writing on food and tourism for more than 20 years. His long-term interest in the social history of food, tourism and leisure has resulted in contributions to educational projects with the National Trust and the use of oral histories in community support groups. This dates from the 1992 World Wildlife Summit Conference in Rio, and Paul's contribution to *Beyond the Green Horizon* (1992). Recent publications include chapters in four textbooks. At present, his research at the University of Exeter mainly focuses on the social history of twentieth-century tourism in the United Kingdom, the evolving relationships between food and tourism, and narratives of tourism.

**Sandra J. Cooper** is a senior lecturer in Culinary Arts and International Hospitality Management at the University of Derby. She is also the faculty learning and teaching advisor. Having completed her professional training at Westminster College Hotel School in London, she has held numerous management positions in the school meal services and contract catering operations, working latterly as area manager and trainer for Sutcliffe Catering and Granada gaining more than 15 years of valuable industry experience in the south of England. Sandra moved from the New Forest to the Peak District to join the University of Derby to coordinate a work-based learning programme supporting collaborative partners delivering FdA in Spa. Alongside her current teaching on a variety of modules in Culinary Arts and International Hospitality Management, she also module leads on nutrition and spa cuisine on the Spa degree programmes. Sandra has a BA in Work-based Learning in Higher Education, an MA in Education, is a senior fellow of the HEA and a member of the Institute of Hospitality.

**Clémence Cornuz** holds an MA in English literature and is a scientific collaborator at Ecole hôtelière de Lausanne (EHL). A member of the Food and Beverage Industry Chair, she is in charge of academic communication and edits the Chair's publications. Clémence also contributes significantly to the literature research for each of the F&B Chair projects.

**Christine Demen Meier**, PhD, is associate professor of Entrepreneurship and Marketing at Ecole hôtelière de Lausanne (EHL). She is also head of the Innovation and Entrepreneurship Department and, since September 2010, holder of the Food and Beverage Industry Chair. Before joining EHL, in 1999, Christine managed and owned several businesses in the hospitality industry. She is currently chair of the Bon Rivage Hotel board of directors (Vaud, Switzerland).

**Justine de Valicourt** received a BSc in biomedical sciences with a minor in nutrition from Université de Montréal in 2007 and carried on with training in the high-culinary arts from the prestigious Institut de Tourisme et d'Hôtellerie du Québec. She finished top of her promotion and first of the national San Pelligrino Almost Famous Chef Competition. In 2010, she received the prestigious Ferran Adria International Fellowship to discover the Catalan culinary traditions and to work with the world leaders of avant-garde gastronomy at El Celler de Can Roca and El Bulli. In 2011–2012, she explored farm-to-table gastronomical options thanks to a Relais et Châteaux Fellowship that brought her to Falsled Kro, Denmark; De Librije, the Netherlands; and Michel and Sébastien Bras, France, at the end of which she spent a couple of months at Alicia Foundation, Spain, a gastronomy and science research institute, to perfect her molecular gastronomy demonstration skills. In 2013, she taught a course at Duke University, USA, about the physics and chemistry of cooking. From May 2013 to April 2014, she worked as a researcher in the Nordic Food Lab in Copenhagen.

**Carolyn Dimitri** is an applied economist with expertise in food systems. An associate professor in the Department of Nutrition, Food Studies and Public Health at New York

University, her current research focuses on urban agriculture, food access in urban areas and the political economies of the National Organic Standard. Prior to joining the NYU faculty, she spent 12 years as an economist with USDA's Economic Research Service, where she gained national recognition for her work on marketing organic food products. She has led numerous large research projects on different aspects of the food system. These projects include a national study of urban farming; an analysis of the manufacture and distribution of organic food products; an assessment of retailing organic food products; and the use of local food in Maryland Schools. She earned her doctorate at the University of Maryland, College Park.

**Gary Elliott** is a lecturer in Wines and Spirits within the Department of Hospitality and Tourism Management, University of Ulster. Gary teaches across a range of modules and levels at both undergraduate and postgraduate level in the area of food and beverage with a keen interest in food/wine tourism and, naturally, wine and spirit studies. Gary delivers a range of WSET (Wine and Spirit Educational Trust) courses both in-house and for the wider licensed trade in Northern Ireland. Gary has contributed many wine articles to the various trade magazines in Northern Ireland. His current research interests include wine tourism, food tourism and wine consumerism.

**Mehmet Ergul**, PhD, is associate professor at San Francisco State University. He earned his PhD from Texas Tech University and has international food and beverage experience in his native Turkey and the USA. His research interests include consumer behaviour, new food product development and entrepreneurship. Mehmet has also completed the USDC-NMFS HACCP Seafood Inspection Certificate programme.

**Josh Evans** is a lead researcher and project manager researcher with the Nordic Food Lab in Copenhagen, Denmark. He took his Bachelor's degree at Yale University where he studied Literature, Philosophy and Food Systems, and worked with the Yale Sustainable Food Project. While writing his Bachelor's thesis on the co-evolutionary issues of European legislation for Protected Designations of Origins of food products, he became interested in microbiota as key mediators between food, people and the environment. At the Lab, he is currently working on insects, Pu-erh style teas and koji and is involved in writing projects. He plans to work with the Lab a while longer, then return to graduate school to pursue his interest in food ethnomicrobiology and history and philosophy of science. He also keeps a blog around food, learning and travel at hearthstrung.wordpress.com.

**Sonia Ferrari** has been associate professor of Tourism Marketing and Place Marketing at the University of Calabria, Italy, since 2005. She has been a researcher in the same university since 1993. She has also taught Management, Service Management, Event Marketing, Marketing of Museums and Tourism Management at the University of Calabria. At the same university she has been president of the Tourism Science Degree Course and president of the Valorizzazione dei Sistemi Turistico Culturali Degree Course since 2007. Her main fields of study and research are: quality in services (also in tourism), tourism marketing, place marketing, event marketing and wellness.

**Roberto Flore** encountered the world of cooking as a child when he was enlisted to help his grandmother in the kitchen. These moments – etched into his memory – have shaped his culinary style and holistic food vision. In a quest to understand the origins of food he obtained his diploma in Management of Marine Parks, Forests and Nature Reserves. After a variety of culinary experiences, he worked at the Four Seasons Milan as a chef de partie. Roberto continued to travel, gaining a wealth of experience. Then, in 2009 he returned to Sardinia to work as a chef. During this period he worked closely with well-known Sardinian producers in order to offer a wide array of local products. In 2013 he gained recognition for his regional cuisine. He also represented Sardinia five times on Italian national television on *La Prova del Cuoco* and competed in the final in May 2014. In 2013 he also completed a stage at Metamorfosi, a one-star Michelin restaurant in Rome. Roberto has collaborated with other international chefs and has exported his signature cuisine around the world. The most predominant feature of Roberto's cuisine is his use of wild herbs, which he collects himself. Now, aged 31 he is the new head chef of the Nordic Food Lab in Copenhagen, Denmark.

**Alissa Folendorf** is an undergraduate student at San Francisco State University, where she is majoring in Anthropology. After her undergraduate study she will continue her education in a Master's programme in the field of Food Studies. Her research interests include nutritional anthropology and the influence of food culture in social, economic, cultural and psychological aspects. In her free time she volunteers in the edible classrooms of public schools and tends to her garden.

**Corazon F. Gatchalian** is a professor of Hospitality Management and former chair of the Department of Hotel, Restaurant and Institution Management, University of the Philippines (UP), where she currently serves as professorial lecturer. She was founding director of UP's Office of Extension Coordination and, for six years, participated in conceptualizing and was responsible for overseeing and coordinating programs and projects involving faculty members of UP and international academic institutions with formal linkages with the university. Corazon served as president of the Asia Pacific Tourism Association (APTA) in 2001 and was an active APTA board member for several years. She was associate editor of the *Asia Pacific Journal of Tourism Research*, an international research publication of APTA. She was president of the Council of Hotel and Restaurant Educators of the Philippines from 2009 to 2010, and for two years, served as member of the Technical Panel for Hotel and Restaurant Management and Tourism, under the Commission on Higher Education in the Philippines. Corazon is a recipient of the outstanding professional achievement award in the field of food service, given by the University of the Philippines Alumni Association. She was also recognized as an outstanding nutritionist dietician by the Nutritionist Dieticians' Association of the Philippines in 2002. Her research interests are in the field of food safety and food service management/entrepreneurship, on which topics she has presented papers in various international conferences. coragatch3@gmail.com

**Pavlos Georgiadis** is a graduate of the University of Edinburgh with a BSc in Biological Sciences/Plant Science and an MSc in Biodiversity and Taxonomy of Plants achieved in the Royal Botanic Garden Edinburgh. He moved to the University of Hohenheim in Stuttgart, for a second MSc in Environmental Protection and Food Production, and is now completing his doctoral studies in the Social Sciences of the Agricultural Sector.

**Monica Gilli** is assistant professor at the University of Milano-Bicocca, where she teaches Sociology of Territory and Tourism. Her research interests are tourism as a factor in urban regeneration and local development, cultural and heritage tourism, museums, the relationship between tourism and identity construction, landscape and sustainability. Her publications include *Authenticity and Interpretation in Tourist Experience* (2009), *The Voyage Out: Sociological Studies* (2012) and, with E. Ruspini, M. Decataldo and M. del Greco, *Tourism, Genres, Generations* (2013).

**Richa Govil** is director of the Rural Innovation and Farming programme of Ashoka: Innovators for the Public, India. She is leading initiatives on topics related to the role of women in agriculture and the intersection of agriculture and nutrition. Richa is also a co-founder of TREE Society, which offers a condensed business management course designed specifically for rural micro-enterprises and farmer–producer companies in India. Prior to Ashoka, Richa served as associate vice-president at Infosys Technologies, as head of Corporate Development, with responsibility for developing global growth strategy. Earlier, as group manager in Infosys Corporate Marketing, she led go-to-market for the industry-award-winning 'Win in the Flat World' initiative to position Infosys as a partner of choice for Global 2000 companies. Previously, Richa was a strategy consultant with Bain and Company in San Francisco. Richa has had long engagement with the development sector through organizations such as Asha for Education, where she served as president and board member. Richa holds a PhD in Physics from the University of California, at Berkeley, USA. She has a Bachelor's degree in Physics and Business Administration, also from UC Berkeley.

**Shirley V. Guevarra** is a professor of Hospitality Management and immediate past chair of the Department of Hotel, Restaurant and Institution Management, University of the Philippines (UP). She also served as director of the UP Business Concessions Office. She is currently a board member of the Asia Pacific Tourism Association (APTA), associate editor of APTA's *Asia Pacific Journal of Tourism Research*, director of the Hotel and Restaurant Association of the Philippines, Associate Division and board member of the Council of Hotel and Restaurant Educators of the Philippines (COHREP). She is also a member of the Board of Overseers of the University Hotel, UP Diliman. Shirley's research projects include inter-disciplinary research on sustainable tourism, homestay, food safety/Hazard Analysis Critical Control Point (HACCP) system, human resource management (training design, organiza-tional values in foodservices), waste management and food and culture/food tourism. She is a recipient of the following distinctions: Best Paper Award, 18th APTA Conference (Taiwan) in 2012; Research Excellence Award, 18th COHREP Conference in 2010; and Best Paper Award, Seminar Series of the Philippine Food and Nutrition Research Institute in 2006. Shirley has local and international publications on food safety/HACCP, environmental management, human resource management and food tourism. shirley_guevarra2001@yahoo.com

**Afton Halloran** is a PhD candidate within the GREEiNSECT research consortium (http://greeinsect.ku.dk), a group of public and private institutions investigating how insects can be utilized as novel and supplementary sources of protein in small- to large-scale industries in Kenya. She formerly worked as a consultant with the Edible Insects Programme at the Food and Agriculture Organization of the United Nations (FAO). She is a co-author on the FAO's most popular publication *Edible Insects: Future Prospects for Food and Feed Security*. Afton holds an MSc in Agricultural Development from the University of Copenhagen where she wrote her thesis on the legitimization and institutionalization of urban agriculture in Dar es Salaam, Tanzania, and Copenhagen, Denmark. Her research interests include urban food systems and policy, rural–urban interactions, undervalued foods, farmer organizations and sustainable diets. As an avid traveller, Afton has been to more than 40 countries and has lived in eight of them.

**Heather Hartwell** is a registered nutritionist. Her work on tourism and well-being is aligned with national research agendas, where it featured in the recent Research Councils UK 'Big Ideas for the Future', identifying the relationship between recreation, leisure and well-being as a key theme for the next 20-year time period. She is editor of the highly acclaimed *Perspectives in Public Health*, a peer-reviewed, practice-based journal, published by Sage.

**Clare Hindley** is a professor in the Language and Communication Department at IUBH School of Business and Management. She has international experience in Europe and South America in the world of business and teaching, a Master's degree in Applied Linguistics and a PhD in Sociolinguistics. Her career includes the academic management of several educational institutions and also training teachers and business professionals. At IUBH she predominantly lectures in research methods and business communication. Her career has been diverse in location and focus, but language, culture and communication have remained the guiding lights. Her research interests include the world of hospitality and tourism with particular focus on education, culture and sociology.

**Ho Weng** graduated from the Institute for Tourism Studies, Macao, majoring in Tourism Business Management.

**Elisabeth Hochwarter** studied Resource Management at the University of Natural Resources and Life Sciences (BOKU) in Vienna. She finished her Master's degree in 2014, analysing the effects of savoury regions in Austria.

**Miles Irving** was introduced to foraging at the age of six by his grandfather. An autumn morning's mushroom foray was the start of an exploration of the edible possibilities of wild nature, which has become the focal point of his life's work. In 2003 he founded a wild food company, Forager, which supplies some of Britain's top chefs; in 2009 his manual of foraging, *The Forager Handbook*, was published – the most comprehensive treatment of British edible wild plants published to date. He continues to work with some of the best chefs in the world exploring wild food not just as a source of delicious flavours but also as a food system second to none in terms of its sustainability. Wild food plants require no inputs in their production, no diesel, no irrigation, no pesticides and no fertilizers!

**Colin Johnson**, PhD, is professor and chair of the Department of Hospitality Management at San Francisco State University. He has taught in seven colleges and universities in the UK, Switzerland and the US. His research interests include internationalization in the hospitality industry, sustainability and social entrepreneurship

**Anders Justenlund** currently holds a dual position as lecturer and business developer in the Department of Hospitality and Experience Management at University College Northern Denmark. He is affiliated with the Center for Research Excellence in Business Models at Aalborg University. Research interests include CSR, sustainability, business model innovation, organizational culture, HRM, change processes and creative new thinking. In 2011, together with his research partner Sofia Rebelo, Anders received the award for best paper from the Council of Hospitality Management Education at the annual research conference in Leeds, United Kingdom. The paper was entitled 'CSR in a hospitality organisation – an analytical framework of understanding'. Anders is active in several international fora and is currently the honorary secretary in the European Council on Hotel, Restaurant and

Institutional Education. He holds a Bachelor's degree in Public Administration and Social Science and a Master's degree in Tourism Development from Aalborg University.

**Peter R. Klosse** is the former professor of Gastronomy at Stenden University, Leeuwarden, and currently professor at the Hotel Management School Maastricht. Jaap Peter Nijboer is one of his students at Leeuwarden. The Foodzone model was developed under his supervision by a group of students at the Hotel Management School Maastricht. Peter is also the owner of Hotel Gastronomique De Echoput and founder of the Dutch Academy for Gastronomy.

**Lam Iok Cheng** graduated from the Institute for Tourism Studies, Macao, majoring in Tourism Business Management.

**Anders Lindén** is a forager at Roland Rittman Ltd., and a farmer, agroecologist and environmental activist. He holds an MSc in Philosophy and Public Policy from the London School of Economics and Political Science, UK, and an MA in Philosophy from the University of St Andrews, Scotland.

**Sandor G. Lukacs de Pereny** holds a Master of International Development from the Graduate School of Public and International Affairs of the University of Pittsburgh thanks to a Fulbright Scholarship and a Full Tuition Remission Fellowship granted by the United States Department of State and the University of Pittsburgh respectively. He also pursued studies at a Master's-level programme in International Relations and Trade at the Institute of Government and Public Administration of the Universidad San Martín de Porres in Lima, Peru. Sandor comes from a tourism, hotel and restaurant management background as he holds a Bachelor's degree in Hotel Engineering from the Université de Toulouse II – Le Mirail in Toulouse, France – a professional title in Hotel Administration from Universidad Tecnológica de Chile in Santiago, Chile. In addition, he pursued various certificate programmes in Peru, India and the United States. In the professional field, Sandor has ten years of experience working in hotels and restaurants, mining and oil camps (in the Peruvian Andes and the Argentinean Tierra del Fuego) and as a university lecturer at Universidad San Ignacio de Loyola and Institut Paul Bocuse. He also has worked as a consultant for the Peruvian Ministry of Trade and Tourism. His topics of interest include rural and sustainable development, entrepreneurship promotion, social responsibility, tourism and international trade.

**Luo Xiao Yan** graduated from the Institute for Tourism Studies, Macao, majoring in Tourism Business Management.

**Carolann Marcus** is currently pursuing graduate studies in International Relations at the Turkeyen campus of the University of Guyana. A Tourism graduate, she worked as product development officer at the Guyana Tourism Authority and as administrative assistant at the Amerindian Peoples Association, an Amerindian advocacy organization in Guyana. She later moved to Barbados where she worked at the consultancy firm of RMJG and Associates and at the Community Tourism Foundation of Barbados. Carolann is of Akawaio ancestry and has a deep research interest in the cultural practices and traditions not only of the Akawaios but also of all peoples who are descendants of the aboriginal nations of Guyana.

**Juline E. Mills** is professor and chair of the Department of Hospitality and Tourism Management at the University of New Haven. She has authored more than 100 scholarly publications in the hospitality and tourism field.

**Christopher Münke** is currently working at the Non-Wood Forest Product Division and the insect for food and feed programme at the Food and Agriculture Organization of the United Nations (FAO). He holds an MSc in Agricultural Development from the University of Copenhagen, Denmark, with a focus on sustainable natural resource management. For his Master's thesis he conducted field research in Cambodia for a value chain analysis on the informal value chain of edible crickets and tarantulas. Prior to this, he studied Regional Development and Innovation in Wageningen, the Netherlands. His study interests are local food systems, food trade, sustainable agriculture and their impact on people's decision-making and livelihoods, especially in rural–urban contexts. During his studies he gained theoretical and practical knowledge around farming/gardening with hands-on experience in the Republic of Ireland, the Netherlands, Laos and Denmark.

**Jaap Peter Nijboer** has recently finished his Bachelor's degree in International Hospitality Management at Stenden University in Leeuwarden, the Netherlands. During this education he specialized in Food and Beverage Management and Gastronomy. Together with a fellow student he conducted research on the way in which the cheese course is served in Dutch top restaurants. Then, Jaap wrote his bachelor's thesis on the conditions for a successful implementation of food self-sufficiency in (Dutch) restaurants. His work as an intern both at Peter Klosse's lectorate of Gastronomy (Stenden University) and in the latter's one-star Michelin restaurant de Echoput broadened his view on culinary homesteading.

**Martyn Pring** is a PhD researcher at the School of Tourism, Bournemouth University. He is a chartered marketer and has an MSc in Tourism Management. Prior to academia he worked across private and public sector marketing management holding a number of senior marketing roles. His current research areas include food tourism, experience management, destination marketing and heritage railways.

**Ulrike Pröbstl-Haider** is professor for Landscape Development, Recreation and Tourism Planning at the University of Natural Resources and Life Sciences in Vienna. She holds a PhD from the Ludwig Maximilian University of Munich, Germany, and a habilitation (venia legendi) from the Technical University of Munich. She teaches undergraduate and graduate courses in Nature Conservation, Rural and Nature-Based Tourism. Since 1988 she has been running her own consulting office for landscape planning, spatial planning and ecological research in Germany. She is a member of the Chamber of Architects in Germany. Her current research addresses landscape development, recreation and tourism planning, forest recreation and protected areas planning. Another focus of her research is the development of environmental assessment and auditing methods as well as climate change adaptation in spatial planning, recreation and nature-based tourism. She has published several books in German and English in the field of spatial and recreation planning. She is editor-in-chief of the *Journal for Outdoor Recreation and Tourism*, published by Elsevier. She is a member of other international professional bodies in tourism and environmental planning.

**Ricardo Radulovich**, PhD, is director of the Department of Agricultural Engineering at the University of Costa Rica and has close to 20 years of experience researching and developing cost-effective and sustainable sea-farming technologies in tropical conditions. After pioneering work growing land crops at sea, irrigated with water distilled or harvested from rain in situ, he moved into producing caged fish and shrimp in polyculture with oysters and mussels. He has, during recent years, advanced cultivation of tropical seaweeds and their use as food. He has recently expanded his work to farming on freshwater bodies, both floating land crops and aquatic plants. His current research projects include establishing at sea the production of caged herbivore tropical fishes fed mostly with seaweeds and efforts to turn some aquatic 'weeds' into full crops for food. For his work he has received grants from the government of Costa Rica, the World Bank, the Bill and Melinda Gates Foundation and Grand Challenges Canada, among others.

**Benedict Reade** is the former head of Culinary Research and Development at the Nordic Food Lab. He started his career washing dishes in a vegetarian diner, followed by education at the culinary powerhouses Ballymaloe Cookery School and the University of Gastronomic Sciences. He has worked as a chef in Scotland, England, Ireland, France and Italy until finding his way to Denmark, joining the MAD Symposium team in 2011. He then moved straight from MAD to carry out his current work at the Nordic Food Lab. A trained chef with an avant-garde angle, he has a deep interest in humans, ecology, travel, biology and culture. Benedict sees taste and smell as our most developed senses – made to navigate toxins and nutrients that bombard our mouths and noses every day. When 1.5 billion are starving and 1 billion are obese but malnourished he asks how developing food education can increase the possibility of a sustainable, delicious future for all.

**Roland Rittman** founded the company Roland Rittman Ltd in 2004 to supply edible wild herbs, berries and mushrooms to Nordic gourmet restaurants, but started as early as 1999 selling wild products on the market square in Lund, Sweden, and to restaurants. Thus he played an important role in putting the wilderness into the Nordic cookery, New Scandinavian cooking or Nordic cuisine movement before and after the introduction of the 'Nordic cuisine manifesto' at NOMA 2004. He has delivered to many restaurants in Scandinavia and the Netherlands. Currently he is selling to gourmet restaurants such as NOMA and AOC (Copenhagen, Denmark), Restaurant Frantzén (Stockholm, Sweden), Bloom (Malmö, Sweden), Restaurant Ask and Sundmans Krog (Helsingfors/Helsinki, Finland) and Maaemo and Grefsenkollen (Oslo, Norway). Further he has been environmental consultant to municipalities in Sweden and has been an engaged environmental activist. He presented his wide experience on foraging at the 3rd MAD Symposium in Copenhagen 2013 under the title 'Go wild'.

**Rodrigues Ng Iris** graduated from the Institute for Tourism Studies, Macao, majoring in Tourism Business Management.

**Nikki Rose** is a Greek-American professional chef, writer and seminar director living in Crete, Greece. She is a graduate of the Culinary Institute of America and has worked in fine dining, culinary education and journalism around the world. Nikki has contributed to academic publications and major media outlets focusing on cuisine, heritage preservation and sustainable tourism. She is founder of Crete's Culinary Sanctuaries, an award-winning programme for best practices in responsible travel. Nikki formed CCS in 1997 to help provide tangible support to residents working on action programmes to protect their cultural and natural heritage. CCS organizes tailored comprehensive seminars for academic institutions and the general public. Nikki and CCS have received awards from *National Geographic*, the United Nations Convention on Biological Diversity, the UN World Tourism Forum for Peace and Sustainable Development, the World Travel and Tourism Council, and have been featured in *National Geographic*, *NPR*, *New York Times*, *Archaeological Institute of America Magazine*, *The Guardian* (UK), *O'Globo* (Brazil), *Australian Gourmet Traveller*, *TV New Zealand*, *Islands Magazine Blue List* and *Lonely Planet*. Nikki is a frequent speaker and adviser for sustainable tourism/culinary heritage projects across the globe. Her book *Crete: The Roots of the Mediterranean Diet* highlights more than 15 years of her work in Crete.

**Laure Saulais** is a research scientist at the Institut Paul Bocuse Food and Hospitality Research Center in Ecully, France, and an associate researcher at the French National Institute for Agricultural Research in Grenoble, France. She has an MSc in Food and Life Sciences Engineering from AgroParisTech, an MSc in Environmental and Natural Resources Economics from Paris X University and a PhD in Economics from the University of Grenoble. Before she joined the Institut Paul Bocuse, she was a postdoctoral fellow at Université Laval (Quebec, Canada). Since she joined the Institut Paul Bocuse in September 2009, she has been taking part in the development of research activities and methodologies, the coordination of projects and the academic activities of the Institut Paul Bocuse. She also teaches courses on experimental economics, and food consumer research in various universities, engineering and business schools in France. Her main area of research is behavioural economics, with a focus on the study of consumer decisions, behaviours and economic preferences related to food in out-of-home contexts. Laure.Saulais@institutpaulbocuse.com

**Josef Schrank** studied landscape planning at the University of Natural Resources and Life Sciences in Vienna. He finished his Master's degree in 2012, looking at opportunities for citizen science in the Nature Park Pöllau valley. Currently he works for the NGO 'Kuratorium Wald' developing an information platform on Natura 2000 in Austrian Forests.

**Jan Arend Schulp** was trained as a biologist at Free University Amsterdam where he took his PhD in 1972. He worked in several fields at Stenden University of Applied Sciences, Leeuwarden, the Netherlands and its predecessors in education, consultancy and research. Most of his activities have been related to food or services, including nutrition, food education, food service and food retailing. At present he is associate professor of Gastronomy at the School of International Hospitality Management. Other relevant skills and experience include vegetable gardening, home cooking and beekeeping.

**Donald Sinclair** is a senior lecturer in Tourism at the University of Guyana and a visiting lecturer at the Suriname College of Hospitality and Tourism. He served for six years as Coordinator for Tourism, Transport, Infrastructure and Communication at the Amazon Cooperation Treaty Organization, headquartered in Brasilia, and has researched and published on the subject of tourism in a number of books and academic journals. He recently co-edited with Chandana Jayawardena an issue of the *Journal of the World Hospitality and Tourism Themes* on the theme of sustainable tourism as a tool for the development of the Amazon rainforest. This foray into sustainable gastronomy varies a research profile that has focused mainly upon sustainable tourism, ecotourism and dark tourism.

**Nicolas Siorak** is a researcher at Ecole hôtelière de Lausanne (EHL). A member of the Food and Beverage Industry Chair, he notably conducts research on sustainable development and food safety in the F&B industry. A member of the GREG, research group in management (CNRS, Grenoble University), he is also consultant for European Union INTERREG projects. Before joining EHL, Nicolas Siorak was lecturer in economics and business management at Grenoble Business School, Wesford.

**Wantanee Suntikul** earned her Master's and PhD in Tourism Studies from the University of Surrey, UK. She is currently teaching at the School of Hotel and Tourism Management at the Hong Kong Polytechnic University. Her core research interests and expertise are in the impact of tourism on cultural tourism destinations and the political and social aspects of tourism development and food tourism. Geographically, her current and recent research and writing has been on South and Southeast Asia. She has been conducting research on Vietnam, Laos, Thailand and Bhutan extensively in the past few years. Wantanee has co-edited two books with Richard Butler entitled *Tourism and Political Change*, published by Goodfellow, and *Tourism and War*, published by Routledge.

**Tim Taylor** has been a lecturer in Environmental and Public Health Economics in the European Centre for Environment and Human Health, part of the University of Exeter Medical School, since 2011. Previously he was a research officer at the University of Bath and a consultant for Metroeconomica Limited in Bath. He holds a PhD in Economics from the University of Bath and is a fellow of the Higher Education Academy. Tim has acted as a consultant to the World Bank and UNEP on issues of sustainable tourism and is an expert in the economic valuation of the environment. Tim is currently supervising five PhD students on topics from positional innovation of the natural environment to the valuation of ecosystem services. He has published in journals including *Ecological Economics*, *Tourism Economics* and the *Journal of Environmental Management*. He lives in Truro, Cornwall with his wife and two sons and enjoys sampling the gastronomy of Cornwall in his spare time.

**John Tredinnick-Rowe** is a final-year PhD student at the University of Exeter Medical School's European Centre for Environment and Human Health. His thesis examines the role of positional innovation of the natural environment in the health and well-being sector (including health tourism). His supervisors are Dr Tim Taylor of the University of Exeter Medical School and Professors Richard Owen and John Bessant of the University of Exeter Business School. He has a background in environmental resource management and agriculture. His research interests include health and well-being service innovation, social innovation, economic anthropology and Green Care. He is the co-author of *The Future of Europe: An Integrated Youth Approach* by the European Free Alliance European Parliamentary Block's think tank, the Centre Maurits Coppieters. He was born and raised in Cornwall, where he lives on the family farm, growing local produce.

**Paul Vantomme** is an agricultural engineer and has worked for FAO since 1978 in forestry projects worldwide. He has coordinated the Non-Wood Forest Products programme at FAO headquarters in Rome since 1996. His focus is to enhance the contribution of forests to food security. He is a co-author on the FAO's most popular publication *Edible Insects: Future Prospects for Food and Feed Security* and *Contribution of Forest Insects to Food Security and Forest Conservation: The Example of Caterpillars in Central Africa*.

**Peter Varga** teaches at the Ecole hôtelière de Lausanne, University of Applied Sciences, in Switzerland. He obtained his BA in International Business Studies from the Oxford Brookes

University; MA in Sociology from the Central European University with the University of Lancaster; doctorate degree in Cultural Anthropology from the University of Guadalajara in Mexico. His research interests lie on three main axes: cultural perspectives of food and eating habits; intercultural communication practices in the hospitality industry; and sociocultural dynamics of current tourism practices in host societies. He carried out extended ethnographic field work in Amazonian indigenous communities on sociocultural impacts of tourism dynamics. Recently he has been conducting applied research on front-desk intercultural competencies in luxury hotels. He lives next to the Lake of Geneva with his wife and his two children.

**Maryam Fotouhinia Yepes** is a registered dietician from McGill University, Canada, with a Master's degree in Dietetics and Human Nutrition from the same university. Her professional experience allowed her to apply her passion for this field as a nutrition communication specialist for the food industry, a clinical dietician for hospitals and clinics as well as a culinary dietician for restaurants and the hospitality industry. She is currently teaching nutrition for hospitality professionals at Ecole hôtelière de Lausanne and conducts research on the role of nutrition information on food decisions at ETH in Zurich. More details available at www.maryamyepes. com.

# PART 1

# Anthropology of food

The sheer novelty and glamor of the Western diet, with its seventeen thousand new food products every year and the marketing power – thirty-two billion dollars a year – used to sell us those products, has overwhelmed the force of tradition and left us where we now find ourselves: relying on science and journalism and government and marketing to help us decide what to eat.

*Michael Pollan,* In Defense of Food: An Eater's Manifesto *(Penguin, 2007)*

Consumer food decisions and the role of history and self-identity form the content of the first chapter. **Alice Brombin** provides a case study of an Italian ecovillage where sustainability combines environmental practice with concern for the land, the self and others. The initiative combines the concept of luxury and simplicity with new interpretations of luxury and individualism, terms both normally associated with the globalized modern world.

The food choices we make are part of our ever-evolving social identity. **Peter Varga** highlights how postmodern societies, for example, use health and wellness to replace the former spiritual and religious taboos on food. Moreover, today's sustainable consumption appears to be based on the search for well-being and personal development. In the past, as today, food choice is an attempt at survival and social-identification; the parameters may change, but objectives remain the same.

The concepts behind consumer food choices have become more public, more debated and correspondingly more complex. **Clare Hindley** contrasts 1980s London and twenty-first-century Germany, highlighting the influences that play a major role in young people's food decisions. Music, politics and role models are just some of the issues forming the framework within which self-identity is sought and moulded.

**Paul Cleave's** examination of regional culinary tastes and fashions in Devon, UK, analyses how the past can help us understand today's hospitality industry. History is seen as an important tool to explain the experiences of today's consumers and producers. Devon provides a vivid example of traditional culinary highlights and local and external interest.

# 1

# "LUXURIOUS SIMPLICITY"

## Self-sufficient food production in Italian ecovillages

*Alice Brombin*

### Introduction

Luxury and simplicity are concepts usually considered contradictory especially in the context of food consumption and food products. The success of Italian culture is undeniably linked to the production of luxury goods known worldwide. Products associated with Italian brands and labels are indicators not only of quality but also of distinction. In the field of food, wine is a good example of these associations. The Pinot Gray, Tuscan Chianti, and Prosecco di Valdobbiadene fall within the category of luxury not only because of the high prices for which they are sold but also for the fame associated with the brand and with a specific design, making these wines immediately recognizable. The consumption of these products requires a distinguished knowledge that is frequently a prerogative of expertise requiring an educated taste. Conversely, simple food is non–label associated and locally produced in farms. It is inexpensive food, carrying with it the ability to enter any household. It is anonymous, with no character or specific taste corresponding to it. Simple food is not associated with luxury, therefore it does not offer any relevant history or reputation to the consumer and is not associated with rituals or narratives that add meaning to personal identity.

The objective of this article is to show how the concepts of luxury and simplicity within the ecovillages assume different meanings respective of those described above and how these categories can be adapted and manipulated according to specific contextual needs. In the ecovillages, luxury and simplicity are not seen in opposition. On the contrary, they shift these categories and offer new frameworks for understanding how the production of food, shared consumption, and communal living contribute to an ethic of care such that simplicity and reciprocity are the new luxury. Simple food and self-production concerns not only the idea of good and healthy eating, it is also linked to a set of practices that help create an aesthetic based on the observation of nature and on the attitude of care. Sustainability is not just about environmental practice but also about the ethos of caring for land, self, and others.

Ecovillages propose creative solutions to develop alternative social microsystems based on self-sufficiency. The goal is not only the maintenance of material needs but also personal satisfaction and happiness, originating from the food that is produced and consumed.

Both anthropological and sociological studies on nutrition recognize the centrality of food in the social field. By adopting a specific diet, each community defines its own way of

3

interacting with nature and territory, revealing criteria and cultural conventions that determine the economy and technology of its own productive system (Poulain, 2008; Douglas, 1999). Everyday life is organized with reference to food and the techniques adopted to produce it, transform it and eat it. For this reason, food is the template for symbolic representations in every culture (Levi Strauss, 2008; Douglas and Isherwood, 1979).

Gastronomy represents a privileged interpretative key for socio-cultural analysis. In this field of studies, a fundamental contribution to the theme of nutrition comes from the sociologist Claude Fischler. According to Fischler, food distinguishes itself from other typologies of consumption because, once incorporated into the organism, it becomes part of the self (Fischler, 1980: 948). Fischler (1980) identifies the increasing influence of the global market on social life and the tendency to consume standardized and anonymous food as distinctive traits of modern society. He coins the concept of "gastro-anomia" to describe the consumers' alimentary anxiety as an oppressive condition resulting from their lack of awareness of the contents of their food. By adopting the principle "I am what I eat," Fischler points out that if you don't know what you are eating, consequently you don't know who you are. This ignorance reflects itself upon the social actors who internalize this unknowing and the related doubts concerning personal identity.

The trend of studies which rises from these ideas (Flandrin and Montanari, 1997; Lupton, 1996; Warde, 1997) proposes an additional body of concepts in which the imaginative and symbolic aspects of alimentary practice are interpreted not only as a means of social identity affirmation (Bourdieu, 1983), but also as variables that are fundamental to the creation of individual identity. Such concepts contribute to overtaking the current perception of gastronomy and taste as "confined in a process of distinction by means of which elites affirm their difference from rising classes" (Poulain, 2008: 147).

Frequently, contemporary society is described as characterized by the growing trend for individualization in the field of alimentary choices, the fragmentation and the simplification of the composition of meals, and the progressive loss of knowledge and control over what is eaten.

However, there is an increasing amount of evidence that points to alternative forms of consumption that underline a critical and responsive approach on the part of the social actor. Alternative food consumption modalities that express the demand for authenticity, tradition, taste, and wellness contribute to restoring and preserving the value of scientifically unmodified, non-industrial local food and cuisine.

These choices also enhance the pleasure of meal sharing, and the importance of intimacy and familiarity in the food preparation and consumption process (Pollan, 2006; Sassatelli, 2004).

In this context, the debate concerning the relationship between nature and science has strong relevance and heavy symbolic significance. Alimentary styles such as veganism and raw-food diets, which utilize nature as a symbol to which the images of purity and goodness are emotionally assigned, are increasingly growing (Lupton, 1996: 139). From this perspective, food is defined as good and healthy if it respects specific characteristics associated with an idea of nature that is often mythicized and uncontaminated: food is healthy if not manipulated by science, if local, and therefore "near" to consumers. This allows them to know its origin and to re-establish the proximity and control over the entire production chain. Conversely, food characterized as "bad" consists of artificial ingredients and processing and evokes the artificial context of culturalized urban life. Those who embrace nature differentiate themselves by a highly emotive ideological position, collocating alimentation and food in an aesthetic and holistic approach that values eating as an expression of a moral, philosophical, and political attitude (Lupton, 1996: 143). The formation of taste is thus the consequence of a continuous process of negotiation and reflection in which the declaration of personal choice has fundamental value (Leonini and Sassatelli, 2008: 118).

Ecovillages are the tangible translation of the concepts expressed above. In Italy, these communities are located mainly in rural settings, the dimensions are generally finite, and they often consist of around 20 to 25 people. The shared goal is to adopt a lifestyle based on self-management, self-sufficiency, and the collectivization of economic resources in order to create economies of subsistence that are sustainable from both an environmental and social point of view. Food and energy self-sufficiency are common goals as well as the establishment of relationships of reciprocity with both the land and surrounding territory. In the ecovillages, consumption dynamics are characterized by a frugal hedonism based on the moral imperative of ethics and sobriety. This entails progressively reducing consumption while fully embracing the principles of reduction—by turning to self-production—when possible. The underlying aim is personal satisfaction and the diffusion of alternative micro-economies (Fabris, 2003; Leonini and Sassatelli, 2008; Latouche, 2007). The will to valorize the local dimension is crucial, not only for what concerns alimentary choices but also for the many movements that insist on local control of cultural resources that see going-back-to-earth and communitarian, auto-managed lifestyles as the best solution to the disrupting tendency of contemporary society (Castells, 1999).

## Ecovillages: new frontiers of sustainability?

By changing the way we cultivate our food, we change our food, our society, our values. Natural farming, which has its origins and its end in respect, is everywhere human and sustainable. The real aim of agriculture is not to grow crops, but the cultivation and perfection of human beings: to be here, to take care of a small field, in the full possession of the freedom and the fullness of every day, daily. This must have been the original way of agriculture.

*(Fukuoka, 1978: 15)*

In modern society, different social movements exist that attempt to gain control over cultural resources that contrast with the large-scale standardized food production system. These ethical and political aspects of consumption gain a high symbolic value. Among these movements, ecovillages seek to regenerate social and natural environments through communal living.

Ecovillages are intentional and experimental communities that embrace environmental sustainability manifested in daily practices through the concept of green consumption, considered the best response to the global ecological crisis and the main indicator of an ecological identity. Environmental ecology is primarily concerned with self-sufficient food production and alternative farming methods, such as permaculture and organic or bio-dynamic farming practices, aimed to achieve a sustainable food style. Moreover, the use of these methods represents a way to criticize the economic logic of equivalent exchange, preferring instead a culture of gifting and the establishment of relations of reciprocity and solidarity on a small scale. These local communities are able to build networks in territories that lead to rational and pragmatic action, both in relation to the way of eating and the use of products, by interacting with related networks, such as groups of joint purchasing.

For ecovillagers, consumption is never separate from production. This logic of eco-compatibility is carried out in several ways: through the preference for local short chain food production, the recovery of native food species, and the possibility of reusing, recovering, and recycling. Therefore, the duties of the consumer come full circle: to him- or herself, to nature, and to the others. These new forms of intentional communitarianism propose the adoption of a lifestyle in which the shared collective dimension of being together paired with an attitude of caring for and attention to the environment—which have strong emotive connections—have fundamental value. To choose to live in an ecovillage requires reflection and pragmatic action, which are the consequences of the necessity to redefine the nature of both individual and collective needs that rise from the tensions and the contradictions that permeate the society we are living in.

It is difficult to describe this particular social phenomenon by using the categories and the conceptual forms particular to the literature quoted thus far. Starting from this premise, it is useful to move towards different theoretical and conceptual formulations in order to interpret and comprehend the nature of the ecovillage movement. This particular kind of intentional communitarianism is distinct from the phenomenon of neotribalism, which tends to be fluid and focused on consumption. A few associations can be made because they share some peculiarities—such as the preference for an "archaic" pattern of socialization centered on micro-policies of communities and the endeavor for "the urgent need for an emphatic society: sharing of emotions, sharing of affections" (Maffesoli, 2004: 18).

From the desire to share common emotions and feelings comes the discovery of a multi-sensory experience in which the body is central to the articulation of food practices. In this sense, it is useful to use the concept of "shared corporeality" (Goodman, 1999; Murdoch, 2001) to describe a relationship in which eco-social production and consumption are deeply interconnected and mutually constructed. In these terms, the sociology of alimentation also offers useful interpretative ideas, as long as it deals with the closed interrelations that exist among the biological, the ecological, and the social. In this regard, Poulain claims that "It is thus the originality of the 'bio-anthropological' connection of a group of humans with its environment to build up the subject-matter of the socio-anthropology of alimentation. Put in this way, the 'social alimentary space' (the representation and the imagery which lie underneath it) is not just a 'total social fact' but a total human fact" (Poulain, 2008: 198). Such interest involves the ecofeminist perspective that emphasizes the idea that interconnection with the natural environment comes from the recovering of direct and concrete experiences through the senses (Mellor, 2006; Shiva, 2002; Stevens, 2012).

The lifestyle adopted in ecovillages attempts to go beyond the anthropocentric vision that places man and nature in a dichotomy. This basis is also the prerequisite on which the philosophy of deep ecology is founded. The latter hopes for the reconciliation of man with nature, starting from acknowledging the intrinsic importance of every being, even those belonging to the non-human sphere (Goldsmith, 1997; Naess, 1973). In contrast with contemporary society dominated by hyper-productive and hyper-consumerist rationalism, deep ecology deviates from the typical ecology subject, moving towards the cult of nature. Ecology is thus translated in a matter of aesthetic sensibility and as such amplifies the emphasis on the spiritual (Lanternari, 2003: 75). This current of thought, in addition to the development of a brand of metaphysics that identifies nature as a being endowed with a conscience, suggests programmatic action with the aim of attaining an economy of self-sufficiency supported by the decentralization of politics that awards local autonomies greater relevance (Naess, 1973; Salleh, 1984). The transition to this type of sustainable agriculture is based on two fundamental elements: the recovery of traditional methods of cultivation and practices, the restoration of an ancient knowledge that has a meter to measure human deeds, and the establishment of sustainable human communities (Drengson et al., 2011). These same principles are the heart of permaculture and synergistic agriculture, which are farming practices widespread among the ecovillages.

Permaculture is an agricultural technique whose name comes from a contraction of the words "permanent agriculture" and "permanent culture," which is based on intensive cultivation for subsistence. It is defined as a design system for creating and managing sustainable human settlements and, at the same time, an ethical and philosophical system and practical approach to everyday life. In essence, permaculture is applied ecology. At the heart of this practice lies the rule: "take your own responsibility" (Reny and Mollison, 2007: 3).

Inside the ecovillages, these kinds of practices described above and shared experiences contribute not only to define a particular food style but also a lifestyle defined as "luxurious simplicity." In this context, the epistemological status of the concept of "luxury" transforms to include the idea of improving well-being and pleasure to enjoying the best. It is no longer a tool used to communicate one's wealth or social status (Bourdieu, 1983; Douglas, 1999).

Beginning with Fabris' redefinition of the concept of luxury (Fabris, 2003: 174–176), we can determine at least five constitutive elements of this process inside the movement of the ecovillages:

- Culture: meant as knowledge of nature, of traditional wisdom, of a shared conception of aesthetics and health; meant also as the experimentation of forms of self-management that implies horizontal and shared policy-making with a focus on the aspect of co-construction between humans and environment.
- Experience: meant as the collective creation and enjoyment of moments and situations that arouse feelings, starting from those coming from the rediscovery of the direct relationship man has with nature and the earth, through the enactment of body awareness and manual abilities.
- Emphasis on the self: meant as giving yourself the best, even by means of the re-appropriation of a conception of time that respects personal and subjective rhythm. In this way, time and spaces are created and conceptualized in a flexible way with relation to specific and personal purposes.
- Pleasure in frugality: meant as a generator of abundance, living simply according to the logic of cooperation and not competition; looking for trusted relationships, empathy, and solidarity, and restoring the logic of gifting and exchange of goods.
- Holism: the experiencing of a circular harmonic dimension that affects all of the aspects of existence, from the direct relation with nature, to interpersonal relations.

The elements described above help to define a vision of luxury that does not concern the possession and accumulation of capital or material culture, and that is not bound to accumulation, excess, and waste, which are distinctive characteristics of the production–consumption dynamic in our society. In this sense, ecovillages illustrate the assertion of Baudrillard (1976: 63) that "in our opulent societies abundance is lost due to a social logic that condemns us to a luxurious and spectacular poverty," we must conclude that mainstream contemporary society satisfies the needs of production and disregards human needs. The self-sufficiency practiced in ecovillages represents the escape from this state of affairs.[1] The case of the ecovillage Garden of Joy presented in the next section shows how luxury primarily concerns the luxury of living. The notion is synonymous with the possibilities to express an informed choice, the choice to live well in a context designed and calibrated to one's own needs and desires resulting in communal ambitions. In this sense luxury is thus defined as *buen vivir*, as good living.

# The Garden of Joy

I wasn't able to tolerate living in the city, the bus stops full of cigarettes, I wasn't able to tolerate even the idea that work, given the economic crisis, had become so pressing at the office. I remember I dreamed the database, I couldn't accept dreaming numbers.

And then I had a really critical time, when I wasn't able to tolerate habits of human beings, the local aperitif, beer, I mean, those conventional ways to meet, to not say anything except banality [. . .] My plan was pretty clear from the beginning, when I decided to come here I decided to change my life. This land doesn't belong only to me, it is also of my sister, we are both owners. The chance I gave to me was utilizing an empty space, in order to give to me, and to anyone who wanted to share this project, the possibility to transform their own lives. And it went well, the first year so many people approached the project, all in one breath, but I realized that I was losing the main goal because of which I came to this place, I mean, those habits started to be recreated here, in respect to drink, to smoke, to eat meat. So there was a very critical moment that has made the number of people who joined the project extremely reduced, because a part of us, I and others, wanted to be much more effective in respect to that it is necessary to keep distance from attachments. First, because they are an obstacle in the pursuit of self-sufficiency, which for me is a matter of well-being and respect for nature. A simple cigarette for me is the equivalent of a whole factory that produces smoke and pollution, I mean the revolution, first you must make it inside you, and then you can do it outside. Recently we had the consensus in respect to the fact that the drug should not enter here, you should smoke out of the Garden, alcohol isn't part of our habits, then we invite people who are coming here, to not choose a bottle of wine as gift, but perhaps a bottle of juice or a pack of rice, or flour.

*(Rosa, 38 years old, Italy)*

The testimony above is of Rosa, who after leaving a good job and a promising career in the fashion industry, decided to return to her native region, Apulia, to establish an intentional community called the "Garden of Joy" within an olive grove owned by her family. The eco-village was established in 2011, inspired by the principles of the Rainbow Family.[2] It started as a self-managed community space to host creative people who want to have experiences of deep connection with nature and community life, pursuing the objectives of self-sufficiency both in food and in energy. The case study presented derives from a still current body of research that started in 2012 and aims to analyze the self-food production practices adopted in the Italian ecovillages that adhere to the RIVE network (Rete Italiana Villaggi Ecologici), the purpose of which is to understand the related symbolic significance and the influence of such practices in the articulation of an eco-sustainable lifestyle.

Currently six people, aged between 21 and 40, are living permanently in the ecovillage. In addition, the community hosts visitors for short and long periods. As a result of regulations adopted by the community that support a very frugal lifestyle and aim to reduce attachment and material needs, the number of members has dramatically decreased compared to the starting point of the project.

The original impulse that gave life to this community experience was the shared desire to distance themselves from the city and the implications of living there. The purpose was to move to a space where the residents felt closer to the land and nature and where they could practice a sober and sustainable lifestyle. The direct aim of this lifestyle is to reduce environmental impact and encourage members to self-sustain and create networks of solidarity within similar realities. Residents who live in the ecovillage do not trade labor for wages, instead they sustain themselves with the activities promoted by the community. The Garden

of Joy offers permaculture and self-construction courses, as well as activities to increase physical and spiritual well-being, such as yoga, shiatsu, and related practices. People who want to attend the courses are not required to pay with money but instead may contribute with voluntary community work or food and goods donations. The ecovillage has no specific tools to publicize these activities besides the visibility given to them on the RIVE website. Word of mouth is the most common tool utilized to bring people to experience the sustainable lifestyle in these communities. In this sense, the presence of short- or long-term guests is essential for the sustenance of ecovillages. Guests help to support the domestic economy by sharing the

community's work and needs. Additionally, connecting with individuals and groups with similar realities is fundamental to the promotion and movement of people to ecovillages. In Apulia, for example, the Garden of Joy remains in contact with the anarchist commune of Urupia and various other small local producers who also utilize alternative agricultural techniques and organic farming.[3]

The ecovillage organization is based on several regulations whose key points mainly concern nutritional taboos that regulate the consumption of food and the intake of several substances—in particular drinking wine, coffee, or alcohol, consuming meat, smoking, and taking drugs are not allowed. Every guest must accept these taboos and adhere to the food style adopted by the community that is vegetarian, nearly vegan. The consumption of eggs is mainly allowed for the guests but dairy products are normally not consumed. This implies that no animal foods can be introduced into the village and there is no possibility of introducing animals for food purposes that implies their killing. Almost all the ecovillage members experienced a raw-food diet for several months and they all agree it is the best way of eating in terms of well-being, nutritional value, and body efficiency. A raw-food diet implies the food is neither cooked nor processed and entails the need to eat six times a day, first fruit and then vegetables.

Following a logic of sustainability, what is ingested has a particular value because—according to a circular conception of the body and vital stages—everything that enters the body is reintegrated into the environment as compost that is used as fertilizer in the gardens. Therefore, it is essential that bodily excrements are healthy and do not contain any chemicals, including medicines, in order not to compromise the food quality. The ecovillage members adopt homeopathy and self-healing treatments and assure they have never been sick since they have been living in the ecovillage thanks to the food quality and the healthy diet they are adopting.

The self-sufficient food production is a central element in the ecovillage life because it puts into practice the community philosophy that aims to adopt a lifestyle that allows each individual to get rid of imagined needs in order to conduct an existence as free as possible from addictions. In this sense, plants are considered the one term of comparison as long as these living organisms are totally self-sufficient.

Following the principles of permaculture, in the ecovillage there are two synergistic gardens in which the vegetables once sown grow freely, without any working of the soil and without the employment of any chemical fertilizer. The goal of this kind of crop is for the gardens to become self-sufficient and self-sowing in five years' time. Wild herbs and spontaneous vegetables are also collected.

## From practice to aesthetics

In the Garden of Joy participants articulated three central tenets of food and feeding practices:

- Aesthetic: adopting the diet practices described above not only allows people the possibility of beauty and good health, but also the fact of being connected to self-production allows them to rediscover body skills and the knowledge related to the recovery of a lost craftsmanship and manual skill. Moreover, re-finding the connection and the relationship with the land is the basis of a path of spiritual research that passes through a comparative approach between men and plants—this also provides an identification with them—according to the principles of deep ecology. The outcome of this work on self and on one's own identity involves a kind of inner rebirth that manifests itself with the adoption of a new name related with the natural world.

- Economy: the village is based on a gift economy. Guests passing through the ecovillage generally choose food as privileged objects of exchange and gift. In turn, the members organize little markets based on voluntary donations in which the main tradable goods are self-produced food or cosmetics, such as olive oil, jams, bread, spontaneous herbs, and natural cleansers and creams made with local herbs and fruits.

- Conviviality and community-building: the most important moments of conviviality are related to the preparation and consumption of food. Sharing meals is central to the empowerment of the community. Guests are generally asked to do voluntary work in the kitchen or garden. Sustainability is not always related to farming practices but also to the way the food is prepared and cooked. Meals are always prepared collectively and mealtime is one of the major rituals and moments of communion. Making a circle by holding hands and singing specific songs is an established practice before meals. For the members, it is a way to thank Mother Earth for the food. Generally, these songs and these circles are made close to the sacred fire, in which only naturally fallen wood and vegetables can be burned. The ritual song has an important symbolic value since it enables people who take part in it to leave the typically historical human dimension, in order to enter the mythical dimension that is represented by the circle. This circle represents Nature in the form of the eternal return, bringing out the intrinsic deity of every human being.

These three tenets help shape an ethical luxury by which luxury means creating a communal dimension primarily based on mutual attention and self-care that consequently translates to the care of others and of the environment. The following quote makes clear the emotional significance that is the basis of communal living:

> Maybe first is the love you can perceive in family relationships, from your mother, your father, your sister, some best friends or your teenage-boyfriend that makes your heart beat fast. It is what generally one calls love. But here, this care is a kind of . . . I'm not even able to define it. There is a care, a sweetness, a closeness of the heart

that you can perceive even through a glance, a look that is deep, I mean, usually we are not used to being seen in that way. Here, the attentions are so true and there is a subtle difference that allows you to perceive slightly different emotions compared with normal conventional relationships, which are more on the surface, in which one doesn't talk about himself, but about other things, about material things and not about how you feel. All these small acts of kindness, of closeness, of sisterhood, sharing . . . make us feel bound by something stronger, a particular kind of bond.

I think it has to deal with the mission that each one of us has. When you have a vision and you want to follow that life style, those choices are shared, you feel closely linked to the others by something that is tight like a blood tie! It is another kind of bond that makes you feel tuned in, on the same boat. Like a particular magnetism.

*(Rosa, 38 years old, Italy)*

It can be said that sustainability does not refer only to a strong environmental sensitivity, nor is it limited to the articulation of food production and consumption practices that are part of the logic of eco-compatibility. Food in the ecovillages is a privileged medium through which sustainability is extended to social relations both inside and outside the community. Sustainability of the relationship first and foremost begins by recognizing the value of the subjects, their specificity, and their different qualities. It means creating the conditions that enable the expression of creative actions in order to achieve a shared goal: self-sufficiency and care of the environment.

A precondition to self-sufficiency is the establishment of networks and connections of mutual support and the investment of time and energy on decision-making in order to create a more horizontal and participatory process, cultivating a dimension of both physical and emotional proximity. Proximity implies attention to the other, both in the case in which "the other" is a human being or a natural element, such as a flower or a plant. This attitude corresponds to an ethic based on the idea of simplicity that becomes the most important living value. Simplicity means taking away what is superfluous, getting rid of attachments that create imagined needs in order to fully enjoy the daily experiences of people and things with which one has decided to share one's own existence. It carries with it the act of experiencing nature starting from contact with the land and physical work in the gardens. Adopting an ethic of simplicity means focusing on what one's own body communicates and on the senses and bodily experiences detected through expressing and sharing emotions. This allows the ability to give new meaning to one's own presence by paying attention to the way in which humans and the environment influence and co-create each other.

This ethic of simplicity translates into an aesthetic that permeates all aspects of life within the ecovillages. Aesthetic is part of everyday life and material beauty is not just about products and goods to be consumed or passively received. Aesthetic is an active engagement with the senses and a creative process that involves interaction with others.

Aesthetic that conveys different aptitudes and individual qualities in a dimension of shared harmony helps to create a communitarian context whose purpose stresses the importance of acceptance of the other and the perceptual and emotional aspects of living together. As Arnold Berleant said, "Social harmony is achieved through taste, by which we mean a developed aesthetic sensibility. This is not just a state of mind: a harmony of the sensuous and the spiritual demands full participation of all aspects of human perception, since the sensuous is as much body as the spiritual consciousness" (Berleant, 2005: 31).

Adopting a shared aesthetic involves integrating the personal and the social. It implies that political and cultural claims are translated into daily opportunities to express themselves and to look for a personal and collective well-being.

Central in this regard is the concept of care. A shared aesthetic is only possible in an environment or context of care, where feelings of empathy and closeness are crucial in relation to the importance given to human relationships. In these terms, it is possible to define an "aesthetic situation" (Berleant, 2005) as the way that art manifestations require reciprocity as much as care manifestations. Through these relationships, a sense of intimacy and closeness is produced. In this perspective, the core concept of luxury embraced by the ecovillages is represented by a shared ethic and aesthetic that enables people to achieve a sense of freedom and personal realization by virtue of the concrete possibility to project and realize their own life according to the meaning they ascribe to it.

## Conclusion

The model proposed by the ecovillages, as an alternative to the contemporary economic system of growth, is based on a lifestyle inspired by an ethic of sobriety and frugality. This lifestyle arises from the will of questioning ourselves about the nature of human needs in order to reduce, or at least reconsider them, given the fragility of our ecosystem and the needs of our planet. These life choices are characterized by a strong eco-pragmatism, which aims to restore a relationship of closeness with the earth, starting from the self-production of food and then recreating a relationship of solidarity and trust at all levels of existence: alimentation, housing, society, interpersonal relationships, and the achievement of a complete self-sufficiency. Nature is considered the fundamental value to build both one's own personal identity and the collective one. As a consequence, environmental sensitivity translates into an orientation towards action that involves all consumption goods (Fabris, 2003: 286). Therefore, happiness and personal satisfaction represent the incarnation of a new contemporary myth. The accomplishment of the *buen vivir* passes through the aesthetic of the everyday in order to obtain a happiness whose fundamental elements are the sharing of emotions and feelings, the emphasis on the collective dimension, and the centrality given to sensorial and bodily experiences (Fabris, 2003: 167; Maffesoli, 2004).

Sensitivity to ecology, defined in its various ways, is more and more widespread in our society. At the same time, it is easy to fall into an ideological trap and be deceived by embracing a strongly romantic concept of nature, considering it as the prime, if not the only, way to free oneself from the constrictions of society.

As sociologist Melucci (2000) points out, nowadays more than ever in the past, society is pervaded by nature because each culture has the irreducible necessity to decide its own limits. Ecovillages recreate and reframe nature in order to render it a matter of choice and moral inquiry. Such a condition is described by Melucci as a paradox that nonetheless expresses an essential need: "we have to culturally become nature, that is to say, we have to go back to our natural roots and preserve our environment by means of cultural choices" (Melucci, 2000: 89).

The community experiences described in this article face the challenges of modernity through the articulation of daily practices that respond creatively to the needs to redefine categories and concepts such as environment, dwellings, nature, time, space, and social relations by assigning new values and meanings. Luxury means having the opportunity to spend one's physical and mental strength to self-produce what one needs, fully satisfying personal desires and ambitions. Luxury means having fresh food on the table in every season, during the whole year, and to share it in a community context, even having the chance to find alternative resources to provide one's own sustenance outside the conventional economic channels whose principles are not embraced by ecovillages.

The phenomenon of ecovillages appropriates some of the contradictory aspects classically ascribed to modernity, converting them into positive elements, into individual and collective tools of growth and enrichment. The main example is the centrality given to individuality that becomes an element of value. In the ecovillages, individuality is enhanced, the uniqueness of the individual and the particular way in which he or she experiences the world become functional instruments to recreate the dimension of community and shared sociality. This is possible in relation to an aesthetic meant as a paradigm through which to interpret the complexity of contemporary life. This aesthetic supports the agency of individuals and groups and enables them to produce concrete practices that are fully included in a horizon of sustainability.

## Notes

1   It is useful to recall Marshall Sahlins' idea (1980) that societies living in an economy of sustenance are the only ones that know and experience real wealth. Sahlins claims that the first source of wealth of "primitives" is having faith. This attitude would be the engine of their economics system: "What founds the trust of the primitives, and makes them live in abundance even in starving conditions is after all the transparency and the reciprocity of social relationships. [. . .] In the economy of the gift and of the symbolic exchange, a small and always finite quantity of goods is sufficient to have a general wealth, since those goods constantly move from one member to the other. Wealth is not funded on goods, but on the concrete exchange among people" (Sahlins, 1968, in Baudrillard, 1976: 62).
2   Rainbow Family is a movement that arose during the 1970s in the United States of America. It is a spontaneous network of individuals and families inspired by the values of non-violence and pacifism. They meet periodically in forests to celebrate nature and the elements that constitute it. The internal organization of these meetings is completely self-managed, there are no official leaders or structure, no official spokespersons, and no membership formalized. The purpose of these meetings, which can last more than a month, is to reconnect humans with nature. Workshops and various kinds of activities are held on these occasions, such as meditation, prayers, or observance of silence. Many of the rituals adopted by the Rainbow Family refer to Native American traditions. The name itself is inspired by an old native prophecy: "When the earth is ravaged and the animals are dying, a new tribe of people shall come unto the earth from many colors, classes, creeds, and who by their actions and deeds shall make the earth green again. They will be known as the warriors of the Rainbow."
3   Qualitative methodology is applied, involving a period of fieldwork and participant observation and collection of oral narratives from people involved in food practices. In addition, an online survey was carried out in order to map all of the ecovillages and intentional communities that are present in Italy.

## References

Baudrillard, J. (1976) *La società dei consumi*, Bologna: Il Mulino.
Berleant, A. (2005) *Ideas for a Social Aesthetic*, in A. Light (2005), *The Aesthetics of Everyday Life*, New York: Columbia University Press.
Bourdieu, P. (1983) *La distinzione. Critica sociale del gusto*, Bologna: Il Mulino.
Castells, M. (1999) *La era de la informacion*, Mexico: Siglo XXI.
Drengson, A., Devall, B., and Schroll, M. (2011) "The deep ecology movement: origins, development, and future prospects (toward a transpersonal ecosophy)," *International Journal of Transpersonal Studies*, 30(1–2): 101–117.
Douglas, M. (1999) *Questioni di Gusto*, Bologna: Il Mulino.

Douglas, M. and Isherwood, B. (1979) *The World of Goods: Towards an Anthropology of Consumption*, New York: Basics Books.

Fabris, G. (2003) *Il nuovo consumatore: verso il postmoderno*, Milan: FrancoAngeli.

Fischler, C. (1980) "Food habits, social change and the nature/culture dilemma," *Social Science Information*, 19(6): 937–953.

Flandrin, J.L. and Montanari, M. (1997) *Storia dell'alimentazione*, Roma-Bari: La Terza.

Fukuoka, M. (1978) *The One-Straw Revolution*, Emmaus, PA: Rodale Press.

Goldsmith, E. (1997) *Il tao dell'ecologia*, Padua: Muzzio.

Goodman, D. (1999) "Agro-food studies in the 'age of ecology': nature, corporeality, bio-politics," *Sociologia Ruralis*, 39(1): 17–38.

Lanternari, V. (2003) *Ecoantropologia*, Bari: Dedalo Edizioni.

Latouche, S. (2007) *La scommessa della decrescita*, Milan: Feltrinelli.

Leonini, L. and Sassatelli, R. (2008) *Il consumo critico*, Bari: Laterza.

Lévi-Strauss, C. (2008) *Il crudo e il cotto*, Milan: Il Saggiatore.

Lupton, D. (1996) *Food, the Body and the Self*, London: Sage.

Maffesoli, M. (2004) *Il tempo delle tribù, il declino dell'individualismo nelle società di massa*, Milan: Guerini e Associati.

Mellor, M. (2006) "Ecofeminist political economy," *International Journal of Green Economies*, 1–2: 139–150.

Melucci, A. (2000) *Culture in gioco*, Milan: Il Saggiatore.

Murdoch, J. (2001) "Ecologising sociology: actor-network theory, co-construction and the problem of human exemptionalism," *Sociology*, 35(1): 111–133.

Naess, A. (1973) "The shallow and the deep, long range ecology movement," *Inquir*, 16: 95–100.

Pollan, M. (2006) *The Omnivore's Dilemma: A Natural History of Four Meals*, New York: Penguin Books.

Poulain, J. (2008) *Alimentazione cultura e società*, Bologna: Il Mulino.

Reny, M. and Mollison, B. (2007) *Introduzione alla permacultura*, Florence: Terra nuova edizioni.

Sahlins, M. (1968) "La première société d'abondance," *Les Temps modernes*, 268.

Sahlins, M. (1980) *L'economia dell'età della pietra*, Milan: Bompiani.

Salleh, A. (1984) "Deeper than deep ecology: the eco-feminist connections," *Environmental Ethics*, 6: 335–341.

Sassatelli, R. (2004) *Consumo, cultura e società*, Bologna: Il Mulino.

Shiva, V. (2002) *Terra madre: Sopravvivere allo sviluppo*, Torino: UTET.

Stevens, P. (2012) "Towards an ecosociology," *Sociology*, 46(4): 579–595.

Warde, A. (1997) *Consumption, Food and Taste*, London: Sage.

# 2

# SPIRITUALITY, SOCIAL IDENTITY, AND SUSTAINABILITY

*Peter Varga*

## Conventional versus sustainable consumerism

Mega food stores, in general, enjoy a steady growth all over the world (Stoeckel, 2008; Agence Bio, 2012). According to Agence Bio, a French organization, today 71 percent of French people opt for sustainably produced food as opposed to only 64 percent in 2011. Eight percent of French people consume organic food on a daily basis and 21 percent occasionally. In fact, around 80 percent of consumers consider that organic food is better for health and the environment. In 2012, 80 percent of "sustainable" consumers preferred to purchase their food in mega food stores rather than in specialized stores or directly from farmers compared to 63 percent in 2011 (Agence Bio, 2012).

Mass-produced conventional food, also called industrial food, has been part of our everyday life in Western societies since the mid-twentieth century, when mass production gradually replaced small-scale businesses through economies of scale. One of the major outcomes of the postwar period was that the production capacities of the food industry, among others, have been growing in quantity and certainly in quality all over the world, too. As a consequence, consumerism as social and economic phenomena appeared where meeting basic alimentary needs is not the major challenge anymore (Smart, 2010). Levine criticized consumerism-related materialism in the twenty-first century as "a shift away from values of community, spirituality, and integrity, and toward competition, materialism and disconnection" (Levine, 2007).

In today's postmodern societies where established social norms, values, and institutions are changing rapidly, we often associate health with our eating habits. Nevertheless, we should not forget that the correlation between food and health was already part of the social and medical thinking of the past. "Dis-moi ce que tu manges, je te dirai ce que tu es" (Tell me what you eat, and I will tell you who you are) said nineteenth-century food scientist Anthelme Brillat-Savarin (Rosen, 2011: 64). A few decades later, Ludwig Andreas von Feuerbach (1863/1864) also believed that "Der Mensch ist, was er isst" (Man is what he eats), referring not only to the nutritional but also the spiritual meaning of our relationship to food (Rosen, 2011: 64).

Generally speaking, today's food consumerism is a result of a strong economic progress and active commercial relationships between countries and regions. Globalization appears in all spheres of human life. According to Giddens (1991: 64), "globalization can thus be defined as the intensification of worldwide social relations which link distant localities in such a way that local happenings are shaped by events occurring many miles away and vice versa." Therefore, in relation to food consumerism, we should be reminded that coffee is not originally from Latin America and cocoa did not exist in the Ivory Coast, neither was the potato part of the Indian "traditional cuisine." These are all results of geopolitical and economic influences decided by the political and economic elite of the Western world (Fumey and Guyau, 2012).

As a consequence, we can say that our eating habits and the symbolical interpretation of the food we consume have been shaped by global dynamics. Therefore, in our quest for understanding spirituality in today's paradoxical association of *sustainable food consumerism*, one should focus on the historical and social dynamics of past societies. In this manner, we can explore the driving forces behind cultural and also individual preferences for particular food items.

## Food and spirituality of the past

Religious food taboos of the past explain how the spiritual relationships between food and humans characterized our connection to the natural and social environments which surrounded us. According to Lévi-Strauss (2013) cooking techniques and consumed food in general demarcate cultures and human interactions in society. In his "culinary triangle" concept, Lévi-Strauss explains that cooking techniques such as roasted, grilled, smoked, and boiled correspond to certain structural developments of the studied culture. In this sense, as a continuation of Strauss' structural approach, postmodern societies can also be analyzed from their current eating habits, such as, for instance, fast food, frozen, and organic products. In fact, the food we consume allows us to understand our cultural materials, social interactions, and symbols that organize the different visions of the world through space and time (Garabuau-Moussaoui, in Duhart, 2005).

Past examples of food spirituality described by Western discourses can be drawn from Marvin Harris, who evoked the idea that spiritual approaches to taboos and eating restrictions always have a materialistic interpretation. In his book *Cows, Pigs, Wars and Witches* (1989) Harris explained that besides the religious/spiritual prohibition of beef in the Indian caste system there was a pragmatic, very much economic-based logic behind it in order to sustain Indian agriculture. Similarly, religious pork prohibition in Muslim and Jewish diets probably correlated both with an environmental incompatibility between man and animal and also with the establishment of social identities that led to an ecological equilibrium among humans and nature in a specific climate (Harris, 1989).

From a sociological perspective, the food that we consume is linked to our social classes, which reflect our tastes, values, and identities (Bourdieu, 1986). In ancient Rome, for example, the passion for some spices such as pepper characterized upper classes that had access to this exotic and expensive delicacy (Gibbon, 2003). Later, in the late Middle Ages, initial social stratification can be explained, among other reasons, by the physical interconnected-ness with the East that was brought into European reach by the Silk Road. Exotic spices such as saffron, cinnamon, cloves, ginger, and nutmeg were popular among medieval lords because they showed prestige and social status (Hobhouse, 1986). The more spices a feudal lord could manifest in the meal in front of his guests, the more his social status was approved by the upper society.

Spices not only meant prestige and social status but also a form of spiritual connection with the new and idealized world where people lived differently from the people in the late

European Middle Ages (eleventh–thirteenth centuries). Therefore, many items and rituals that originated in the East (the American continent was unknown at the time) fulfilled a rather latent ceremonial function in the ideological and spiritual openings of the European aristocrats. Consuming spices and exotic items was considered luxurious and only accessible to rich people who deliberately maintained their social and economic privileges through these exotic items. It is not without reason that it was the Spanish royal family who financed Christopher Columbus' first voyage to discover new trade routes to the Far East where the exotic and treasured spices originated (Schivelbusch, 1992).

As Schivelbusch (1992) pointed out in his book *Tastes of Paradise*, the growing spice trade with Asia resulted in a saturated market in Europe in the seventeenth century. As a consequence, European upper classes started to search for new tastes and rituals to sustain social differences. During the eighteenth-century Enlightenment period, cocoa, coffee, and tea were some of the food items that served not only to distinguish social classes but also as a spiritual and intellectual boost for social change in general in European societies. Coffee, for instance, "served" as a spiritual panacea for all kinds of medical problems in the seventeenth century, despite the fact that it was not approved by the medical sciences of the time. Notwithstanding, this previously unknown drink in Europe became a major foodstuff of the future upper and upper-middle classes due to its manifest and also latent functions. Coffee not only kept people awake, but it also meant discipline and success in contrast to the laziness, illiteracy, and poverty of the masses. Thus, coffee contributed to the intellectual and social emergence of the bourgeoisie by symbolically establishing social distinction. To a certain extent, it also triggered the gender struggle for equal rights among women who previously did not have the right to consume it (Fernández-Armesto, 2004).

Nevertheless, the spiritual depreciation of formerly cherished exotic spices and food items was unavoidable. The very expensive chocolate, for example, as a solely religious and upper-class beverage of the seventeenth century has become a morning drink for today's children. The function of traditional British tea-time as a social ritual among upper-class members, which can be associated with Asian spirituality, has been gradually replaced by another popular drink: coffee. Today's coffee-drinking lifestyle is endlessly reinterpreted in society through the media. Coffee symbolizes harmony, seduction, romanticism, semi-individuality, self-identity, meditation, efficiency, and friendship, among others. In fact, coffee is appreciated in any situation and in any moment, exactly as it was perceived during its initial phase in the seventeenth-century European societies (Schivelbusch, 1992).

As a result, coffee is living its renaissance from a spiritual and also from an economic perspective today because it fulfills a practical and symbolic role in today's societies. It does not only help us in our daily routine tasks, but it also provides us with a fashionable touch, due to the multitude of varieties, to find the most pertinent reason behind one's choice to consume it. Today's famous coffee advertisements hint that personality, identity, and even spirituality are shaped by the type of coffee one consumes. To a certain extent it is similar to people's preference for organic food nowadays. Since conventional food production has been broadly criticized in Western societies, people look for answers and solutions that meet their expectations regarding health, morality, and identity.

## Spirituality of sustainable food

The question of why individuals and, in a larger context, particular social groups in society favor certain foodstuffs today seems interesting to evoke. Indeed, neo-diffusionist theory would interpret it in a way that Western eating habits, among other cultural manifestations, have infiltrated most of the world's cultures. As a consequence, concerning the "McDonaldization of society" (Ritzer, 2012), global Western foods such as fast food and Coca-Cola symbolize a West-centric progress and belonging. The cultural discourse theory would criticize the unequal diffusion of scientific knowledge about today's Western food consumerism in the world (Shi-xu, 2012). From this perspective, the tendency to buy and consume sustainable and organic food seems to be mainly part of Western urban societies due to their increasing health concerns and their decreasing physical connection with food production and farming in general (Macleod and Carrier, 2010).

Ironically, in developing economies, low-scale, non-certified organic food production is basically accessible for an important part of the rural population due to farmers' familiarity with traditional growing methods and also due to the lack of financial incentives to obtain economies of scale through advanced technologies (FAO, 2013). In this context, sustainable food does not seem to attract the same interest in the developing world as in the developed economies. In Western countries, it seems to be a sustainable movement, while in developing societies, mainly in traditional agrarian societies, it seems to be a standard aspect of human subsistence.

The concepts of sustainability and sustainable development in general have become a strong discourse in Western societies since the late 1980s when they were first defined by the Brundtland Report (United Nations World Commission on Environment and Development, 1987). As a consequence, economic and political decisions started to pay attention to sustainable issues that affect humans' social actions. For example, the question of the growing number and varieties of available food on supermarket shelves opened discussions about the origin and reliability of our consumed food (Agence Bio, 2012; Watson and Caldwell, 2005).

Reconsidering Harris' cultural materialistic perspective, which was evoked previously, in today's postmodern societies, one can uphold the notion that sustainable discourses are comparable to religious food taboos. The food people consume symbolizes the individual's striving for survival and social identification, such as it did in the past. In today's Western societies, sustainable food production and consumption has undoubtedly attracted a growing interest in the past decades; nonetheless, sustainable and organic food in general, often imported and not subsidized, is still rather expensive compared to conventional food in Western societies (Kittler et al., 2011).

From these perspectives, today's sustainable/organic food dynamics could remind us of the late Middle Ages and the Renaissance when the European social transformation was strongly influenced by imported food items, such as spices and vegetables. Today's sustainable trend for healthy food in Western societies is comparable to the search for exotic products by the aristocrats of the European Renaissance because many of today's organic foods have their origins in the developing and exotic world. Therefore, Delia Chiaro's expression "taste of otherness" can also be interpreted in the way that sustainability and spirituality are tied together, thus prestige that determines social status also continues to depend on our choices and eating behaviors, exactly as occurred in the Renaissance (Chiaro, 2008).

## Postmodern sustainability?

Denison Nash (2001) defends the idea that the Western cultural influence in developing countries goes beyond physical borders. One of the major agents of this cultural "neo-colonization" is tourism, which allows values and norms of Western societies to invade visited cultures and overtake traditions and authenticity. Part of this unidirectional social phenomenon is the Western extension of eating customs. Even though there is less fascination for exotic and faraway foodstuff in Western societies, as opposed to past centuries, consumers are still influenced by the fact that certain foodstuffs can only have exotic origins. Most of the tropical fruits for instance cannot be harvested in the European continental climate. As a consequence, many of the food items we have on the market spiritually connect us with other cultures and regions of the world.

According to food historian Fernández-Armesto (2004: 19), postmodern individuals strive for narcissism and "romantic primitivism [that] allies with ecological anxiety." Certainly, today's Western food-related sustainable discourses mainly rest on health and environmental awareness due to the fact that religious food taboos do not guide us anymore. Instead, our individual choices enable us to interpret food in an imagined way such as, for instance, a guarantee of a long and healthy existence. In this sense, our individualized eating habits replace supernatural divinities to influence our human experience. As a consequence, contemporary spirituality can also be characterized as a holistic New Age movement that seeks a complete human experience where mind, body and spirit are all interconnected (Spring, 2004). Food can be considered as one of the basic elements of this quest in Western societies.

Borrowing from the French philosopher Roland Barthes' psycho-sociological approach to food consumption (Counihan and Van Esterik, 2008), one of the elements one should consider when trying to understand the growing interest in sustainable food is the previously discussed economic and technological progress that enables us to consume basically whatever we want, whenever we wish. The exoticism of the past remains in today's Western societies but it is progressively experiencing the same path as any other previously mentioned items that were facing a symbolic depreciation. Former luxurious food items and substances became available on a daily basis to everyone in today's societies. On the other hand, as mentioned previously, labeled, organic, and—in this case—sustainable food is often more expensive than its conventional counterpart. Accordingly, labeled/sustainable food is not easily available for all social classes on a daily basis in Western societies, which justifies past dynamics on social status and symbolic separation of urban upper-middle classes even in postmodern societies where people build their identities through the perception that others have of them.

Barthes also applies the concept of communication that connects us with the food we consume to the society we live in. By choosing sustainable food, people may also express a form of intellectual and spiritual distinction that is based on financial and cultural capitals (Bourdieu, 1986). The individual or collective identity that is created by a sustainable choice might attract approval or disapproval from our fellow citizens; nevertheless it demarcates the social relationships and the expectations of people with sustainable preferences. If we connect this dimension with the previously mentioned idea of "neo-colonization" (Nash, 2001), we can correlate spiritual and also internal colonization of new segments in Western societies, based on economic and/or cultural capitals, which tend to differentiate their identity from other segments and justify this difference through their eating habits and choices.

From the anthropological perspective of embodiment, consuming sustainable and, in this context, probably healthier food guarantees one a daily interconnectedness with nature that seems to be increasingly appreciated by the upper-middle classes of postmodern, urban populations (Macleod and Carrier, 2010). This spiritual quest for natural and healthier food can be connected to eighteenth-century Renaissance philosophical movements, such as Rousseau's idea of the Noble Savage, when the individuals who were closely related to nature were more cherished than the ones who were socially and politically polluted in European urban areas. Today, the collective trust of Western societies in large-scale, industrial food production seems to be affected by the increasing detachment of their practices from nature (McMillan and Coveney, 2010; Shiva, 2013). Nevertheless, due to the increased access to information, upper-middle classes in Western societies gain knowledge and understanding of Western eating habits and their enigmatic impacts on our most precious individual treasury: health.

A puzzling element of our cognitive connection to food is the way consumerism generates specific desires when faced with a multitude of choices through advertisements. Today's elderly generations can easily recall, for instance, the theatrical symbiosis established by multinational companies, between nature, adventure, virility, and cigarettes. Due to scientific results and political engagement, the younger generations can only find evidence of this former spiritual invasion of the individual through vintage archives on the web.

In fact, conventional food advertising is perpetually invading our private space because ads find new means of communication often in a still uncontrollable way on the web. There are some sustainable trends these days, which focus on food labels; however, companies often generate a sort of inauthentic authenticity by attracting consumers' attention to the place and context of production (Cohen, 1988). French-made cheese, Argentinian beef, real hamburgers, or farmer-made items have the goal of convincing consumers about the authenticity and realness of the specific product. Stiles et al. (2011) explain this phenomenon with the concept of "ghost of taste," when people associate an imagined truthfulness of the advertised food product with its origin, such as a farmer's photo on a meat package. This spiritual interconnectedness with the unreal characteristics of the offered item can also remind us of a sort of "hyperreality" (Baudrillard, 1995), where consumers imagine the non-existent synergies of the way and place of production with health and nature that gratify one's spiritual fulfillment.

Local and global food dynamics (Stiles et al., 2011) can justify this imagined unreal-reality because consumers are unable to track down the details of pre-purchasing phases. Certainly, eco-labeled items provide information on the origins of the food; however, this information is often limited to the place of production and not to its social and cultural contexts. The image we associate with the eco-labeled food in postmodern consumerism is a moral guarantee of our altruism with others and also with ourselves.

Barthes also evokes the circumstantial adjustment between substance and function in food consumerism (Counihan and Van Esterik, 2008). As in the past, today's food-eating habits contribute to a more functional objective that is self-identification in a society where a rising individualism requires a growing material excuse for socialization and prestige. Coffee breaks replaced tea breaks in most Western societies. Elderly Chinese people observe new generations' preference for coffee, a drink that did not touch Chinese society notably until the 1980s. In this sense, cultural colonization, mentioned previously, is a real global phenomenon. The way individuals identify themselves is highly correlated to the items we consume today. The image of products, such as coffee, justifies a dynamic professional and personal life that fits with postmodern expectations. If a further step is needed for self-identification, then sustainability fulfills the gap because it is new, trendy, perceptible, and healthy.

## Conclusion

The question whether sustainable food consumerism will be maintained as a marginal demand in postmodern societies or will become a global norm cannot be answered yet. If today's spiritual, ecological, and social attachment to sustainable food consumption becomes a norm in Western societies, it will create a global challenge for the food industry and for the political legislation behind it. Since religious doctrines seem to have a reduced influence on our individual food choices, the unconventional scientific understanding of our eating habits will probably contribute to better health awareness in society. Victor Lindlahr, in 1942, already advocated this idea: "ninety per cent of the diseases known to man are caused by cheap foodstuffs. You are what you eat" (Rosen, 2011: 64).

Therefore, the food we consume determines our health and indirectly our role and interactions in society. If health, both physical and mental, stays a primary driving force in increasingly educated societies, social pressure will probably lead to a more reliable food supply for the masses. Nevertheless, if sustainable food is available for all, privileged social classes will probably look for other salient alimentary symbols to identify themselves. We can only hope that they will stay within a controllable and sustainable limit that will not jeopardize future generations' subsistence.

# References

Agence Bio (2012) *10e Baromètre Agence BIO 2012*, www.agencebio.org/sites/default/files/upload/documents/4_Chiffres/Dossier_Presse_AgenceBIO_06022013.pdf.

Baudrillard, J. (1995) *Simulacra and Simulation (The Body, In Theory: Histories of Cultural Materialism)*, Michigan: University of Michigan Press.

Bourdieu, P. (1986) "The forms of capital," in J. Richardson (ed.), *Handbook of Theory and Research for the Sociology of Education*, New York: Greenwood, pp. 241–258.

Chiaro, D. (2008) "A taste of otherness: eating and thinking globally," *European Journal of English Studies*, 12(2): 195–209.

Cohen, E. (1988) "Authenticity and commoditization in tourism," *Annals of Tourism. Research*, 15: 371–386.

Counihan, C. and Van Esterik, P. (eds.) (2008) *Food and Culture: A Reader*, 2nd edn, New York and London: Routledge.

Duhart, F. (2005) "Des perspectives originales pour l'anthropologie de l'alimentation," *Ethnologie française*, 35(1): 161–163.

FAO (2013) *Organic Agriculture*, www.fao.org/organicag/oa-faq/oa-faq5/en.

Fernández-Armesto, F. (2004) *Near Thousand Tables: A History of Food*, New York: Free Press.

Fumey, G. and Guyau, L. (2012) *Géopolitique de l'alimentation*, Paris: Éditions Sciences humaines.

Gibbon, E. (2003) *The Decline and Fall of the Roman Empire*, New York: Modern Library.

Giddens, A. (1991) *The Consequences of Modernity*, Cambridge: Polity Press.

Harris, M. (1989) *Cows, Pigs, Wars and Witches: The Riddles of Culture*, New York: Vintage Books.

Hobhouse, H. (1986) *Seeds of Change: Five Plants that Transformed Mankind*, California: Perennial Library, University of California.

Kittler, P.J., Sucher K.P., and Nelms, M. (2011) *Food and Culture*, 6th edn, Wadsworth: Cengage Learning.

Levine, M. (2007) "Challenging the culture of affluence: schools, parents, and the psychological health of children," *Independent School Magazine*, 67(1): 28–36.

Lévi-Strauss, C. (2013) "The culinary triangle," in C. Counihan and P. Van Esterik (eds.), *Food and Culture*, 3rd edn, New York and London: Routledge, pp. 40–47.

Lindlahr, V. (1942) "You are what you eat," *Journal of Living*.

Macleod, D. and Carrier, J. (2010) *Tourism, Power and Culture: Anthropological Insights. Tourism and Cultural Change*, Bristol: Channel View Publications.

McMillan, J. and Coveney, J. (2010) "What took you so long? Sociology's recent foray into food," *Health Sociology Review*, 19(3): 282–284.

Nash, D. (2001) *Anthropology of Tourism*, Bingley: Emerald Group Publishing.

Ritzer, G. (2012) *The McDonaldization of Society: 20th Anniversary Edition*, 7th edn, Thousand Oaks, CA: Sage.

Rosen, J.S. (2011) *Food for the Soul: Vegetarianism and Yoga Traditions*, Santa Barbara, CA: Praeger Publishers Inc.

Schivelbusch, W. (1992) *Tastes of Paradise: A Social History of Spices, Stimulants, and Intoxicants*, New York: Vintage Books.

Shiva, V. (2013) *Making Peace with the Earth*, London: Pluto Press.

Shi-xu (2012) "Why do cultural discourse studies? Towards a culturally conscious and critical approach to human discourses," *Critical Arts: South-North Cultural and Media Studies*, 26(4): 484–503.

Smart, B. (2010) *Consumer Society*, Thousand Oaks, CA: Sage.

Spring, J. (2004) *How Educational Ideologies Are Shaping Global Society: Intergovernmental Organizations, NGOs, and the Decline of the Nation-State*, New York: Routledge.

Stiles, K., Altiok, O., and Bell, M. (2011) "The ghosts of taste: food and the cultural politics of authenticity," *Agriculture and Human Values*, 28(2): 225–236.

Stoeckel, A. (2008) *High Food Prices: Causes, Implications and Solutions. Rural Industries Research and Development Corporation*, www.rirdc.gov.au (accessed November 17, 2013).

United Nations World Commission on Environment and Development (1987) *Our Common Future*, Oxford: Oxford University Press.

Watson, J.L. and Caldwell, M. (2005) *The Cultural Politics of Food and Eating*, Oxford: Blackwell.

# 3

# 'SUSTAINABLE FOOD': WHOSE RESPONSIBILITY IS IT ANYWAY?

## A personal commentary

### *Clare Hindley*

> It shouldn't be the consumer's responsibility to figure out what's cruel and what's kind, what's environmentally destructive and what's sustainable.
> *Jonathan Safran Foer,* Eating Animals *(Little, Brown and Company, 2009)*

'Sustainable' and 'food' are well-established entries in a standard dictionary (Oxford Dictionaries, n.d.), but 'sustainable food' has yet to earn its place. The combination of the two ideas is left to the individual. This could partly in itself offer the definition, as the consumer is indeed faced with a broad and sometimes unclear concept accompanied by a seemingly unending string of decisions and considerations when trying to consume and/or purchase sustainable food (Tobler et al., 2011). Certainly dictionaries play less of a role in defining each individual's world than the media and in fact our assessment of 'sustainable' and 'food' are both heavily influenced by our media consumption (Wansink and Sobal, 2007, Greenslade, 2011).

In 1980s London, being sustainable meant reading *The Guardian* newspaper, riding a bicycle, shopping at a wholefood (organic) shop and being vegetarian (Rieff, 2005; Robinson, 2010). Somehow, maybe apart from riding a bicycle and reading *The Guardian*, the items were not really separable. Wholefood shops did not really seem to stock much, if any, meat; organic intrinsically meant vegetarian. Choosing to be vegetarian meant an initial step towards rescuing mankind from its seemingly inevitable destruction of the planet, but was naturally also influenced by the desire to fit into the peer group of 20-somethings in London. There was a certain knowledge that destroying the rainforest, the Amazon in particular, meant eating tofu was better than eating meat, but the exact link wasn't spontaneously clear. Somehow it was connected to Live Aid and the knowledge that tofu rather than meat could 'save the world'. Living in London also involved eating at Cranks and marvelling at what one could do without meat and with brown rice and lentils. The later demise of this extremely successful restaurant chain in London in 2001 with a concept referred to as 'anachronistic' (Pook, 2001) maybe showed that this image did stay stuck in the 1980s too long. What we never questioned was that the tofu had travelled halfway round the globe, presumably leaving its trail of transportation pollution, in contrast to some of the meat that was local produce. 'Sustainability' and 'food miles' had not yet become common parlance (McKie, 2008). Rye bread from Germany was simply perceived as more politically correct than the local baker's produce. Organic carrots from Italy were undeniably more exotic and certainly more morally correct than non-organic carrots from down the road. Shunning the supermarkets was an integral part of seeking organic food as none or at least very few stocked organic produce. However, the belief in tofu was only carried out to the full by those who 'went the whole way' and became vegans. The majority were not really disciplined enough to renounce leather bags and shoes not to mention honey and milk chocolate. We all knew what 'fruit-arians' were, had toyed with the idea, but knew problems would arise when we still wanted to go home to mum for some good home-cooking. We were aware of the food crisis with regard to certain African nations suffering from famine but the fact that supermarkets in the UK were already throwing away food simply because it was past its sell-by date or blemished had not seeped through yet (Rubin, 2002). The word 'sustainable' was not part of our vocabulary, but we were creating our own definitions of what later would be called sustainable.

These definitions and somewhat vague ideas were heavily influenced by particular concrete events. 'Those years of the late 70s and early 80s [were] extraordinarily exciting. England was being convulsed by a social, cultural and political counter-revolution' (Cowley, 2009). The decision to become vegetarian was not just a dietary decision; it was a clear political, social and moral positioning influenced by a desire to 'react'. 'For much of Britain, including London, the 1980s was a brutal decade of poverty and unemployment, to say nothing of strikes, riots and bombings' (Harris, 2006). In 1980s UK there was definitely a lot to react to: Margaret Thatcher, the miners' strike, the Falklands War, Brixton and Toxteth riots, IRA bombs, not to mention the more international concerns of Apartheid and Reagan's Central American policies (a close ally of Thatcher). Of course, choosing to be vegetarian was not expected to change the political course of Britain, but it was a way of positioning ourselves and showing a willingness to take responsibility. In this whirlwind of social, cultural and political changes famine, music and fur stand out as particularly symbolic in the decision to be a 1980s (sustainable) vegetarian.

Famine was a concept everyone was conscious of, but it didn't affect us directly until 13 July 1985. On this day nearly 2 billion people 'woke up with one purpose. Nearly a third of humanity knew where they were going to be that day. Watching, listening to, attending: Live Aid' (Jones in Bainbridge, 2013). 'Live Aid was the day that pop stars started having to be role models' (Bainbridge, 2013). Despite the fact that Live Aid was an initiative to raise money to alleviate the famine in Ethiopia, it provided the motivation to think about and review our own consumption. Linked to this was that eating less or, ideally, no meat could feed more people. The impact of Live Aid cannot be overstated and Dylan Jones (in Bainbridge 2013) refers to it as the time 'when a nation's attitudes and expectations were somehow captured and changed forever'. We watched, we sang, we donated and we took it upon ourselves to change the world.

Music was, of course not only Live Aid and the bands represented there. The 1980s saw the rise of many bands including the British band, The Smiths, with their 'Meat is Murder' single advocating vegetarianism. 'Meat Is Murder's sinister opening, full of strange noises that conjure up an abattoir, moves into a terrible, beautiful melody. "The carcass you carve with a smile, it is murder . . . And the turkey you festively slice, it is murder" ' (Viner, 2011). Morrissey, the lead singer, was very vocal about his vegetarianism and was renowned also for voicing his political beliefs. 'Around the time of the release of Meat Is Murder, Morrissey's interviews were becoming increasingly political as he trashed the Thatcher administration and campaigned for vegetarianism' (Erlewine, n.d.). Thus the link between politics, music and diet was made.

The 1980s also saw the establishment of many animal rights initiatives. There was 'a widespread shift in thinking about how we ought to treat animals. Britain . . . played an important role in this area of . . . moral concern' (Singer, 2001). 'In the 1980s, experimentation on animals became a "hot topic" as cosmetics companies testing their products on animals suddenly became a big "no no" ' (Ethical Consumer, n.d.). The anti-fur campaigns, although not directly linked to vegetarianism, were part of the animal welfare movement. With slogans such as 'It takes up to 40 dumb animals to make a fur coat. But only one to wear it' (Lynx anti-fur poster, 1984) and posters showing animals caught in steel traps, the public was beginning to see fur in a new way (Anti-Fur Movement, 2012). 'The anti-fur organisation in 1985, enlist[ed] top models of the day, musicians and photographers to their cause with a series of high-profile adverts and publicity stunts [. . .] made not wearing fur trendy and [gave] pariah status to anyone who chose to ignore the message' (EADT, 2012). Such widespread campaigns and such a clear message left a lasting impression and were another building block in the creation of 'sustainability'.

These events, influences and personalities were a significant part of the formation of our individual ideals and beliefs. Human welfare issues, environmental concerns and even political opinions and musical tastes were relatively easily aligned. The path forward seemed clear. The question, however, arises as to whether this is simply a personal interpretation, a capital city issue, only the UK or possibly a wider European movement.

Education played no or a very limited role in developing our ideas. Girls still had home economics/domestic science as a compulsory school subject and certainly no one discussed where the food came from, the role of meat in our diet or the impact of our consumption on the environment. Working in a small town in southern Spain in the 1980s, vegetarian cuisine in restaurants meant accepting the meat casserole and simply taking the meat out. The only wholefood shop was a tiny room that closed during my stay. Germany, famous in the UK for the green movement, was not much different. Traditional cuisine amounted to variations of meat and two veg and the vegetarian option was simply two veg (Hughes, 2013). 'Until very recently chefs in Germany showed very little creativity in vegetarian cooking and the vegetarian option in restaurants amounted to very little more than a . . . vegetable plate, with or without egg' (Puskar-Pasewicz, 2010: 118). However, the Bioladen (wholefood store) was already well-established with the same link to vegetarianism as in the UK, despite the fact that animal welfare was not as widely discussed.

Nowadays the millennials and generation Z face other challenges. It's simply not so easy to eat sustainably. Schools, at least in Germany, in subjects such as food science, economics, politics and social science deal specifically with related topics. Children aged 14–15 carry out projects on, among other things, sustainable winter sports, sustainable energy production, sustainable clothing production and sustainable food. Presentations are given, papers written and debates held to actively prepare and encourage pupils to make the decisions the twenty-first century demands. Even children's TV includes daily 'science' programmes discussing the same and more. The internet – well known for its easy access to information but also its inability to sort 'useful' from 'overload' and 'inaccurate' – provides another source of info inundating the (future) consumer with factors that 'should' all be part of the purchasing decision (Confino, 2010).

The result: a 15-year-old German standing in the local supermarket making a mature decision to act responsibly and put their understanding of sustainability into practice and asking simply: which product is more sustainable? The local carrots or the Israeli organic carrots? What matters most, the food miles, the organic product, fair trade or the support of the local producer? How can it be that the haricot beans are imported from Tanzania, doesn't Africa have a food shortage? Does purchasing the Tanzanian beans support the local community there; surely it is ridiculous to import beans from so far away when so many farmers in Germany produce them? The issue is not helped by another customer saying that we should buy local produce to stop 'all those foreigners stealing our jobs'. That doesn't really support the first attempt at making a sustainable decision. The bananas are easier as thankfully there are no German bananas! However, there's still the issue of organic bananas, non-organic bananas or non-organic/fair trade bananas. It's best not to delve too deeply into the numerous discussions on how fair 'fair trade' actually is (Organic Consumers Association, 2005; Elliott, 2012). The confectionery section offers the next challenge, with the choice of organic, organic/fair trade, non-organic/fair trade or non-organic produce. Again a difficult decision – probably organic/fair trade means we've made the most sustainable decision, but in this case personal experience has established this particular chocolate doesn't actually taste that good. Should the consumer forget their maturing culinary tastes and eat chocolate they don't like just to be sustainable? The decision is not made easier by the fact that currently labelling is not the food industry's most renowned trait and can we really believe what is in the product anyway? As Alan Reilly, chief executive of the Food Safety Authority of Ireland, stated: 'The most important ingredient in food is trust, and once consumers lose that, it takes a long time to get it back' (Reilly, 2013).

The final criterion is then simply the 'best before' date, often seen as a line not to be crossed (Stillman, 2011). The media is awash with information on the global food crisis, but surely this means there isn't enough food for the world, not that here in Europe people should maybe consider that the yoghurt they won't touch because today is its sell-by-date will later the same day be on the mountain of 'unwanted/unneeded' food disposed of daily. Thank goodness the multi-buy, three for the price of two craze has not hit Germany yet. As once the initial purchasing frenzy is over it becomes clear that a two-person household doesn't actually want three for the price of two – they want two, as otherwise the third will simply be thrown away (Smithers, 2013) and join the supermarket mountain. Does this mean, when confronted with bulk-buying offers, in order to be sustainable the menu for the week should already be clear to avoid overbuying? Thank goodness a 14–15-year-old does not have yet to take the price into consideration and 'sustainable packaging' will only be discussed in next term's curriculum.

Despite my long career as a 1980s sustainable, organic, fair trade, bike-riding, *Guardian*-reading vegetarian, I can't really help generation Z's decision except to say that we had it easier. Maybe van Vark (2013b) is right in stressing that 'Customers want food they can trust and expect retailers to do the ethical and environmental thinking for them'. For various reasons, the individual often does not want to tackle these decisions and the pressure is indeed on the retailers to do the ethical and environmental thinking for them. 'For retailers, this mainstreaming of sustainability throughout the system will be a challenge [. . .], but it's one they can't shy away from' (van Vark, 2013a). Even the individual who willingly faces the challenge of seeking out 'sustainable food' can be overwhelmed with the multitude of ethical and environmental issues involved.

Despite the dictionary's difficulty with 'sustainable food', it does offer a definition of 'food for thought' defined as 'something that warrants serious consideration' – maybe this would be a suitable entry for 'sustainable food', just leaving it open to interpretation as to who is responsible for this 'serious consideration'.

# References

*Online newspapers and blogs are the primary sources for the above text, based on these information channels being highly influential on consumer attitudes and behaviour.*

Anti-Fur Movement (2012) 'The rise of the Anti-Fur Movement', www.allisonsmf.wordpress.com.

Bainbridge, L. (2013) *'The Eighties: One Day, One Decade* by Dylan Jones – review', www.theguardian.com/books/2013/jul/08/one-day-decade-dylan-jones-review.

Beckett, A. (2013) *'Bang! A History of Britain in the 1980s* by Graham Stewart – review', www.theguardian.com/books/2013/jan/17/bang-history-britain-1980s-review.

Confino, J. (2010) 'Does the tidal wave of information on the web create more informed citizens?', www.theguardian.com/sustainability/blog/media-literacy.

Cowley, J. (2009) 'England was convulsed by a social and political revolution', www.theguardian.com/books/2009/apr/19/1980s-cultural-history.

EADT (2012) 'How Lynx set the fur flying', www.eadt.co.uk/news/features_2_483/how_lynx_set_the_fur_flying_1_1184497.

Elliott, K.A. (2012) 'Is my fair trade coffee really fair?', www.cgdev.org/doc/full_text/policyPapers/1426831/Is-My-Fair-Trade-Coffee-Really-Fair.html.

Erlewine, S.T. (n.d.) 'The Smiths artist biography', www.allmusic.com/artist/the-smiths-mn0000899530/biography.

Ethical Consumer (n.d.) 'Animal testing', www.ethicalconsumer.org/shoppingethically/ourethicalratings/animalrights.aspx.

Foer, J.S. (n.d.) www.goodreads.com/quotes/tag/sustainability.

Greenslade, R. (2011) 'How newspapers, despite decline, still influence the political process', www.theguardian.com/media/greenslade/2011/jun/21/national-newspapers-newspapers.

Harris, J. (2006) 'So the 1980s were one long orgy of champagne and shoulder pads? What about the riots, poverty and bombings?', www.theguardian.com/commentisfree/2006/apr/26/bookscomment.workandcareers.

Hughes, J. (2013) 'The best countries in the world to be vegetarian', www.theguardian.com/lifeandstyle/wordofmouth/2013/sep/23/best-countries-to-be-vegetarian.

McKie, R. (2008) 'How the myth of food miles hurts the planet', www.theguardian.com/environment/2008/mar/23/food.ethicalliving.

Organic Consumers Association (2005) 'Nestlé reported to UK Advertising Standards Authority over dishonest Fairtrade product advertisement,' www.organicconsumers.org/fair-trade/nestle.cfm.

Oxford Dictionaries (n.d.) www.oxforddictionaries.com.

Pook, S (2001) 'Cranks vegetarian restaurants to close', www.telegraph.co.uk/news/uknews/1365608/Cranks-vegetarian-restaurants-to-close.html.

Puskar-Pasewicz, M. (2010). *Cultural Encyclopedia of Vegetarianism*, Santa Barbara, CA: ABC-CLIO.

Reilly, A. (2013) 'The horsemeat scandal erupts', www.theguardian.com/world/2013/dec/29/2013-eyewitness-accounts-horsemeat-scandal-erupts.

Rieff, D. (2005) 'Cruel to be kind', www.theguardian.com/world/2005/jun/24/g8.debtrelief.

Robinson, J. (2010) 'BBC marks 25th anniversary of Live Aid with Bob Geldof drama', www.theguardian.com/world/2010/jul/14/bob-geldof-live-aid-bbc2.

Rubin, G. (2002) 'It ain't pretty and it ain't so tasty either', www.theguardian.com/money/2006/jul/02/observercashsection.theobserver2.

Searle, A. (2013) 'Journey through London subculture is a fascinating ragbag bursting with life', www.theguardian.com/culture/2013/sep/12/journey-london-subculture-fascinating-ragbag.

Singer, P. (2001) 'Animal rights: the right to protest', www.utilitarianism.net/singer/by/20010121.htm.

Smithers, J. (2013) 'UK supermarkets face mounting pressure to cut food waste', www.theguardian.com/business/2013/oct/21/uk-supermarkets-pressure-cut-food-waste.

Stillman, J. (2011) 'The kids are risk averse: will the recession scar gen Y?', www.cbsnews.com/news/the-kids-are-risk-averse-will-the-recession-scar-gen-y/.

Tobler, C., Visschers, V.H.M. and Siegrist, M. (2011) 'Organic tomatoes versus canned beans', *Environment and Behavior*, 43(5): 591–611.

van Vark, C. (2013a) 'Shoppers stick to ethical principles despite financial pressures', www.theguardian.com/sustainable-business/shoppers-stick-to-ethical-principles.

van Vark, C. (2013b) 'Sustainable food chains make business sense and consumers happy', www.theguardian.com/sustainable-business/sustainable-food-chains-make-business-sense.

Viner, K (2011) 'My favourite album: *Meat Is Murder* by the Smiths', www.theguardian.com/music/musicblog/2011/oct/14/meat-murder-smiths.

Wansink, B. and Sobal, J. (2007) 'Mindless eating: the 200 daily food decisions we overlook', *Environment and Behavior*, 39(1): 106–123.

# 4

# FOOD FOR THOUGHT

## Culinary heritage, nostalgia, and food history

*Paul Cleave*

## Introduction

Our food, how and what we eat is constantly changing. Food historians have documented the evolution of our diets (Drummond and Wilbraham, 1957; Spencer, 2002; Tannahill, 1973), suggesting that change is stimulated by many factors: political, social, economic, and ethical. These are complemented by Visser (1991: 345), who draws on examples of culinary tradition in the consumption of special, celebratory meals and day-to-day eating. Spang (2000: 2) identifies the origins of modern commercial hospitality, and the restaurant as a space of urban sociability since emerging in the late eighteenth century. Learning from the past and the experiences of others develops our understanding of society and the evolving role of gastronomy.

This chapter proposes that an appreciation of food history in the context of Lashley's (2007) domains of domestic and commercial hospitality is significant in future gastronomic/culinary development. Drawing on the valuable work of late nineteenth- and early twentieth-century food writers – for example, Newnham-Davis (1912, 1914), Hartley (1979), White (1932), and the English Folk Cookery Association in the 1930s – it includes examples of European hotels and restaurants. These provide a framework for investigation, and demonstrate how foods are influenced by other cultures and traditions, and are subsequently presented to the visiting public.

Utilizing the timescale of a century, the changing experience of hospitality will be employed to show how food is subject to trends and fashions and that, as our taste and life-styles change, so does food consumption. Examples from the early twentieth century demonstrate how culinary taste is influenced by world events and technology, and that the experience of eating away from home has evolved. This is an important period in the historiography of gastronomy and hospitality. The public were becoming accustomed to travel for leisure, whether on a day excursion, staying at a holiday camp, or on a European tour (Graves and Hodge, 1941: 380–381). Trends in leisure consumption are identified by Pimlott (1976: 241–242), who suggests that, by the early twentieth century, holidaymaking had become a cult and was for many associated with the prevailing attraction of health resorts and an interest in fitness (Fortescue-Fox, 1938). Hall and Gössling (2013: 10–14), assert that there is an increasing public and academic interest in local foods, sustainability, and food tourism. A growing world population and changes in dietary preference are contrasted with the prolif-eration of local food systems. These are characterized by a close relationship between producer and consumer. The origins and logic of farmers' markets, Slow Food, and sourcing local produce and suppliers can be detected in examples from our collective culinary history. This chapter explores origins and influences of current trends in sustainable food production and consumption.

## Food consumption: eating away from home

As the public became accustomed to travel for leisure and pleasure in the early twentieth century, food and hospitality became an important component of the experience. Guide books – for example, Muirhead's, *The Blue Guides, England* (1939) – provide details of food and hospitality provision, indicating an interest in regional food that would later contribute to the emergence of food tourism. Hall and Sharples (2003) include in their definition of food tourism: visiting food producers, food festivals, and restaurants, with food as the primary motivating factor for travelling to the destination. Earlier generations, too, had demonstrated an interest in food and travel.

Writing soon after the end of World War I, Rey (1920: iv–v) acknowledges that French cuisine is '*de rigueur*' at all the first-class hotels and restaurants. Menus, it is suggested, at these establishments were always written in culinary French, some of the terms considered irksome, even to epicures with some knowledge of French. The encyclopaedia reflects on the social mores of the day regarding dining out, for example lavish dinners with extensive menus. However, it does indicate an interest in traditional food. There are few references to regional specialities, but readers are advised that the United Kingdom has some appetizing national dishes, for example Irish stew and haggis. The average Englishman, Rey (1920) concludes, does not think he has made a good dinner unless he has partaken of a 'large joint of meat, a pie, or pudding, Cheddar or Stilton cheese, accompanied by a good supply of wine or beer'.

In the United Kingdom, consumption of local food, including that produced in the Empire, was encouraged through initiatives such as the National Mark scheme, introduced in 1928. Walter Elliot, Minister of Agriculture and Fisheries, writing in the foreword to *National Mark Recipes* (Anon, 1935: 6), described the National Mark in terms of its standardization, and guar-antee of food quality. The food produced in Britain was considered to be of a high standard (Herbodeau and Thalamas, 1955: 2). In purchasing National Mark produce, consumers were advised that they were helping to 'restore prosperity to our oldest industry – agriculture'. Trewin (2010) suggests that by the late twentieth century, consumers were again encouraged to demand local and home-grown produce in order to revive agricultural and artisan food production.

Looking at food through the lens of history provides an insight into the experiences of consumers and producers. This is evident in the reflections of Lieutenant Colonel Newnham-Davis, food writer, gourmet, and gastronomic correspondent of *The Pall Mall Gazette*. In the early twentieth century, Newnham-Davis compiled two comprehensive restaurant guides, *The Gourmet's Guide to London* (1914) and *The Gourmet's Guide to Europe* (1912). These are significant in that they present in detail the restaurant and culinary landscape of the belle époque, an era of conspicuous consumption, eating out in public, and leisured travel. Newnham-Davis' narratives may be contrasted with the trend for more modest hospitality outlets, notably, cafés and tea rooms (Kinchin 1991, 1998; Cleave, 2011). Shaw et al. (2006) identify tea shops as significant social spaces for women, encouraging eating out in public. Examples of restaurants and tea rooms show that the public were becoming accustomed to and aspiring to eating out for pleasure, entertainment, and experience, at home and abroad.

In *The Gourmet's Guide to London*, Newnham-Davis (1914: 313–319) visits the Cavendish Hotel. This was run by Mrs Lewis, 'A great British woman cook', with a female kitchen brigade. He provides details of the 'splendid, airy and spacious' kitchen, where he met Margaret, the cook who was to prepare his lunch. After the meal of grilled oysters on celery root, followed by a quail pudding (invented by Mrs Lewis, and a favourite of her patron, King Edward VII), he resumed his tour of the kitchens where coffee was served. Here, backstage, Newnham-Davis discussed changes in gastronomy with Mrs Lewis, who informed him that, in her experience, diners had become more demanding, discerning, and knowledgeable about their food.

In contrast, *The Gourmet's Guide to Europe* (1912) identifies a wide range of hotels, restaurants, and cafés, where, when eating out in Imperial Europe on the eve of World War I, a universal culinary French terminology was used in most establishments.

It is interesting to note that, in the Berlin chapter, Newnham-Davis informs readers that the city is plentifully supplied with restaurants. These are differentiated as: the *classic* restaurant, the *hotel* restaurant, and *restaurants of the people*. Borchardt's, shown in Figure 4.1, whose patrons included Prussian royalty, aristocrats, and diplomats, is described as a *classic* restaurant with the dignity and atmosphere of a classic restaurant in any capital (Newnham-Davis, 1912: 216–217). Its public dining room of crimson silk and dark wood, an ample menu of German dishes, the great variety of the lunchtime cold buffet, and admirable wine cellars, are praised. The classic dish, *Schnitzel Holstein*, is said to have been created at Borchardt's for Friedrich Von Holstein. The original restaurant was destroyed during World War II, but almost half a century later the culinary landmark reopened in an adjacent building.

Similarly, another gastronomic legacy is identified in the *Hotel Adlon* (Newnham-Davis, 1912: 221), one of Europe's leading luxury hotels of the belle époque. Destroyed at the end

*Figure 4.1* Postcard, Borchardt's, Berlin, c. 1900.
*Source:* author's collection.

of World War II, it was symbolically rebuilt on its original site following the reunification of Germany in the 1990s. It is portrayed in the context of a *hotel* restaurant, 'mightily gorgeous with its marble and gilding', and it is noted the Kaiser had paid the chef, M. Bodart, the compliment of visiting his kitchen. The *Cafe Josty*, described by Hessel (2010) as belonging to the old times, and reawakened almost 80 years after it had closed, marks a nostalgic return to another era, one evocative of the gastronomic, cultural, social, and artistic past of the city.

Examples from Newnham-Davis' guides not only introduced his readers to some of the best hotels and restaurants in Europe, but also invited them to learn about the patrons, chefs, and waiters who contributed to their success. Newnham-Davis encouraged potential diners to discover more about their gastronomic encounter, and to search for regional food and specialities. This heralds consumers' interest in exploring further the elements of Goffman's (1959) front-stage and backstage social interaction – in the context of the theatrical environment of hospitality provision. The influential *Gourmet's Guides* (Newnham-Davis, 1912, 1914) identify the chef as a celebrity, the importance and social status of place, and that travel has influenced the foods we eat.

London too has recently revived one of its former luxury restaurants, Boulestin, 70 years after the death of its founder, Xavier Marcel Boulestin. Its revival draws attention to Boulestin as an influential food writer, restaurateur, and first (BBC) television chef in 1937 (Parkin, 1981). Houston-Bowden (1975: 44) suggests that the instantaneous success of the original restaurant is attributed, in part, to Boulestin's policy of running an authentic French restaurant with Parisian atmosphere, and an *a la carte* menu, The new Boulestin menu uses traditional recipes inspired by the past, but presented in a contemporary style. Boulestin not only encouraged the British public to dine in his restaurant, but also to prepare similar, classic French dishes in their homes through demonstrations, and numerous cookery books, for example *Simple French Cooking for English Homes* (1923) and *What Shall We Have Today?* (1931). Burnett (2004: 198) describes him as the 'culinary icon of the age', influential through his writing, restaurant, cookery school, and television appearances, a celebrity model that would be developed by subsequent generations.

These examples, perhaps, affirm the public's interest in and affiliation to the culinary past. Wechsberg (1953: 110) reflects on the influence of some of Europe's leading restaurants in the turbulent period following World War II. He notes that Gundel's in Budapest had combined the very best of Hungarian ingredients (sourced from local markets by its patron, Charles Gundel) and culinary traditions, with the techniques and influence of French haute cuisine.

The celebrities, grand hotels, cafés, and conspicuous consumption of a former era appear to have a relevance to the present and a new generation of diners. Examples from Europe provide a perspective of regional differentiation, but could be applied to other areas. It is interesting to note the nostalgia for another age and to understand in some way the longing for a previous era. Hotels, restaurants, and hospitality outlets are important in illustrating the evolution of eating out and the evolving interest in food through the twentieth century.

Contemporary records of chefs and hoteliers tell us much about the way our interests in food have evolved. Two influential figures from the nineteenth century, Escoffier (Herbodeau and Thalamas, 1955) and Ritz (1981: 60) – who is said to have realized the power of imagination and value of illusion early in his career – are important in developing an awareness of culinary influences and a gastronomic heritage that, today, in its diversity includes versions of everyday dishes of peasant origin and culinary creations of Michelin star chefs and restaurants.

Grand hotels encouraged dining out for pleasure and many resort hotels provided dinner dances and entertainment. However, during the inter-bellum and the depression, in the period between the two World Wars, some establishments encouraged business with relatively modest charges. Lyons, famous for its tea shops offered its customers a competitively priced dinner dance menu (see Figure 4.2). Lyons' menu, with its caviar, *hors d'oeuvre*, and jellied consommé, is typical of the food served in hotels at that time, and would have been considered sophisticated (Spencer, 2002), stimulating a buoyant demand from aspiring middle-class customers (Burnett, 2004: 193). Simon (1930: 13) describes the impact of Lyons as significant in terms of popular catering provision and encouraging the public to eat out for enjoyment and leisure.

*Figure 4.2* Lyons' menu, souvenir postcard, 13 August 1931.
*Source:* author's collection.

## Regional food and local specialities

It is important that the simple dishes and local foods that are examples of the ordinary and commonplace in a local diet are not overlooked. In the context of tourism these are frequently transformed into the extraordinary as foods are re-localized, and tourists search for the authentic, regional, and local specialities. Towner (1995) suggests that, in tourism, the everyday and seemingly mundane experience, including food, is often discounted. Although in the environment of tourism and hospitality these are often overshadowed by elaborate, Michelin-starred food experiences, they both have their place.

Numerous traditional English recipes were collected by Florence White, and published as *Good Things in England* (1932). This was important gastronomic and cultural research as it stimulated an interest in gastronomic regional differentiation and food heritage. It was followed in 1935 by White's and the English Folk Cookery Association's (EFCA) *Good Food Register*, a booklet for travellers interested in regional cookery. It listed catering establishments serving regional dishes. For example, the Royal Clarence Hotel in Exeter, Devon (believed to be England's first hotel) was apparently noted for its 'Dripping Cake', a simple fruit cake made with fat from the roasted joint and served for afternoon tea.

The EFCA were concerned that many traditional dishes and regional specialities would be lost if not recorded and brought to the attention of the public and the catering industry. Mennell (1985: 221), indicates that, in England, industrialization and urbanization had disrupted the transmission of rural lore and traditions, including food.

The work of the EFCA is important at a time when the many sectors of the hospitality and catering industry were still under the influence of Escoffier, a man of vision and a perfectionist (Herbodeau and Thalamas, 1955), and classic French cuisine. At this time Dorothy Hartley was travelling the country gathering material for *Food in England* (1979). Together, Hartley's and the EFCA's work recorded dishes and culinary skills that were disappearing. Some of these have now experienced a renaissance, such as regional cheeses, artisan bakers, and rare breeds. The emergence of local food groups – for example farmers' markets and Slow Food – who are keen to return to traditional methods of production has also contributed to the renewed interest in regional and traditional food. Dougherty et al. (2013: 1–3) suggest that such groups are significant in current models of local food tourism networks, encouraging food consumption by a host and visiting market. Farmers' markets, local restaurants, and speciality food shops are identified as key actors in the network.

## Case study: Devon, the south-west of England

It is interesting to note that historically there has been an interest in the food of the locals, rustics, and peasants in the south-west of England. This was noted by numerous travellers (Fiennes, 1984; Defoe, 1962; Mavor, 1798) who demonstrated a public interest in the routine and ordinary food, in addition to that produced in hotels and restaurants. In contrast to many urban developments, with a concentration of city hotels and restaurants, the south-west of England is a region with a long tradition of food production and tourism. Its history, climate, landscape, and agriculture contributed to its appeal as a tourist destination. Trewin (2010) indicates a renewed and specialized 'food' interest in the county that draws on elements of its culinary and agricultural past. A similar situation could be found in other areas, for example Italy, and France (Croce and Perri, 2010).

The county of Devon's culinary past is influenced by its agriculture, and that it is a maritime county. Both have contributed to its appeal as a tourist destination. Harris (1907: 65) describes Devon as the land of junket and cream, and as apple country. He suggests that the Phoenician tin traders taught the old people the secret of making clotted cream (Harris, 1907: 35). Trewin (2010: 16) identifies a diversity of landscapes in the county, two contrasting coastlines, moorland, and lush farmland contributing to a wide range of local ingredients, including fish, meat, and dairy produce. These are apparent in its agricultural history and culinary traditions, and in the legacy of its hotels, restaurants, and commercial hospitality.

The Imperial Hotel in Torquay (Figure 4.3) provides an example of a nineteenth-century outpost of commercial hospitality. It dates from the development of the south-west of England as a fashionable tourist destination. A resort benefitting from a mild climate and lush vegetation, it was frequently equated with the south of France, Monte Carlo, and the Riviera. Boxer (1994: 9) indicates that the rapid development of the 'grand hotel' in the nineteenth century

*Figure 4.3* Imperial Hotel, Torquay, postcard c. 1890.
*Source:* author's collection.

revolutionized our social life. This is, in part, due to the influential partnership of hotelier Cesar Ritz and chef Auguste Escoffier, whose work in many of Europe's grandest hotels left enduring global gastronomic influences; food, modernity, innovation, management, and, later, the trend for celebrity chefs and hoteliers. The influence of Escoffier and Ritz is evident in the style and ambience of the Imperial, and the hotel soon became widely known for its food, service, and luxury.

A leading article in *Picture Post*, 1947, describes the Imperial in terms of complicated machinery designed for luxurious comfort and pleasure. Journalist Marjorie Beckett (1947: 11–12) indicates the importance of such establishments in raising standards in the industry, and that well-run hotels like the Imperial are the universities of the hotel profession, exemplars of good food, service, and hospitality education. Lethbridge (2003: 148–149) states that the Imperial followed a pattern of greatness and unostentatious splendour found in other smart resorts. The Imperial Hotel was important in the development of Devon as a place to visit for good food and eating out. Denes (1982: 97) traces the gastronomic tradition of the Imperial back to the nineteenth century, the time when Torquay was regarded as a resort for the upper classes and visiting aristocracy.

The county is now promoted as a food destination. Enhanced provenance of foodstuffs, competitive advantage, history, and tradition in the context of food are used in marketing the county. *Visit Devon* (2012) encourages local and sustainable food consumption thus:

> When people mention Devon holidays, the first thing they tend to think of are the beaches and the rolling countryside. However, there is another aspect of Devon that has been gathering steam over the last few years. The West Country has established itself as one of the prime gastronomic hotspots of the UK.

Tourists are advised that they will find excellent, fresh, locally sourced ingredients and a wide range of superb places to eat in the county.

## Food souvenirs: taking food home

An important aspect of travel and tourism is the souvenir. These are frequently food-based and enable consumers to extend, relive, and share their food experiences at home in the domestic hospitality domain. There are many opportunities for consumers to purchase food souvenirs. Farm shops, farmers' markets, food festivals and fairs, inspired by examples of regional pannier markets, and livestock fairs in many cases are now transformed for the visiting public, encouraging consumption of local produce. They have, in many instances, become food-themed events, celebrating and showcasing new and traditional regional foods, chefs, and producers.

As food is not only consumed in commercial outlets but is frequently purchased as a souvenir gift and memento, it often becomes a touchstone of memory (Morgan and Pritchard, 2005) and associated with its place of production. Croce and Perri (2010) allude to the trend for food-focused visits and souvenir opportunity with the example of vineyard visits and wine souvenirs. Fudge, a confectionery product originating from America, is popular with tourists in the south-west of England. The addition of clotted cream and butter give it a local appeal, and added value, although its connection to place (Devon) is attributed to the addition of Devonshire dairy products (Cleave, 2013). Menus and postcards have also served as souvenirs, and now digital images are used as a means of recording foods consumed, perhaps the current version of the postcard and photographic image. Figure 4.4 shows a range of rustic dishes considered

*Figure 4.4* Postcard, 'A Devon Welcome', c. 1920.
*Source:* author's collection.

typical fare of the period. A combination of nostalgic, stereotypical bucolic imagery, and range of traditional dishes listed in the local dialect would appeal to the tourist market.

## Conclusion

This chapter has demonstrated the influence of the culinary and gastronomic past. It has identified the domains of domestic and commercial hospitality, developing an understanding of the differences and commonalities of the two. What has gone before influences the present and the future. Memories of food are evocative and frequently stimulate a culinary longing for food from the past. This is often what is perceived to be authentic, whether a peasant dish, regional speciality, or the ambience of a grand hotel, restaurant, or café. Schouten (2006: 191) states that souvenirs as well as experiences are conceived as being authentic when they reflect the perceived core values of the destination visited. We can learn from what has gone before, the legacy of the past, elements of which are sometimes incorporated in a new style and presentation.

Croce and Perri (2010) suggest that in the late twentieth century, in our food and eating habits, there was a return to natural and authentic foods, with traditional recipes revisited and an interest in native species, organic farming, regional products, and sustainability. Archival and contemporary data provide the researcher with numerous examples of the evolution of gastronomy, hospitality, and food consumption.

Looking at the food consumed by the public away from home, eating for pleasure and leisure, and investigating a specific region, destination, or location we discover the culinary influences that have shaped its evolution. Our food production and consumption is evolving, and reflects changes in lifestyle, ingredients, knowledge, and culinary aspirations. By developing our appreciation of the past we are better able to understand the present, and plan for the future.

# References

Anon (1935) *National Mark Recipes*, London: Ministry of Agriculture and Fisheries.

Beckett, M. (1947) 'Above stairs and below stairs in a Grand Hotel', *Picture Post*, 56(9): 7–13.

Boulestin, X.M. (1923) *Simple French Cooking for English Homes*, London: Heinemann.

Boulestin, X.M. (1931) *What Shall We Have Today?* London: Heinemann.

Boxer, A. (1994) 'The rise of the grand hotel', *Convivium*, 2(2): 7–23.

Burnett, J. (2004) *England Eats Out – 1830–Present*, London: Pearson/Longman.

Cleave, P. (2011) *Deller's Cafes, Petits Propos Culinaire*, Totnes: Prospect Books.

Cleave, P. (2013) *Sugar Heritage and Tourism in Transition, Wrapped in Devonshire Sunshine*, Bristol: Channel View.

Croce, E. and Perri, G. (2010) *Food and Wine Tourism*, Wallingford: CABI.

Defoe, D. (1962) *Tour Through the Whole Island of Great Britain*, London: Dent.

Denes, G. (1982) *The Story of The Imperial, the Life and Times of Torquay's Great Hotel*, Plymouth: Latimer Trend.

Dougherty, M.L., Brown, L.E. and Green, G.P. (2013) 'The social architecture of local food tourism: challenges and opportunities for community economic development', *Journal of Rural Social Sciences*, 28(2): 1–27.

Drummond, J. and Wilbraham, J. (1957) *The Englishman's Food, Five Centuries of British Diet*, London: Jonathan Cape.

Fiennes, C. (1984) *The Illustrated Journeys of Celia Fiennes, 1688–1712*, Exeter: Webb and Bower.

Fortescue-Fox, R. (1938) *British Health Resorts, Spa, Seaside, Inland, Including the British Dominions and Colonies: Official Handbook*, London: J. & A. Churchill Ltd.

Goffman, F. (1959) *The Presentation of Self in Everyday Life*, Garden City, NY: Doubleday.

Graves, R. and Hodge, A. (1941) *The Long Week-end: A Social History of Great Britain, 1918–1939*, London: Readers Union Limited/Faber and Faber Limited.

Hall, C.M. and Gössling, S. (2013) *Sustainable Culinary Systems, Local Foods, Innovation, Tourism and Hospitality*, London: Routledge.

Hall, C.M. and Sharples, E. (2003) *Food Tourism Around the World*, London: Butterworth-Heinemann.

Harris, J.H. (1907) *My Devonshire Book*, Plymouth: The Western Morning News Company Ltd.

Hartley, D. (1979) *Food in England*, London: Macdonald and Jane's.

Herbodeau, E. and Thalamas, P. (1955) *Georges Auguste Escoffier*, London: Practical Press Ltd.

Hessel, F. (2010) *Spazieren in Berlin*, Berlin: Bloomsbury Taschenbuk.

Houston-Bowden, G. (1975) *British Gastronomy, the Rise of the Great Restaurants*, London: Chatto & Windus.

Kinchin, P. (1991) *Tea and Taste: The Glasgow Tea Rooms 1875–1975*, Wendlebury: White Cockade.

Kinchin, P. (1998) *Taking Tea with Mackintosh*, Warwick: Pomegranate Europe Ltd.

Lashley, C. (2007) 'Discovering hospitality, observations from recent research', *International Journal of Culture, Tourism and Hospitality Research*, 1: 214–226.

Lethbridge, H.J. (2003) *Torquay and Paignton, the Making of a Modern Resort*, Chichester: Phillimore and Co. Ltd.

Mavor, W. (1798) *The British Tourists, or Traveller's Pocket Companion, Through England, Wales, Scotland, and Ireland*, London: Newberry.

Mennell, S. (1985) *All Manners of Food*, Oxford: Blackwell.

Morgan, N. and Pritchard, A. (2005) 'On souvenirs and metonymy: narratives of memory, metaphor, and materiality', *Tourist Studies*, 5: 29–33.

Muirhead, L.R. (1939) *The Blue Guides, England*, London: Ernest Benn Limited.

Newnham-Davis, Lieut. Col. (1912) *The Gourmet's Guide to Europe*, 3rd edn, London: Grant Richards Ltd.

Newnham-Davis, Lieut. Col. (1914) *The Gourmet's Guide to London*, London: Grant Richards Ltd.

Parkin, M. (1981) *A Salute to Marcel Boulestin and Jean-Emile Labourer*, London: Michael Parkin, Fine Art Limited.

Pimlott, J.A.R. (1976) *The Englishman's Holiday*, 2nd edn, Hassocks, Sussex: Harvester Press.

Rey, J. (1920) *The Modern Caterer's Encyclopaedia*, London: Carmona and Baker.

Ritz, M.L. (1981) *Cesar Ritz*, Paris: Bodley Head/Ritz Hotel.

Schouten, F. (2006) 'The process of authenticating souvenirs', in *Cultural Tourism in a Changing World: Politics, Participation and (Re)presentation*, Clevedon: Channel View Publications.

Shaw, G., Curth, L.H. and Alexander, A. (2006) 'Creating new spaces of food consumption: the rise of mass catering and the activities of the Aerated Bread Company', in J. Benson and L. Ugolini (eds.), *Cultures of Selling*, Aldershot: Ashgate.

Simon, A. (1930) *The Art of Good Living*, London: Constable.

Spang, R. (2000) *The Invention of the Restaurant*, Cambridge, MA: Harvard University Press.

Spencer, C. (2002) *British Food, an Extraordinary Two Thousand Years of History*, London: Grub Street with Fortnum and Mason.

Tannahill, R. (1973) *Food in History*, St Albans: Paladin.

Towner, J. (1995) 'What is tourism's history?', *Tourism Management*, 16: 339–343.

Trewin, C. (2010) *The Devon Food Book*, Chard, Somerset: Flagon Press.

*Visit Devon* (2012) www.visitdevon.co.uk.

Visser, M. (1991) *The Rituals of Dinner*, Toronto: HarperCollins.

Wechsberg, J. (1953) *Blue Trout and Black Truffles*, London: Victor Gollancz Ltd.

White, F. (1932) *Good Things in England*, London: Jonathan Cape.

# PART 2

# Local food initiatives

The first supermarket supposedly appeared on the American landscape in 1946. That is not very long ago. Until then, where was all the food? Dear folks, the food was in homes, gardens, local fields, and forests. It was near kitchens, near tables, near bedsides. It was in the pantry, the cellar, the backyard.

*Joel Salatin,* Folks, This Ain't Normal: A Farmer's Advice for Happier Hens, Healthier People, and a Better World *(Center Street, 2012)*

The euphoria at what the global can offer is waning and people are returning to local environments for the 'authentic' experience. The opportunities, experiences and products that global offers are being questioned, as local is perceived as the more sustainable option.

This chapter begins with **Sean Beer**'s examination of local purchasing decisions and the justification behind them. Is local always the most sustainable solution? The search for the authentic may be based on some outdated concept of what authentic is and a sustainable future requires a clear definition of authenticity.

Several international case studies highlight the role of local food in creating a sustainable food environment and consolidating local identity. The Kartoffelkombinat in Munich, Germany, is community-supported agriculture in a metropolitan context. **Thomas Berron** describes the collective aims to maintain a sustainable, self-organized community and local food supply culture. The community and farmers restore traditional connections and jobs and money remains in the local community.

**Richa Govil** presents a case study of women farmers in rural India who are encouraged to use local resources as the most efficient way to feed the population. Despite India's booming economy, poverty and malnutrition remain severe problems in rural communities. The local food programme aims to improve the production of women farmers and increase their nutrition-seeking behaviour.

In Guyana, major fast food chains are well established and increasingly part of the landscape. **Donald Sinclair and Carolann Marcus**, however, show that evidence exists that Aboriginal cuisine and culinary practices will survive due to the strength and tenacity of ancestral traditions. Food can express cultural resistance and also be used to cement identity.

Thai cookery courses in Chiang Mai, Thailand, are examined in their role of sustaining local food culture and disseminating it beyond the local context. **Wantanee Suntikul,**

**Rodrigues Ng Iris, Ho Weng, Luo Xiao Yan, Lam Iok Cheng and Chan Weng San** show that gastronomic experiences are increasingly important in motivating tourists to travel to particular destinations and are even a part of experiencing local food.

Cornwall, UK, provides an example of entrepreneurship in local food and beverage for **John Tredinnick-Rowe and Tim Taylor**. The roles of brand symbolism and conscientious consumers are analysed along with aspects such as using strong local identity as a marketing tool. The heritage of a region is clearly used to build the future.

# 5

# DOES THE PURSUIT OF LOCAL FOOD DESTROY OUR ENVIRONMENT?

## Questions of authenticity and sustainability

*Sean Beer*

> The destiny of nations depends on the manner in which they feed themselves.
> *(Brillat-Savarin, 2009 [1825])*

## Introduction

There is a well-established mantra within the 'environmental movement' that local is good (whatever local means). This is particularly so with food and drink. If food and drink can be sourced locally this is considered to be more sustainable (whatever that means) than sourcing it from a distance; possibly the other side of the world (Germov and Williams, 1999). Primarily this is based on the perceived increase in carbon emissions associated with transporting food long distances, the premise that underpins concepts such as food miles. 'Eating and drinking the local' is seen as something that is good to do from an environmental (and other) perspective(s), something that is sustainable (Beer et al., 2012).

At the same time, among some people, there is a real drive to pursue authentic experiences; again particularly with regard to food and drink. Some local people and tourists will try to seek out the food and drink that is distinctive and peculiar to the area in which they live or which they visit (Beer, 2008). This pursuit of the authentic is often seen as something good to do, something sustainable. This is almost taken as a given, but potentially this argument is fundamentally flawed.

First, we need to decide what is meant by local and sustainable. Second, it may well be that 'local' food and drink has a much larger carbon footprint than food that has been transported from the other side of the world. Third, depending on how supply chains are constructed, it may well be that the economic benefits are overestimated. Finally, the pursuit of the authentic may well be based on pursuing some sort of preindustrial ideal that seeks to conserve communities in aspic rather than allow them to develop and embrace change. Possibly food producers and others involved in tourism become actors living out an historical drama rather than living in a vibrant, developing community. While the tourist pursues what Nietzsche (1991 [1882]; 1997 [1909]), Heidegger (1962) and Sartre (1948) might have considered to be the authentic life, the communities that they visit are forced to live in an unauthentic way in order to survive.

In this chapter I explore these issues from a postmodern perspective, examining the interplay of these various ideas in an attempt to, as Bernstein (1983) said, move beyond objectivism and relativism towards praxis. I will also discuss the need for a new 'open authentic approach' to research in this area that is underpinned by concepts of a social justice that goes beyond some of the reductionist approaches that are currently used to justify policy.

## What is local?

If we look back in history, originally our ancestors had very short food supply chains (they ate what they hunted and gathered). These supply chains gradually lengthened with the ongoing process of specialization and aggregation within the food supply chain. In the late twentieth century, for a variety of reasons, these extended global food supply chains began to be viewed with increasing scepticism. This led to individuals seeking out food that had been produced more locally (geographically closer to home) and in ways with which they had more sympathy; and herein lies a tension, particularly with regard to academic interpretations of this movement; 'local food' is not just about food that is produced locally.

This tension can be considered threefold and relates to place, purpose and process. The word 'local' implies a short supply chain; a close proximity of production to consumption; but local might be 10 metres (my back garden) or 1,000 miles (if I lived in Australia). This 'local' production may be for a whole series of different reasons or purposes (political, economic, social/cultural and environmental) combined or otherwise and may be implemented through a whole series of different processes. The definition of each of these elements can vary from case to case, although the term 'local food' may be used as a catch-all for this movement, or localness may be a component of a variety of other terms used to describe food movements that question the modern global food supply chain. Allen et al. (2003: 63) talk about 'multiple and conflicting meanings' and Feagan (2007: 24) endeavours to tease out 'the diverse respatialization threads among (such) food system permutations', to unravel this meaning.

The debate around this concept of localness led the Food Standards Agency in the UK to commission a report on the subject (COI, 2007). The report is wide-ranging but, with specific reference to the term 'local', results were interesting. Most respondents (40 per cent) said that local food was food produced within a ten-mile radius of their home; however, 20 per cent defined it as being produced within their county, 15 per cent from their or a neighbouring county and 20 per cent as being produced within the region. Feagan (2007: 23) states that:

> Being conscious of the constructed nature of the 'local', 'community' and 'place' means seeing the importance of local social, cultural and ecological particularity in our everyday worlds, whilst also recognizing that we are reflexively and dialectically tied to many diverse locals around the world.

We are local and at the same time global. It is difficult to see how these two perspectives can be effectively reconciled/honoured and it may well be that the term 'local' can really only be defined by the individual(s) that use(s) it. The conclusion must be that the concept of localness is complicated.

## What is sustainable?

There has already been extensive discussion of the nature of sustainability in other chapters within this book giving rise to a common theme of the triple bottom line. This implies that sustainability should have social, economic and environmental dimensions. The phrase was first thought up by John Elkington in 1994 (see Elkington 1994, 1998). This sort of focus is all very well but there is a secondary question: what does the consumer perceive as being sustainable? Many authors have examined the rise of the ethical consumer. Newholm and Shaw (2007) provide a very good overview of many of the issues. There seems to have been a rise in ethical consumption in the late twentieth century, of which green consumerism can be seen to be a part (Atkins and Bowler, 2001; Germov and Williams, 1999; Mepham, 1996; Schlosser, 2002; Smith, 1994; Wilson, 2008).

Risk mediation has been suggested by some as a basis for this development (Beck, 1992; Harrison et al., 2005; Parkins and Craig, 2006) and food has been the subject of a whole variety of ongoing concerns and specific scares, which may also have sensitized the consumer to thinking about the provenance of their food. Other authors have argued that when consumers are freed from the basic difficulty in obtaining protein and calories, as a result of an increase in income, they may start looking at other things to do with where their food comes from, ethical concerns and environmental impact forming part of this (Brooker, 1976; Dickinson and Carsky, 2005; Hansen and Schrader, 1997). The situation is potentially complicated.

## Why is local food seen as being sustainable?

Suspending any feelings that the concepts of localness and sustainability may be too complicated to easily reconcile, we can return to the popular idea that consuming local food can make a major contribution to sustainability. A good example of such ideas can be found in the Friends of the Earth (2000) publication, *The Economic Benefits of Farmers' Markets*. Traditionally farmers sold their produce through local produce markets. These went out of fashion with the development of specialist retailers, but came back in fashion in the early 1990s in the UK and slightly earlier in the USA. At these markets, local food producers can sell their produce direct to consumers. Farmers' markets are considered to deliver many benefits for sustainability, some of which are summarized in the second column of Table 5.1. FARMA (the UK National Farmers' Retail and Market Association) develop this in a slightly more marketing orientated way with their 21 (actually 18) reasons to support local foods (FARMA, 2013).

## Why is it that local may not be as sustainable as we think?

The sorts of discourses indicated by the two examples above are the received wisdom of the local food movement. Academics have found the growth in the local food movement of great interest. Ilbery and Maye (2005) cite eight themed sections and special editions of journals looking at developments in 'local', 'alternative', or 'traditional/speciality' foods (*British Food Journal*, 105(8), 2003; *Environment and Planning A*, 35(3), 2003; *International Planning Studies*, 4(3), 1999; *Journal of Rural Studies*, 19(1), 2003; *Sociologia Ruralis*, 40(2), 40(4), 2000, 41(1), 2001, 42(4), 2002). Growth in local food was seen as an important development for the EU rural development regulation (1257/99). However, much of this discourse has not challenged the basis upon which the claims for the sustainability of local food are made. These do deserve to be critically evaluated and in Table 5.1 I have taken the key points from the two sources outlining the benefits of local food production cited above (Friends of the Earth, 2000; FARMA, 2013), combined them and posed critical responses to these key points. Three points need to be made to put this in context. First, these challenges are based on more than 30 years' experience working with local food producers and championing local food. Thus

*Table 5.1* Challenges to the perceived benefits of local foods as put forward by Friends of the Earth (2000) and FARMA (2013)

| Interest group | | Critical response |
| --- | --- | --- |
| Benefits for Farmers | A different source of income. | Yes, but also an additional set of costs and if resources are focused on local supply they must be removed from whatever was being done before. |
| | Greater control over their 'economic lives'. | The producer does move from a few large volume customers to more, smaller volume customers. |
| | Higher prices for the farmer (removal of 'middlemen'). | Higher prices but what of costs and also the benefit for the consumer? |
| | Farmers diversify their skills. | Yes. |
| | Increased networking opportunities. | Yes, there may be. |
| Benefits for the local economy | More money is spent in the local economy and it circulates there longer. | Possibly, although there may also be substantial out flows of funds to investors such as banks. |
| | Knock-on spending to other shops on market days. | Possibly, but that spend may have taken place regardless and money may not be being spent in local shops as it is spent in the market. |
| | An outlet for local produce for other businesses. | Yes, but it would be expensive. |
| | Reinforce local job and business networks. | Yes. |
| Benefits for consumers | They enjoy the atmosphere of the market, meet nice people. | There may be and there may not. |
| | Consumers get freshest, healthy produce at competitive prices, good value for money. | It may be or it may not, supermarket chains can produce excellent outcomes. In terms of being good value for money this depends on an individual's definitions of good value. |
| | Increased choice. | Compared to 24,000 lines in a small, modern supermarket? Also some outlets such as farmers' markets may be monthly, so where does the choice go? |
| | Help develop community cohesion. | They can do, but the politics of local food can be divisive. |
| | Food is fully traceable. | Not necessarily, potentially it can be less traceable than supermarket-purchased food, particularly when we are dealing with products other than fresh fruit, vegetables and meat. |
| | Able to try something new. | More able than in a small supermarket with 24,000 lines? |
| | Purchasing is an education. | It may be. |
| | Retains seasonality. | Seasonality is duplicated in supermarkets, although they provide food in and out of season. Whether this is sustainable or not is another question. |

| Benefits for the environment | Less food miles. | Only because 'food miles' is a catchy but flawed concept. See discussion. |
|---|---|---|
| | Less packaging. | Compared to what? |
| | Less waste – for consumer and farmer. | In what way? If it is not processed then the consumer must prepare the food and there will be additional waste. |
| | Keeps the countryside looking beautiful. | What is beauty? Small farms, or wilderness with no farms and food produced somewhere else? |
| | Important outlet for those selling organic or less intensively produced food. | Yes potentially for small-scale producers; this is to do with size not really method of production. |

the comments are ethnographic in nature. Second, this experience was gained largely in the UK and the UK local food sector and may be different to the sector in other countries. Finally, and this is particularly evident in farmers' markets, many of the producers are not farmers and are not using local ingredients to make their local products, but these products are processed locally.

From this it can be seen that many of the economic, social and environmental benefits are open to challenge, which is not a bad thing. This also represents a potential opportunity for research as there is a dearth of refereed research that examines some of these issues in detail. I would, however, like to look in a little more detail at two issues that have received some attention: environmental sustainability in terms of carbon footprint and economic sustainability.

## Environmental sustainability in terms of carbon footprint

One of the most important supposed benefits of local food consumption is that of reduced carbon footprint. This ethos is summarized in the concept of food miles. The idea is fairly simple. The food miles for an individual product are the miles that it travels from producer to consumer. The food miles for a dish would be the total miles that the ingredients had travelled. Thus if I am a consumer in the UK eating a lamb chop from New Zealand (a cut of meat cut perpendicularly to the spine containing part of a rib and part of a vertebra), it has travelled 11,619 food miles (18,809km). For a typical UK meal this might be:

| | |
|---|---|
| New Zealand lamb chop | 11,690 miles (18,809km). |
| Kenyan green beans | 4,237 miles (6,817km). |
| Sweet potatoes from the USA | 3,666 miles (5,898km). |
| Bottle of wine from Australia | 10,554 miles (16,981km). |
| **Total** | **30,147 miles (48,505km).** |

These figures were calculated using the food miles calculator at www.foodmiles.com. They are based on the direct distances between countries and do not include other associated mileage. Unfortunately the concept of food miles is fundamentally flawed in two ways. First, not all food miles are equal. For example, transport by air, road and ships are all different in terms of their carbon contribution. Second, the contribution from one lamb chop travelling 11,690 miles from New Zealand on a boat is very different to the contribution when it is shared by another 99,999 lamb chops. Third, the carbon footprint of a foodstuff produced in one country may vary considerably to that when it is produced in another country. Therefore, returning to the lamb chop produced in New Zealand, the ability of New Zealand to grow grass and the systems used to transform that into meat mean that there will be minimal use of fertilizer and additional feeds. This will mean that the production of greenhouse gases (focusing principally on carbon dioxide in this case) will be far less than the cost of shipping that meat from New Zealand and will not wipe out the production advantage (AEA Technology, 2008; AEA Environment, 2005; Stocks, 2009). Similar comparisons could be drawn for fruit and vegetables produced in different countries and imported into the UK.

Such research led the UK Department for International Development (DFID) and Defra to state that:

> Food miles alone, or the distance food has travelled is an incomplete way of judging whether the food we eat is sustainable. Research shows that distance travelled is, on its own, not a reliable indicator of the environmental impact of food transport.
>
> *(DFID, 2010)*

The second consideration has to be the food that is being consumed. Not all food types are equivalent in the amount of greenhouse gases that they produce. According to the Intergovernmental Panel on Climate Change (IPCC, 2007), the principal global warming agents are nitrous oxide, methane and carbon dioxide. Over a 20-year period, methane is potentially 72 times as powerful as carbon dioxide and nitrous oxide 289 times as powerful (IPCC, 2007). This is important because the production of different types of foodstuff produces different amounts of these global warming gases. Fruit and vegetables tend to be quite low. According to Carlsson-Kanyama and González (2009), cooked soya beans imported from overseas had total emissions of 0.92kg carbon dioxide equivalent over 100 years, potatoes 0.45kg and fresh carrots 0.42kg. When fruit or veg were airfreighted from abroad, this did raise the value: fresh tropical fruit imported to Sweden by plane producing emissions of 11.0kg carbon dioxide equivalent. Production of meat produces high values. Cooked fresh domestic chicken produced 4.3kg carbon dioxide equivalent and domestic cooked cod 8.5kg. Ruminant livestock fared the worst, with domestic cooked beef scoring 30.0kg as a result of high levels of methane production, a by-product of their bacteria-based digestive system. The ways in which these calculations are put together is complicated and there are many assumptions (see Fuentes and Carlsson-Kanyama, 2006). Because of these considerations, possibly we should not be asking whether we should be consuming home-produced lamb or New Zealand lamb, but should we be consuming home-produced chicken or New Zealand lamb?

## Economic sustainability

Local food supply chains are seen to be of value economically and primarily for two reasons. First, they represent an additional (diversified) source of income for farmers and growers, who on the whole have historically struggled to make good standards of living. Second, local food is seen as a way of retaining economic value in the community. On the first point, it cannot be argued that, for some individual farmers and growers, developing new local supply chains has been an economic lifeline. This has been especially so for small farmers; however, in terms of the broad agricultural community these people are very much in the minority. There are many reasons why this may be the case, but two factors are particularly important. First, the local food market in the UK is a niche market. Local food is consumed by middle-class 'foodies' and does not form the bulk of even their food consumption. Second, there is a structural problem in developing local food supply chains beyond niche markets and that is that the necessary infrastructure no longer exists. The food supply chain has been redesigned to focus on providing food through large-scale retailers and the food service industry, thus we have seen the decline in small-scale food processing facilities and abattoirs, for example (Taylor, 2006).

The benefit of retaining value within the local economy also needs to be questioned. A study by the New Economic Foundation (Boyde, 2001) estimated that for every pound spent in a local organic box scheme, £2.59 was generated for the local economy compared with £1.40 of every pound spent at a supermarket. Without wishing to get into detailed economic discussion, these figures are crudely what economists call a multiplier. The idea of a multiplier effect is that for every pound spent in an economy there will be knock-on spending within that economy as a result of the initial spend. The degree to which this takes place is called the multiplier effect. For farmers' markets a number of studies have put the multiplier at between 1.58 and 1.78 (see Otto and Varner, 2005; Myers, 2004 and Henneberry et al., 2009). Thus it can be seen that, potentially, local food can make a very positive contribution to the local economy; however, what is not sometimes considered is that if resources are moved from one type of supply to another, economic benefits may be lost from the old chain as well as gained in the new; there may be increased sales at the farmers' market but decreased sales in local grocery stores. There is a need for some far more extensive economic modelling in order to understand this situation better. In particular, depending on how these local supply chains are constructed, it may well be that much of the economic benefit leaves the immediate area and moves to external investors. The conclusion must be that the concepts of environmental and economic sustainability when applied to local food are complicated.

## What has this to do with authenticity?

In the introduction I indicated that I wanted to tie in this discussion of the sustainability of local food with ideas of the consumption of authentic food. This is important, particularly in the context of local food, as the idea that 'this is an authentic product' is an important part of the sales pitch. The academic discussion of authenticity is complicated, and has been best developed within the tourism literature. Many commentators (Chhabra, 2008; Cole, 2007; Wang, 2007) trace the initial genesis of this discussion to MacCannell (1973, 1976), which seems to establish a basis for an objective truth upon which authenticity is based, where authenticity is a self-explaining concept that is fully genuine and trustworthy, and a tourist experience of authenticity that is in some way staged. Thus the tourist experiences a perform-ance of authenticity that is put on by the host. This harks back to Smith's (1977) discussions of the relationship between the self (the tourist) and the other (the host) and was developed further by Cohen (1988, 1989, 2001, 2007) in looking at the way that authenticity might emerge as a result of this interaction, or might actually become negotiated and agreed (Bruner, 1994; Hughes, 1995). I consider that Cole (2007) provides a useful overview of authenticity in that she considers that authenticity is a Western cultural notion, with no objective quality, that is socially constructed and therefore negotiable, and that this negotiation often leads into a complex process of potentially positive and negative exploitation. However, the picture is still not coherent, as at the same time she maintains that within the literature there is a notion that there is a primitive other pre-modern world that is considered authentic, either because it is objectively so (cool, after the scientific philosophy of Karl Popper (1959 [1934], 1963), for example) or because this is socially constructed in some way (hot, after the sociology of

Durkheim (2012 [1893]), for example Selwyn (1996)). I could also discuss existential authenticity, focusing on the lived experience of individuals at particular times and in particular places citing philosophers such as Heidegger and Sartre and academic papers by Wang (1999), Steiner and Reisinger (2006) or more recently Brown (2013). The conclusion is that the concept of authenticity is complicated and much contested.

There is yet another tension that arises between the idea of local food and authenticity. Various discourses on localness link the idea of localness to that of authenticity and the idea of place to authenticity. In certain circumstances, governments will seek to give special credence to certain food products; something that could be considered a form of authentication. The European Union sets out definitions of the nature of specific foods using a certification scheme (Defra, 2013; EU, 2013). Thus certificates of Protected Designation of Origin (PDO), Protected Geographical Indication (PGI) and Traditional Specialty Guaranteed (Certificate of Specific Character, CSC) are used to set out a legal definition of a whole series of different products. These certificates may record geographic areas of production (comparable to the French *Terroir* system), ingredients and production methods. This whole system is based on the idea of place, the locale, even if it is not your locale. This authentication is important as it adds 'societies' weight and authority to the process and this has significant commercial value. It also harks back to a 'time' possibly a pre-modern time (Cole, 2007) and, in doing so, our ideas of authenticity become shackled and people and communities are conserved in aspic rather than allowed to develop and embrace change, to perceive things in different ways.

## Conclusion

In this chapter I have explored some of the ideas relating to localness, sustainability and authenticity in the context of food. Defining all three terms is problematic; none of them have a stable meaning. I have shown that the received wisdom that local food is sustainable needs to be challenged, in order for more sustainable systems to be developed as at present the predominantly uncritical approach to this assumption is creating an illusion of progress. In all this I think that there is a need for more honesty. I believe that there is a need for a new 'open authentic approach' to research in this area that is underpinned by concepts of social justice that go beyond some of the reductionist approaches that are currently used to justify policy. We should be looking at the broader ways that individuals and communities define authenticity that are not necessarily tied in time and space in order to help people really engage with food, and in that way confront individuals with the implications of their actions. This is not about objectivism and the power of authority on the one hand and existentialism and the freedom of the individual on the other. It is about a middle way, what Bernstein (1983) might have called 'praxis'. It is by this route that we will determine a more sustainable future.

## References

AEA Environment (2005) *The Validity of Food Miles as an Indicator of Sustainable Development*, http://webarchive.nationalarchives.gov.uk/20130123162956/http:/www.defra.gov.uk/evidence/economics/foodfarm/reports/documents/Foodmile.pdf (accessed 1 October 2013).

AEA Technology (2008) *Comparative Life-cycle Assessment of Food Commodities Procured for UK Consumption Through a Diversity of Supply Chains*, http://randd.defra.gov.uk/Default.aspx?Menu—enu&Module—ore&Location–one&ProjectID=15001&FromSearch=Y&Publisher=1&SearchText=FO0103&SortString=ProjectCode&SortOrder=Asc&Paging=10#Description (accessed 1 October 2013).

Allen, P., FitzSimmons, M., Goodman, M. and Warner, K. (2003) 'Shifting plates in the agrifood land-scape: the tectonics of alternative agrifood initiatives in California', *Journal of Rural Studies*, 19: 61–75.

Atkins, P. and Bowler, I. (2001) *Food in Society: Economy, Culture, Geography*, London: Arnold.

Beck, U. (1992) *Risk Society: Towards a New Modernity*, London: Sage.

Beer, S.C. (2008) 'Authenticity and food experience – commercial and academic perspectives', *Journal of Foodservice*, 19: 153–163.

Beer, S.C., Murphy, A. and Shepherd, R. (2012) 'Food and farmers' markets', in C. McIntyre (ed.), *Tourism and Retail*, London: Routledge.

Bernstein, R.J. (1983) *Beyond Objectivism and Relativism: Science, Hermeneutics, and Praxis*, Philadelphia: University of Pennsylvania Press.

Boyde, T. (2001) *Cusgarne Organics Local Money Flows*, London: New Economics Foundation.

Brillat-Savarin, J. (2009 [1825]) *The Physiology of Taste*, London: Everyman.

Brooker, G. (1976) 'These self-actualising socially-conscious consumers', *Journal of Consumer Research*, 3(2): 107–113.

Brown, L. (2013) 'Tourism: a catalyst for existential authenticity', *Annals of Tourism Research*, 40: 176–190.

Bruner, E. (1994) 'Abraham Lincoln as authentic reproduction: a critique of postmodernism', *American Anthropologist*, 96: 397–415.

Carlsson-Kanyama, A. and González, A.D. (2009) 'Potential contributions of food consumption patterns to climate change', *American Journal of Clinical Nutrition*, 89: 1704–1709.

Chhabra, D. (2008) 'Positioning museums on an authenticity continuum', *Annals of Tourism Research*, 35(2): 427–447.

Cohen, E. (1988) 'Authenticity and commoditization in tourism', *Annals of Tourism Research*, 15(3): 371–386.

Cohen, E. (1989) 'Primitive and remote: hill tribe trekking in Thailand', *Annals of Tourism Research*, 16(1): 30–61.

Cohen, E. (2001) 'Ethnic tourism in South East Asia', in C.B. Tan, C.H. Cheung and Y. Hui (eds.), *Tourism, Anthropology and China*, Singapore: White Lotus.

Cohen, E. (2007) ' "Authenticity" in tourism studies: Apres la lute', *Tourism and Recreation Research*, 32(2): 75–82.

COI (2007) *Local Food: Omnibus Research Report*, London: Food Standards Agency.

Cole, S. (2007) 'Beyond authenticity and commodification', *Annals of Tourism Research*, 34(4): 943–960.

Defra (2013) *Farm Shops and Farmers Markets*, www.gov.uk/farm-shops-and-farmers-markets (accessed 1 October 2013).

DFID (2010) *Joint DFID Defra Position on Food Miles*, www.docstoc.com/search/joint-dfid-defra-position-on-food-miles (accessed 1 October 2013).

Dickinson, R. and Carsky, M. (2005) 'The consumer as economic voter', in H. Harrison, T. Newholm and D. Shaw (eds.), *The Ethical Consumer*, London: Sage, pp. 25–36.

Durkheim, E. (2012 [1893]) *The Division of Labour in Society*, trans. G. Simpson, Eastford, CT: Martino Fine Books.

Elkington, J. (1994) 'Towards the sustainable corporation: win-win-win business strategies for sustainable development', *California Management Review*, 36(2): 90–100.

Elkington, J. (1998) *Cannibals with Forks: the Triple Bottom Line of 21st-Century Business*, Gabriola Island, Canada: New Society Publishers.

EU (2013) *Geographical Indications and Traditional Specialities*, http://ec.europa.eu/agriculture/quality/schemes/index_en.htm (accessed 23 July 2014).

FARMA (2013) *21 Reasons to Support Local Foods*, www.farma.org.uk/index.php?option=com_content&view=article&id=9:about-local-foods&catid=10:about (accessed 1 October 2013).

Feagan, R. (2007) 'The place of food: mapping out the "local" in local food system', *Progress in Human Geography*, 31(1): 23–42.

Friends of the Earth (2000) *The Economic Benefits of Farmers' Markets*, www.foe.co.uk/resource/briefings/farmers_markets.pdf (accessed 1 October 2013).

Fuentes, C. and Carlsson-Kanyama, A. (2006) *Environmental Information in the Food Supply System*, Stockholm: Swedish Defence Research Agency.

Germov, J. and Williams, L. (1999) *A Sociology of Food and Nutrition: The Social Appetite*, South Melbourne, Victoria: Oxford University Press.

Hansen, U. and Shrader, U. (1997) 'A modern world of consumption for a sustainable society', *Journal of Consumer Policy*, 20(4): 443–469.

Harrison, R., Hewholm, T. and Shaw, D. (2005) *The Ethical Consumer*, London: Sage.

Heidegger, M. (1962) *Being and Time*, trans. J. Macquarrie and E. Robinson, Oxford: Blackwell.

Henneberry, S.R., Whitacre, B. and Agustini, H.N. (2009) 'An evaluation of the economic impacts of Oklahoma farmers markets', *The Journal of Food Distribution Research* 40(3), http://purl.umn.edu/99760 (accessed 1 October 2013).

Hughes, G. (1995) 'Authenticity in tourism', *Annals of Tourism Research*, 22: 781–803.

Ilbery, B. and Maye, D. (2005) 'Food supply chains and sustainability: evidence from specialist food producers in the Scottish/English borders', *Land Use Policy*, 22: 331–344.

IPCC (2007) *Working Group I. Climate Change 2007: The Physical Science Base*, www.ipcc.ch/ipccreports/ar4-wg1.htm (accessed 4 November 2010).

MacCannell, D. (1973) 'Staged authenticity: arrangements of social space in tourist settings', *The American Journal of Sociology*, 79(3): 589–603.

MacCannell, D. (1976) *The Tourist: A New Theory of the Leisure Class*, New York: Schocken Books.

Mepham, B. (1996) *Food Ethics*, London: Routledge.

Myers, G.S. (2004) *Howard County Farmers' Market Economic Impact Study 2004*, Howard County: Howard County Economic Development Authority, Agricultural Marketing Program.

Newholm, T. and Shaw, D. (2007) 'Studying the ethical consumer: a review of research', *Journal of Consumer Behaviour*, 6: 253–270.

Nietzsche, F. (1991 [1882]) *The Gay Science: With a Prelude in Rhymes and an Appendix of Songs*, trans. W. Kaufmann, New York: Random House.

Nietzsche, F. (1997 [1909]) *Thus Spoke Zarathustra: A Book For All and None*, trans. W. Kaufmann, Ware: Wordsworth Editions Limited.

Otto, D. and Varner, T. (2005) *Consumers, Vendors, and the Economic Importance of Iowa Farmers' Markets: An Economic Impact Survey Analysis*, Ames: Iowa State University.

Parkins, W. and Craig, G. (2006) *Slow Living*, Oxford: Berg

Popper, K.R. (1959 [1934]) *The Logic of Scientific Discovery*, London: Hutchinson & Co.

Popper, K.R. (1963) *Conjectures and Refutations*, London: Routledge & Keegan Paul Limited.

Sartre, J.P. (1948) *Existentialism and Humanism*, trans. P. Mairet, Eyre: Methuen.

Schlosser, E. (2002) *Fast Food Nation: What the All-American Meal is Doing to the World*, New York: Penguin.

Selwyn, T. (1996) 'Introduction', in T. Selwyn (ed.), *The Tourist Image: Myths And Myth Making in Tourism*, Chichester: Wiley, pp. 1–32.

Smith, D. (1994) *Food Watch*, London: HarperCollins.

Smith, V. (1977) *Hosts and Guests: The Anthropology of Tourism*, Oxford: Blackwell.

Steiner, C. and Reisinger, Y. (2006) 'Understanding existential authenticity', *Annals of Tourism Research*, 33(2): 299–318.

Stocks, C. (2009) 'Imported food could be greener than local, says DEFRA', *Farmers Weekly Interactive*, 27 July, www.fwi.co.uk/Articles/2009/07/27/116850/Imported-food-could-be-greener-than-local-says-DEFRA.htm (accessed 1 October 2013).

Taylor, D.H. (2006) 'Strategic considerations in the development of lean agri-food supply chains: a case study of the UK pork sector', *Supply Chain Management: An International Journal*, 11(3): 271–280.

Wang, N. (1999) 'Rethinking authenticity in tourism experience', *Annals of Tourism Research*, 26(2): 349–370.

Wang, Y. (2007) 'Customized authenticity begins at home', *Annals of Tourism Research*, 34(3): 289–804.

Wilson, B. (2008) *Swindled: From Poison Sweets to Counterfeit Coffee – the Dark History of the Food Cheats*, London: John Murray.

# 6

# BACK TO THE ROOTS – WHEN HIP MEETS SUSTAINABLE

## A case study of the Kartoffelkombinat in Munich

*Thomas Berron*

### Introduction

Germany has one of the most competitive grocery markets in the western hemisphere, because food is very low-priced. How can a CSA-oriented project like the Kartoffelkombinat be en vogue while other consumers cover their nutritional needs in the cheapest possible way? Which aspects need to be taken into consideration, when it comes to setting up a local food supply structure? Is this an idea limited to Munich or could it be replicated anywhere a community desires an unconventional diet and unconventional grocery shopping?

This chapter aims to demonstrate one of many ways to set up a regional, seasonal food supply structure in a metropolitan area. By illustrating the structure and function of the Kartoffelkombinat, different challenges will be described while strengths, weaknesses, opportunities and threats are analysed. This paper is merely a fraction of the work that has gone into setting up the Kartoffelkombinat. It is intended as an overview and maybe even an inspirational read, showing a different path to becoming an entrepreneur. The idea and its implementation need to be groundbreaking.

### What is CSA?

In order to understand the Kartoffelkombinat it is essential to understand the CSA concept: CSA implies that the members financially commit to the farm for an entire vegetation period (often one year). This enables the farmer to plan ahead since he knows exactly how many depend on him or her and how much money he or she has available.

The *European Handbook on Community Supported Agriculture* defines a CSA as 'a partnership between a farm and consumers, where the risks and the rewards of farming are shared' (Community Supported Agriculture for Europe, 2013: 6).

Given this fixed client base, the farmer grows as many vegetables as necessary to feed the community. He or she will do it in such a way that they produce the highest quality in the most sustainable way possible. However, the currencies exchanged between the farmer and the community are various, from produce, an event location or place of knowledge to money, labour and other specific expertise from the members of the CSA – depending on what the individual member can provide.

The term 'community-supported agriculture' was coined in the 1980s, when the bio-dynamic farming principles of the German philosopher and anthropologist Rudolf Steiner were applied in the United States by a German (Trauger Groh) and a Swiss farmer (Jan Vander Tuin), who created the first CSA (Adam, 2006: 1).

## Why did people come up with CSAs?

Rudolf Steiner and his approach to life and agriculture laid the foundation for the CSAs we know today. Originally known for his anthroposophical theories and biodynamic practices, Steiner inspired people to think in closed cycles and value the soil, the plants and the people in ways he thought suited them the most (McFadden, 2004).

Over time, the concept of CSA became an elaborate approach to solve the problems of industrialised food production. It originated way back in the day when it seemed to be the most common thing in the world to take care of the person who supplies your food. When trading started to pick up and globalisation made the world a denser and more closely connected place, certain shifts in the food structure became apparent: the production was moved to places where the principles of economies of scale and cheap labour applied. It became more affordable to import food than to grow it a mile from home. Supply outbalanced the demand while cheap labour and subsidies resulted in a plummeting of prices.

However, a growing number of people decided to rediscover their local farms. Food scandals, piles of grocery waste, lack of trust in the grocery industry and a growing awareness regarding health and diet are some of the aspects causing this.

Further, when talking to the members of a CSA venture, they seem to look for something to add to their everyday life, striving for meaning and finding it in something often referred to as 'honest work' or 'getting their hands dirty'. Many reminisce, thinking of times when they were working on their grandfather's farm or visiting friends in rural areas. In essence, the members enjoy switching jobs for a couple of hours and grounding themselves while reconnecting with nature, the earth and fresh produce.

## Why did Daniel and Simon start the Kartoffelkombinat?

In the summer of 2011, Daniel and Simon decided to launch the Kartoffelkombinat (English: potato cooperative) in Munich, Germany. They had met through colleagues and decided to set a higher standard for themselves and their families' dietary habits. They were being fed, but were fed up nonetheless. Subsequently, they began to rethink their personal role in the food system. Grocery stores were no longer an option for fulfilling this particular demand for local, high-quality produce. Offering the same assortment year round without regard to the carbon footprint made them realise that the upscale food industry was producing inferior goods while hurting local farmers and their foreign colleagues alike. And if they felt this way about their food, others might, too.

The Kartoffelkombinat is a big leap towards a local, sustainable, self-organised community and local food supply structure. In this day and age, where you can ignore or condemn the way your food is produced, Daniel and Simon chose to look closely at how they could create a model that reaches people in the city and connects them to the agricultural folk that work hard to produce their food.

In a more holistic perspective, their aim was to pave the way towards the 'good life' where future generations had opportunities their parents always sought, not solely paying for the previous generation's sins but reconnecting with the country, the soil and the people who produce the food we eat.

## What are the goals of the Kartoffelkombinat?

The Kartoffelkombinat is strongly influenced by the concept of CSA. Yet, there are slight variations and specifics that Daniel and Simon emphasise. In order to make the Kartoffelkombinat strategy more comprehensible the following guidelines were solidified in a mission statement. These distinguish the Kartoffelkombinat from other merchants or farms using the delivery box system.

- Supply food for the members of the cooperative.
- Supervise cultivation, processing and distribution.
- Fair pay for all employees and helpers involved.
- Transparent decision-making process as a registered cooperative.
- Product and service tailored to the metropolitan area of Munich.
- Affordability for the members.
- Additional value, such as events, workshops, sense of community.

## How does the Kartoffelkombinat work?

There seems to be a certain predicament in our society. People seem to buy what they want and what they know in a store that is convenient and often close to home. The closer a store is to full supply for its customers, the better. However, some supermarkets sporadically offer fresh, local, seasonal produce. This is not necessarily to the supermarket's credit. It is simply reacting to the demand of their customers.

Further, the German grocery market is one of the most competitive in the world (Knorr and Arndt, 2003: 16–17). A country with a notorious propensity to save (on food) and being the origin of grocery discounters such as Aldi, Lidl, etc. made it unfeasible (among other reasons) for the largest grocer in the world, Walmart, to last in Germany (Handelsblatt, 2002). Does this seem like a desirable, competitive environment?

The aim of the Kartoffelkombinat is not to steal customers from grocery stores but rather to offer an alternative and make fresh local produce as accessible as possible. And this is the main service the Kartoffelkombinat is providing: pairing CSA with a customer-oriented food supply system. In addition to high-quality, organic produce, this is a popular culinary trend in Munich, where the Kartoffelkombinat is a registered cooperative. Daniel and Simon make up the executive board. A board of directors reviews the executives' actions.

Being a registered cooperative entitles the members to participate in the decision-making process. However, to join the Kartoffelkombinat in the first place, they have to purchase a cooperative share (currently €150, January 2014). If, for any reason, a member decides to leave the cooperative, his money will be refunded entirely without interest. He or she may do so twice a year (July and December). This is in line with the growing cycle: plant something now, harvest it in a couple of weeks or even months.

The cost for a share is set deliberately at a medium level. Daniel and Simon want people to join easily while still thinking twice about their commitment. In times of financial hardship, the members are not obliged to contribute to a compulsory call for funds.

For some people it is a bit of a stretch to switch their current habit of shopping and cooking to a weekly box delivery system. Hence, there is a six-week testing phase that does not require the purchase of a cooperative share. If the testing period was a success, the purchase of the share is mandatory.

Members will receive a box with fresh produce every week except during the Christmas holidays. In return, they make a financial contribution of €68 per month (January 2014). The first €68 payment of six is due in February, the second in July. This covers the expenses and other fixed costs the farmer has in advance.

Even though the vegetable box appears to be the main reason to join the Kartoffelkombinat, there is a loophole in leaving the opportunity to contribute to the cause without receiving the vegetables from the farm. People who live too far away, have food allergies or maybe grow their own food might not want or need these vegetables. But they could still be interested in participating in the other activities the Kartoffelkombinat has to offer. Therefore, these people pay a fee of €30 (January 2014) or higher in order to use the services such as the library, the cinema or the academy.

## SWOT analysis of the Kartoffelkombinat

The SWOT analysis (strengths, weaknesses, opportunities, threats) is a helpful tool to clarify a business' strengths and weaknesses. This is an internal view and evaluation of core competences and services. However, there are also external factors that help position the enterprise within the market and the competition, exposing potential opportunities and threats (Goodrich, 2013). What is the unique selling proposition of the Kartoffelkombinat? Which areas need improvement or need to be re-evaluated? Which other areas could the Kartoffelkombinat tap into? Are other competitors threatening the future of the Kartoffelkombinat?

### *Strengths – what is the Kartoffelkombinat's unique selling proposition (USP)?*

The Kartoffelkombinat appeals to the public for various reasons. By cutting out the middle man and sharing value on every level in the process, every stakeholder gains.

Farmers no longer need to carry the risk of production all by themselves. They get paid in advance and get the money to continue farming. The collaboration with the Kartoffelkombinat could also be the answer to a very important question for a farmer: Is a willing and capable successor available? If not, having an organisation such as the Kartoffelkombinat might offer a solution to that predicament.

By becoming a partner in the Kartoffelkombinat model small farms will be able to remain competitive in the sense that 'the vegetables lose their price but regain their worth' (Gartencoop Freiburg, 2012), while the farm specialises in certain varieties and offers produce for the cooperative. With smaller sustainable farms in place a good contribution to the conservation of the environment is made.

Members receive fresh, high-quality produce that has not been contaminated by chemicals or pesticides. Also, the associates regain their personal economical sovereignty through trust and transparency alike, gaining knowledge about growing and processing food that would otherwise continue to vanish. Since everything is seasonal, there is a certain anticipation and excitement when the harvest of speciality items is approaching, such as the first picking of the tomatoes. To align oneself with the changing seasons and its harvest is something that many people have forgotten to do.

If you are in need of a decent workout or if you are just bored with your job, feel free to roll up your sleeves and contribute your service to the farm for a nice round of weeding or spreading manure with a pitchfork.

The members' contribution ensures fair pay for the farmer and all the employees involved. When a job covers salary, food and community – that is when it starts to be fun! New job opportunities and challenges arise and need to be met, which is a very exciting prospect for the employees.

All stakeholders form a cooperative that increases their sense of doing something good for the self, the community and the environment.

The cooperation of a farmer such as Sigi Klein with almost 30 years of experience with two men like Daniel and Simon with an extraordinary vision and an extensive marketing background makes for a powerful combination that is bound to stir up the way people view food, farmers and agriculture. This is a win–win–win situation all around. The era of 'farmer wants a wife' is over. Nowadays, the community wants a farmer.

## Weaknesses – disadvantages to doing it the Kartoffelkombinat way

After all the information above the reader might be wondering about the disadvantages of the Kartoffelkombinat. So far, it seems like this is a great idea and a good deal for the farmers and members. There are, however, certain challenges that should be addressed in this part. If a farming enthusiast, for whatever reason, wants to set up his or her own CSA model, he or she might encounter certain speed bumps along the way.

There are various ways to set up a CSA. Sometimes, the founding fathers look for the members first before they set out to find a piece of land and start growing vegetables. All the necessary initial investments (tractor, green house, etc.) are divided by the number of members. This defines the amount for the co-operative share (often much higher than €150). Then, they hire a farmer (or they might be farmers themselves) to run the agricultural side of things. Competence and expertise are divided and clear and the CSA model and mindset is 100 per cent incorporated into the farm.

The Kartoffelkombinat is growing into an existing farming structure that specialises in selling to wholesalers and running its own farm shop. The owner Sigi Klein has been managing the farm for almost 30 years as the sole proprietor. He has a lot of experience, also in regard to packaging, transport and other box delivery systems. Simon and Daniel have unconventional ideas and confidence in their venture. And even though everyone has the same goal, everyone has a slightly different way of going about achieving it. Naturally, there is an adjustment period.

Dwight Eisenhower, the 34th President of the United States of America, said during an address at Bradley University, Peoria, Illinois, 1956: 'Farming looks mighty easy when your plough is a pencil, and you are a thousand miles from the corn field.' What he presumably meant by this is there are many variables when growing vegetables. You do not simply put seed in the ground and a couple weeks later you harvest it. Further, it is very difficult to squeeze a tomato plant into an Excel spreadsheet and predict the amount of kilograms the farmer will harvest in different growth periods. Hence, there is no way to give the members the exact same share. There will always be too much or too few of something. Therefore, it is crucial to become familiar with the basic principles of farming and create a framework that allows some 'wiggle room' and flexibility regarding farming variables.

In comparison to other box delivery systems, the Kartoffelkombinat has set very strict guidelines on how they choose to do business. While this is a great way to create a unique selling proposition, it may hinder other efforts. An example: in order to launch a real alternative supply structure, Daniel and Simon wanted to be part of a fully self-sustainable system that does not borrow any credit capital. All the money has to come from either within the cooperative or from sponsorships and donations. So the 'leverage effect' might not apply to the Kartoffelkombinat but in case the financial system crashes, the members are covered. Other possible but currently not realisable tasks are box delivery with emission-free cars or bikes, or turf-free farming. These are aspects that the Kartoffelkombinat is currently working on. However, it is more about continually working towards these goals than going the 'all or nothing' route.

Complexity and bureaucracy should also be mentioned here. While other types of business ownership allow more security and less calibration in the administration and decision-making process, the registered cooperative is indispensable for a transparent, self-sovereign structure.

In December 2012 the Kartoffelkombinat consisted of approximately 80 members. Only one year later, it had grown to 380 members. This is quite a significant jump. While it seems very tempting to 'storm the gates' and do everything at once, it is vitally important to let the different parts grow consistently. The farm is capable of providing the quantities of vegetables; packaging and delivery needed to grow accordingly. The off-season is a great time to direct resources into refining the overall infrastructure.

There are various challenges but none of them are so severe that the future of the Kartoffelkombinat is in danger. These are points to consider if the aim is to set up a similar business combining proven traditional methods and new innovative ideas.

## *Opportunities – CSA of unlimited possibilities*

The Kartoffelkombinat is in the process of a friendly takeover of the farm Sigi Klein, which was mutually agreed upon at the beginning.

A next step could be to take another farm under the Kartoffelkombinat's wing. In order to be compatible, the additional farm ought to offer slightly different produce (open land instead of green house, stored instead of fresh fruit and vegetables, etc.). Not only would this split the risk of production, it would also increase the width of the assortment. Synergy emerges as the executive board incorporates the new farm into the marketing strategy.

Other possibilities are to diversify the portfolio and offer additional products such as preserves, processed food (e.g., flour, pasta), beer or clothing. The risk is very low, because the members of the cooperative will be able to decide in advance whether they want to purchase these products or not. In order to cover the cost of production, packaging, logistics, etc., interested members will be able to pay another share for the Kartoffelkombinat Pasta cooperative, limiting the liability in case things do not work out. With an increasing client base there are various ways to 'play-test' additions to the scenario without endangering the main business.

Since the Kartoffelkombinat is on its way to becoming one of the most significant CSAs in Germany, it could offer consulting services such as a CSA consultancy in regard to branding, bureaucracy and community-building. Some farmers might have great produce and a beautiful farm, but lack time or expertise in marketing and community-building. Others might not have a farming background but are well-equipped in the marketing department. The Kartoffelkombinat can offer a step-by-step guide on how to handle the bureaucracy and challenges they have faced themselves.

## Threats – 'sowing is not as difficult as reaping' (Goethe)

There are different threats that immediately come to mind when talking about competitors: other box delivery systems, farmers markets, organic grocery stores and regular supermarkets with a partially organic assortment. There are also more indirect threats, such as farm shops and other social or ecological organisations.

Given a fixed household budget there are limited projects that can be supported. But the so called 'threats' are not really competition. It is more about creating fundamental change, even on a political level. The more sustainable, organic projects that are out there, the better. So to lure the customers of another project into the Kartoffelkombinat is not a real source of business; it is rather another potential partner to collaborate with and share expertise and experience.

## Conclusion

The Kartoffelkombinat took the concept of a traditional CSA and added its own twist to it. Its success is based on the conviction of Simon and Daniel and the members. Having the idea of a food supply structure and developing it while establishing a community of like-minded people might seem like an uphill battle at first. But the more people join in, the more momentum is being created. This cooperative has made local, organic food accessible to almost 400 homes. If forecasts and news articles are any indication, the organic trend will continue and change the way we experience food and agriculture in the long run. 'People will always need food' is a common saying. However, people should also talk about food and how it is produced. Food scandals, obscured labelling and employee exploitation are only some of the symptoms. Why not change the way of thinking in regard to food? A couple of folks from Munich are doing it right now. And so can you.

## References

Adam, K. (2006) *Community Supported Agriculture*, http://attra.ncat.org/attra-pub/csa.html (accessed 26 December 2013).

Community Supported Agriculture for Europe (2013) *European Handbook on Community Supported Agriculture*, http://future-farmers.net/2013/10/04/european-handbook-on-community-supported-agriculture-csa-is-out-and-available-for-free-download/ (accessed 14 October 2013).

Eisenhower, D. (1956) *Address at Bradley University, Peoria, Illinois, 25 Sept 1956*, www.eisenhower.archives.gov/all_about_ike/quotes.html and also www.ranker.com/list/notable-and-famous-farming-and-farmers-quotes/reference (accessed 16 December 2013).

Gartencoop, Freiburg (2012) *Die Strategie der krummen Gurken*, www.gartencoop.org/tunsel/film (accessed 15 May 2013).

Goethe, J.W. (n.d.) *Famous Farming and Farmers Quotes*, www.ranker.com/list/notable-and-famous-farming-and-farmers-quotes/reference (accessed 16 December 2013).

Goodrich, R. (2013) 'SWOT analysis: examples, templates and definition', *Business News Daily*, www.businessnewsdaily.com/4245-swot-analysis.html (accessed 11 November 2013).

Handelsblatt (2002) *Wal-Mart wagt zweiten Anlauf in Deutschland*, www.handelsblatt.com/archiv/nach-einer-reihe-grober-managementfehler-wal-mart-wagt-zweiten-anlauf-in-deutschland/2183544.html (accessed 26 December 2013).

Knorr, A. and Arndt, A. (2003) 'Why did Wal-Mart fail in Germany', *Materialien des Wissenschaftsschwerpunktes: 'Globalisierung der Weltwirtschaft'*, 24.

McFadden, S. (2004) *Community Supported Agriculture*, http://solutions.synearth.net/2004/02/working-together-658/ (accessed 16 November 2013).

## Additional information

www.kartoffelkombinat.de
http://future-farmers.net/2013/10/04/european-handbook-on-community-supported-agriculture-csa-is-out-and-available-for-free-download
www.dhbw-mosbach.de/studienangebote/food-management.html
www.attrac.ncat.org
www.nal.usda.gov/afsic/pubs/csa/csa.shtml

# 7

# NUTRITION IN RURAL INDIA

*Richa Govil*

## Introduction

Malnutrition (or more precisely, "undernutrition") rates in India are alarming, with 39 per cent of women aged 15–49 and 47 per cent of children under three reported as undernourished in rural areas (NFHS, 2007). The direct causes of undernourishment are inadequate dietary intake and diseases that diminish the human body's ability to absorb nutrients (UNICEF, 2011). Inadequate dietary intake and diseases are, in turn, caused by poor access to affordable food and clean water, sanitation, health services and inadequate care of individuals within a household, as shown in Figure 7.1.

Underlying these household characteristics are the systemic causes that drive undernutrition, such as income poverty, lack of sufficient capital, or the poor quality of human, physical and natural resources. Social and cultural factors also play a critical role in determining the intra-household distribution of scarce resources and services. For example, the patriarchal tradition of women eating last in the household results in persistent inadequate nutrition for female members of the family whenever the supply of nutritious foods (which are typically more expensive) is limited.

Undernutrition among children is measured against international World Health Organization (WHO) standards for height-for-age, weight-for-age and weight-for-height. The latest year for which comprehensive national level data is available in India is 2005–2006, and it shows that in rural India, where the majority of the Indian population resides, 47 per cent of children under three years of age do not achieve height standards and are considered stunted (NFHS, 2007).

Undernutrition among adults is typically measured against international standards for Body Mass Index (BMI), and currently stands at 39 per cent and 33 per cent for women and men respectively in rural India (NFHS, 2007). Across the country (urban and rural), while the prevalence of undernutrition per most indicators has been declining, the decline has been very slow and not commensurate with the rapid economic growth during the same period (Deaton and Dreze, 2009). This raises serious academic and practical concerns about the best approaches for addressing undernutrition.

In addition, iron deficiency is alarmingly high across the country, with about 81 per cent of the children (aged 6–35 months), about 58 per cent of adult women and 28 per cent of adult men in rural India suffering from anaemia (NFHS, 2007).

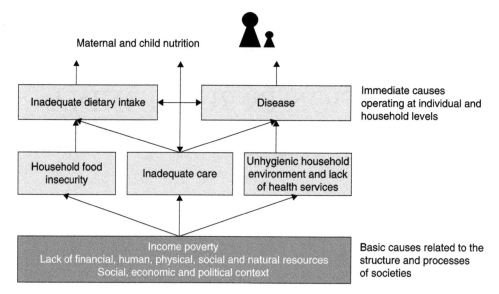

*Figure 7.1* Causes of undernutrition.

Adapted from UNICEF (2011).

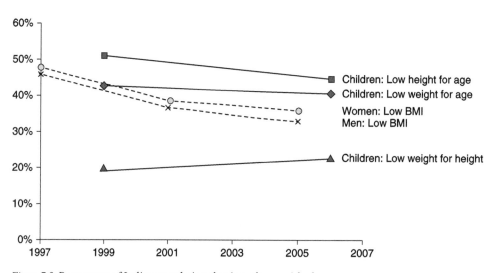

*Figure 7.2* Percentage of Indian population that is undernourished.

*Source:* Deaton and Dreze, 2009.

*Note:* Children under age of 3; Children's undernourishment measured against new WHO standards.

As mentioned above, there are many direct and indirect factors that cause undernutrition, including water, sanitation and maternal care. However, the scope of this chapter is limited to dietary intake. We will examine national trends pertaining to undernutrition and dietary intake, and household-level trends regarding dietary habits from a household study. In doing so, we will cover both supply- and demand-side factors. In this chapter, we will focus on women's nutrition because their undernutrition level is worse than that of men and also because their health status affects that of their children during pregnancy and early child-hood, thus multiplying its (negative) impact.

Undernutrition and dietary intake levels vary across different states within India. These differences and the social and economic factors that influence them are beyond the scope of this chapter.

## Food expenditure and dietary intake

Food consumption and nutrition trends in India pose a puzzling scenario. There has been a significant reduction in self-reported hunger: the National Sample Survey shows that the percentage of households reporting insufficient food for "two square meals a day" dropped in rural India from 18.5 per cent in 1983 to 2.4 per cent in 2005 (Saxena, 2011). Yet, the propor-tion of the population getting the FAO minimum of 1,800 calories per day was 40 per cent in 2009–2010 (Himanshu and Sen, 2013). Thus while abject hunger may not be an issue on average, sufficiency of quantity continues to be an issue. In fact, the current challenge in India is less about hunger per se and more about sufficient intake of calories and micro-nutrients required by the human body for health and vitality.

Surprisingly, despite economic growth and reduction of poverty, the per capita consump-tion of calories and protein has been decreasing in India. Between 1988 and 2005, while real per capita expenditure increased by 15 per cent, real expenditure on food remained stable despite an increase in real cost of calories (Figure 7.3).

The per capita consumption of calories dropped by around 10 per cent and proteins slightly more, while per capita consumption of fats increased by about 25 per cent (Figure 7.4). This reduction in caloric intake is despite increase in food production outstripping population growth as shown in Figure 7.5 (FAO, 2014). Therefore it is instructive to understand the various factors that drive dietary intake in rural India.

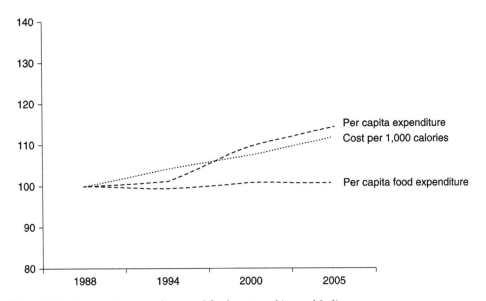

*Figure 7.3* Real per capita expenditure and food cost trend in rural India.

*Source:* Adapted from Deaton and Dreze, 2009.

*Note:* 1998 normalized to 100.

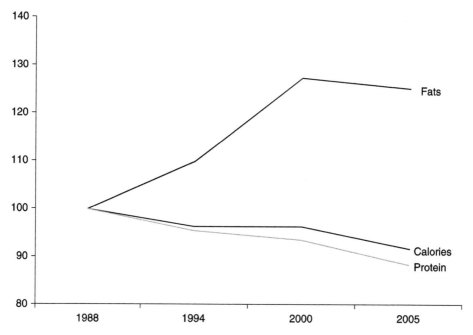

*Figure 7.4* Per capita consumption trends in rural India.

*Source:* Adapted from Deaton and Dreze, 2009.

*Note:* 1998 normalized to 100.

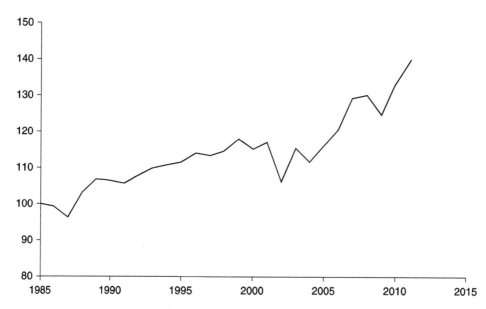

*Figure 7.5* Food production index per capita (FAO, 2014).

*Source:* Adapted from FAOSTAT, 2014.

*Note:* 1985 normalized to 100.

## Food intake of women in rural India

It is important to pay special attention to the nutritional status of women for multiple reasons. First, women in India show much higher prevalence of undernourishment than men. Second, nutritionists have long recognized that the best time to address the nutritional needs of an individual is during the first 1,000 days of life, from conception to approximately three years of age. Third, women are typically the ones who buy and prepare food for the family. Thus their choices (and limitations) usually determine household nutrition.

While national statistics are useful for understanding macro trends in consumption, primary field surveys are a good source of information about micro-level behaviours and preferences of the population. The author was engaged in such a field survey of rural women in the Indian state of Karnataka (Ashoka, 2013). This paper will rely extensively on insights from this survey.

The survey obtained more than 1,500 responses from young mothers and pregnant women in three rural districts in the state of Karnataka, India. The women were engaged in a variety of occupations such as cultivation, livestock keeping, agricultural labour (at farms owned by others), etc. The age of respondents ranged from 16 to 47, with an average of 24 years. All women surveyed were either pregnant or had children under the age of four.

The survey was conducted in a state where rice is a staple, and it is not surprising that 99 per cent of women reported consuming it "the previous day".

Seventy-three per cent of women reported consuming millets the previous day. Millets are "coarse cereals" such as sorghum (jowar), finger millet (ragi) and bajra (pearl millet). Millets are part of the traditional Indian diet, particularly in rural areas. Typically millets are more nutritious than rice or wheat and therefore their consumption is of particular interest from a nutrition perspective.

Ninety-three per cent of the women reported consuming pulses and beans on the day prior to the survey. Pulses, such as lentils, are a good source of protein, and therefore also of interest from a nutrition perspective.

Roughly half the respondents reported eating green leafy vegetables, which are a rich source of iron vitamins and other nutrients and often recommended by doctors for pregnant women. However, further probing revealed that the women consider any green-coloured vegetables such as gourds to be "green leafy vegetables". Therefore this number is likely to be an overstatement of the degree of consumption of greens, which are an important source of micro-nutrients including iron.

Almost half the respondents (46 per cent) reported eating fruits at least twice a week. However, with the exception of bananas, fruits are rarely consumed because of their expense and inconvenience. Due to high perishability, poor rural households typically buy them in smaller quantities once a week.

Focus group discussions revealed that women prefer buying vegetables over fruits not only because fruits cost roughly twice as much per kilogram as vegetables, but also because even small quantities of vegetables can be shared more easily among family members.

A very small percentage of surveyed women had consumed either chicken or eggs during the previous day; the majority consumed them only once or twice a month.

The survey did not find an appreciable difference between food items consumed by women and the rest of the family. However, focus group discussions and field visits highlighted that within a household, women eat last (after children and male members) and therefore if only a limited quantity of an item is available they eat whatever is left, if anything at all.

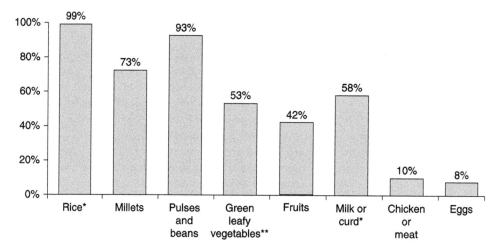

*Figure 7.6* Food items consumed by young mothers.

*Source:* Ashoka Nutrition Survey, 2013. Survey of 1,500+ pregnant women and mothers of young children in 3 districts in Karnataka, India.

*Note:* ★ Data from only 2 districts. ★★ Some respondents interpreted "green leafy vegetables" as any vegetable green in colour. Therefore this data is likely to overrepresent consumption of green leafy vegetables.

> Mahalaxmi (composite profile) is a landless, daily wage labourer in Raichur district of Karnataka. She belongs to a scheduled caste and lives in a "kutcha" (semi-permanent or temporary) house with her husband and three children. She works on other farmers' fields for daily wages during sowing, weeding and transplanting seasons. She does not earn enough money to buy fruits and vegetables on a regular basis.
>
> She says she can afford a quarter litre of milk daily but the local dairy refuses to sell her such a small quantity.

## Source of food in rural India

The majority of the food consumed in rural households is bought from the local markets. The Ashoka household survey also reflects this (Figure 7.7).

While 77 per cent of households purchase rice, 23 per cent grow some or all of the rice they consume. In addition, 73 per cent of respondents reported buying at least some quantity of rice through the Public Distribution System (PDS). The PDS is a food security system established by the government of India that distributes highly subsidized food to poor households through a network of PDS shops.

Millets present an interesting case. Since millet value chains and market linkages tend to be underdeveloped compared to rice, a greater percentage (29 per cent) of households report growing some or all the millets they consume. In addition, approximately 2 per cent of households report sourcing millets through exchange (barter).

Overall, around 15–30 per cent of the women in the survey reported that they consume rice, millets and/or milk from self-grown produce, consistent with the national average.

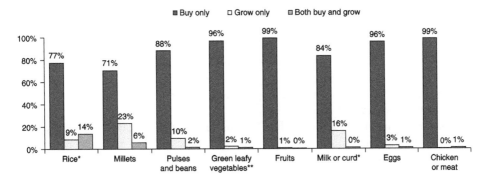

*Figure* 7.7 Source of food.

*Source:* Ashoka Nutrition Survey, 2013. Survey of 1,500+ pregnant women and mothers of young children in 3 districts in Karnataka, India.

*Note:* Data for small percentage of respondents who source food through exchange (barter) excluded from analysis. They represent 2% of millet consumers and <1% of consumers of pulses & beans. ★ Data from only 2 districts. ★★ Some respondents interpreted "green leafy vegetables" as any vegetable green in colour. Therefore this data is likely to overrepresent consumption of green leafy vegetables.

Nationally, households which produce a commodity (e.g., vegetables) consume much more of that commodity than non-producers (NSSO, 2013). For example, vegetable producers consume 30–60 per cent more vegetables than non-producers.

In the Ashoka survey, farmer households that produced a certain food item consistently reported consuming the food item more frequently than those households who do not produce the item. For example, producers of millets, which as described earlier are traditional staples, reported consuming millets more frequently than non-producers: 90 per cent of producers reported consuming millets almost daily (at least five times per week), compared to only 77 per cent of non-producers.

Previous research also supports this conclusion: "With very few exceptions, home garden programs increased the consumption of fruit and vegetables; aquaculture and small fisheries interventions increased the consumption of fish; and dairy development projects increased the consumption of milk" (Masset et al., 2012). The World Bank also views agriculture as a critical pathway to achieving reduction in undernutrition (World Bank, 2013). A recent study comparing performance of different states in India showed a strong link between adult nutrition and agricultural performance (Gulati et al., 2012). It found that improving agricultural productivity can be a powerful tool for reducing undernutrition in rural areas.

Thus, agriculture is recognized as an effective means for reducing undernutrition in rural areas, even though less than a third of the households grow any food for consumption. Producers increase not only the supply of food items grown for their own households, but also the local availability of those foods for the village or village cluster.

## Women farmers: where food production and consumption converge

Women farmers form a critical link between agriculture, household income and nutritional status. Nationally, women constitute 37 per cent of the agriculture workforce of India and are engaged in agricultural activities such as cultivation, livestock rearing and working as agricultural labourers on other people's farms (Census of India, 2014). These women farmers offer a particularly effective path to achieving better nutrition (Herforth and Harris, 2013). There are many reasons for this:

1. Households in which women do agriculture work, are among the poorest households in the country. Therefore targeting women farmers self-selects the most marginalized households.
2. As mentioned earlier, households that produce a commodity (e.g., vegetables) consume more of that commodity than non-producers.
3. Women are more likely to be involved in consumption farming and livestock than men. Almost all women who engage in any kind of agricultural activity produce some food items for household consumption (Ashoka, 2013). Women's involvement in production is higher for nutrient-rich produce such as vegetables, millets and dairy. Therefore it is logical to target women farmers when aiming to achieve better nutrition through agriculture.
4. Increasing total household income does not necessarily increase the nutritional status of the household. However, increasing women's income can have as much as 11 times the impact on children's nutrition and health than increasing men's income (World Bank, 2009).

We present a framework (Figure 7.8) to depict the multiple ways in which women farmers and their activities are intricately tied to household income and nutrition. First and foremost, women farmers contribute labour to household agriculture activities through the crops or livestock they produce (bottom layer of Figure 7.8).

If this produce is nutrient-rich, it contributes to the availability of nutritious foods for the household and 1.3 to 1.6 times greater consumption of the produced items (for vegetables; even higher for milk). The increased income leads to increased calorie consumption though

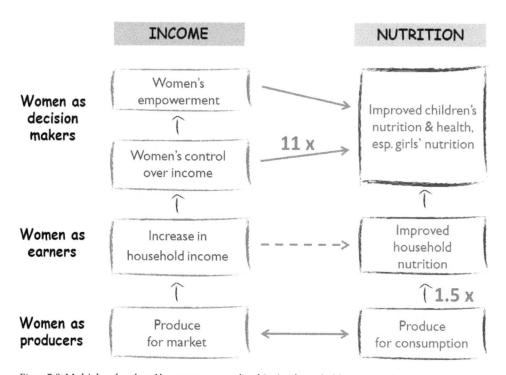

*Figure 7.8* Multiple roles played by women towards achieving household income and nutrition outcomes.

it does not necessarily lead to increased nutrition (Deaton and Dreze, 2009). Frequency of consumption of most foods increases with self-reported income: this is particularly true for green leafy vegetables, fruits, milk or curd and soft drinks (Ashoka, 2013).

As mentioned earlier, increasing women's income has a much higher impact on child education and health compared to men's income. This makes it imperative to improve women's influence over income and expenditure, especially in patriarchal societies in India. Improvements in women's empowerment also have a strong impact in investment in children's education and health, especially for female children.

## Increasing demand for nutritious foods

The discussions so far point towards an opportunity to tackle undernourishment by creating agricultural interventions targeted at women who engage in farming activities, whether as part of market-oriented agriculture or vegetable gardens. Such interventions operate at multiple levels. They increase the supply of nutritious foods for the household and possibly for the local community in the village or village cluster. The market-oriented programmes also increase household income through better market linkages, and sometimes incorporate programme elements that increase women's control over the earned income.

However, for improving nutrition, increasing the supply of nutritious food is not enough; it is equally important to increase demand for nutritious foods, which we discuss next.

In the West, there has been an increased awareness of nutritious diets to address "overnutrition" and obesity. For most of the rural population of India the challenge is the opposite, namely to address "undernutrition", as discussed above. However, both challenges require the creation of mechanisms which drive people to seek and incorporate more nutritious foods in their regular diet.

But changing human habits, especially those related to dietary intake, is incredibly difficult. Knowing that we must eat a nutritious diet and acting upon that knowledge are two very different things.

In the Ashoka survey, more than 97 per cent of the women knew that millets are more nutritious than rice, yet fewer women report consuming millets at least five times per week (81 per cent compared to 99 per cent for rice). Thus in rural India, just as in the West, awareness of nutrition value does not necessarily lead to healthy dietary practices.

There are innumerable studies in psychology, decision science and behavioural economics that highlight the fact that human behaviours and habits are not always rational decisions and are influenced by many other factors. In fact, by some estimates, up to 45 per cent of our daily actions are driven by behaviours repeated in the same location, in other words, habits (Neal et al., 2006). Studies designed to evaluate whether habits or explicit behavioural intentions are better predictors of future behaviour show that, regardless of people's intentions, strong habits tend to predominate in contexts such as riding bicycles, voting in national elections, drinking milk, eating snack food, watching TV, exercising and purchasing fast food (Wood et al., 2014).

This fact has both positive and negative implications: While it is very difficult to change behaviours, it is possible to do so if we use well-tested behaviour change principles. For example, one study focused on impulse buys of junk food by children in the school cafeteria. By replacing chips and snacks at the cash register with fruits, researchers observed an increase in purchase of fruits and a decrease in purchase of unhealthy snacks (Just and Wansink, 2009). Such behavioural techniques have been shown to work in other contexts such as helping people increase their savings over time. Behavioural economists Richard Thaler and Shlomo Benartzi created a programme called Save More Tomorrow, under which participants signed up to increase future contributions to savings with every pay rise. At the time of commitment, the future contribution percentages were recorded and automatically came into effect, with the possibility of opting out. In this case, procrastination and inertia led to no request for changes at the time of the rise, and therefore, increased savings (Karlan and Appel, 2011).

Despite such research and pilots, the development sector in India and elsewhere still relies almost exclusively on conventional approaches, such as awareness campaigns, for creating positive behaviours. A handful of social entrepreneurs do recognize this gap and are creating innovative programmes to drive change. However, to create lasting change, such techniques need to be studied in the context of developing countries and then deployed on a larger scale.

## Conclusion

As described earlier, a large percentage of India's population, especially women and children, suffer from undernutrition, which in part is due to inadequate dietary intake. While supply-side challenges can be addressed through agricultural interventions designed to improve productivity and market-linkage, there is an equally important need to drive nutrition-seeking behaviour among undernourished populations.

Women farmers offer a particularly interesting leverage point, not only because they are highly undernourished, but also because they are producers of some of the most nutritious produce available in rural areas, such as millets, vegetables and milk.

Some of the specific opportunities include providing better agricultural information to women farmers, especially on more nutritious produce. Providing women farmers productivity improvement support for produce grown for consumption is as essential as for produce intended for the market. And development of better tools and equipment designed for women farmers and the activities they do can help free up women's time for health and nutrition related activities. Creating better market linkage for crops cultivated by women farmers, and helping increase their influence and control over the income is an effective method for directing more of the household income towards health and nutrition.

In addition, there are many other approaches that can be leveraged for improving the supply of nutritious produce. As noted earlier, the majority of rural inhabitants purchase the food they eat. Therefore it is essential to fix supply chain issues that limit the availability of perishable produce such as milk and vegetables in rural areas, especially those that are not produced locally. There is also a need to increase the variety of nutritious foods available through India's Public Distribution System. The 2013 Food Security Act, which incorporates millets as a subsidized food item in the PDS, is a step in the right direction.

Equally important, it is essential to drive nutrition-seeking behaviours not only through awareness-building but also through state-of-the-art behavioural techniques.

## Acknowledgements

The survey cited in this paper was conducted as part of the author's work at Ashoka: Innovators for the Public, India. The author thanks Garima Rana for conducting the field research and rigorous analysis of findings. She thanks Archana Sinha for survey execution and analysis inputs and Siddharth Dixit for validation.

# References

Ashoka (2013) *Agriculture and Nutrition Surveys*, unpublished, Ashoka Innovators for the Public.

Census of India (2014) *Census of India: Primary Census Abstract Highlights*, www.censusindia.gov. in/2011census/PCA/PCA_Highlights/pca_highlights_india.html (accessed 14 February 2014).

Deaton, A. and Dreze, J. (2009) "Food and nutrition in India: facts and interpretations", *Economics and Political Weekly*, 44(7): 44–65.

FAO (2014) *FAOSTAT*, http://faostat.fao.org/site/612/DesktopDefault.aspx?PageID=612#ancor (accessed 3 February 2014).

Gulati, A., Ganesh-Kumar, A., Shreedhar, G. and Nandakumar, T. (2012) "Agriculture and malnutrition in India", *Food and Nutrition Bulletin*, 33(11): 74–86.

Herforth, A. and Harris, J. (2013) *From Agriculture to Nutrition: Pathways and Principles, Feed the Future, Agriculture-Nutrition Global Learning and Evidence Exchange (AgN-GLEE)*, Feed the Future.

Himanshu and Sen, A. (2013) "In-kind food transfers – II: impact on nutrition and implications for food security and its costs", *Economics and Political Weekly*, 48(47): 60–73.

Just, D.R. and Wansink, B. (2009) "Smarter lunchrooms: using behavioral economics to improve meal selection", *Choices*, 24(3): 1–7.

Karlan, D. and Appel, J. (2011) *More Than Good Intentions*, New York: Penguin.

Masset, E., Haddad, L., Cornelius, A. and Isaza-Castro, J. (2012) "Effectiveness of agricultural interventions that aim to improve nutritional status of children: systematic review", *BMJ*, 344: d8222.

Neal, D.T., Wood, W. and Quinn, J.M. (2006) "Habits – a repeat performance", *Current Directions in Psychological Science*, 15(4): 198–202.

NFHS (2007) *Key Indicators for India from NFHS-3*, National Family Health Survey, India, IIPS, www. rchiips.org/nfhs/pdf/India.pdf (accessed 3 February 2014).

NSSO (2013) *Public Distribution System and Other Sources of Household Consumption, 2009–2010*, New Delhi: Government of India.

Saxena, N.C. (2011) *Hunger, Under-Nutrition and Food Security in India*, CPRC India Working Paper 44.

UNICEF (2011) *Conceptual Framework for Nutrition*, www.unicef.org/nutritioncluster/files/ Module5CausesOfMalnutritionTechnicalNotes.pdf (accessed 17 January 2014).

Wood, W., Labrecque, J.S., Lin, P.Y. and Rünger, D. (2014) "Habits in dual process models", in J.W. Sherman, B. Gawronski and Y. Trope (eds.), *Dual Process Theories of the Social Mind*, New York: Guilford Press.

World Bank (2009) *Gender in Agriculture Sourcebook*, New York: World Bank.

World Bank (2013) *Improving Nutrition through Multisectoral Approaches*, New York: World Bank.

# 8

# ABORIGINAL FOOD

## Traditional dishes surviving in the fast food era

*Donald Sinclair and Carolann Marcus*

### Introduction

The focus of this study is the menus that are rooted in the ancestral traditions of the people that comprise modern-day Guyana, the styles of food preparation that have survived through time, been passed on principally through oral transmission and have left an indelible print upon even the most sophisticated modern Guyanese dish. Aboriginal food finds a place in these ancestral traditions, embracing recipes and cooking methods that go back centuries, are just as popular and appealing today and are a feature of mainstream culinary practice. There is a manifest strength and persistence in this Amerindian culinary tradition in Guyana that serves as a tool for the enhancement of the indigenous cultural identity. In the context of this article, the survival and persistence of Amerindian food and Amerindian culinary tradition must be seen essentially as the triumph of 'the bush'. In terms of the anthropology of food, the pattern that emerges is of an interior culinary tradition that survives and coexists with 'coastal' and foreign concoctions of more recent vintage. This theme of a triumphant interior tradition will underlie the discussion in the section that follows.

### Guyana – brief background

Guyana (formerly British Guiana) lies on the north-eastern coast of South America, occupying an area of 214,970km² (83,000 square miles). The country shares borders with Brazil to the south, Venezuela to the west, Suriname to the east and it abuts the Atlantic Ocean to the north-east. The official language is English, although some Amerindians, especially those residing in the remote interior locations, speak their indigenous languages. The total population, as recorded in the census of 2002, is 751,233. The capital city is Georgetown, situated on the north-eastern Atlantic coast (Daniels, 2010).

From the standpoint of the thematic of this chapter it is important to observe that the colony of British Guiana was the object of a colonial exploitation that was concentrated largely and almost exclusively on the coastal lowland and the area immediately behind the sand and clay region. Alvin Thompson writes: 'Attention was paid by the European class almost exclusively to those areas of the country and those aspects of the economy that could produce relatively quick and large scale profits' (Thompson, 1987: 15). The colonial export economy, narrowly based upon plantation sugar production, needed only a network of productive sugar estates to sustain it. In a paradoxical way, inattention to the interior areas meant the retardation of development in those regions (predominantly inhabited by indigenous populations) but it also facilitated a consolidation of the cultural forms and traditions of the interior and its forest peoples. Hence rituals, dialects, customs and traditions flourished by virtue of the neglect of the coastal masters. In this matrix Amerindian cultural traditions prospered.

## Amerindian cultural traditions in Guyana

The phenomenon of cultural retention among the Amerindian peoples of Guyana is indeed a paradox. A largely coastal colonial and postcolonial agenda nurtured an attitude towards the interior that was a mix of disdain, fear and reverence. The 'bush' and its people held secrets, dangers and mysteries that were often impenetrable by or incomprehensible to the coastal intelligence. The post-independence and late twentieth-century rush to the interior, with the single objective of the pursuit of wealth through mineral extraction, implied a small paradigm shift in developmental thinking – the interior was now the theatre for a frenzied materialism. Lesley Potter notes:

> Many of Guyana's development efforts in the interior over the one hundred and fifty years have been based on exploitation of extractable resources. The activities and those pursuing them, have been very often transitory in nature. It is this fact which, perhaps, has enabled the Amerindians to survive, a survival regarded by some observers as an accident of history.
>
> *(Potter, 1993: 3)*

Although, as would be inevitable, the Amerindians were themselves part of this exploitation of mineral resources, their cultural traditions and practices persisted with varying degrees of integrity. Among those traditions were the culinary practices and menus that the Amerindians have now bequeathed to Guyana as part of an eclectic mix of national dishes (Bennett, 1977; Fox and Hall, 1978). Before that legacy is understood it is useful to understand the social background of the progenitors of that legacy – the Amerindians themselves.

The Amerindians of Guyana are referred to as the First Peoples of the country, attesting to their having descended from the original inhabitants of Guyana. Although the Amerindians of Guyana can boast of a natural increase in their population, the story of their survival through the ages is a complex plot of periodic devastations due to wars, exploitation and strange diseases to which they had no immunity. The fact that much of this history bears no permanent visual record has impacted our complete and comprehensive understanding of the challenges that, historically, confronted the Amerindians, and of the creative ways in which they responded to such challenges (Potter, 1993).

The Amerindian population can be grouped into three broad language systems – Arawak, Carib and Warrau, and further sub-divided into seven tribes or nations – Akawaio, Arekuna, Carib, Macusi, Patamona, Waiwai and Wapisiana. The Carib, Akawaio, Arekuna and Patamona tribes live in the river valleys of west Guyana. Two Amerindian groups live in the savannah region of Rupununi: the Macusi in the northern half and the Wapisiana in the south. The Waiwai live in the southernmost point near where the Essequibo River rises (Fox and Danns, 1993: 13).

Although significant settlement can be observed in areas or villages officially designated as Amerindian villages, the process of population diffusion has resulted in Amerindians being scattered in all parts of Guyana, pursuing a variety of occupations and educational goals no different from any other of the six races that comprise the Guyana population; intermarrying with other races and practising cultural forms that are indistinguishable from the dominant coastal expressions. It is largely in the more settled populations of the interior that one finds the greatest persistence and retention of ancestral cultural traditions and practices. These forms are manifested in some principal ways.

## Language

In Guyana English (and varieties thereof) is the official language but there also exists a rich profusion of native dialects, languages and vernaculars. Amerindian languages are spoken. To assist the process of language retention a number of dictionaries were recently handed to the Walter Roth Museum of Anthropology in Guyana for distribution to Amerindian communities.

## Craft

Few craft shops in Guyana would run the risk of omitting works of Amerindian weaving, basketry or woodwork from their display spaces. Many Amerindian communities produce a very wide and exquisitely crafted assortment of mats, wooden kitchen utensils, personal jewellery items, furniture, clothing, headwear and footwear, ornaments and other souvenir items for sale to both locals and tourists alike. For many craft is the medium through which the creative talent of the Amerindians finds its most visible expression. Works of Amerindian craft are often a feature of display stands at tourism fairs and other expos attended by both government and private sector representatives.

## Folklore and legends

The Amerindians of Guyana, being the First People and descendants of the original inhabitants of the country, lay claim to a rich store of legends, myths and folklore (Ridgwell, 1972). Some of these legends have been put to verse or song and now form part of a national repertoire of folk songs and legends. Among the most popular of the Amerindian legends is that of Old Kaie, the Patamona chief who is believed to have gathered all his belongings and paddled to his death over the majestic Kaieteur Falls as a sacrifice to his people. Apart from this famous legend there exists a rich store of tales of mythical beings who performed mysterious feats deriving from their innate powers and gifts.

## Medicinal lore

The medicinal lore of the Amerindians constitutes a substantial segment of their intellectual property that has been gaining respectability and attracting growing scientific interest in recent times. Engagement with the 'bush' for centuries has produced an orally transmitted (and now increasingly recorded) pharmacopeia of herbal remedies, potions, stimulants, suppressants and prophylactics. Through this vehicle an important strand of Amerindian culture is preserved and disseminated.

## Amerindian food

As the central focus of this chapter, the theme of Amerindian food will receive much more comprehensive treatment in the ensuing sections. Amerindian cuisine and culinary practices have now entered the Guyana culinary mainstream, enriching the national store and consolidating the strength of the Amerindian culinary component. But first, some thoughts about the positive national context in which Amerindian cultural traditions now find fertile ground.

## *National context*

The past three decades in Guyana have seen widespread and unprecedented recognition being accorded to the rights and welfare of the indigenous people. The passage of the Amerindian Act of 2006 enshrined into law a number of measures aimed at safeguarding Amerindian rights in such issues as environmental protection, mining and forestry, intellectual property, land titles and village administration (Nokta, 2011). There is an entire month – September – designated as Amerindian Heritage Month and an increasing number of agencies, both at the local and international level, have shown willingness to make funding available for projects aimed at improving the welfare of the Amerindian Peoples of Guyana. Given this supportive national (and international) environment Amerindian cultural traditions enjoy a speciality of place that more than assures their longevity.

## Food and cultural identity

Few modern consumers, hearing the terms 'pizza', 'taco', 'lasagna', 'seviche', 'roti', 'chow mein' or 'croissant', would be in any doubt as to the national identities associated with those foods. In reality, each of the mentioned items has long transcended its specific national or cultural context and now occupies a place in that culinary kaleidoscope we call the modern restaurant menu. Food can be a means of branding cultures and nations. According to Happel (2012: 176): 'The production, conservation and consumption of foods were, thus, important activities that determined social identity and values of the indigenous Andean community before and after the Spanish conquest.' Those Andean societies were predominantly agriculture-based and the Inca rulers consumed a fare that derived almost exclusively from the agricultural labours of the indigenous populations.

Perhaps nowhere is the branding power of food more noticeable than in the proliferation of 'ethnic' restaurants encountered in most modern cities. Such proliferation results in consumers opting to eat Mexican or Chinese, Italian or Vietnamese, Indian or Lebanese or Caribbean. Each choice or culinary preference is informed by a clear sense of menu, preparation, spicing, even ambience. These associations are possible thanks to the weight of culinary tradition that has gone into the branding of each ethnic or national or cultural variety. Such terms as 'fine dining' or '*haute cuisine*' would of course fuse national culinary particularities into the cosmopolitan, eclectic menus of the modern restaurant, placing the world on your plate.

As is the case with any branding scenario, some brands are stronger than others; some better-known and more enticing than others. The relatively low profile that indigenous foods and preparations may enjoy, both in Guyana and internationally, is by no means any indication of the extent to which such foods reflect, and indeed reinforce, cultural identity. In the perspective of Counihan (1999) food is a window to the complex constituents of human life and culture. For many scholars (Lappé and Collins, 1986; Fischler, 1988) food cannot be confined to the domains of the nutritional or agricultural sciences and in fact is at the centre of a number of anthropological, political and sociological discourses relating to gender, power, access to power and exercise of power. Food of the Amerindians in Guyana is as much a cultural marker and an indication of an identity brand as is the case with the more universally popular and familiar culinary varieties consumed in the developed world. The persistence of the Amerindian brand results largely from the fact that the Amerindian cultural tradition is a tradition that is autochthonous and one that evolved over centuries in relative isolation from other culinary influences.

## Food in traditional Amerindian society

Indigenous people of the Americas populated the New World long before Columbus arrived. In the case of Guyana, they came first to this region about 12,000 years ago (Daniels, 2010). They were hunters and gatherers and their daily diet consisted of fish and game, nuts, roots and berries. As time went by, they practised subsistence farming and included cassava, yams, sweet potatoes, corn, plantains, bananas, pineapples, etc. in their diet (Bennett, 1977).

Traditionally, food played a significant role in the Amerindian society. It was there for kayap (communal work – land for a farm had to be cleared, a church needed to be built, etc. If it was a community project, each family would bring food and drink to be consumed at lunch time or after the work was done. If it was one family's plot of farm land that had to be cleared, that family would provide meals and/or drinks for those who came to help them). It was also used in religious ceremonies and it was celebrated after a harvest (Moses, interview).

Today, much as it was in years gone by, food is an integral part of religious ceremonies and community festivities (Yde, 1965). The Young Cassava Festival, also known as Young Crop, is observed annually on the first Saturday in June. Special food is prepared and it must be blessed by the priest, Piai'chang (pee-eye-shang), before consumption. Young cassavas are used to make bread that is much smaller than those made for everyday use. Usually, the entire cassava plant is uprooted during reaping, but for the Young Crop, the soil is parted and one or two roots are cut off (the others are left to mature and are celebrated later in the year). These are taken to a designated Young Crop cassava bread maker. This is usually a woman, a spinster, who makes bread for the entire community. Maum birds and Silabey fish are roasted and casiri (cassava drink), sugarcane juice and/or pineapple drink are made the day before the festival. After dances and prayers, canapé-sized cassava bread topped with roasted Maum and/or Silabey along with the drinks are served to the gathering much like communion in modern churches.

The other cassava festival is more of a thanksgiving for an abundant crop. This is celebrated annually on November 30. The cassavas that were left to mature after the Young Crop roots were harvested are now ready for reaping. The men of the village go out hunting and fishing sometimes for up to one week to amply supply fish and game for the celebrations. Fermented drinks are made in abundance and it is not uncommon to see drunken villagers napping against a wall or under a tree (Moses, interview).

Traditionally, the daily diet consisted of fish or meat tuma pot (a spicy dish made from the juice of the bitter cassava, fish or meat and hot peppers) with cassava bread or farine and casiri. Usually, men were the hunters/fishermen while women did the cooking. For celebrations, meat was caught well in advance and smoked as a way of preserving it; cassava bread and farine were made and stored and beverages were made and left to ferment.

Since all the groups did not dwell in the same geographical space, their daily diets differed due to the availability of ingredients. For the riverain groups, fresh fish and meat were abundant. For those further inland, smoked or dried meats and fish were consumed. Also, myths determined what got eaten and by whom. For example, some groups believed that if a woman ate big fish while pregnant her baby would be born unusually big; due to their fast sprouting, mushrooms would make children grow quickly so parents would touch the soles of babies' feet with them, then sauté and serve; turtle would make those who consumed it move slowly and get rough, scaly skin; pregnant women should not eat crawling animals or their babies would be born with a deformity, among others.

## Religious and social considerations

In traditional Amerindian society religious beliefs also determined what got eaten and what was shunned. For instance, Adventists do not eat wild hog, un-scaled fish and shellfish because in the Old Testament eating these things was forbidden since they were deemed unclean. Persons who practise the Alleluiah religion do not eat un-scaled fish because the skin is smooth like a human's, and wild cow or bush cow is not eaten because its ribs are like a man's. Eating these animals was forbidden by Makonaima (mah-koo-nye-mah) the Great Spirit who created the earth.

Regardless of group or location, cassava (cassava bread, farine, cassareep, cassava water and tapioca) and hot peppers were staples. All of the traditionally used foods are still eaten in Amerindian villages today and even though foods from the coastland are becoming increasingly popular, the myths and old wives' tales are still prevalent.

Class considerations are seldom involved in the consumption of foods in the Amerindian society, but traditionally, men are usually given their meals first or a special portion is set aside for them. The other family members eat what is left. This is so because it is mainly the men who hunt and fish so setting aside a special portion is in acknowledgement of their efforts.

Young children are given a special tuma that is made with bigger, less bony fish and small, mildly spicy peppers. They are usually seated at a different table from adults to allow the grown-ups to discuss the day's happenings in private.

It is expected that visitors should bring a gift of food for the Toshau (village leader and head of the village council). Usually, it is smoked fish or meat if the journey is on foot (these are easy to transport and would not spoil on the journey), and farm produce (fruits, plantains, yams) if it's by canoe or other mode of transport (Moses, interview).

Intoxicating drinks are used every day and for a variety of purposes, usually at meal times, during work breaks, celebrations, religious ceremonies or just to quench a thirst on a hot day. Children are given the drinks 'fresh' – in the unfermented stage, or pineapple or banana drink, but sometimes if there is nothing else, they're allowed to drink it after it has been fermented.

## Popular Amerindian dishes and their preparation

*The information in this section was gathered in an exclusive interview with Betty Moses, elder of the Akawaio tribe in the Mazaruni region of Guyana.*

Cassareep – the juice collected from the grated cassavas during the cassava bread process – is boiled for hours until it thickens and becomes dark brown. Cassareep is the key ingredient in the absolutely indispensable Guyanese dish called 'pepper pot' (a rich, spicy kind of meat stew served at Christmas), but it can also be used year round in stews, gravies and sauces.

## Pepper pot dish

Tuma or atchee – this spicy dish is made from boiled cassava juice, peppers, usually fish or if available, wild meat. The cassava juice is boiled to remove the toxins and before it thickens to form cassareep, fish or meat and hot peppers are added. It is eaten with cassava bread or farine.

## Tuma in the pot

Farine – made differently depending on the region, and mainly eaten in Regions Eight (Potaro/Siparuni) and Nine (Upper Takatu/Upper Essequibo) – is made from cassava and done through a similar process to cassava bread. In Region Seven – Cuyuni/Mazaruni – the cassavas are scraped to remove the skin, washed, grated, squeezed in a matapee and sifted. The couscous is then placed in a large pan – think giant wok – and parched until light brown. The result is fine grains that can be best described as coarse cream of wheat. This is usually eaten with broth or made into porridge.

In Regions Eight (Potaro/Siparuni) and Nine (Upper Takatu/Upper Essequibo), the process is slightly different. When the cassavas are brought from the farm, they are left in the warishi (woven basket used to fetch farm produce and carried on the head and back) and soaked in water for about one week. By this time, they are quite soft. The skin is removed and the cassava is pounded with a mortar and pestle, squeezed in a matapee, sifted and toasted in a large pan. The grains are much coarser and harder than the farine from Region Seven. It is usually eaten with tasso (sun dried beef or other meat), roasted and/or smoked meats, broths and stews.

Casiri/Bashwar – this potent drink is made from a certain species of bitter cassava. The cassavas are washed, scraped and grated before being boiled on low heat for many hours, sometimes even one day to remove the naturally occurring toxins. Purple sweet potatoes are added for colour and to aid the fermentation process. This mixture is poured into a barrel or large bucket, covered and left to ferment for about three days. For religious celebrations, the drink is consumed after one or two days of fermentation.

Piwari – this intoxicating drink is made from toasted cassava bread. The specially made thin cassava bread is toasted until brown, crumbled and placed in a barrel or large bucket with water and sugarcane juice or sugar (to aid fermentation). It is covered and left to ferment for up to three days before it is strained and sweetened.

Traditionally and before sugar crystals were available, a purple variety of sweet potato or sugarcane juice was used to sweeten drinks. The potatoes were peeled, boiled and crushed before being added to the drinks. The sugarcane juice was extracted by grinding the canes with stones and collecting the juice in a gourd or other container then adding to the mix.

It is said that an older, toothless woman would chew bits of cassava bread and spit it in the piwari to aid fermentation. This myth is perpetuated among coastland dwellers, but this writer knows of no one who has ever actually seen this occur. Regardless of linguistic group or residence, the ever versatile cassava is a staple in the Amerindian diet. It is used for bread, farine, casiri, piwari, tuma pot, tapioca, porridge and cassareep (while this isn't a dish, it deserves mention because Christmas in Guyana, celebrated by all Guyanese, would not be the same without it).

Cassava bread – this is usually made within 24–72 hours of harvesting to prevent the roots from spoiling. After the cassavas are reaped from the family farm, they are washed and scraped to remove thin bark and underlying skin. They are washed again to remove any bits of skin that might be present, and then hand grated. The couscous, or grated cassava, is then placed in a matapee (not to be confused with the Zimbabwean musical instrument of the same name), which is an ingenious woven basket sieve in the shape of a cylinder with loops at each end. It is hung securely from a rafter, using the top loop. Grated cassava is placed inside the matapee from the top. A pole is placed in the lower loop and, with the aid of someone sitting on the pole, the matapee is stretched downward and the juice is squeezed out leaving the grated, almost dry couscous inside. The liquid extracted by this squeezing action is collected in a basin or bowl positioned underneath the matapee. The liquid is used to make cassareep, the remaining meal to make cassava bread.

The couscous is then put to dry for a day or two, sifted through a sieve and placed on a baking pan and shaped into circles to make the bread. Once removed from the pan, the bread is usually placed on the roof of the kitchen to dry further then stored. For a softer, more pliable bread (arasucca), the couscous is not left to dry. This kind of bread is eaten with roasted fish or meats.

Owing to the increased interest in gold-mining, some traditional farming communities no longer maintain farms and are unable to adequately supply the demands for cassava bread. As a result, they bring their cassavas from the coastland or even the ready-made cassava bread from predominantly Afro-Guyanese communities on the coast. Despite the adjustments that, in these traditional farming communities, are made necessary by twenty-first-century economic and social conditions, Amerindians in Guyana are committed to the preservation of their culinary traditions and traditional foods. Also, any of Guyana's larger hotels (for example the Pegasus, the Princess, the Opus, Brandsville hotel) offer Aboriginal food as part of their menus. In the interior resorts it is accepted that Aboriginal food would be served, or even prepared by an Amerindian. At official state lunches 'pepper pot', the Aboriginal staple, enjoys the status of an iconic Guyanese dish. The food preparations described above do not exist in some kind of culinary periphery; they are integral to Guyanese cuisine and have demonstrated their survivability and resilience even in the face of a proliferation of fast food preparations.

## Conclusion

For the Amerindians of Guyana a centuries-long engagement with the land, played out in relative isolation from coastal populations, forged a symbiosis of man and nature that sustained human livelihood, nurtured their belief systems and promoted cultural continuity. Modes of dress, religious rituals, hunting and rearing practices all consolidated themselves as part of the man–nature continuum. So did culinary and medicinal practices, reflecting the Amerindian knowledge of the terrestrial world they inhabited and their mastery of its culinary and medicinal applications. The foods and culinary preparations that arose as a result of the Amerindians' centuries-old understanding of and adaptation to their environment assumed the status of cultural property, inseparable from the evolution and identity of the Amerindians themselves.

Understanding Amerindian food and culinary preparation is to understand the Amerindian relationship with, and mastery of, the environment. For example, the famous Amerindian 'pepper pot' is famous for its shelf longevity – a fact that relates directly to the need on the part of the Amerindians to make the best use of time and resources by concocting a dish that would be 'renewable' and 'sustainable' with minimum repeat cooking. This dish (pepper pot) has now passed into the culinary mainstream of Guyana, and is precious to culturally diverse palates, but its roots in Amerindian culture are known and celebrated. Such mainstreaming sustains the culinary item as a projection of a minority culture surviving amidst the pervasive fast food constructs emanating from the growing number of international fast food chains making their presence felt in Guyana. Food therefore becomes cultural resistance and a means of reinforcing and consolidating a brand and an identity.

## References

Bennett, L. (1977) 'Some meals and beverages used by Guyanese Arawaks', *Bulletin of the Amerindian Languages Project*, 14.

Counihan, C.M. (1999) *The Anthropology of Food and Body: Gender, Meaning and Power*, New York: Routledge.

Daniels, S. (2010) *Some Notes on the Amerindians of Guyana Then and Now*, Georgetown: Walter Roth Museum of Anthropology.

Fischler, C. (1988) 'Food, self and identity', *Social Science Information*, 27: 275–293.

Fox, D. and Danns, G (1993) *The Indigenous Condition in Guyana. A Field Report on the Amerindians of Mabura*, Turkeyen: University of Guyana.

Fox, D. and Hall, J. (1978) 'Some traditional meals of the Akawaios of Guyana', *Bulletin of the Amerindian Languages Project*, 2(4).

Happel, C.A.C. (2012) 'You are what you eat: food as expression of social identity and intergroup relations in the colonial Andes', *Cincinnati Romance Review*, 33: 175–193.

Lappé, F.M. and Collins, J. (1986) *World Hunger: Twelve Myths*, New York: Grove Press.

Nokta, S. (2011) *Compilation of Data for Amazon-Caribbean Tourism Trail*, Brasilia: ACTO.

Potter, L. (1993) 'The Amerindians of Guyana and their environment', *History Gazette*, 2–21.

Ridgwell, W.M. (1972) *The Forgotten Tribes of Guyana*, London: Tom Stacey.

Thompson, A. (1987) *Colonialism and Underdevelopment in Guyana 1580–1803*, Bridgetown: Carib Research and Publication.

Yde, J. (1965) *Material Culture of the Wai Wais*, Ethnographics Series, 10. Copenhagen: National Museum of Denmark.

# 9

# SUSTAINING AND SPREADING LOCAL FOOD CULTURE THROUGH COOKING CLASSES

## A Case Study of Chiang Mai, Thailand

*Wantanee Suntikul, Rodrigues Ng Iris, Ho Weng, Luo Xiao Yan, Lam Iok Cheng, and Chan Weng San*

## Local food and tourism

Tourism connected to food has been referred to alternatively as food tourism, culinary tourism, or gastronomy tourism (Karim and Chi, 2010). Culinary activities at a tourism destination are sometimes classified as a component of cultural tourism (Corigliano, 2002; Richards, 1996). Food is an intrinsic component of a destination's image and an important motivator in the decision to visit a particular country (Boyne et al., 2002; Henderson, 2004; Karim, 2006),

In the context of tourism, "local cuisine" refers to a selection of products that represent the culture of a destination (Sims, 2008). In addition, the cultural value of food is about identifying and communicating cultural expressions, about symbols and images of idealized realities (Bertella, 2010; Richards, 2002; Tellstrom et al., 2005). Local food can reflect a distinctive national or cultural identity (Du Rand et al., 2003a, 2003b; Riley, 2000), promote national cuisine to foreign tourists, and contribute to a destination's competitive advantage (Sims, 2008). By saving resources and energy required for transport and preservation, local food can also contribute to sustainable tourism (Sims, 2008).

The use of locally sourced food products can be beneficial for guests as well as hosts (Boniface, 2003; Torres, 2002). The purchase and consumption of local food can connect tourists with the places where food is produced and the local food producers. This type of connection can be an important part of the touristic experience (Sims, 2008). López-Guzmán and Sánchez-Cañizares (2012) identify tourists who are interested in local food products as an emerging new tourism niche. Urry (1994) and Wang (1999) have shown that the food and drink of a place are part of the iconography of what tourists perceive as the "typical" aspects of that place.

Local food reflects local identity and authenticity through branding and marketing strategies while building connections between consumers and producers (Hall and Wilson, n.d.). Thus, local food can be a tool to integrate tourism development through its capacity for typifying the place and culture. Local food has been recognized as a substantial part of the local culture and tasting local food is an essential part of creating a tourism experience as it serves as both a cultural activity and a form of entertainment (Kim et al., 2009; Kivela and Crotts, 2006; Kim and Eves, 2012).

Local food is an important manifestation of a place's intangible heritage, contributing to tourists' sense of authenticity in their experience of a place (Okumus et al., 2007). Local food experiences have been shown to help sustain tourism development, contributing to maintaining a place's identity (Knowd, 2006; Gössling et al., 2011). Cooking classes at a tourism destination not only support the preservation of traditional cooking methods and cuisines, but also contribute to the sustainability of local culture and promote agriculture in the local area. Sims (2008) stated that "consumer demands for foods perceived to be 'traditional' and 'local' can also be viewed as linked to a quest for authenticity."

Reynolds (1994) argued that "food is perhaps one of the last areas of authenticity that is affordable on a regular basis for tourists." However, due to the mutual effect of globalization and localization, local food is changing. It has been argued that food producers tend to ignore traditional cuisine authenticity in order to appeal to tourists' dining preferences (Du Rand et al., 2003a, 2003b; Steinmetz and Milne, 2010).

## The development of Thai food tourism

Thai dishes have become popular outside Thailand in the past few decades, having become a truly global cuisine known around the world. The Tourism Authority of Thailand launched the "Amazing Thailand" marketing campaign in 1994, which contributed to an increase in the number of tourists to Thailand from 5.7 million in 1993 to around 7 million in 1995. This raised the tourists' demand for Thai food and Thai ingredients and more tourists became interested and know about Thai food. In a survey (cited in Sirijit, 2005) investigating familiarity with ethnic foods, Thai food was the fourth most mentioned cuisine, behind Italian, French, and Chinese.

When prepared and served outside Thailand, Thai food is often adapted to local dining customs and taste preferences, and availability of ingredients. In order to appeal to an international market, overseas Thai restaurants tend to create menus similar to those already known internationally. Even the Thai government has encouraged overseas Thai restaurants to use standard menus. Thus, as Thai food continues to be popular in the global market, it cannot avoid transformation, hybridization, and "creolization" (Sirijit, 2005). Cooking classes in Thailand are one way in which knowledge of Thai food is passed on and spread globally.

## Methodology

This study investigates the role of cooking classes in Chiang Mai in sustaining and spreading Thai food culture. The research was the final assignment of the fourth-year undergraduate subject "Seminar on Tourism and Hospitality" at the Institute for Tourism Studies (IFT) in Macao. This course involves a study trip to a foreign country. In 2013, the students from IFT went to Chiang Mai, Thailand, to conduct research in collaboration with Chiang Mai Rajhabat University. The IFT students were divided into groups of five, joined by Thai students from the host university. The research topic and research design were identified before arriving in Chiang Mai. The IFT students spent one week in Chiang Mai collecting primary and secondary data on various research projects.

For data collection, qualitative and quantitative methods were used. A survey questionnaire was distributed to 105 tourists participating in cooking classes at nine cooking schools

in Chiang Mai, and in-depth interviews were conducted with the owners/managers of these schools during a field study in March 2013.

The questionnaire attempted to measure the tourists' perspective on the cooking classes of Chiang Mai. The survey was divided into two sections. Section 1 was designed to explore the factors motivating respondents to join the cooking classes. Section 2 consists of four sub-sections: learning/food culture, authenticity, teaching method, and inheritance/spread. Respondents were asked to rate their level of agreement on a Likert scale ranging from 1 = strongly disagree to 5 = strongly agree.

The semi-structured interviews were designed to explore the principles on which the cooking schools operate, as well as the perception of the owners/managers of the schools on the role of their schools in sustaining and spreading Thai food culture.

The following sections present the findings of the research. The next part is an analysis of the interviewed cooking school participants' opinions and the following parts analyze the point of view of those running the cooking classes.

## Cooking participants' perspectives

Table 9.1 shows the demographic profile of the respondents. The proportion of females to males was higher than 2:1. The majority (55.2 percent) were aged 21–30. Most (58.1 percent) had a bachelor's degree as their highest academic achievement and most (67.6 percent) were

*Table 9.1* Demographic characteristics of interview sample

| Gender | frequency | | Age | frequency | |
|---|---|---|---|---|---|
| Male | 33 | 31.4% | <21 years | 16 | 15.2% |
| Female | 72 | 68.6% | 21–30 years | 58 | 55.2% |
| Employment Status | frequency | | | | |
| Employed | 71 | 67.6% | 31–40 years | 20 | 19.0% |
| Unemployed | 34 | 32.4% | >40 years | 11 | 10.5% |
| Nationality | frequency | | Education | frequency | |
| Asia Pacific | 41 | 39.1% | High school or lower | 27 | 25.7% |
| Americas | 27 | 25.7% | Bachelor's degree | 61 | 58.1% |
| Europe | 37 | 35.2% | Master's or Higher | 17 | 16.2% |

employed. The largest number of respondents (39.1 percent) were from the Asia Pacific region, although those from Europe accounted for a comparable portion (35.2 percent) and over a quarter (25.7 percent) came from the Americas.

Table 9.2 illustrates that recommendations from others, the price of the cooking class, and the reputation of the school were the main factors influencing respondents' choice of a particular cooking class. The results could be seen as indicating that the expectations of the participants and the offerings of the instructors are aligned. The price set by the cooking school was accepted by the respondents as being requisite to the services provided. Cooking school owners or instructors were concerned with maintaining the reputation of their school by providing high-quality service to earn positive responses from their participants and encourage participants to recommend their school to others.

Table 9.3 summarizes the primary source from which respondents obtained information about the cooking class. With advances in technology, people have become accustomed to getting information from the Internet rather than other channels, as reflected in the 48.6 percent of respondents who became aware of the cooking classes from websites and 21 percent from travel blogs. Other popular channels for respondents were friends and relatives, guide books, and tour operators.

A regression analysis to test the relationship between replies to the statement "The cooking class makes use of local Thai ingredients" and replies to the statement "I will be able to/I am able to distinguish and select Thai ingredients after taking the cooking class" revealed a

*Table 9.2* Reasons for selecting cooking school

| Factor | Frequency | Percentage |
|---|---|---|
| Recommendations | 23 | 21.9% |
| Price of the course | 21 | 20.0% |
| Reputation of the school | 20 | 19.0% |
| Dishes offered by the school | 19 | 18.1% |
| Convenience | 13 | 12.4% |
| Qualifications of cooking instructor | 7 | 6.7% |
| Other | 2 | 1.9% |

*Table 9.3* Primary source of information on cooking schools

| Source | Frequency | Percentage |
| --- | --- | --- |
| website | 51 | 48.6% |
| friends/relatives | 29 | 27.6% |
| travel blogs | 22 | 21.0% |
| guide books | 22 | 21.0% |
| tour operator | 20 | 19.0% |
| television | 11 | 10.5% |
| magazines | 8 | 7.6% |
| hotel/motel | 5 | 4.8% |
| other travelers | 2 | 1.9% |
| poster/banner/ad | 2 | 1.9% |
| brochure | 1 | 1.0% |

p value of 0.00, indicating a strong correlation between perceived authenticity of the ingredients and confidence in selecting ingredients.

The questions were divided into four clusters addressing the perceived authenticity of the cooking class, the teaching method, the understanding of Thai food culture gained through the class, and the contribution of the course to dissemination of Thai food culture, respectively. One-sample t-tests (Tables 9.4–7) show that all the variables are significant (p value < 0.05). The responses to all but three of the 17 questions had a mean value between 4.00 and 4.50, indicating a general attitude of agreement, tending towards strong agreement, with the statements posed.

The cooking instructors claimed that they maintain authenticity of Thai food when teaching Thai food culture and cooking skills to their participants. Respondents indicate a strong awareness of this fact, accompanied by an impression of the teacher as being knowledgeable and meticulous about authenticity (Table 9.4). The perspectives from cooking instructors and the respondents are consistent on the maintaining of authenticity.

The teaching method in class described by the cooking instructors was more or less the same for all of the schools. The participants also reported that the content in class was effectively conveyed to the participants, which can contribute to sustaining Thai food culture.

The cooking instructors mentioned that they introduced Thai food culture to participants during the cooking demonstration. Table 9.6 outlines the respondents' opinions on the understanding of Thai food gained through the course, which corroborates the statements of the cooking instructors.

*Table 9.4* Authenticity

| | Mean | Sig. |
| --- | --- | --- |
| The cooking class makes use of local Thai ingredients. | 4.50 | 0.00 |
| The instructor has a deep knowledge of Thai food. | 4.47 | 0.00 |
| As far as I know, my cooking instructor maintains the authentic taste of the dishes that he/she teaches us. | 4.23 | 0.00 |
| The authenticity of the food is most important for me. | 4.07 | 0.00 |
| Taking this cooking class is one of the most authentic experiences I have had in Chiang Mai. | 3.90 | 0.00 |

*Table 9.5* Teaching method

|  | Mean | Sig. |
| --- | --- | --- |
| The instructor pays attention to each participant. | 4.46 | 0.00 |
| The teaching method is effective. | 4.40 | 0.00 |
| The instructor and I can communicate smoothly. | 4.30 | 0.00 |
| The instructor's language is understandable. | 4.29 | 0.00 |

*Table 9.6* Understanding of Thai food culture

|  | Mean | Sig. |
| --- | --- | --- |
| The cooking instructor introduces not only cooking, but also Thai food culture. | 4.08 | 0.00 |
| I understand Thai food culture much better after this class. | 4.08 | 0.00 |

*Table 9.7* Dissemination of Thai food culture

|  | Mean | Sig. |
| --- | --- | --- |
| This cooking class helps me to know more about Thai food culture. | 4.33 | 0.00 |
| This cooking class makes me more interested in Thai food culture. | 4.20 | 0.00 |
| I will spread Thai food culture to my friends/relatives/colleagues. | 4.10 | 0.00 |
| I will continue to practice cooking Thai food in my home country. | 4.07 | 0.00 |
| I would like to attend more Thai cooking classes in the future. | 3.92 | 0.00 |
| After taking this cooking class, I am likely to visit Thai restaurants more frequently in my home country. | 3.73 | 0.00 |

Findings pertaining to the dissemination of Thai food culture by participants after the cooking class are shown in Table 9.7. The table demonstrates that respondents feel strongly that their interest in and knowledge of Thai food culture had increased because of the cooking class, and that they intend to take this knowledge back to their home country to prepare Thai food at home and spread the knowledge to others.

A regression calculation of the relationship between the factors related to teaching method and those related to understanding of Thai food culture results in a p value of 0.00, showing a high degree of relation between these factors. In other words, the perceived quality of the teaching methods relates strongly to the understanding of Thai food culture the respondents felt they had acquired. Likewise, a p value of 0.00 was also found in a regression calculation between teaching method and dissemination of Thai food culture, showing a link between opinions about the teaching quality and the desire and preparedness to spread the knowledge and practice of Thai cooking in one's country of residence.

## Cooking school owners' perspective

### *Reason for opening a cooking school*

The interviewed cooking school owners reported different reasons for deciding to open a cooking school. For the majority of respondents, one of the main reasons was that they had long previous experience in working at cooking schools and considered that they were know-ledgeable enough in running a cooking school and teaching cooking classes to open their own business.

Some respondents were more interest-oriented in operating cooking schools. They opened cooking schools because they love cooking. One stated that he opened the school because his wife loved cooking. Some respondents established their cooking schools at the suggestion of potential customers who wanted to learn Thai cooking.

On the other hand, some of the interviewees tended to be more business-oriented. As Thai cuisine is famous around the world and there is a high demand for Thai cooking classes among tourists, they considered a cooking school to be a good business venture in Chiang Mai.

### The "most important thing" in operating a cooking school

When asked to name the "most important thing" in operating a cooking school, three themes dominated interviewees' replies. The first is *service quality*. Some respondents mentioned that this was the most important factor in running cooking schools, because they thought that by providing high-quality service to the customers, they would encourage participants to become repeat guests and to recommend the cooking school to others, by word of mouth and by online forums such as TripAdvisor.

The second one is to *spread the Thai food culture*. Some interviewees revealed that they would like to spread the traditional, seasonal, and healthy Thai cuisine to the participants. These cooking school owners wanted more people to know more about Thai food culture and cook in the traditional Thai way, so as to sustain Thai cuisine and even spread to other countries.

The third one is *personal interest*. Reiterating a point made above, they opened cooking schools to pursue their love of cooking and enjoy the process.

## Common themes among owners

The following common themes emerged from the interviews with the cooking school owners/managers.

### Cuisine design for participants

Most of the interviewees indicated that they would design the menus prepared in the classes according to customers' expressed preferences; hence the classes would provide a variety of alternatives for customers to select. They also considered the popularity of the different dishes, and some said that they conducted research online to identify which dishes are popular. Some declared that they choose relatively simple dishes for the classes, for the participants to acquire basic skills upon which they could build in the future. Additionally, one respondent stated that he would not let former participants take a class of the same cuisine as the class they had already studied, as he would like to let his participants gain wider techniques and ideas about cooking.

### Origin of the ingredients

Regarding ingredients, the majority of respondents purchase from local markets in Chiang Mai. During the ingredients purchase and selection process, the instructors take participants along, so as to teach them how to select and distinguish different Thai ingredients. Thus, the cuisine would be more authentic by using original Thai ingredients. Moreover, some interviewees even have their own gardens, which are planted with ingredients for the cooking classes to use. They take participants to visit the garden to introduce them to the ingredients. Therefore, the beginning of most classes takes place at markets or gardens. However, one owner stated that Thai cuisine was infused with different countries' cultures, and to truly reflect Thai cuisine, it is necessary to purchase ingredients from different places, and some ingredients used in her classes were brought from abroad, such as a curry from Burma, which is not produced in Thailand.

## Authenticity of cuisine taste

In terms of taste, all of the owners/managers insisted that their recipes were in traditional Thai style and authentic. They teach participants how to make Thai cuisine in the original taste. Afterwards, the participants can adjust the taste to their own liking, since not all of them can accept the original strong, spicy flavor. However, one respondent emphasized the principle of "stay Thai," and would not let participants reduce the spiciness of the dishes, so as to let the participants understand what is real Thai. On the other hand, some respondents are willing to make arrangements for customers. For instance, if the customer is a vegetarian, he will create a vegetarian version.

## Teaching style and process

Most of the interviewees explained that at the beginning of the class, they start with an explanation of the fundamental theories and principles of Thai cuisine, such as the introduction of Thai ingredients. That is why they take the participants to the markets or private gardens. Besides, some of them also teach participants about Thai culture and history. Afterwards, they do live demonstrations of preparation and cooking techniques for the participants to learn and observe; then the participants start to make their own dishes.

## Introduction to Thai culture and history during the class

Besides food-related knowledge, the majority of the interviewed cooking school owners also introduce Thai cultural and historical knowledge to the participants during classes. Furthermore, some also explain how to eat in Thai style, the origins and histories of different Thai cuisines, seasonal food, and even recommend sauces to participants.

## Dissemination of Thai cuisine knowledge

All of the respondents were confident that their participants continued to practice cooking in Thai style in their home countries, since some participants would remain in contact with them, mostly through email but in some cases by phone. Normally, the participants contacted them to ask questions regarding cooking Thai food, such as where to buy ingredients or what kind of ingredients to use to replace the ones that they could not get in their hometown. Some ask for more recipes.

## Conclusion

This study has revealed a number of ways in which cooking classes in Chiang Mai contribute to the sustaining and dissemination of Thai food culture around the world. There was substantial alignment between the intentions of the cooking school owners and the factors motivating participants to join the cooking classes. A love of cooking and a respect for Thai culture characterized both of the groups, and members of both groups also assigned high value to maintaining the authenticity of the cuisine. Owners are gratified by spreading awareness of the Thai culinary arts, while tourists return home with a new set of skills and cultural knowledge.

The trend of increasing interest in cooking classes in Thailand can be seen as a new wave in the globalization of Thai food. Following the proliferation of Thai restaurants around the world in the past few decades, tourists are traveling to Thailand in increasing numbers to experience Thai food at its source, and are acquiring the skills and knowledge to distinguish and appreciate authentic Thai cuisine and to prepare this food at home upon their return. Whether to stick with the authentic recipes they learned or to adapt the cuisine to their own taste will be a personal choice for each of them.

The results of the survey questionnaire show that participants gain confidence in their knowledge of the authentic preparation of Thai cuisine and their desire to bring it back to their country of residence. First, respondents considered that they could easily distinguish the Thai ingredients after the cooking class through ingredient selection. Second, most of the respondents agreed that the cooking classes maintain the authenticity of Thai food culture. Third, since the cooking instructors would introduce Thai culture in class, respondents would better understand the relationship between traditional Thai food and Thai culture. Fourth, the teaching method was seen as effective in delivering Thai food cooking skills and culture.

Cooking school owners and operators were found to have chosen that vocation out of personal interest. The study also identified a common concern among cooking school owners for the preservation and dissemination of authentic Thai cuisine. Involving participants in acquiring ingredients, in the traditional venue of the market or the garden, reinforces the understanding and appreciation of the ingredients and their link to Thai culture. While trying to accommodate the wishes and the preferences of their participants, the owners insist on maintaining authenticity of ingredients and preparation method. The practices discussed in the preceding section constitute a shared set of tactics on the part of cooking class instructors in Chiang Mai for making the knowledge of authentic Thai cuisine preparation available to tourists, thereby facilitating both the spread of Thai cuisine around the world and also the spread of an appreciative and aware audience for authentic Thai cuisine.

# References

Bertella, G. (2011) "Knowledge in food tourism: the case of Lofoten and Maremma Toscana," *Current Issues in Tourism*, 14(4): 355–371.

Boniface, P. (2003) *Tasting Tourism: Travelling for Food and Drink*, Ashgate: Burlington.

Boyne, S., Williams, F., and Hall, D. (2002) "The Isle of Arran taste trail," in A.M. Hjalager and G. Richards (eds.), *Tourism and Gastronomy*, London: Routledge, pp. 91–114.

Corigliano, A. (2002) "The route to quality: Italian gastronomy networks in operation" in A.M. Hjalager and G. Richards (eds.), *Tourism and Gastronomy*, London: Routledge, pp. 166–185.

Du Rand, G., Heath, E., and Alberts, N. (2003a) "Role of local and regional food in destination marketing: a South African situation analysis," *Journal of Travel and Tourism Marketing*, 14(3/4): 97–112.

Du Rand, G., Heath, E., and Alberts, N. (2003b) "The role of local and regional food in destination marketing: a South African situation analysis," in C.M. Hall (ed.), *Wine, Food, and Tourism Marketing*, New York: The Haworth Hospitality Press, pp. 77–96.

Gössling, S., Garrod, B., Carlo, C., Hille, J., and Peeters, P. (2011) "Food management in tourism: reducing tourism's carbon 'food print'," *Tourism Management*, 32: 534–543.

Hall, M. and Wilson, S. (n.d.) *Scoping Paper: Local Food, Tourism and Sustainability.*

Henderson, J. (2004) "Food as a tourism resource: a view from Singapore," *Tourism Recreation Research*, 29(3): 69–74.

Hjalager, A.M. and Johansen, P.H. (2013) "Food tourism in protected areas – sustainability for producers, the environment and tourism?" *Journal of Sustainable Tourism*, 21(3): 417–433.

Karim, S. (2006) *Culinary Tourism as a Destination Attraction: An Empirical Examination of the Destination's Food Image and Information Sources*, unpublished PhD, Oklahoma State University.

Karim, S. and Chi, C. (2010) "Culinary tourism as a destination attraction: an empirical examination of destinations' food image," *Journal of Hospitality Marketing & Management*, 19(6): 531–555.

Kim, Y. and Eves, A. (2012) "Construction and validation of a scale to measure tourist motivation to consume local food," *Tourism Management*, 33: 1458–1467.

Kim, Y.G., Eves, A., and Scarles, C. (2009) "Building a model of local food consumption on trips and holidays: a grounded theory approach," *International Journal of Hospitality Management*, 28: 423–431.

Kivela, J. and Crotts, J.C. (2006) "Tourism and gastronomy: gastronomy's influence on how tourists experience a destination," *Journal of Hospitality and Tourism Research*, 30(3): 354–377.

Knowd, I. (2006) "Tourism as a mechanism for farm survival," *Journal of Sustainable Tourism*, 14(1): 24–42.

López-Guzmán, T. and Sánchez-Cañizares, S. (2012) "Gastronomy, tourism and destination differentiation: a case study in Spain," *Review of Economics & Finance*, 1: 63–72.

Okumus, B., Okumus, F., and McKercher, B. (2007) "Incorporating local and international cuisines in the marketing of tourism destinations: the cases of Hong Kong and Turkey," *Tourism Management*, 28: 253–261.

Reynolds, P.C. (1994) "Culinary heritage in the face of tourism," in C. Cooper and A. Lockwood (eds.), *Progress in Tourism, Recreation and Hospitality Management*, 6: 189–194.

Richards, G. (1996) "The scope and significance of cultural tourism," in G. Richards (ed.), *Cultural Tourism in Europe*, Wallingford: CAB International, pp. 19–45.

Richards, G. (2002) "Gastronomy: an essential ingredient in tourism production and consumption?" in A.M. Hjalager and G. Richards (eds.), *Tourism and Gastronomy*, London: Routledge, pp. 3–20.

Riley, M. (2000) "What are the implications of tourism destination identity for food and beverage policy? Culture and cuisine in a changing global marketplace in strategic questions," in R. Woods (ed.), *Food and Beverage Management*, London: Butterworth Heinemann, pp. 187–194.

Sims, B. (2008) "Food, place and authenticity: local food and the sustainable tourism experience," *Journal of Sustainable Tourism*, 17(3): 321–336.

Sirijit, S. (2005) *The Globalization of Thai Cuisine*, paper presented at the Canadian Council for Southeast Asian Studies Conference, York University, Toronto, October 14–16.

Steinmetz, R. and Milne, S. (2010) *Food, Tourism and Destination Differentiation: The Case of Rotorua, New Zealand*, unpublished Master of Philosophy thesis, Auckland University of Technology.

Suntikul, W (2012) "Food induced tourism and the globalization of Thai cuisine," *2nd Interdisciplinary Tourism Research Conference in Turkey*, pp. 1040–1051.

Tellstrom, R., Gustafsson, I.-B., and Mossberg, L. (2005) "Local food cultures in the Swedish rural economy," *Sociologia Ruralis*, 45(4): 346–359.

Torres, R. (2002) "Toward a better understanding of tourism and agriculture linkages in the Yucatan: tourist food consumption and preferences," *Tourism Geographies*, 4(3): 282–306.

Urry, J. (1994) *Consuming Places*, London: Routledge.

Wang, N. (1999) "Rethinking authenticity in tourism experience," *Annals of Tourism Research*, 26(2): 349–370.

# 10

# THE USE OF LOCAL CULTURE AND SUSTAINABILITY IN LOCAL FOOD AND BEVERAGE ENTREPRENEURSHIP

## Case studies in Cornwall

*John Tredinnick-Rowe and Tim Taylor*

### Introduction

Local food has become an important area for entrepreneurs seeking to exploit market opportunities presented by consumer preferences for traceability, quality and ethics – be they environmental (e.g., organic, eco-labels) or social (e.g., fair trade). This chapter attempts to explore the linkages between local identity and sustainability in facilitating innovation in the food and beverage sector, drawing on the specific case study of Cornwall in the United Kingdom.

Innovation in the food and beverage industry can be measured by the tracking and analysis of design patents (Alfranca et al., 2002; Rama, 1996; Rama et al., 2003). The driving force behind this is to track the deepening effect of historical layers of innovation, illustrating a trajectory within the industry, such as increased technical accumulation (Alfranca et al., 2002). But this typically focuses on multinational corporations with the capacity to register legal paperwork and does not focus on local food and beverage production, nor the social side of innovation due to the neo-Schumpeterian slant in the literature (Alfranca et al., 2002).

Cornwall is a county located in the far south-west of the United Kingdom. It is home to 532,300 people (Cornwall Council, 2013b), of whom 73,200 self-identify themselves as Cornish according to the 2011 census (Cornwall Council, 2013a). The Cornish are recognised as an ethnic minority by the European Framework for Protection of National Minorities. In 2005 the UK government included the Cornish Language (Kernewek) under Part II of the European Charter for the Protection of Regional or Minority Languages. Statistics do not exist currently for the exact number of speakers. The Cornish National Minority Report 2 states 'conservative estimates put the number of fluent speakers at around 300, and those with some knowledge of the language at between 4,000 and 5,000' (Saltern, 2011). The language is however dominant in place names and other toponyms, and surnames in the region, including bi-lingual street signage in some districts. Hence it should be clear that Cornwall has a distinct ethno-linguistic heritage that renders it distinct from the rest of the United Kingdom.

The food and beverage sector in Cornwall is a key contributor to the economy. In 2011 the agri-food sector accounted for 63,700 jobs and was significantly more important in terms of job provision in Cornwall than in the rest of the country. In economic terms it was estimated that the Cornish agri-food sector is worth £1.4 billion (University of Exeter Centre for Rural Policy Research, 2011). The industry is inextricably linked to the tourism sector in the region, which helps to boost the food sector. Cornwall has a number of legally recognised products under the European Union regulation No 510/2006 on Protected Geographical Indications and Protected Designations of Origin. Some of the notable produce are Cornish pasties (DEFRA, 2011b), Cornish pilchards (DEFRA, 2011a) and clotted cream (Alexander, 1997).

In this context, a number of companies have innovated, drawing on the cultural identity of Cornwall in their marketing. In this chapter, we examine the behaviour of three Cornish companies in terms of positional marketing and innovation. We show that innovation is all about context, and the processes of culturally anchoring a product are key to successful local food and beverage entrepreneurship. The key relationship between local production and sustainability is discussed.

The chapter is structured as follows. First, an overview is given of the concepts of social innovation and entrepreneurialism. Second, we discuss the crucial role of context for successful innovation. Third, we present case studies of innovation in the food and beverage sector. Fourth, we present some discussion of the lessons arising from the case studies for successful innovation around local food and beverage. Finally, we present some conclusions and areas for future research.

## Social innovation and entrepreneurialism

The definition and categorisation of innovation has a history that stretches from Say (1821) and his work on invention through to Schumpeter (1934b) and, more recently, Linton (2009), who has conducted a meta-study of innovation typologies. First we must define the concept of innovation itself. There are many definitions of innovation but van de Ven (1986) provides a broad summary:

> The process of innovation is defined as the development and implementation of new ideas by people who over time engage in transactions with others within an institutional context . . . From a managerial viewpoint, to understand the process of innovation is to understand the factors that facilitate and inhibit the development of innovations. These factors include ideas, people, transactions, and context over time.
>
> *(van de Ven, 1986: 591)*

The OECD also defines innovation as an iterative process initiated by the perception of a new market and/or new service opportunity for a technology-based invention that leads to development, production and marketing tasks striving for the commercial success of the invention (OECD, 1991).

More succinctly Tidd and Bessant (2009) state that innovation is driven by the ability to see connections, to spot opportunities and take advantage of them. One clear distinction to make is between innovation and invention as Cavalli (2007: 959) highlights:

> The difference from invention to innovation, thus, is to be found in the acknowledgment that innovation is primarily a social fact (sales and marketing are clearly not technical aspects), whereas invention remains a technical fact.

This is also echoed in the way van de Ven (1986) talks of transactions with others within an institutional context: 'it is the social and institutional nature that defines innovation'. The work on characterising innovation has become incrementally more accepting of the social dimension involved in the innovation process. This has aided its application to the service economies that typify food and beverage industries such as restaurateurs, hoteliers and mobile food outlets. One system that is of particular interest, due to its unique blend of social and technical aspects, was that developed by Tidd and Bessant (2009), and it is in this system that we find more of a concrete description of how social forms of innovation can be expressed. This framework is called the '4Ps' typology and in brief it characterises all forms of innovation space in which businesses operate, which are outlined by Tidd and Bessant (2009) as:

- Product: what a business offers the world.
- Process: how businesses create and deliver that product.
- Position: where a business targets its products and the story it tells about them.
- Paradigm: how a business frames what it does.

The 4Ps function as a framing device as in the practical application of innovation the terms tend to overlap. For example, the growing popularity of foraging for restaurant food – such as René Redzepi at Noma – as a tourist activity could be seen as both a new product and a new process innovation (Weston, 2011).

Positional innovation is one of the lesser studied members of the innovation family. Bessant (2003) characterises positional innovation as a change in the context in which an innovation is applied and it is probably the most applicable form of innovation when analysing local food and beverage production. A classic illustration of this is Häagen-Dazs repositioning ice cream as a luxury item at a time when ice cream was seen as a product for children (Tidd and Bessant, 2009). However there is a disparity in the study of innovation in that the majority of papers focus on the innovation of processes, products or paradigms, leaving the study of positions to play the laggard (Francis and Bessant, 2005). If we look at Schumpeter (1934b) his concept of 'economic innovation' has criteria for defining innovations that do not really consider the social or positional dimension, but that focus on process, product and paradigms. The use of concepts from social science (such as place, identity and culture) in innovation, particularly in the creative industries, only took place in the latter stages of the twentieth century (Cavalli, 2007).

We can at this point see the movement also of social scientists such as Elizabeth Hirschman into studying innovation as a social phenomenon. Hirschman talks of symbolic innovations as 'those which result from the reassignment of social meaning to an existing product' (Hirschman, 1982: 537). This was used in conjunction with reference group theory,[1] and as a concept has all the hallmarks of positional innovation. The term 'symbolic innovation' has all but disappeared in favour of 'positioning' or 'repositioning'. Economic anthropologists such as Bourdieu and Darbel (1966) analysed entrepreneurial activity and Bourdieu went on to create the notion of symbolic economies. Symbolic economies involve the construction of economic action from individual up to a market place through social action and networks, or 'the economy of the offering' (Bourdieu, 1998). This approaches a better characterisation of the networks and actions that exist in small or family firms that characterise local gastronomy. This synergy between the social world and innovation is shown in the context of local food in Figure 10.1.

The consequence for the historical lag in innovation towards the social and intangible aspects of innovation is that until relatively recently entrepreneurial food and beverage

*Figure 10.1*　The mixture of resources needed for marketing innovation in the local food sector (Doyle, 1997).

activity would have only been analysed and consciously expressed through new physical products and physical processes. The acceptance and ability to operationalise new developments through psychological and sociological aspects – such as marketing, package design or how to network effectively – have not been studied closely (Heck et al., 2008). This chapter aims in some small way to reconcile this position.

## Context – the mother of all (successful) innovation

When considering entrepreneurial activity, it is essential to recognise that all success is specific to the time and culture context within which it is placed, and that *innovation is fundamentally about interaction with context*. There needs to be the correct social and, in other cases, technical conditions for innovations to take root. If this is not the case, there will be no existing market for the entrepreneur to exploit and also none can be created until a technical or societal shift occurs. In regard to the public accepting the works of the artist Duchamp, Bourdieu said 'for Duchamp to be Duchamp, the field had to be constituted in such a way that he could be Duchamp' (Bourdieu, 1998: 112). Just as many artists who were obscure when alive become popularised once dead, innovations that are too radical and pre-empt the market in which they would be successful are likely to fail. In regard to food and beverage innovations, if the social conditions are not appropriate, the innovation will not take off at that time. For example

*Table 10.1* Linking history and typical food products in Cornwall

|  | Pre-industrial | Industrial | Post-industrial |  |
| --- | --- | --- | --- | --- |
| 1) Classic | Documented history of existence/ reputation | Creation of producer association/product specifications | Strong reputation/ renown, PDO-eligible | E.g., clotted cream and pasties |
| 2) Appropriations | Origins in wide spread artisanal activity | Many small producers eclipsed by industrial activity; few persisted through entrepreneurship | Remaining producers appropriate previously shared know-how | E.g., Fal oysters |
| 3) Re-inventions | Origins in wide spread artisanal activity | Practice dies out in face of industrialisation | Practices revived in face of revalorisation Practices invented in face of revalorisation | E.g., Cornish Yarg and Cornish sea salt |
| 4) Nineteenth-century specialities | Origins in artisanal activity | Branding of specific products to capture tourist/ gift markets | Products retain strong speciality/gift symbolism | E.g., Cornish clotted cream fudge |
| 5) Industrial Other | Origins in medical/ apothecary practices | Products gain renown through industrial-scale manufacture | Products often have strong markets close to local origin | E.g., Cornish mead |

*Source:* Based on Tregear (2003).

serving foraged food in world-class restaurants such as Noma would have been highly unlikely in an era when foraging was associated with poverty rather than quality.

In addition to the context-specific innovations, it is to be noted that the ideas also tend to be recyclable. Hirschman (1982) noted how wire-rimmed eyeglasses had two *diffusion cycles*, initially in the 1920s and again in the 1960s. The 'new' market may well have large amounts of historicity about it, something Jameson called 'nostalgia for the present' (Jameson, 1989). The idea is perhaps best described by Brown and Patterson (2001: 164):

> The past is not only inexhaustible and infinitely recyclable but it is readily rearranged ... this tendency to connect the unconnected, that is the hall mark of post-modernism.

How historic, regional and artisanal properties of food have proven to be successful innovations and how they transit into current products is illustrated by Table 10.1.

## Case studies: Cornwall and food and beverages

Trewin et al.'s *Gourmet Cornwall* situates Cornish food in its cultural and historical context, illustrating the iconographic nature; whether it be derelict mine-scapes or bearded fishermen from a Stanhope Forbes painting (Trewin et al., 2005). This typical character of Cornish cuisine illustrates how very hard it is to isolate the food from the culture and people that give it legitimacy.

Cornwall has been and continues to be one of the poorest areas of the United Kingdom with wages approximately 25 per cent lower than the national average (Gerard, 2008) and this along with its unique geological and geographic characteristics and the peninsula's maritime and mining history have shaped its gastronomy. The food is simple and robust, designed to give farmers, fishermen and miners enough energy to continue working. Typical examples of Cornish food include: fish and crab dishes, especially pilchards, which come from the fishing tradition; pasties – a distinctly Cornish D-shaped beef and vegetable pie traditionally eaten by miners; clotted cream, ice cream and cheese relating to the dairy farming tradition; and cakes and biscuits – saffron cake, hevva cake and Cornish fairings. There is also a tradition in brewing beer and mead – a fortified honey-wine often flavoured with fruit.

The contemporary food industry in Cornwall has its links to the traditional cuisine in that it utilises the local ingredients but in different ways, such as the trends in *haute cuisine* and the growing demand for responsibly and sustainably sourced products (Everett and Aitchison, 2008). In this context, there have been numerous efforts to draw on the cultural context of Cornwall to position products in the food and beverage market. In this section, we explore lessons from three of these – Tregothnan tea, St Austell Brewery and Cornish Sea Salt.

## Tregothnan tea

Tregothnan is a family-run estate, belonging to the Viscount of Falmouth, home to the Boscawen family since 1335. Tregothnan is the only wholesale grower and producer of tea in the British Isles (Invest in Cornwall, 2012). The Tregothnan estate has been selling tea since 2005 (Tregothnan Estate, 2012b). The tea operation took five years to set up and cost £2.6 million (Gerrie, 2011). The tea plantation is currently 50 acres (BBC, 2012) although the estate itself is 26,000 acres (Artfact, 2012). It currently exports half of its 10-tonne production of tea per annum (BBC, 2012). The estate in 2011 turned over £1.1 million from its tea production (Gerrie, 2011).

The estate has a number of revenue streams beyond tea. The estate is also the only Manuka honey producer found outside of New Zealand using its own Manuka bushes and Cornish bees. Tregothnan is part of Energy Share, a community-based carbon reduction scheme, in an attempt to reduce its carbon footprint (Energy Share, 2012). In addition the estate is Forest Stewardship Council-certified in its charcoal production (Forest Stewardship Council, 2012).

The current head of the family, the Honourable Evelyn Boscawen, has stated that she is committed to sustainability on the estates (Tregothnan Estate, 2012a, 2012b). The company comes with a certain pedigree in that it is owned by a family that has been seated in that location since 1335. As such, the emphasis on local products and branding is an obvious choice, as is the rhetoric of sustainability when selling to ABC1[2] demographics capable of purchasing responsibly made products. In terms of the move to tea production, Jonathon Jones, Tregothnan commercial and garden director, stated:

> English tea-drinking is not just about the drink, but it's the whole lifestyle and culture. We recognised that there was a whole host of marketing opportunities around tea-drinking and we could sell in the other Tregothnan products that make English tea-drinking great.
>
> *(Export Cornwall, 2010)*

*Figure 10.2*   Tregothnan tea.

*Source:* Alex Smalley.

The branding of Tregothnan builds on the heritage aspect (see Figure 10.2). As a signatory to the UK Trade & Investment's Passport to Export programme, Tregothnan is pursing the revenue that comes from a thriving export market with 50 per cent of its products being exported (BBC, 2013). The company is also exporting to China and India (BBC, 2013). The reality from this case study seems to be that the sophistication associated with sustainability and local products can open new markets especially in BRIC countries with growing middle classes. Entrepreneurial activity in local food and beverage production uses the symbolic capital of localism and sustainability as a lifestyle marketing tool – and a very lucrative one in this case.

There are, of course, natural tensions between trade and the environment. The transportation of goods and the carbon emissions associated with such trade may conflict with the environmental ethos of companies trading in local food. It needs to be realised that sustainability also implies economic and social considerations – and Tregothnan has certainly been effective in developing a viable brand and in terms of job creation. By use of positional innovation, drawing on the Cornish identity in branding and appropriate marketing, Tregothnan have managed to complete one of the ultimate business challenges in selling tea to the Chinese.

## St Austell Brewery

Cornwall has a strong brewing tradition. One of the main local breweries is the St Austell Brewery, founded in 1851 by Walter Hicks, who chose to mortgage his farm to raise the start-up capital. The company remains a private, family-run business, one of only 30 independently family-owned breweries in Britain. The brewery started a chain of pubs in 1863, which currently consists of 169 pubs largely across Cornwall, Devon and the Isles of Scilly. The Brewery has more than 1,000 employees (including part-time staff) and turnover was £90 million in 2011 (St Austell Brewery, 2011; Business Cornwall, 2008).

The St Austell Brewery has a long heritage of innovation, both process innovation as far back as 1876 in terms of making use of new technology such as the telephone, and product innovation – brewing new beers and securing sole agency to distribute Coca-Cola in Cornwall in 1955. The brewery also claims to have been home to one of the earliest examples of female entrepreneurial activity in the beverage industry from 1911 to 1939 when it was controlled by Hester Parnell.

In terms of environmental credentials, the company states that it is committed to being 'one of the UK's greenest brewers' (St Austell Brewery, 2012) – and it has won a number of awards including being Overall Winner in the Cornwall Sustainability Awards in 2009.

The current managing director of the company is also the chairman of Clean Cornwall – a partnership between local business, community groups and public sector organisations committed to reducing litter in Cornwall (Cornwall Council, 2009). The company is currently working towards achieving the Carbon Trust Standard, which certifies organisations that are committed to ongoing carbon reduction targets. It is part of a Hospitality Carbon Reduction Forum and has a 12-point environmental plan (St Austell Brewery, 2006).

In terms of product innovation, the brewery has been resurrecting old recipes from history. It re-launched, on St Patrick's day, the 1913 Cornish Stout also meant to commemorate Cornwall's Celtic heritage (*Western Morning News*, 2013). The company has considered regional variation in raising brand awareness through corporate sponsorship of sporting activity. It is pragmatic in sponsoring the most popular sport in the particular region in question. The real ale industry is not noted as a hotbed for innovation or sustainability; however, a commitment to local traditions and sustainability has undoubtedly had a positive impact on the performance of the business and in their branding they exploit their Cornish heritage (see Figure 10.3).

## Cornish Sea Salt

Established in 2004, producing salt on the site of an iron-age sea salt works, the Cornish Sea Salt company continues the tradition of salt manufacture in the peninsula. The company has 23 employees and a projected turnover of £1.2m per annum (Hurley, 2011). It is one of only two British sea salt companies (IFDE, 2013). The company needed £800,000 in initial investment (Hurley, 2011).

It has been endorsed by celebrity cooks such as James Martin, Hugh Fearnley-Whittingstall, Nathan Outlaw and Rick Stein. The company's products can also be found in most supermarkets and also high-end stores such as Harrods, Fortnum & Mason, Selfridges and Waitrose. The company currently also exports to Ireland, Spain, Germany, Sweden, Norway, America, Australia, Saudi Arabia and Indonesia (Cornish Sea Salt, 2010). An example of the product is given in Figure 10.4.

John Steel, chairman of Cornish Sea Salt, describes the business as an 'emotional entrepreneur story rather than a commercial one' (Hurley, 2011) and describes the owner as a man with guts and possessed of an idea – although not a particularly solvent one from a bank's perspective, as it took, as is typical with capital intensive start-ups, a good few years to generate a profit.

*Figure 10.3*   A bottle of St Austell Brewery's Ale.

*Source:* Alex Smalley.

*Figure 10.4*   A pot of Cornish Sea Salt.

*Source:* Alex Smalley.

The company is legally bound to work responsibly as it operates in a marine conservation area and Site of Special Scientific Interest (Cornwall Council, 2010). This very-low-tech industry aids the creation of a sustainable product, as there is almost no artificial chemical element to the process at all, just filtration and UV light (Cornish Sea Salt, 2013). The business has made strenuous efforts to reduce energy use in its building design including green building materials, rain water harvesting, using waste heat from machines to heat the facility itself and matching the external render of the facility to the rock colour behind it so that it blends into the natural setting reducing its visual impact (Cornwall Council, 2010). Tony Fraser started the company through a fascination with the history of local salt produced by fishermen to preserve their catch (Hurley, 2011). The local culture and history seems more relevant to driving the initial conception of the entrepreneur and also again – cultural distinction of products are aimed at the ABC1 demographic of Harrods, Fortnum & Mason, Selfridges and Waitrose and devotees of the Hugh Fearnley-Whittingstall school of cooking.

The use of local product orientation and corporate sustainability measures could be a technique to access a market and, in the case of Cornish Sea Salt, bringing new people to an existing market (Hurley, 2011), which – given the size of their exports to countries including Ireland, Spain, Germany, Sweden, Norway, America, Australia, Saudi Arabia and Indonesia – has succeeded (Cornish Sea Salt, 2010).

## Discussion

The case studies and the wider context in Cornwall provide some interesting lessons for potential entrepreneurs in the food and beverage sector. Here we highlight some of these.

### *Significant investment capital is needed*

As is typical of entrepreneurial ideas in other sectors, our case studies illustrate that substantial investment and patience are required before you go to market. There is also need for capital along the way, to allow the firm to invest in new technologies such as telephones and cars to expand delivery networks. The availability of capital, be it from private sources or from banks, is an important enabling factor for innovation in the food and beverage sector.

### *The role of the evolution of the conscientious consumer in driving localism*

The forms of social innovation that give context to entrepreneurship have specific narratives that anchor them in a context. These narratives help to describe how patterns of entrepreneurial activity have come to evolve. In the food and beverage sector some of the strongest narratives are sustainability and transparency – for which local production functions as proxy. This has been driven by waves of food-related crises such as CJD/BSE (Beck et al., 2007; Sharpley and Craven, 2001), causing a growing appetite for sustainable, transparent and traceable production that feeds directly into the desire (and the narrative) of locally and regionally produced food. It is a classic example of Schumpeter's concept of creative destruction (Schumpeter, 1934b) where 'discontinuities', namely crises, provide fresh opportunities for creative solutions by entrepreneurs (Schumpeter, 1934a). It is these crises in the food industry that raised the awareness of ABC1 consumers. This has subsequently caused an increasing number of entrepreneurs in the food and beverage sector to use more local and regional branding strategies predicated on the idea that local is sustainable and transparent in comparison to multinational produce. This is perhaps best reflected in the use of local produce in the marketing of food in restaurants and local organic food in supermarkets.

## The role of brand symbolism and consumer attitude

The role of the brand symbolism is worth noting, and how it interacts with other sociological and entrepreneurial theory. Product success holds that a belief in the value of a product quite often involves an element of wilful misrecognition. The purchaser of an item is often wilfully misrecognising the faults or inconsistencies in an item in order to feel part of a select socio-economic group, with a particular behaviour pattern (Bourdieu, 2005). The role of social capital in driving behaviour is perhaps best represented by the Tregothnan tea case, where consumers in China are purchasing British tea to present an association with a particular identity. Another example is given by local food, which may not be produced in the most environmentally friendly way if the product in question is not suited for local growing, but is perceived as being 'greener' compared to imported foods – people allow themselves an element of conscious misrecognition to pursue a chosen lifestyle.

This unconscious choice-making is alluded to by Sarup (1993) and Bourdieu (1992) and can be termed 'learned ignorance'. As such to invite people in a direct conscious manner to account for their behaviour is somewhat misguided if we accept Bourdieu's position that many choices are not made consciously.

## 'Local washing' and cultural identity

From a public relations or marketing point of view, the actuality of a product's sustainability or locality of production is far removed from the perception of it; most of the product is processed at an unconscious, more symbolic, level by the consumer. As such there is the potential to capture market share through what may be termed 'local wash', where products may be identified as 'Cornish' but not have any cultural, historical or geographic connection to Cornwall. This has not been the case in the case studies discussed, but the need for Protected Designation of Origin (PDO) and Protected Geographical Indication (PGI) for products such as Cornish pasties, Cornish clotted cream and Cornish pilchards shows that, in the absence of appropriate regulation, such local identities can be misappropriated.

## Conclusion

Given the limited number of case studies here it would be unadvisable to make anything other than naturalistic generalisations between the case studies. It should also be stated that themes discussed are clearly not the only factors at work in how consumers make choices or how entrepreneurs innovate. The trend towards individualism is not discussed, for example. However there seems to be an interaction between locality, transparency and sustainable gastronomy.

The use of sustainable processes in local food and beverage production is most likely driven by motivations to reduce operational cost through energy reduction and take advantage of benefits from eco-labelling and so create a brand that is attractive to ABC1 demographics.

Local culture and sustainable business practices have a significant role to play in local food and beverage entrepreneurism. When consistently applied throughout a business's practices, cultural anchoring could be the driver for sustainable food production and sustainable consumption. The use of strong local identity in marketing products to other regions and nations offers potential for economic sustainability. There is a strong business case to look to the past, to the heritage of a region, to help build for the future – be it in terms of recreating old recipes of ales or building on the heritage of the use of salt in preserving fish. There is also a strong case for looking at the particular advantages given by the geography and climate of a region in developing new products. Cornwall has a distinct cultural and gastronomic history, and its food and beverage industry is exploiting this resource to satisfy consumer demand for sustainable and traceable food.

## Acknowledgements

John Tredinnick-Rowe acknowledges funding for his PhD studentship from the European Social Fund Convergence Program for Cornwall and the Isles of Scilly.

Tim Taylor acknowledges funding from the European Centre for Environment and Human Health, part of the University of Exeter Medical School, which is supported by investment from the European Regional Development Fund 2007 to 2013 and the European Social Fund Convergence Program for Cornwall and the Isles of Scilly.

## Notes

1 Reference group theory is a term coined by social psychologist Herbert Hyman (1960), which seeks to explain how individuals come to view themselves as groups, and how the barriers of those groups are formed and defined.
2 ABC1 refers to National Readership Survey demographic categories; crudely put, ABC1 makes up a customer segment from upper class to lower-middle class. In regard to food, ABC1 consumers' trends are not just based on greater affluence but also on factors such as a greater awareness of health issues and ethics

## References

Alexander, N. (1997) 'Objects in the rearview mirror may appear closer than they are', *The International Review of Retail, Distribution and Consumer Research*, 7(4): 383–403.
Alfranca, O., Rama, R. and von Tunzelmann, N. (2002) 'A patent analysis of global food and beverage firms: the persistence of innovation', *Agribusiness*, 18(3): 349–368.
Artfact (2012) *Lot 933: W. A. Beckwith, London a fine Cased Composed Pair of 15-Bore Pinfire Double-Barrelled Sporting Guns*, www.artfact.com/auction-lot/w.-a.-beckwith,-london-a-fine-cased-composed-pair-276-c-bd5576e78f.
BBC (2012) *Tregothnan Estate Tea Harvest 'Boosted' by Rain*, www.bbc.co.uk/news/uk-england-cornwall-19243550.
BBC (2013) *Cornwall Tea Producer Plans to Grow Exports to China*, www.bbc.co.uk/news/uk-england-cornwall-20911983.
Beck, M., Kewell, B. and Asenova, D. (2007) *BSE Crisis and Food Safety Regulation: A Comparison of the UK and Germany*, working paper, Department of Management Studies, University of York.
Bessant, J. (2003) *High Involvement Innovation: Building and Sustaining Competitive Advantage Through Continuous Change*, Chichester: John Wiley & Sons.
Bourdieu, P. (1992) *The Logic of Practice*, Cambridge: Polity Press.
Bourdieu, P. (1998) 'The economy of symbolic goods', in *Practical Reason: On the Theory of Action*, Stanford, CA: Stanford University Press, pp. 92–126.
Bourdieu, P. (2005) *The Social Structures of the Economy*, Cambridge: Polity Press.
Bourdieu, P. and Darbel, A. (1966) 'La fin d'un malthusianisme', in G. d'Arras (ed.), *Le partage des bénéfices, expansion et inégalités en France*, Paris: Éditions de Minuit, pp. 135–154.

Brown, S. and Patterson, A. (2001) *Imagining Marketing: Art, Aesthetics and the Avant-garde*, New York: Routledge.

Business Cornwall (2008) *St. Austell Brewery Signs Sponsorship Deal with Exeter City FC*, www.business-cornwall.co.uk/latest-news/st-austell-brewery-signs-sponsorship-deal-with-exeter-city-fc-123.

Cavalli, N. (2007) 'The symbolic dimension of innovation processes', *American Behavioral Scientist*, 50(7): 958–969.

Cornish Sea Salt (2010) *Cornish Sea Salt*, www.cornishseasalt.co.uk/upload/images/inline/content/CornishSeaSalt.pdf.

Cornish Sea Salt (2013) *How Cornish Sea Salt is Produced*, [online], available: http://www.cornishseasalt.co.uk/discover/how-cornish-sea-salt-is-produced/.

Cornwall Council (2009) *Cornwall Council Puts on its Rubber Gloves to Help Clean Cornwall*, www.cornwall.gov.uk/default.aspx?page=18242.

Cornwall Council (2010) *Cornwall Sustainable Building Guide Case Study: Cornish Sea Salt*, www.cornwall.gov.uk/default.aspx?page=21590.

Cornwall Council (2013a) *2011 Census: Cornish Identity*, www.cornwall.gov.uk/default.aspx?page=26948.

Cornwall Council (2013b) *Population*, www.cornwall.gov.uk/default.aspx?page=22137.

DEFRA (2011a) Council Regulation (EC) No 510/2006 on Protected Geographical Indications and Protected Designations of Origin, 'Cornish Sardines'.

DEFRA (2011b) Specification Council Regulation (EC) No 510/2006 on Protected Geographical Indications and Protected Designations of Origin, 'Cornish Pasty'.

Doyle, P. (1997) *Twelve Marketing Case Studies: The Contribution of Marketing to the Innovation Process*, London: The Marketing Council.

Energy Share (2012) *Tregothnan*, www.energyshare.com/tregothnan.

Everett, S. and Aitchison, C. (2008) 'The role of food tourism in sustaining regional identity: a case study of Cornwall, south west England', *Journal of Sustainable Tourism*, 16(2): 150–167.

Export Cornwall (2010) *A Cornish Estate Owned by Descendants of Earl Grey – Namesake of the Famous Upmarket Tea – is Selling the English Tea-drinking Lifestyle to Customers in Japan*, http://community.businessanswers.info/community/exportcornwall/case-studies/tregothnan.

Forest Stewardship Council (2012) *Certificate Code: CU-FM/COC-806720 Tregothnan Kent Estate and Tregothnan Cornwall Estate Woodlands*, http://cogent.controlunion.com/cusi_production_files/SISI_files/FL_011110032127_Tregothnan_Kent_Estate_and_Tregothnan_Cornwall_Estate_Woodlands_MainASSESS_2009-01-PS_PUBSUM.pdf.

Francis, D. and Bessant, J. (2005) 'Targeting innovation and implications for capability development', *Technovation*, 25(3): 171–183.

Gerard, J. (2008) 'Southern discomfort', *New Statesman*, p. 25.

Gerrie, A. (2011) 'All the tea in Cornwall: we drink tea by the gallon, and now at last we're growing it in Britain', *The Independent*, 26 May.

Heck, R.K.Z., Hoy, F., Poutziouris, P.Z. and Steier, L.P. (2008) 'Emerging paths of family entrepreneurship research', *Journal of Small Business Management*, 46(3): 317–330.

Hirschman, E.C. (1982) 'Symbolism and technology as sources for the generation of innovations', *Advances in Consumer Research*, 9: 537–541.

Hurley, J. (2011) 'Cornish Sea Salt makes the case for boosting export sales', *The Telegraph*, 11 October.

Hyman, H.H. (1960) 'Reflections on reference groups', *Public Opinion Quarterly*, 24(3): 383–396.

IFDE (2013) *Award-winning Cornish Sea Salt Co Makes Waves at IFE 2013*, www.ife.co.uk/page.cfm/action=press/libID=1/libEntryID=100.

Invest in Cornwall (2012) *Tregothnan Tea*, www.investincornwall.com/key-sectors/case-study/food-drink/tregothnan-tea.

Jameson, F. (1989) 'Nostalgia for the present', *The South Atlantic Quarterly*, 88(2): 527.

Linton, J.D. (2009) 'De-babelizing the language of innovation', *Technovation*, 29(11): 729–737.

OECD (1991) *The Nature of Innovation and the Evolution of Product System, Technology and Productivity: The Challenge for Economic Policy*, Paris: OECD.

Rama, R. (1996) 'Empirical study on sources of innovation in international food and beverage industry', *Agribusiness*, 12(2): 123–134.

Rama, R., Alfranca, O. and von Tunzelmann, N. (2003) 'Competitive behaviour, design and technical innovation in food and beverage multinationals', *International Journal of Biotechnology*, 5(3): 222–248.

Saltern, I. (2011) *Including the Cornish – A Unique Case for Recognition: Cornish National Minority Report 2*, Cornwall: Azook Community Interest Company.

Sarup, M. (1993) *An Introductory Guide to Post-Structuralism and Post-Modernism*, 2nd edn, Hemel Hempstead: Harvester Wheatsheaf.

Say, J.B. (1821) *A Treatise on Political Economy; or, the Production, Distribution, and Consumption of Wealth*, Philadelphia: J.B. Lippincott and Company.

Schumpeter, J. (1934a) *Capitalism, Socialism and Democracy*, 6th edn, Abingdon: Routledge.

Schumpeter, J. (1934b) *The Theory of Economic Development, Harvard Economics Series*, Cambridge, MA: Harvard University Press.

Sharpley, R. and Craven, B. (2001) 'The 2001 foot and mouth crisis – rural economy and tourism policy implications: a comment', *Current Issues in Tourism*, 4(6): 527–537.

St Austell Brewery (2006) *Environmental and Energy Management Review*, St Austell Brewery.

St Austell Brewery (2011) *St Austell Brewery: The Company*, www.staustellbrewery.co.uk/company. html.

St Austell Brewery (2012) *Our Commitment to the Environment*, www.staustellbrewery.co.uk/company/ environment.html.

Tidd, J. and Bessant, J. (2009) *Managing Innovation: Integrating Technological, Market and Organizational Change*, 4th edn, Chichester: John Wiley & Sons.

Tregear, A. (2003) 'From stilton to Vimto: using food history to re-think typical products in rural development', *Sociologia Ruralis*, 43(2): 91–107.

Tregothnan Estate (2012a) *It's official – 60 Royal Woodlands fit for The Queen*, http://tregothnan.co.uk/ news-events/news/its-official-60-royal-woodlands-fit-for-the-queen.

Tregothnan Estate (2012b) *Tea at Tregothnan*, http://tregothnan.co.uk/tea-plantation-bar/tea-at -tregothnan.

Trewin, C., Woolfit, A. and Davenport, P. (2005) *Gourmet Cornwall*, Cornwall: Alison Hodge Publishers.

University of Exeter Centre for Rural Policy Research (2011) *A Review of Cornwall's Agri-Food Industry: Final Report*, University of Exeter Centre for Rural Policy Research.

van de Ven, A.H. (1986) 'Central problems in the management of innovation', *Management Science*, 32(5): 590–607.

Western Morning News (2013) *Century-old Cornish Stout Recipe to be Brewed Once Again*, www.thisiscornwall. co.uk/Century-old-Cornish-stout-recipe-brewed/story-18390643-detail/story.html#axzz2Op Op2Dc1.

Weston, N. (2011) 'Foraging without damaging', *The Guardian*, 11 March.

# PART 3

# Food movements

The average person is still under the aberrant delusion that food should be somebody else's responsibility until I'm ready to eat it.

*Joel Salatin*, Folks, This Ain't Normal: A Farmer's Advice for Happier Hens, Healthier People, and a Better World *(Center Street, 2011)*

Food movements and initiatives are increasingly changing the landscape of food production and consumption. This chapter analyses their impacts and feasibility on both a local and global scale. **Maryam Fotouhinia Yepes** examines vegetarianism and veganism as public awareness increases of the environmental impacts of meat production and consumption. The negative effects on the environment combined with increasing obesity and health problems have led to interest in plant-based alternatives to meat. The hospitality industry is expected to react and play an important role in environmental and public health issues.

**Jan Arend Schulp** presents a case study on locavorism in the Netherlands, examining the options local food presents and asking the question whether the Netherlands could feed itself. Imports and domestic transportation are considered along with the real outcomes of urban framing. The analysis concentrates on the issue of whether locavorism can really work.

**Sandra J. Cooper** work focuses on spas as an important part of the hospitality industry that have so far concentrated on healthy lifestyles rather than food choices. As spa customers provide a clientele open to advice in lifestyle and nutrition, their role as a forerunner in sustainable food is analysed. Spas can potentially play a significant role in education and the use of seasonal and local food.

The Slow Food movement is used to exemplify how local food initiatives and community agriculture can impact on a global scale. **Alissa Folendorf, Colin Johnson and Mehmet Ergul** show how the Slow Food movement and the right to good, clean, fair food philosophy form the basis for slowing down body and mind in today's fast-paced society.

# 11

# VEGETARIANISM FOR PUBLIC HEALTH AND FOR THE ENVIRONMENT

## Major F&B implications

*Maryam Fotouhinia Yepes*

## Introduction

Successful hospitality professionals of the next generation, not only will understand the impact of their daily decisions on the environment and their clients' health, but will also take an active role in reducing their $CO_2$ footprint while protecting their clients from chronic diseases. These will partly be the result of the growing consumer demand for transparency, and partly due to the new rules and regulations that will require the hospitality professional to meet industry standards implemented by law and other regulatory bodies.

Adding vegan items to the menu allows hospitality professionals to reach a variety of growing markets such as those with cholesterol or heart problems, the lactose intolerant, certain religious groups, athletes and the growing environmentally conscious consumer segment.

This chapter provides an overview of the driving forces behind these changing trends. It highlights some of the existing scientific evidence related to the environmental implication and health consequences of a meat-based diet. It also provides practical and clear suggestions on how to offer balanced and healthy vegetarian alternatives to reduce the $CO_2$ footprint while giving tasty and delicious menu options to your clients.

## Environmental implications of a meat-based diet

Based on a recent multidisciplinary research project at Cornell's Atkinson Centre for a Sustainable Future, it was calculated that land required to support a typical omnivore diet is 3,370m$^2$ compared to a vegetarian diet, which uses a mere 890m$^2$ of annual production. Of those 3,370m$^2$, 2,950m$^2$ of agricultural land is needed annually to nourish and house farm animals such as cows, pigs and sheep, while approximately 270m$^2$ is needed to support ovo-lacto vegetarians (Friedlander, 2013). Another similar study looking into the $CO_2$ intensity comparison of various food products indicated beef as the most expensive food product in terms of $CO_2$ emission for every 100 calories produced (Stec and Cordero, 2008) (see Figure 11.1).

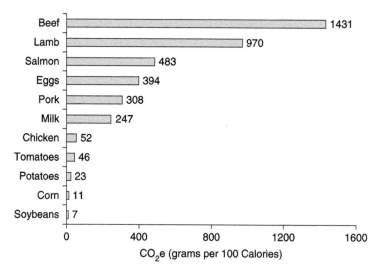

*Figure 11.1* Comparison $CO_2$ emission of various products.

*Source:* Stec and Cordero (2008).

According to a report from the United Nations Environment Program (UNEP-GEAS, 2012), the International Panel of Sustainable Resource Management has estimated that 10–35 per cent of all global greenhouse gas (GHG) emissions in industrial agriculture result from meat production. These GHG emissions are generated partly during the production of animal feed, but mainly are the result of ruminants, particularly cows, emitting methane, which is 23 times more potent as a global warming agent than carbon dioxide. According to Steinfeld et al. (2006), emissions from livestock constitute nearly 80 per cent of all agricultural emissions.

The above findings in combination with statistics on global population growth (expected to reach 10.2 billion by 2050, leading to a 70 per cent increase in food demand) are alarming for the sustainability of our natural resources (UN, 2004). The UN agency has warned that meat consumption is set to double by the middle of the century, which is an alarming concern for governments across the world. UN officials urged a reduction in meat consumption to reduce the global impacts of global warming (UNEP-GEAS, 2012).

These concerns are leading increasing numbers of people to choose vegetarianism or to reduce their meat consumption as an approach to protect the environment and our natural resources for future generations.

## Health implications of plant-based diet

Globally about 35 per cent of adults are overweight, with half a billion of them obese (WHO, 2011). The causes of obesity are multifaceted (Kopelman and Dietz, 2010) but calorie-rich diets combined with sedentary lifestyles are major risk factors. Today's agricultural system has resulted in increased access to energy and fat-dense meat and dairy products, as well as highly processed sugar-dense foods, all GHG-intensive foods that are also linked to an increased risk of obesity (Popkin and Gordon-Larsen, 2004).

In an official position paper, the Academy of Nutrition and Dietetics have stated that in all stages of life, a planned vegetarian diet is 'healthful, nutritionally adequate, and provides health benefits in the prevention and treatment of certain diseases' (ADA, 2009). Most recent scientific population studies comparing a whole grain diet to a meat-based one also identify better health indicators for diets high in whole grain than those high in red meat products (Montonen et al., 2013).

It is important to note that any diet can result in weight gain or poor health if the calories consumed exceed the calories burned in physical activity. Therefore a vegetarian diet is not a guaranteed approach to weight loss and great health. However, it is more difficult to over-consume calories from plant-based sources than animal-based sources, since they are naturally very low in calories and fat, very high in water and fibre and overall more satiating foods. Plant-based diets are also very high in vitamins, minerals and phytochemicals. These natural properties of plant-based products lead to generally better health for vegetarians over the long term.

## Vegetarian diet variety

Aside from environmental or health reasons, there are many other motives for individuals to choose a meat-free or animal-free diet, such as religious, ethical or animal rights reasons. Together, all these motives are leading to a rise in the number of people choosing full-time or part-time vegetarian diets.

There are no scientific classifications of vegetarianism as many of these diets are based on individual choices. In general vegetarian diets can be grouped into the following categories, based on the food groups included in the diet (Table 11.1).

In addition to the below categories, there is also the raw-food approach, which is a vegan diet emphasizing raw food or foods heated to temperatures below 45 °C to better preserve their nutritional properties. The raw vegan diets are generally very rich in nutrients since the vitamin and mineral losses that normally occur during processing and cooking are avoided and therefore foods' natural properties are preserved.

## Nutritional consideration of a vegetarian diet

While diets free of animal products are naturally very nutrient dense, if not carefully planned, vegetarian, and most specifically vegan diets, can lead to nutritional deficiencies. Over the long term, vegan diets avoiding all animal products risk developing deficiencies in four major nutrients: iron, calcium, vitamin D and vitamin B12, as these nutrients are found mainly in animal products, in easily absorbable forms and in high quantities.

*Table 11.1* food groups included (✓) or excluded (x) among different vegetarian/vegan diets

|  | Beef, pork, chicken, fish or other animal flesh | Eggs and other egg-based products | Milk, cheese, yoghurt and other dairy products | Honey, gelatine, other animal products |
| --- | --- | --- | --- | --- |
| Vegan | x | x | x | x |
| Lacto-vegetarian | x | x | ✓ | ✓ |
| Ovo-vegetarian | x | ✓ | x | ✓ |
| Lacto-ovo vegetarian | x | ✓ | ✓ | ✓ |

*Source:* Vegetarian Society (www.vegsoc.org).

Vegans avoiding all animal products are at a higher risk of nutrient deficiency than vegetarians and need to carefully plan their meals to ensure the highest nutritional quality for each meal. They often need to rely on vitamin and mineral supplements for B12 as it is the only nutrient found solely in animal products and our bodies are not capable of producing it on their own. This essential nutrient is responsible for many daily metabolic and cellular operations and a long-term B12 deficiency can result in chronic fatigue, anaemia, depression or even irreversible neurological damage.

Calcium and vitamin D are mainly found in dairy products and together these nutrients function in bone health as well as body fluid balance and many important cellular functions. To ensure the daily calcium requirement and to prevent calcium deficiencies vegans must ensure the calcium content of each meal is at its highest, by incorporating calcium-rich plant products such as green leafy vegetables, beans and certain cereals or seeds. Vitamin D, on the other hand, is a nutrient that our body is capable of producing by itself, with the help of the sun's UV rays. Vitamin D deficiency can be avoided with sufficient sun exposure on a daily basis as well as incorporating certain vitamin D-fortified foods such as breakfast cereals and fortified breads.

Iron is another important nutrient that is involved in major cellular functions as well as oxygen transport in blood. Iron deficiencies can lead to chronic fatigue and difficulty in concentration. Women and growing children require higher daily iron intakes so veganism among these groups must ensure adequate iron content at every meal. Iron found in plant products such as green leafy vegetables, whole grain cereals and many nuts and seeds is not as easily absorbed by the body due to the high fibre content of these foods. Certain food combinations can increase the iron bio-availability of these plant-based iron sources. To enhance nutritional bioavailability of iron-rich beans or vegetables, they need to be combined with acidic or vitamin C-rich foods. In general, consuming citrus fruits at the same time as iron-rich plant foods will enhance iron absorption. An example of such combinations is the traditional spinach salad topped with tangerines, which takes into account this complementary principle of enhanced iron absorption of spinach in the presence of vitamin C-rich tangerines.

## Protein quality of foods

Proteins in foods are composed of building blocks called amino acids. In total the body requires 20 major amino acids in the right quantity for its regular physiological functions as well as for the immune system and its many components. Many of these amino acids are considered essential nutrients, because the body is not capable of producing them on its own, and thus it is essential that the diet provides the required amount of these amino acids on a daily basis.

Animal products are considered an excellent source of high quality protein because they contain all these essential amino acids in high quantity and in accessible form. Plants, on the other hand, while they remain an excellent source of protein, may be missing, or have only very limited quantities of, these essential amino acids. Collectively all the essential amino acids can be found in different plant sources, but individually many plants contain variable amounts of these essential nutrients. However, when carefully combined they can provide complete protein quality with all the essential amino acids, similar to that of animal products.

As a general rule, the essential amino acids missing in seeds and cereal products are found in abundance in beans; and the missing amino acids in beans are found in abundance in seed and cereal products. Therefore carefully combining any foods from these three food groups can provide a complementary complete protein with similar quality and quantity to any animal protein. While it is not required to eat these complementary proteins during the same meal, it is recommended to include recipes containing them as a means to ensure sufficient intake of these amino acids on a regular basis.

Certain plant protein such as soy beans, hemp seed, chia seeds, amaranth, buckwheat, quinoa and their derivatives have higher sources of all essential amino acids and do not need to be complemented with other cereals or seeds. Soy and hemp milks are recommended on a daily basis to ensure a regular supply of all amino acids for vegans and most vegetarians.

It is worth highlighting that germination and sprouting of grains increases their amino acid availability and results in a higher quality protein. Those on raw vegan diets rely mainly on germination to ensure sufficient supply of essential amino acids. Germination activates the enzyme required for plant growth, and during this activation process, it provides a high quality amino acid profile for vegans eating mainly a raw food diet, as it enhances the nutritional bioavailability of these foods and renders them more digestible.

## Vegetarian menu planning

Chefs and food and beverage professionals are often required to include vegetarian dishes on their menu, in response to the growing demand for dishes without meat or animal products. These items must be well-planned with the help of a nutrition expert or an informed chef to ensure a complete amino acid profile as well as high quantities of vitamins and minerals required for a balanced vegetarian meal.

Before planning recipes and incorporating these meat-free dishes on the menu, two important questions must be addressed.

### 1. Is it a vegetarian dish?

If the aim is to create a vegetarian dish it can include dairy and/or eggs, which are animal products and contain all essential amino acids and are complete protein sources. Therefore complementary proteins are not necessary. However, certain flexibility in the recipe can be incorporated to allow the replacement of dairy with eggs or vice versa to respond to the different demand of lacto- or ovo-vegetarians.

### 2. Or is it a vegan dish?

If the aim is to make a vegan dish, careful planning is required not to include any animal products or by-products, while providing a nutrient-dense, high-quality protein source using only plant-based products. This can be achieved by respecting the complementary protein rule explained earlier. Therefore any cereal or seed can be selected and combined with any bean or legume and the final dish will be a high-quality protein. Table 11.2 offers some examples:

During menu development, it is important to plan a few dishes that can be easily turned into a vegetarian dish, which can be achieved by replacing the meat with plant-based meat substitutes such as tofu or other soy-based patties and vegetarian sausages made with a combination of grains and beans. For example, when preparing spaghetti sauces, sauces without meat or dairy can be prepared in advance to add more variety while increasing the vegetarian options on the menu. Also using vegetable broth instead of meat broth as a base in all main

*Table 11.2* Other considerations to increase vegetarian options on your menu

| High-protein plant foods | Complementary foods | Menu items examples |
| --- | --- | --- |
| **Beans and legumes:** lentils, chick peas, kidney beans, lima beans or any other beans | **Grains or cereals:** wheat, oats, quinoa, corn, rice, barley or any other cereal products<br><br>**OR**<br><br>**Nuts and seeds:** almonds, peanuts, walnuts, cashew, sunflower seeds, flaxseeds or other seeds | Stir fry vegetables with green soybeans served with brown rice and sesame seeds<br><br>Lentil-walnut loaf with cashew gravy sauce<br><br>Fried tofu cubes on mixed salad and peanut-coconut dressing |

dishes can allow for quick substitutions of the final ingredients and offer more vegetarian menu options.

There are numerous pre-made soy-based meat substitutes such as soy burgers and crumbles, vegetarian deli slices and sausages and other meat replacers that can offer an attractive centrepiece to a vegetarian dish. There are also a number of dairy and egg substitutes on the market for those difficult vegan recipes. Soy, rice or almond milk as well as certain sea vegetables offer excellent nutrient-dense substitutes to dairy or egg products. Many food distributors now offer a variety of non-dairy cheeses, which can add lots of possibilities to transform recipes to a vegan version.

Many chefs are inspired by ethnic cuisine, which offers many delicious options for well-balanced vegetarian recipes. Asian or South American cooking traditionally offers many vegan or vegetarian solutions for adding diversity to any menu.

## Conclusion

The market for healthy vegetarian dishes remains one of the fastest growing markets in all categories of restaurants, and as eating away from home continues to rise, today's food and beverage professionals have an advantage when expanding the vegetarian options on their menu. Adding more vegetarian or vegan options attracts not only the health- and environmentally conscious consumer, but also appeals to clients with hypertension, elevated cholesterol or other forms of heart disease, as well as those suffering from lactose intolerance or those who choose a meat-free diet for religious or cultural beliefs.

Keeping in mind the environmental impact of meat production, the restaurant industry can play a major role in protecting the future of the planet by offering tasty and attractive alternatives to meat-based dishes and encouraging even non-vegetarians to eat meat-free dishes more often. Such initiatives also encourage the food industry to create and offer more alternatives to animal products; already there is a growing variety of meat substitutes that are identical to meat products and behave similarly in traditional meat-based recipes. Supporting these industries by offering more vegetarian and vegan dishes on the menu allows for the growth of such industries while significantly reducing the damage caused by meat production to our environment while protecting the consumer from the negative long-term health impact of meat consumption.

The hospitality industry plays a crucial role in two of the most critical global issues and by incorporating and promoting tasty plant-based items they can perform an important part of their social responsibility with regard to the environment and public health issues at the same time.

# References

ADA (2009) 'Position of the American Dietetic Association: vegetarian diets', *Journal of the American Dietetic Association*, 109(7): 1266–1282.

Friedlander, B. (2013) 'Adding veggies to your diet helps cut global warming', *Cornell Chronicle*, http://news.cornell.edu/stories/2013/05/adding-veggies-your-diet-helps-cut-global-warming.

Kopelman, P.G.C. and Dietz, W.H. (2010) *Clinical Obesity in Adults and Children*, 3rd edn, Cambridge: Blackwell.

Montonen, J., Boeing, H., Fritsche, A., Schleicher, E., Joost, H.G., Schulze, M.B. and Pischon, T. (2013) 'Consumption of red meat and whole-grain bread in relation to biomarkers of obesity, inflammation, glucose metabolism and oxidative stress', *European Journal of Nutrition*, 52(1): 337–345.

Popkin, B.M. and Gordon-Larsen, P. (2004) 'The nutrition transition: worldwide obesity dynamics and their determinants', *International Journal of Obesity and Related Metabolic Disorders*, 28(3): S2–9.

Stec, L. and Cordero, E. (2008) *Cool Cuisine: Taking the Bite Out of Global Warming*, Utah: Gibbs Smith.

Steinfeld, H., Gerber, P., Wassenaar, T., Castel, V., Rosales, M. and de Haan, C. (2006) *Livestock's Long Shadow: Environmental Issues and Options*, Rome: FAO.

UN (2004) 'World Population to 2300', in *Department of Economic and Social Affairs, Population Division*, New York: UN.

UNEP-GEAS (2012) 'Growing greenhouse gas emissions due to meat production', www.unep.org/pdf/UNEP-GEAS_OCT_2012.pdf.

WHO (2011) 'WHO global report on noncommunicable diseases', www.who.int/nmh/publications/ncd_profiles2011/en/index.html.

# 12

# REDUCING THE FOOD MILES

## Locavorism and seasonal eating

*Jan Arend Schulp*

## Introduction

Today, most consumers eat food that has travelled far to their plate. The 'food mile' is a measure for the travel distance from farm to plate. Transport from all over the world uses up fossil fuels and adds to the $CO_2$ emissions. Causing food miles, therefore, adds to one's ecological footprint (Martinez et al., 2010; Rees, 1992). On the other hand, the environmental impact depends on more variables than just distance (Pirog and Benjamin, 2003); the food mile concept is not as straightforward as it looks at first sight!

The alternative for eating foods from far away is: eating the food grown nearby, the *local* food: being a *locavore*. In this chapter, the possibilities and the limitations of locavorism will be explored. The focus will be on the Netherlands, and to a lesser extent on Germany. The chapter opens with some examples in food retailing and restaurants at the high end of the market.

## Locavorism: some examples from the high end of the market

In the Netherlands and in Western Europe in general 'eating locally' is on the increase, at least at the high end of the market. Even if the concern about climate change is growing, in the cases below, reducing the carbon footprint plays a secondary role with the entrepreneurs.

Restaurant Piloersemaborg, Den Ham, the Netherlands, sources most ingredients from very near, throughout the province of Groningen. It is the philosophy of chef Dick Soek that the guests should 'consume Groningen' – very much like the central philosophy of Hall et al. (2003). Freshness is very important; therefore, every day small quantities of ingredients are fetched or delivered in many different delivery van drives. This might result in a relatively high carbon footprint, in spite of the short distances covered.

In the Restaurants of Stenden University, Leeuwarden, the concept of these learning company restaurants is geared towards sustainability, including reduction of $CO_2$ emissions. Locavorism has a central position: using mainly seasonal and local products, mostly vegetables, combined with small quantities of animal products. The use of seasonal food requires less imported fresh products and greenhouse vegetables, thus reducing the carbon footprint of the restaurants. Additionally, the philosophy of Albert Kooy (2006), chef-professor, involves respecting the seasons and the Dutch culinary heritage for their own sake. The criterion for local food is: grown in the Netherlands or nearby. Not everything is sourced as near to the restaurants as possible. Instead, one main supplier is used who sources practically all his products throughout the Netherlands: *national*, not *local* sourcing. Efficient logistics contributes to the reduction of emissions. Fish and shellfish come, by a local supplier, from small and ecologically responsible fishers. Wines are mainly from Germany and France, not from the 'new wine countries'.

Restaurant De Gulle Waard, Winterswijk, sources locally, from the Achterhoek region and adjacent parts of Germany for a couple of reasons. In the first place, the chef-owner Nel Schellekens wants to stimulate the regional economy. A considerable part of the wines served come from this region in which wine-growing has started only recently. In the second place, it is about doing justice to each individual animal that has been slaughtered for food. She works with animals that have lived for some other objective first (milk, eggs, grazing of nature reserves) and that may be useless in the context of industrial meat production (older male goats, young male kids, outsize chickens). Her style of meat production is what McGee (2004: 135) calls the 'rural style'. Another consequence of her respect for the killed animals is that all parts are used. Reduction of food miles is in her philosophy in the backseat, although it is an automatic consequence of her approach.

The Bäuerliche Erzeugergemeinschaft Schwäbisch Hall (BESH) started with saving a local breed of pig, the Schwäbisch Hällisches Landschwein or Mohrenköpfle. It was under threat of extinction in spite of its fantastic meat quality, because it was ill adapted to the industrial methods of pork production. The BESH is Rudolf Bühler's creation, who established it for the breeding, processing and marketing of this breed. Meanwhile, many other producers of regional products have joined (local breeds of beef, geese, sheep, goat and many fruit, dairy, vegetables, snails and cereal producers). In Wolpertshausen, the BESH exploits a 950m$^2$ supermarket, combined with a good and affordable restaurant, completely based on regional products. Again, the primary objective is not to reduce food miles (BESH, n.d.).

Marqt is a supermarket chain with eight branches in the west of the Netherlands. The supermarkets sell mainly fresh products produced by environmentally responsible suppliers from nearby (although wines can come from as far as Argentina). In other words: a locavore supermarket.

## Can the Netherlands be fed from home production?

Partial locavorism at the high end of the market seems successful in the Netherlands. But does this mean that complete locavorism for everyone in the country is possible and desirable? In sparsely populated regions, the yield of the land nearby is sufficient to sustain the population. For big cities and agglomerations, food must be imported from far away.

We conduct a thought experiment: would it be possible to feed the Dutch population with nothing but locally produced cereals? The yield of cereals in the Netherlands is 9,300kg/ha (2009), the population 17 million and the energy requirement per person 2,500 kcal/day. Then, 5,610km$^2$ would be enough to supply everyone with enough calories. The total agricultural area in the Netherlands in 2010 was 19,000km$^2$. Superficially, therefore, the Netherlands would be able to feed itself, with more than 14,000km$^2$ remaining for dairy, meat, oil, wine, potato and vegetable production. However, the enormous agricultural yields are only possible by extensive use of chemical fertilizers, pesticides and fuels for heavy agricultural machines, much of these imported. In 1920, mainly horse-drawn tools and farm manure were used, and then the cereal yield was a scanty 2,000kg/ha. Under these conditions, for 17 million people to grow 2,500 kcal/day in cereals, 26,000km$^2$ of agricultural area would be needed. Actually, during the German occupation (1940–1945), the Netherlands had to feed itself – compulsory locavorism! This was possible, but only under conditions of extreme austerity – for the then population of around 9 million!

Therefore, from a quantitative perspective, complete locavorism is impossible for a densely populated area like the Netherlands or for any metropolitan area in the world.

Certain imported food items will not grow in the country itself: spices, coffee, tea, cocoa, wine, olive oil, citrus fruits, etc. Nevertheless, these foods are part of the food culture of a country and therefore their absence would mean real austerity. Not importing them would only be acceptable under extreme emergency.

Therefore, also from a qualitative perspective, total locavorism is impossible and unacceptable.

## Importing fresh fruits and vegetables: bad ecology, bad gastronomy

During the 1950s and 1960s in Western Europe, prosperity increased, and people used part of this income to go on holiday. They made their acquaintance first with the Mediterranean regions and subsequently with tropical destinations. Here, they acquired the taste of exotic foods and back home they wanted to continue the holiday feeling: eating the authentic food from their holiday destination. The proliferating supermarkets were eager to please and started selling broad assortments of imported wines, cheeses, olive oils and increasingly also fresh fruit and vegetables. The latter categories were meant to enable the customers to have all fruits and vegetables all the year round: the supermarkets abolished the seasons. Increase of conditioned transport by road, rail and air stimulated this development. Transport costs were high, but wages in exporting countries low. This is also why living animals for slaughtering are transported all over Europe: meat products are made at the lowest cost, without considering animal well-being.

All of this resulted in low consumer prices, at the same time putting many local producers in the importing countries out of business.

Abolishing the seasons: it sounds attractive but it is not. Asparagus from Chile and strawberries from Spain are available around Christmas, but they lack crispness and taste. Imported peaches from Southern Europe are picked very unripe. And ripe they never will be. The risk of throwing out fruits because they rot before they ripen is placed with the consumers. Exporters, wholesalers and supermarkets refuse to take the risk of throwing out fruits because they are over-ripe. Pears and apples can be imported during the months of scarcity in Europe and not of a very good quality. Thanks to sophisticated ripening techniques, the quality of these fruits is acceptable to most customers . . . until they are confronted with home-grown fruits, freshly picked at an optimal level of ripeness. Then, the consumers become aware of the full potential of these fruits.

Similar remarks can be made about vegetables. Green beans from Egypt, Ethiopia or Senegal generally lack crispness. All vegetables start to deteriorate soon after harvesting: peas and corn lose their sugar; leafy vegetables become limp, etc. Eating freshly picked vegetables is one of the main attractions of having a vegetable garden of one's own, and commercially grown vegetables from nearby are generally superior to what has travelled far.

## Meat products: food miles and more

Increasingly, meat is traded all over the world. Excesses and scandals are by no means rare; see the most recent scandal of mixing horsemeat in products that allegedly contained 100 per cent beef (Lawrence, 2013). Companies from France, the Netherlands, Romania and the UK were involved, illustrating the real Europe-wide character of meat commerce, and the concomitant lack of transparency. Considerable numbers of animals are involved: for 2010, the PVE (Dutch organization for meat and egg producers) registered an export of live animals: 12 million pigs, 60,000 head of cattle, 120,000 calves and 220,000 sheep and goats (PVE, n.d.). In spite of detailed European and national regulations concerning duration of transport, resting time, eating and drinking, many transgressions do occur (Regulation EU nr. 1 2005, 22 December 2004). Here, incurring food miles is combined with diminishing animal welfare.

Although the Netherlands produces great amounts of meat (total value of the export in 2011: €7.5 billion), imports are also quite considerable (2011: €4 billion). Again, the Netherlands incurs food miles in order to arrive at low prices.

## Urban farming?

Politicians and idealists continuously plead for urban farming. Sometimes, the suggestion is made that cities might produce all of their own food (for one example, involving high-tech solutions, see www.innovatienetwerk.org).

Actually, it would be impossible to grow enough food in any big city or agglomeration. If, for example, each Amsterdam household had an allotment garden of 200m$^2$, enough for a competent gardener to cover 70 per cent of the need of vegetables and 20 per cent of fruits (author's own 31-year experience), it would take 72km$^2$ out of a total area of the municipality of 219km$^2$. That is not realistic. Apart from the need of area, an allotment garden makes many requirements upon the gardener: skills, available time and fitness. At present, Amsterdam has approximately 6,000 allotment gardens, occupying approximately 1.5–2km$^2$. The importance of urban farming is in the sphere of social and pedagogical issues: advancement of social cohesion, better understanding of food production, a better understanding of food quality and more appreciation and respect for professional agriculturalists. The yield in terms of food is thrown into the bargain (Schulp, 2012). Oil, dairy, meat, the bulk of the potatoes and the cereals must be produced outside the urban areas, although hopefully not too far away.

New high-tech concepts are around for efficient vegetable growing that might fit in an urban context. LED lighting is applied with only those wavelengths that are actually used by plants for photosynthesis. Even if an extra energy conversion, from electricity to light, is involved, the efficiency in using the photons for photosynthesis, the avoidance of waste heat thanks to LED light and the avoidance of diffused light makes up for this loss. Moreover, this technique can be applied in high-rise buildings. The beds can be piled up in a way that is only limited by the height of the plants, provided that occasionally they can be moved for operations on the plants (seeding, planting, harvesting). Even in this way, it will be impossible to grow enough calories for the whole population (cereals, potatoes, oil). It is a far cry from the more romantic idea of urban farming, but it does save food miles, and it is also sustainable.

Even farther removed from romanticism is the idea of transferring the meat production to the urban regions. Due to the vagaries of history, the production of pork, chicken and eggs is concentrated in the southern and eastern sand regions of the Netherlands. Originally, the animals were fed the potatoes and cereals from the farmers' own production. For today's immense numbers of animals, this is not possible any more. The animals are fed with imported feed that is put ashore in Rotterdam, transported to the industrial farms, from where the animals are transported to the slaughterhouses elsewhere in the Netherlands or far into

Europe. The idea is advanced to limit the food miles for the animal feed and at the same time reduce food miles plus stress for the animals, by locating the slaughterhouse next to the pig sheds by relocating the whole industry in urban areas, in the immediate proximity of the harbours, for example, on the Maasvlakte, municipality of Rotterdam. Rearing of the animals can be done in high-rise buildings; slaughtering and further processing can take place next-door; industrial processing of manure is economical due to economies of scale. The animal welfare in this situation can improve as compared to the existing situation. For this reason, even organizations campaigning for animal welfare are not opposed to this new approach (Varkensflats, n.d.).

## Recommendations: what can be done instead of importing?

The recommendations apply both to private households, and therefore, to the food retailing business, and to the food service industry. Not all these recommendations are easy to realize, given the present-day context.

First, make fresh, local food attractive to the consumers. Take care of freshness, the right stage of ripeness, attractive presentation and realistic prices. In principle, this is possible: see the introductory cases. But realization at a larger scale might be problematic. Take the field of fresh fruit and vegetables. Here, the supermarkets are dominant; in 2012, their market share in the Netherlands was 86.6 per cent. Specialist shops had 4.2 per cent and the remaining 9.3 per cent is for street markets, farm door sales, etc. (Vers Awards, 2012). Working with fresh vegetables and fruits requires more expertise at the shop floor than the supermarkets are willing to pay for. Also, it might involve decentralized stocking of the supermarkets, thus upsetting the logistic system. Only if supermarkets of the Marqt type develop into a serious threat might the big chains be willing to partially reconsider their policy. Here might be a chance for the specialists indeed when they focus on fresh products from nearby at the right stage of ripeness.

Second, highlight and celebrate the seasonality of food, as is the custom already for new herring and asparagus: there's a whole culture of asparagus festivals, asparagus queens, asparagus dinners, asparagus peeling competitions and so on. Partly the supermarkets already participate in touting the arrival of these. However, why not extend this to the first green kale and sauerkraut, or the first really fresh strawberries? The big supermarket chains may have no problem with this kind of propaganda, but at the same time they will be eager to keep their green beans from Senegal in every season. Again, specialist shops may play a more important role here. Additionally, customer education is necessary, to make green beans in December accepted as not a very good idea, because of the poor taste and texture. Organizations such as Slow Food and Eurotoques might play a role in this, in connection with food events like the 'Week van de Smaak' (Week of Taste).

Third, make consumers aware that importing 'authentic' food from abroad is not always a good idea. Brie in its own region is infinitely superior to anything you find imported in the Netherlands. The Dutch cheese assortment has strongly increased in the past 20 years; new cheeses have been developed and old cheeses, like North Holland Meshanger, have been revived. Just one of the new cheeses, Petit Doruvael, resembles the French Port Salut, but has higher flavour intensity. In other words: better use is being made of the full potential of Dutch agriculture and traditional food trade. Why import Parma ham when Ganda ham from Ghent is available? The Netherlands has no great tradition in dried meats like the Italians have. But since the arrival of airing cupboards, good artisanal butchers produce dried items like coppa and pancetta that can stand the comparison with excellent Italian products. And after all, one traditional Dutch dried meat product does exist: the Naegelholt, comparable to the best Bressaola. Again, the specialist shops and restaurants will have to do the work and from the big supermarket chains not much can be expected.

In the three above recommendations, specialist shops together with supermarkets based on organic agriculture or locavore concepts have to do the pioneering work. A lack of strategic orientation and general commercial expertise and skills makes it difficult for them to fulfil this task, but education and cooperation, for example using franchising formats, could enable them.

Urban agriculture also might be a good way to stimulate locavorism and therefore to reduce food miles. Not indeed, by directly providing much food for the stomach, but certainly by providing food for thought: when our super-fresh, home-grown vegetables are so very good, why shouldn't it be true for our other types of food as well: cheese, meat, eggs, oil? An educated taste and expertise in food with a broad group of consumers may ultimately lead to more local eating and fewer food miles.

## Conclusion

A shift from indiscriminate food imports to locavorism means: *better ecology and better gastronomy*. It fosters food awareness, enjoyment of the true tastes and experiencing and enjoying the seasons. But do not impose, from mistaken locavore dogmatism, unnecessary austerity on the population. Don't rob them of tea, coffee and chocolate. This will turn out to be counterproductive. But certainly, there is a future in moderate locavorism.

## References

BESH (n.d.) www.besh.de.
Cavagnaro, E. and Gehrels, S.A. (2009) 'Sweet and sour grapes: implementing sustainability in the hospitality industry – a case study', *Journal of Culinary Science & Technology*, 7(2–3): 181–195.
Hall, C.M., Sharples, L., Mitchell, R., Macionis, N. and Cambourne, B. (2003) *Food Tourism Around the World – Development, Management and Markets*, Oxford: Butterworth Heinemann.
Kooy, A. (2006) *De Nieuwe Nederlandse Keuken*, Zutphen: Kunstmag.
Lawrence, F. (2013) 'Horsemeat scandal: timeline – ten key moments of revelation in the investigation', *The Guardian*, 10 May.
Martinez, S., et al. (2010) *Local Food Systems: Concepts, Impacts, and Issues*, ERR 97, US Department of Agriculture, Economic Research Service.
McGee, H. (2004) *On Food and Cooking – The Science and Lore of the Kitchen*, New York: Scribner.
Pirog, R. and Benjamin, A. (2003) *Checking the Food Odometer: Comparing Food Miles for Local Versus Conventional Produce Sales to Iowa Institutions*, www.leopold.iastate.edu/pubs/staff/files/food_travel072103.pdf.
PVE (n.d.) www.pve.nl.
Rees, W.E. (1992) 'Ecological footprints and appropriated carrying capacity: what urban economics leaves out', *Environment and Urbanisation*, 4(2): 121–130.
Schulp, J. (2012) 'Eten van de stad?' *Slow Food Magazine*, 2012–2013: 26–28.
Varkensflats (n.d.) www.dierenwelzijn-nederland.nl/varkensflats.htm.
Vers Awards (2012) www.gfk//joop_holla_-_vers_awards_2012.pdf.

# 13

# SPA CUISINE

## An opportunity for the hospitality industry?

*Sandra J. Cooper*

## Introduction

Consideration of nutrition and eating a healthy diet has never been more topical than it appears to be now. Food consumption patterns in Europe and the USA over the past two decades have been raising concerns about the possible health risks related to diet (Chern and Rickertsen, 2003). The NHS Information Centre (2012) supports this alarming increase by updating the diagnosis of obesity as a major increase from 22,878 in 2000/2001 to 211,783 in 2010/2011; hence hospital admissions also increased with primary and secondary diagnosis.

To remain healthy, all of the essential nutrition must be present in certain minimum quantities in people's diet (Webb, 2008). An inadequate food intake can result in a shortage of these nutrients and can lead to adverse symptoms. Poor nutrition habits can lead to long-term health problems and being overweight and obese is one of those symptoms, which can contribute to a range of conditions such as coronary heart diseases (CHD), diabetes, cancer and respiratory disease (British Nutrition Foundation, 2013). In 2006, 24 per cent of adults (aged 16 or over) in England were classified as obese (NHS Information Centre, 2012), representing an overall increase from 15 per cent in 1993. The need to control obesity is repeatedly referenced by the media and government but there is only very little success in dealing with the problem (Wiseman, 2002).

Another concern is a new 'fad' diet – programmes to lose weight quickly. The reason for choosing the 'fad' diet might be medical, such as food intolerance, doctor recommendations or an eating disorder. The 'fad' diet is often portrayed by celebrities and endorsed by medical professionals as being significantly sound and proven (British Nutrition Foundation, 2013). Unfortunately this leads to disappointment, as the weight that people lose applying one of these diets usually goes straight back on when they stop (Webb, 2008). Furthermore there have been many cases where women attempted dieting, even when they were at their medically correct weight. Being under incredible pressure from society to be thin, it is often hard to keep self-esteem and body image at satisfying levels and the media – in the form of magazines, tabloids and television – appear to support this image by providing the illusion of the perfect human being (Webb, 2008).

Food choices are often determined by a variety of reasons such as availability, income, culture, demographic changes, social interactions, medical purposes, food presentation, body weight and image, as well as a lack of knowledge about nutrition (Mann and Truswell, 2007; Anderson and Morris, 2002). There are various reasons as to why individuals choose the food they consume including feelings, desires and conditioned responses (Keegan, 2002). Each individual has certain characteristics that they attach to the cultural and social meanings of food. Eating then focuses on social values, meanings and beliefs rather than on dietary requirements and nutritional values (Murcott, 1982). In the Western world, hunger is not a driving force to consume food, unfortunately stress features more prominently and it is inevitable that feelings and desires will dominate the choices made.

Although individuals recognise what is required for a healthy balanced diet, many would rather eat takeaways as the *Daily Mail* (2011) interprets 'they can't be bothered to cook'. Many individuals have chaotic and hectic lifestyles; Macrae (2009) suggests that doctors, lawyers and other professionals are eating more takeaway food, which contains almost 1,400 calories in one dish, almost three-quarters of a woman's daily allowance, leaving little room for healthy options. With the government and many food establishments using calorie counting as a way to help broaden the awareness of consumption, producing calorie information on menus has been used as a way to provide control to consumers, who now have more information about what they eat. Yet two ingredients exist more in takeaway food than in any other provision, monosodium glutamate and salt.

## Monosodium glutamate

Monosodium glutamate (MSG) is an additive that stimulates our fifth sense umami, which allows us to enhance the flavours. It is widely used in Chinese takeaways as the umami tricks the customer's tongue, allowing them to believe they are eating a more robust, hearty meal. Neurosurgeon expert Dr Blaylock explains: 'MSG overexcites your cells to the point of damage or death, causing brain damage to varying degrees and potentially even triggering or worsening learning disabilities, Alzheimer's disease, Parkinson's disease' (Mercola, 2009). The Global Healing Center (2012) claims it could potentially increase health risks such as 'diabetes, adrenal gland malfunction, seizures, high blood pressure, excessive weight gain, stroke and other health problems'. Yet the Food and Drug Administration (2011) stated in 1969 that MSG was 'generally recognised as safe' and this statement still stands today. MSG can be bought in Asian supermarkets and online by any individual, allowing the public to believe this additive is safe to use and does not contain any harmful effects.

## Salt

There are many risk factors that contribute towards getting coronary heart disease; excessive amounts of salt intake could trigger high blood pressure, which is one of the major causes of coronary heart disease. Research released by the British Heart Foundation (2012) states 'that half of all the takeaway pizzas surveyed contain the entire daily salt recommendation per pizza'. Health experts recommend adults should consume less than 6g of salt a day as the NHS (2011) states '75% of the salt we eat is already in everyday foods such as bread, breakfast cereal and ready meals'. A survey by Siemens and the Stroke Association conducted on 3,000 people reported that a staggering '64 per cent of people told researchers they were unconcerned about their salt intake, while 57 per cent said they had no idea how much they were eating' (Hope, 2009). Foods people may think are healthy, usually turn out to be unhealthy due to the ingredients within them, often due to the way items are packaged and advertised within the media. Many ingredients are hidden in products, making them seem healthier than they are.

## The concept of spa cuisine

Originally perceived as health food or hippie food in the 1970s to 1990s, Magnum-Copelli (2008) suggests that the new millennium identifies spa cuisine as the new organic food/ wholeness phenomenon, where only fresh, organic, seasonal, local and nutritious food is prepared and served. Yet the food is more than that; it is artistically designed and presented to keep you healthy and vibrant as well as stimulating the mind.

The term 'spa cuisine' was originally coined by the Four Seasons Restaurant in Manhattan in 1983 where they provided special 'fitness' or spa menus with the emphasis on beautiful, healthy food as a collaboration between chef Seppi Renggli and Dr Myron Winick and Joyce Leung from the Institute of Human Nutrition at Columbia University (*Los Angeles Times*, 1986; Cydadiet.org, n.d.).

No one definition can encompass the basic principles of spa cuisine; James Boyce, executive chef at Montage Resort and Spa, Laguna Beach, suggests that it is nutritionally dense, low-calorie foods to shed unwanted pounds but also a lighter style of dining. Chris Swensen, chef de cuisine at La Quinta Resort and Club, La Quinta, says 'spa cuisine is natural, healthy, and light. Our menu items contain a lot of vegetables with moderate levels of protein and carbohydrate' (Healing Life Styles, n.d.). Yet according to spa cuisine guru, Hunter Reynolds, cited by Magnum-Copelli (2008), this new food preference is 'essentially taking our food preparation and cooking methods back to the simpler and less refined ways of the past'.

It is clear that hospitality professionals are not only recognising this trend that is being demanded by hungry spa-goers but are embracing the opportunity to prepare nutritional meals for their guests, that are exciting, fun and full of flavour.

## Satisfying our needs

Rolfes et al. (2010) explains how as food enters the gastrointestinal (GI) tract, hunger diminishes, which is when 'satiation' develops. This state of satiation is developed as receptors in the stomach stretch and hormones become active; the person begins to feel full and, in response, stops eating. As humans, nutrients and energy are vital in order to satisfy the feeling of hunger, but eating is not solely triggered through hunger, but also when we are bored, anxious and, most commonly, stressed. Repeat eating to relieve stress can further lead to overeating and weight gain (Food Standards Agency, n.d.).

Sustaining the body's state of satiation and satiety depends primarily on the nutrient composition of the meal. Protein is considered to be the most satisfying, such as poultry, fish or meat. High-fibre foods fill the stomach and delay the absorption of nutrients; for this reason, eating high contents of fruit and vegetables within a meal or prior to a main meal can help reduce a person's portion size by providing satiation faster. In contrast, fat has less effect on the feeling of satiation, therefore leading to over-consumption. Foods that are high in fat content are flavourful, as a result stimulating and enticing the appetite to eat more. High-fat foods are also energy dense, thus delivering higher calorie content. These fatty food options are what people tend to go for when undergoing stress, boredom or anxiety, as cortisol levels are raised, which can trigger a binge. When stressed, men opt for salty, fatty foods such as pizza and crisps, whereas women opt for sweeter fatty food options such as chocolate and cakes (Macrae, 2009). Yet the common denominator in both of these food cravings is fat, which naturally appeals to the chemical cells in the brain through taste and smell. Fats alleviate anxiety by triggering the body to release endorphins, which counteracts the negative reaction of stress. Studies indicate that 61 per cent of consumers would choose the restaurants that are transparent about their food ingredients (World Menu Report, cited in Stamford, 2011). However, with 57 per cent uninterested in the fat content, and 69 per cent not wanting to know how many calories are in the food, it is not surprising that this has had little impact on the rising levels of obesity.

## Role of governments

Food-based dietary guidelines are designed to educate the general public, using a basic framework in order to propose meal plans on how to eat healthier food groups in the correct proportions rather than their nutrients value (EUFIC, 2008). This is specially designed for 19 countries within Europe, addressing suggested healthy eating plans. The World Health Organization (WHO) convey the characteristics of the food based dietary guidelines as presented:

- The expression of the principles of nutrition education mostly as foods;
- Intended for use by individual members of the general public;
- If not expressed entirely as foods, written in language that avoids, as far as possible, the technical terms of nutritional science.

(WHO, cited in EUFIC, 2008)

WHO cited by the NHS Information Centre (2012) predicts that by 2015 there will be 2.3 billion overweight adults in the world including 700 million obese and it is clear that the initiatives discussed are having little impact. Governments have a part to play and can influence dietary choices by changing the prices of various foods, the provision of information concerning the diet and health as well as education and support for health and nutrition research (Stuart, 2010). Their role could be to modify the food choices in a delicate policy issue, and to encourage these changes by educating the people on how to make healthy choices (Webb, 2008). Therefore, government and customers will continue to pressurise the hospitality industry to provide more nutritional details on menus. Calories alone are not sufficient as is evident and there are concerns about the cost of nutritional analysis, particularly for small catering operators, which would have to be passed on to customers. Other concerns are for the provision of significant training of chefs, school teachers, community leaders and spa managers before this will take place (Stamford, 2011).

On the other hand, the UK government is still providing licences to open fast food outlets and takeaway businesses for new and existing operators. They are allowing them to keep operating until late night as the UK Premises Licence Experts (n.d.) state 'the government felt it necessary' to provide late-night refreshments for individuals who may have been drinking and to also protect local residents from the 'potential for disorder, nuisance and disturbance'. This dilemma may be another contributing factor towards obesity statistics rising.

Nutrition as a base theory concentrates on a balanced diet by understanding what benefits and disadvantages eating certain food items have on the body. A well-known method of understanding what different foods need to be consumed on a regular basis is the 'food pyramid', produced by the United States Department of Agriculture in 1992 as a guide to healthy eating but later revised in 2005. This offers a pictorial representation of the proportion of foods in each group that an individual should consume on a daily basis.

Different countries have adapted these guidelines to meet their individual needs and focus on the primary diet within their borders and there are many different images produced. Representations such as the 'Eatwell Plate' designed by the UK Food Standards Agency (FSA) also provide an indication of the foods that are deemed acceptable within a balanced diet. It is also designed to suit most people, including people of ethnic origin, healthy or overweight and also vegetarians. Although the 'Eatwell Plate' may provide a visual presentation of a balanced diet, its simplicity does not display the fat, sugar or salt content of the products. Interestingly, different countries recommend different portions of each food groups with some quite specific measurements, such as the Chinese Food Guide Pagoda available from the Chinese Nutrition Society.

## Farm-to-spa movement

'The farm-to-table movement has inspired a new movement called "farm-to-spa" wherein spas use locally sourced ingredients for their spa treatments', Allie Hembree, public relations manager at the International Spa Association (ISPA) announced in September 2013. An increasing interest in sourcing, preparing and cooking, along with consumer demands for food traceability, food miles and nutrition is having an impact globally. The Euromonitor International's study entitled *Understanding the Global Consumer for Health and Wellness 2012* highlights that health and wellness packaged food is a $628 billion market, more than ten times bigger than the spa industry. This growing trend has been embraced by some spas to explore a partnership with local farmers to provide the best quality of food possible to spa guests.

The April 2013 issue of *Pulse* magazine published an article entitled 'Farm-to-spa movement: building partnerships with local farmers', which stated 'the farm-to-table movement has helped spark interest in the idea of sustainable agriculture and partnerships with local growers. Spas were among the early champions of this movement, serving up spa cuisine with ingredients either grown from the spa's or resort's backyard or sourced directly from nearby farms.' The concept was initially focused for use within their products, but has been recognised as an opportunity to establish a fundamental theme throughout the spa. The Sundara Inn and Spa in Wisconsin, USA, is just one example of a spa that has adopted the local and organic theme through its entire business. It is a member of the Orange Cat Community Farm and sources all the organic products it uses for treatments and cooking from here, as well as harvesting from its own organic herb garden.

The spa industry is reporting that 87 per cent of travellers want healthier food (Spafinder, 2014) and are responding to this demand. Headlines under the banner of 'Healthy hotels' in the Spafinder 2014 Trends Report quote 'a key element that's part of a wider 2014 trend: grab-and-go healthy food markets vs. stuffy, eat-too-much restaurants'. They also outline examples of guest consultations with the spa director to create their own salads, smoothies and bespoke meals.

In essence, sourcing food from local producers who care about sustainable issues can have wide-reaching benefits and enhance the guest experience. Sourcing locally ensures a much fresher product and a longer shelf-life from the produce because of the limited distance travelled; plus a significant reduction on the business's carbon footprint. It can also be suggested that local ingredients can create a more authentic spa experience for guests by using ingredients unique to the region or community. This will appeal to an increasingly popular group of individuals looking for a more genuine approach to their experience. These initiatives will support the local economy and provide local jobs to the community. This will also help broaden the marketability of other local products and encourage other tourist activities such as healthy, gourmet dining at local restaurants.

## Spa client profile

The Day Spa Association (cited in Kelleher, 2003) claims that the majority of clients visiting the day spas are women (70–80 per cent) aged 31 to 40, whereas the male clients are the minority (10–30%). Typical day spa clients are the baby boomer population seeking to improve their appearance and preserve their health; they are looking to enhance their lifestyle and beauty and associate the spa with escapism and relaxation (Kim, 2010)

According to the British International Spa Association (2011), the key findings from the online satisfaction questionnaire were that relaxation is the number one reason to visit a spa (91 per cent), followed by ridding the body of toxins (56 per cent), then discounts (81 per cent) and spa gifts (65 per cent). In general, the number of clients is often inconsistent with respect to healthy eating. This might be due to a busy lifestyle and pursuing a career, which often leads to increased physical and emotional stress (Theberge, 2005). It may be easier to purchase ready-prepared meals, rather than prepare healthy dishes, because of lack of time and a hectic schedule. Although, there is nothing wrong with it once in a while, in a long-term period, it can have a significant impact on a diet's healthfulness and results in the risk factors (Theberge, 2005).

The Academy of Nutrition and Dietetics celebrates March as National Nutrition Month and is a long-standing promoter of healthy living and wellness, recognising that spas are focusing on the healthful benefits of utilising local and sustainable foods within their facilities. 'The number one reason globally that men and women go to a spa is to learn how to manage their stress. We know that in order to lead a life of wellness, one must incorporate a diet rich in fruits and vegetables, so it only makes sense that spas are encouraging a more well-rounded approach to a healthy lifestyle', said International SPA Association President Lynne McNees (ISPA, 2014). Yet it is clear that the spa industry can also play a vital part in promoting sustainable food.

## Discussion/recommendations/conclusion

Reinforcing the views of Kelleher (2003), spa clients are seeking to enhance their lifestyle and, although not consciously considering nutrition, are open to positive suggestions and education on their lifestyle (Mintel, 2009). Food fanatics and spa wellness devotees are generally willing to pay high prices for high standards together with individuality, providing a unique experience for clients and inevitably gaining competitive advantage. Intelligently and carefully designed food that is both bold and imaginative can appeal to each of the body's senses, providing fragrant aromas, together with contrasting yet complementary flavours and textures. Flavour is important to all consumers and the combination of spices and seasonings supports this making the food so vibrant, incorporating sweet, sour, salted and hot flavours.

Since the early twentieth century, the attention and craze for 'superfoods' has grown dramatically. No technical definition exists and an internet search will reveal well over 10 million results. The European Food Information Council (EUFIC, 2008) suggests that 'generally speaking, superfoods refer to foods — especially fruits and vegetables — whose nutrient content confers a health benefit above that of other foods'. After just one report on a new food that claims to cure cancer or reduce heart disease the public are persuaded and drawn into a health-obsessed lifestyle. The *Daily Telegraph* (2011) highlighted a survey conducted by YouGov which stated that 61 per cent of candidates admitted purchasing, eating, or drinking specific food just because they were labelled a 'superfood'. According to a report from the NHS (2012) the EU has now banned the use of the word on product packaging unless the claim is backed up by convincing research.

Other foods provide nutrients just as valuable as those found in 'superfoods', for example carrots, apples and onions are packed with health-promoting nutrients such as beta-carotene, fibre and the flavonoid quercetin. Wholegrain varieties of cereal-based starchy foods such as bread, rice and pasta are also high in dietary fibre; in adults, dietary fibre intake should be at least 25g per day. Many studies evidence the huge health benefits due to the chemical contained in chillies known as capsaicin, with such physiological processes including the reduction of appetite, increasing metabolism, lowering cholesterol and reducing pain (Bhumichitr, 2005). First, they reduce your appetite and, second, they can aid in the effectiveness of insulin, helping the body to burn fat rather than store it, thus improving the metabolic rate. Bhumichitr (2005) further claims that the red chilli boosts the activity of the sympathetic nervous system, thereby minimising hunger. One theory for this is that the area of the brain involved is rich in nerves sensitive to capsaicin triggering a response to reduce hunger. A World Cancer Research Fund (WCRF) review found that eating greens reduces cancer risk and studies show that oily fish may reduce age-related macular degeneration (a common eye disorder that limits vision).

A recent BUPA survey reports that many believe that there are more health benefits to 'superfoods' than eating a balanced diet (*Daily Telegraph*, 2011). Food companies are labelling certain foods as 'super', giving the impression that other foods are not as healthy. Yet this is not the case; it appears that a lot of the foods we eat have 'super' properties and it is not just 'superfoods' that are beneficial to our health. Nevertheless they can help promote healthier eating and are often referred to in spa menus.

## The culinary and spa experience

The *European Spa Magazine* (2012) identifies the significant and fast-growing trend of combining 'creative culinary and spa experiences', which had previously been dissociated. The growing trend specifically targets the crossover demographic of people who are both food fanatics and spa wellness devotees. Furthermore, it conveys the image portrayed when five-star foods interlink with five-star spas, representing an exceptional experience.

A current growing trend in spas is to offer guests an experience to harvest and help cook their food, by attending cooking classes, visiting wineries and restaurants, all incorporated into their daily spa experience of treatments (*European Spa Magazine*, 2012). More spas worldwide are continuing to accommodate their guests' unique food demands in order to provide an idealistic package for clients' personal needs. This focuses specifically on dietary requirements such as vegetarian, vegan, lactose intolerance and gluten-free dining. This makes it a fast-growing necessity for spa marketers to understand nutrition and its effect on the organisation as a whole in order to create a successful menu, portraying the image they desire from the food they are providing. Spafinder (2014) further report that at Amangalla Spa in Sri Lanka, the chef escorts guests to local markets to select fresh ingredients and then they travel together to a local village to learn how to cook their purchases in clay-pot curries. As they point out 'wellness culinary tourism adventures are especially hot . . .'

To support this trend, spa therapists should have the necessary knowledge of nutrition to reinforce its benefits and provide clientele with knowledge of the psychology of food, enabling an understanding of the body's hunger and assisting in recommendations to individual dietary requirements to help benefit the clients' overall experience by way of health and wellness. Miraval Resort and Spa in Arizona, USA, offer a cooking demonstration of spa fare, incorporating local, fresh ingredients, allowing guests the taste of the wholesome foods available during their spa stay.

Emphasis is on farm-to-table, farm-to-spa and slow real food, which a small handful of hotels are embracing to meet the needs and demands of the spa consumer. Education has a large part to play in this culture change, with therapists getting more involved in the well-being of the whole body, including the menu; chefs are preparing food that meets the demands of a busy lifestyle with the appropriate nutrition to complement it. The ethos of back-to-basics food is not new to the hospitality industry but the opportunity to embrace the partnership of healthy eating and well-being is a welcome one that can support a more sustainable industry. Providing dishes and menus that highlight health benefits, reduce the fat, salt and sugar in food and keep the flavours and taste will satisfy all. Nutrition plays an enormous role in our lives, affecting all aspects of our health and well-being. The initiatives highlight a commitment to sustainability through a guarantee to use seasonal organic food and promoting local food from local producers to provide a high-quality product that combines flavours, taste and nutrition.

# References

Anderson, A. and Morris, S. (2002) 'Changing fortunes: changing food choices', *Nutrition & Food Science*, 30(1): 12–15.

Bhumichitr, V. (2005) *A Taste of Thailand: The Definitive Guide to Regional Cooking*, London: Chrysalis Books.

British Heart Foundation (2012) www.bhf.org.uk/ThinkFit/resources_and_events/news_and_updates/takeaway_pizzas_shockingly_sal.aspx (accessed 21 September 2013).

British International Spa Association (2011) *Exceeding Client Expectations for Better Client Retention*, www.spaassociation.org.uk (accessed 29 June 2013).

British Nutrition Foundation (2013) www.nutrition.org.uk (accessed 19 February 2014).

Chern, S. and Rickertsen, K. (2003) *Health Nutrition and Health Demand*, Oslo: Norwegian Agricultural Economics Research Institute.

Chinese Nutrition Society (2014) *Chinese Food Guide Pagoda*, www.cnsoc.org/en/nutrition.asp?s=9&nid=806 (accessed 1 April 2014).

Cydadiet.org (n.d.) www.cydadiet.org (accessed 14 April 2014).

*Daily Mail* (2011) 'The average Briton eats 2,500 takeaways in their lifetime (. . . that's 46 per year)', www.dailymail.co.uk/news/article-2074180/Average-Briton-eats-2-500-takeaways-lifetime-thats-46-year.html#ixzz29BebYKQ6 (accessed 20 October 2013).

*Daily Telegraph* (2011) www.telegraph.co.uk/health/healthnews/8836177/Superfoods-encourage-unhealthy-eating.html (accessed 21 March 13).

EUFIC (2008) www.eufic.org/page/en/nutrition/understanding-food (accessed 30 January 2014).

*European Spa Magazine* (2012) www.europeanspamagazine.com/index.html (accessed 23 April 2013).

Food and Drug Administration (2011) *Select Committee on GRAS Substances (SCOGS) Opinion: Monosodium L-glutamate*, www.fda.gov/Food/FoodIngredientsPackaging/GenerallyRecognizedasSafeGRAS/GRASSubstancesSCOGSDatabase/ucm260903.htm (accessed 21 September 2013).

Food Standards Agency (n.d.) www.food.gov.uk (accessed 22 May 2013).

Global Healing Center (2012) *The Harmful Effects of Monosodium Glutamate: MSG*, www.globalhealing-center.com/nutrition/msg-toxins (accessed 21 September 2013).

Healing Life Styles (n.d.) www.healinglifestyles.com/index.php/ten-spa-chefs1 (accessed 14 April 2014).

Hope, J. (2009) 'Salt warning to the takeaway generation: Teens risk health by eating one ready-meal a day', *Daily Mail*, www.dailymail.co.uk/news/article-1228709/Salt-warning-takeaway-generation-Teens-risk-health-eating-day.html (accessed 21 September 2013).

ISPA (2014) www.experienceispa.com (accessed 14 April 2014).

Keegan, L. (2002) *Healing Nutrition*, 2nd edn, Canada: Thomson Learning.

Kelleher, M.R. (2003) The Day Spa Association: A Blueprint for Success, https://courseresources.derby.ac.uk/webapps/portal/frameset.jsp?tab_tab_group_id=_3_1&url=%2Fwebapps%2Fblackboard%2Fexecute%2Flauncher%3Ftype%3DCourse%26id%3D__25725_1%26url%3D (accessed 3 November 2012).

Kim, S., et al. (2010) *A Predictive Model of Behavioural Intention to Spa Visiting: An Extended Theory of Planned Behaviour*, International CHRIE Conference – Refereed Track, http://scholarworks.umass.edu/refereed/CHRIE_2010 (accessed 15 December 2013).

*Los Angeles Times* (1986) http://news.google.com/newspapers?nid=892&dat=19861021&id=2exSAA AAIBAJ&sjid=QIIDAAAAIBAJ&pg=6877,4492510 (accessed 14 April 2014).

Macrae, F. (2009) 'Middle classes hooked on takeaways as hectic lifestyles turn Britain into "fast food nation" ', *Daily Mail*, www.dailymail.co.uk/news/article-1185100/Middle-classes-hooked-takeaways-hectic-lifestyles-turn-Britain-fast-food-nation.html (accessed 12 November 2013).

Magnum-Copelli, D. (2008) *Spa Cuisine: Food for Thought*, www.professionalbeauty.com.au/2008/10/28/spa-cuisine-food-for-thought/ (accessed 14 April 2014).

Mann, J. and Truswell, S. (2007). *Essentials of Human Nutrition*, 3rd edn, New York: Oxford University Press.

Mercola (2009) *MSG: Is This Silent Killer Lurking in Your Kitchen Cabinets?*, http://articles.mercola.com/sites/articles/archive/2009/04/21/msg-is-this-silent-killer-lurking-in-your-kitchen-cabinets.aspx (accessed 21 September 2013).

Mintel (2005) *Impact of Diets Eating Out*, http://academic.mintel.com (accessed 21 June 2013).

Mintel (2009) *Salons and Spas – UK November 2009*, http://academic.mintel.com (accessed 2 February 2014).

Mintel Oxygen (2009) *The Media and Food: Does the Media Really Influence What People Eat?*, http://academic.mintel.com/display/394627 (accessed 1 November 2013).

Murcott, A. (1982) 'The cultural significance of food and eating', *Proceedings of the Nutrition Society*, 41(2): 203–210.

NHS (2011) *Salt: The Facts*, www.nhs.uk/Livewell/Goodfood/Pages/salt.aspx (accessed 21 September 2013).

NHS (2012) *Food Labels: Traffic Light Colour Coding*, www.nhs.uk/Livewell/Goodfood/Pages/food-labelling.aspx (accessed 21 September 2013).

NHS Information Centre (2012) *Statistics on Obesity, Physical Activity and Diet: England, 2012*, www.ic.nhs.uk/webfiles/publications/003_Health_Lifestyles/OPAD12/Statistics_on_Obesity_Physical_Activity_and_Diet_England_2012.pdf (accessed 30 October 2013).

*Pulse Magazine* (2013) http://viewer.zmags.com/publication/29fc6223#/29fc6223/37 (accessed 21 March 2014).

PureSpa, Edinburgh (2012) *Natural Nutrition*, www.purespauk.com/natural-nutrition.htm (accessed 7 February 2014).

Rolfes, S., Pinna, K. and Whitney, E. (2010). *Understanding Normal and Clinical Nutrition*, 8th edn, Pacific Grove, CA: Pacific Grove Brooks/Cole.

Spafinder (2014) *Spafinder Trends Report 2014*, www.globalspaandwellnesssummit.org/images/stories/pdf/2014-trends-report.pdf (accessed 7 February 2014).

Stamford, J. (2011) 'Is it time for nutritional information on menus?', *Caterer and Hotelkeeper*, 17 February, www.caterersearch.com (accessed 3 May 2013).

Stuart, A.S. (2010) 'The relationship between mandatory and other food label information', *British Food Journal*, 112(1): 21–31.

Theberge, C. (2005) *Diet and Nutrition for the Hardworking Women*, www.nafwa.org (accessed 21 November 2013).

UK Premises License Experts (n.d.) www.ukpremiseslicense.co.uk/premises-license-faqs (accessed 2 February 2014).

USDA (n.d.) www.choosemyplate.gov/food-groups/downloads/MyPlate/ABriefHistoryOfUSDAFoodGuides.pdf (accessed 7 January 2014).

Webb, G. (2008) *Nutrition: A Health Promotion Approach*, New York: Oxford University Press.

Wiseman, G. (2002) *Nutrition & Health*, New York: Taylor & Francis.

# 14

# DISCUSSIONS ON SLOW FOOD AND SAN FRANCISCO

*Alissa Folendorf, Colin Johnson, and Mehmet Ergul*

## Introduction

Forecasts predict that the world population will increase by 50 percent from 6 billion in 2000 to 9 billion people by 2042 (US Census Office, 2014). This has led to much debate and controversy on the part of agriculture and food-producing companies as to the way to feed the additional populace.

On the agricultural side this has resulted in giant monocultures of soy and corn, along with enormous feedlots or factory farms housing thousands of cattle, pigs and chickens. Proponents of industrial agriculture and genetically modified organisms (GMOs) argue that this is the most effective way to ensure that so many millions more do not go hungry each day.

On the demand side of the industrial agricultural equation there are increasing levels of obesity in many developed economies, often attributed to a more sedentary lifestyle and the increased consumption of the so-called "Western diet" (highly processed food high in sodium, sugar and fat) that has been distributed by global fast food brands such as McDonald's, Kentucky Fried Chicken, and Taco Bell. Technology, for its part, is seemingly and ineluctably demanding that people spend more and more of their time being "productive" in their working lives and, therefore, with less time or inclination to spend in more traditional tasks such as preparing and cooking food.

The Slow Food movement is a direct response to many of these trends.

Cultures around the world are often adapting to the forces of globalization as economic development continues in emerging economies. This results in conflict with traditional values, especially concerning methods of preparing and cooking food and beverages. The model from major companies that establish production bases in emerging economies is often of productivity at all costs and the message is that to live a life that is anything but fast-paced seems counterproductive. This emphasis on speed, however, comes with certain costs, which are often costs on the health of the producer. Increasing stress results in many diseases and the erosion of existing cultural norms.

Slow Food, therefore, is in opposition to the fast-paced lives that people in the developed and developing world are or are becoming accustomed to. This chapter outlines the philosophy of the Slow Food movement from the beginning of the organization to the current movement. The chapter will focus on San Francisco's approach to initiating a community response around Slow Food principles and then examine how conscious food choices affect the overall health of the body and mind. The chapter also discusses some of the current arguments against the Slow Food movement.

## The philosophy of Slow Food

Slow Food was started as a grassroots movement in 1986 by Carlo Petrini and other activists to "defend the regional traditions, good food, and gastronomic pleasures and the slow pace of life" in response to the McDonald's corporation's attempt to open a chain restaurant at the entrance of Rome's historically famous Piazza de Spagna (Petrini, 2001). The characteristics that defined the Slow Food mission were in contrast to the idea of a society driven by global markets and capitalism, or the "fast way." By 1989 the international Slow Food movement was officially founded in Paris, France. The organization transformed from a small grassroots effort whose mission was to bring awareness to the public regarding the detrimental effects of global corporations into an international organization dedicated to the preservation of traditional foods and agricultural customs. According to the Slow Food website (Slow Food USA, 2014b), there are currently 100,000 participating members of Slow Food in more than 150 countries. These members participate through regional local chapters of Slow Food otherwise known as a *convivia*.

Members of Slow Food seek to preserve and maintain the rich cultural traditions of food preparations and practices that have been passed down through generations. One example is the development of the Ark of Taste, which was created to classify and direct people to the heirloom varieties of fruits and vegetables as well as heritage breeds of animals that are endangered due to the rise of large-scale agribusiness. The beliefs of a traditional system are a counterargument to the fast food industry's standards of preparation and practices. Globalization has transformed food necessity into a commodity and in the process has destroyed the natural elements of food cultivation and cultural significance. Slow Food believes global enterprises that condone fast food will inevitably destroy the Earth along with the traditional family meal, the community and cultural value with it.

The three main principles of Slow Food philosophy are:

1. Good: a fresh seasonal diet that satisfies the senses and is part of the local culture.
2. Clean: food production and consumption that does not harm the environment, animal welfare, or human welfare.
3. Fair: accessible prices for consumers and fair conditions and pay for producers.

These three unifying principles establish the foundation of Slow Food and what it means to act and think *slowly* and locally in a global world. The foundations do not just emphasize Slow Food's philosophy of nutrition but also how one can create a lifestyle statement through food choices (Richards, 2002).

## What does it mean to be good?

The role of *good* in the Slow Food movement means that regional and local foods are consumed within the seasonal time frame that nature has allowed for them. Industrial agriculture has manipulated seasonal produce that is now distributed throughout the year to large chain grocery stores. Consumers today often do not know the seasonal nature of the produce they consume; instead they buy produce at any time of the year, regardless of season. Along with the production of these foods throughout the year, the traditional methods of preparation have been transformed into frozen and pre-packaged meals. Processed foods now line the supermarket and household shelves, consisting of many foods that have lost their natural taste and are depleted of their nutritional content.

Local foods and regional cuisines imply particular access to resources that are dependent on climate and geography (Mintz, 1986). The available resources provide a structure for the culture producing the customs and habits that define their traditions. Eating locally produces a system that adheres to the patterns of nature. Local cuisine relies on the raw materials, but also on the techniques and methods used in preparation and cooking (Mintz, 1986). The regional raw materials and cooking techniques used produce flavors and tastes that make the region unique. Packaged and processed foods produced by fewer and fewer people due to the reliance on factories and machines have eliminated the original taste with bi-products that are not only potentially harmful but that also manipulate the authenticity of the real cuisine. By eating *good* food, consumers are proactively seeking authentic and real taste that can only be found in seasonal and local cuisines. Eating *good* is embracing the pleasure of taste that real food has to offer while nourishing the body to make us stronger and healthy. In the United States the typical food item has been transported an average distance of 1,500 miles (Kingsolver et al., 2007). The local meal has been replaced with aged produce grown by conventional methods that produce unclean and unsafe foods for consumers and often unsafe working conditions for producers.

## The cleaner the better

The mission of *clean* food means that good, fresh, seasonal foods are clean and safe to consume. Eliminating the use of harmful herbicides, pesticides, and artificial fertilizers prevalently used in conventional agriculture practices means that food will be safe and *clean* to consume. These three harmful chemical products pollute the air, water, and degrade the soil, which is the key to producing healthy and nutritious produce. Conventional agricultural practices in theory produce abundant crop yields that feed a sufficient amount of the world's population; yet, they are also contributing to the loss of biodiversity and creating vast ecological problems (Hazell and Wood, 2008). The methods used in conventional farming are not sustainable to the growing food needs of the population, which are estimated to be doubled by 2050 (Kremen and Miles, 2012). Sustainable agriculture practices such as composting, adding animal manure, and intercropping are all beneficial contributors to diverse microbial and invertebrate communities, producing a rich and complex soil system yielding larger crop production (Vandermeer, 1992).

Large-scale livestock facilities or concentrated animal feeding operations also harm and create below-standard working conditions for the producers as well as living conditions for the animals. The ecological damage that is done to produce animal protein for human consumption has had detrimental effects on the Earth's land, not to mention the land needed to grow feed for these animals. Global corporations are deforesting ancient jungles in order to raise more cattle. Not only are these corporations destroying habitats on six continents, they are also removing native plants and animals that are essential to regional cuisines (Rifkin, 1992). The organic materials left from waste run-off seep into clean and fresh groundwater, which becomes unfit for consumption by both humans and animals. The large-scale production of animals creates unethical, crowded living conditions spreading diseases and viruses to other animals as well as humans. The World Watch Institute (2013) reports that from 1999 to 2009, 75 percent of new diseases that affected humans originated in animals or from animal products.

Conventional and large-scale farming is increasingly problematic to the Earth and to humans. Slow Food promotes the production of clean and ethical foods that do not destroy the geological structure of the Earth or the biology of the human body. The consumption of clean food promotes a sustainable agriculture system and can help improve the overall health of the world's population. Slow Food's commitment to *clean* food benefits not only their members, but also the community and the world. Slow Food emphasizes that we as consumers must make ethical purchasing decisions supporting sustainable agricultural practices, producers, animal welfare, and human health.

## How being fair can benefit us all

In order to bring *good* and *clean* food to local communities producers must ensure that the food is accessible and available to all, including covering the costs associated with the producer. Carlo Petrini is quoted in *Eating Planet-Nutrition Today: A Challenge for Mankind and for the Planet*, arguing for the fair pay of farmers who produce the food supply:

> Farmers should be repaid for the many services that they perform for society and for the earth, not just for the products that they put on the market. This money pays for certain values, not just for the price of a product. Farmers are responsible for both the beauty and wellbeing of the land used for food production, and this is a service for which they should be compensated when consumers buy the food they grow.
> *(Barilla Center For Food and Nutrition and Worldwatch Institute, 2012: 106–107)*

Healthy and real food must also be accessible to all consumers; it does not seem equitable that in grocery stores today highly processed synthetic foods are cheaper for the consumer than fresh, nutrient-rich foods. If consumers choose to keep buying cheap processed food over real foods then large corporations will have access to the entirety of the global market, which will increase unclean and unsustainable food and agricultural practices. This is not reasonable either to the consumer who seeks to eat fresh produce but cannot because of financial constraints or to the Earth on which our food grows. There is an increasing need for greater awareness on the part of the consumer to be aware of true costs behind the production and distribution of foods and the contribution to the fair price of produce and products from local farmers.

Slow Food philosophy states that we as consumers need to take value in the food we eat. The more we value what we are putting into our bodies the more we will value the Earth, the producers, the community, and ourselves. The active awareness of our own community engagement will lead to fair agriculture practices and a stronger local economy. Local farms and producers depend on the community and Slow Food actively seeks to establish a relationship between the farmer and the consumer to set fair standards for all.

## The Ark of Taste

To value *good, clean* food we must celebrate the production of unique regional foods and their foundation to create cultural diversity. With the rise of industrial agriculture, landscapes that were once home to a large gene pool of fresh produce are being replaced with monoculture crops such as corn, soy, and wheat replacing these heirloom and native varietals. Slow Food introduced the Ark of Taste at the first gathering of Salone del Gusto in Turin, Italy in 1996

(Slow Food Foundation). The Ark of Taste is a catalogue of once-abundant crops from across the globe that are now near extinction due to globalization. With the help of the active communities globally, Slow Food can record and save the seeds that not only represent food as consumption but food as a means of culture and diversity. The Ark represents ancient knowledge of plants, animals, and nature that are rapidly disappearing right before our eyes. The preservation of these traditional foods and the methods in preparation are essential to the biodiversity of our Earth and to future generations. The dependency of the once-abundant foods is important in understanding our past generations, their history, and survival.

The Ark of Taste is reawakening people to the negative effects of monoculture cropping that started in the 1960s with the green revolution (Letourneau et al., 2011). The gene pools of these diverse crops are essential to the production of food worldwide. These plants and animals enable the soil to gain nutrients that are not available from monoculture cropping. Integrating a diverse ecological landscape inhibits beneficial microorganisms that increase crop yield, act as natural herbicides and pesticides, and as pollinators. Although the collection and cultivation of seeds and breeding of regional animals has been present for many generations, the Ark of Taste is a mode in which global awareness can be spread and acknowledged. By saving heritage breed animals and heirloom crops we are saving the world's cultures, biological traits, and the Earth.

*Convivia*, the local Slow Food chapters, and Salone del Gusto, the exhibition of foods and their producers held biennially in Turin, Italy, are examples of how Slow Food preserves and brings awareness to the Ark of Taste. By celebrating the taste of the foods producers and consumers are able to share in the experience of eating and finding unique products. These events and the catalogue curated by Slow Food enable there to be a market for local native foods not sold in commercial grocery stores. Education and awareness is raised through the participation in these events and creates an economy for unique and diverse food products, which is what is meant by "eco-gastronomy" (Pollan, 2003).

The entire collection of the Ark of Taste can be found on the Slow Food Foundation website, www.slowfoodfoundation.com. There are currently more than 1,600 products from across the globe in the catalogue. Slow Food encourages everyone to contribute and participate in the preservation of these foods, whether it is varieties of fruit, breeds of animals, cured meats, cheese, or sweets.

## San Francisco, California, and the Bay Area: a case study in the importance of Slow Food in community

The 1960s in California brought a counterrevolution to the growing capitalist markets, which fought to change the political system. This movement was also focused on the stewardship of the land, the revival of fresh foods in the community, and the national awareness of the suffering and unfair working conditions of the farm workers. In 1965, Fred Rohé opened New Age Natural Foods in San Francisco, the first natural food store in the United States, and a year later César Chávez and Dolores Huerta marched from Delano, California, 340 miles to the state capital in Sacramento fighting for fair labor practices for farm workers. These two events would bring national attention to California and to the growing concerns of industrial agriculture production (University California Santa Cruz, 2010). The 1970s would bring the farm-to-table movement back into discussion with the opening in Berkeley, California, of famed restaurant Chez Pannise by Alice Waters, who is an activist of the Slow Food movement food policy and one of the most influential figures in American cooking (Kahn, 2013).

Today, San Francisco and Bay Area agriculture produce an abundance of vegetables, fruits, meat, dairy, and wines attracting people from across the globe to enjoy the plentiful diversification of products, engage in the local economy, and create a relationship with the producer. The engagement of consumers who are actively interested in locally grown foods, ecosystem services, and agritourism is contributing to the philosophy of Slow Food (Unger and Lyddan, 2011).

## San Francisco Slow Food chapter

According to the San Francisco chapter of Slow Food, the organization started in the late 1980s shortly after the creation of Slow Food International (Slow Food San Francisco, 2013). One of the contributing factors to this was the wealth of cultures (especially immigrant) and the engagement in cultural cuisine and tradition that were brought with them. The connection to their heritage and history are exactly what Slow Food International seeks when gathering producers for Terra Madre, another event held in Turin, Italy, every two years. San Francisco and the Bay Area "echo in the spirit" of Terra Madre, as Eleanor Bertoni writes in *The Slow Food Guide to San Francisco and the Bay Area* (Brackett et al., 2005). With the diversity of agricultural produce, artisan products, and world-renowned chefs, the feeling of a world event such as Terra Madre seems to be right in the backyards of many San Franciscans.

In 2008 Slow Food Nation was held over Labor Day weekend in San Francisco, an event that attracted more than 50,000 Slow Food activists, according to Slow Food USA (2014a). This event showcased the philosophy of the Slow Food movement in lectures with food visionaries and notable journalists, a marketplace to showcase the teeming food products of California and the nation, exhibitions, and even a tasting hall dedicated to letting the attendees experience the taste and emotional satisfaction that Slow Food offers. The event even took to the streets of San Francisco by transforming the lawn in front of City Hall into a ¾-acre edible garden, in which the harvested foods were donated in partnership with local food banks to those who do not have access to clean, healthy, organic foods.

Slow Food San Francisco held the Childhood Obesity Bay Area Conference to promote good health in children and raise awareness of the growing epidemic in America of childhood obesity and malnourishment. Since 2011, this conference brings together stakeholders from across the medical field, food industries, activists, and technology companies to promote the awareness and innovation of insight into the crucial area of interest (San Francisco Health Improvement Partnership, online, 2014). The conference addresses solutions to childhood obesity and brings immediate attention to those children and families at risk. The convening of these conferences is important today, especially with the growing commercial industry of fast foods. Slow Food San Francisco is bringing awareness to the necessity of real foods in children's diets and in their school lunches. The contributions raised are donated to Slow Food San Francisco's Garden Program. This program is implemented in public schools in San Francisco to teach children the value of locally produced, sustainable seasonal foods through hands-on education in outdoor classrooms.

## Edible Schoolyard: bringing awareness to classrooms

Alice Waters and other food activists have also brought awareness of the education and accessibility of food to children. In 1995 the Edible Schoolyard Project started at Martin Luther King Jr. Elementary School in Berkeley as an outdoor classroom engaging children in the participation of growing, producing, harvesting, and social responsibility of food. Not only does this program connect the community, it allows for the access of *good, clean, fair* food to children and their families. This program established a blueprint for edible gardens in schools nationally and internationally. The engagement of children in outdoor classrooms, hands-on learning, and community involvement teach them the benefits of growing their own food or buying it from local farms, teaching them how to be activists in stewarding the Earth and having the power to make changes. Edible Schoolyard, in the philosophy of Slow Food, is committed to social justice and community engagement centered around a sustainable accessible food network.

## Criticisms of Slow Food

Despite the many positive aspects of Slow Food highlighted in the chapter, it should be noted that there are criticisms of the Slow Food movement. Among others Simonetti (2012) gives specific and more general philosophical arguments against Slow Food.

Some of the most obvious may be that, despite Slow Food seeking to attack the fast food movement, fast food in fact has always existed. Also at a more philosophical level it may be seen that Slow Food seeks to give a kind of idealization of an imaginary past (Simonetti, 2012: 179) and that the movement attempts to denigrate progress while offering no real option in terms of increasing agricultural output so that food security could be offered to the vastly increased population mentioned at the beginning of this chapter.

Simonetti (2012), however, may also seem to be disingenuous in that, while it may be true that fast food has always been around, it has certainly not existed on the scale or scope of the massive industrial agricultural enterprises present today. Another aspect that is often overlooked is that the vast agricultural production currently in use is often not to feed humans, but rather to produce cereal that is then fed to animals, or used for other purposes than feeding mankind.

## Conclusion

The importance of Slow Food San Francisco and the Slow Food movement internationally brings together like-minded individuals who share a commitment to the preservation of the food system through diversity, value, and taste. The Slow Food International movement is an international organization that works on a community level to collectively advocate the promotion of the *clean, good, fair* philosophy of food. By building a stronger community around the most crucial component of human life, Slow Food is able to create a network through politicians, activists, community gardens, classrooms, and world-renowned food visionaries and chefs addressing the issues of food sustainability, preservation, and bringing food back into the dinner table conversation. The Ark of Taste and the continuation of the saving and cataloguing of crops, animal breeds, cooking methods, and recipes is becoming more and more critical to the food supply on a daily basis when looking at the infrastructure of the global food industry. The continuation of sustainable agriculture practices develops a cycle of appreciation that is deeper than the roots of the plants themselves but in the community, environment, and self. The simple act of slowing the body and mind down from the fast-paced world is enough to change the world, yet not enough people are doing this simple task. In the commitment to a slower life there would be less global disaster and more global prosperity. Slow Food is committed to global prosperity and the right to *good, clean, fair* food for all.

# References

Barilla Center For Food and Nutrition and Worldwatch Institute (2012) *Eating Planet—Nutrition Today: A Challenge for Mankind and for the Planet 2012*, Parma: Barilla Center For Food and Nutrition.

Brackett, S., Moore S., and Downing, W. (2005) *The Slow Food Guide to San Francisco and the Bay Area: Restaurants, Markets, Bars*, White River Junction: Chelsea Green Publishing.

Cooking Up a Story (2007) *Slow Food Nation: An Evening With Carlo Petrini*, www.youtube.com/watch?v=ECzTRG7tjV0.

Hazell P. and Wood, S. (2008) "Drivers of change in global agriculture," *Philosophical Transactions of the Royal Society B*, 363: 495–515.

Kahn, H. (2013) *Alice Waters Makes the World a More Edible Place*, New York: Dow Jones & Company, http://online.wsj.com/news/articles/SB10001424052702303376904579137630815409064.

Kingsolver, B., Hopp, S.L., and Kingsolver, C. (2007) *Animal, Vegetable, Miracle*, New York: HarperCollins.

Kremen, C. and Miles, A. (2012) "Ecosystem services in biologically diversified versus conventional farming systems: benefits, externalities, and trade-offs," *Ecology and Society*, 17(4): 40.

Letourneau, D.K., Armbrecht, I., Salguero Rivera, B., Lerma, J.M., Carmona, E.J., Daza, M.C., Escobar, S., Galindo, V., Gutiérrez, C., López, S.D., Mejía J.L., Rangel, A.M.A., Rangel, J.H., Rivera, L., Saavedra, C.A., Torres, A.M., and Trujillo, A.R. (2011) "Does plant diversity benefit agroecosystems? A synthetic review," *Ecological Applications*, 21: 9–21.

Mintz, S. (1986) *Sweetness and Power: The Place of Sugar in Modern History*, New York: Elisabeth Sifton Books.

Petrini, C. (2001) *Slow Food: The Case for Taste*, New York: Columbia University Press.

Pollan, M. (2003) *Michael Pollan Talks Turkey, San Francisco: Mother Jones and the Foundation for National Progress*, www.motherjones.com/politics/2003/05/michael-pollan-turkey.

Richards, G. (2002) "Gastronomy: an essential ingredient in tourism production and consumption," in A.M. Hjalger and G. Richards, *Tourism and Gastronomy*, London: Routledge.

Rifkin, J. (1992) *Beyond Beef*, New York: Penguin.

San Francisco Health Improvement Partnership (2014) "3rd Annual Childhood Obesity Conference Bay Area," San Francisco: The Healthy Communities Institute and the Hospital Council of Northern & Central California Online, www.sfhip.org/index.php?module=PostCalendar&func=view&Date=&tplview=&viewtype=details&eid=198&print=.

Simonetti, L. (2012) "The ideology of Slow Food," *Journal of European Studies*, 42(2): 168.

Slow Food San Francisco (2013) "About," www.slowfoodsanfrancisco.com/about.

Slow Food USA (2014a) "Convenings," www.slowfoodusa.org/convenings.

Slow Food USA (2014b) "History," www.slowfood.usa/history.

Unger. S. and Lyddan, K. (2011) "Sustaining our agriculture bounty: an assessment of the current state of farming and ranching in the San Francisco Bay Area," *American Farmland Trust, Greenbelt Alliance, Sustainable Agriculture Education*.

University California Santa Cruz (2010) *Timeline: Cultivating a Movement, An Oral History Series on Organic Farming and Sustainable Agriculture on California's Central Coast*, Santa Cruz: University California Santa Cruz, http://library.ucsc.edu/reg-hist/cultiv/timeline.

US Census Office (2014) www.census.gov/population/international/data/idb/worldpopgraph.php.

Vandermeer, J.H. (1992) *The Ecology of Intercropping*, Cambridge: Cambridge University Press.

Worldwatch Institute (2013) *Rising Number of Farm Animals Poses Environmental and Public Health Risk*, Washington, DC: Worldwatch Institute, www.worldwatch.org/rising-number-farm-animals-poses-environmental-and-public-health-risks-0.

# PART 4

# Social pillar/social entrepreneurship

Entrepreneurs with a social mission: a species known as social entrepreneurs.

*The editors*

Sustainable employment practices are not only about stewarding the environment but also about caring for both unskilled workers and the company directors alike in an equitable manner that strives to achieve fairness of financial advantage and well-being for all. Indeed, employment is viewed as therapeutic activity by a growing group of social entrepreneurs who demonstrate how employment can have a remedial effect on those on the margins of society.

This chapter starts with a discussion by **Gaurav Chawla** on the relevance of ethical employment from a sustainability standpoint within the global catering industry. Ethical employment practices are very relevant in today's business world because of consequent organizational benefits such as greater employee engagement, creativity and lower staff turnover. Practical guidance is offered on ethical employment-related issues in the catering sector, based on the five pillars established in ISO 26000:2010 standards and a ten-point framework, based on the Global Reporting Initiative. The author argues that sustainable development in industry and the wider community must include ethical employment practices.

The benefits of sustainable entrepreneurship in Peru are highlighted in a case study by **Sandor G. Lukacs de Pereny** on the cocoa bean industry in San Martín. Small-scale farmers have been incorporated into the local economy through participative decision-making processes concerning cultivation, processing and commercialization of cocoa. Local businesses that have benefited from combining modern technological innovation with their own ancestral knowledge are identified. The way the cocoa bean entrepreneurs of San Martín continue to reach better markets with better prices through social inclusive job-creation is described.

The potential restaurant catering operations have in the rehabilitation process of UK prisoners is explored by **Sonja Beier**. In HM Prison, The Verne a unique social entrepreneurship model has been developed to assist prisoners in their rehabilitation process. In addition to acquiring practical catering skills they acquire socialization skills and the desire to fully integrate into society through customer interactions, teamwork and responsibility.

# 15

# ETHICAL EMPLOYMENT IN THE CATERING INDUSTRY

*Gaurav Chawla*

## Introduction to ethics

The principles of sustainable living are firmly entrenched within ethics, as ethical behaviours form the building blocks of human society. According to Aristotle, who laid the foundations of ethics more than 2,000 years ago, virtuous behaviour – such as generosity, justice and charity – benefits the individual and society alike. But how can something as subjective and personal as ethics be defined? In a more general sense, 'ethics', as defined by the Oxford English Dictionary, refers to the distinction between right and wrong, thereby guiding behaviour. Clearly, this definition is very abstract. However, it can help us understand the concept of business ethics, defined as a framework of values such as integrity, trust and fairness, to guide the actions of all within the organisation.

Although the study of ethics in an organisational context is not new, the field is constantly evolving and such issues are gaining prominence on the business agenda. The latter part of the nineteenth century witnessed the success of noted industrialists (they are household names even today – Cadbury, Lever and Rowntree to name a few) who also were active philanthropists. Their vision prompted the establishment of many non-profit organisations promoting ethical business in the early twentieth century, most notable among these being the Ethics Resource Centre (1922), the International Business Ethics Institute (1994) and the Society for Business Ethics (1980). These developments, coupled with widespread condemnation of unethical practices (in internationally publicised cases such as Nike, Enron and Union Carbide India Limited), renewed interest in managing businesses ethically. Although critics such as prominent economist Milton Friedman reject the idea of business ethics altogether, the same is increasingly being embedded in all aspects of business and many modern enterprises such as Marks & Spencer, Ben and Jerry's, IBM and Hewlett-Packard pride themselves on their ethical model of business management.

Ethics is about conduct – right or wrong, virtuous or vicious, worthy of praise or blame. It is a lot more than a prescriptive code of conduct, it is a way of life and a way of doing business.

## Understanding employment ethics

It is evident that business ethics is a rather broad study area. Therefore, this chapter focuses exclusively on a key agenda, namely employment-related ethics. Research establishes that businesses are increasingly becoming aware of the need to ensure that their dealings support the common good. Employment ethics therefore is a key dimension of strategic management. Employment ethics can be defined as those organisational practices that are aimed at humanising the workplace by promoting employee welfare (Institute of Business Ethics, 2013). Prominent scholars articulate employee rights to liberty, safety and respect as the most compelling agendas concerning employment ethics (Beauchamp and Bowie, 2004; Rowan, 2000). In other words, ethical employment can be viewed as how the business values its employees, while observing human rights. Winstanley and Woodall (2000) break away from a universalistic approach and focus on the needs and circumstances of individuals in their conceptualisation. To summarise, ethical employment is grounded within principles of inclusivity, opportunity, welfare and equity. Storey (2007) advocates justice and equity are also fundamental in matters of employment-related ethics. Clearly, the scope of ethical labour practices is vast, and encompasses all aspects of managing employees – from recruitment and promotion to disciplinary and grievance procedures; termination and redundancies; training and skills development; work conditions; and health and safety.

One might justifiably ask why should a for-profit venture concern itself with ethics and welfare? Is the government and its elected representatives not responsible for managing such issues? The answer is twofold; first, it is the right thing to do. Second, the sustained success of any business depends upon its employees. Olssen and Peters (2005) argue that we are living in the age of 'knowledge capitalism', and knowledge (possessed by employees) is the most significant form of global capital. In other words, intellectual capital represented by employees is a major part of a company's value. This argument assumes greater importance in the context of tourism, hospitality and leisure enterprises, as the industry by its very nature is people-intensive. The core product of any catering establishment is the guest experience, which primarily depends upon interactions between customers and employees. Effective management of human capital therefore is understood to be a core business function. Barber et al. (2011: 8) observe that 'the hospitality industry is dependent for its survival on the availability of high quality personnel to deliver, operate and manage the service offering'. Their skills, knowledge and experience are fundamental for organisational success, but also their commitment towards the organisation, which can be enhanced through ethical labour practices.

## Ethical employment and sustainability's triple bottom line

Sustainability as a global agenda has long been associated with environmental concerns and natural resource management. John Elkington (1997) led the way in understanding sustainability as a multifaceted concept and famously coined the 'triple bottom line', arguing that the performance of any business must be measured based not only on the profit (economic) dimension, but also planet (environmental), and people (social) bottom lines. The US Environmental Protection Agency (2008) further clarifies that 'sustainability permits fulfilling the social, economic and other requirements of present and future generations'. Evidently, socio-economic concerns are assuming heightened importance within sustainability discourse. A closer examination of sustainability's triple bottom line highlights some important points – most notably equity, opportunity, inclusivity and justice. This value set is clearly grounded within employment ethics. In other words, it is the ethical obligation of every organisation to contribute towards sustainable development. Ethics and sustainability can therefore be envisioned as two sides of the same coin.

> The creation of jobs, as well as income are among an organisation's most important economic and social contributions. Meaningful and productive work is an essential element in human development. Ethical and responsible labour practices are essential to justice, stability and peace.
>
> *(ISO, 2010: 34)*

## How ethical is employment in the restaurant sector?

Before we discuss ethical employment in detail, it is important to audit the current state of employment practices within the food and beverage (F&B) service industry. The industry presents a unique case, due to its sector-specific characteristics. In general, labour practices in catering establishments are informal and flexible due to the small size of their operations. The smaller size of operations presents many opportunities for ethical labour practices, as managers have more immediate control over the business' activities. This also allows operators to have close contact with the employees and the local communities. On the other hand, the industry often models employment policies on outdated models and is less than strategic in its approach (Cairncross and Kelly, 2008; Enz, 2009). Very often, employment practices are based on short-term orientation, rather than longer-term benefits. This has earned the sector a less than favourable image for attracting talent, but also created chronic problems of staff turnover and skills shortage. Another consequence is that employment in the restaurant sector is not seen as a serious career option. A multitude of factors contribute to these issues including:

- Shift work and long working hours (resulting in poor work–life balance).
- Poor remuneration (very often matching or marginally exceeding the legal minimum pay regulations, and often topped up with tips as fair compensation).
- Lack of training (even when training is provided, it is mostly Taylorist, aimed at improving productivity and makes little contribution to individuals' growth and progression).
- Limited developmental opportunities such as promotions or career growth.
- Exploitative policies – absence of overtime pay, annual leave, access to gratuities, etc.

In addition, dictatorial and authoritarian employment practices within the industry are often reported, earning the restaurant sector a notorious reputation (Poulston, 2008). Low level of unionisation, and lack of stable employment (owing to widespread use of seasonal, temporary and part-time contracts) have further compounded the problem. Unsurprisingly, Tseng et al. (2010) suggest that many small and medium-sized enterprises (or SMEs – most dining establishments will fall into this category) really struggle to do business sustainably. Could ethical employment offer a solution to these chronic industry-wide issues and promote long-term sustainability of the industry?

> Marriott International widely publicise their Global Employment Principles with the aim of attracting the best talents. Their underlying philosophy is simple 'we take care of our associates (employees), so they can take care of our guests'.
>
> *(Marriott, 2012)*

## Benefits of ethical employment

Professor Lynn Sharp Paine (2003) of Harvard Business School reports that ethical employment practices can result not only in greater employee engagement and creativity, but a range of business benefits such as:

- Employees are more supportive of management decisions that have been reached through a fair process.
- Employees are more likely to engage in discretionary behaviour to benefit the organisation when they perceive that the business operates ethically.
- Greater sense of pride and ownership among the workforce.
- More effective teamwork and sharing of knowledge within a positive work environment, where mutual respect and trust are unifying factors.
- Ability to attract and retain employees. Research suggests that companies' ethical reputation is increasingly playing a key role when prospective employees evaluate their job options.

It is evident that ethical labour practices can lower operating costs (by lowering staff turnover, and all its associated costs such as recruitment and training), enhance productivity and build an organisation's image (through recognition and awards such as Best Employers in Hospitality Awards, 100 Best Corporate Citizens, American Business Ethics Awards). Research also suggests that ethical labour practices have the potential to induce customer loyalty and provide greater access to capital as more and more investors are keen to work with ethical companies. In short, ethical employment can make perfect business sense too!

> Accor's initiative 'Take Off' was introduced in 2012. The programme aims to help Accor employees gain formal hospitality qualifications at world leading hotel schools. Take Off helps Accor staff grow and develop their careers, broadens their horizons and provides a platform to enhance their talents.
>
> *(Accor, 2013)*

## Barriers to ethical employment

Proponents of ethical employment present a strong case, although implementation is often fraught with complexities. Consequently, the catering industry has been slow to embrace and adopt such policies. A recent study by the International Labour Organization (2010) establishes that dining services work within the confines of thin profit margins, and often find themselves looking for an equilibrium between justice and efficiency. Operational costs indeed remain a prime concern, and ethical business practices can be seen as an additional burden. Usually, it is difficult to recover the investment by charging customers more for services. Apart from financial concerns, smaller establishments such as restaurants are stretched for investment of time and effort. The issue is further compounded with a lack of expertise. Independent restaurant operators are rarely known to invest in hiring specialists, who could offer guidance in matters of ethical employment.

Measurability of ethics and related issues presents another challenge (Turker, 2009). Benefits resulting from ethical employment practices are often non-quantifiable and therefore ethical concerns may not always find relevance in business strategy. Operators are reluctant to engage unless they can see favourable (and preferably immediate) returns on their investments. Other key problems are related to unfavourable attitudes (some just do not believe that ethics and business can coexist). Conflicts of interest can also arise within different stakeholders, and managing resulting issues is problematic.

Despite these real barriers and impediments, Sparrow and Cooper (2003) contend that ethical employment practices can lessen the impacts of stress, ill health and poor life quality. This in turn can address many other problems such as absenteeism, job dissatisfaction, staff turnover, engagement and presenteeism (lack of psychological availability at work). In other words, benefits achieved can clearly outweigh the costs involved.

> McDonald's and Subway, leading fast food operators have been heavily criticised for offering 'zero hour contracts' to their employees. The direct implication of such contracts is that work is offered as per the needs of the organisation and cannot be guaranteed. Consequently, employees cannot rely on a stable or secure income. Such employment practices are increasingly being reported and seriously questioned by stakeholders.
>
> *(Hall, 2013)*

## Ethical employment in practice

> Studies of workflow suggest there is five times more opportunity to experience joy in the workplace on a daily basis than in the home environment if it is a workplace that is in tune with the needs of the soul . . . Once we have a community of fully nurtured souls, the possibility of creativity is limitless. Everyone in the workplace will be tapped into his own power source as well as being part of a larger community of effort and partnership.
>
> *(Wright and Smye, 1996: 248–249)*

It is clear by now that, by definition, ethical employment is about giving people's jobs more meaning, by making them more satisfying and fulfilling. Effective implementation demands that these principles are understood, appreciated and willingly honoured by all employees. Inclusion of ethics into any business practice (more so employment, which permeates all aspects of a labour-intensive industry such as catering) may imply a complete cultural change. Stredwick (2005) offers some guidance, and establishes that the following conditions must be satisfied if the organisation is to embrace ethical practices:

- Supported and led by top management.
- Inclusive, involves all stakeholders.
- Based on clear goals and standards.
- Allows dialogue about ethical scenarios, effectively communicated to all in the organisation.
- Promotes mechanism for reporting of ethical code violation.
- Embraces culture that rewards ethical conduct.
- Linked to business strategy.

ISO 26000 guidelines by the International Organization for Standardization (ISO, 2010) offer very clear directions in matters of ethical employment. Although the standards address sustainability issues in general, they also include detailed guidance on ethical employment.

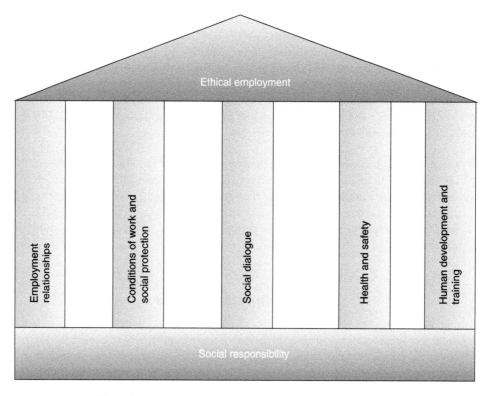

*Figure 15.1*   Five pillars of ethical employment (ISO 26000).

The standards are widely used internationally across industries. ISO 26000 guidelines on ethical employment are based on five main pillars, as depicted in Figure 15.1.

Each of these five pillars will now be discussed in detail.

## Pillar 1: Employment relationships

The objective of employment should be human development, and must improve standards of living through secure and decent work. The employment relationship confers rights and responsibilities on both employees and employers in the interest of the organisation and society. In this respect, businesses are expected to:

- Provide secure work, rather than part-time and seasonal employment contracts. Although short-term contracts are the norm in the industry owing to seasonality of the business, secure work provides for stability.
- Mitigate adverse effects in its operations, such as closures or reduction of hours. This can be achieved by providing timely and transparent information, offering employment in other units (where applicable) or offering assistance in finding alternative employment.
- Offer equal opportunities without discrimination on grounds of gender, race, disability, sexual orientation, marital/family status or religion. In other words, all employment decisions must be based solely on the requirement of the job.

- Maximise opportunities for local employment. This will not only result in an authentic hospitality experience, but also stimulate a ripple effect (or multiplier effect in economic terms), further contributing to better quality of life for the community as a whole.
- Work with and support suppliers who also observe ethical employment practices. The principles of ethical labour practices are not limited to the organisation, but extend to suppliers and subcontractors also.

## Pillar 2: Conditions of work and social protection

Conditions of work include wages, working time, rest periods and holidays, disciplinary practices and welfare matters. These impact the quality of life of workers and their families and also their social and economic development. Social protection implies that organisational policies must offer employees security in the event of reduction of income due to injury, maternity or illness, etc. Enterprises therefore must endeavour to:

- Allow observance of national or religious customs and traditions where possible. This might relate to planning staff meals (kosher, Islamic, vegetarian choices) or when designing uniforms, for instance.
- Permit work–life balance. This can be achieved through family-friendly policies, such as childcare options, offering flexible working hours, paternity/maternity leave, etc. It also applies to shift planning – for example, straight instead of split shifts.
- Compensate for overtime and additional work. Although overtime is almost unavoidable given the nature of catering operations, it must not be forced and employees must be offered a choice in this matter. Where applicable, fair wages or compensation must be paid.
- Provide equal pay for equal work –remuneration must only be based on the value of work, irrespective of all other factors.
- Provide paid day(s) off work and annual holidays. This is crucial for psychological and physiological well-being.

## Pillar 3: Social dialogue

Social dialogue includes all types of negotiation, consultation or exchange of information between employers and employees on matters relating to social and economic concerns. This pillar of ethical labour practices is based on the understanding that employers and employees have both competing and mutual interests. Therefore, the needs and priorities of both parties must be taken into account; ensuring outcomes that are meaningful and longer lasting. Operators should:

- Provide healthy opportunities for social dialogue between employees and employers, based on democratic principles. Although the catering industry is fragmented, employees must be afforded freedom to join unions to advance their interests without fear of bias.
- Create platforms for discussions when changes in operations (franchising, closures or acquisitions, for example) profoundly impact employees. This will allow implications to be jointly examined and help mitigate any adverse impacts.
- Provide access to decision-makers and information, allowing employees to have a true and fair picture of the organisation's activities. Transparency of information is crucial from an ethical standpoint.

- Consider participating in employees' organisations to enhance opportunities for social dialogue.

## *Pillar 4: Health and safety at work*

This dimension of ethical employment refers to maintaining the highest degree of physical, mental and social well-being, while ensuring protection from risks to health, both physiological and psychological. Health and safety concerns may arise from dangerous equipment, processes and substances. It is critical that the organisation:

- Provides adequate training about potential hazards, risks and emergency procedures. These could include certified courses such as the Occupational Health & Safety Standard (OHSAS).
- Records and investigates all health and safety incidents to prevent reoccurrence.
- Provides safety equipment needed. This may include appropriate uniforms, cooking and storage equipment for instance.
- Ensures elimination of psychological hazards (leading to stress and illnesses). This could be done by planning regular shift patterns, providing counselling services and organising diversity management programmes, for example.
- Considers needs of special groups including pregnant women, disabled and younger employees. The nature of work allocated needs to consider each special case.

## *Pillar 5: Human development and training*

Human development refers to the process of enlarging people's choices by expanding human capabilities. It includes providing access to opportunities for being creative, promoting self-respect, and enhancing a sense of belonging (to the community) and contributing (to the society). The business can achieve this by:

- Promoting continued employability. This can be done by investing in formal hospitality education, investing in partnership projects with employees and stimulating entrepreneurship. It is common to sell company shares to employees (in larger catering operations) as this allows them greater control over operations and promotes engagement with the business.
- Promoting diversity and fighting discrimination. This ensures equity and fairness, and can be achieved by diversity management training. Given the international nature of the industry, this is critical for organisational success.
- Providing access to skills development, training and opportunities for career advancement within the organisation. This is based on principles of lifelong learning and can afford better life quality for those concerned.

## Code of ethics – Darden Restaurants

Darden is the world's leading chain of fine-dining restaurants. They own and manage more than 2,000 restaurants and employ more than 200,000 staff. The company proudly expresses its commitment to ethical labour practices through its code of ethics, presented below:

- **Integrity and fairness** – we trust each other to always do the right thing, to be open, honest and forthright with ourselves and others, to demonstrate courage, to solve without blame and to follow through on all our commitments.
- **Respect and care** – we reach out with respect and have a genuine interest in the well-being of others. We know the importance of listening, the power of understanding and the immeasurable value of support.
- **Diversity** – even though we have a common vision, we embrace and celebrate our individual differences. We are strengthened by a diversity of cultures, perspectives, attitudes, and ideas. We honour each other's heritage and uniqueness.
- **Always learning, always teaching** – we learn from others as they learn from us. We learn. We teach. We grow.
- **Being of service** – we treat our people as special and appreciated by giving, doing more than expected, anticipating needs, and making a difference.
- **Teamwork** – by trusting one another, we bring together the best in all of us and go beyond the boundaries of ordinary success.
- **Excellence** – we have a passion to set and to pursue, with innovation, courage and humility, ever higher standards.

*Darden Restaurants (2013)*

## Evaluating ethical performance

Audits are no longer limited to the accounts offices, but all aspects of business are now subject to auditing. After all, how can any enterprise be sure of its success without evaluating performance? Social audits are tools to identify, measure and evaluate the impacts, communicate performance internally and externally, and make improvements in areas of ethical practices. Evaluating ethical practices is complex, as measurement of non-financial data such as welfare is problematic.

There are many ways of measuring and evaluating ethical performance, but the Global Reporting Initiative (GRI, 2013) framework is most commonly used. GRI has created a set of key performance indicators (KPIs) so that businesses are able to measure their own ethical performance. Their reporting framework is periodically updated to reflect the most relevant challenges organisations are facing. At the time of writing, GRI 3.1 guidelines were in use. Although our list is far from exhaustive, following are ten core KPIs as far as ethical labour practices are concerned. These could easily be measured at the unit level, and can provide insights into how fair and inclusive employment practices really are.

1. Total workforce by employment type, contract type and region must be recorded. This helps the business promote inclusivity and support primary and secondary employment within the local communities.
2. Employee turnover, with additional information such as gender and age, must be reported. Exit interviews can further highlight key issues, which can be suitably addressed.
3. Range of benefits provided to full-time versus part-time/temporary employees must be documented. It is essential that the organisation achieves parity in this respect.
4. Detailed records of occupational health and safety programmes must be kept. Training must be provided to all concerned and the content of such training courses and frequency needs to be evaluated.

5.  Education, training and counselling programmes in place for employees and their dependants must also be reported. Details such as types of training provided, number of employees allowed access to hospitality courses, the impact on their promotion prospects within the organisation and opportunities for continued growth need to be detailed.
6.  Statistics of average hours of training per employee per year, by employment type must be maintained. This is a clear indicator of investment the organisation makes to develop its employees.
7.  Other details such as rates of injury, work-related fatalities, lost days and absenteeism must be recorded as these can indicate health-and-safety-related matters.
8.  Statistics of employees receiving regular performance and career development reviews must be made available within the public domain. This can indicate provision of opportunities for growth and development.
9.  Indicators of diversity (such as age, gender, minority groups, etc.) must be chronicled. Commitment to diversity is a hallmark of ethical labour policies.
10. Ratio of wages and salaries to male and female employees must also be reported. This is grounded within principles of equal pay for equal work and indicates equity and fairness.

---

### Case study – Starbucks

Starbucks, the world's leading chain of coffeehouses has earned itself a distinct reputation for its ethical employment policies. This has also earned the company numerous awards. Ethisphere's list of the 'World's Most Ethical Companies' featured Starbucks for the seventh time in 2013.

Starbucks employees are called 'partners'. The company is committed to creating a positive work environment for all – based on principles of respect, trust and dignity. They promote diversity, exceed accepted safety norms for the industry, have clear wage and hour rules, empower their partners and provide a comprehensive benefit package.

According to Starbucks, this is a part of the company's strategic objective and will ensure the long term success of the business.

*(Starbucks, 2013)*

---

## Conclusion

Although business ethics is a vague and abstract agenda, it now occupies a prominent position within business strategy, rather than being purely seen as an interesting alternative. Ethical employment refers to management's concern for employee welfare, by offering opportunities for growth, fulfilment and development; and by providing meaningful work. Inclusivity and societal well-being are the foundational principles of employment ethics. In the age of knowledge capitalism, ethical employment practices can ensure the success of the business by creating a positive image, enhancing customer loyalty and increasing staff productivity.

Our discussions so far have comprehensively established that ethical employment can significantly impact the long-term sustainability of the organisation, local communities and the wider society. The ground realities, however, are far from ideal, especially in the catering industry, which seems to be lagging as far as embracing ethical employment is concerned. Organisational policy initiatives are often seen as ranging from symbolic devices to counteract poor public image, to addressing short-term recruitment and retention difficulties, through to pioneering efforts aimed at establishing a new order in the workplace. It is a challenging task, as building culture grounded in ethics demands that ethical dealings are integrated within all business practices and strategy. Ethics need to be seen as part and parcel of business policy and not as an entirely different realm of activity. ISO 26000 standards offer comprehensive guidelines on ethical employment. Although measurability of ethical performance is problematic, the Global Reporting Initiative offers detailed advice on creating self-evaluation mechanisms for organisations of all sizes.

It is crucial that employers understand that the job is also a means for many to integrate and find their place within society. Smola and Sutton (2002) refer to the new working philosophy, as employees are increasingly looking for association of self-worth with one's job. Scholarship of psychological contracts also points out the expectations employees have of businesses and the resultant obligations towards well-being of employees. Other commentators extend the concept of ideological contracts that connect personal values to those of the organisation; and allow reciprocal interactions between the two parties to exchanges that contribute to a valuable cause (Vantilborgh et al., 2012). Giele's (1995) comments echo with the fundamentals of sustainability, as she argues that the organisation must not only concern itself with the welfare of the present workforce, but invest in the development of future generations also. This will not only raise the image of careers in the catering sector, but also secure future sustainability of the industry and our society.

# References

Accor (2013) *Welcome to Take Off! The Accor Student Challenge*, www.accortakeoff.com/Pages/Form/Contest/Home.aspx (accessed 11 August 2013).

Barber, N., Deale, C. and Goodman, R. (2011) 'Environmental sustainability in the hospitality management curriculum: perspectives from three groups of stakeholders', *Journal of Hospitality and Tourism Education*, 23(1): 6–17.

Beauchamp, T.L. and Bowie, N.E. (2004) *Ethical Theory and Business Practice*, 7th edn, Englewood Cliffs, NJ: Prentice-Hall.

Cairncross, G. and Kelly, S. (2008) 'Human resource development and casualization in hotels and resorts in eastern Australia: getting the best to the customer?', *Journal of Management and Organisation*, 14(4): 367–384.

Darden Restaurants (2013) *Our Culture*, www.darden.com/careers/culture.asp (accessed 11 August 2013).

Elkington, J. (1997) *Cannibals With Forks: The Triple Bottom Line of 21st-Century Business*, Oxford: Capstone Publishing Limited.

Enz, C. (2009) 'Key issues of concern in the lodging industry: what worries managers', *Cornell Hospitality Report*, 9(4): 1–17.

Giele, J. (1995) 'Women's changing lives and the emergence of family policy', in T. Gordon and K. Kauppinen-Toropainen (eds.), *Unresolved Dilemmas: Women, Work and the Family in United States, Europe and the Former Soviet Union*, Aldershot: Avebury.

GRI (2013) *Sustainability Reporting Guidelines*, www.globalreporting.org/resourcelibrary/G3.1-Guidelines-Incl-Technical-Protocol.pdf (accessed 29 August 2013).

Hall, J. (2013) 'They won't be lovin' it', *The Independent*, 6 August, www.independent.co.uk/news/uk/home-news/they-wont-be-lovin-it-mcdonalds-admits-90-of-employees-are-on-zerohours-contracts-without-guaranteed-work-or-a-stable-income-8747986.html (accessed 10 August 2013).

Institute of Business Ethics (2013) *Frequently Asked Questions*, www.ibe.org.uk/index.asp?upid=71&msid=12#1 (accessed 11 August 2013).

International Labour Organization (2010) 'Developments and challenges for the hospitality and tourism sector', *Global Dialogue Forum for the Hotels, Catering, Tourism Sector*, Geneva, 23–24 November, http://t20.unwto.org/sites/all/files/docpdf/gdfhts-r-2010-08-0058-1l-en.pdf (accessed 11 August 2013).

ISO (2010) *Guidance on Social Responsibility*, ISO 26000 International Standard.

Marriott (2012) *Business Conduct Guide*, www.marriott.co.uk/Multimedia/PDF/Corporate Responsibility/Marriott_Business_Conduct_Guide_English.pdf (accessed 4 August 2013).

Olssen, M. and Peters, M.A. (2005) 'Neoliberalism, higher education and the knowledge economy: from the free market to knowledge capitalism', *Journal of Education Policy*, 20(3): 313–345.

Paine, L.S. (2003) *Value Shift: Why Companies Must Merge Social and Financial Imperatives to Achieve Superior Performance*, New York: McGraw-Hill.

Poulston, J. (2008) 'Hospitality workplace problems and poor training: a close relationship', *International Journal of Contemporary Hospitality Management*, 20(4): 135–144.

Rowan, J.R. (2000) 'The moral foundation of employee rights', *Journal of Business Ethics*, 24(2): 355–361.

Smola, K.W. and Sutton, C.D. (2002) 'Young workers' work values, attitudes and behaviours', *Journal of Occupational and Organisational Psychology*, 74(4): 543–558.

Sparrow, P.R. and Cooper, C.L. (2003) *The Employment Relationship: Key Challenges for Human Resources*, Burlington: Butterworth-Heinemann.

Starbucks (2013) *Facts about Starbucks and Our Partners*, www.starbucks.co.uk/about-us/company-information/business-ethics-and-compliance (accessed 23 August 2013).

Storey, J. (2007) *Human Resource Management: A Critical Text*, 3rd edn, London: Thomson Learning.

Stredwick, J. (2005) *An Introduction to Human Resource Management*, 2nd edn, Burlington: Butterworth-Heinemann.

Tseng, Y.F., Wu, Y.J., Wu, W. and Chen, C. (2010) 'Exploring corporate social responsibility education: the small and medium-sized enterprise viewpoint', *Management Decision*, 48(10): 1514–1528.

Turker, D. (2009) 'Measuring corporate social responsibility: a scale development study', *Journal of Business Ethics*, 85(4): 411–427.

US Environmental Protection Agency (2008) *Sustainability: Basic Information*, www.epa.gov/sustainability/basicinfo.htm (accessed 14 July 2013).

Vantilborgh, T., Bidee, J., Pepermans, R., Willems, J., Huybrechts, G. and Jegers, M. (2012) 'Effects of ideological and relational psychological contract breach and fulfilment on volunteers' work effort', *European Journal of Work and Organisational Psychology*, November: 1–14.

Winstanley, D. and Woodall, J. (2000) *Ethical Issues in Contemporary Human Resource Management*, Basingstoke: Palgrave.

Wright, L. and Smye, M. (1996) *Corporate Abuse*, New York: Macmillan.

# 16

# THE PERUVIAN CACAO VALUE CHAIN'S SUCCESS

## Fostering sustainable entrepreneurship, innovation, and social inclusion

*Sandor G. Lukacs de Pereny*

### Introduction

A sour-bitter Aztec beverage was the first taste the Spanish had of *Theobroma cacao*. The conquistadores decided to take the tasty beans of this tropical fruit to Europe where they introduced their own adaptation of the ancient ceremonial drink to the French. Soon, its fruity aromas, buttery texture, and exotic flavor conquered the old continent's palate. Yet, the Swiss claim themselves as the alchemists of that irresistible balance between sugar, milk, and "cocoa," the Anglicized word for cacao "derived from the *Nahuatl* word *Cacahuatl*" (Bingham and Roberts, 2010: 19). As a result, they created a well-rounded, sweet, toasted, and creamy solid dark bar. This is the brief story of how *Xocolatl* became "chocolate."

The world loves chocolate and the artisanal chocolatiers and massive candy-bar manufacturers are aware of it. Chocolate is perhaps one of mankind's most valued gastronomic creations, comparable only to bread or coffee. Indeed, "few foods inspire such passion in people as chocolate" (Wallenstein, 2009: 80). Certainly, consumption and sales are the most reliable indicators supporting the previous statement. For instance, in 2011, the German, the French, and the American per capita consumption—expressed in cacao beans—ranged between 3.5kg and 4.0kg. (ICCO, 2012b). Similarly, in November 2011, the chocolate confectionery industry sold more than US$100 billion for the first time in history (ICCO, 2012b). The emerging Chinese middle-class boosted sales since it has become a very attractive and profitable market for the chocolate manufacturers and cacao bean producers (MINCETUR, 2007). The latter represents a huge, economically relevant sector composed of approximately 5–6 million farmers producing almost 90 percent of the world's cacao beans (WCF, 2012). Likewise, 40–50 million people directly depend on cacao for their livelihood (WCF, 2012).

World production (2011/2012) reached 3.98 million metric tons (MT) (WCF, 2012) whereas Africa was responsible for 73 percent (2.80 million MT), Asia and Oceania 14 percent (0.62 million MT), and the Americas 13 percent (0.56 million MT) (ICCO, 2012b). Within the American region, Brazil and Ecuador (the top producers) generated 0.23 million MT and

*Figure 16.1* Organic cacao from San Martín, Peru.

*Source:* Lukacs de Pereny (2011).

0.13 million MT respectively followed by the Dominican Republic (0.05 million MT) and Peru (0.04 million MT) (FAO, 2011). Peru's case, despite its comparatively low production, is interesting given that within a decade, this country has become the world's second largest organic cacao producer (Diario Gestión, 2013). Peru has also been recognized for its rich-aromatic, organic cacao mostly cultivated in San Martín—the leading cacao region—which accounts for 32.6 percent of the national share (UNODC, 2011). One must embrace that organic cacao markets have few buyers, very high standards (e.g., product and sanitary certifications), and only represent a small fraction (0.5 percent) of the whole cacao market (estimated in 15,500 tons of certified product) (ICCO, 2012a).

Hence, organic markets are strongly competitive because it is generally difficult for the small-scale producers to meet those requirements, yet not for San Martín's cacao farmers. They have been able to access them and hence become part of the cacao global value chains (GVC). This seems hard to believe, especially because 20 years ago, this former unproductive region was populated by scattered subsistence-farmers, drug cartels, and terrorist groups. Cocaine production, extortion, and state absence better describe San Martín's past economic, political, and social contexts. Nevertheless, today this region stands as a world-class example of sustainable entrepreneurship, innovation, and social inclusion. Cacao beans stand as an example of how a gastronomic product was cultivated to harvest sustainable development.

The present case study intends to provide an analysis of how San Martín's small-scale cacao farmers reached the world cacao markets despite the previously mentioned adverse backgrounds. In this view, I will employ the governance of global value chains (GVC) theory as my framework (Gereffi et al., 2005) given that it focuses on all the different stages, actors, and outputs within a production value chain. Additionally, I will incorporate several scholars' work plus other scientific, gastronomic, and statistical references. In terms of organization, I will first explain the rationale—and relevance—behind this case study. This will lead to a brief description of the GVC's framework. Third, I will present the region San Martín (in terms of data and contexts). Fourth, I will argue why the Peruvian cacao has a comparative advantage and how this (plus other factors) has allowed Peruvian cacao producers to access specific market niches. Fifth, I will identify who the main actors are (with particular emphasis on the main stakeholders, the small-scale farmers), their roles, power, and interactions. Sixth, I will briefly elaborate on three major concepts: sustainable entrepreneurship; innovation; and social inclusion, since these concepts best summarize the success of the present case study. I will end my work by delivering my personal remarks in the conclusions section. Finally, it is worth mentioning that my article presents two limitations. The first one is related to updated statistical-data availability. As a matter of fact, some sources range between one and ten years old. The second limitation is that there is neither specific research nor conclusive statistical data to support that San Martín's cacao sector has directly contributed to improving the rural peasants' quality of life expressed in the Human Development Indicators (HDI) (e.g., economic, health, and education indicators). This said, let's begin with the topic's rationale.

## Rationale

What assets or resources do people in the rural areas possess besides land, crops, cattle, and other minor animals? I believe most of them will have neither bank accounts nor documented properties nor university education. Thus, what other sorts of capital do they have?

Culture, in the form of ancestral knowledge and traditions, is perhaps one of their most valued resources. Undoubtedly, this sort of intangible asset has been often ignored or put in second place. However, we must embrace the true potential of such cognitive capital. For instance, the Amazon native communities know which types of plants alleviate certain types of symptoms. Accordingly, the indigenous Quechua communities know thousands of existing varieties of potatoes they have been keeping for centuries (CIPOTATO, 2011). Likewise, San Martín's farmers know the natural-ancestral ways to grow one of the world's top-notch cacao bean's wild organic varieties. All this knowledge has benefitted both the pharmaceutical and food industries, just to mention two.

Peru is one of the top ten flora and fauna "megadiverse" countries worldwide; it has the second largest Amazon rainforest (16 percent); 84/117 world habitats; plus 28 different micro-climates (Brack and Mendiola, 2000). Ergo, by combining ancestral knowledge with natural diversity, rural peasants can participate in the economy dynamic that perhaps might not solve all poverty-related problems, but can contribute to reducing them. This is not a personal enlightened discovery since organic crop production, biocommerce, and tourism (including gastronomy) already exist. In my opinion, the true challenge relies on *how* to match supply and demand concerning profitable segmented niches hungry for high value added products where Peru can be competitive. Yet, "[H]ow can economic actors gain access to the skills, competences and supporting services required to participate in global value chains? What potential is there for firms, industries, and societies from the developing world to 'upgrade' by actively changing the way they are linked to global value chains?" (Gereffi et al., 2001: 3). The idea is to support local entrepreneurship through investment and training as Hjalager and Richards (2011: 207) point out: "[T]he contention that local food production systems, if financially viable, can contribute towards maintaining local economies, societies, cultures, and environments provides positive encouragement for looking closely at the role of food both in the tourism industry and within local economies."

## The governance of the global value chains (GVC) framework

Understanding how a market operates requires the identification of basic features such as who the actors are (e.g., clients and/or producers); what are the driving forces (e.g., political and/or economic); and what are the resulting interactions (e.g., profit and/or social benefit)? Such is the case of those sectors producing for global markets, a complex enchainment of inter-twined processes entailing time and resources. These structures are called global value chains (GVC) (Gereffi et al., 2005). Similarly, "Global value chain research and policy work examine the different ways in which global production and distribution systems are integrated, and the possibilities for firms in developing countries to enhance their position in global markets" (Gereffi et al., 2005: 1). However, GVC are strongly influenced by their actors and their interactions. Clearly, some of them will concentrate more power than others and therefore will *govern* (rule, dictate, and/or influence the market). This is called the *governance* of GVC, "a central concept to value chain analysis. Governance can be defined as a non-market coordination of economic activity" (Gereffi et al., 2001: 4). Consequently, this framework is pertinent because it provides a broad structural approach on "how to include micro, small-and-medium-sized producers and firms into the value chain" (Bamber and Fernandez-Stark, 2012b: 41) by assessing their economic relevance in developing economies. Gereffi et al. (2005) consider their work as a means to boosting employment creation, expanding economic development, triggering industrial upgrading, and increasing poverty alleviation through more effective policies. For Humphrey and Schmitz (2001), producers first need to know *what* to do, *how*, *when*, and *how much* to produce before finding a client and becoming suppliers. Bamber and Fernandez-Stark (2012) refer to the Four-Pillar Model of Value Chain Inclusion, which relates to access to markets, training, finance, and coordination and collaboration-building. In their turn, Gereffi et al. propose five global value-chain governance types: markets; modular; relational; captive; and hierarchy (2005) (see Annexes 1 and 2).

## The cacao value chain (CVC)

The CVC is basically the same among all cacao bean-growing countries. This is: growing, harvesting, fermenting, and drying the beans before commercializing—shipping—them to chocolate manufacturers, who elaborate a wide array of sub-products (e.g., chocolate, cacao butter, and cacao powder) (see Annex 3). Nevertheless, some cacao bean-producing countries are investing in infrastructure, technology, and human capital in order to locally process their own beans (value added). Their intention is to break the perpetuity of the classical Wallerstein's commodity chain model: "talking of commodity chains means to talk of an extended social division of labor which, in the course of capitalism's historical development, has become more and more functionally and geographically extensive, and simultaneously more and more hier-archical" (Wallerstein 1983: 30). In this regard, the CVC allows us to fully examine "the labor inputs, technologies, standards, regulations, products, processes, and markets in specific industries and locations, thus providing a holistic view of industries both from the top down to the bottom up" (Gereffi and Fernandez-Stark, 2011).

## Region San Martín

Located in the north central part of the Peruvian Amazon rainforest (Annex 4), San Martín has a population of 794,730 inhabitants and three minor ethnic groups, Quechua Lamista, Aguaruna, and Chayahuita (INEI, 2007).

San Martín is essentially a natural-resource dependent economy (55.5 percent of its population work in natural-related activities) (MINAG, 2012b). In 2006 approximately 58.1 percent of the economically active population (EAP) worked in agriculture. Yet, in 2008, it dropped to 46.8 percent due to 2007's world financial crisis (MINTRA, 2013). From 2001 to 2012 extractive activities decreased (−9.3 percent) while local trade increased (+2.2 percent) (MINAG, 2013). The unemployment rate reached 1.8 percent in 2001 (Peru: 5.1 percent). A decade later it slightly increased to 2.2 percent (Peru 3.7 percent) (MINAG, 2013). The labor force (aged 15 to 44) counted for 76.4 percent in 2001 and 69.2 percent in 2012. However, it is interesting to note that the EAP aged 45 to 64 increased by 6.2 percent within the same period (from 18.7 percent to 24.9 percent) (MINAG, 2013). This can be explained by an increase in agricultural investment and agriculture-related activities (MINAG, 2012a).

In 2011, illiteracy rates reached 2.67 percent (MINTRA, 2013). In 2001, 51.1 percent and 31.6 percent of the EAP affirmed to have concluded primary and secondary school respectively. In 2012, this proportion dropped to 35.6 percent and 38.1 percent respectively (INEI, 2013) since children are traditionally a source of labor.

Complementarily, Table 16.1 provides data related to the Human Development Index (HDI) with regard to San Martín and other Peruvian regions for 2010.

By 1986, two terrorist groups, Sendero Luminoso and Movimiento Revolucionario Túpac Amaru (MRTA) (Túpac Amaru Revolutionary Movement) had total control in San Martín through extortion, corruption, and assassination mechanisms (UNODC, 2011). Meanwhile, Peruvian and Colombian drug cartels were installing themselves in the region. A symbiotic cash-for-security relation emerged between both illegal actors. As a result, San Martín

*Table 16.1* Human Development Index (HDI) comparison between San Martín and other Peruvian regions

| Item | Rank | Amazonas | Rank | Cajamarca | Rank | San Martín | Rank | Huánuco | Rank | Pasco | Rank | Junín |
|---|---|---|---|---|---|---|---|---|---|---|---|---|
| Inhabitants | 19 | 389,700 | 4 | 1,359,023 | 13 | 669,973 | 12 | 730,871 | 21 | 266,764 | 8 | 1,091,619 |
| HDI | 17 | 0.5535 | 19 | 0.54 | 14 | 0.5735 | 21 | 0.5311 | 13 | 0.5752 | 10 | 0.5922 |
| Literacy | 17 | 87.40% | 21 | 80.90% | 13 | 90.80% | 20 | 83.20% | 14 | 90.50% | 11 | 91.60% |
| Education | 23 | 77.80% | 24 | 75.70% | 21 | 79.60% | 22 | 78.60% | 14 | 85.60% | 10 | 86.40% |
| Life expectancy | 16 | 68.9 | 13 | 69.4 | 9 | 70.9 | 19 | 68 | 15 | 69.3 | 12 | 69.8 |
| Educational achievement | 19 | 84.2094 | 24 | 79.10% | 14 | 87.10% | 21 | 81.70% | 12 | 88.90% | 10 | 89.90% |
| Per capita family income | 19 | 215.3 | 17 | 216.7 | 20 | 211.1 | 23 | 157.8 | 14 | 239.8 | 9 | 306.6 |

*Source:* adapted from UNODC (2011).

became Peru's second coca bush-producing region (+25,000ha, 1992) (UNODC, 2011). De Soto best summarizes the previous context: "No group—aside from terrorists—is better positioned to sabotage capitalist expansion" (De Soto, 2000: 156). Indeed, rural peasants were paid by drug cartels to grow coca bushes since "for small farmers in some areas of the developing world, money advanced by drug traffickers is practically the only credit available" (De Soto, 2000: 154). However, during the 1990s, the Peruvian government carried out an aggressive military strategy seeking to recover several *zonas liberadas* (free zones) claimed by both terrorist groups and narc cartels. Moreover, in 1992, Sendero Luminoso's leader Abimael Guzmán was captured and imprisoned. This final coup triggered the slow yet continuous dilution of these illegal actors. Consequently, hundreds of peasant coca bush farmers found themselves with no buyers and an uncertain future. In this regard, cacao crops played a crucial role. Local farmers switched from coca to cacao due to the economic benefits derived from adequate government policy incentives and international agencies' alternative crop programs.

## The Peruvian cacao's comparative advantages

The "unquestionable" Mesoamerican origin of cacao still haunts scientists, gastronomists, and gourmands. However, Motamayor et al. (2008) identified the *Sphaerocarpum* subspecies as a South American native variety, while, according to Zhang et al. (2006), *Theobroma cacao* is indigenous to the Amazon region of South America. Even Peru also has its own native varieties of cacao. Additionally, the Peruvian Amazon hosts a large number of diverse cacao populations and genetic diversity (Zhang et al., 2006) (Annex 5). Moreover, Bartley (2005: 325) posits that in the Amazon "cultivation has been practised for centuries." Arévalo (2011) goes even further. His findings are related specifically to San Martín. He posits that several genetic experiments carried out with regional samples have shown that the material has a promising genotype endemic to San Martín.

Cacao is classified by gastronomists and connoisseurs according to its aroma, taste, texture, and fat content (essential for top chocolate manufacturing). Genetic richness doesn't only ensure excellent organoleptic characteristics but can also boost productive yields. For instance, in Tocache, the average output is 3,800kg/ha, while Indonesia and Colombia reach 1,000kg/ha and 400kg/ha respectively (Gobierno Regional de San Martín, 2009). Genetics also matter when referring to plagues. For example, Ecuador's current *Nacional cacao* variety originally succumbed to a voracious plague in the early 1900s and it is currently commercialized as a non-pure variety. Yet, the Peruvian *Nacional* variety remained untouched. This explains why today 186 Peruvian farmers depend on the export of exclusive pure and rare genetic varieties—for example, to the Swiss market (*New York Times*, 2012). Genetics can also provide health benefits such as flavonoids and polyphenols (antioxidants) present in dark chocolate (Gutiérrez, 2002; Wallenstein, 2009; IICO, 2005). China is also "moving towards the consumption of dark, high fat content chocolate. This trend opens large growth opportunities for Peruvian cacao, in the race to compete on an equal footing with *cacao* from major traditional producing countries" (MINCETUR, 2007: 11).

The ICCO identifies another consumption trend related to the increasing demand for organic cacao due to consumers' health and environmental concerns. Organic products are characterized for having minimal human intervention as they are only cultivated within areas nourished with natural compost and rain water (Lukacs de Pereny, 2011). The fine cacao market "accounts for 10% of the world's harvest" (MINCETUR, 2007: 5). Clearly, Peru's chances of matching Ghana's production volume are inversely proportional to the latter trying to match Peru's quality. Pietrobelli and Rabellotti (2006) suggest that a country

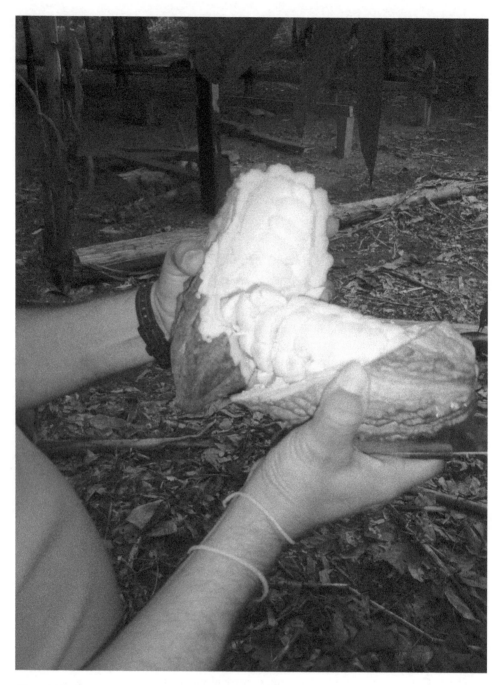

*Figure 16.2*   Premium wild raw cacao fruit from San Martín.

*Source:* Lukacs de Pereny (2011).

*Figure 16.3* San Martìn's wild cacao is cultivated employing natural composting—an ancestral technique.

*Source:* Lukacs de Pereny (2011).

specialized in a specific product should "decommodify it" through market *differentiation*. This implies that "the protection of *intellectual property* rights from multinational enterprises to other partners" (Arzeni, 2008: 74) is key to preserving these comparative advantages. Quality also depends on ancestral knowledge (e.g., plant identification). Hjalager and Richards (2011) contend that consumers are seeking new identities and security in today's turbulent world and thus, heritage and nostalgia—in the form of tourism—can fulfill those expectations where food stands as a quest for identity. Both authors claim that "gastronomy, although rooted in regional and local produce, is more than produce alone. This is reinforced by the World Intellectual Property Organization . . . in the suggestion that, rather than being limited to agricultural products, geographical indications can also relate to the specific qualities of a product that are due to human factors found in the place of origin" (Hjalager and Richards, 2011: 161).

## Stakeholders

Wallerstein's historical capitalism refers to a widespread commodification of processes, not only exchange-related ones, but production, distribution, and investment processes too (Wallerstein, 1983). A market function can be divided into *primary activities* (firms accomplish their role by satisfying their clients' needs) and the *support activities* (related to control and business development). Both activities comprise upward, suppliers and, downward, distribution channels. Therefore, "the representation of value creation as a chain, i.e. a sequence of activities performed one after the other, was essentially based on a manufacturing/retail view of industry" (Arzeni, 2008: 15–16). Hence, understanding *how* the market operates means understanding *who* is involved in making it work. The actors' roles and influence within the GVC directly impact both output and consumption. From an agricultural and scientific approach, Bhullar and Bhullar (2013) posit that a new understanding for institutional development includes psychologists, sociologists, political scientists, training specialists, and educators' expertise to obtain a holistic approach to tackle "the problems caused by the global industrial system of which science itself forms the basis" (Bhullar and Bhullar, 2013: 34). Similarly, the "inclusion of the stakeholders affected as well as the presence of respect for the government and its laws are necessary" (Edenhofer et al., 2012: 224). Precisely, small-scale farmers are the most important actors in this study case. Weersink and Herath state that they "play a critical role in modern, high-value agro-food chains for a variety of reasons, including policy changes, labor intensity, and land ownership structures" (cited in Bamber and Fernandez-Stark, 2012b: 9). Finally, Bair (2005) offers a succinct comparison by contrasting the different existing chain frameworks (Annex 5).

## The Peruvian CVC

In 2011, Peru produced 56,500 tons of cacao allowing 30,000 and 150,000 direct and indirect jobs respectively (Diario Gestión, 2013). The productive CVC in San Martín currently employs more than 6,000 producers with an average output of 836kg/ha (24 MT) within harvested 24,543ha and an estimated commercial value of US$52.5 million (Arévalo, 2011: 13) (exchange rate US$1 = PEN S/.2.80 as of October 30, 2013). Arévalo (2011) underlines that 55.7 percent of the small-scale producers' income comes from cacao bean production (Annex 6). Peru's fine cacao production represented 20 percent (2010) and 36 percent (2013) of the world's production (América Economía, 2010/2013). In 2012, the main export markets were the Netherlands (30.4 percent), Belgium (18.6 percent), the US (17.0 percent), and Switzerland/Italy (11 percent each) (APPCACAO, 2012). One of the major problems small-scale cacao bean farmers have ever faced is middlemen intervention. In 1982, Hopkins and Wallerstein claimed that there was one expanding economy (due to globalization) in "the form of various 'national' (and 'colonial') economies related to 'international' trade ... more global in scope" (Hopkins and Wallerstein, 1982: 11). In this same way, Gereffi et al. (2001) point out the "downside" of globalization including falling prices and low profit despite a product/process upgrading. In this view, the International Fund for Agricultural development (IFAD) has carried out several projects to reduce transaction costs between "rural producers and private-sector intermediaries" (IFAD, 2003: 10). These included the participation of different stakeholders such as associations and cooperatives (IFAD, 2003).

## San Martín's CVC stakeholders: a brief analysis

There are two types of stakeholder dimensions: the *primary* (small-scale producers, associations, middlemen, cooperatives, brokers and firms); the *secondary* (local, regional, central government, institutions, and IOs); plus four criteria: *function, relevance, power,* and *interaction* (UNODC, 2011) (Annexes 7 and 8). Now, it is time to go back to apply the governance of GVC's framework to illustrate San Martín's case.

*Figure 16.4*   The Pineda family: organic cacao farmers of Shilcayo island in San Martín, Peru.

*Source:* Lukacs de Pereny (2011).

First, small-scale producers were supported and trained in cacao bean growing, production, and commercialization. Ancestral knowledge was combined with innovation and technology (e.g., plague control). As a consequence, productivity yields skyrocketed. Second,
cacao farmers received advice regarding how to constitute an association/cooperative plus
other legal and phytosanitary training. Thus, producers switched from individual production
units to integrated structures (Annex 1).

Third, with regard to the governance of GVC's framework (Annex 2), I consider that, by
taking into consideration the previous arguments, the small-scale farmers have transited from
a *hierarchy* type of governance influence (characterized by a high degree of power asymmetry)
to a *captive* one (in which one lead firm has captive suppliers) to a current *relational governance*
network (where there is mutual and frequent information and knowledge exchange).
Cooperatives and associations like the Peruvian Cacao Association (APPCACAO) (Annex 9)
allowed farmers to increase their negotiation power and income. In order to synthesize the
key facts that led to the strengthening and development of the San Martín CVC, I have elaborated in Table 16.2, based on the multiple gathered sources.

## Fostering sustainable entrepreneurship (SE), innovation, and social inclusion

This last section describes the results and achievements of this case study. I will focus on what
I believe have been the model's three pillars to then enumerate the most relevant facts, results,
and achievements.

*Table 16.2* Key facts that contributed to San Martín's cacao activity

| Who | Issue | When | What and How |
|-----|-------|------|--------------|
| The Peruvian government | Terrorist groups (Shining Path and MRTA) and drug cartels operating in San Martín | Between the early 1980s and the mid-1990s | Military presence: pacification actions and intensive coca bush eradication plus alternative economic plans for farmers (e.g., cacao and palm oil crops) |
| San Martín regional government | Local farmers lacking financial resources and technical support | Late 1990s to present | Financial support and technical assistance to foster local farmers' cacao production |
| United States Agency for International Development (USAID) | Local farmers lacking financial resources | 2013 to present | USAID invested US$90 million in a 30,000ha cacao project in San Martín |
| Peruvian Ministry of Agriculture (MINAG) | Local farmers lacking technical support | Mid-2000s to present | The MINAG provided technical support to local farmers on how to prune, fertilize, and naturally deal with plagues |
| Small-scale producers | Poor local farmer networking and bargaining power | Early 2000s to present | Small-scale producers organized themselves and constituted cacao associations and cooperatives |
| Peruvian Gastronomy Society (APEGA) | Local farmers lacking access to markets and consumers | Late 2000s to present | APEGA, through different gastronomic events, acknowledged the importance of Peruvian cacao as a national emblematic product. This allowed local farmers to participate in fairs like Mistura |

## SE: business, social needs, and the environment

Societies, in order to be sustainable, need to integrate social needs and economic opportunities into their environmental limitations (Agyeman et al., 2002, as cited by Blewitt, 2008). SE "address the most urgent and ecological challenges" (Weidinger et al., 2013: 109) (e.g., deforestation, illegal mining, and drug production; MINAM, 2013). The CVC becomes a sustainable form of business since it exports exactly what it urges be preserved. Ergo, sustainable development focuses on "the needs of this and future generations, while preserving natural resources" (Weidinger et al., 2013: 55). Moreover, Schaltegger and Wagner (2011) propose four different types of entrepreneurship (SE included) (Annex 10).

## Innovation for sustainability

Innovation, in Schumpeter's words, is "a new combination of production factors" (Schumpeter, 1982, as cited by Weidinger et al., 2013: 106) to cope with technological changes and international competition's intensity (Gereffi et al., 2005). For instance, San Martín has 4,435ha that can produce 500 tons of cacao thus benefitting 1,100 families (Arévalo, 2011). However, this will only be possible as long as improved plant materials, pest control, and bean quality standards are ensured (Bartley, 2005) via innovation. Weidinger posits that innovation is central to economic growth since knowledge-based economies rely on R&D for human capital development (Weidinger et al., 2013). Peru ranks 118/144 in company spending on R&D and 120/144 on scientists and engineer availability (WEF, 2013). "[W]ithout innovation neither broad-based development in poor countries would be possible" (Edenhofer et al., 2012: 101). In this view, I highlight the creation of the Cacao Center for Innovation and Technology (Cacao-CITE San Martín) created in December 2010 (Gobierno Regional de San Martín, 2009). Pietrobelli and Rabellotti (2006: 282) argue that "new methods, inputs, and machinery are introduced through interactions between suppliers and research labs, which carry out the majority of the research activity."

## Social inclusion: linking small-scale farmers to global markets

Good governance needs to be inclusive (Hoggett, 2001, as cited by Blewitt, 2009). Allowing rural peasants to become part of the economy is part of a fair trade approach. As Jaffee contends, "fair trade is about reinserting noneconomic values—morality, decency, sustainability, community—into market transactions" (Jaffee, 2007: 24) while politics are becoming increasingly sensitive (Dryzek, 1996, as cited by Blewitt, 2009). Hence, government policies are oriented towards developing high-value agricultural products with net higher prices and income (Weinberger and Lumpkin, 2007, as cited by Bamber and Fernandez-Stark, 2012b). Positive externalities can result in broadening the benefits of a *social inclusion* development approach. For instance, San Martín's regional government has created the "Cacao Route," a tourism initiative benefitting 2,000 peasants while attracting a potential 1.2 million tourists to the region (Agencia Andina de Noticias, 2013). Definitely, the "modern status conscious traveler is likely to seek out the local cuisine, very often the 'traditional' or 'peasant' food not supplied by the mainstream tourism industry" (Hjalager and Richards, 2011: 40). In order to better convey the different elements that contributed to San Martín's CVC success, I have synthesized a series of relevant facts, results, and achievements comprised in Annex 11.

## Conclusion

The governance of GVC is a useful tool to identify actors, actions, and outputs. My research has sought to analyze San Martín's CVC stakeholders by amalgamating different contexts and combining theory with data. Now, I will address my conclusions in the form of three major remarks.

First: for the past decade, Peru has been experiencing a true gastronomic boom. Both national identity and traditions have been revalued, and greater attention has been given to cultural assets and biodiversity. Consequently, Peruvian chocolatiers and cacao producers have reached higher market niches. Cacao has become a premium gastronomic product since quality is Peru's main comparative advantage as "the key to sustainable inclusion in any value chain is competitiveness; that is, the ability to provide the desired quantity and quality of a specific product in a more economical and timely manner than other suppliers" (Bamber and Fernandez-Stark, 2012a: 3). In my opinion, San Martin's CVC will face two main challenges: monocropping and a primary-export-oriented dependency. The main reason for both is price volatility. For instance, between 1980 and 2000, 18 major export commodities' prices fell by 25 percent (Jaffee, 2007) while cacao prices have been prone to volatility despite a spiking 30-year historical US$3,625/tons (2010), which dramatically fell to US$2,200/tons

(2011) (ICCO, 2012b). Nevertheless, installing cacao refinery plants *in situ* could strengthen the product's competitiveness.

Second: building human capital—through training and education—has propelled a new class of visionary, organized, and sustainable entrepreneurs in San Martín in lieu of the former uninformed and scattered rural peasants. I believe that social inclusion stems from sharing and exchanging mutual knowledge and information. Strong public–private alliances like Alianza Cacao reinvigorate the markets' trust in both the State's and corporate sector's role.

Third: this is a case concerning entrepreneurial sustainability through gastronomy. One must understand the existing relation a specific society has with a specific product. Such is the case of San Martín and cacao. There is an identity, a tradition, and a hope beyond mere business and economic development. I believe that small-scale farmers felt they were finally listened to and consequently, their opinion and knowledge were taken into consideration, which is embedded within a community participatory approach. This has been a successful case, yet some questions arise. For instance, how to avoid land degradation? (More farmers are attracted by the benefits of the cacao market, compared to other crops.) Or how to ensure continuous training and technological support to an increasing Peruvian cacao labor force? Certainly, San Martín has done a good job in terms of sustainable entrepreneurship and commercialization of a high-quality product. The Peruvian government's current role is to implement this case's findings and lessons in other communities with

*Figure 16.5* Peru's high-quality chocolates also include local products such as fruits and liquors.

*Source:* Lukacs de Pereny (2011).

*Figures 16.6 and 16.7* Peruvian cacao producers participating in commercial events like Mistura, Peru's most important gastronomic fair.

*Source:* Lukacs de Pereny (2011).

Sandor G. Lukacs de Pereny

potential and unique products (e.g., camu-camu in Amazonas; native potatoes in Huancavelica, among others).

I want to conclude my work by citing the powerful words of Geister Cachique, a rural farmer from Las Mercedes (San Martín) who used to cultivate cocoa for several years. But, in 2011, he started growing cacao and was taught better pruning and fertilizing techniques. As a result, he managed to double his productivity and increase his income (due to higher market prices for his organic beans). When the NGO Technoserve interviewed him he said: "Most of all, I want them (referring to his family) to be proud because this money will be earned with dignity and free from violence . . . I am working to send my children to college" (Technoserve, 2013). Gastronomy for development.

# References

Agencia Andina de Noticias (2013) *Ruta Turística del Cacao proyecta atraer 1.2 millones de visitantes al 2016*, www.andina.com.pe/espanol/noticia-ruta-turistica-del-cacao-proyecta-atraer-12-millones-visitantes-al-2016-473365.aspx#.U1Ncffl5N1Y (accessed September 3, 2013).

AGRODASAM (2013) *Serie Histórica de Superficie Existentes, Cosecha y Producción de los Cultivos Permanentes y Semipermanentes*, San Martín: Gobierno Regional de San Martín, www.agrodrasam.gob.pe (accessed September 17, 2013).

América Economía (2010/2013) *Perú exporta un 20% del cacao fino a nivel mundial*, www.americaeconomia.com/negocios-industrias/peru-exporta-un-20-del-cacao-fino-nivel-mundial/, http://www.americaeconomia.com/negocios-industrias/preven-que-produccion-de-cacao-en-el-peru-crezca-20-nivel-nacional (accessed September 6, 2013).

APEGA (2013) *El Boom Gastronómico Peruano 2013*, Lima: APEGA, http://apega.pe/descargas/contenido/boom_gastronomico_peruano_al_2013_web.pdf (accessed September 10, 2013).

APPCACAO (2012) *Datos Estadísticos de Cacao Peruano – Junio 2012*, San Martín: APPCACAO, www.appcacao.org/index.php?option=com_content&view=article&id=610&Itemid=100029 (accessed September 27, 2013).

Arévalo, E. (2011) *Identificación del Cacao Criollo como Producto Nativo de la Biodiversidad de San Martín y Evaluación de su Potencialidad Regional*, Lima: Perúbiodiverso, http://perubiodiverso.pe/assets/Identificaci%C3%B3n-del-cacao-nativo-San-Mart%C3%ADn.pdf (accessed September 8, 2013).

Arzeni, S. (2008) *Enhancing the Role of SMEs in Global Value Chains*, Paris: OECD, www.oecd-ilibrary.org/industry-and-services/enhancing-the-role-of-smes-in-global-value-chains_9789264051034-en (accessed October 9, 2013).

Bair, J. (2005) "Global capitalism and commodity chains: looking back, going forward," *Competition & Change*, 2: 153–180, http://spot.colorado.edu/~bairj/Research_&_Publications_files/Global%20Capitalism%20and%20Commodity%20Chains%20Looking%20Back%20Going%20Forward.pdf (accessed September 13, 2013).

Bamber, P. and Fernandez-Stark, K. (2012a) *Conversion to Organic Cacao Cultivation in Peru*, North Carolina: Center on Globalization, Governance & Competitiveness, Duke University, www.cggc.duke.edu/pdfs/Duke_CGGC_Cacao_case_Paru.pdf (accessed September 17, 2013).

Bamber, P. and Fernandez-Stark, K. (2012b) *Basic Principles and Guidelines for Impactful and Sustainable Inclusive Business Interventions in High-Value Agro-Food Value Chains*, North Carolina: Center on Globalization, Governance & Competitiveness, Duke University, www.cggc.duke.edu/pdfs/CGGC-IDB_%20Basic_Principles_and_Guidelines_for_Impactful_and_Sustainable_Inclusive_Business_Interventions_inHigh-Value_Agro-Food_Value_Chains_May_1_2012.pdf (accessed September 17, 2013).

Bartley, B. (2005) *Genetic Diversity of Cacao and its Utilization*, Oxfordshire: CABI Publishing.

Bhullar, G. and Bhullar, N. (eds.) (2013) *Agricultural Sustainability: Progress and Prospects in Crop Research*, California: Elsevier.

Bingham, A. and Roberts, J. (2010) *South and Meso-American Mythology A to Z*, New York: Chelsea House.

Blewitt, J. (2008) *Understanding Sustainable Development*, London: Sterling.

Brack, A. and Mendiola, C. (2000) *Ecología del Perú*. Lima: Bruño.

Central del Café y Cacao del Perú (2011) *Exportaciones Nacionales de Cacao*, Lima: Central del Café y Cacao del Perú, http://cafeperu.org.pe/cafe/images/stories/actividades/pdf/estadisticas%20cacao.pdf (accessed September 18, 2013).

CIPOTATO (2011) *Catálogo de Nuevas Variedades de Papa*, http://cipotato.org/publications/pdf/005909.pdf (accessed September 19, 2013).

De Soto, H. (2000) *The Mystery of Capital: Why Capitalism Triumphs in the West and Fails Everywhere Else*, New York: Basic Books.

Diario, Gestión (2013) *Perú es el segundo productor mundial de cacao orgánico*, http://gestion.pe/economia/peru-segundo-productor-mundial-cacao-organico-2013475 (accessed September 18, 2013).

Edenhofer, O., Wallacher, J., Lotze-Campen, H., Reder, M., Knopf, B., and Müller, J. (eds.) (2012) *Climate Change, Justice and Sustainability: Linking Climate and Development Policy*, Heidelberg: Springer.

FAO (2011) *Faostat*, http://faostat.fao.org/site/567/default.aspx#ancor (accessed September 12, 2013).

Gereffi, G. and Fernandez-Stark, K. (2011) *Global Value Chain Analysis: A Primer*, North Carolina: Center on Globalization, Governance & Competitiveness, Duke University, www.cggc.duke.edu/pdfs/2011-05-31_GVC_analysis_a_primer.pdf (accessed September 19, 2013).

Gereffi, G., Humphrey, J., Kaplinsky, R., and Sturgeon, T. (2001) *Introduction: Globalisation, Value Chains and Development*, Sussex: Institute of Development Studies Bulletin 32.3, www.ids.ac.uk/files/dmfile/gereffietal323.pdf (accessed September 16, 2013).

Gereffi, G., Humphrey, J., and Sturgeon, T. (2005) "The governance of global value chains," *Review of International Political Economy*, 12:78–104, www.tandfonline.com/doi/pdf/10.1080/09692290500049805 (accessed September 12, 2013).

Gobierno Regional de San Martín (2008) *Plan Regional de Desarrollo Social Integral de la Región San Martín 2009–2011*, San Martín: Gobierno Regional de San Martín, www.regionsanmartin.gob.pe/gerencias/grdesarrollosocial/Descargas/Planes/PlanDesarrollo20092011.pdf (accessed September 19, 2013).

Gobierno Regional de San Martín (2009) *Plan Estratégico Sectorial Regional Agrario 2009–2015*, San Martín: Gobierno Regional de San Martín-MINAG, www.regionsanmartin.gob.pe/administracion/documentos_transparencia/doc_transparencia13.pdf. (accessed September 27, 2013).

Gutiérrez, B. (2002) *Chocolate, Polifenoles y Protección a la Salud*, Buenos Aires: Latin American Journal of Pharmacy, www.latamjpharm.org/trabajos/21/2/LAJOP_21_2_3_1_S2133VGV50.pdf (accessed September 8, 2013).

Hjalager, A.M. and Richards, G. (eds.) (2011) *Tourism and Gastronomy*, London: Routledge.

Hopkins, T. and Wallerstein, I. (1982) *World Systems Analysis: Theory and Methodology*, California: SAGE Publications Inc.

Humphrey, J. and Schmitz, H. (2001) *Governance in Global Value Chains*, Sussex: Institute of Development Studies Bulletin 32.3, www.ids.ac.uk/files/dmfile/humphreyschmitz32.3.pdf (accessed September 16, 2013).

ICCO (2005) *Inventory of Health and Nutritional Attributes of Cocoa and Chocolate*, London: ICCO, www.icco.org/about-us/international-cocoa-agreements/cat_view/30-related-documents/35-health-nutrition.html (accessed September 2, 2013).

ICCO (2012a) *Cocoa Market Update*, London: ICCO, http://worldcocoafoundation.org/wp-content/uploads/Cocoa-Market-Update-as-of-3.20.2012.pdf (accessed October 14, 2013).

ICCO (2012b) *The World Cocoa Economy: Past and Present*, London: ICCO, www.icco.org/about-us/international-cocoa-agreements/cat_view/30-related-documents/35-health-nutrition.html (accessed September 4, 2013).

IFAD (2003) *Market Access for the Rural Poor in Order to Achieve the Millennium Development Goals*, Rome: IFAD, www.ifad.org/gbdocs/gc/26/e/markets.pdf (accessed September 14, 2013).

INEI (2007) *Censos Nacionales 2007: XI de Población y VI de Vivienda*, http://censos.inei.gob.pe/censos2007 (accessed September 17, 2013).

INEI (2013) *Evolución de la Pobreza Monetaria 2007–2012*, Informe Técnico, Lima: INEI, www.pcm.gob.pe/wp-content/uploads/2013/05/Informe-de-Pobreza-2012_01.pdf (accessed September 8, 2013).

Jaffee, D. (2007) *Fair Trade: Coffee, Sustainability, and Survival*, California: University of California Press.

Lukacs de Pereny, S. (2011) *Cultura Alternativa, Cultivo de Progreso: Cacao por Coca*, www.chefandhotel.cl/images/Revista46.pdf (accessed September 4, 2013).

MINAG (2012a) *Cacao Perú: Un campo Fértil para sus Inversiones y el Desarrollo de sus Exportaciones*, Lima: MINAG, www.salondelcacaoychocolate.pe/2012/archivos/ficha_cacao.pdf (accessed October 1, 2013).

MINAG (2012b) *Plan Estratégico Sectorial Multianual 2012–2016*, Lima: MINAG, www.minag.gob.pe/portal/download/pdf/marcolegal/normaslegales/resolucionesministeriales/2012/mayo/pesem2012-2016.pdf (accessed September 18, 2013).

MINAG (2013) *Valor Bruto de la Producción Agropecuaria Julio 2013*, Lima: MINAG, www.minag.gob.pe/portal/download/pdf/herramientas/boletines/boletineselectronicos/VBP/2013/VBP-julio-2013.pdf (accessed October 29, 2013).

MINAM (2013) *Cuarto Informe sobre la Biodiversidad Biológica 2006–2009*, www.minam.gob.pe/diversidadbiologica/wp-content/uploads/sites/21/2013/10/Cuarto-Informe_Convenio-de-Diversidad-Biologica.pdf (accessed September 8, 2013).

MINCETUR (2007) *Cacao in Peru, a Rising Star*, Lima: MINCETUR, www.peru.org.tw/web/data/file/userfiles/files/Cacao%20Peru%20Promperu.pdf (accessed September 8, 2013).

MINTRA (2013) *Estadísticas Laborales*, www.mintra.gob.pe/mostrarContenido.php?id=93&tip=9 (accessed September 9, 2013).

Motamayor, J., Lachenaud, P., da Silva e Mota, J., Loor, R., Kuhn, D., et al. (2008) *Geographic and Genetic Population Differentiation of the Amazonian Chocolate Tree* (*Theobroma cacao*), www.plosone.org/article/info%3Adoi%2F10.1371%2Fjournal.pone.0003311 (accessed September 14, 2013).

*New York Times* (2012) "Rare cacao beans discovered in Peru," www.nytimes.com/2011/01/12/dining/12chocolate.html?_r=0 (accessed September 10, 2013).

Pietrobelli, C., and Rabellotti, R. (2006) *Upgrading to Compete: Global Value Chains, Clusters, and SMEs in Latin America*, Washington: Inter-American Development Bank.

Schaltegger, S. and Wagner, M. (2011) "Sustainable entrepreneurship and sustainability innovation: categories and interactions," *Business Strategy and the Environment*, 20: 222–237, http://onlinelibrary.wiley.com/doi/10.1002/bse.682/pdf (accessed September 4, 2013).

Technoserve (2013) *Sustainable Support for Smallholder Farmers in Peru*, www.technoserve.org/our-work/stories/sustainable-support-for-smallholder-farmers-in-peru (accessed September 22, 2013).

UNODC (2011) *Perú: Monitoreo de los Cultivos de Coca 2010*, Lima: UNODC-DEVIDA, www.unodc.org/documents/crop-monitoring/Peru/Peru-cocasurvey2010_es.pdf (accessed September 8, 2013).

Wallenstein, G. (2009) *The Pleasure Instinct*, New Jersey: Wiley.

Wallerstein, I. (1983) *Historical Capitalism*, Norfolk: Verso.

WCF (2012) *Committed to Cocoa-Growing Communities*, Washington: WCF, http://worldcocoafoundation.org/wp-content/files_mf/2012wcfbrochure.pdf (accessed September 18, 2013).

WEF (2013) *The Global Competitiveness Report 2012–2013*, www3.weforum.org/docs/WEF_GlobalCompetitivenessReport_2012-13.pdf (accessed September 16, 2013).

Weidinger, C., Fischler, F., and Scmidpeter, M. (2013) *Sustainable Entrepreneurship Business Success through Sustainability*, London: Springer.

Zhang, D., Arévalo, E., Mischke, S., Zúñiga, L., Barreto, A., and Adriazola del Aguila, J. (2006) "Genetic diversity and structure of managed and semi-natural populations of cocoa (Theobroma cacao) in the Huallaga and Ucayali Valleys of Peru," *Annals of Botany*, 98: 647–655.

**Annex 1**

*Five global value chain (GVC) governance types*

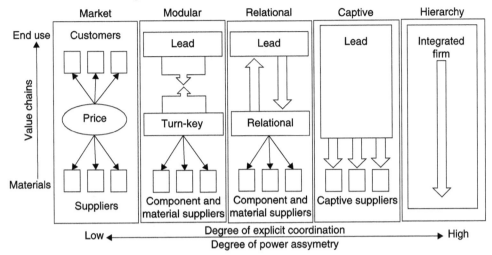

*Source:* adapted from Gereffi et al. (2005).

## Annex 2

### Five global value chain (GVC) governance types

| Market | Modular | Relational | Captive | Hierarchy |
|---|---|---|---|---|
| Market governance involves transactions that are relatively simple. Information on product specifications is easily transmitted, and suppliers can make products with minimal input from buyers. These arms-length exchanges require little or no formal cooperation between actors and the cost of switching to new partners is low for both producers and buyers. The central governance mechanism is price rather than a powerful lead firm. | Modular governance occurs when complex transactions are relatively easy to codify. Typically, suppliers in modular chains make products to a customer's specifications and take full responsibility for process technology using generic machinery that spreads investments across a wide customer base. This keeps switching costs low and limits transaction-specific investments, even though buyer–supplier interactions can be very complex. Linkages (or relationships) are more substantial than in simple markets because of the high volume of information flowing across the inter-firm link. Information technology and standards for exchanging information are both key to the functioning of modular governance. | Relations governance occurs when buyers and sellers rely on complex information that is not easily transmitted or learned. This results in frequent interactions and knowledge sharing between parties. Such linkages require trust and generate mutual reliance, which are regulated through reputation, social and spatial proximity, family and ethnic ties, and the like. Despite mutual dependence, lead firms still specify what is needed, and thus have the ability to exert some level of control over suppliers. Producers in relational chains are more likely to supply differentiated products based on quality, geographic origin or other unique characteristics. Relational linkages take time to build, so the costs and difficulties required to switch to a new partner tend to be high. | In these chains, small suppliers are dependent on one or a few buyers that often wield a great deal of power. Such networks feature a high degree of monitoring and control by the lead firm. The power asymmetry in captive networks forces suppliers to link to their buyer under conditions set by, and often specific to, that particular buyer, leading to thick ties and high switching costs for both parties. Since the core competence of the lead firms tends to be in areas outside of production, helping their suppliers upgrade their production capabilities does not encroach on this core competency, but benefits the lead firm by increasing the efficiency of its supply chain. Ethical leadership is important to ensure suppliers receive fair treatment and an equitable share of the market price. | Hierarchical governance describes chains characterized by vertical integration and managerial control within lead firms that develop and manufacture products in-house. This usually occurs when product specifications cannot be codified, products are complex, or highly competent suppliers cannot be found. While less common than in the past, this sort of vertical integration is still an important feature of the global economy. |

*Source*: adapted from Gereffi et al. (2005).

# Annex 3

## *Summary of the process of transforming cocoa beans into chocolate*

**Step 1**: The cocoa beans are cleaned to remove all extraneous material.

**Step 2**: To bring out the chocolate flavor and color, the beans are roasted. The temperature, time and degree of moisture involved in roasting depend on the type of beans used and the sort of chocolate or product required from the process.

**Step 3**: A winnowing machine is used to remove the shells from the beans to leave just the cocoa nibs.

**Step 4**: The cocoa nibs undergo alkalization, usually with potassium carbonate, to develop the flavor and color.

**Step 5**: The nibs are then milled to create cocoa liquor (cocoa particles suspended in cocoa butter). The temperature and degree of milling varies according to the type of nib used and the product required.

**Step 6**: Manufacturers generally use more than one type of bean in their products and therefore the different beans have to be blended together to the required formula.

**Step 7**: The cocoa liquor is pressed to extract the cocoa butter, leaving a solid mass called cocoa presscake. The amount of butter extracted from the liquor is controlled by the manufacturer to produce presscake with different proportions of fat.

**Step 8**: The processing now takes two different directions. The cocoa butter is used in the manufacture of chocolate. The cocoa presscake is broken into small pieces to form kibbled press-cake, which is then pulverized to form cocoa powder.

**Step 9**: Cocoa liquor is used to produce chocolate through the addition of cocoa butter. Other ingredients such as sugar, milk, emulsifying agents and cocoa butter equivalents are also added and mixed. The proportions of the different ingredients depend on the type of chocolate being made.

**Step 10**: The mixture then undergoes a refining process by traveling through a series of rollers until a smooth paste is formed. Refining improves the texture of the chocolate.

**Step 11**: The next process, conching, further develops flavor and texture. Conching is a kneading or smoothing process. The speed, duration and temperature of the kneading affect the flavor. An alternative to conching is an emulsifying process using a machine that works like an egg beater.

**Step 12**: The mixture is then tempered or passed through a heating, cooling, and reheating process. This prevents discoloration and fat bloom in the product by preventing certain crystal-line formations of cocoa butter developing.

**Step 13**: The mixture is then put into molds or used for enrobing fillings and cooled in a cooling chamber.

**Step 14**: The chocolate is then packaged for distribution to retail outlets.

*Source:* International Cocoa Organization.

**Annex 4**

*Geographic and genetic population differentiation of the Amazonian*
*chocolate tree (*Theobroma cacao L*)*

*Source:* Motamayor et al. (2008).

**Annex 5**

*Contending chain frameworks*

| | Commodity chains | Global commodity chains | Global value chains |
|---|---|---|---|
| Theoretical foundation | World–systems theory | World–systems theory Organizational sociology | International business literature Global commodity chains |
| Object of inquiry | World–capitalist economy | Inter-firm networks in global industries | Sectoral logistics of global industries |
| Orienting concepts | 1. International division of labor<br>2. Core-periphery, semi-periphery<br>3. Unequal exchange<br>4. Kondratieff cycles | 1. Industry structure<br>2. Governance (PDCC/ BDCC distinction)<br>3. Organizational learning/ Industrial upgrading | 1. Value-added chains<br>2. Governance models (modular, relational, captive)<br>3. Transaction costs<br>4. Industrial upgrading and rents |
| Intellectual influences | 1. Dependency theory<br>2. Structuralist development economics | 1. MNC literature<br>2. Comparative development lit. | 1. International business/ Industrial Organization<br>2. Trade economics<br>3. Global/international production networks/ systems |
| Key texts | Hopkins & Wallerstein (1977: 1986)<br>Arrighi & Drangel (1986)<br>Arrighi (1990)<br>*Review*, 23(1), 2000 | Gereffi & Korzeniewics (1994)<br>Appelbaum & Gereffi (1994)<br>Gereffi (1999)<br>Bair & Gereffi (2001) | Humphrey & Schmitz (2000)<br>*IDS Bulletin* 29(1), 2000<br>Sturgeon (2002)<br>Gereffi et al. (2005) |

*Source:* adapted from Bair, 2005.

# Annex 6

## *San* Martín's cacao *production statistics*

### Characteristics of *San Martín's* small *cacao* producers

| Characteristics | Tocache | Mariscal Cáceres | Bellavista | El Dorado | Lamas | San Martín | Average |
|---|---|---|---|---|---|---|---|
| % of producers as current members of organizations | 23.10% | 48.00% | 50.00% | 52.00% | 55.30% | 33.30% | 43.60% |
| Cooperative member | 19.20% | 48.00% | 33.30% | 52.00% | 22.00% | 0.00% | 29.10% |
| Producers' association member | 3.90% | 0.00% | 16.70% | 0.00% | 33.30% | 33.30% | 15.50% |
| Spends less than US$105 per month | 53.80% | 80.00% | 64.50% | 47.80% | 44.40% | 50.00% | 56.80% |
| Spends between US$105 and US$175 per month | 23.10% | 20.00% | 25.00% | 30.40% | 22.20% | 50.00% | 28.50% |
| Spends more than US$175 per month | 23.10% | 0.00% | 14.50% | 21.70% | 17.80% | 0.00% | 12.90% |
| Income below US$105per month | 53.80% | 24.00% | 31.30% | 91.00% | 38.90% | 33.30% | 45.40% |
| Income between US$105 and US$175 per month | 23.10% | 44.00% | 41.70% | 39.10% | 27.80% | 66.70% | 40.40% |
| Income over US$175 per month | 23.10% | 28.00% | 25.00% | 21.70% | 27.80% | 0.00% | 20.90% |
| Sells *cacao* | 76.90% | 92.00% | 47.20% | 34.80% | 33.30% | 50.00% | 55.70% |

### *Cacao* harvested hectares

| Hectares harvested | Producers' average |
|---|---|
| 0.5 | 3.00% |
| 1 | 32.70% |
| 1.5 | 6.10% |
| 2 | 13.50% |
| 3 | 8.40% |
| 4 | 7.70% |
| 5 | 3.30% |
| 6 | 3.30% |
| 8 | 3.80% |
| 11 | 3.80% |
| Non-harvested | 14.50% |

### *Cacao* production yield

| Yield kg/HA | General average |
|---|---|
| 200–300 | 26.70% |
| 301–400 | 26.10% |
| 500–600 | 18.30% |
| 600–700 | 1.30% |
| 900–1000 | 1.30% |
| None | 26.50% |

*Source:* adapted from Arévalo, 2011.

**Annex 7**

*The cacao chain actors' relations*

| Actors | Function | Relevance | Power | Interaction |
|---|---|---|---|---|
| **Primary** | | | | |
| Small producers | High-priced market products | Low | Low | Conflict |
| Small producers in cooperatives and associations | Adequate prices and transparent management | Medium | Medium | Committed to transparency |
| Storage businesses | Buys products at their lowest possible price | Medium | Medium | Conflict |
| CACAO CP Association | Access to export markets | Medium | Medium | Partnership |
| APCU Association | Access to export markets | Medium | Medium | Partnership |
| Tocache Agroindustrial Cooperative | Access to efficient management niche markets and associate fidelity | Medium | Medium | Partnership |
| ASPROC NBT | Access to efficient management niche markets and associate fidelity | Medium | Medium | Partnership |
| Oro Verde Cooperative | Access to efficient management niche markets and associate fidelity | High | High | Partnership |
| APOCAGRO Cooperative | Access to efficient management niche markets and associate fidelity | High | High | Partnership |
| Cooperativa de Ahorro y Crédito Norandino | Credit offer and recovery | High | Medium | Partnership |
| SUMAQAO Broker | Quality product | Medium | Medium | Partnership |
| PRONATEC Company | Quality product | High | High | Partnership |
| Epico Company | Quality product | High | High | Partnership |
| BARRY CABELLAU Company | Organic quality product | High | High | Partnership |
| ALTER ECCO Company | Organic quality product | High | High | Partnership |
| ICAM Company | Organic quality product | High | High | Partnership |
| TRADING ORGANIC Company | Organic quality product | High | High | Partnership |
| TCHO Company | Organic quality product | High | High | Partnership |
| **Secondary** | | | | |
| UNODC | Alternative development promotion | High | High | Partnership |
| USAID (PDA) | Alternative development promotion | High | High | Partnership |
| DEVIDA | Alternative development promotion | High | High | Partnership |
| Local Governments | Local economic development | Medium | Medium | Concertation |
| Regional Government | Local economic development | High | High | Concertation |

*Source:* adapted from UNODC (2011).

## Annex 8

### *Productive coffee and* cacao *chain structure*

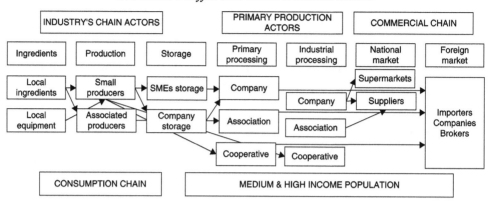

*Source:* adapted from UNODC (2011).

## Annex 9

### *San Martín's cacao production statistics (2010)*

| Provinces | HA | Harvested HA | Production (MT) | New HA | Average yield (kg/HA) |
|---|---|---|---|---|---|
| Rioja | 223 | 208 | 164 | 2 | 787 |
| Moyobamba | 369 | 246 | 213 | 58 | 867 |
| Lamas | 3,462 | 2,873 | 2,454 | 397 | 854 |
| San Martín | 2,545 | 2,315 | 1,876 | 488 | 811 |
| El Dorado | 1,284 | 1,150 | 1,012 | 63 | 880 |
| Picota | 561 | 403 | 299 | 29 | 742 |
| Bellavista | 1,688 | 1,237 | 1,111 | 329 | 899 |
| Huallaga | 4,522 | 2,685 | 2,032 | 567 | 757 |
| M. Cáceres | 7,424 | 6,287 | 5,612 | 972 | 893 |
| Tocache | 9,469 | 7,138 | 6,226 | 2,197 | 872 |
| Total | 31,547 | 24,543 | 24,543 | 5,132 | 836 |

| Location | Cacao Ha (3×3m) | Productivity (kg/HA) | Participation % | Economic value | Labor days | Number of workers |
|---|---|---|---|---|---|---|
| Bellavista | 791 | 94,894 | 17.80% | 474,468 | 47,477 | 198 |
| El Dorado | 13 | 1,609 | 0.30% | 8,043 | 804 | 3 |
| Huallaga | 899 | 107,886 | 20.30% | 539,428 | 53,943 | 225 |
| Lamas | 248 | 29,705 | 5.60% | 148,523 | 14,852 | 62 |
| Mariscal Cáceres | 1,042 | 124,985 | 23.50% | 624,923 | 62,492 | 260 |
| Moyobamba | 301 | 36,174 | 6.80% | 180,872 | 18,087 | 75 |
| Picota | 72 | 8,625 | 1.60% | 43,123 | 4,312 | 18 |
| Rioja | 218 | 26,116 | 4.90% | 130,579 | 13,058 | 54 |
| San Martín | 493 | 59,214 | 11.10% | 296,070 | 29,607 | 123 |
| Tocache | 358 | 42,980 | 8.10% | 214,902 | 21,490 | 90 |
| Total | 4,435 | 532,186 | 100.00% | 2,660,929 | 266,093 | 1,109 |

| Production process | Grain | Cacao liquor | Cacao paste/ powder | Butter | Liquid chocolate | Cholocate-bar units (100 gr.) |
|---|---|---|---|---|---|---|
| Final product MT/unit | 500 MT | 400 MT | 212 MT | 188.7 MT | 650 MT | 6.5 million |
| Residual product | | | | | | 74.2 MT (*cacao* powder) |
| Estimated price | Organic *cacao* US$ 3,000 to US$4,000 Wild *cacao* US$4,000 to US$5,000 | | | | | Organic *cacao* between €2 and €3, Wild *cacao* between €6 and €8 |
| Organic *cacao* exports' income | US$1,500,000 | | | | | €13,000,000 |
| Wild *cacao* exports' income | US$2,000,000 | | | | | €39,000,000 |

*Source:* adapted from Arévalo, 2011.

**Annex 10**

*The linkage between sustainability and sustainable entrepreneurship*

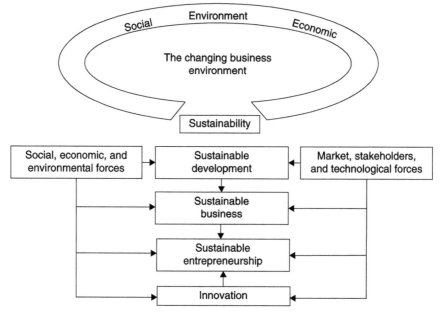

*Source:* adapted from Weidinger et al. (2013).

*Characterization of different kinds of sustainability-oriented entrepreneurship*

| | Ecopreneurship | Social entrepreneurship | Institutional entrepreneurship | Sustainable entrepreneurship |
|---|---|---|---|---|
| Core Motivation | Contribute to solving environmental problems and create economic value | Contribute to solving societal problems and create value for society | Contribute to changing regulatory, societal, and market institutions | Contribute to solving societal and environmental problems through the realization of a successful business |
| Main goal | Earn money by solving environmental problems | Achieve societal goal and secure funding to achieve this | Changing institutions as direct goal | Creating sustainable development through entrepreneurial corporate activities |
| Role of economic goals | Ends | Means | Means or ends | Means and ends |
| Role of non-market goals | Environmental issues as integrated core element | Societal goals as ends | Changing institutions as core element | Core element of integrated end to contribute to sustainable development |
| Organizational development challenge | From focus in environmental issues integrating economic issues | From focus on societal issues to integrating economic issues | From changing institutions to integrating sustainability | From small contribution to large contribution to sustainable development |

*Source:* adapted from Schaltegger and Wagner (2011).

## Annex 11

### *Facts, results, and achievements of San Martín's cacao success*

| Item | Actor/s | Issue/Subject | Achievements | Facts/Results | Source |
|---|---|---|---|---|---|
| 1 | *Región San Martín* | Cacao production share national market | Share increased from 1997 to 2001 | From 12% to 37% | UNODC, 2011 |
| 2 | | *Cacao* products and subproducts exports | | In terms of exports: *cacao* beans (52.69%); *cacao* butter (25.2%); and *cacao* powder (12.45%) | *Central del Café y Cacao del Perú*, 2011 |
| 3 | | Cooperatives and associations' network | Contracts without middlemen intervention | They will sell directly to the *Chocolatiers de France* (4,000 chocolate artisans) | *Agencia Andina*, 2013 |
| 4 | | Tocache Agroindustrial's cacao beans | Obtained *"2009 Salon du Chocolat Award"* | Award for the best aromatic *cacao* beans in Paris | Reuters, 2010 |
| 5 | | *Cacao* production yield | Yield increased from 2001 to 2010 | From 1,814 MT to 20,999 MT (1,057% increase) | *Gobierno Regional de San Martín*, 2011 |
| 6 | National *cacao* producers | Imitation of *San Martín's* cacao success | National production increased | Production and sales increased by 323% and 527% respectively | *Central del Café y Cacao del Perú*, 2011 |
| 7 | | *Cacao* exports | Exports increased from 2005 to 2011 | From US$36 million to US$119 million (183% increase) | MINCETUR, 2012 |
| 8 | | *Cacao* production yield | Yield increased from 1997 to 2011 | From 584kg/HA to 858 kg/HA (Peru: 600kg/HA). 146.92% increase in 14 years | *Gobierno Regional de San Martín*, 2012 |
| 9 | | New markets access | National producers are offering their products online | The most utilized commercial website is www.alibaba.com | *Diario El Comercio*, 2012 |
| 10 | Peruvian Government | Signature of multiple FTAs | Access to larger and wealthier markets | Most relevant FTAs: The United States, China, and the European Union (EU) | MINCETUR, 2014 |
| 11 | World *Cacao* market | *Cacao* beans price increase | *Cacao* producers increased their profit | Beans price rose from US$0.94kg to US$2.18 kg (232% increase in four years) | *Gobierno Regional de San Martín*, 2012 |

(*continued*)

## Annex 11 (Continued)

| Item | Actor/s | Issue/Subject | Achievements | Facts/Results | Source |
|------|---------|---------------|--------------|---------------|--------|
| 12 | *San Martín* small-scale farmers | Technical and agricultural cooperation | Organization of the first *Cacao* tree pruning techniques seminar | Courses delivered by Edil Sandoval (Peru's most competitive *Cacao* producer) from *Tocache* | *Inforegión*, 2013 |
| 13 | Public–private partnerships | *Alianza Cacao* (Cocoa Alliance) | Constitution of a national public–private alliance | Promotion of (new) 28,000 HA of *cacao*; benefitting 10,000 families; creating 18,000 jobs | *Agencia Andina*, 2012 |
| 14 | The German Cooperation Agency (GIZ) | Sustainable Rural Development Program (PDRS) | *San Martín's* CVC marginal gross profit increased from 2009 to 2011 | From US$7,720 to US$ 577,617 respectively. Moreover, 70 producers did business with 4 private companies | GIZ, 2013 |
| 15 | Ibero-American Program of Science, Technology, and Development | Science and innovation | First forum focused on *San Martín's cacao* | Scientific studies on *San Martín's cacao* DNA | CYTED, 2012 |
| 16 | Multiple | *Cacao* fairs, markets, and commercial events | A participation increase in commercial gastronomic and food events | Choco Expo Perú, *Cacao* and Chocolate Exposition, *Mistura*, ExpoAlimentaria, *Salon International de l'Alimentation*, and *Salon du Chocolat*, among others | *Diario Gestión*, 2013 |

# 17

# AN ANALYSIS OF THE POTENTIAL RESTAURANT OPERATIONS HAVE FOR REHABILITATING OFFENDERS

## A case study of Her Majesty's Prison, The Verne

*Sonja Beier*

## Introduction

To counteract high recidivism rates among ex-offenders, the British government has been working on reforming rehabilitation practices in British prisons. Simultaneously, a couple of notable prison establishments across the country have developed their own rehabilitative methods. HMP (Her Majesty's Prison) The Verne offers prisoners a qualification in catering at its jailhouse café while serving their sentences, and exposes them to controlled contact with the public. The café represents a training facility for "suitably risk-assessed prisoners to obtain an NVQ (national vocational qualification) level 2 in Catering" with the goal of giving the prisoners "experience and qualifications that will hopefully reduce reoffending" (McGowen, cited in Kitching, 2011). Since December 2011, the jailhouse café has been open to the public and is today run by the social enterprise Expia CIC, a community interest company that recently opened another jailhouse café at HMP Guys Marsh, the north Dorset prison (This is Dorset, 2012). Two other prisons in Great Britain that follow the trend of rehabilitation through hospitality are HMP High Down in Surrey and HMP/YOI Askham Grange in York. This paper analyses how hospitality can foster offender rehabilitation by comparing the industry's nature with what is needed for rehabilitation.

## Methodology

Since the research aims to analyse why hospitality can potentially foster rehabilitation, a case study approach was chosen because it enables the researcher "to expand and generalize theories" (Yin, 2009: 15) and "can provide a source of new hypotheses" (Saunders et al., 2003: 93). Due to the lack of prior research on this topic, an exploratory design was chosen as it enables the researcher to become more acquainted with the topic (Babbie, 2004). In order to define the nature of hospitality, academic journal articles were reviewed for defini-tions. To find out how a guided restaurant operations experience can prepare prisoners for life upon release, face-to-face interviews with prison staff and prisoners were chosen as the data collection method. An application for research at the three prisons in Britain was denied by the National Offender Management Service (NOMS) but HMP The Verne gave local approval to conduct research at The Verne.

Subsequently, interviews with five staff members, one guest, and 11 prisoners took place at the café. As it provided a casual setting, it was considered important for prisoners to relax and avoid feelings of interrogation. Simultaneously, prisoners could reflect in situ about the interview topic. In order to protect identity, prisoners are not listed by name, but referred to as prisoner A, prisoner B, etc. Interviews with the following staff members were conducted:

- Michelle Preston, business and community partnerships manager
- Diane James, chief executive Expia CIC
- Mark Glenn, offender supervisor
- Simone McManus, outreach officer
- Jim McGowen, head of reducing reoffending

The collected data were analysed inductively using "consistencies and differences" in answers to "identify themes or patterns" (Taylor-Powell and Renner, 2003: 2).

## The nature of restaurant operations

In order to better evaluate if and why the hospitality industry is suitable for the rehabilitation of ex-offenders, it is necessary to explore the sector's nature. Considering the literature available on this topic, this paper describes the nature of work and identifies three dimensions characteristic to the industry, including economic, social and philosophic dimensions.

Narrowed down to a very simple understanding, the hospitality industry's main purpose is the provision of food, drink and accommodation to travellers (Brotherton and Wood, 2000). Gradually hospitality work has evolved to also "include a range of, arguably, sophisticated generic skills covering areas such as communications, languages, and information technology, as well as emotional and aesthetic labour inputs" (Baum, 2006: 131). Especially demanding in hospitality is the phenomenon of so-called "emotional labour" (Tesone and Ricci, 2006: 67), which "requires one to induce or suppress feeling in order to sustain the outward countenance" (Hochschild, 1983: 7).

Moreover, hospitality work is described as a "dichotomy between the employees' hard work and the expected outcome of their efforts, which is mostly other people's pleasure" (Pizam and Shani, 2009: 144). Further aspects in association with hospitality work are for example "exceptional unbalanced working hours", the "harsh work conditions", and "relatively low wages" (Pizam and Shani, 2009: 144). Evidence exists that the industry has a clear commercial purpose, which is of utmost importance since hospitality is "a source of revenue for the state, for individuals and, indeed, businesses" (O'Gorman, 2009: 786). In the United Kingdom, 2.44 million jobs are directly linked to the hospitality industry (Oxford Economics, 2010), representing "one of the UK's largest sectors and employing over two million people" (Pearson Education, 2013).

In addition to the economic dimension, there is clear evidence of a distinct social nature which, first, distinguishes it from other service sectors and, second, benefits society in ways beyond the generation of financial profit. The main distinguishing factor of restaurants and the hospitality industry in general is that it has the stated aim of "generating happiness in people's life" (Pizam and Shani, 2009: 142) and is designed to "enhance the mutual wellbeing of all parties concerned" (Brotherton, 1999: 168). This unique feature of the industry is reflected in the high degree of social interaction, and the need for willingness to understand and please fellow humans. This is shown in the "relative long-term interaction between guests and employees" and the "need to truly understand and comprehend the customers" (Pizam and Shani, 2009: 142). Consequently, the hospitality industry seems to be "much more people-oriented than other industries" (Pizam and Shani, 2009: 142). The hospitality experience is considered the root of social interaction and a contributor to the "development of the societies" (O'Gorman, 2005: 148) because it strengthens relationships and can bridge the gap between strangers (Selwyn, 2000). The reason is that "relationships between households and friends were developed through mutual hospitality between the original partners, and then subsequently given to their descendants and their wider circle of friends" (O'Gorman, 2005: 148). Thus, hospitality is contagious; people transmit hospitality towards others in business contexts and personal situations that they have experienced in an organized hospitality event.

Finally, Pizam and Shani (2009: 146) conclude that "hospitality work was characterized as calling for a high degree of collaborations and teamwork, which consequently involve a high degree of solidarity between employees". These statements hint at a social dimension being characteristic for the hospitality industry but some assign an even deeper meaning to hospitality by calling it a philosophy. To begin with, hospitality is associated with the word "natural" (O'Connor, 2005: 269). Hospitableness is "printed onto our character or personality at birth, almost genetically" (O'Connor, 2005: 269). Consequently, if hospitality is natural then it must be unconditional. Unconditional hospitality simply is the "workplace version of the cordial and generous behaviour we naturally offer our family and friends" (Herbst, 2001: 18). In true hospitality "it doesn't matter who the guest is, nor their apparent status in life" (Herbst, 2001: 142). Interestingly, Pizam and Shani (2009: 143) conclude that hospitable behaviour is considered "as a virtue that differentiates it from other forms of service providing" and thus support the philosophic dimension of the industry, while simultaneously indicating that this is a trait unique to the hospitality business. In summary, hospitality comprises the provision of food, drink and accommodation and is complemented by "hospitable behaviour" (Brotherton, 1999: 170).

## Hospitality as a motor for rehabilitation

To find out if hospitality can support the process of rehabilitation it is necessary to uncover what is fundamental to rehabilitation in general. Important for rehabilitation is the opportunity to work during incarceration, a good education and the development of personal skills. This is because many prisoners originate from poor backgrounds and unstable family conditions with a low educational background, some of them without a "legitimate social network" (Coyle, 2008: 226). Offenders often lack the skills needed in order to "function in the family, community, and workplace" (Coffey and Knoll, 1998: 11). Escapes from prisons can best be prevented if prisoners are offered opportunities "to participate in constructive activities and prepare them for release" (Coyle, 2008). This view is supported by the belief that properly designed "education programs in correctional facilities and communities can provide individuals involved in the criminal justice system with the academic instruction, vocational training, and cognitive and life skills they need to succeed in today's economy" (Brazzell et al., 2009: 2).

Other factors contributing to rehabilitation are the maintenance of family connections during incarceration (Johnston and Hamilton-Grey, 2010). With regard to this, Coffey and

Knoll (1998: 8) are convinced that individuals require so-called survival skills, which include "knowledge about budgeting, leases, credit, insurance, taxes, and other daily living areas" and in order to be "an effective spouse and parent" offenders need knowledge about "personal relationships, parenting, health, and nutrition". Regarding job life, "the person needs a number of social skills" that, apart from "filling in applications, interviewing" or "work ethic", include knowing "how to get along with peers, deal with supervisors and other authority figures, and provide timely, responsible, and consistent work performance" (Coffey and Knoll, 1998: 8–9). With regard to society it is crucial to know how to "get along with people", to be able to resolve conflicts and be familiar with "mediation" (Coffey and Knoll, 1998: 8–9).

In summary, education is fundamental for different areas in life but for true reintegration into society, social skills such as communication are even more important. These ideas are supported by the theory of desistance, which explains why people desist from crime. According to this theory, criminal behaviour is related to people's "ties to family, employment or educational programmes" (McNeill, 2006: 46) and the existence of these ties fosters criminal desistance. For example marriage increases social stability (Gibbens, cited in Sampson and Laub, 1992) and hence desistance because "more is at stake" (Laub et al., 1998: 225). Being a father and carrying responsibility for children is "an important turning point toward desistance and motivator for change" (Moloney et al., 2009). Other factors contributing to desistance are hope and motivation. For example Burnett and Maruna (2004: 395) suggest that "the level of prisoner optimism might have an impact on their success upon release". Hope is referred to as the desire to change and as the "perceived ability" to do so (Burnett and Maruna, 2004: 396). It seems that people who are more confident regarding their ability to change are less likely to return to crime. An interesting factor that is suggested to contribute to desistance from crime was found in giving something to society. Burnett and Maruna (2006: 101) report the positive effects when prisoners are "placed in roles of service to others". The authors report that prisoners placed in voluntary work expressed "satisfaction, even joy, they experience in the course of contributing to the well-being of others" (Burnett and Maruna, 2006: 95).

The final principle Maruna (cited in McNeill, 2006: 46) mentions is based on how people's perception of themselves and their identity changes, which influences "changing motivation, greater concern for others, and more consideration of the future". It is believed that offenders who change their perception of themselves, between the "old me", the offender, and the "new me", a caring person, are more likely to desist (Burnett and Maruna, 2006: 94). Consequently, desistance theory supports the importance of work, education and family bonds as identified before (e.g., Coffey and Knoll, 1998) and furthermore introduces the idea of sense of self.

## Findings

HMP The Verne is a category C prison, which means that prisoners enjoy more freedom than, for instance, at a category A prison, the strictest prison category. According to Michelle Preston, the goal of the café is "to provide a learning and working environment within the community for suitably risk assessed prisoners to refresh old skills, learn new ones, and become work ready". All prisoners who work at the jailhouse café do so voluntarily after completing a risk assessment as explained by Preston and Glenn. Interviews revealed that prisoners adopt an array of skills that can be divided into vocational skills, social skills and family skills. Additionally, the programme leads to prisoners finding or shaping their identity.

Regarding vocational skills, Preston explains that prisoners are educated in customer service, front of house hospitality, hygiene, health and safety or barista training. Diane James adds being on time and Jim McGowen mentions that prisoners develop a sense of responsibility. This idea is supported, for example, by prisoner A, who observed that prisoners manage the café on their own.

An important feature of the programme at The Verne is the possibility to receive a qualification. Mark Glenn mentions that, upon release, prisoners face the problem of carrying the stigma of being a prisoner and having a criminal record, which represents a barrier to gaining employment. This is also important from the prisoners' point of view. Many of them use the opportunity to gain a qualification even if they do not pursue a career in catering. Some consider the NVQ as a back-up option for their time after release. An interesting idea that evolved during interviews was the transferability of skills that prisoners adopt. Glenn explains that at the café prisoners learn a lot of skills, such as timeliness or the ability to deal with complaints, which are also applicable to job settings other than restaurants.

In addition to vocational skills, an array of social skills that prisoners adopt could be identified, which according to McGowen are fundamental since many prisoners spend years separated from society, having no visitors at all. One example is the idea of emotional control. Glenn mentions that prisoners' problem-solving skills are not very good and they often show their emotions by shouting. Prisoner B has the feeling that some people "want to check you out", but he recommends being polite, showing a happy demeanour and being pleasant. Prisoner D mentions that at the café "you cannot swear", because it is a public place and "you need to respect the public". One word, which was mentioned repeatedly, was "teamwork". According to prisoner I, good service requires teamwork, and prisoner B believes that cooperation is key and that without teamwork everything would fall apart. Prisoner C also mentions teamwork and unity as a prerequisite for good service. When asked about the meaning of "good customer service", many prisoners point out the importance of some sort of interaction or communication with guests and mention "naturalness". For example, prisoner B recommends: "If you are not used to dealing with people then just be yourself and be natural." He thinks guests need to have the feeling that "you are being yourself". Prisoner H adds that good customer service requires courtesy and politeness and prisoner I believes in patience. In order to provide good customer service, communication among co-workers is key (prisoner B). Prisoner F shows how the programme helps him: "I'm interacting with people and I have the feeling I can do it." Moreover, prisoner B mentions the aspect of becoming familiar with guests. He says that, since the café has some regular guests, the opportunity exists to become familiar with them, which for him creates a comfortable working environment. Prisoner D says: "The programme is good; it brings you back to the community and to normal people."

Another interesting result of the interviews was the impact the café work might potentially have on family life. "Dad can now cook a cake", a prisoner's child said, according to Diane James. Expia's chief executive believes that cooking skills must help family life because they give prisoners an insight into what their partner usually does for the family. Interestingly, family is the reason why prisoner D chose to work at the café in the first place: "I have a wife and children and I want to be able to cook when I get home." Prisoner C, who also works in the kitchen, believes that he does not want to work in catering later, but that cooking skills are important for his family life. Preston believes that cookery and other elements of hospitality can be excellent life skills, and result in an individual becoming more involved in family life. Preston also suggests potential future economic and health benefits to prisoners who eventually cook at home rather than eating out. Prisoner D confirms that the programme helps to get back to the family. He says that his kids love it. In general most prisoners report that family members admire their working at the café. In summary, interviews revealed that prisoners adopt an array of social or interpersonal skills including emotional control, teamwork, communication with both guests and also other prisoners, courtesy, politeness, patience, helpfulness and attentiveness. Moreover, the café work equips prisoners with cooking skills, which increase their ability to care for themselves and their families. Regarding the social impact of the jailhouse café, Diane James tries to get to the heart of the issue. She explains that the café is "a very pleasant and normal part of life, which people enjoy and where you see society around you". She adds that the café offers a great possibility for people who have been marginalized from society to gradually re-enter society.

Maybe the most important fact about the programme's impact on prisoners is what McManus reports. Apparently prisoners transfer the behaviour they adopt at the café into the prison because they are "more articulate". Many discussions revealed that prisoners develop self-esteem and confidence through working at the café. James explains that if prisoners at their point of release do not have any self-confidence, they will probably end up back where they came from. James explains that prisoners who work at the café have been through the prison system for a long time and need time to get used to looking people in the eyes. Regarding the situation inside the prison, Glenn adds that prisoners either behave like "I'm the biggest person in the world" or they are very reserved in order to avoid being picked on by others. James noticed that, through working at the café, prisoners have returned to the same level of confidence and self-esteem as before. Prisoner C gives evidence for this since he says the work fosters his self-esteem and mentions that having people ask who has cooked the food and the comments in the visitors' book make him proud. Prisoner D also explains that it was challenging for him to show confidence when he started to work at the café. And he confirms that if customers like the food it makes him happy and increases his level of confidence. Prisoner D also likes that the programme is a "confidence-builder". He believes communicating with the public contributes to this, and that the communication as such is important because it assists people in losing their prejudice towards prisoners. Prisoner A believes that the catering facility is a great opportunity for prisoners because it is good for them to be trusted.

James describes how some prisoners have never been praised before and that some say that nobody has ever been "nice to them". At the café, prisoners receive immediate feedback for their work. The visitors' book, which consists of many positive guest experiences, is "a good tool" for learning, as prisoner I mentions. Prisoner K adds that the book offers constructive feedback and prisoner J calls it "my credentials" and says customer feedback has a lot of weight for him. When asked why they chose to work at the café, many prisoners mentioned being with "normal people" or feeling that they could behave normally. Prisoner G chose to work at the café because it was a chance to escape the prison walls, to have breathing space and to "be with normal people". When inside the prison, prisoner G explains that he has to be careful not to upset other prisoners and rather behave "like a robot or an actor", but with the guests he can just be himself. Prisoner B sums this up by saying: "I've forgotten what it's like to talk to normal people." Being with "normal people" also seems to be important for prisoners because it diminishes people's prejudice. For instance, prisoner F believes: "The café offers an opportunity to gain good knowledge, but more importantly it changes the public's view on prisoners." Prisoner G underlines this point because he believes that the best thing about the programme is that people may find potential in prisoners and that they reduce their prejudices. Preston also thinks that café guests might leave with a different mindset and develop a new view of prisoners. Finally, prisoner B summarizes the café as a good idea, and says "here are normal people at the café". He adds that the visitors' book makes him feel like an individual delivering good service, because the comments people leave show that they remember him as an individual as opposed to a random prisoner. In summary, interviewees mentioned various factors somehow related to identity. First of all it was observed that prisoners regain their level of confidence and self-esteem. Second, prisoners' motivation to work at the café results from the possibility of being with "normal people" and of behaving normally. Finally, prisoners enjoy being perceived as a person and not only as a prisoner. Their identity is not reduced to being a criminal but to a skilful individual.

Considering interview outcomes and findings from the literature review hospitality restaurant operations seem to answer the objectives of a rehabilitation programme.

## Conclusion/recommendations

Although case studies cannot be generalized and other factors in addition to catering experience might ultimately lead to rehabilitation, interviews revealed that prisoners adopt numerous skills essential for rehabilitation and therefore suggest the applicability of hospitality restaurant operations as a rehabilitation tool.

One of the main reasons is the possibility for offenders to receive a qualification in catering, which opens the possibility to work in an industry that in Britain alone represents one fifth of all employment opportunities. Additionally, the transferability of hospitality skills to other jobs was pointed out. Second, prisoners are equipped with an array of social skills including responsibility, communication, interaction with people and teamwork, which are fostered through the nature of work the hospitality industry demands. This mainly results from the high degree of customer interaction representing the core of hospitality. Customer interaction also enables prisoners to be perceived as a "normal" person and a skilful individual and lose the stigma of the prisoner, hence increasing their employability and self-confidence. It allows them to build relationships with the public and potential employers.

The main reasons why prisoners chose to work at the café were the belief that it enables them to (re)connect with their families due to adopted cooking skills and the wish to be around "normal people". Here, hospitality again responds to the idea of strengthening family bonds and therefore improving rehabilitation. The wish to be with "normal people" and especially the statement that prisoners can act naturally with them suggests that they show their true selves. Perception of self was also found to contribute to desistance from crime. It seems that hospitality allows prisoners to find their way back not only to family and society, but most importantly to themselves. This is the point where rehabilitation should start in the first place.

Finally, and this might be the most promising result regarding rehabilitation, it was outlined that prisoners transfer the behaviour adopted at the jailhouse café to the prison wing. If prisoners can transfer what they have learned at the café into the prison setting, they might also transfer this behaviour to their life after release.

This study suggests that hospitality has a strong potential to contribute to prisoner rehabilitation. However, conclusions drawn from interviews are based on a point in time where prisoners are still serving their sentences. Therefore, the effect on prisoners after release could not be explored within this study and must be further investigated.

## References

Babbie, E. (2004) *The Practice of Social Research*, 10th edn, Belmont, CA: Wadsworth.

Baum, T. (2006) "Reflections on the nature of skills in the experience economy: challenging traditional skills models in hospitality", *Journal of Hospitality & Tourism Management*, 13(2): 124–135.

Brazzell, D., Crayton, A., Mukamal, D.A., Solomon, A.L. and Lindahl, N., (2009) *From the Classroom to the Community: Exploring the Role of Education During Incarceration and Re-entry*, www.urban.org/UploadedPDF/411963_classroom_community.pdf (accessed 5 June 2013).

Brotherton, B. (1999) "Towards a definitive view of the nature of hospitality and hospitality management", *International Journal of Contemporary Hospitality Management*, 11(4): 165–173.

Brotherton, B. and Wood, R.C. (2000) "Defining hospitality and hospitality management", in C. Lashley and A. Morrison (eds.), *In Search of Hospitality – Theoretical Perspectives and Debates*, Oxford: Butterworth Heinemann, pp. 134–156.

Burnett, R. and Maruna, S. (2004) "So 'prison works', does it? The criminal careers of 130 men released from prison under home secretary Michael Howard", *Howard Journal of Criminal Justice*, 43(4), http://onlinelibrary.wiley.com/doi/10.1111/j.1468-2311.2004.00337.x/pdf (accessed 5 July 2013).

Burnett, R. and Maruna, S. (2006) "The kindness of prisoners: strength-based resettlement in theory and in action", *Criminology and Criminal Justice*, http://rethinking.catalystdemo.net.nz/eserv/rcp:178/Burnett_Maruna_The_kindness_of_pris.pdf (accessed 10 May 2013).

Coffey, O.D. and Knoll, J.F. (1998) *Choosing Life Skills: A Guide for Selecting Life Skills Programs for Adult and Juvenile Offenders*, http://eric.ed.gov/?id=ED418367 (accessed 13 June 2013).

Coyle, A. (2008) "The treatment of prisoners: international standards and case law", *Legal and Criminological Psychology*, 13(2), http://internationalhumanrightslaw.net/wp-content/uploads/2011/01/The-treatment-of-prisoners-International-standards-and-case-law.pdf (accessed 13 June 2013).

Herbst, L., (2001) "Unconditional hospitality", *Lodging Hospitality*, 57(1): 18.

Hochschild, A.R. (1983) *The Managed Heart: Commercialization of Human Feeling*, Berkeley, CA: University of California Press.

Johnston, J. and Hamilton-Grey, S. (2010) *Can Rehabilitation be Designed into a Prison?* www.insidetime.org/articleview.asp?a=716&c=can_rehabilitation_be_designed_into_a_prison (accessed 7 May 2013).

Kitching, L. (2011) *Portland's Jailhouse Cafe to Open its Doors in New Scheme*, www.dorsetecho.co.uk/news/9373370.Portland_s_Jailhouse_cafe_to_open_its_doors_in_new_scheme (accessed 16 May 2013).

Lashley, C. and Morrison, A. (eds.) (2000) *In Search of Hospitality – Theoretical Perspectives and Debates*, Oxford: Butterworth Heinemann.

Laub, J.H., Nagin, D.S. and Sampson, R.J. (1998) "Trajectories of change in criminal offending: Good marriages and the desistance process", *American Sociological Review*, 63(2), www.jstor.org/discover/10.2307/2657324?uid=3737864&uid=2&uid=4&sid=21102543206913 (accessed 16 May 2013).

McNeill, F. (2006) "A desistance paradigm for offender management", *Criminology and Criminal Justice*, http://crj.sagepub.com/content/6/1/39 (accessed 16 May 2013).

Moloney, M., MacKenzie, K., Hunt, G. and Joe-Laidler, K. (2009) "The path and promise of fatherhood for gang members", *British Journal of Criminology*, http://bjc.oxfordjournals.org/content/49/3/305.short (accessed 16 May 2013).

O'Connor, D. (2005) "Towards a new interpretation of 'hospitality' ", *International Journal of Contemporary Hospitality Management*, 17(3): 267–271.

O'Gorman, K.D. (2005) "Modern hospitality: lessons from the past", *Journal of Hospitality & Tourism Management*, 12(2): 141–151.

O'Gorman, K.D. (2009) "Origins of the commercial hospitality industry: from the fanciful to factual", *International Journal of Contemporary Hospitality Management*, 21(7): 777–790.

Oxford Economics (2010) *Economic Contribution of UK Hospitality Industry*, www.bha.org.uk/wp-content/uploads/2010/10/BHA-Economic-Contribution-of-UK-Hospitality-Industry-Final-.pdf (accessed 10 July 2013).

Pearson Education (2013) *NVQ (NQF) Hospitality and Catering*, www.edexcel.com/quals/nvq/hos-cat/Pages/default.aspx (accessed 10 July 2013).

Pizam, A. and Shani, A. (2009) "The nature of the hospitality industry: present and future managers' perspectives", *Anatolia: An International Journal of Tourism & Hospitality Research*, 20(1): 134–150.

Sampson, R.J. and Laub, J. H. (1992) "Crime and deviance in the life course", *Annual Review of Sociology*, 18(1): 63–84.

Saunders, M., Lewis, P. and Thornhill, A. (2003) *Research Methods for Business Students*, 3rd edn, Harlow: Pearson Education.

Selwyn, T. (2000) "An anthropology of hospitality", in C. Lashley and A. Morrison (eds.), *In Search of Hospitality – Theoretical Perspectives and Debates*, Oxford: Butterworth Heinemann, pp. 134–156.

Taylor-Powell, E. and Renner, M. (2003) *Analyzing Qualitative Data*, http://learningstore.uwex.edu/assets/pdfs/g3658-12.pdf (accessed 17 May 2013).

Tesone, D.V. and Ricci, P. (2006) "Toward a definition of entry-level job competencies: hospitality manager perspectives", *International Journal of Hospitality & Tourism Administration*, 7(4): 65–80.

This is Dorset (2012) *Mat Follas Helps to Launch Guys Marsh Café Project*, www.thisisdorset.co.uk/Mat-Follas-helps-launch-Guys-Marsh-caf-project/story-17620042-detail/story.html#axzz2Tda8Mrsq (accessed 10 May 2013).

Yin, R.K. (2009) *Case Study Research: Design and Methods*, 4th edn, Thousand Oaks, CA: Sage Publications.

# PART 5

# Food innovation/future

What are we eating tomorrow? Yesterday's leftovers.

*The editors*

The quest for new sources of protein has never been stronger. Faced with a multiplicity of obstacles for producing enough meat and fish to feed a burgeoning planet population, a group of food scientists, botanists and chefs are coming up with practical and tasty solutions. Foods that neither gastronomes nor environmentalists would have imagined a generation ago are coming to our tables. Insects, vegetable proteins, forgotten wild plants and seaweeds are without doubt the new foods of the future.

Edible insects provide an intriguing case of giving gastronomic value to neglected and underutilized ingredients. While many have been and remain a part of traditional diets in many areas of the world, in others they have been largely overlooked or abhorred. This growing interest in the potential of edible insects is explored and its place in sustainable food systems for the future is explained by **Afton Halloran, Christopher Münke, Paul Vantomme, Benedict Reade and Josh Evans**. Edible insects serve as a model in enhancing our exposure to the wider edible landscape.

For millions of people worldwide all manner of wild plants, animals and fungi make up part of the daily diet because of either tradition or necessity. These foods in varied ecosystems offer a vivid array of unique flavours, textures and aromas, and together represent the seasonality and biodiversity of different regions. The article by **Christopher Münke, Afton Halloran, Paul Vantomme, Josh Evans, Benedict Reade, Roberto Flore, Roland Rittman, Anders Lindén, Pavlos Georgiadis and Miles Irving** describes how ethnobotanical knowledge that stretches down through the ages can now be more widely diffused. Examples from Sardinia, Denmark and Sweden of foraging are presented.

The growing supply and variety of foods from both fresh water and saltwater aquaculture are explored during a time of dwindling global fish stocks by **Ricardo Radulovich**. Microalgae, like spirulina and others, are already significant food supplements and aquatic plants like water hyacinth are becoming the focus of research for use as food. The increasing quantity of aquatic plant production used directly as food and for the production of hydrocolloids such as carrageen is described. This article describes how the sea and lakes are becoming more like immense aquacultural fields.

**Benedict Reade, Justine de Valicourt and Josh Evans** highlight another important development in terms of food for the future in the form of fermented foodstuffs that offer a wide range of tastes, flavours and textures. The phenomenon of fermentation long predates human existence, yet over millennia of experimentation humans have developed methods for harnessing the power of microbes to transform foods for preservation and taste. The principles of fermentation are introduced and illustrations are made of how the ancestral craft of fermentation is reconciled with laboratory experimentation to produce delicious results.

# 18

# BROADENING INSECT GASTRONOMY

*Afton Halloran, Christopher Münke, Paul Vantomme,*
*Benedict Reade and Joshua Evans*

## Introduction

In recent years there has been a trend among chefs to diversify their ingredients and techniques, drawing inspiration from other cultures and creating new foods by blending this knowledge with the flavours of their local region. Edible insects, with their plethora of taste, aromatic, textural and visual characteristics, is an example of an area of nature that requires further gastronomic exploration. Many parts of the world consume insects, neither as a novelty nor as a fall-back famine food (FAO, 2013). Insect-consuming populations often eat them as a delicacy, seeing each insect as an ingredient in its own right – not collectively as 'insects', as it is easy for many uninitiated to do. Many of these insects frequently fetch higher prices than other meat sources in the market, and it is this approach of investigating insects as a delicious gastronomic product that interests us. Indeed, if people might be expected to adopt a new food, it is necessary that it tastes good!

Despite the diversity of insect flavours, those who do not eat insects often react adversely when confronted with a six-legged meal. The universal emotion of disgust is something that has only recently been studied. Nonetheless, it is understood that disgust (lit. 'bad taste') most likely originates from a rejection response that protects the body from potentially harmful foods. The sensation most distinctly associated with disgust is nausea, which inhibits the body from ingesting food; in a sense, disgust becomes 'a guardian to the temple of the body' (Rozin et al., 2008: 764).

Because some insects live in contact with rotting flesh or faeces, in general they are often associated with filth and unsanitary conditions even though many are in fact quite clean (DeFoliart, 1999). Moreover, some arthropod species like spiders invoke mixed sensations of fear and disgust, despite the fact that they are seldom of danger to humans (Rozin et al., 2008). Humans are omnivores who make choices of what to eat based partly on experience (Rozin, 2002). In addition to biology, culture also plays a major role in food selection (Rozin, 1984). Thus, given that most human–food relationships are acquired, they may also be altered both positively and negatively. Cuisines, as systems of selecting and preparing food, emerge out of geography, climate, culture, disposition and other factors, and can also change through social needs and advances in technology (Rozin, 2002).

Developing broader culinary roles for insects is one way to change the disgust that many Westerners commonly associate with them. Chefs and other gastronomic leaders thus play an integral role in broadening the perception of what is edible and (re-)introducing ingredients, like insects, into delicious foods. To illustrate this process, Nordic Food Lab (NFL) describes their gastronomic innovation through their experiments with three different kinds of insect: ants (wild), grasshoppers (domesticated) and bees (semi-domesticated).

These three categories (wild, semi-domesticated and domesticated) are considered in relation to the methods for their harvest and sustainable management. Wild insects are collected from wild sources, which are often not monitored and can therefore be more prone to over-harvesting. Wild gathering therefore requires strong knowledge about the ecology and biology of the species in order to minimize the impact on a specific area's population (Yen, 2009). Ants, as described in the following by Nordic Food Lab, are in principle wild, but can be semi-domesticated by creating favourable conditions. Semi-domestication allows a more consistent supply, while keeping insects in their natural habitat or a habitat closely mimicking their natural environment. This technique is mostly used for species that cannot be taken completely out of their environment as they are too difficult to be domesticated fully (FAO, 2013). In order to provide a sufficiently consistent supply of insects for gastronomic institutions, farmed insects are an option for species that can live outside of their natural habitat and are relatively easy to breed in captivity relative to the initial cost of investment (FAO, 2013). However, in order to be utilized for human consumption, farmed insects have to be produced in hygienic and food-safe conditions.

The objective of this chapter is to discuss the growing interest in the potential of insects as food. Moreover, we describe how edible insects can help secure sustainable food systems for the future. Furthermore, we use insects as a case to explore the potential of diversified, wild and undervalued food sources. This is done by analysing how insects can be shifted from the category 'inedible' to edible and integrate them as a valued component of a cuisine, rather than just a novelty food or gimmick.

## Ants

Many societies around the world eat ants. In Mexico the larvae of (*Liometopum* sp.) are known as escamoles and consumed as a delicacy at celebrations. In Colombia and other countries, (*Atta laevigata*) is valued for its large abdomen, hence its Spanish name, hormigas colunas, translated literally as 'big-arsed ants'. In Denmark we (NFL) have been working with two species of ant: the smelling carpenter ant (*Lasius fuliginosus*) and the common wood ant (*Formica rufa*). These two ants have interesting organoleptic characteristics, one quite different from the other – this diversity is the key to developing gastronomic context for insects in a region, where each species can be recognized for its particular qualities. Many ants produce formic acid as a defence mechanism, which gives them acidity. Because of their big taste and small size, we use both these species mainly in the context of a spice or seasoning. The wood ant has quite a straight and sharp acidity with the aroma of charred lemon, while the smelling carpenter ant has a gentler acidity and a pronounced aroma of kaffir lime. It seems as well that different populations can express different aromas. This aromatic diversity arises from the ants' use of pheromones for communication, which humans experience as a myriad of aromas, similar to those of other herbs and spices (Morgan, 2009).

There has arisen one potential food safety concern regarding ants. Some of the wood ants can harbour a parasitic flatworm called a lancet liver fluke (*Dicrocoelium dendriticum*) that is potentially parasitic to humans (Cengiz et al., 2010), so it is necessary to ensure the ants are safe before consumption. We are currently investigating different treatments that make the ants safe for consumption, like thorough freezing.

Because the formic acid in the ants can be distilled at Nordic Food Lab relatively easily, we decided to make a gin by infusing the ants into alcohol, then distilling the alcohol under a strong vacuum to collect a concentrate of the aromatic mixture. The gin has a distinct note of nasturtium seed spice, which leaves a tingle on the tip of the tongue. It is completely delicious.

## Grasshoppers/locusts

Grasshoppers are commonly farmed around the world and for that reason make an interesting case study due to their relatively wide accessibility (Hanboonsong et al., 2013; FAO, 2013). They are also notable as locusts so often decimate human crops, especially in Africa. Most farming of grasshoppers takes place to provide pet reptiles with feed, so pet shops are often a good source for these food-grade insects. As with any food, the sourcing of the product must be undertaken carefully. We choose locusts that have been fed only grass which has not been exposed to synthetic pesticides or fertilizers. The locusts are then purged (kept without food) for 24 hours before we freeze them. They can also be blanched for five minutes and kept at 5–7 °C – a technique that has proven to keep the insects microbially stable for two weeks (Belluco et al., 2013). The insects are excellent toasted in a tiny amount of oil on medium heat, or roasted in butter in the oven. The most appropriate preparation technique is largely informed by the developmental stage of the insect. Locusts in the third or fourth instar (developmental stage) tend to be optimal for eating whole, as the wings are not fully developed but the main body has reached a size which gives some amount of substance. With larger locusts we have experimented with making a salt-rich fermentation using a barley *koji* moulded with *Aspergillus oryzae* to create a umami-tasting sauce, much like a fish sauce but without fish. We call the sauce 'grasshopper garum'. Our recipe is as follows:

---

### Nordic Food Lab's grasshopper garum

800g whole grasshoppers (usually adult *Schistocerca gregaria* or *locusta migratoria*)
225g of pearl barley *koji* made with *Aspergillus orzyae*
300g of filtered water
240g of salt

Place everything in a blender and mix.
Incubate at 40 °C for ten weeks.

---

It is interesting to remember that in some places in the world people get a considerable amount of their protein from fish sauce. In the Philippines, for example, up to 18 per cent of daily protein may be obtained through fish sauce. When considering the immense biomass in a swarm of locusts, perhaps this incredibly damaging force to agriculture should instead be harvested, processed and used as human food and animal feed which can be used to provide valuable nutrition to people who have been ravaged by such a plague.

# Bees

Bee larvae are particularly interesting because unlike ants, which we harvest wild, and grasshoppers, which are often farmed, bee larvae are the young of the semi-domesticated honeybee (*Apis mellifera*), which are often a by-product of beekeeping, as a result of a strategy to regulate the Varroa mite population in a hive. The larvae are an easy target for the mite, and the drones in particular attract the highest concentration of mites because of their extended developmental period, staying in the larval stage for a few days longer than worker bees. Once the queen lays the eggs in the comb, the individual hexagonal cells are sealed with wax until the larvae pupate and hatch – but not before the mites find their way into the cells too. Since the drones attract the greatest number of mites, beekeepers use drone brood as a sort of decoy, drawing the mites into the cells then removing the brood to keep overall mite levels low – they remove about one-third of a hive frame per week during the season. This technique, called the 'safe strategy', was devised by the Danish Beekeeping Association (Danmarks Biavlerforening) as a way to contain Varroa mite populations without using chemical pesticides.

The mite harms the bee by biting holes in the bee's tissue which cannot heal, opening their circulatory system to the environment. It then serves as a vector for viruses to attack the weakened bee. So why do we eat the drone brood if it is covered with Varroa mite? In fact, the mite itself poses no threat to other organisms. The drones would almost all die anyway, as only a few of the many thousands are needed to inseminate the queen, so we are in some sense helping our apian friends by consuming the most serious threat to their population.

The fat and protein composition of the larvae is high, which lends itself to techniques that highlight its savoury taste such as a bee larvae granola. In addition it has a delicate flavour and a fragile texture, for which we have developed a bee larvae ceviche. The following recipes containing bee larvae have been developed by the Nordic Food Lab:

---

### Bee larvae granola

750g oats/seeds/nuts (rough ration: five parts rolled oats; two parts sesame seeds; two parts
    sunflower seeds; one part pumpkin seeds)
250g bee larvae
100g honey
5g salt
**sometimes a pinch of fennel seed or tiny amount of crushed juniper berry is nice

Let bee larvae thaw.
Blend until smooth with honey and salt.
Mix through dry ingredients on a baking tray.
Spread thin and bake at 160 °C for 16 minutes or until golden.
Toss through some birch syrup for added sweetness and clump-ability.
Stir at minutes 5, 10, 13, 16 or as needed; for more clumps, stir less.
For extra bee effect, mix in some dehydrated whole larvae for texture after cooked and cooled.

---

*Figure 18.1*  Revisiting the utterly familiar with beekeeping by-products – bee larvae granola with bee larvae yoghurt. Photo by Josh Evans.

---

**Bee larvae ceviche**

15g bee larvae
100ml rhubarb vinegar
3g lemon thyme
5g freeze-dried lingonberries
3g red oxalis stems
5g søl salt

Pick lemon thyme leaves and chop dried lingonberries and oxalis stems very finely.

Take the bee larvae from the freezer and defrost for three minutes. Add them to the vinegar and season with salt. Wait another three minutes.

Take the bee larvae out from the vinegar and dress them with the other ingredients (stems, lingonberries and lemon thyme).

---

## Market development

Despite the growing interest in entomophagy there are still many challenges that influence the widespread adoption of insects as food. First, the lack of regulations governing insects as food and feed at national, regional, and international levels affects the market availability of edible insects. In Europe, legislation for insects as food is a relatively grey area as insects are not explicitly mentioned in general food regulations. Under Regulation (EC) 258/97, novel food and ingredients that were not consumed 'to a significant degree' before 1997 may have to undergo an authorization before entering the market. As proposed in the new draft Novel Food Regulation 872 (COM, 2007), a legally recognized novel food needs evidence for its significant consumption in Europe before 1997, or proof that it has been and continues to be part of the normal diet for at least one generation in a large part of the population of a given country outside Europe. As suggested by Gradowski et al. (2013), scientific evidence should be used where no official regulations exist.

Second, supply chains are relatively undeveloped. With relatively few producers compared to other food sources/ingredients, insects as an ingredient are difficult to come by. Current trade in edible insects in developing countries is usually specific to migrant communities in Europe or North America, or through the development of niche markets for exotic foods (FAO, 2013). Despite these challenges, edible insects in the food sector is growing quickly and gaining more and more interest in the Western world.

## Conclusion and discussion

Entomophagy has gained a flush of attention recently due to the arguments for their nutritional potential and supposed sustainability benefits. These are interesting ideas but they are not enough to ensure the preservation of the crucial bio- and cultural diversity on which truly sustainable food systems rely. Insects as delicacies in their cultural, ecological and gastronomic contexts contribute to traditional diets around the world. They also provide an example for better understanding of agro-ecologic and sustainable food systems, as well as the benefits, and limits, of related traditional knowledge. Ultimately, they can only be a 'sustainable' ingredient in the context of the larger ecological–gastronomic system. Moreover, they should not be seen as a 'future food', out of any gastronomic context, for the sake of 'pushing the boundaries'. Instead they should be investigated and shared as a delicious ingredient which celebrates the diversity of life in our edible landscape.

The adoption of insects within contemporary food cultures thus relies on collaboration between foragers, producers, food scientists, gastronomic leaders, policymakers, consumers and media – bringing together ecology, psychology, gastronomy, social economics and knowledge from diverse traditional food cultures to further the contextual understanding and culturally appropriate use of insects as a sustainable, nutritious and delicious ingredient.

## References

Belluco, S., Losasso, C., Maggioletti, M., Alonzi, C.C., Paoletti, M.G. and Ricci, A. (2013) 'Edible insects in a food safety and nutritional perspective: a critical review', *Comprehensive Reviews in Food Science and Food Safety*, 12(3): 296–313.

Cengiz, Z.T., Yilmaz, H., Dülger, A.C. and Çiçek, M. (2010) 'Human infection with *Dicrocoelium dendriticum* in Turkey', *Annals of Saudi Medicine*, 30(2): 159.

COM (2007) *872 Final. Proposal for a Regulation of the European Parliament and of the Council on Novel Foods and Amending Regulation (EC) No XXX/XXXX* [common procedure] (presented by the Commission).

DeFoliart, G.R. (1999) 'Insects as food: why the Western attitude is important', *Annual Review of Entomology*, 44: 21–55.

FAO (2013) *Edible Insects: Future Prospects for Food and Feed*, Rome: FAO.

Gradowski, N., Klein, G. and Lopez, A.M. (2013) 'European and German food legislation facing uncommon foodstuffs', *Comprehensive Reviews in Food Science and Food Safety*, 53(8): 787–800.

Hanboonsong, Y., Jamjanya, T. and Durst, P. (2013) *Six-legged Livestock: Edible Insect Farming, Collecting and Marketing in Thailand*, Bangkok: FAO, Regional Office for Asia and the Pacific.

Morgan, D.E. (2009) 'Trail pheromones of ants', *Physiological Entomology*, 34(1): 1–17.

Rozin, P. (1984) 'The child's conception of food: the development of food rejections with special reference to disgust and contamination sensitivity', *Journal of Child Development*, 55(2): 566–575.

Rozin, P. (2002) 'Human food intake and choice: biological, psychological, and cultural perspectives', in H. Anderson, J. Blundell and M. Chiva (eds.), *Food Selection: From Genes to Culture*, Paris: Danone Institute, pp. 7–24.

Rozin, P., Haidt, J. and McCauley, C.R. (2008) 'Disgust', in M. Lewis, J.M. Haviland-Jones and L.F. Barrett (eds.), *Handbook of Emotions*, 3rd edn, New York: Guilford Press, pp. 757–776.

Yen, A.L. (2009) 'Entomophagy and insect conservation: some thoughts for digestion', *Journal of Insect Conservation*, 13: 667–670.

# 19

# WILD IDEAS IN FOOD

*Christopher Münke, Afton Halloran, Paul Vantomme, Josh Evans,*
*Benedict Reade, Roberto Flore, Roland Rittman, Anders Lindén, Pavlos*
*Georgiadis and Miles Irving*

## Introduction

Foraging for all manner of wild plants, animals and fungi and their products makes up part of the traditional diets of approximately 300 million worldwide (Bharucha and Pretty, 2010). Furthermore, their relevance in the global food supply is often underestimated, as policies and statistics at national and regional levels tend to neglect their importance for food sovereignty and food culture (Bharucha and Pretty, 2010). Foraged plants often grow spontaneously and many exist independent of human interaction (Heywood, 1999).

Foraging, or 'searching widely for food or provisions' (Oxford English Dictionary, 2013), is an interactive and intimate activity. Foraged foods can convey distinctiveness of local identity, representing ethnicity, culture, landscape, social context, connection to nature and stories of survival and wealth (Hall et al., 2003; Timothy and Amos, 2013). Moreover, foraged foods – gathered from varied and robust ecosystems – hold a vivid array of unique flavours, textures and aromas, and together represent the seasonality and biodiversity of different regions. Historical ethnobotanical surveys on wild plants estimate that approximately 7,000 species have been a part of human diets over time (Grivetti and Ogle, 2000). For example, more than 1,100 edible mushroom species are known worldwide (FAO, 2004).

Diversification of food sources promotes ecologically resilient and nutritious food systems; thus, foraged foods offer a great opportunity to broaden culinary horizons while simultaneously promoting diverse foodscapes. Wild foods are invariably more diverse than farmed foods, especially considering that 75 per cent of human food is derived from just 12 plants and five animals (Jaenicke and Höschle-Zeledon, 2006).

From elderflowers (*Sambucus nigra*) to samphire (*Salicornia europaea*) to wood sorrel (*Oxalis acetosella*), this diversity provides the opportunity to emphasize and celebrate locality by strengthening the sensory connection of the eater to their surroundings through food. In some areas of the world wild gathered foods risk disappearing from human diets (Leonti et al., 2006). On the other hand, foraging in forests, fields, lakes and by the sea is experiencing a gastronomic revival and is regaining significance in contemporary food culture, nutrition paradigms, local economies and society at large. This resurgence is due in part to the interest in wild products by some of the world's leading chefs, such as Michel Bras (Bras, Aveyron,

France), Rene Redzepi (Noma, Copenhagen, Denmark), Alex Atala (DOM, São Paulo, Brazil) and many others.

In order to exemplify this ecological diversity and interaction with foraged foods in gastronomy, we provide four cases, each with a different theme (ethnobotanical knowledge, entrepreneurship, natural resources and conservation), from different parts of the globe: the Mediterranean island of Sardinia, southern Sweden, England and the Yunnan Province in China. These cases valorize the heritage of foraged foods and show how local knowledge renders products accessible to modern gastronomic entrepreneurs and chefs while drawing from a region's historical, geographical and social diversity (Hall et al., 2003).

Most wild-harvested products are accessed through traditional ecological knowledge of edible species, which provides further reason to preserve and enhance this knowledge before it vanishes. Indigenous knowledge accumulated over generations serves as the basis of agriculture, food production, human and animal health, as well as natural resource management decision-making (Slikkerveer, 1994). To exemplify the importance of interconnected knowledge systems, chef and forager Roberto Flore presents his approach to gastronomy, and its relation to the protection of biodiversity and food sovereignty in Sardinia.

## *Wild idea #1:* Sardinia – handing down a family history through food: the tale of a chef-forager

### *Roberto Flore, Sardinian chef*

'Chef-forager' is a relatively unknown term, and for some it may even seem like a new food fad. However, in reality it describes the genuine awareness of how to handle food through a greater contact with nature and the rediscovery of a region's own flavours.

The term 'foraging', when translated into the Sardinian language, is *'erbuzzae'*, meaning the act of collecting wild herbs. Through my work, foraging, culinary research and interpretation I have the possibility of engaging in one of the most ancient of human activities: the collection of wild species. Since prehistoric times – when farming and agricultural systems were yet to develop – human beings foraged for seeds, fruits and herbs, which were used to feed, to heal and to perform spiritual rites. These practices still affect our everyday lives, even if now in a limited way. In Sardinia, wild species such as Mastic (*Pistacia lentiscus*), Myrtle (*Myrtus communis*), wild fennel (*Foeniculum vulgare*) and borage (*Borago officinalis*) have created a sound foundation for our historical and cultural heritage and are still used in most communities. As such, their protection needs to be ensured. The knowledge of wild herbs is often transferred orally to young people using the specific names in the Sardinian language, as their names in Italian are often not known. Plant names are often used as place names to identify where a given species prevails. This gives a clue as to what kind of vegetation, such as trees, shrubs, fruits and herbs, one can find in a given place. The names of wild plant species are also used to define the physical and psychological characteristics of a person. From these multiple significances it is easy to see the importance of wild herbs in our culture.

My training was born in the arms of my grandmother. She taught me how to cook and recounted to me how she had survived World War II nourished only by self-made foods, wild herbs and fruits. These stories have changed my perspective on food and cooking. Even as a child I was very aware of the origins of my food, as I was often foraging for it myself. The story of my family has been passed down through food; as a result food for me has always provoked strong emotions, which then feed my passion for food and cooking. For me the act of cooking is far more complex than just feeding people: a plate of food becomes a means to inspire young people or to illustrate to conscious travellers the image of '*la mia Sardegna*'. Therefore, it is essential to use high-quality local products and to fight for the preservation of small-scale producers. In this respect my former training as an agricultural technician has helped me become closer to producers and understand the quality of their products. The knowledge that I have accumulated has allowed me to interact with international colleagues who have a similar vision and allows me to promote local development in a global context.

Roberto Flore's example illustrates a sharing of knowledge based on a traditional understanding of the diversity of food resources. These resources play an important role in times of crisis, but even more so they play a role in the preservation of knowledge and culture, which shapes the identity of place (Fischler, 1988). Consumers often look for 'authentic' experiences associated with local, traditional foods and the history of an area, and are taken up by many marketing and branding initiatives in order to promote regional products (Sims, 2009). Shaping or creating an identity can be a spontaneous or a deliberate process, but often contains elements of both.

The arrival of fresh, wild products on our plates can be achieved in a variety of ways. In recent years there has been an increase in commercial foraging enterprises that supply wild food to restaurants, such as herbs, mushrooms, berries, fruits and nuts (Luczaj et al., 2012). Wild food enthusiasts have applied their knowledge to promote local food systems by enabling the provision of these foods to importers, wholesalers, greengrocers and restaurants.

The Swedish professional foragers of Roland Rittman Ltd. present their experiences as entrepreneurs, and their work that contributed to the expansion of New Nordic cuisine.

### Wild Idea #2:    Sweden – Roland Rittman and the Yellow Archangel

#### Roland Rittman and Anders Lindén – professional foragers, Sweden

This is the story of how wild tastes arrived on the plates of Noma in Copenhagen, considered the world's premier restaurant 2010–2012 according to 'The World's 50 Best Restaurants'. Our narrator is Roland Rittman, former teacher, field-biologist and environmental activist who has played a significant role in bringing these flavours to market.

'It all started with a modest sale of mushrooms at the farmers market in Lund some 15 years ago. I gradually expanded the assortment with classic weeds such as nettles (*Urtica dioica*). Shortly thereafter, I built up the courage to enter a restaurant kitchen for the first time in my life and I was over the moon when I left the building with my crates empty. At this point, I extended the hobby of foraging to an activity of survival! There was no grand plan for my little enterprise or any idea where it would lead. However, something fundamentally changed when I decided to take my wagon across the bridge from Skåne, Sweden to Copenhagen, Denmark, where I came into contact with René Redzepi. The culinary chemistry between my products and René was considerable and his enthusiasm stimulated my continued rediscovery of tastes from the wild. To the people involved in my company, foraging as a profession has meant a lot of hard work and weekly deliveries to Copenhagen but it has also given us many precious hours in the forests and on the beaches of our beautiful province. Among our current selection of more than 30 wild products, there is one herb that holds a special place in my heart.

During the mild winters of the early years, I foraged for Yellow Archangel (*Lamiastrum galeobdolon*) among magnificent columns of Beech (*Fagus sylvatica*) and as dusk fell over the forest, roe deer (*Capreolus capreolus*) frequently joined me at a distance. These gastronomes often just pick the very best shoot of a plant before moving on to a different taste, utilizing up to three quarters of available herbs depending on the season. Now that is curiosity for flavour worth aspiring to! I knew that this type of ecosystem had been providing for humans and other wildlife for thousands of years and I never felt lonely as I navigated from one natural treasure to the next. Two close relatives of the Yellow Archangel, White Deadnettle (*Lamium album*) and Purple Deadnettle (*Lamium purpureum*) were already known as herbaceous delicacies. Deadnettles do well with scallops or flatfish and René created a dish combining Yellow Archangel with blood sausage. These herbs were also used in sweeter contexts such as in Quince (*Cydonia oblonga*) marmalade. The results were well-received and as Noma grew in reputation, *Lamiastrum* from our humble forests came to populate plates across the region. Through successful relationships with Noma, many wild herbs now have the attention of the gastronomic world and they have made a contribution to establishing Copenhagen as the deepest taproot of the New Scandinavian Kitchen/Nordic Cookery/Nordic Cuisine.'

'Wild' as a theme and a source of inspiration for chefs involves different techniques aside from wild gathering to ensure a stable supply. Beyond the image of collecting rare species from the wild, cultivating wild plants within agricultural food systems is not yet fully acknowledged (Luczaj et al., 2012).

Prior to the dawn of agriculture, 'weeds' as we know them did not exist as such (Harlan, 1992). After all, the category of 'weeds' is much more cultural than botanical, as evidenced by the varying value of these plants as either unwanted pests or desired herbs. The same wild plants can be seen both as a detriment to agricultural systems and demanding removal, and as an edible and delicious resource – depending on history, culture and the individual forager. Although highly dependent on species, some wild plants can be semi-domesticated for commercial use. Some farmers and gardeners, such as Søren Wiuff and Søren Espersen in Denmark, produce food in this grey area between 'wild' and 'cultivated', letting wild plants grow alongside planted crops, and transplanting wild species into fields without selecting seed. Here the United Kingdom's leading professional forager recounts his experience with the inclusion of a wild resource in the broader agricultural paradigm.

### Wild Idea #3:   United Kingdom – searching for fat hen (*Chenopodium album*)

#### *Miles Irving – Forager Ltd.*

The search for uses for our edible wild plants is a bit like the Greek god Janus, with one face to the future and one face to the past. We look back to see where plants have been used in the past, and this can provide a starting point for using them now. However, it is not a process of nostalgic primitivism that limits us to these historic uses. With all the resources of our contemporary cosmopolitan context at our disposal, we can forge a future that develops the possibilities of these plants beyond only what has been done before. We have techniques, technology and the ability to learn and communicate far beyond those our ancestors possessed. With this in mind, we are presently exploring the possibilities of various edible weed seeds with a strong history of use, but a future of use that we believe is even stronger.

This year we have homed in on fat hen (*Chenopodium album*), a plant whose place in the culture of rural Suffolk was strong enough to give its name – '*melde*' – to several towns and villages, for example Milden and Melbourne (the original Melbourne being a Cambridgeshire village). Seeds of fat hen have been found in the stomach of several of the mummified peat bog men as well as on many sites of ancient settlement (Glob, 1969). However, the culture of using edible weeds along with the crop they share ground with has long since disappeared in Europe, despite being alive and well in most parts of the world where subsistence farming is still practised. For a farmer, fat hen, with its ability to produce as many as 50,000 seeds from a single plant, is public enemy #1. Yet fat hen shares the nutritional profile of its South American cousin quinoa (from which it is virtually indistinguishable to the untrained eye prior to flowering), having very high levels of calcium, vitamin A and protein. Farmers invest considerable resources trying to get rid of it, which only goes to prove its superior vitality as compared to the much less resilient cultivars with which it competes for ground. We think it wiser to work with the one that flourishes in spite of opposition!

This year we have harvested 20kg or so of ripe fat hen seeds. There are challenges with the processing of them – the seed coats are heavy in saponins, the removal of which demands repeated washings. At least some of what remains of this black outer coating should probably also be removed to allow the seed to swell, as mechanically prepared quinoa does, when cooked. But these are mere technical problems. It may be that fat hen seeds were abandoned precisely because earlier technologies could not solve these problems efficiently, so that large grass grains such as wheat and rye came to predominate. With all the technical tools available to us now, however, we are sure that processing fat hen seed quickly and efficiently will be just a matter of tracking down the right equipment and techniques. The first part of the processing is already happening: every year tons of fat hen seed gets processed through combine harvesters where it occurs as a weed in organic grain crops. Some of this gets sold as bird seed but often it is thrown away. This is a momentous step because we are edging a food production system back towards the wild by purposefully including a wild resource in the agricultural regime. This act, even just for this plant, has global implications: either fat hen or one of its close relatives is a prolific weed on every continent. The potential is vast.

Wild edible plant species grow within a diverse array of terrestrial and aquatic ecosystems. While these ecosystems are often defined by their resiliency, human pressures such as overharvesting, unsustainable forestry practices, introduction of invasive species and urbanization affect the biodiversity and population dynamics of wild edible plants (Heywood, 1999). As another example, Pavlos Georgiadis explains the importance of the wild edible golden orchid in Yunnan Province and the threat of overharvesting and habitat destruction.

## *Wild Idea #4:*   China – the wild edible golden orchid

### *Pavlos Georgiadis*

Orchids (*Orchidaceae*) are the largest plant family, comprised of more than 40,000 known species. Several orchid species are traded as ornamental plants by virtue of their wide diversity of conspicuous floral patterns and arrangements. Many species from several genera have been used for a long time in the preparation of herbal treatments, especially in traditional Chinese medicine (Ye and Zhao, 2002) and Ayurveda (Georgiadis, 2007). Ethnobotanical research in Xishuangbanna of Yunnan Province in China has revealed that orchids might have more to offer than just a showy image and medicinal properties, but also are elements of indigenous food culture, what can be called 'ethnogastronomy'.

Embodying the powerful spirit of nature, life, balance and love, the 'golden orchid' (*Dendrobium chrysotoxum*) possesses the rare ability to induce the balance between yin and yang, a natural duality forming the guiding philosophical principle in traditional Chinese medicine. This beautiful epiphyte has thus become highly sought after, with its stems corresponding to the (*Herba dendrobii*), the most commonly used herbal material in Chinese medicine (Li et al., 2005). These stems are still dried and sucked as cough drops as they are believed to induce the production of body fluids and to strengthen the immune system.

A rare 'golden tea' is also prepared from the flowers of *D. chrysotoxum*, which are carefully harvested from its bright-yellow racemes, followed by sun-drying. A dozen dried flowers are infused into a glass of hot water and drained three times to yield a golden-yellowish concoction with a smooth texture and warm, woody flavour reminiscent of wild forest honey. A larger dosage of flowers yields a stronger concoction with a more intense taste, while the dehydrated flowers can be ingested directly, in salads or preserved in marmalades. This special tea is prescribed by local healers to lower blood pressure, strengthen the immune system, enhance reproduction capacity, and to induce a calm sleep, free of bad dreams. Recent studies have revealed an array of beneficial substances present in this orchid (Gong et al., 2004; Yang et al., 2004), especially polysaccharide with anti-oxidant, anti-hyperglycemic and immune stimulation properties (Zhao et al., 2007).

Overharvesting due to high demand as well as habitat destruction from ecologically ill-conceived development activities in this global biodiversity hotspot (Myers et al., 2000) are threatening the existence of *D. chrysotoxum*. Once abundant in the wild, its occurrence is now limited, growing in support structures atop traditional homes in tropical forest communities around the Mekong River basin in southern China, Thailand and Myanmar. Scientific evidence and increased recognition for its anti-diabetic properties may hold the key for the conservation of this beautiful orchid. Research and development in emerging fields of gastronomy for the creation of premium products based on edible *D. chrysotoxum* should aim for the valorization of its organoleptic and medicinal properties in innovative food concepts. A moderate demand from high-end gastronomy can be met by sustainable production through tissue culture inside the orchid's natural habitat, as part of adapted agroforestry systems and/or recovery initiatives for restoring native biodiversity in the tropical mountain forests of Xishuangbanna and neighbouring regions.

This research was funded by the Faculty of Agricultural Sciences, University of Hohenheim and the Fiat Panis Foundation, Ulm, Germany. Thanks are due to the TianZi Biodiversity Research & Development Center, Jinghong.

The case by Pavlos Georgiadis brings to our mind that wild edible plants are not just edible but they also can have an ornamental function and be valued for medicinal properties, which are deeply embedded into local culture. However, this multiple function can increase demand and threaten the wild population. Setting up sustainable harvesting standards in combination with breeding and domestication, therefore, can ensure future supply and protection of some species, which are under pressure.

## Conclusion

The untamed and fluid nature of 'wild' foods brings a myriad of flavours, textures and aromas that represent the seasonality and biodiversity of different regions. Wild plants have always comprised an important component of traditional diets, and continue to do so in many countries. These wild foods are uniquely adapted to specific agro-ecological niches, do not require inputs such as fertilizers to grow, and often have multiple uses (Jaenicke and Höschle-Zeledon, 2006).

With an increasing interest from leading chefs, as well as consumers, many wild foods are undergoing an important revalorization. The establishment of strong relationships between chefs and foragers helps to preserve, record, spread and build upon traditional knowledge, as well as to tell a story through specific gastronomic experiences. Nonetheless, the increased interest in wild foods must go hand-in-hand with sustainable harvesting practices in order to conserve wild populations. It is thus of crucial importance that the value of these resources becomes more deeply understood – allowing gastronomic enterprises to continue exploring the potential of these diverse and delicious wild resources while ensuring that they continue to thrive in the ecologies where they originate.

## References

Bharucha, Z. and Pretty, J. (2010) 'The roles and values of wild foods in agricultural systems', *Philosophical Transactions of the Royal Society B*, 365(1554): 2913–2926.
FAO (2004) *Wild Edible Fungi: A Global Overview of their Use and Importance to People*, Rome: FAO.
Fischler, C. (1988) 'Food, self, identity', *Social Science Information*, 27(2): 275–293.
Georgiadis, P. (2007) *Local Plant Knowledge for Livelihoods: An Ethnobotanical Survey in the Garhwal Himalaya, Uttarakhand, India*, Weikersheim: Margraf Publishers.
Glob, P.V. (1969) *The Bog People: Iron-Age Man Preserved*, New York: Faber and Faber.
Gong Y.Q., Fan, Y., Wu, D.Z., Yang, H., Hu, Z.B. and Wang, Z.T. (2004) 'In vivo and in vitro evaluation of erianin, a novel anti-angiogenic agent', *European Journal of Cancer*, 40(10): 1554–1565.
Grivetti, L.E. and Ogle, B.M. (2000) 'Value of traditional foods in meeting macro- and micronutrient needs: the wild plant connection', *Nutrition Research Reviews*, 13: 31–46.
Hall, C. (2013) 'Why forage when you don't have to? Personal and cultural meaning in recreational foraging: a New Zealand study', *Journal of Heritage Tourism*, 8(2–3): 224–233.
Hall, C., Sharples, L., Mitchell, R., Macionis, N. and Cambourne, B. (eds.) (2003) *Food Tourism Around the World: Development, Management and Markets*, Oxford: Butterworth Heinemann.
Harlan, J.R. (1992) *Crops & Man*, 2nd edn, Madison, WI: American Society of Agronomy, Crop Science Society of America, Inc.
Heywood, V. (1999) *Use and Potential of Wild Plants in Farm Households*, FAO Farm Systems Management Series 15, Rome, Italy: FAO.
Jaenicke, H. and Höschle-Zeledon, I. (2006) *Strategic Framework for Underutilized Plant Species Research and Development*, Rome: ICUC, Colombo and Global Facilitation Unit for Underutilized Species.
Leonti, M., Nebel, S., Rivera, D. and Heinrich, M. (2006) 'Wild gathered food plants in the European Mediterranean: a comparative analysis', *Journal of Economic Botany*, 60(2): 130–142.
Li, T., Wang, J. and Lu, Z. (2005) 'Accurate identification of closely related *Dendrobium* species with multiple species-specific gDNA probes', *Journal of Biochemical & Biophysical Methods*, 62: 111–123.

Luczaj, L., Pieroni, A., Tardío, J., Pardo-de-Santayana, M., Sõukand, R., Svanberg, I. and Kalle, R. (2012) 'Wild food plant use in 21st century Europe: the disappearance of old traditions and the search for new cuisines involving wild edibles', *Acta Societatis Botanicorum Poloniae*, 81(4): 359–370.

Maurizio, A. (1927) *Die Geschichte unserer Nahrungspflanzen*, Berlin: Von den Urzeiten bis zur Gegenwart. Verlagsbuchhandlung Paul Parey.

Myers, N., Mittermeier, R.A., Mittermeier, C.G., da Fonseca, G.A.B. and Kent, J. (2000) 'Biodiversity hotspots for conservation priorities', *Nature*, 403: 853–858.

Oxford English Dictionary (2013) 'Foraging', www.oxforddictionaries.com/definition/english/forage (accessed 5 November 2013).

Sims, R. (2009) 'Food, place and authenticity: local food and the sustainable tourism experience', *Journal of Sustainable Tourism*, 17(3): 321–336.

Slikkerveer, L. (1994) *Indigenous Agricultural Knowledge Systems in developing Countries: A Bibliography*, Indigenous Knowledge Systems Research and Development Studies No. 1. Special Issue: INDAKS Project Report 1 in collaboration with the European Commission DG XII. Leiden Ethnosystems and Development Programme (LEAD).

Timothy, D.J. and Amos, S.R. (2013) 'Understanding heritage cuisines and tourism: identity, image, authenticity, and change', *Journal of Heritage Tourism*, 8(2–3): 99–104.

Yang, H., Chou, G.X., Wang, Z.T., Hu, Z.B. and Xu, L.S. (2004) 'Two new fluorenones from *Dendrobium chrysotoxum*', *Journal of Asian Natural Products Research*, 6(1): 35–38.

Ye, Q.H. and Zhao, W.M. (2002) 'New alloaromadendrane, cadinene and cyclocopacamphane type sesquiterpene derivatives and bibenzyle from *Dendrobium nobile*', *Planta Medica*, 68: 723–729.

Zhao, Y., Son, Y.O., Kim, S.S., Jang, Y.S. and Lee, J.C. (2007) 'Antioxidant and anti-hyperglycemic activity of polysaccharide isolated from *Dendrobium chrysotoxum* Lindl', *Journal of Biochemistry & Molecular Biology*, 40(5): 670–677.

# 20

# FOODS FROM AQUACULTURE

## Varied and growing

*Ricardo Radulovich*

## Introduction

Thousands of years ago hunting and gathering evolved into agriculture, a most powerful, controlled food-production strategy that greatly enhanced the natural productivity of the land. Nowadays aquaculture, already a global industry with far-reaching international trade, is becoming the evolution from just fishing and recollecting in the aquatic environment towards more controlled aquatic food production. This is happening as a response to dwindling fisheries and increasing demand for aquatic food. Of course, this change of paradigm is afforded by technology and as problems and opportunities arise, scientific and engineering solutions allow the continuous growth of the industry—to yet unpredictable levels.

The sustainability of this rapid growth of aquaculture varies among the different production options. Although naturally the eco-friendliness of producing filter-feeding shellfish and seaweed at sea is very high, effects on environment and biodiversity from large and intensive fish and shrimp farming operations can be significant. Also, there are threats from external variables, among them climate change, including ocean acidification, but also freshwater shortages and limited supply of fishing catch that is used in feed. Yet the industry is striving to guarantee its sustainability, realizing the implications of growth in a changing world, controlling its own negative externalities and promoting positive ones, while moving some operations offshore, developing new feeds and clean production technologies, and establishing standards and certifications that guarantee best practices and product quality. These issues will be discussed throughout this chapter and a final section contains key references and links to sites dealing with sustainability and certification.

Unlike agriculture, which almost totally replaced hunting and gathering, given the vast expanses of the ocean and of some lakes, as well as the myriad of freshwater bodies that are traditionally fished, at least for the time being fishing and recollecting from the aquatic environment will continue until eventually, perhaps, controlled food production through aquaculture will largely overtake the more unpredictable fishing and recollection—which, together, are known as 'capture'—from the sea and other water bodies.

In fact, what may well happen, and is already happening, is that fisheries themselves will evolve towards incorporating or even becoming one or more forms of aquaculture. An example of this are current methods of aquaculture-assisted fisheries, which consist of releasing laboratory-raised or laboratory-manipulated fish fingerlings, lobster juveniles, or bivalve seeds to restock populations that eventually will be captured (or recaptured)—in a sort of sea ranching. The other way around, fisheries-assisted aquaculture is in fact a major form of aquaculture whereby juveniles of some species (that are hard to reproduce or to be raised from larvae) are captured and grown in controlled conditions such as cages or ponds. Such is the case for, for example, milkfish, tuna, eel, and spiny lobster farming.

Other major aspects of this food-production revolution are that close to 85 percent of world aquaculture is produced in Asia, particularly in China (De Silva and Davy, 2010), and while 87 percent of capture fisheries (of which 85 percent is fish) is marine and only 13 percent inland, this is not the case in aquaculture, where 70 percent is inland fish or freshwater production and only 30 percent of production is marine, of which 76 percent is of mollusks (FAO, 2012). In the case of seaweeds, which are often treated separately from fisheries and aquaculture, although their harvest from the natural environment is recollection and their cultivation is a type of aquaculture, close to 99 percent of the—rapidly growing—production comes from only seven Asian countries. All this indicates, among other considerations, that there is extraordinary room for growth outside of Asia, that mollusks, crustaceans, and seaweeds are becoming far more available, and that freshwater fish will continue to dominate markets, at least for some years to come—something that renders the term "seafood" inappropriate and favors the term "aquatic food," leaving "seafood" for the increasingly more expensive true food from the sea, whether captured or cultured.

A distinction between capture and cultured fish production may also be in order, particularly for marine fishes since long-favored properties such as flavor, meat firmness, and oil content may differ significantly. For example, in controlled-feeding conditions, salmon do not naturally develop a typical flesh color and must be fed with colorants. A similar case may be made for meat firmness and even its red color for active swimmers like tuna, which is not fully developed in controlled conditions. This, coupled to some limitations to the expansion of marine fish farming, which will be discussed below, indicate that choice-captured marine fishes, such as tuna, sea bass, grouper, snapper, and others, may become increasingly more costly products. However, this may be offset, at least partly, as captured seafood becomes more under scrutiny for a variety of reasons, including limitations in traceability given the fact that it is almost impossible to know what fish have eaten and thus accumulated without testing.

World fisheries' capture of fish, mollusks, crustaceans, and other creatures, grew to circa 90 million tons (MT) around 1990 and has stagnated since then, particularly in the marine sector. The FAO (2012) considers that 87 percent of the world's fishing stocks are either fully (57 percent) or over- (30 percent) exploited. As a response to this, animal aquaculture grew at a rate of 8.8 percent per year since 1970 from 2.6 MT to 66.7 MT in 2012, when it reached 73 percent of the tonnage produced by capture (Table 20.1). In fact, it is considered that, in a few years, overall fish food production via aquaculture will surpass that from fisheries.

Mollusk production via aquaculture (Table 20.1), which is mostly marine bivalves, has more than doubled that from capture, while crustaceans and others (like sea urchins) are already similar in quantities between capture and aquaculture. In the years to come, supply of marine mollusks, crustaceans, and others from aquaculture will continue to grow and dominate the market, abundantly providing the commonly consumed oysters and shrimps as well as many other species.

However, the situation is far from static and both freshwater and marine aquacultures are evolving fast, in a rather fierce competition with other food sectors and under heavy attack from environmental and biodiversity concerns. For example, Duarte et al. (2008) describe the recent domestication of hundreds of freshwater and marine animals and marine plants,

*Table 20.1* Comparison between capture and aquaculture production (data in million tons)

| Group | 1970 | | | 2012 | | |
|---|---|---|---|---|---|---|
| | *Capture* | *Aquaculture* | *% aquac./capture* | *Capture* | *Aquaculture* | *% aquac./capture* |
| Fin fish | 50.6 | 1.5 | 3.0 | 77.5 | 44.2 | 56.9 |
| Mollusks | 2.7 | 1.1 | 40.7 | 6.9 | 15.2 | 219.7 |
| Crustaceans | 1.9 | 0.01 | 0.5 | 6.3 | 6.5 | 103.7 |
| Other | 0.2 | 0.0 | 0.0 | 0.6 | 0.8 | 133.3 |
| Total | 55.4 | 2.6 | 4.7 | 91.3 | 66.7 | 73.0 |
| | Harvested | Cultivated | % | Harvested | Cultivated | % |
| Seaweeds | 0.9 | 1.0 | 108.6 | 0.8 | 20.9 | 2635.2 |

Data from FAO (www.fao.org/fishery/topic/16140/en).

and the FAO (2012) states that about 600 aquatic species are raised in captivity, including frogs and reptiles, in about 190 countries. This large variation, of course, places importance on paying attention to the different species being produced and marketed, perhaps expecting that as the industry and markets mature there will be a reduction in the number of species being cultured, leaving fewer "winners" or predominant species. Or perhaps not, and variation will continue to cater for ever growing sophisticated markets. As already evidenced for major groups in Table 20.1, production through aquaculture for some individual species is also much higher than their capture counterpart. For example, aquaculture supplies almost 100 percent of the total production of Atlantic salmon and oysters.

The often-forgotten dark horse of aquaculture is seaweed cultivation, yet it may soon grow to become the main form of aquatic food production (because seaweeds, just as crops on land, are, through biosynthesis, the true producers of food, while animals really only transform existing food—albeit into a higher quality). With an exponential rate of growth, in which tropical countries have grown the fastest in the past two decades, already 21 MT of fresh seaweeds are produced in the world via cultivation, representing 96 percent of the world's production of seaweeds, compared to 0.8 MT harvested from the wild. In 1970 production via cultivation was equivalent to that from harvest, yet in 2012 cultivated production was 26 times that from natural harvests (Table 20.1). Thus, with seaweeds in particular, aquaculture is making the strongest difference between captured and cultured. According to Chopin (2012: 24), "The use of seaweeds as sea vegetables for direct human consumption [represents] 76% of the tonnage and 88% of the value." Yet this is not the case for tropical seaweed cultivation, which is still mostly for hydrocolloids, with recent efforts toward their use as food (e.g., Lee, 2008; Radulovich et al., 2013).

Besides the many achievements and the extremely large potential, there are, of course, many problems related to aquaculture that must be considered, yet most of these pertain to aquatic food production in general, whether natural or partly controlled. Given the nature of the aquatic environment, water and whatever is dissolved or suspended in it (e.g., chemicals, microbes, silt) travels with waves, tides, and currents. Aquaculture, however, since it normally entails keeping what is being produced in one place, while feeding it and caring for it, allows for better traceability and control than fisheries. Even little- or non-moving animals like bivalves are subjected to moving waters that require constant monitoring to know what they brought with them. Complete control through intensive, self-contained recirculating aquaculture systems makes a difference in this respect—yet, to an extent, this takes the "zest" away.

Among undesirable situations, toxins in the marine environment, produced, for example, by dinoflagellates that cause ciguatera (ciguatoxins and others) or by some phytoplankton blooms (e.g., red tides) must be considered as they accumulate permanently in carnivorous fishes (up the trophic chain) and temporarily in filter feeders like bivalves, respectively. In freshwater environments, although not excluding marine ones, parasites and pathogens that affect humans find ideal vectors in fish and plants. Adding to chemical contaminants from industry and agriculture, heavy metals from natural sources prove a concern. Besides mercury, which accumulates in fish oil, arsenic—common in waters near volcanoes—can accumulate in aquatic organisms, including, for example, clams that inhabit muddy bottoms (like the geoduck clam, *Panopea generosa*, from the Pacific Northwest of the USA) and some seaweeds (like hijiki, a species of *Sargassum* from the coasts of Japan). Spoilage from poor post-harvest handling of produce, normally a problem in fisheries related to the time elapsed from catch to port and to poor facilities aboard, is far more controlled in aquaculture since harvest can be better synchronized with rapid and even live transport to adequate processing and storage plants. Also, in general, harvest and slaughter from aquaculture tends to be more humane than what many fisheries offer.

Increases in greenhouse gases, besides indirectly raising ocean temperature and promoting sea-level rise, directly promote ocean acidification, which decreases the strength of the calcareous shell of mollusks—something that is already affecting production in many sites. These processes may emphasize the shift from fisheries into aquaculture for a variety of species in order to maintain and increase supply, since species to be farmed can be largely chosen and established according to varying conditions. Complementarily, aquaculture may implement some measures designed to counteract these effects, such as, for example, shifting production to less-affected areas and providing an adequate environment during the initial stages of bivalve development for proper shell-setting.

In general, implementation of good practices, usually as part of certification programs that aim at guaranteeing the quality and safety of aquatic foods, is gaining importance. These programs range from registering aquatic production to the most advanced certifications, such as best practices, HACCP, organic, and kosher (e.g., to be kosher, fish species must have both fins and scales, therefore all other aquatic animals like catfish, eels, shrimps, and oysters, as well as sturgeon's caviar, are not), and can be public and/or private. Some of the major organizations and programs related to aquaculture and certification are referenced at the end of this chapter.

Compliance with a variety of other requirements, some of which reflect societal trends, can also be of relevance to aquaculture products, similar to when tuna fisheries had to adapt to exclude dolphins, and shrimp fisheries now adapt to excluding turtles and abandoning bottom trawling. One factor that leads to criticism of the culture of carnivore fishes such as salmon and tuna, as well as other marine and even choice freshwater species and crustaceans, is that their feeds are largely based on fish meal and oil, for which a sizable share of capture fisheries is devoted (indeed, turning them into luxury products). While fish meal can be more easily replaced with other sources of protein, to date fish oil has proven irreplaceable if quality of fish meat is to be maintained—although important efforts are being made to achieve substitution. The main problem is that substituting fish meal and oil in aquaculture feed may lead to these fish and shrimp being so different to the point of having a significantly different nutrition profile than their wild counterparts (e.g., see Toppe et al., 2012; Bowyer et al., 2013). This issue is threatening the sustainability of this branch of the industry.

An interesting spin-off from this situation is that fish oil from forage fish and krill (a shrimp) are being offered as nutritional supplements on their own, rich with omega 3s and antioxidants and free of bioaccumulation of mercury and other contaminants suffered by high trophic level fish. Oil from microalgae is also being used in this manner.

The use of chemicals and pharmacological products to produce fish (like hormones, antibiotics and parasiticides) is a significant concern that must be more openly publicized. Another important issue is whether species being cultured are native or not, or of too-narrow a genetic makeup, or even if they have been genetically modified, since their inevitable escape can affect native biodiversity. Overall, green or eco-friendly aquaculture, although more costly, is better positioned, particularly for higher markets.

Thus, as capture dwindles, controlled food production in aquatic environments is undergoing rapid evolutionary processes to complement and even substitute fisheries to a large degree. Of course, in many ways, products from aquaculture are not the same as those from fisheries, and this entails an adaptation challenge to the food industry. Many of the limitations regarding the choice of species being farmed or, rather, not farmed, have to do mainly with the inability to reproduce the species, at least with the regularity and reliability needed to establish a farming operation. As these limitations and others are slowly overcome, more species with high market demand are beginning to be farmed on significant scales, to the point where economic factors will become the major determinant. In the meantime, of course, production will continue to be dominated by those species that are easy to reproduce or their reproduction has already been mastered, like most of the freshwater fishes. Reproduction, and with it farming, of several marine species like salmon and many bivalves has already been mastered.

On the other hand, capture of juveniles or seed from the wild affords considerable—although in most cases limited—farming, as is the case for eels, tuna, and lobster. The culture of milkfish (*Chanos chanos*) in onshore ponds and waterways, however, traditionally conducted in Asia by capturing millions of fingerlings from the coastal sea, is an example of a sizable aquaculture option that developed without mastering reproduction—although currently great effort is being devoted to mastering milkfish reproduction in order to guarantee sustainability.

It is, however, important to consider that aquaculture is, overall, a young industry that is constantly striving to improve and adapt. Therefore, what may be true today can rapidly change, so far usually for the best. Excellent examples of this are the appearance of newcoming species, in both marine and freshwater environments. While most farmed fish species grow at rates of around 1kg/year or even less, newcomer cobia (*Rachycentron canadum*), a tropical marine fish, can grow up to 4kg/year. A freshwater species from the Amazon, *Arapaima gigas*, can grow much faster (reputedly, up to 20kg/year) and is becoming an important substitute for other freshwater species. All of this, of course, must be at some point compared to animal production on land. For example, chicken grow to 3kg in six weeks, explaining some differences in prices. On the other hand, as some problems are being identified, like the cases of arsenic accumulation or ocean acidification mentioned above, it is important for those involved in aquatic food products to keep abreast of developments.

After these introductory notes, the rest of this chapter is devoted to describing in some more detail the main and most interesting species being farmed within each major group. After that follows a brief section of concluding remarks describing current developments, some of which may determine the future of the industry.

## Fish

As pointed out, the major difference to date is that the most common fish being cultured are freshwater species produced in freshwater ponds, although increasingly intensively in tanks and caged in large water bodies such as lakes. A reason for this is that aquaculture began in freshwater. Comparatively, considering reproduction, management, feed requirements, and harvest, it is far easier to produce fish in freshwater ponds than at sea.

As seen in Table 20.2, three types of freshwater fish dominate production worldwide: carps, tilapias, and catfishes. Most production comes from Asia and their price is comparatively low—although some tend to be marketed at higher prices. However, to any fish connoisseur, their taste and other characteristics are rather bland, yet this freshwater fish production satisfies the most basic market demands for fish meat.

An important characteristic of the main cultured freshwater fish species is that they are mostly of low to medium trophic level—omnivorous and some even herbivores or to a degree filter feeders—so their feed is often low cost and to a large extent produced *in situ* (through fertilization of ponds, adding chemical fertilizers or agricultural residues that promote the growth of plankton and from that a vigorous trophic chain, something called "green water"

*Table 20.2* Main or most interesting fish species in aquaculture.

**Freshwater**

Carps: family *Cyprinidae*, several species: silver, grass, common, bighead, and rohu carps.

Tilapias: several species, main one being farmed is Nile tilapia, *Oreochromis niloticus*; others, *Tilapia* spp.

Catfishes: important species, pangasiid or pangasius catfishes (*Pangasius* spp., *Pangasianodon* sp.), channel catfish (*Ictalurus punctatus*) and European catfish (*Silurus glanis*).

Other interesting groups of freshwater fishes are:

Trout (several species, among them the rainbow trout, *Oncorhynchus mykiss*), relatively important in colder freshwater production.

Sturgeons (family *Acipenseridae*, at least two important genera, *Acipenser* spp. and *Huso* spp.), which are also a subtropical to colder water group of slowly growing species (taking from five to eight years to reach maturity), produced both for meat and for their roe, which is made into caviar. Their aquaculture is growing and already caviar prices have fallen to about a third of their past peak. Some expect that in a few years close to 100 percent of the world's caviar will be from aquaculture.

Arapaima (*Arapaima gigas*), mentioned above, a fast-growing species from the Amazon, is gaining terrain.

Barramundi or Asian seabass (*Lates calcarifer*), produced in Asia, Australia and New Zealand, both in freshwater and seawater.

Eels (*Anguilla* spp.), the farming of which is growing, even though due to their complex lifecycle they are not bred in hatcheries but they are recollected from the wild in an early stage known as glass eel for the stocking of aquaculture ponds or recirculating tanks.

**Seawater**

Salmon[1] (Atlantic salmon, *Salmo salar*, also Pacific and Coho salmons, *Oncorhynchus* spp.).

Milkfish (*Chanos chanos*), produced mostly in Asia.

Cobia (*Rachycentron canadum*), a tropical species that is gaining terrain.

Tuna (*Thunnus* spp.), several species are being farmed, both bluefin and yellowfin, capturing juveniles and raising them in pens at sea. Breeding efforts are under way.

Grouper (several genera in the subfamily *Epinephelinae*, mainly *Epinephelus* spp.), there is already a long tradition of farming groupers in Asia and other regions.

Grey mullet (*Mugil cephalus*), traditionally grown in onshore ponds.

Several other species, including snappers, sea bass and sea bream.

The FAO provides factsheets on 64 cultured aquatic species at www.fao.org/fishery/culturedspecies/search/en.

aquaculture (see Neori, 2011)). Thus (excepting tilapia in intensive production) they do not require to any large extent fish meal and oil in their diet as carnivores do. In that sense freshwater fish production is quite sustainable, and several advanced production, harvest, and postharvest techniques make it financially viable as well—including, for example, the all-male production techniques for tilapia.

However, since besides exchange requirements water is lost from ponds by evaporation and seepage, freshwater fish require thousands of liters of water for each kilogram produced. This very high water requirement has slowed down the expansion of freshwater aquaculture and, together with many complications arising from any large industry—including market saturation and many quality-related considerations, such as releases of polluted water from ponds—has increasingly placed freshwater aquaculture in a state of controversy. The usually unreported use of antibiotics and other chemicals in overly intensive freshwater fish production, as well as other unhygienic conditions, must be considered and reliable certifications are essential if quality is to be guaranteed.

In spite of the many limitations already discussed, marine fish production is, nonetheless, gaining momentum and technology is facilitating its growth. The main or most promising marine species being farmed to date are shown in Table 20.2, where most of them are notably carnivorous and high up in the trophic chain—mainly because of their high value that makes their costly and risky farming at sea financially viable (which is not exempt from similar problems to freshwater aquaculture, such as, for example, parasites). Exceptions to the carnivore rule are traditional production of milkfish and grey mullet in onshore salt- and brackish-water ponds. Due to ease of reproduction and high market prices, the first group of marine species to be grown in caged farming directly at sea was salmon (mainly Atlantic salmon, but others as well, like Pacific and Coho salmons). Many attempts have followed with other species, yet to date reproduction and high-quality feed remain a limiting factor. Although reproduction has been achieved to a large extent beyond doubt for a few species (e.g., cobia mentioned above, groupers and others like snappers), some marine fish farming operations rely entirely on the capture of juveniles from the wild—being in that sense a "fattening" or ranching operation. Tuna is a good example of this, although efforts to reproduce them are under way.

Besides active research towards finding suitable oils to replace that from fish in feed, perhaps from seaweeds or even from microalgae, a tendency may be to culture "down the trophic chain" (analogous to "fishing down the trophic chain"), growing omnivores, "forage" fish like filter feeding sardines, anchovies, and menhaden, and herbivore fishes like rabbit fish, instead of the more tasty and nutritionally superb yet very expensive, although perhaps unsustainable, carnivores like salmon and tuna.

While for several reasons marine aquacultured choice fish and even crustaceans may differ in several characteristics from their natural counterparts, this is not at all the case for bivalves, which get their feed from passing water. Size is another concern. For example, many aquacultured fish species are grown to a minimal profitable size, like plate-sized, harvesting as soon as possible in order to decrease risk and guarantee profit. On the other hand, besides being stagnated or dwindling, so their continued supply at best will remain similar to present levels, marine fisheries are not without quality problems that go well beyond poor post-harvest handling. A balance is certainly hard to achieve and a dynamic posture on fish will guarantee the best choices.

## Crustaceans

Production of marine crustaceans through aquaculture has grown in the last years to the point that it has now surpassed capture. It has centered for decades now on shrimp farming in onshore ponds with sea- or brackish water. Catering mainly to USA, European, and Japanese markets, this industry grew mostly in Asia and Latin America to an annual production of 6.5 MT in 2012, already 103.7 percent that of capture crustacean fisheries which have stagnated at around 6 MT since 1998 (Table 20.1).

Most crustacean aquaculture is based on two species of marine shrimps, *Penaeus vannamei* (Pacific white shrimp) and *Penaeus monodon* (giant tiger prawn). Both belong to the *Penaeidae* family, from which several other *Penaeus* species are also farmed (like the Indian white shrimp, *Penaeus indicus*), some in growing quantities.

Given the size of the industry, shrimp farming in many thousands of hectares of onshore ponds has been related to several environmental problems. To begin with, it has been established by destroying mangrove forests and other natural coastal formations (something for which there is probably no way back). The other major environmental problem is the disposal of effluent waters loaded with nutrients and organic matter. While also plagued by production variability due to diseases that can wipe out entire areas, as well as toxins that may develop in pond water, the industry is evolving towards certified better farming practices and growing more in intensive production than in new farming areas. That, together with the alternative of farming shrimp in cages at sea that has been recently developed (e.g., Radulovich, 2010), coupled to an increased interest in growing shrimp in tanks using recirculating methodologies (something that allows the industry to be established in just about any location), guarantees a stable and growing supply of shrimp.

Moreover, improved shrimp-farming techniques allow the production of larger shrimp, since limitations in size have normally been due to poor conditions related to crowding and low oxygen in onshore ponds.

Aquaculture of crabs, mainly also in onshore ponds with sea- or brackish water, is in second place in importance, although far less sizable than shrimp. Besides the sturdiness of the crab and fast growth rates for meat, this has the incentive of the soft-shell crab upper-end market, and the supply is growing. Crab species being cultured include the blue crab (*Callinectes sapidus*) and the mud crab (*Scylla serrata*). Some freshwater crabs are also produced but in limited amounts.

Lobster aquaculture is placed in a distant third place, limited because of complicated reproduction from complex developmental stages. Spiny lobster (*Panulirus* spp.) is being produced in cages or ponds, taking juveniles from the wild. Ongoing efforts allow that lobster aquaculture may become more common in the future, not only as reproduction in hatcheries develops, but also as restocking efforts increase opportunities to obtain juveniles from targeted areas.

There is considerable farming of freshwater prawns, mainly the giant river prawn, *Macrobrachium rosenbergii*, grown mainly in China but other places as well, such as in the USA.

## Mollusks

The surprising winners in animal aquaculture, so far and compared to their captured counterpart, have been marine mollusks (*phylum Mollusca*), particularly bivalves (order *Bivalvia*) like mussels and oysters, though there are other important *Mollusca* groups described below. As indicated earlier, close to 100 percent of the oysters being marketed worldwide come from marine aquaculture—most of it directly at sea—and the trend continues with sophisticated techniques (such as, for example, triploid and tetraploid oysters). Although some freshwater bivalves are cultured, this is an extremely small fraction compared to marine production.

Historically for centuries cultured in Europe, as seen in Table 20.1, already in 1970 mollusk culture at sea represented 40.7 percent of what was recollected from the wild (1.1 over 2.7 MT), while in 2012 the aquacultured tonnage of mollusks more than doubled what is recollected (15.2 over 6.9 MT). This is largely due to a combination of ease of reproduction (in some cases, like with mussels, it only requires keeping ropes near spat fall areas where they get covered with juveniles that settle on them) and of farming (including the advantage that they are mostly immobile), greatly aided by the fact that bivalves don't need to be fed since they are filter-feeders—indeed lowering costs and simplifying an operation. All these great advantages lead to this branch of the industry growing, with many species being produced (described in Table 20.3), and it will probably be some time until the market saturates. What used to be expensive oysters and other bivalves are becoming far more common and affordable.

Important issues already mentioned are that bivalves, as filter-feeders, will also take in a variety of contaminants that may accumulate, some permanently, others temporarily. Another issue also discussed above is that ocean acidification is making it hard for mollusks to construct their calcareous shells. The main point, however, is that the industry may have a low ceiling related to how much bivalves will be incorporated into diets in spite of price and supply—dictated by some inelasticity of demand that may have to be modified.

Aquatic gastropods are another major branch of the *Mollusca* phylum. They are called univalves or snails. Although there are many freshwater species, some of which are edible and a few are cultured (like the applesnail, *Pomacea canaliculata*, considered an invasive pest),

*Table 20.3* Main bivalve groups and species being cultured

Mussels (family *Mytilidae*): blue mussel, *Mytilus edulis*, Mediterranean mussel, *Mytilus galloprovincialis*, and New Zealand greenshell mussel, *Perna canaliculus*, among others.

Oysters (family *Ostreidae*): particularly the Pacific or Japanese oyster, *Crassostrea gigas*, already produced in nearly 100 countries, and others like the American or Atlantic oyster, *Crassostrea virginica*, the European flat oyster, *Ostrea edulis*, and the rock oyster, *Saccostrea glomerata*.

Clams (true clams belong to the *Veneridae* family, which are "infauna" in that they live buried in mud or sand): included are hard clam, *Mercenaria mercenaria*, Manila clam, *Tapes philippinarum*, grooved-shell clam, *Ruditapes decussatus*, littleneck clam, *Protothaca staminea*, and the Japanese clam, *Venerupis japonica*.

Other "clams" (from different families but sharing the "infauna" characteristic): the sizable Pacific geoduck clam, *Panopea abrupta* (family *Hiatellidae*); the surf clam or macha, *Mesodesma donacium* (family *Mesodesmatidae*); and the large group of the razor clams (family *Pharidae*), among which the Atlantic Jackknife, *Ensis directus*, the Chinese razor clam, *Sinonovacula constricta*, the razor shell, *Ensis arcuatus*, and the pod razor, *Ensis siliqua* are cultured.

Scallops (family *Pectinidae*): with several species being cultured, such as Yesso scallop or Japanese scallop, *Patinopecten yessoensis*, the Pacific scallop, which is a hybrid, *Patinopecten caurinus* x *yessoensis*, the giant or sea scallop, *Placopecten magellanicus*, the Northern Bay Scallop, *Argopecten irradians*, the Chilean scallop, *Argopecten purpuratus*, and the great scallop, *Pecten maximus*.

Ark clams or blood cockles (family *Arcidae*): extensively cultured is the blood cockle, *Anadara granosa*, although there are several other *Anadara* spp. being farmed.

True cockles (family *Cardiidae*): some are cultured to an extent, among them the common cockle, *Cerastoderma edule* and the basket cockle, *Clinocardium nuttalli*.

the majority of the interest is on sea snails. Two gastropod seafood groups that are being cultured are the abalone (several species of the genus *Haliotis* are being farmed, from cold to tropical waters), which is gaining terrain and feeds on seaweeds, and the conch, of which the Queen conch (*Lobatus gigas*) is a major representative already being farmed in the Caribbean.

Within yet another group of *Mollusca*, the cephalopods (octopi, squids), the farming of octopus (several species of the genus *Octopus*) is proceeding at speed given high market demand, and soon there may be stable supplies of this otherwise overfished group.

## Echinoderms

The phylum *Echinodermata* is composed of marine animals of which sea urchins and sea cucumbers are being farmed due to increasing demand and thanks to the development of technology.

Sea urchin roe is a luxury food product and their culture in both cold waters (e.g., the green sea urchin, *Strongylocentrotus droebachiensis*) and tropical waters (e.g., the tropical sea urchin, *Tripneustes gratilla*) is proving easy. Moreover, they feed mostly on seaweeds, therefore in some ways lowering production costs and making them less dependent on external feed sources.

Sea cucumbers (class *Holothuroidea*), of which the harvested product is referred to as *bêche-de-mer*, have a strong market in China and, while overfishing has depleted populations, this has promoted a growing aquaculture. Interestingly, since sea cucumbers are mostly bottom-dwellers and detritus eaters, they can be grown together with other species, like in shrimp ponds or fish cages, feeding on refuse and leftovers. Several species are being produced, including the Japanese sea cucumber, *Stichopus japonicus*, the sandfish, *Holothuria scabra*, the greenfish, *Stichopus chloronotus*, and the prickly redfish, *Thelenota ananas*.

## Reptiles and amphibians

These two groups are cultured in a very limited manner, all cases in freshwater. Among them alligator farms are famous and their viability depends on production for leather and tourism rather than for meat. Another aquatic reptile being cultured for food, mainly in China, is the soft shell turtle (*Trionyx sinensis*). Within amphibians, some frog species (*Rana* spp.) are being produced for their legs, although their production in controlled conditions is difficult, in many ways due to their need to be fed live feed.

## Seaweeds (macroalgae)

A very strong newcomer into marine aquaculture and increasingly as a food is seaweeds (formally known as macroalgae, singular "macroalga"). While in 1950 cultivated tonnage was 10.4 percent of that harvested from the wild (0.03 vs. 0.33 MT), in 2012 cultivated tonnage was more than 26 times that harvested from the wild (20.9 vs. 0.8 MT), most of it used as food. While only seven countries in Asia produced 98.9 percent of the world's seaweed output, already a total of 31 countries and territories reported significant seaweed farming in 2010 (FAO, 2012). One hundred and forty-five seaweed species are known to be used for food and 101 species for hydrocolloid production (Zemke-White and Ohno, 1999). These are agar, alginate, and carrageenan, commonly used in the food industry as thickeners and for water retention (Bixler and Porse, 2011).

Classified as red, brown, and green, there are estimated to be between 8,000 and 10,000 seaweed species worldwide (Lüning, 1990; Thomas, 2002). Consumption of seaweeds by man is ancient practice. There is evidence that they were used for food and medicine more than 14,000 years ago in southern Chile (Dillehay et al., 2008). An early report from Hawaii (Reed, 1907) describes not only that "many tons of these seaweeds are gathered and eaten," but that they were cultivated by reseeding them in different locations to increase their abundance. Nutritional properties of seaweeds include high protein content of adequate digestibility and a balanced amino acid composition, polyunsaturated fatty acids, vitamins (including B12 precursor), and high fiber and mineral content (e.g., Black, 1952; McDermid and Stuercke, 2003; MacArtain et al., 2007; Matanjun et al., 2009; Van Ginneken et al., 2011).

The growing interest in cultivated seaweeds for human food has resulted in a variety of recent publications. Among these, Lee (2008), Mouritsen (2013), and Radulovich et al. (2013) describe the use of seaweeds as food, while Winberg et al. (2011), Radulovich et al. (2013), and Redmond et al. (2014) describe cultivation methods.

## Microalgae

Several microalgae types and species are being cultured worldwide for food and other uses. The activity originated with the well-known spirulina, which is a cyanobacteria also known as blue-green algae, and is now placed in the genus *Arthrospira* (*maxima* and *platensis*). Spirulina is very high in protein of adequate amino acid distribution and provides several other nutritional benefits, including high-quality oil. Other important microalgae being cultured for food or food supplements, among them polyunsaturated fat (including omega 3s) and antioxidants, are, for example, *Chlorella vulgaris* and *Dunaliella salina*. Their high productivity, however, although initially leading people to believe that they would be an answer to growing food and even fuel limitations, requires some stringent conditions that greatly increase costs. Therefore, their use as "food" in general is restricted at present, while their use as food complements and as sources of nutraceutical compounds may grow.

## Other plants

Freshwater bodies, like lakes and dams, are now eliciting increased interest for controlled food production, with caged fish aquaculture and aquaculture-assisted fisheries among them. Yet perhaps the most promising techniques are based on plants. Besides what is being termed "aquatic agriculture," growing land plants in floating conditions (related in a sense to "aquaponics," which is hydroponics using the water from controlled freshwater fish aquaculture), there are some direct efforts at cultivating aquatic plants (which like seaweeds carry the misnomer of "aquatic weeds") beyond growing them on freshwater aquaculture ponds as animal feed.

Several of these species, including some freshwater green macroalgae, tend to grow fast and have an excellent nutritional composition. In particular, water hyacinth (*Eichornia crassipes*) is the fastest growing, has a very wide distribution, and is well known for blocking waterways and surfaces. However, water hyacinth, but others as well, accumulate small and sharp crystals of calcium oxalate in their tissue, presumably as a defense mechanism against herbivory, something that renders them inedible. Some recent efforts aim at either learning how to make aquatic plants edible or identifying or even forging strains through genetic means that are low in or have no calcium oxalate. If these attempts are successful, the world can count on a highly productive new aquatic crop.

# Conclusion

Aquatic food production is already a global food industry and it certainly is growing in the number of cultured species, quantities produced, and quality. Moreover, given that 70 percent of the planet's surface is covered by water, while land food production is increasingly limited by water availability, aquatic foods may well be more important in the years to come, perhaps to the point of becoming a second agriculture (e.g., see Radulovich, 2011). In fact, once sizable portions of these water surfaces begin to be properly used, mostly the ocean but also lakes and other freshwater bodies, there will probably be no shortage of food at the world level that some fear. However, for this to be true, production must be based on new aquatic plant growth, which will be the food in itself or the feed to grow aquatic animals. Seaweeds, of course, are first in line, and there is ample room for selection and improvement in turning them into more palatable and useful crops.

Regarding animal aquaculture, freshwater production of fish will continue to dominate for some time, probably until marine aquaculture takes over. Most likely, however, the long-term emphasis on fish production will shift to lower-trophic animals that do not require feeds heavy in fish meal and oil to develop properly—except, of course, as far as the adaptation to alternative feed sources will allow. This will also be true to an extent for crustaceans, which are carnivores to a large extent. Bivalve production, however, will continue to grow unfettered until it eventually reaches some limitations, like market saturation.

Integrated strategies to manage fisheries, aquaculture, and conservation together will probably provide new avenues to recover and perhaps increase fisheries while sustainably increasing areas for aquaculture. This will provide a continued and increasing supply of aquatic meat and plant products that will affect eating habits and food supply in novel ways. Moreover, possibilities based on the extensive marine biodiversity go far beyond commonly known and farmed species, with growing applications of genetic engineering and marine biotechnology in a range of products, such as nutraceuticals (see, e.g., OECD, 2013).

Overall, it may well be that we are entering an aquatic age and we must, simply, evolve.

# Links to aquaculture organizations and certification

Additional to each country's associations and other organizations, some of those with international involvement are:

> The World Aquaculture Society, www.was.org.
> The European Aquaculture Society, www.easonline.org.
> The Global Aquaculture Alliance, www.gaa.org.

## *For quality concerns and certifications*

Alongside each country's regulations for production and import/export, there are several private (some public/private) efforts to guarantee sustainability and standards being applied to fishery and aquaculture products.

* The Norwegian Ministry of Fisheries and Coastal Affairs (2009) provides an excellent example of a strategy at the national level to achieve environmental sustainability of their aquaculture industry.

- The FAO (www.fao.org) has been greatly involved in the issue and is the leading world authority. There is a recent FAO publication on aquaculture standards and certifications, freely available online (FAO, 2011). In another FAO document, Toppe et al. (2012) address biosecurity concerns related to aquatic foods.
- The World Fish Center (www.worldfishcenter.org) and the Network of Aquaculture Centres in Asia-Pacific (www.enaca.org) are two additional organizations involved in better management practices and certification issues. Certification of aquaculture, however, is not without critique (e.g., see Bush, 2013).

The following sites are devoted to aquaculture certification:

- Best Aquaculture Practices (BAP) certifications, through the Global Aquaculture Alliance (www.gaa.org), the Aquaculture Certification Council, www.responsibleseafood.org, and www.aquaculturecertification.org.
- Aquaculture Stewardship Council (ASC) standards and certifications, www.asc-aqua.org.
- Organic aquaculture certification, www.naturland.de.
- Perdikaris and Paschos (2010) provide an interesting short review of organic aquaculture.

## Note

1 Salmon spp. begin and end their life in freshwater, living at sea in-between.

## References

Bixler, H.J. and Porse, H. (2011) "A decade of change in the seaweed hydrocolloids industry," *Journal of Applied Phycology*, 23: 321–335.

Black, W.A.P. (1952) "Seaweeds and their value in foodstuffs," *Proceedings of the Nutrition Society*, 12: 32–39.

Bowyer, J.N., Qin, J.Q., and Stone, D.A.J. (2013) "Protein, lipid and energy requirement of cultured marine fish in cold, temperate and warm waters," *Reviews in Aquaculture*, 5: 10–32.

Bush, S.R., Belton, B., Hall, D., Vandergeest, P., Murray, F.J., Ponte, S., Oosterveer, P., Islam, M.S., Mol, A.P.J., Hatanaka, M., Kruijssen, F., Ha, T.T.T., Little, D.C., and Kusumawati, R. (2013) "Certify sustainable aquaculture?" *Science*, 341: 1067–1068.

Chopin, T. (2012) "Seaweed aquaculture provides diversified products, key ecosystem functions. Part II: recent evolution of seaweed industry," *Global Aquaculture Advocate*, 14(4): 24–27.

De Silva, S. and Davy, F.B. (eds.) (2010) *Success Stories in Asian Aquaculture*, Ottawa: Springer/NACA/IDRC.

Dillehay, T.D., Ramírez, C., Pino, M., Collins, M.B., Rossen, J., and Pino-Navarro, J.D. (2008) "Monte Verde: seaweed, food, medicine and the peopling of South America," *Science*, 320: 784–786.

Duarte, C.M., Marba, N., and Holmer, M. (2008) "Rapid domestication of marine species," *Science*, 316: 382–383.

FAO (2011) *Private Standards and Certification in Fisheries and Aquaculture*, FAO Fisheries and Aquaculture Technical Paper 553, Rome: FAO.

FAO (2012) *The State of World Fisheries and Aquaculture 2012*, Rome: FAO.

Lee, B. (2008) *Seaweed Potential as a Marine Vegetable and other Opportunities*, RIRDC Publication No. 08/009, Australia.

Lüning, K. (1990) *Seaweeds: Their Environment, Biogeography, and Ecophysiology*, New York: J. Wiley and Sons.

MacArtain, P., Gill, C.I.R., Brooks, M., Campbell, R., and Rowland, I.R. (2007) "Nutritional value of edible seaweeds," *Nutrition Reviews*, 65(12): 535–543.

Matanjun, P., Mohamed, N., Mustapha, M., and Muhammad, K. (2009) "Nutrient content of tropical edible seaweeds, *Eucheuma cottonii, Caulerpa lentillifera* and *Sargassum polycystum*," *Journal of Applied Phycology*, 21: 75–80.

McDermid, K.J. and Stuercke, B. (2003) "Nutritional composition of edible Hawaiian seaweeds," *Journal of Applied Phycology*, 15: 513–524.

Mouritsen, O.G. (2013) *Seaweeds, Edible, Available and Sustainable*, Chicago: University of Chicago Press.

Neori, A. (2011) " 'Green water' microalgae: the leading sector in world aquaculture," *Journal of Applied Phycology*, 23: 143–149.

Norwegian Ministry of Fisheries and Coastal Affairs (2009) *Strategy for an Environmentally Sustainable Norwegian Aquaculture Industry*, Oslo: NMFCA.

OECD (2013) *Marine Biotechnology: Enabling Solutions for Ocean Productivity and Sustainability*, Paris: OECD Publishing.

Perdikaris, C. and Paschos, I. (2010) "Organic aquaculture in Greece: a brief review," *Reviews in Aquaculture*, 2: 102–105.

Radulovich, R. (2010) "Caged production experiments conducted with shrimp in Costa Rica," *Global Aquaculture Advocate*, 13(4): 82–83.

Radulovich, R. (2011) "Massive water gains from producing food at sea," *Water Policy*, 13: 547–554.

Radulovich, R., Umanzor, S., and Cabrera, R. (2013) *Algas Tropicales: Cultivo y Uso como Alimento*, San Jose: University of Costa Rica Press, www.maricultura.net.

Redmond, S., Green, L., Yarish, C., Kim, J., and Neefus, C. (2014) *New England Seaweed Culture Handbook*, Connecticut: Connecticut Sea Grant.

Reed, M. (1907) *The Economic Seaweeds of Hawaii and their Food Value*, Ithaca, NY: Cornell University Library Digital Collections.

Thomas, D.N. (2002) *Seaweeds*, London: Natural History Museum.

Toppe, J., Bondad-Reantaso, M.G., Hasan, M.R., Josupeit, H., Subasinghe, R.P., Halwart, M., and James, D. (2012) "Aquatic biodiversity for sustainable diets: the role of aquatic foods in food and nutrition security," in B. Burlingame and S. Dernini (eds.), *Sustainable Diets and Biodiversity: Directions and Solutions for Policy, Research and Action*, Rome: FAO, pp. 94–101.

Van Ginneken, V.J.T., Helsper, J.P.F.G., de Visser, W., van Keulen, H. and Brandenburg, W.A. (2011) "Polyunsaturated fatty acids in various macroalgal species from north Atlantic and tropical seas," *Lipids Health Disease*, 10: 104–112.

Winberg, P., Skropeta, D., and Ullrich, A. (2011) *Seaweed Cultivation Pilot Trials*, RIRDC Publication No. 10/184, Australia.

Zemke-White, W.L. and Ohno, M. (1999) "World seaweed utilization: an end-of-century summary," *Journal of Applied Phycology*, 11: 369–376.

# 21

# FERMENTATION ART AND SCIENCE AT THE NORDIC FOOD LAB

*Benedict Reade, Justine de Valicourt and Josh Evans*

## Nordic Food Lab

The Nordic Food Lab (NFL) is a self-governed foundation based in Copenhagen, Denmark. The aim of NFL is to investigate food diversity and deliciousness and to share the results in an open-source format. We combine scientific and cultural approaches with culinary techniques from around the world to explore the edible potential of our region. We are intent on challenging and broadening tastes while generating and adapting practical ideas and methods for those who make food and those who enjoy eating.

Food fermentation, as a highly diverse and complex set of phenomena, is ripe for this sort of interdisciplinary, practical study. Our aim is to understand the science and craft behind the exceptional results obtained by the very best food producers and, by analysing and experimenting with this knowledge, to figure out how it can be reapplied to food production in new ways.

## Fermentation definition

A biochemist might define fermentation as 'a process performed by microorganisms that transforms sugars into energy in the absence of oxygen'. Others adopt broader definitions of fermentation, including both the metabolic processes of microorganisms (with or without oxygen), and also the action of chemicals they produce (particularly enzymes, organic acids, gases and volatile compounds) of either plant or animal origin on a substrate (Nout, 2005). For the good of this text, food fermentation will be broadly defined as the metabolic processes of microorganisms as applied to food substrates for preservative, gastronomic, health and other benefits.

During the production of fermented foods, there are often other physical and chemical transformations that are not directly related to the microbes' metabolism yet nonetheless affect the outcome of the final product. Examples include hydrolysis of macromolecules by enzymatic activity, oxidation from light or air, transformation by heat, and moisture loss. These processes are important in the production of certain foods, for example Maillard reactions in soy sauce and cured meats, or enzymatic and oxidative processes in various teas. While these processes are not direct results of fermentation itself, it is important to realise that

*Figure 21.1*   The Nordic Food Lab.

they may both affect and be affected by fermentation kinetics and are often vital to the organoleptic characteristics of the finished food product. A holistic understanding of fermented foods must also include these processes, along with the myriad other factors that affect the fermentation environment and thus the ultimate quality of the food.

## Main functions of fermentation with a focus on sustainability

### *Preservation*

This is the function most often cited for the development of fermented food traditions. Many fermentative processes produce organic acids, ethanol or carbon dioxide or other biopreservatives such as nisin, which help to make the food pathogenically stable (Ross et al., 2002). These compounds make the environment difficult to inhabit for unwanted microorganisms, allowing the desirable microbes to become and remain dominant instead of pathogenic competitors. These fermentative processes often take place 'spontaneously' by naturally present microorganisms; many fermentation techniques thus likely began as chance discoveries, and were subsequently developed into more refined practice (McGovern, 2010). Fermenting edible substrates often requires little to no further temperature treatment – such as freezing, refrigeration, dehydration (hot or cold), pasteurisation or sterilisation – for preservation, and therefore fermented foods can often be made with a relatively low energy consumption. Fermentation techniques are thus ideal for remote areas and much of the developing world, and also for lowering energy consumption worldwide – many fermentation processes even generate energy. Fermentative food preparations also have applications during a glut of a certain type of food. A clear example of this is when many cabbages are ready at the same time – if one makes sauerkraut, possibly without even the addition of salt, the cabbages can be eaten all year long.

### Flavour

Food fermentations usually contain organic acids. Especially when one considers the origins of fermentation as soured/alcoholic beer prototypes/porridges and early breads (Braidwood et al., 1953), the added sour taste would have served an important role in augmenting an essentially bland diet. During fermentation, the breakdown of complex carbohydrates into sugars, proteins into peptides and free amino acids, and lipids into fatty acids and aromatic molecules gives a much wider range of tastes, aromas and textures than would be available in the ingredients in their unfermented state. As flavour is the body's way of recognising nutrients in the environment (Morini, 2007), it is unsurprising that this point of flavour development is intrinsically linked to the bioavailability of nutrients – as explored in brief below.

### Health

There is an exponentially broadening picture of how microbes and fermented foods affect our health. Microbes break down molecules in the foods we eat, such as lactose in dairy products and inulin and other less-digestible fibres in vegetables. Fermentation can also enhance vitamin and essential amino acid content as well as produce beneficial antimicrobial compounds. This increase in bioavailability of nutrients means that foods that would otherwise be quite poor in nutrients can become very dense, just through the action of microbes and time. They detoxify certain foods like cassava, whose cyanogenic glycosides are rendered harmless in fermentations. This detoxification leads us to broaden our food choices, as some foods that would otherwise be poisonous can be rid of toxins. Increasing the diversity of our food choices has repeatedly been shown to increase the sustainability of food systems by broadening our reliance on any one food, thus lowering specific pressures on natural resources and bolstering ecological resilience (Burlinghame and Dernini, 2012).

In many cases, fermented foods provide both probiotic and prebiotic functions (Cutting, 2011; Moslehi-Jenabian et al., 2010). The microbes themselves in unpasteurised foods sometimes come to populate our gastrointestinal tract, providing numerous benefits while reproducing and living in our bodies. Having a healthy ecology of bodily microbes is essential to sustaining human health; microbes living in our large intestine outnumber human cells in a healthy human body by around 10:1, providing essential and diverse roles such as heightened immune-responses, digestion and homeostasis (Wallace et al., 2011).

## Classification

Classification of fermented foods can be done by different means – for example, by substrate, by classical microbial nomenclature, by human culture or geographical origin, by techniques used in production (such as inoculation method) or, as is most frequently done, a mixture of these methods.

At NFL we use a variety of methods to classify our fermentations, but perhaps the most useful is simply the name of the final product that our ferment aims to emulate. However, things quickly become complicated when we start to carry out processes that, at least to our knowledge, have never been carried out before. At this point a small amount of knowledge of the microbiology of similar fermented foods helps. For example, we know a bit about sauerkraut, and we would like to carry out a similar process on some apples. We know that in the sauerkraut we are trying to emulate, the dominant form of fermentation is 'lactic acid fermentation', so we call our apples 'lacto-fermented apples'. This kind of classification removes the problem of identifying the often incredibly complex microbial ecologies inside the food stuff and allows us to describe new products by 'functional similarity' to existing techniques and traditions, rather than mainly by specific microbial ecologies.

## Classification by inoculation method

There are three main ways we can begin the process of fermenting.

### *Backslopping*

Backslopping has historically been the principal method for inoculation. Backslopping is the process of using an already successful ferment to inoculate a new one. The assumption is that the existing 'good' microbes will colonise the newly available nutrients, reproducing and generating a more-or-less similar culture. Good examples are sourdough bread mothers and some traditional vinegars. Methods of perpetuated ferments such as *nuka* or various brines into which typically vegetable substrates are submerged are similar in their ecology. This gives rise to mixed, but very stable ecology of microbes in the food (Vogel and Ehrmann, 2010). Some ferments use multi-stage backslopping methods, which can be very complex (Chen et al., 2008). Continual selection of successful ferments means that, over time, microbes are selected for beneficial characteristics. This symbiotic evolution also in turn affects human development (McGovern, 2010). This coevolution is a fascinating area of study.

## *Wild-type fermentations*

Wild-type fermentations use the microorganisms found naturally on the substrate and in the surrounding environment. Often, but not always, these ferments are begun by changing the substrate's physical and chemical conditions to select for a certain type of microbe that might already be found in its naturally occurring mix. For example, adding salt to cabbage selects for lactic acid bacteria (LAB) and against many pathogens. This method gives the least consistent and most surprising results (Katz, 2013).

## *Pure strain inoculation*

Pure strain inoculation involves the addition of one or more known strains of microbes. This method has only been available since the laboratory cultivation of microbes became a developed and affordable technique. This process is used in almost all industrial-scale food fermentations. Many different species can be used for inoculation, a good summary of which can be found in Bourdichon et al. (2012). Although some results may lack character, this reliability can give the opportunity for perfecting recipes and technique over many batches.

## Foods by applied microbial family

### *Bacteria*

#### *Lactic acid fermentation*

LAB are a broad category of microbes found in many foods including pickled vegetables like kimchi and sauerkraut, sourdough, salami, soy sauce, and fermented dairy products such as cheese, *villi* or *trahanas*. Their unifying characteristic is their ability to produce lactic acid as the main product of their metabolism of glucose thus creating an acidic environment. By lowering pH, lactic acid protects the food against most pathogenic bacteria and gives these foods their characteristic sour flavour.

The fermentation can be homolactic or heterolactic. Homolactic fermentation transforms one molecule of glucose into two molecules of lactic acid, while heterolactic fermentation transforms one molecule of glucose into one molecule of lactic acid, one molecule of ethanol, and one molecule of carbon dioxide. This heterolactic fermentation explains the light effervescence of some acidified foods.

Homolactic fermentation:   glucose = 2 lactic acid + energy
$$C_6H_{12}O_6 = 2\ C_3H_6O_3 + 2\ ATP$$
Heterolactic fermentation:   glucose = lactic acid + ethanol + energy
$$C_6H_{12}O_6 = C_3H_6O_3 + C_2H_5OH + CO_2 + 2\ ATP$$

To ferment many vegetables using LAB, little more is needed than to add salt. Salt draws moisture out of the vegetable matter by osmosis, which produces a brine: the submerged vegetables are then in the necessary oxygen-poor (but not completely anaerobic) environment in which LAB thrive. LAB fermentations can occur across a wide range of salinity, from 0 per cent (many dairy products like yoghurt and sour cream) to 25 per cent (certain seafood sauces in East Asia). We have found 2–2.5 per cent salt of the total weight of substrate to be a good minimum salt concentration to experiment with. This can be achieved by

*Figure 21.2* Fermenting vegetables.

adding 2.5g of salt to 100g of substrate or with brine by adding 5g salt to 100g water, and 200g substrate.

LAB are microaerophiles, meaning that they like to be in the presence of small amounts of oxygen, but not too much. They are also typically mesophilic, meaning that they like to ferment at room temperature or slightly warmer. For this reason we carry out much of our lactic fermentations in vacuum bags, which have been sealed just before reaching full vacuum.

If a heterolactic fermentation occurs, then $CO_2$ production may cause the bag to explode – keep a close eye! It should also be noted that excessive use of plastic vacuum bags is not a sustainable practice; old-fashioned brining, which we also utilise, is much less wasteful.

As the pathogenic microbe *Clostridium botulinum* cannot produce toxins below pH 4.2, this is generally regarded as a safe final acidity if it is reached quickly. Ferments can frequently be cooled down to slow or stop the microbial activity at pH 4.6 and the pH will continue to drop for a period, reaching a final pH of 4.2.

While we enjoy lacto-fermenting all manner of vegetables and dairy (Reade, 2013), other exciting experiments involving LAB include various fermented sauces. Incidentally, they are also a perfect example of a mixed microbial culture in action. Fermented sauces such as fish sauce and other protein-rich sauces are made partly through a process of lactic acid and some-times alcoholic fermentations. These occur alongside the enzymatic breakdown of proteins (proteolysis). In the case of fish sauce, added salt prevents the growth of undesired microbes so halophilic (*halo* – salt, *philic* – liking) LAB can dominate the substrate. Through osmosis, the salt draws water from the fish, creating a brine in which proteolysis occurs. Enzymes of the fish's flesh and digestive tracts flow into the brine and proteolysis causes the solution to become a 'soup' of free amino acids giving the sauce its characteristic umami taste.

## *Acetic acid fermentation*

Vinegar, a solution of acetic acid and water and hopefully some residual sugar and aromatic compounds, is often considered a poor cousin in the realm of fermented foods. Yet when made with the right knowledge and aims, vinegar can be a high-quality and valuable product, as in the case of *Aceto Balsamico Tradizionale di Modena,* which reaches prices in excess of €1/ml.

As ethanol is a product of a first fermentation mostly done by yeast, vinegar is a product of a double and mixed fermentation. Vinegar can be obtained from any raw material that has undergone an alcoholic fermentation. A good vinegar is normally achieved from an alcohol concentration of 5–9 per cent; however both stronger and weaker solutions can produce excellent results. In an acetic fermentation, acetic acid bacteria (AAB) convert ethyl alcohol (ethanol) into acetic acid, the essential characteristic of vinegar. This occurs in the presence of oxygen:

$$\text{ethanol} + \text{oxygen} = \text{acetic acid} + \text{water} + \text{energy}$$
$$C_2H_5OH + O_2 = CH3COOH + H_2O + 8\text{–}13 \text{ ATP}$$

Classic vinegars as we know them in the West are made by a number of methods. These can be divided roughly into two groups: slow, traditional techniques where attaining a finished vinegar may take from one month to many years; and rapid techniques, which make vinegar from 'wine' in as little as six hours.

AAB will proliferate much more easily if some vinegar is mixed in with the alcoholic ferment, thereby acidifying the wine and creating an environment where the AAB thrive. This addition is normally carried out using a mature batch of unpasteurised vinegar made from the same source (backslopping!). If this is done with unpasteurised vinegar it is also a means by which to inoculate the 'wine' with the correct AAB strains. As AAB are ubiquitous, if an alcoholic solution of appropriate concentration is left open to the air, it will eventually turn to vinegar, regardless of inoculation.

The most famous slow method of vinegar production is the Orleans method. Barrels are half-filled with a mixture of around 80 per cent wine and 20 per cent live, unpasteurised vinegar, and fermentation is carried out by the AAB, which, in warm conditions, will metabolise all the alcohol in a 9 per cent ethanol wine in one to three months. When fully acidified, the vinegar is siphoned off, leaving around 12L inside a 225L barrel. This is then again half-filled with fresh 'wine', allowing the maximum surface area to be exposed to air. To make sure the AAB have as much oxygen available as possible, holes are drilled through the ends of the barrel which are then covered with muslin. This same process can be carried out at home with a large, wide-mouthed jar covered in muslin – a great way to use leftover wine.

We are experimenting with the traditional method for balsamic vinegar production, except using quinces instead of grapes as the initial substrate. The result is an intense, resinous vinegar that has beautiful notes of dried figs and sherry. Another successful recipe involves elderflower wine macerated with elderberries and then left to oxidise into vinegar, creating a sweeter, layered elder vinegar with good aging potential. We have also experimented with rapid aeration methods that can give us vinegar in four to five days and from less traditional ingredients that have less residual sugar to start with, such as herbs, roots, mushrooms and trees. While the rapid method works well for prototyping and industrial production, the slow methods will invariably yield the most complex and delicious final products.

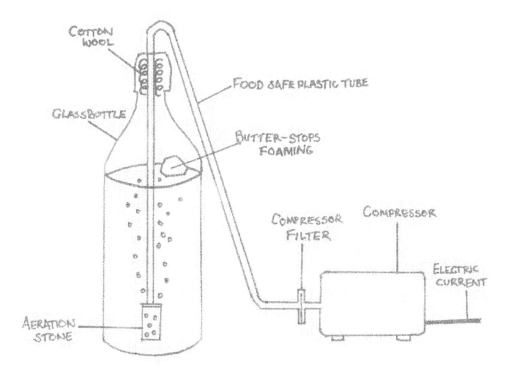

*Figure 21.3* Vinegar aeration system.

## Alkaline fermentations

A lesser-known group of fermentations, alkaline fermentations involve aerobic endospore-forming bacteria (AEB). These foods provide protein-rich, low-cost condiments for millions of people in south-east Asia and Africa (FAO, 1998). The *Bacillus* genus, with *B. subtilis* as the most common species, is capable of hydrolysing proteins into amino acids and ammonia. The ammonia increases the alkalinity up to a pH of 9, protecting the food against bacterial spoilage and giving the characteristic ammoniated smell. This type of fermentation normally uses legumes or seeds, as they are rich in proteins (Wang and Fung, 1996; Parkouda et al., 2009). Well-known examples of alkaline fermentations include Japanese *natto*, the rind on washed-rind cheeses and West African *dawadawa* or *soumbala*. NFL has not yet experimented very much with alkaline fermentation – it is a vast world yet to explore.

## Fungi

### Yeast

Many yeasts are able to produce energy in both aerobic and anaerobic conditions. In food, yeasts are primarily used under anaerobic conditions which will yield ethanol and $CO_2$. Yeasts thus give rise to almost all alcoholic beverages (the Mexican drink *pulque* is an exception, as most of its alcohol is produced by a bacterium, *Zymomonas mobilis* (Steinkraus, 1983)). Leavened bread is also made using yeast (*Saccharomyces cerevisiae*) – the $CO_2$ creates the bubbles in the bread, and the alcohol evaporates during baking.

The skins of sugary fruits are typically covered in a thin layer of wild yeasts (and other microbes). This means that as the fruit ripens, these yeasts consume available sugars. To make a wild-fermented alcohol, it is often enough just to leave the juices of sugar-rich fruits in contact with the skins for a while – this brief contact should be enough to initiate alcoholic fermentation. Once the yeasts begin transforming the sugars an airlock system should be used, allowing $CO_2$ to escape without allowing oxygen to enter.

The most commonly domesticated yeast is *Saccharomyces cerevisiae*, naturally found on fruit skins and other sugar-rich material. Due to their variations in alcohol tolerance and enzyme production, different strains of *S. cerevisiae* produce varying quantities of ethanol and $CO_2$ and at different speeds, which has given rise to different applications in baking and brewing since ancient times (it is also likely that different human activities have in turn selected for these functional differences, enhancing naturally occurring variation). Yeasts also play a role in the fermentation of dairy products such as kefir, as well as in cacao and coffee (Boekhout and Robert, 2003: 24). The genus *Saccharomyces* also contains other species (e.g., *S. bayanus* and *S. pastorianus*) that play an important part in processes of making bread, beer, wine and other alcohols. There are in addition many other yeasts involved in the fermentation of various other foods and drinks (Querol and Fleet, 2006).

## *Filamentous fungi/moulds*

A huge diversity of fungi are involved in fermented dairy production (Ropars et al., 2012). Fermented meat products are similarly complex (Spotti and Berni, 2007) and although we experiment with both meat and dairy, much of our exploration into the realm of filamentous fungi has been elsewhere.

As discussed earlier, fish guts offer one source of proteolytic enzymes for the production of umami-rich, protein-based sauces. Another way of harnessing hydrolytic enzymes comes from filamentous fungi (mould) grown on cooked grains or pulses. *Koji* in Japan, *nuruk* and *meju* in Korea, *qu* in China – these mould-based techniques are loosely but functionally related. The most common fungus used in this technique, and the predominant one in Japanese *koji*, is *Aspergillus oryzae. A. sojae, Monascus purpureus* and other species are also used (Steinkraus, 2004). The mould produces many hydrolysing enzymes that can break down proteins, fats and starches (Chen et al., 2008). The umami taste arises through the breaking down of proteins into their building blocks of amino acids, thus creating free glutamic acid, the main molecule that bonds with the umami taste buds and enriches the flavour. Umami can also be found in other ferment-ations where some proteins are hydrolysed, such as in old cheeses, cured meats and fish sauce. Some of our most delicious recipes have been a sauce fermented in the soy sauce style with barley koji and yellow peas; a miso made in a similar fashion; Roman-style garums made with all manner of animal proteins including pheasant, hare, grasshopper and wax moth larvae; and 'koji-chovies' – herrings fermented to achieve an effect similar to anchovies. Although their traditional analogues may not have involved koji, at NFL all of these projects do so.

In addition to umami applications, mould-based saccharification processes also form the basis of grain-based wines such as *makgeolli, sake, amazake* and *li* (Shurtleff and Aoyagi, 2012).

Beyond its use for saccharification and proteolytic breakdown, we have also been experi-menting with *koji* technology for its flavour development. Growing koji on barley and other grains yields a range of fruity, nutty and mushroomy flavours. Resulting koji can then be roasted, allowing us to obtain a whole range of toasted flavours akin to chocolate or coffee. We are currently developing versions of these products involving blends of fermented and unfermented Nordic ingredients, which are mixed with roasted *kojis*.

Another application of filamentous fungi involves the mould *Aspergillus niger*, the predominant fungus in Pu-erh tea which gives it many of its mossy, earthy characteristics. We are currently investigating the use of this mould on Nordic plant parts to produce fermented tisanes that evoke Pu-erh in method but have ultimately their own character.

## Very mixed fermentations

Most traditional food fermentations contain many species of microorganism. These microbial ecologies develop and can be highly stable, such as in the case of sourdough mothers (Vogel and Ehrmann, 2010), or they may fluctuate as populations of different species rise and fall. One example would be the *moromi* stage of a soy sauce ferment. First, the salt in the *moromi* brine kills off species (such as the *koji* moulds), which are not tolerant to the changed osmotic pressure. Next, halotolerant yeast (*Zygosaccharomyces rouxii*) species that create alcohol begin to thrive, and as they consume available sugars, a species of LAB (*Tetragenococcus halophilus*) begins to acidify the solution as the yeasts subside (Steinkraus, 2004).

A further example of a mixed fermented food is kombucha. Kombucha is a beverage typically made with black tea, sweetened with 5–15 per cent sucrose, and set to ferment at 25–30 °C for 10–12 days with a symbiotic culture of bacteria and yeasts (SCOBY) (Sreeramulu et al., 2000; Dufresne and Farnworth, 2000). Inoculation of new batches uses either about 10 per cent of kombucha from a previous batch, or a piece of the mother. The brewing vessel is covered with a clean, coarsely woven cloth to keep out insects and debris while allowing aeration (Greenwalt et al., 1998).

The jellyfish-like mother produced by *Acetobacter xylinum* is often called 'tea fungus' (Mo et al., 2008).

*Figure 21.4*   Kombucha mother.

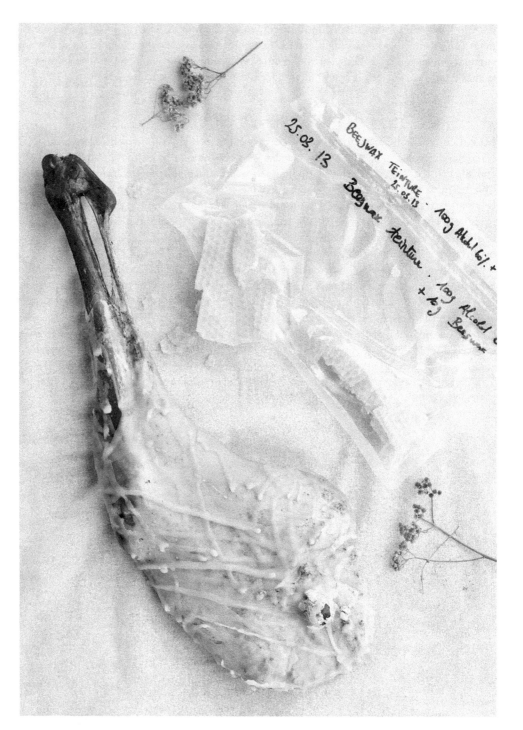

*Figure 21.5* Venison Fenalår.

Although much superstition surrounds the presence or absence of the mother, the functional microbes are present also in the liquid and the floating membrane is in fact only a visible manifestation of the yeast–bacteria symbiosis – the *zoogleal mat* (Jayabalan et al., 2010; Sreeramulu et al., 2000). The cellulose is a secondary metabolite of the fermentation, similar in structure to a 'mother of vinegar' (Jayabalan et al., 2010). The exact microbial composition depends on the source, condition and treatment of the kombucha culture (Sreeramulu et al., 2000).

We have experimented quite extensively with kombucha, exploring flavouring agents and different fermentable substrates. Particularly interesting and successful recipes have included kombuchas of juniper wood, boletus mushrooms, lemon verbena and carrot.

## Fenalår

Fenalår is an old Norwegian tradition for preserving sheep's leg. We have taken this tradition and elaborated it quite a bit, mixing in mummification techniques and other layers of fermentation to yield a product that is as complex as it is unique and delicious. We undertake the process on a leg of roe deer. The process involves rubbing the venison leg with yoghurt whey; leaving it at 5 °C overnight; rubbing the leg with juniper dust and salt (around 2 per cent of weight); leaving it at 2 °C for seven days; rubbing the leg with spruce resin tincture; hanging the leg at 2 °C for four days; placing the leg in a cold smoker for four days; removing and hanging for two months; dipping into rendered deer fat; leaving a further two months; dipping into melted beeswax; leaving a further two months; then removing the wax, slicing thinly and enjoying. This is a very mixed fermentation that likely involves LAB, yeasts, enzymatic breakdown of proteins and fats, oxidation, moisture loss, surface moulds of varying descriptions and the production of a whole host of secondary metabolites – and is a perfect example of complex microbial ecology in action.

## Conclusion

Microbes are one of the most powerful tools we have to create foods that are diverse, delicious, nourishing and speak genuinely of their place in the world. We have been evolving alongside microbes since before our emergence as a species and will continue to do so into the future. Engaging in the fermentation of food is one of the most exciting ways to engage directly in this coevolution. Using scientific methods to learn more about the complexity of microbial ecology in fermented foods, paired with a gastronomic sensibility and a desire to eat well, allows us to experiment, keeping food traditions alive and exploring ways to situate them in contemporary food systems and cultures.

We are continually discovering new applications for pure strain microorganisms and wild mixed ecologies, and new techniques to make the most of traditional and innovative tools and techniques. Visit our website, www.nordicfoodlab.org, for more information on all of the above and to follow our ongoing research.

## References

Boekhout, R. and Robert, V. (2003) *Yeasts in Food: Beneficial and Detrimental Aspects*, Hamburg: Behrs Verlag.

Bourdichon, F., Casaregola, S., Farrokh, C., Frisvad, J.C., Gerds, M.L., Hammes, W.P., Harnett, J., Huys, G., Laulund, S., Ouwehand, A., Powell, I.B., Prajapati, J.B., Seto, Y., Schure, E.T., Van

Boven, A., Vankerckhoven, V., Zgoda, A., Tuijtelaars, S. and Hansen, E. (2012) 'Food fermentations: microorganisms with technological beneficial use', *International Journal of food Microbiology*, 154: 87–97.

Braidwood, R.J., Sauer, J.D., Helbaek, H., Mangelsdorf, P.C., Cutler, H.C., Coon, C.S., Linton, R., Steward, J. and Oppenheim, A.L. (1953) 'Symposium: did man once live by beer alone?', *American Anthropologist*, 55(4): 515–526.

Burlinghame, B. and Dernini, S. (eds.) (2012) *Sustainable Diets and Biodiversity: Directions and Solutions for Policy, Research and Action*, Rome: FAO.

Chen, F., Li, L., Qu, J. and Chen, C.X. (2008) 'Cereal vinegars made by solid-state fermentation in China', in L. Solieri and P. Giudici (eds.), *Vinegars of the World*, Milan: Springer-Verlag Italia, pp. 243–260.

Cutting, S. (2011) 'Bacillus probiotics', *Food Microbiology*, 28: 214–220.

Dufresne, C. and Farnworth, E. (2000) 'Tea, kombucha, and health: a review', *Food Research International*, 33: 409–421.

FAO (1998) *Fermented Fruits and Vegetables: A Global Perspective*, www.fao.org/docrep/x0560e/x0560e10.htm.

Greenwalt, C.J., Ledford, R.A. and Steinkraus, K.H. (1998) 'Determination and characterization of the antimicrobial activity of the fermented tea kombucha', *LWT – Food Science and Technology*, 31: 291–296.

Jayabalan, R., Malini, K., Sathisshkumar, M., Swaminathan, K. and Yun, S.-E. (2010) 'Biochemical characteristics of tea fungus produced during kombucha fermentation', *Food Science and Biotechnology*, 19: 843–847.

Katz, S. (2013) *The Art of Fermentation*, White River, VT: Chelsea Green Publishing.

McGovern, P. (2010) *Uncorking the Past: The Quest for Wine, Beer, and Other Alcoholic Beverages*, Berkeley, CA: University of California Press.

Mo, H., Zhu, Y. and Chen, Z. (2008) 'Microbial fermented tea – a potential source of natural food preservatives', *Trends in Food Science & Technology*, 19: 124–130.

Morini, G. (2007) 'Molecular aspects of taste', *Gastronomic Sciences*, 2: 42.

Moslehi-Jenabian, S., Pedersen, L.L. and Jespersen, L. (2010) 'Beneficial effects of probiotic and food borne yeasts on human health', *Nutrients*, 2(4): 449–473.

Nout, M.J.R. (2005) 'Food fermentation: an introduction', in M.J.R. Nout, W.M. De Vos and M.H. Zwietering (eds.), *Food Fermentation*, Wageningen: Wageningen Academic Publishers, pp. 13–21.

Parkouda, C., Nielsen, D.S., Azokpota, P., Ouoba, L.I.I., Amoa-Awua, W.K., Thorsen, L., Hounhouigan, J.D., Jensen, J.S., Tano-Debrah, K., Diawara, B. and Jakobsen, M. (2009) 'The microbiology of alkaline-fermentation of indigenous seeds used as food condiments in Africa and Asia', *Critical Reviews in Microbiology*, 35(2): 139–156.

Querol, A. and Fleet, G.H. (eds.) (2006) *The Yeast Handbook, Vol 2: Yeasts in Food and Beverages*, Berlin: Springer-Verlag.

Reade, B. (2013) 'Bog butter: a gastronomic perspective', in M. McWilliams (ed.), *Wrapped and Stuffed Foods: Proceedings of the Oxford Symposium on Food and Cookery 2012*, Devon: Prospect Books.

Ropars, J., Cruaud, C., Lacoste, S. and Dupont, J. (2012) 'A taxonomic and ecological overview of cheese fungi', *International Journal of Microbiology*, 155(3): 199–210.

Ross, R.P., Morgan, S. and Hill, C. (2002) 'Preservation: past present and future', *International Journal of Food Microbiology*, 79: 3–16.

Shurtleff, W. and Aoyagi, A. (2012) *History of Koji – Grains and/or Soybeans Enrobed with a Mold Culture (300BCE to 2012)*, www.soyinfocenter.com/pdf/154/Koji.pdf.

Spotti, E. and Berni, E. (2007) 'Starter cultures: molds', in F. Toldrá (ed.), *Handbook of Fermented Meat and Poultry*, Iowa: Blackwell.

Sreeramulu, G., Zhu, Y. and Knol, W. (2000) 'Kombucha fermentation and its antimicrobial activity', *Journal of Agricultural and Food Chemistry*, 48: 2589–2594.

Steinkraus, K. (1983) 'Lactic acid fermentation in the production of foods from vegetables, cereals and legumes', *Antonie van Leeuwenhoek*, 49: 337–348.

Steinkraus, K. (ed.) (2004) *Industrialization of Indigenous Fermented Foods*, 2nd edn, New York: CRC Press, pp. 1–97.

Vogel, R.F. and Ehrmann, M.A. (2010) 'Sourdough fermentations', in L. Cocolin and D. Ercolini (eds.), *Molecular Techniques in the Microbial Ecology of Fermented Foods*, Berlin: Springer-Verlag, pp. 119–144.

Wallace, T., Guarner, E., Madsen, K., Cabana, M.D., Gibson, G. and Hentges, E. (2011) 'Human gut microbiota and its relationship to health and disease', *Nutrition Reviews*, 69(7): 392–403.

Wang, J. and Fung, D.Y.C. (1996) 'Alkaline-fermented foods: a review with emphasis on pidan fermentation', *Critical Reviews in Microbiology*, 22: 101–138.

# PART 6

# A sustainable restaurant system

Manger est une nécessité, mais manger intelligemment est un art.
(To eat is a necessity, but to eat intelligently is an art)

*Duc François de La François La Rochefoucauld*

The restaurant industry is a cornerstone of the development of sustainable food and beverage principles and practices. But what is 'sustainable food and beverage'? In juggling the economic, environmental and socio-cultural pillars, this section seeks to provide some guidance and possible answers to the greatest challenges ahead for this industry so heavily reliant on agricultural and human resources.

Sustainable food and beverage is often associated with organic and fair-trade ingredients. However, this view on sustainable food and beverage is one-sided – if not outdated. Along with sustainable restaurant indicators, there are five general 'ingredients' necessary to create a sustainable restaurant: culture, health, nature, quality and profit. **Elena Cavagnaro** discusses those five ingredients in detail via three best industry practices.

Health and nutrition has become a new responsibility of the foodservice sector as meals consumed away-from-home are on the increase. However, responsibility is a double-edged sword: on the supply side this may translate into offering healthier options, while on the demand side, consumers are the ones making the food choices. To help making those choices, the nature, type, display and diffusion of information methods play an important role. **Laure Saulais** also presents the multiple barriers to improving nutritional quality in foodservice.

'You are only as sustainable as your supply chain' – for many restaurants, buying products from small, local suppliers is the most straightforward way to make a supply chain more sustainable. However, shortening a supply chain is far from the only (or best, for that matter) way to 'greenify' procurement: using the appropriate technology, collaborating with suppliers, and optimising stock management are also crucial. **Christine Demen Meier, Nicolas Siorak, Stéphanie Bonsch Buri and Clémence Cornuz** examine different modalities of sustainability that are incorporated in supply-chain management, as well as the 'green initiatives' taken by chain-affiliated as well as independent restaurants.

An alternative of outsourced food procurement is to rely on self-sufficiency. However, the implementation of complete food self-sufficiency in restaurants is a complex and idealistic idea that is proven unfeasible if practised in a single, closed restaurant. However, with close cooperation between a series of restaurants with a supply chain consisting of one large mixed farm or a network of farms, self-sufficiency may be a possibility. **Jaap Peter Nijboer, Peter R. Klosse and Jan Arend Schulp** introduce the Foodzone model, which is designed as a management tool to be used by chefs and restaurant-owners to decide on and assess the level of self-sufficiency and buying locally.

Beyond environmental issues, corporate social responsibility (CSR) is widely adopted by restaurant businesses; however, the interpretation of CSR depends on the individual restaurant concept. **Anders Justenlund** reflects on how CSR could be applied to existing or future business models, by applying the Osterwalder and Pigneurs' *Business Model Canvas*. Four examples of socially responsible and sustainable restaurant practices where CSR is an integrated part of the business strategy are discussed.

Nevertheless; does the *sustainable restaurant* actually exist? **Charles Barneby and Juline E. Mills** discuss what the true meaning of sustainable restaurant may be, from the sourcing of the cutting board to the table on which the food is served. Current standards and flaws in measuring restaurant sustainability are presented and the future of restaurant sustainability is discussed.

# 22

# SUSTAINABLE RESTAURANT CONCEPTS, FOCUS ON F&B

*Elena Cavagnaro*

## Introduction

Sustainability in food and beverage (F&B) is often associated with the use of organic and fair-trade ingredients. A recent survey in the Netherlands has shown that sometimes this is not the case: when asked to describe a 'sustainable deep-fried potato', the majority of respondents referred not to the potato or the oil in which it is fried, but to the paper or plastic disposable in which it is offered.[1]

This rather astonishing answer might reflect the fact that the interest for sustainability in restaurants in general and food and beverage in particular is quite recent (Cavagnaro and Gehrels, 2009). However, the understanding of both academics and professionals involved in this field is more articulated than a reference to organic and fair-trade ingredients, as this contribution intends to show.

Already in 2006, in discussing sustainable food procurement, Rimmington et al. (2006) observed that, in defining what constitutes sustainable food, at least nine aspects should be covered (see Table 22.1).

Interestingly, in this list there is no explicit reference to organic food, although (as Rimmington et al. note) this is implicit in the second aspect. Fair-trade issues are addressed in aspects three and nine.

Some of the aspects of sustainable food procurement proposed by Rimmington et al. overlap. For example, aspects two and three both deal with providing full and trustworthy information to customers, while aspects one and four both refer to locally sourced food – an aspect that has implications for transportation as well (aspect six). A certain degree of overlap is unavoidable when looking at sustainability criteria. Yet the question arises whether it would be possible to develop a more compact list of basic aspects of sustainable F&B.

In a landmark article in 2010, Legrand et al. proposed an integrated approach to sustainable restaurants involving not only F&B, but also the seating, design and construction of the premises; the furniture, fixtures and fittings; energy and waste; and community engagement. For each of these five categories, indicators were proposed on the basis of an extensive literature review. The indicators were then tested on four London restaurants professing to be sustainable. Of the 32 individuated indicators, almost half pertain to the F&B domain (15 indicators). These were also the indicators that were most easily recognized

*Table 22.1* Sustainable food aspects (from Rimmington et al., 2006)

1. Select food produced locally.
2. Give customers the possibility of making an informed, sustainable choice by providing appropriate menu information and food offerings.
3. Avoid the purchase of foods that have been produced using processes that excessively damage human health and/or the environment.
4. Explore ways to source from smaller local or regional suppliers.
5. Process food by using resource efficient facilities.
6. Choose the most sustainable form of transport.
7. Source animal food from farmers that comply with standards such as the one developed by the World Organisation for Animal Health.
8. Assure that food offered to consumers is prepared with the minimum amount of additives, including salt and sugar, and provide information to customers on additives.
9. Address in a corporate code of practice the issues embraced by the International Labour Organization.

during the test, thus confirming the centrality of F&B in developing a sustainable restaurant concept.

In Legrand et al. (2010) F&B indicators' list, alongside organic and fair-trade food products, relevance is given to: sourcing locally and choosing seasonal produce; to the offer of a vegetarian choice and vegan wines on the menu; to attention for the dietary goals and guidelines of the country the restaurant is located in; and to involvement of staff through training and transparent communication with guests.

Although there are some differences in the indicators described in Rimmington et al. (2006) compared to Legrand et al. (2010), it is evident that both support the conclusion that sustainability applied to F&B cannot be reduced to the use of organic and fair-trade ingredients. It is therefore mandatory to keep exploring the boundaries of sustainable F&B in a restaurant context. This is exactly the aim of the next section of this chapter. Before proceeding further, however, it is essential to briefly clarify the understanding of sustainability on which this contribution is based.

Sustainability is a means to reach the goal set by the WCED or Brundtland commission back in 1987: a better quality of life for present and future generations. This goal can only be achieved through a better distribution of resources among and in-between generations, and by remaining inside the limits of the Earth's capacity to sustain life (WCED, 1987; Cavagnaro and Curiel, 2012). In further elaborations of the concepts highlighted in the Brundtland report, sustainability has been described as value creation on an economic, social and environmental dimension both at the level of society and at the level of organizations (Earth Summit II, 1997; Elkington, 1998).

As Legrand et al. correctly state, 'the relationship that restaurateurs have toward environmental challenges and societal concerns is one of a rather remote and intangible nature' (2010, 167). It is therefore useful to remember that there are natural limits that have a clear impact on restaurants' operations. Among these, let us quote here the scarcity of fresh water resources; the decreasing availability of nutrients – such as nitrogen and phosphate – that are essential for modern agriculture; the land's declining fertility; and the limited capacity of the Earth to cope with pollution and waste. As recent research has shown, most of these limits have been exceeded already (Rockström et al., 2009). Restaurants are not only affected by these limits, but also impact on them. Consider for example the case of food waste. While it is true that the main food wasted is in manufacturing and households, it has been estimated that at least 14 per cent of food waste in Europe occurs in food services and catering (Bio Intelligence Service, 2010).

From a social perspective, labour conditions – both of own personnel and of people employed all along the food supply chain – are considered one of the most pressing issues involved in sustainable F&B. Yet, as will be shown below, less evident aspects, such as respect for a country's culinary tradition, have commanded increasing attention.

Finally, the financial perspective should not be forgotten. It has been observed that many restaurants survive only thanks to the number of hours invested in them by the owner, chef and other personnel. This is of course unhealthy, both for the people involved and for the long-term survival of the restaurant. A healthy financial situation is an essential dimension of sustainability. Not considering it will threaten the organization's continuity, even if the social and environmental dimensions are properly accounted for. In other words, every proposition for implementing sustainability in restaurants should take three dimensions into account: the social, the environmental and the economic.

## Five 'ingredients' for sustainable restaurants

Sustainability applied to F&B covers, as has been shown, a broad field ranging from the way food and beverage is produced, sourced, packaged and transported, to the way food ingredients are processed in the kitchen; from respect for the culinary tradition of a country to respect for the people producing our food and wines; from the design of the restaurant premises to energy and waste reduction in the whole food supply chain.

It is a rich and complex field, and this may be daunting for those restaurateurs who are looking for a blueprint on how to implement sustainability in their premises. From a managerial perspective, what is needed are simpler guidelines that still reflect the environmental, social and economic dimension of sustainability.

In the F&B domain, such a guideline has been developed by Albert Kooy, executive chef at Restaurant@Stenden in the Netherlands, in the form of *Five Ingredients for Better, Fresher, Healthier and More Just Food* – the title of his 2013 book. Kooy is a cook and, as he states in the book's introduction, it is as a cook that he is concerned about food. The point Kooy wishes to make is that contemporary patterns of food production and consumption are unhealthy, both for us and for the Earth. The only way forward, in his opinion, is to better understand what we eat and then choose accordingly. To this end, he has developed the 'five ingredients' to which the title of his book refers – these are thus not only applicable to restaurants but also to day-to-day food choices of each of us.

The five 'ingredients' or components that Kooy proposes as a guideline for sustainable food can be summarized using the following five terms: culture, health, nature, quality and profit. Let's briefly consider these ingredients one by one.

Culture asks for respect of the culinary heritage of the region in which the restaurant is situated by using local and seasonal ingredients, and by designing new recipes taking into account this heritage. Although it should be recognized that culinary traditions keep evolving, the bottom line is that a guest should be able to recognize the region and the season from the dish served.

It cannot be doubted that 'local' has become a trend in restaurants. The US National Restaurant Association has even pronounced it to be *the* trend of US 2012 restaurants (Sloan et al., 2013). The appeal of locally sourced food ranges from its freshness, to the opportunity of differentiating from competitors by offering produce that is special to one area.

'Local' is of course a broad concept, and has to be operationalized, for example by referring to climate areas where fruit and vegetables are open-grown or by mileages (see

*Figure 22.1* An Albert Kooy dish: spaghetti with cockles from the Waddenzee.

*Source:* the author.

Chapter 25 in this book). It is widely recognized that not all ingredients can be sourced locally. Even looking from a quite broad regional perspective, by considering for example Europe as a region, coffee, tea, chocolate and several spices cannot be produced 'locally'. Kooy proposes as a rule to use 80 per cent local and 20 per cent imported ingredients.

As a component of sustainable F&B, culture touches both on the social (culinary heritage) and on the environmental (local, seasonal, open-grown) dimension of food sustainability.

The second and third ingredients for sustainable restaurants – health and nature – can be discussed together. The first refers to our personal health, the second to Earth's. Our health is best served by reconsidering the role that meat and vegetables take in a typical restaurant menu (and in many homes, see Tukker et al., 2009). The principal role is usually for meat, while vegetables are considered background actors. A healthy human diet is based on the reverse choice; in Kooy's proposition this means designing dishes around the formula: 80 per cent vegetables and 20 per cent meat.

Considering the impact of meat production on Earth's resources, this choice is also the most environmentally friendly.[2] And, looking at the relative costs of meat and vegetables, this choice is the most sensible from a financial perspective as well.

Similar outcomes are also achieved by reducing portions; restaurant portions often exceed by far the calories needed daily, and lead either to overeating or to avoidable waste.[3] What is not wasted has not to be bought, and thus reducing portions is a sustainable choice financially as well. This may free resources that could be used for buying organic food and beverages, even though these are more expensive than non-organic ones.

In line with Rimmington et al., Kooy's sustainable F&B manager or restaurateur avoids additives and an inappropriate use of salt and sugar.[4] He or she prepares dishes starting from

*Table 22.2* Kooy's five ingredients and the three sustainability dimensions

| | Ingredient | Key words | Sustainability dimension |
|---|---|---|---|
| 1. | Culture | Culinary heritage; local, seasonal, open-grown | Social and environmental |
| 2. | Health | 80 per cent vegetable and 20 per cent meat; no additives | Social and financial |
| 3. | Nature | 80 per cent vegetable and 20 per cent meat; full animal; local; organic | Environmental |
| 4. | Quality | Respect for products and producers (fair trade) | Social |
| 5. | Profit | Profit for all stakeholders | Financial |

fresh ingredients and not from pre-packaged components (Pollan, 2009). Finally, she or he utilizes the whole animal – including 'odd bits' such as the head and offal. In this way a restaurateur realizes a positive outcome both for the planet and the profit dimension of sustainability.

The fourth ingredient for a sustainable restaurant asks for respect. Respect for the quality of the products and for the people producing them, all over the world. This includes, but is not limited to, choosing products from so-called developing countries with a fair-trade logo. Choosing fair trade is a common recommendation in sustainable F&B. A fair price is an essential element of the social or people dimension of sustainability, as long as the premium price that is paid reaches the producers as it should. Moreover, as Kooy justly notes, it should be remembered that also in the so-called developed countries farmers and other employees in the food chain are often not properly rewarded for their work. Local farmers in developed countries in general, and local farmers producing organically in particular, are often unable to sustain their business due to the low prices paid on the market. This issue should get the same attention from a sustainable restaurateur as fair-trade issues in developing countries.

The last ingredient of a sustainable restaurant is profit. Of course profit is needed for the survival of a business. Yet the profit Kooy refers to here is the result of all the above and consists of creating value for all stakeholders including suppliers, guests, the Earth and the restaurateur.

The five components of sustainable F&B in restaurants proposed by Kooy are easy to remember, and not difficult to operationalize as will be shown in the next section. Moreover, they are in line with authoritative academic literature, such as that discussed in the introductory section, and influential policy documents, such as the report written by Lang et al. (2011) for the Sustainable Development Commission (see Table 22.2).

## Retaurateurs in action for sustainable F&B

While the previous section has shown the components of a sustainable restaurant from a theoretical point of view, this section presents three best practices showing innovative ways found by entrepreneurs to engage with sustainability.

The first best practice illustrates Albert Kooy's work at Stenden University of Applied Sciences. He has used the 'five ingredients' described above to design the menu of both the Stenden canteen and restaurant. At the time of writing (October 2013), Stenden Canteen has received a nomination as the best Dutch canteen, even though traditional canteen food such as deep-fried frites and beverages with high sugar content are banned. Moreover, it has to be noticed that students of the Stenden Hotel Management School form the canteen and restaurant staff. Students are very dedicated, but not professional staff. That they can prepare dishes based on the 'five ingredients' serves to demystify the idea that cooking from fresh, seasonal ingredients and using the whole animal is only for the happy few who master difficult cooking techniques.

All 'five ingredients' are applied to the Stenden restaurant and canteen. Yet, it can be said that the central concept in the new (autumn 2013) restaurant menu is the concept of 'no waste' and the use of alternative ingredients, such as jellyfish and grasshoppers. More traditional dishes, such as entrecote, are also offered; but then the guest has to pay a premium price. This turns the traditional idea that organic food is expensive upside-down: it is meat that is expensive, not organic food.

Stenden has campuses also outside the Netherlands, in Qatar, South Africa, Thailand and Bali (Indonesia). Together with the local chefs, Kooy is devising menus that respect the 'five ingredients' of a sustainable F&B offer.

The second-best practice refers back to the use of the whole animal. Not wasting any part of an animal makes sense both from an economic and an environmental perspective. Waste is economically unsound, because what is wasted has to be bought in advance and affects the environment negatively because – in the case of meat – more animals are needed, and more animals means more farm land needed to grow the cereals that will feed them; more manure and so on (see the discussion in Sloan et al., 2013, on agricultural inputs to the Western diet). The impact of farming on natural resources such as water, its contribution to greenhouse gas emissions and the manure overshoot are some of the issues that call if not for a reduction of meat consumption, at least for a better use of the animals we breed and kill for human consumption. If we look back to traditional cuisine, nothing of an animal was wasted. Respect for the life taken, regard for the work involved in breeding an animal and economic considerations led to the use of the whole animal. With affluence, consumers started to choose only those parts of an animal that were considered more 'noble'. One of the consequences of this trend is that some animal parts – such as tongue, heads and offal – have quite disappeared from our kitchen. They seem even to be considered not suitable for human consumption.[5]

Fortunately, a movement is developing that wishes to bring back less noble animal parts to our menu. This counter-tendency can be illustrated by the success of Toronto-based cookbook author Jennifer McLagan. She has recently (2011) published a cookbook with the title *Odd Bits: How to Cook the Rest of the Animal*, after having written a book on the use of bones and fat in cooking. In the introduction, McLagan notices that those parts that were considered the most special and expensive, such as the tenderloins and the racks, are now common and cheap thanks to modern industry production methods and because they are easy to cook. And then she states:

> I'm not interested in these cuts and you won't find them here. This book is about the rest of the animal; the pieces we once enjoyed and relished but no longer bother with. Unfamiliar and odd, they have become the 'odd bits' [. . .] They are all animal parts we have forgotten not only how to cook but also how to eat.
>
> *(McLagan, 2011: 1)*

McLagan is very conscious of the need to choose the whole animal from a sustainability perspective. She is also deeply concerned with animal welfare. As she puts it:

> Those of us who care about what we eat – and we should all care – must demand that the animals we eat are raised naturally and humanely, treated with respect in both life and death. This is the only way a thinking carnivore can continue to eat meat.
>
> *(McLagan, 2011: 2)*

As she herself recognizes, McLagan is not the only one interested in the use of the whole animal. In her introduction she quotes Fergus Henderson, the chef-owner of St John

Restaurant in London. In 1999 Henderson published the award-winning book *Nose to Tail Eating – A Kind of British Cooking*. This book soon became a cult-item and, as reminded by Anthony Bourdain in his introduction to the 2004 edition, was instrumental in bringing back to restaurant menus neglected bits of animal.

Among the restaurants that are digging into this trend are restaurants such as The Black Hoof and The Beast – maybe not surprisingly both based in Toronto.

Looking further at waste minimization, an interesting concept is that of Spirit, a self-service restaurant located in Rotterdam. Self-services and buffets increase the post-preparation waste: it has been reckoned that almost 10 per cent of what a guest puts on his plate is not eaten (Bio Intelligence Service, 2010). Daniël Saat, Spirit chef and developer of its concept, recognized that the main driver behind this behaviour is the fixed price paid by guests. As is widely known, one of the main motivators of people behaviour is the desire to guard resources that have been acquired, including financial resources. This desire often works against sustainable choices (Lindenberg and Steg, 2007). Spirit bends this mechanism so that it has a positive and not a negative impact on food waste: they let their guests pay per eaten gram of food. The idea is simple: after serving themself, the guest weighs his/her plate, and pays for the exact amount of what s/he has chosen. As Saat puts it, this concept has proven a good way to engage guests in waste minimization and is moreover fair both for big and for small eaters. Spirit is successful, and has already enlarged its premises to cater for the increasing demand. Its simple and innovative concept, united to a menu consisting exclusively of vegetarian dishes prepared with organic and seasonal ingredients, has received attention from the SKAL Foundation (a non-profit inspection body for organic production in the Netherlands), making Spirit the only restaurant in Rotterdam that is certified by SKAL.[6] In this respect as well, Spirit forms a best practice for sustainable restaurateurs.

## Conclusion

Sustainable F&B goes much further than the use of organic and fair-trade products. This may be challenging for restaurateurs and chefs, but offers also ample opportunity for their creativity and innovation, as has been shown in the last section. A major challenge is surely constituted by the risk to cater only for a very limited niche. Clear and transparent communication with guests is a must for each sustainable entrepreneur, and even more so for outspoken sustainable restaurateurs who with their menu offer, almost by definition, challenge the F&B habits of their clients.

This said, it should also be remembered that to become fully sustainable, a restaurateur should go beyond F&B and strive to create value on the environmental, social and economic dimension of all choices connected with the restaurant.

## Notes

1 Personal communication by Eveline de Kruif (KHN – Dutch Category Organizations for Hotels, Restaurants and Caterings, September 2013).
2 Meat and dairy account for 24 per cent of the environmental impact of Europeans' consumption patterns (Tukker et al., 2009).
3 In so-called developed countries, but also in some developing countries, obesity and weight problems have become serious health issues, with daunting financial consequences. It has for example been estimated that obesity and weight issues would cost the UK National Health Service £50 billion in 2050 (see Lang et al., 2011).
4 Inappropriate here means the use of salt and sugar where they are not required for the execution of a recipe (such as sugar in a mayonnaise) or their excessive use where they are required (such as sugar in a jam). On the risks connected with a too high consumption of salt, see Lang et al. (2011).

5  To illustrate this point, it may be useful to relate here an incident that happened to the father-in-law of the author. Wishing to cook a typical Italian dish ('rigatoni con la pajata') he went to a Dutch butcher and asked for veal bowel. Unsure about the particulars of preparing it, he asked the butcher about the cooking time. The answer was: 'You do not need to cook it; just throw it in their bowls, and the dogs will eat it.' To the butcher, offal was by definition not for human consumption.
6  Information from the best practice on Spirit comes from research carried out by students from the five Dutch hotel management schools during the Hospitality Excellence Program patronized by KHN (Dutch Category Organizations for Hotels, Restaurants and Caterings) in February–June 2013. These students worked under the supervision of Dr Elena Cavagnaro.

# References

Bio Intelligence Service (2010) *Preparatory Study on Food Waste Across EU27*, Technical Report 2010–054 to the European Commission, Directorate C – Industry, SP: European Community.

Cavagnaro, E. and Curiel, G.H. (2012) *The Three Levels of Sustainability*, Sheffield: Greenleaf.

Cavagnaro, E. and Gehrels, S. (2009) 'Sweet and sour grapes, implementing sustainability in the hospitality industry – a case study', *Journal of Culinary Science and Technology*, 7(2–3): 181–195.

Earth Summit II (1997) *Programme for the Further Implementation of Agenda 21*, Outcome of the General Assembly Special Session to Review Progress on Implementation of Agenda 21, New York: UN, www.earthsummit2002.org/toolkits/Women/un-doku/un-conf/ES2chap1.htm (accessed 30 March 2011).

Elkington, J. (1998) *Cannibals with Forks: The Triple Bottom Line of 21st-Century Businesses*, Gabriola Island, BC: New Society Publishers.

Henderson, F. (1999, 2004) *Nose to Tail Eating – A Kind of British Cooking*, London: Bloomsbury Publishing.

Kooy, A. (2013) *5 ingrediënten voor beter, verser, gezonder en eerlijker eten*, Zutphen, Netherlands: KMuitgevers.

Lang, T., Dibb, S. and Reddy, S. (2011) *Looking Back, Looking Forward: Sustainability and UK Food Policy 2000–2011*, London: Sustainable Development Commission.

Legrand, W., Sloan, P., Simons-Kaufmann, C. and Fleischer, S. (2010) 'A review of restaurant sustainable indicators', in J.S. Chen (ed.), *Advances in Hospitality and Leisure*, Volume 6, Bingley: Emerald Group Publishing Limited, pp. 167–183.

Lindenberg, S. and Steg, L. (2007) 'Normative, gain and hedonic goal frames guiding environmental behavior', *Journal of Social Issues*, 65(1): 117–137.

McLagan, J. (2011) *Odd Bits: How to Cook the Rest of the Animal*, Berkeley: Ten Speed Press.

Pollan, M. (2009) *In Defence of Food*, London: Penguin.

Rimmington, M., Carlton Smith, J. and Hawkins, R. (2006) 'Corporate social responsibility and sustainable food procurement', *British Food Journal*, 108: 824–837.

Rockström, J., Steffen, W., Noone, K., Persson, Å., Chapin, III, F. S., Lambin, E. F., Lenton, T. M., Scheffer, M., Folke, C., Schellnhuber, H. J., Nykvist, B., de Wit, C. A., Hughes, T., van der Leeuw, S., Rodhe, H., Sörlin, S., Snyder, P.K., Costanza, R., Svedin, U., Falkenmark, M., Karlberg, L., Corel, R.W., Fabry, V.J., Hansen, J., Walker, B., Liverman, D., Richardson, K., Crutzen, P. and Foley, J.A. (2009) 'A safe operating space for humanity', *Nature*, 461: 472–475.

Sloan, P., Legrand, W. and Chan, J.C. (2013) *Sustainability in the Hospitality Industry: Principles of Sustainable Operations*, Oxford and New York: Routledge.

Tukker, A., Bausch-Goldbohm, S., Verheijden, M., de Koning, A., Kleijn, R., Wolf, O. and Pérez Domíngues, I. (2009) *Environmental Impacts of Diet Changes in the EU*, Seville: European Commission Joint Research Centre Institute for Prospective Technological Studies.

WCED (1987) *Our Common Future*, Oxford: Oxford University Press.

# Additional information

Restaurant@stenden (former restaurant.nl), www.stendenrestaurant.com/RestaurantNL
Saint John Restaurant, www.stjohngroup.uk.com
Spirit, www.spiritrotterdam.nl
Stenden Canteen, www.stendencanteen.com/the-canteen
The Beast, http://thebeastrestaurant.com
The Black Hoof, http://theblackhoof.com

# 23

# FOODSERVICE, HEALTH AND NUTRITION

## Responsibility, strategies and perspectives

*Laure Saulais*

## Introduction

For the foodservice sector, whose mission is to provide meals outside the home, the health of consumers is becoming a new responsibility – and a new challenge. The alarming rise of chronic diseases associated with nutritional imbalance is a collective concern worldwide. Overweight or obese people amounted to 47.3 per cent of French adults in 2012 (Inserm et al., 2012) and 68 per cent of American adults in 2007–2008 (Flegal et al., 2010).[1]

The foodservice sector has been blamed for its role in the obesity epidemics, with quick-service restaurants in the front line (Lake and Townshend, 2006; Prentice and Jebb, 2003). One of the difficulties in assessing the contribution of foodservice to this phenomenon, however, lies in the variety of activities covered by this industry[2] and, in particular, the heterogeneity of the offer – from sandwiches to gastronomy. However, there is a general consensus that away-from-home (AFH) foods[3] play an important role in the diet (Lachat et al., 2012), with a variable contribution across countries and age groups. Adults in the US obtain up to 32 per cent of their daily calorie intake from AFH sources (Lin and Morrison, 2012). European adults eat between 12 and 28 per cent (depending on country and gender) of their daily calories outside their home (Orfanos et al., 2007). In a context of rapid evolution of eating habits and forms of consumption (Grunert, 2013), the number of eating-out occasions is increasing in most countries (Lin et al., 1999; Laisney, 2012; Lachat et al., 2012) and, consequently, so does the contribution of AFH food to diet (Martinez-Palou and Rohner-Thielen, 2011). This trend raises concerns in the public health community, as AFH eating has been associated in many studies with higher energy intake, excessive fat and salt intake, and poorer nutritional quality of the diet (Lachat et al., 2012; Larson and Neumark-Sztainer, 2011; Myhre et al., 2013; Park et al., 2009). In other words, eating out more seems to lead to eating more. Other epidemiological studies have directly linked consumption outside the home and body mass index (Naska et al., 2011; Bezerra et al., 2012; Bes-Rastrollo et al., 2010).

Some specific characteristics of the AFH food offer have been particularly pointed out in this phenomenon. The first characteristic is the nutritional quality of the food offered: several studies, indeed, report larger portion sizes and a poorer nutritional quality of AFH food (Lin and Morrison, 2012; Nielsen and Popkin, 2003; Prentice and Jebb, 2003). Another characteristic is the context in which the food is offered. A greater availability of energy-dense foods, a lower availability of healthy options, and a lack of information about the contents of the products, have indeed been highlighted (Lachat et al., 2009, 2012).

Obesity is a multifactorial problem, and preventing it requires combining multiple levels and scales of action. Interventions may target the offer itself, the context, but also consumers and their behaviours. Actions may be undertaken on a large scale (e.g., with health education programmes), or locally, with actions at the point of choice.

At the restaurant level, improving the nutritional quality of meals consumed by restaurant customers can be achieved either by changing the offer, or by guiding consumers' choices. The rest of this chapter discusses these approaches and the possible barriers to the implementation of such actions.

## On the supply side: offering healthier options

Eating meals prepared out of home makes it more difficult for consumers to control the nutritional content of dishes and, therefore, to eat healthily (Lachat et al., 2009).

For foodservice professionals, two levels of action can be considered when looking at the challenge of offering healthier meal options: the dish level (i.e., modifying the recipe, for instance by substituting saturated fat with unsaturated fats, by reducing sugar content or adding dietary fibres) and the assortment level (i.e., offering smaller portions or adding to the menu healthier options that were previously unavailable, for instance increasing the number of fruits on offer for dessert).

For instance, in the 'Better Life Menu' programme in Canada, recipes of usual dishes were modified to contain a maximum of 30 per cent energy from fat (10 per cent from saturated fat), and polyunsaturated or monounsaturated fats were used for sauces, salad dressings and cooking. This dish-level intervention was coupled with assortment-level changes, such as an increased availability of lower-fat products and a decrease in portion sizes. Regular customers of a worksite cafeteria decreased their saturated fat and protein intake by 3 per cent, while carbohydrate intake increased by 7 per cent of total energy (Dubois et al., 1996).

The reference to define healthy food is generally official nutritional standards. In an effort to translate these standards into actions for foodservice professionals, the European FOOD programme[4] developed a guide providing simple advice, such as preferring steam cooking to frying, or seasoning with spices rather than salt.

Quantifying the direct nutritional impact of offer modification is difficult. Because of the variety of foodservice activities, and the diversity of actions, meta-analyses are limited. Nevertheless, a recent review of six studies in workplace restaurants found some (although limited) evidence of a weak but positive behavioural effect of such interventions (alone or combined with nutrition education). Improvements concerned mainly fruit and vegetable consumption (Geaney et al., 2013).

Strategically, improving the offer can be an added-value for foodservice companies, who may communicate about their commitments. In 2013, the major European quick-service restaurant company Quick publicly announced[5] the signature of a charter with the French Health Ministry,[6] with commitments to improve the dietary quality of its offer.

## On the demand side: changing food choices behaviours

While an essential step towards the improvement of meals, changing the offer is a 'one size fits all' approach. Restaurant customers, on the other hand, have varied nutritional needs, but also varied motives for having a meal, and different representations and knowledge regarding healthy eating. Another approach to improving the quality of the meals eaten by restaurant customers is to help them make better choices for themselves among a variety of options, either by providing information to consumers, or by changing the way food options are presented.

## Information-based strategies

Providing information to consumers is probably the most widespread approach for healthy AFH eating. These information-based strategies rely on the assumption that informing consumers allows them to make better choices.

Different approaches are possible, as summarized below (Figure 23.1). Actions are differentiated in terms of *the nature of the information diffused* (they either provide consumers with general knowledge and recommendations about healthy eating or display specific information about the products on offer), and in terms of *means of diffusion* (information is most commonly displayed at the point of choice, but may also appear outside the restaurant). Outside the eating location, the development of the internet has allowed the emergence of new vectors of information. Major quick-service restaurant chains such as McDonald's or Kentucky Fried Chicken provide nutritional information on their products on their websites. In 2013, McDonald's also started implementing QR codes on packaging, which direct consumers to the nutritional values of the dish (Johnson, 2013). Augmented reality should also, in the near future, open new opportunities for providing customized product information.

## General information

The objectives of such programmes are generally defined in the long term. They aim to educate consumers about nutrition, to remind them of healthy practices and/or to improve

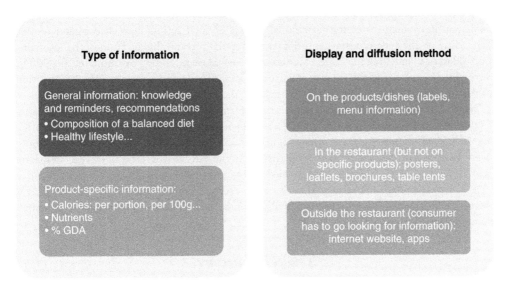

*Figure 23.1* A typology of information-based strategies in foodservice settings.

*Source:* the author.

knowledge and awareness of the importance and conditions of healthy eating, in the hope of changing attitudes and intentions, and, eventually, behaviours. They may combine several types of tools (e.g., training, information, coaching) and be deployed in different locations (beyond the point of choice and consumption).

While education and awareness-raising are not the primary missions of the foodservice sector, restaurants can be good settings for such programmes. This holds especially true when customers are regular, allowing for longer exposure to messages.

Since these programmes primarily target knowledge and satisfaction, only a few studies have assessed their direct impact on food intake or choices, with non-significant, weak, or partial effects (Fitzgerald et al., 2004; Steenhuis et al., 2004). Conversely, the impact on customer attitudes, awareness and satisfaction is generally positive. For instance, the TrEAT Yourself Well social marketing campaign targeted restaurant diners in California through media advertising, on-site promotion and various community events. A survey demonstrated a positive effect on beliefs and attitudes towards healthy eating (Acharya et al., 2006).

Because of this seemingly low direct impact on behaviours, general information is often combined with other actions and different levels of information, mixing, for instance, information on nutrition, physical activity and nutritional content (Sorensen et al., 1992; Holdsworth et al., 2000). Because of this multi-component approach, these programmes may be quite costly to implement. The heterogeneity of approaches also makes the assessment of their efficiency quite difficult.

## Product-specific information

Most of the time referred to as 'calorie posting' or 'nutrition labelling', product-specific information strategies consist in providing descriptive, factual information on the nutritional contents of the dishes or products sold. Unlike in the packaged foods sector,[7] this practice is recent in the foodservice sector. Mandatory calorie labelling was only extended to chain restaurants in New York City in 2008, and in all US chain restaurants in 2010.[8] In Europe, voluntary initiatives have recently emerged – notably in the major quick-service restaurant chains.

Scientific evaluations of the nutritional impact of such actions have had mixed results, depending on the type of restaurant, the target population, and the duration of the intervention (Harnack and French, 2008; Holdsworth and Haslam, 1998; Seymour et al., 2004). Several studies also find the success of such operations to depend upon the initial motivation of participants to eat more healthily (Harnack et al., 2008; Dumanovsky et al., 2011).

Much like general information, nutritional information generally improves customer satisfaction, attitudes towards nutrition and calorie information, perceived benefit of the programme and perceived usefulness of the information. However, it should be noted that this has only been measured in US populations. Whether the same effects would be observed elsewhere, with different dietary practices and knowledge about nutrition, remains largely unknown.

Lastly, while providing information to customers appears to increase their satisfaction, it is unclear whether this information is actually used to make choices, or if consumers simply value information.

## Choice architecture

Information-based strategies rely on the premise that consumers call upon rationality to make decisions. Thus, providing information to consumers should improve the quality of their decisions. This assumption is challenged by recent advances in behavioural sciences, which provide evidence that the environment of choice, or the way the choice task is structured (called the 'architecture of choice'), also affects decisions. Since the works of Kahneman and Tversky on dual-process reasoning systems (Kahneman, 2003; Tversky and Kahneman, 1974, 1981, 1986), it has been hypothesized that rationality is bounded, and that decisions are subjected to biases. Decisions involve two systems of reasoning: a fast and automatic system (system 1) that relies on emotions and intuition, and a slow and reflexive system (system 2) that relies more heavily on thinking and rationality (Kahneman, 2011). Food choices involve intuitions and emotions, and may thus rely on system 1 (Köster, 2009). They may also be biased in an automatic way by the context of choice. As these biases are predictable, the environment can be manipulated to orient consumers towards choices considered as healthier (Ariely, 2009).

Approaches using changes in the choice environment, popularized under the term 'nudge' since the works of Thaler and Sunstein (2008), have recently generated considerable interest from the Public Health sector. Specific government departments, such as the British behavioural insights team (referred to as the 'Nudge Unit'), were created in the USA and the UK in order to explore such avenues for public action. In the foodservice sector, some experiments were conducted to test the effect of environmental changes on the nutritional quality of meals, with promising results (Downs et al., 2009).

'Nudging' restaurant customers towards healthier choices in AFH settings can take many forms. Using the MINDSPACE framework (Dolan et al., 2012), Figure 23.2 presents examples of successful nudges tested in AFH settings.

One of the most frequently encountered approaches is the *use of labels* to signal healthy items on menus (or in a cafeteria display line) to simplify the information-processing task performed by consumers. Nutrients and calories are factual indicators, but restaurant customers eat dishes, not nutrients. Therefore, they may not be able to process information at the nutrient level, especially since dishes may contain both healthy and unhealthy nutrients. By placing the focus on a single attribute, labels reduce the parameters of the decision. They also 'prime' consumers with unconscious cues. Labels are often displayed with accompanying posters, which describe the programme. While the criteria of selection for labelled items vary, they most frequently target low-fat products, or products that are rich in dietary fibres. The intervention may consist either in labelling already existing products, or in developing new dishes meeting the criteria. It is however unclear whether these actions have beneficial effects on consumer choices. Sales of labelled items increase, in most studies, for at least a subset of the targeted offer. However, the impact on actual individual food intake is unclear (Dubbert et al., 1984; Steenhuis et al., 2004; Hoefkens et al., 2011).

Nudges are promising. From an operational point of view, they seem relatively straightforward and inexpensive to implement. Yet, to our knowledge, their actual monetary cost has never been evaluated. Furthermore, at this point, data is insufficient to demonstrate their effectiveness and their applicability to a variety of AFH contexts and populations. However, some robust effects can be drawn from experiments in other public health fields (Dolan et al., 2012). Further research should therefore be carried out in order, first, to strengthen the existing data on the effectiveness of such approaches in AFH settings and, second, to enable their operational development in the foodservice sector.

In particular, the menu card is the main medium of choice at the restaurant, and thus embodies both a critical point of the choice architecture and an apparently simple way to explore the operational level. An experiment showed, for instance, a link between the menu position of an item and its sales (Dayan and Bar-Hillel, 2011). Other behavioural levers, identified and tested in other areas of public health (Blumenthal-Barby and Burroughs, 2012; Johnson et al., 2012; Thaler et al., 2010) could be explored in the design of menu cards

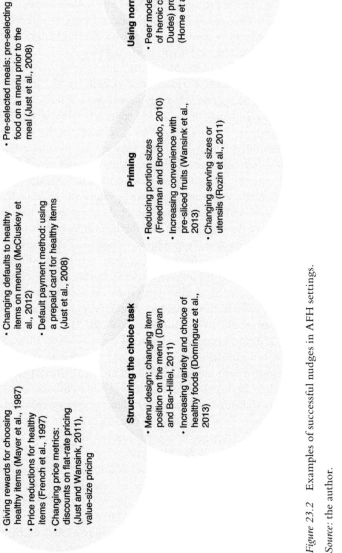

**Creating incentives**
· Giving rewards for choosing healthy items (Mayer et al., 1987)
· Price reductions for healthy items (French et al., 1997)
· Changing price metrics: discounts on flat-rate pricing (Just and Wansink, 2011), value-size pricing

**Using defaults**
· Changing defaults to healthy items on menus (McCluskey et al., 2012)
· Default payment method: using a prepaid card for healthy items (Just et al., 2008)

**Committing**
· Pre-selected meals: pre-selecting food on a menu prior to the meal (Just et al., 2008)

**Using saliency**
· Increasing the availability of healthy options (French et al., 2004)
· Increasing the visibility of/ access to healthy food (Rozin et al., 2011)
· Attribute parsimony: labelling healthy items or both healthy and unhealthy items (Levy et al., 2012)

**Structuring the choice task**
· Menu design: changing item position on the menu (Dayan and Bar-Hillel, 2011)
· Increasing variety and choice of healthy foods (Domínguez et al., 2013)

**Priming**
· Reducing portion sizes (Freedman and Brochado, 2010)
· Increasing convenience with pre-sliced fruits (Wansink et al., 2013)
· Changing serving sizes or utensils (Rozin et al., 2011)

**Using norms and messengers**
· Peer modelling: Showing videos of heroic characters (Food Dudes) promoting healthy foods (Horne et al., 2009)

*Figure 23.2*　Examples of successful nudges in AFH settings.

*Source*: the author.

promoting healthiest choices. For example, the menu categories (usually structured as 'appetizers, main dish, dessert') could be modified to guide towards healthy choices, using research on partitioning and variety-seeking behaviours which shows that consumers tend to evenly allocate their choices within a set of categories (Johnson et al., 2012; Read et al., 1999).

## Diffusion

The diffusion of nutritional strategies within the foodservice sector is very heterogeneous. In France, major companies are the most active. All major collective catering companies have developed nutrition and health programmes in the past decade (such as Sodexo's *Programme Equilibre*, launched in 2003, which became the *Boost&Moi* programme in 2012, or the *Démarche Equilibre* by Elior, started in 2004). These programmes rely on a multitude of tools acting both on the quality of the offer and diffusion of information to consumers (through brochures, posters, animations, etc.). Some of the tools and messages of these programmes have obtained a certification from the National Health and Nutrition Program (PNNS). The fast food industry, meanwhile, has started to display product-specific information: for example, McDonald's France provides the energy values of some sandwiches, and has a website where customers can view their energy needs and calculate the nutrient and energy contents of their meals. In traditional commercial catering, conversely, whether chain or independent, initiatives remain scarce.

The existence of a legal framework, and its nature, determines partly the level of involvement of foodservice actors, and institutional and commercial foodservice are affected differently by regulations. In France for instance, as early as 2001, official recommendations were established by the GEMRCN[9] for institutional foodservice. In 2010, a statutory obligation was introduced for the implementation of nutritional recommendations for institutional meals in schools, universities, kindergartens, health care institutions, social and medico-social institutions and prisons.[10] Similarly, voluntary standards became statutory in England for schools in 2008, and should be implemented in the four UK countries by September 2013 (Adamson et al., 2013). The existence of a framework does not, however, fully guarantee the implementation of related actions. Obligations may be perceived as frustrating or confusing by foodservice professionals (Almanza et al., 1997), slowing down their implementation. In France, a debate regarding the obligation to apply nutrition standards in collective catering settings has opposed, in 2013, public health actors with operators arguing that standards were too difficult to meet (Société Française de Santé Publique, 2013).

Regarding commercial foodservice, with the exception of the recent US regulations for chain restaurants, there is little regulation worldwide regarding nutrition, either on the nature of the offer or on the information provided to consumers.

The impulse to change may thus rely for a large part on voluntary commitment from the foodservice sector. Indeed, most of the programmes described in this chapter were developed primarily for commercial purposes, in response to consumer demand for a healthier food offer, for more information or, in the case of contract catering, as an asset in business-to-business negotiation. Consequently, the success of the programmes in actually improving diets is generally a secondary objective, which is not systematically evaluated.

## Barriers to improving nutritional quality in foodservice

A few studies have shed some light on potential obstacles to implementation of nutrition actions, which may also explain the limited development of such programmes, especially in independent restaurants.

## *Beliefs and motivation*

In the absence of legal obligation, foodservice professionals need to be convinced that consumers are looking for balanced meals or that they value nutrition information. Among potentially precluding beliefs about consumers' expectations is the assumption that consumers are more attracted to unhealthy food and find, on the contrary, healthy food to be devoid of taste.[11] Restaurant owners may also have beliefs about the definition of healthy food, which may drive the choice of actions to implement (Vyth et al., 2012).

## *Lack of nutritional expertise*

Developing nutrition strategies calls upon an expertise that may not be part of the training of foodservice professionals. For instance, product-specific information labelling requires a nutritional evaluation of the dishes' content. While major chains may afford a dietician and the adequate technical capacity for measurement, it may not be the case with independent restaurants. Restaurant-specific challenges may arise such as the frequency of menu renewal, or the lack of structural flexibility for the supply of adequate ingredients (Lachat et al., 2010), which may lead to improper or partial application of nutritional standards. In a recent study in the top 400 US chain restaurants, most main dishes complied with recommendations regarding daily energy needs, but not regarding nutrients, specifically sodium and fat (Wu and Sturm, 2013). Lastly, restaurant owners may have trouble following recommendations while trying to address a heterogeneous demand (Vermeer et al., 2010).

## *Time and human resources*

A lack of operational feasibility may also slow down the implementation of such programmes. Notably, the perceived added workload, the lack of financial resources or time, and more generally the fear of a cost premium related to the programme, constitute barriers to the implementation of such procedures (Vyth et al., 2012; Almanza et al., 1997). Facing these obstacles, the main determinants of professional involvement in nutrition programs are the ease of implementation of the actions (Vermeer et al., 2010), the adaptation of the measures to the local culture and constraints (Lachat et al., 2010), as well as the possibility to communicate about the implementation (Vyth et al., 2012). The results of the European FOOD programme, in which questionnaires were handed out to restaurant owners, corroborate these findings and show that time and budget, beyond the lack of expertise of Chefs about nutrition, remain, in independent private restaurants in particular, powerful barriers to implement changes to a more balanced diet. These practical barriers to implementation may appear even when there is either motivation (commercial), a framework or even a legal obligation to implement the programs. For instance, a study on the application of GEMRCN recommendations in France reported that secondary state schools complied, on average, with only half of the provided guidelines (Bertin et al., 2011).

## *Perceived costs and benefits*

Although a strong determinant of the implementation of nutritional action, the financial impact of such programs – whether positive or negative – is hard to assess. For instance, the implementation of nutritional labelling involves some supplementary costs (nutritional evaluation of dishes, cost of the communication tools, etc.). The resulting benefits of such programmes are, however, difficult to ascertain. While most studies report a demand for information and an overall positive effect of such programmes on customer satisfaction (Josiam and Foster, 2009; Alexander et al., 2010), the direct impact on willingness-to-pay and on demand is unclear and context-dependent. Regarding the cost of changing the quality of the offer, likewise, little evidence is available in the literature. In a study of the implementation of the GEMRCN in French school canteens, Darmon et al. (2010) find that restaurants that had started following the recommendations had reduced their costs, due to the recommended reduction of portion sizes. However, the same study revealed that there were no differences in costs between sites applying or not the recommendations at the same time period.

## Conclusion

Achieving sustainability in foodservice requires taking into account the ecological, economic and social aspects of this activity. One of the key aspects in this equation is to preserve the health of consumers, by ensuring that they can eat healthily. While the strategies described in this chapter could all potentially contribute to this objective, their implementation is not straightforward.

On the supply side, the increased awareness of cooks, the growing pressure from the market to produce healthier food, as well as the slow emergence of a regulatory framework may contribute to improving the nutritional quality. However, many barriers, which we described above, exist, and the path to success may not be linear.

It has been demonstrated that customers tended to greatly underestimate their calorie consumption in the restaurant (Burton et al., 2006). This result, put into perspective with those on the effect of menu information and phrasing on the judgement and choices of consumers (Wansink et al., 2001, 2005), seems to support the idea of the appropriateness of nutrition information on menus. But studies directly assessing the effects of point-of-purchase information on food choices show that these effects depend on context, customer characteristics (especially their motivation), and the nature of the information available.

Point-of-purchase information, therefore, may need to be complemented by longer-term health promotion and education programmes. Such an approach would go beyond the normal scope of action of the foodservice sector, and require collaboration between foodservice professionals and other actors, such as public health professionals. But it may demonstrate more efficiency in the long run. A 2010 review listed 16 British studies evaluating the effect on nutrition-related variables of interventions to promote health in the workplace. The results indicate a positive, but weak, effect on eating behaviours and on the nutritional status of employees. The authors, however, noted the low robustness of the results of available studies, and specifically, the lack of financial and acceptability assessment of interventions (Mhurchu et al., 2010).

Another promising approach is the modification of the choice environment through nudges, which have contributed to highlight the importance of the choice setting on behaviours, and the impact of the strategic choices of foodservice professionals on consumer health. One striking example is the impact of portion sizes and value-size pricing on food choices (Pratt et al., 2007; Vermeer et al., 2009; Freedman and Brochado, 2010). However, setting up nudges in a foodservice environment raises the delicate question of how to determine what the 'better choices' should be for consumers. This normative aspect of nudges, which has been the topic of much debate in the literature, relates to important ethical questions about the extent to which public health actors, but also foodservice professionals, should intervene in consumers' food and health-related choices (Blumenthal-Barby, 2013; Selinger and Whyte, 2011; Quigley, 2013).

Ultimately, despite the need to strengthen current knowledge about possible actions, there are many ways in which foodservice can be an agent of health and nutrition promotion, and a vector of good practices, information and education.

## Notes

1 Adults were aged 18 or over for the French figures, 20 or over for the USA.
2 The definition of the scope of activity of the foodservice sector, in itself, is debated (Edwards, 2013), which may substantially affect the evaluation of this contribution.
3 Lin et al. (1999) propose to distinguish home and away-from-home foods on the basis of the location where they are obtained (as opposed to where they are eaten): away-from-home (AFH) foods covers any food prepared outside the home and consumed without any additional culinary preparation by the consumer, whether it is consumed outside the home, in a restaurant, or at home.
4 The FOOD (Fighting Obesity through Offer and Demand) project (2009–2011) was a multi-partner project which received funding from the European Union, in the framework of the Public Health Programme.
5 Press release, 3 June 2013: 'Quick, 1ère enseigne de restauration rapide à signer une 'Charte d'engagements volontaires de progrès nutritionnel' avec les Pouvoirs Publics', http://groupe. quick.fr/fr/une-histoire-de-gout/quick-1ere-enseigne-de-restauration-rapide-signer-une-charte-dengagements-volon (accessed 8 November 2013).
6 The French programme for nutrition and health (PNNS) has set up charters (*Chartes d'engagements volontaires de progrès nutritionnel*), which are signed on a voluntary basis by food or foodservice companies committing themselves to improve the nutritional quality of their offer. The Quick charter signed in 2013 can be found on the website of the Health Ministry: www.sante.gouv.fr/ IMG/pdf/Quick.pdf (accessed 8 November 2013). Four axes of improvement were defined: fat, sugar, salt and fibres. Examples of commitments found in the charter are the increase from 15 per cent to over 50 per cent of the dietary fibres content in bread utilized for the burgers, or the reduction of sugar content in sodas by 100 per cent.
7 Packaged foods sold in retail have been subjected to mandatory labelling in many countries for several years (Hawkes, 2004). In the USA, 'nutrition facts' have been mandatory for packaged foods since 1990.
8 According to the Patient Protection and Affordable Health Care Act, US chain restaurants with more than 20 locations must disclose calorie information for standard menu items and make nutrient information available on demand. (*HR- 3590 Patient Protection and Affordable Health Care Act – Sec. 4205: Nutrition Labeling of Standard Menu Items at Chain Restaurants*, www.govtrack.us/congress/ bills/111/hr3590/text.)
9 The acronym GEMRCN stands for '*Groupe d'étude des marchés de restauration collective et nutrition*' (Study Group on the Markets for Public Catering and Nutrition). This study group defined recommendations for the composition and structure of institutionalized meals (e.g., standards regarding the frequency of some dishes in the menu, the quantities and portion sizes).
10 An application decree (Décret no. 2011-1227 du 30 septembre 2011 relatif à la qualité nutritionnelle des repas servis dans le cadre de la restauration scolaire) for this obligation, based on the previously established GEMRCN standards, came into effect for all school food services from 1 September 2012, followed by other decrees for the other sectors (effective in 2013).
11 The question of whether such assumptions are founded is debated in the scientific community. Studies about this so-called 'unhealthy = tasty' effect find contradictory results: some authors find that food labelled as 'less healthy' is expected by US consumers to be tastier, more enjoyable, and preferred in choice tasks (Raghunathan et al., 2006), while the assumption is not verified by other authors – for instance in the French population (Werle et al., 2012).

## References

Acharya, R.N., Patterson, P.M., Hill, E.P., Schmitz, T.G. and Bohm, E. (2006) 'An evaluation of the "TrEAT Yourself Well" restaurant nutrition campaign', *Health Education & Behavior*, 33: 309–324.

Adamson, A., Spence, S., Reed, L. Conway, R., Palmer, A., Stewart, E., McBratney, J., Carter, L., Beattie, S. and Nelson, M. (2013) 'School food standards in the UK: implementation and evaluation', *Public Health Nutrition*, 16(6): 968–981.

Alexander, M., O'Gorman, K. and Wood, K. (2010) 'Nutritional labelling in restaurants: whose responsibility is it anyway?', *International Journal of Contemporary Hospitality Management*, 22: 572–579.

Almanza, B.A., Nelson, D. and Chai, S. (1997) 'Obstacles to nutrition labeling in restaurants', *Journal of the American Dietetic Association*, 97: 157–161.

Ariely, D. (2009) *Predictably Irrational*, New York: HarperCollins.

Bertin, M., Lafay, L., Calamassi-Tran, G., Voltier, J.-L. and Dubuisson, C. (2011) 'School meals in French secondary state schools: compliance to national recommendations and schools catering patterns', *Revue d'épidémiologie et de santé publique*, 59(1): 33–44.

Bes-Rastrollo, M., Basterra-Gortarim F.J., Sánchez-Villegas, A., Marti, A., Martínez, J.A. and Martínez-González, M.A. (2010) 'A prospective study of eating away-from-home meals and weight gain in a Mediterranean population: the SUN (Seguimiento Universidad de Navarra) cohort', *Public Health Nutrition*, 13: 1356–1363.

Bezerra, I.N., Curioni, C. and Sichieri, R. (2012) 'Association between eating out of home and body weight', *Nutrition Reviews*, 70(2): 65–79.

Blumenthal-Barby, J.S. (2013) 'Choice architecture: a mechanism for improving decisions while preserving liberty?', in C. Coons and M. Weber (eds.), *Paternalism?: Theory and Practice*, Cambridge: Cambridge University Press.

Blumenthal-Barby, J.S. and Burroughs, H. (2012) 'Seeking better health care outcomes: the ethics of using the "nudge" ', *The American Journal of Bioethics*, 12: 1–10.

Burton, S., Creyer, E.H., Kees, J. and Huggins, K. (2006) 'Attacking the obesity epidemic: the potential health benefits of providing nutrition information in restaurants', *American Journal of Public Health*, 96: 1669–1675.

Darmon, N., Allegre, L., Vieux, F., Mandon, L. and Ciantar, L. (2010) 'Nutrition standards for schools in France: what impact on meal costs?', *Cahiers de Nutrition et de Diététique*, 45(2): 84–92.

Dayan, E. and Bar-Hillel, M. (2011) 'Nudge to nobesity II: menu positions influence food orders', *Judgment and Decision Making*, 6: 333–342.

Dolan, P., Hallsworth, M., Halpern, D., King, D., Metcalfe, R. and Vlaex, I. (2012) 'Influencing behaviour: the mindspace way', *Journal of Economic Psychology*, 33: 264–277.

Domínguez, P.R., Gámiz, F., Gil, M., Moreno, H., Zamora, R.M., Gallo, M. and de Brugada, I. (2013) 'Providing choice increases children's vegetable intake', *Food Quality and Preference*, 30: 108–113.

Downs, J.S., Loewenstein, G. and Wisdom, J. (2009) 'Strategies for promoting healthier food choices', *American Economic Review*, 99(2): 159–164.

Dubbert, P.M., Johnson, W.G., Schlundt, D.G. and Ward Montague, N. (1984) 'The influence of caloric information on cafeteria food choices', *Journal of Applied Behavior Analysis*, 17(1): 85–92.

Dubois, A., Strychar, I.M., Champagne, F., Leblanc, M.P. and Tremblay, C. (1996) 'The effect of a worksite cafeteria program on employees' dietary fat intakes', *Journal of the Canadian Dietetic Association*, 57(3): 98–102.

Dumanovsky, T., Huang, C.Y., Nonas, C.A., Matte, T.D., Bassett, M.T. and Silver, L.D. (2011) 'Changes in energy content of lunchtime purchases from fast food restaurants after introduction of calorie labelling: cross sectional customer surveys', *BMJ: British Medical Journal*, 343.

Edwards, J.S.A. (2013) 'The foodservice industry: eating out is more than just a meal', *Food Quality and Preference*, 27(2): 223–229.

Fitzgerald, C.M., Kannan, S., Sheldon, S. and Eagle, K.A. (2004) 'Effect of a promotional campaign on heart-healthy menu choices in community restaurants', *Journal of the American Dietetic Association*, 104(3): 429–432.

Flegal, K.M., Carroll, M.D., Ogden, C.L. and Curtin, L.R. (2010) 'Prevalence and trends in obesity among US adults, 1999–2008', *JAMA: The Journal of the American Medical Association*, 303(3): 235–241.

Freedman, M.R. and Brochado, C. (2010) 'Reducing portion size reduces food intake and plate waste', *Obesity*, 18: 1864–1866.

French, S.A., Jeffery, R.W., Story, M., Hannan, P. and Snyder, M.P. (1997) 'A pricing strategy to promote low-fat snack choices through vending machines', *American Journal of Public Health*, 87(5): 849–851.

French, S.A., Story, M., Fulkerson, J.A. and Hannan, P. (2004) 'An environmental intervention to promote lower-fat food choices in secondary schools: outcomes of the TACOS Study', *American Journal of Public Health*, 94(9): 1507–1512.

Geaney, F., Kelly, C., Greiner, B.A., Harrington, J.M., Perry, I.J. and Beirne, P. (2013) 'The effectiveness of workplace dietary modification interventions: a systematic review', *Preventive Medicine*, 57(5): 438–447.

Grunert, K. (2013) 'Trends in food choice and nutrition', in M. Klopi, A. Kuipers and J.-F. Hocquette (eds.), *Consumer Attitudes to Food Quality Products*, Wageningen: Wageningen Academic Publishers, pp. 23–30.

Harnack, L.J. and French, S.A. (2008) 'Effect of point-of-purchase calorie labeling on restaurant and cafeteria food choices: a review of the literature', *International Journal of Behavioral Nutrition and Physical Activity*, 5: 51.

Harnack, L.J., French, S.A., Oakes, J.M., Story, M.T., Jeffrey, R.W. and Rydell, S.A. (2008) 'Effects of calorie labeling and value size pricing on fast food meal choices: results from an experimental trial', *International Journal of Behavioral Nutrition and Physical Activity*, 5, 63.

Hawkes, C. (2004) *Nutrition Labels and Health Claims: The Global Regulatory Environment*, Geneva: World Health Organization.

Hoefkens, C., Lachat, C., Kolsteren, P., Van Camp, J. and Verbeke, W. (2011) 'Posting point-of-purchase nutrition information in university canteens does not influence meal choice and nutrient intake', *The American Journal of Clinical Nutrition*, 94(2): 562–570.

Holdsworth, M. and Haslam, C. (1998) 'A review of point-of-choice nutrition labelling schemes in the workplace, public eating places and universities', *Journal of Human Nutrition and Dietetics*, 11: 423–445.

Holdsworth, M., Haslam, C. and Raymond, N.T. (2000) 'Does the heartbeat award scheme change employees' dietary attitudes and knowledge?', *Appetite*, 35: 179–188.

Horne, P.J., Hardman, C.A., Lowe, C.F., Tapper, K., Le Noury, J., Madden, P., Patel, P. and Doddy, M. (2009) 'Increasing parental provision and children's consumption of lunchbox fruit and vegetables in Ireland: the Food Dudes intervention', *European Journal of Clinical Nutrition*, 63(5): 613–618.

Inserm, Kantar Health and Roche (2012) *ObEpi 2012 – Enquête épidémiologique nationale sur le surpoids et l'obésité*, www.roche.fr/home/recherche/domaines_therapeutiques/cardio_metabolisme/enquete_nationale_obepi_2012.html (accessed 9 September 2013).

Johnson, E.J., Shu, S.B., Dellaert, B.G.C., Fox, C., Goldstein, D.G., Häubl, G., Larrick, R.P., Payne, J.W., Peters, E., Schkade, D., Wansink, B. and Weber, E.U. (2012) 'Beyond nudges: tools of a choice architecture', *Marketing Letters*, 23: 487–504.

Johnson, L. (2013) 'QSRs' appetite for QR codes shows no signs of waning', *Mobile Marketer*, 29 July, www.mobilemarketer.com/cms/news/software-technology/15835.html (accessed 5 November 2013).

Josiam, B. and Foster, C. (2009) 'Nutritional information on restaurant menus: who cares and why restaurateurs should bother', *International Journal of Contemporary Hospitality Management*, 21: 876–891.

Just, D.R. and Wansink, B. (2011) 'The flat-rate pricing paradox: conflicting effects of "all-you-can-eat" buffet pricing', *Review of Economics and Statistics*, 93: 193–200.

Just, D.R., Wansink, B., Mancino, L. and Guthrie, J. (2008) *Behavioral Economic Concepts to Encourage Healthy Eating in School Cafeterias: Experiments and Lessons from College Students*, Economic Research Report No 68, Washington, DC: US Department of Agriculture.

Kahneman, D. (2003) 'A perspective on judgment and choice: mapping bounded rationality', *The American Psychologist*, 58(9): 697–720.

Kahneman, D. (2011) *Thinking, Fast and Slow*, New York: Farrar Straus and Giroux.

Köster, E.P. (2009) 'Diversity in the determinants of food choice: a psychological perspective', *Food Quality and Preference*, 20: 70–82.

Lachat, C.K., Huybregts, L.F., Roberfroid, D.A., Van Camp, J., Remaut-De Winter, A.M., Debruyne, P. and Kolsteren, P. (2009) 'Nutritional profile of foods offered and consumed in a Belgian university canteen', *Public Health Nutrition*, 12(1): 122–128.

Lachat, C.K., Naska, A., Trichopoulou, A., Engeset, D., Fairgrieve, A., Marques, H.Á. and Kolsteren, P. (2010) 'Essential actions for caterers to promote healthy eating out among European consumers: results from a participatory stakeholder analysis in the HECTOR project', *Public Health Nutrition*, 14(2): 193–202.

Lachat, C., Nago, E., Verstraeten, R., Roberfroid, D., Van Camp, J. and Kolsteren, P. (2012) 'Eating out of home and its association with dietary intake: a systematic review of the evidence', *Obesity Reviews*, 13(4): 329–346.

Laisney, C. (2012) 'L'évolution de l'alimentation en France', *Centre d'Etudes et de Prospective*, 5: 1–25.

Lake, A. and Townshend, T. (2006) 'Obesogenic environments: exploring the built and food environments', *Journal of the Royal Society for the Promotion of Health*, 126: 262–267.

Larson, N. and Neumark-Sztainer, D. (2011) 'Young adults and eating away from home: associations with dietary intake patterns and weight status differ by choice of restaurant', *Journal of the American Dietetic Association*, 111(11): 1696–1703.

Levy, D.E., Riis, J., Sonnenberg, L.M., Barraclough, S.J. and Thorndike, A.N. (2012) 'Food choices of minority and low-income employees: a cafeteria intervention', *American Journal of Preventive Medicine*, 43(3): 240–248.

Lin, B.H. and Morrison, R.M. (2012). *Food and Nutrient Intake Data: Taking a Look at the Nutritional Quality of Foods Eaten at Home and Away From Home*, Economic Research Service, Washington, DC: US Department of Agriculture.

Lin, B.H., Frazao, E. and Guthrie, J. (1999) *Away-From-Home Foods Increasingly Important to Quality of American Diet*, Agricultural Information Bulletin No. 479, Washington, DC: US Department of Agriculture.

Martinez-Palou, A. and Rohner-Thielen, E. (2011) *From Farm to Fork – Food Chain Statistics*, Eurostat, http://ec.europa.eu/eurostat/statistics-explained/index.php/From_farm_to_fork_-_food_chain_statistics (accessed 21 January 2015).

Mayer, J.A., Brown, T.P., Heins, J.M. and Bishop, D.B. (1987) 'A multi-component intervention for modifying food selections in a worksite cafeteria', *Journal of Nutrition Education*, 19(6): 277–280.

McCluskey, J.J., Mittelhammer, R.C. and Asiseh, F. (2012) 'From default to choice: adding healthy options to kids' menus', *American Journal of Agricultural Economics*, 94: 338–343.

Mhurchu, C.N., Aston, L.M. and Jebb, S.A. (2010) 'Effects of worksite health promotion interventions on employee diets: a systematic review', *BMC Public Health*, 10: 62.

Myhre, J.B., Løken, E.B., Wandel, M. and Anderden, L.F. (2013) 'Eating location is associated with the nutritional quality of the diet in Norwegian adults', *Public Health Nutrition*, 17(4): 915–923.

Naska, A., Orfanos, P., Trichopoulou, A., May, A.M., Overvad, K., Jakobsen, M.U., Tjønneland, A., Halkjær, J., Fagherazzi, G., Clavel-Chapelon, F., Boutron-Ruault, M.C., Rohrmann, S., Hermann, S., Steffen, A., Haubrock, J., Oikonomou, E., Dilis, V., Katsoulis, M., Sacerdote, C., Sieri, S., Masala, G., Tumino, R., Mattiello, A., Bueno-de-Mesquita, H.B., Skeie, G., Engeset, D., Barricarte, A., Rodríguez, L., Dorronsoro, M., Sánchez, M.J., Chirlaque, M.D., Agudo, A., Manjer, J., Wirfält, E., Hellström, V., Shungin, D., Khaw, K.T., Wareham, N.J., Spencer, E.A., Freisling, H., Slimani, N., Vergnaud, A.C., Mouw, T., Romaguera, D., Odysseos, A. and Peeters, P.H. (2011) 'Eating out, weight and weight gain: a cross-sectional and prospective analysis in the context of the EPIC-PANACEA study', *International Journal of Obesity*, 35(3): 416–26.

Nielsen, S.J. and Popkin, B.M. (2003) 'Patterns and trends in food portion sizes, 1977–1998', *JAMA: The Journal of the American Medical Association*, 289: 450–453.

Orfanos, P., Naska, A., Trichopoulos, D., Slimani, N., Ferrari, P., van Bakel, M., Deharveng, G., Overvad, K., Tjønneland, A., Halkjaer, J., Santucci de Magistris, M., Tumino, R., Pala, V., Sacerdote, C., Masala, G., Skeie, G., Engeset, D., Lund, E., Jakszyn, P., Barricarte, A., Chirlaque, M.D., Martinez-Garcia, C., Amiano, P., Quirós, J.R., Bingham, S., Welch, A., Spencer, E.A., Key, T.J., Rohrmann, S., Linseisen, J., Ray, J., Boeing, H., Peeters, P.H., Bueno-de-Mesquita, H.B., Ocke, M., Johansson, I., Johansson, G., Berglund, G., Manjer, J., Boutron-Ruault, M.C., Touvier, M., Clavel-Chapelon, F. and Trichopoulou, A. (2007) 'Eating out of home and its correlates in 10 European countries: the European Prospective Investigation into Cancer and Nutrition (EPIC) study', *Public Health Nutrition*, 10(12): 1515–1525.

Park, H.R., Jeong, G.O., Lee, S.L., Kim, J.Y., Kang, S.A., Park, K.Y. and Ryou, H.J. (2009) 'Workers intake too much salt from dishes of eating out and food service cafeterias: direct chemical analysis of sodium content', *Nutrition Research and Practice*, 3(4): 328–333.

Pratt, C.A., Lemon, S.C., Fernandez, I.D., Goetzel, R., Beresford, S.A., French, S.A., Stevens, V.J., Vogt, T.M. and Webber, L.S. (2007) 'Design characteristics of worksite environmental interventions for obesity prevention', *Obesity*, 15(9): 2171–2180.

Prentice, A.M. and Jebb, S.A. (2003) 'Fast foods, energy density and obesity: a possible mechanistic link', *Obesity Reviews*, 4(4): 187–194.

Quigley, M. (2013) 'Nudging for health: on public policy and designing choice architecture', *Medical Law Review*, 21(4): 588–621.

Raghunathan, R., Naylor, R.W. and Hoyer, W.D. (2006) 'The unhealthy = tasty intuition and its effects on taste inferences, enjoyment, and choice of food products', *Journal of Marketing*, 70: 170–184.

Read, D., Loewenstein, G. and Rabin, M. (1999) 'Choice bracketing', *Journal of Risk and Uncertainty*, 19(1–3): 171–197.

Rozin, P., Scott, S., Dingley, M., Urbanek, J.K., Jiang, H. and Kaltenbach, M. (2011) 'Nudge to nobesity I: minor changes in accessibility decrease food intake', *Judgment and Decision Making*, 6(4): 323–332.

Selinger, E. and Whyte, K. (2011) 'Is there a right way to nudge? The practice and ethics of choice architecture', *Sociology Compass*, 5: 923–935.

Seymour, J.D., Yaroch, A.L., Serdula, M., Blanck, H.M. and Khan, L.K. (2004) 'Impact of nutrition environmental interventions on point-of-purchase behavior in adults: a review', *Preventive Medicine*, 39(S2): 108–136.

Société Française de Santé Publique (2013) Les sociétés savantes et associations d'experts en nutrition demandent que soient maintenues les normes sur l'équilibre nutritionnel en restauration scolaire, http://www.sfsp.fr/activites/detail.php?cid=243 (accessed 21 January 2015).

Sorensen, G., Morris, D.M., Hunt, M.K., Hebert, J.R., Harris, D.R., Stoddard, A. and Ockene, J.K. (1992) 'Work-site nutrition intervention and employees' dietary habits: the Treatwell program', *American Journal of Public Health*, 82(6): 877–880.

Steenhuis, I.H.M., van Assema, P., van Breukelen, G., Glanz, K., Kok, G. and de Vries, H. (2004) 'The impact of educational and environmental interventions in Dutch worksite cafeterias', *Health Promotion International*, 19(3): 335–343.

Thaler, R. and Sunstein, C. (2008) *Nudge: Improving Decisions about Health, Wealth, and Happiness*, New Haven, CT: Yale University Press.

Thaler, R., Sunstein, C. and Balz, J. (2010) *Choice Architecture*, http://ssrn.com/abstract=1583509 (accessed 21 January 2015).

Tversky, A. and Kahneman, D. (1974) 'Judgment under uncertainty: heuristics and biases', *Science*, 185: 1124–1131.

Tversky, A. and Kahneman, D. (1981) 'The framing of decisions and the psychology of choice', *Science*, 211: 453.

Tversky, A. and Kahneman, D. (1986) 'Rational choice and the framing of decisions', *Journal of Business*, 59(4): S251–S278.

Vermeer, W.M., Steenhuis, I.H.M. and Seidell, J.C. (2009) 'From the point-of-purchase perspective: a qualitative study of the feasibility of interventions aimed at portion-size', *Health Policy*, 90(1): 73–80.

Vermeer, W.M., Steenhuis, I.H.M. and Seidell, J.C. (2010) 'Portion size: a qualitative study of consumers' attitudes toward point-of-purchase interventions aimed at portion size', *Health Educucation Research*, 25(1): 109–120.

Vyth, E.L., Van Der Meer, E.W.C., Seidell, J.C. and Steenhuis, I.H.M. (2012) 'A nutrition labeling intervention in worksite cafeterias: an implementation evaluation across two large catering companies in the Netherlands', *Health Promotion International*, 27(2): 230–237.

Wansink, B., Painter, J. and Van Ittersum, K. (2001) 'Descriptive menu labels' effect on sales', *Cornell Hotel and Restaurant Administration Quarterly*, 42: 68–72.

Wansink, B., van Ittersum, K. and Painter, J.E. (2005) 'How descriptive food names bias sensory perceptions in restaurants', *Food Quality and Preference*, 16: 393–400.

Wansink, B., Just, D.R., Hanks, A.S. and Smith, L.E. (2013) 'Pre-sliced fruit in school cafeterias: children's selection and intake', *American Journal of Preventive Medicine*, 44(5): 477–480.

Werle, C., Trendel, O. and Ardito, G. (2012) 'Unhealthy food is not tastier for everybody: the "healthy = tasty" French intuition', *Food Quality and Preference*, 28(1): 116–121.

Wu, H.W. and Sturm, R. (2013) 'What's on the menu? A review of the energy and nutritional content of US chain restaurant menus', *Public Health Nutrition*, 16(1): 87–96.

# 24

# SUSTAINABLE SUPPLY CHAINS AND ENVIRONMENTAL AND ETHICAL INITIATIVES IN RESTAURANTS

*Christine Demen Meier, Nicolas Siorak,*
*Stéphanie Bonsch Buri and Clémence Cornuz*

## Introduction

A development is sustainable when it 'meets present needs without compromising the ability of future generations to meet their own needs' (World Commission on Environment and Development, 1987: 27). In effect, such a development has three dimensions: environmental, economic and social (Elkington, 1998). Chou et al. (2012: 703) define the first dimension thus: 'environmental innovation or green innovation refers to those environmental practices incorporated into company policies to guide products, productions and management'. The two other aspects entail that sustainable organisations must consider their impact on social communities and seek at least a minimum of profitability (Elkington, 1998).

Several elements motivate a shift towards more sustainable restaurant practices. They can be classified as either external or internal to food service outlets. External pressure comes from consumers, regulators or simply the evolution of standards within a profession; this is particularly the case in the food service industry. For instance, the increasing consumer demand for more authenticity and fresher products encourages restaurants to use less processed items (Demen Meier et al., 2013). On the other hand, valuing sustainability and pursuing profitability are internal pressures. These two types of pressure often interact; for instance, increasing raw food material and energy prices – which follow a sustained upward trend (Portier, 2013; Info Energie Rhône-Alpes, n.d.) – can prompt restaurant managers to manage their intermediate consumption more efficiently in order to avoid financial losses.

In restaurants, sustainable practices can notably be implemented in the purchasing process and the supply chain. *Supply chain* generally refers to the companies – suppliers and logistics providers – 'that work together to deliver a value package of goods and services to the end customer' (Maloni and Brown, 2006: 36). Handfield and Nichols (1999: 2) define sustainable supply chain management in the following way:

> The supply chain encompasses all activities associated with the flow and transform-
> ation of goods from raw materials stage (extraction), through to the end user, as well

as the associated information flows. Material and information flow both up and down the supply chain. Supply chain management (SCM) is the integration of these activities through improved supply chain relationships to achieve a sustainable competitive advantage.

Krause et al. (2009: 18) state that 'a company is no more sustainable than its supply chain', but only chained restaurants and major outlets can implement supply chain management processes; for independent restaurants, actions favouring a greener production primarily concern the purchasing function. Leenders and Fearon (2008) define purchasing as the function that reaches outside the boundaries of the firm to acquire goods and services in support of the operations; this entails that the sustainable actions undertaken by a restaurant depend on the intensity and depth of the relationships it establishes with its suppliers.

To analyse to what extent restaurants are able to implement and favour sustainable procurement and better practices, this chapter will first explore how they implement short supply chains and greener procurement. The second part of the chapter will focus on waste management and the ways it is improved by restaurant outlets. To conclude, ethical practices will be discussed.

## Short supply chain and green procurement

There are several ways for restaurants to adopt greener procurement practices: selecting suppliers that use more sustainable methods, implementing purchasing processes, adopting shorter supply chain practices and, for bigger companies, creating an entirely new sustainable supply chain. One of the easiest practices is the selection of branded products that either are sustainable or indirectly benefit from sustainable actions.

An important added value of these approaches is the improvement of traceability, which meets customers' awareness and need for information. The latter is increased by 'e-word of mouth' and customer reviews on social media. They tend to stress the quality of food products (including their freshness and their origin) and have a direct impact on restaurant sales (Zhang et al., 2010).

Before discussing the different ways in which a restaurant can make its purchases or supply chain greener, one must remember that most food service operations are small, independent restaurants. According to Euromonitor International (2013), in Asia-Pacific, Western and Eastern Europe, the Middle East and Africa, the sales value of independent restaurants is over 80 per cent of the total sales value. While the sales value of restaurant chains is over 50 per cent in North America, it is only 25 per cent worldwide. Consequently, most of the progress towards a more sustainable industry will be made by small structures adopting better practices according to their means.

## Collaboration with local producers and short supply chains

The length of a supply chain does not refer to the geographical distance between the producer and the consumer, but to the number of intermediaries between production and the final consumer (European Commission, 2000). The ecological nature of products issued from short supply chains is therefore debatable. Indeed, a distributor or a restaurant buying products directly from foreign producers (rather than from a local but multi-stage supply chain) will be responsible for the carbon dioxide emissions produced to transport these goods.

Nevertheless, shortening the supply chain by reducing the number of intermediaries strengthens the relationship between the producer, the final user and the customers. It also tends to reduce the degree of product processing, and consequently the quantity of

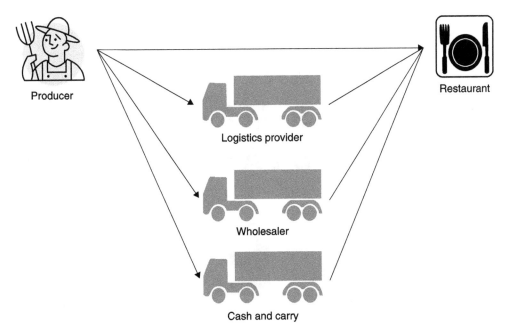

*Figure 24.1*   Supply chains in foodservice.

preservatives used. According to Earth Markets (n.d.), short supply chains generally favour local food networks and are 'alternative strategies enabling producers to regain an active role in the food system'.

In Europe, for both independent and chained restaurants, national governments and the European Commission support initiatives favourable to local products and local food systems. For instance, in France and Italy, companies in charge of the catering in schools and universities must use local and organic products (Ministère de l'agriculture, de l'agroalimentaire et de la forêt, 2011; Clément, 2010). Moreover, the European Commission has financed numerous projects favouring local food systems and supply across Europe (Community Research and Development Information Service, n.d.).

## Differences between independent and chained outlets

### *Independent restaurants*

As stated above, most restaurants are small outlets. Professional associations encourage and help these outlets to have more direct suppliers. For instance, numerous associations of kitchen chefs showcase dishes made with local products.

The association Jeunes Restaurateurs d'Europe ('Young European Chefs'), which has more than 350 members in 12 European countries, highlights the importance of local and artisanal supply. The French association Maîtres Restaurateurs ('Master Restaurateurs'), which was founded in 2007 and has almost 3,000 members, also promotes the use of local products: members must use fresh and local ingredients, and buy others (charcuterie, for example) from small, independent producers. The certification this association delivers is the only nationally recognised title for kitchen chefs in France.

ASSOCIATION FRANÇAISE DES MAÎTRES RESTAURATEURS

CHEFS COLLABORATIVE

Finally, in the USA, the powerful association Chefs Collaborative is committed to promoting greener practices and providing educational resources to food service professionals.

It is becoming easier for restaurants to find local products. For instance, Metro Cash & Carry, the worldwide leading wholesaler for professionals, has implemented strategies to offer local products to its customers. In Canada, Metro aims to showcase local and regional products and to improve their availability in each of its shops. To do so, the company works in collaboration with local associations and producers to meet the requirements of the catering profession (Hauguel, 2013). In Europe, Metro has adopted a similar strategy to satisfy restaurateurs' demand for more sustainable products: according to Regis Bertrand, manager of the Bercy shop (in Paris, France), the increase in local and seasonal offers is linked to the customers' interest in traceability and in regional products (Huijgen and Lentschner, 2013).

## Chained restaurants

Chained restaurants have the critical size to implement efficient short supply chains. McDonald's, for example, has an integrated model in most countries, thus establishing long-term collaborations with suppliers of meat, lettuce, milk, bread, etc. Moreover, menu items are adapted to each country by using regional products, such as cheese in France. Starbucks has established short supply-chain processes as well, buying coffee beans directly from agricultural producers. Controlling the whole supply chain in this way enables the business to track and quantify greenhouse gas emissions at every step of production and delivery. These data allow Starbucks to reduce the main sources of carbon dioxide emissions and have a greater impact on climate change mitigation.

Implementing a sustainable supply chain also makes companies responsible for negative externalities. For instance, Starbucks is responsible for non-ecological practices in agricultural areas where forests were cut in the past to implement coffee farms. To make up for this, the company has invested in forest protection and conservation and gives farmers incentives to benefit from forest carbon markets (Starbucks, 2012).

The fact that customers expect more information and traceability is an important motivation to improve restaurant supply chains. Major restaurant chains face much pressure in this regard: unsustainable practices and low product quality would most likely be widely publicised and could impact the whole company.

## Selection of sustainable products

The easiest way for restaurants to greenify procurement is to purchase more environment-friendly products. Indeed, in order to reduce the carbon footprint of their dishes, buying local products is necessary. The fact that, in the USA, fruits and vegetables travel on average 2,400km before being consumed shows how much progress can be made in this regard. Buying local products also gives restaurateurs the opportunity to communicate on the origin of ingredients on the menu, which is a marketing argument.

The concerns about carbon dioxide emissions motivate an increased and more precise use of certifications, such as Appellation d'Origine Contrôlée (AOC, 'Controlled Designation of Origin'), which is common in France, Italy, Germany and Switzerland.

Another easy way for restaurants to make their purchases more sustainable is to work with sustainable suppliers. A study conducted by the F&B Chair of Ecole Hôtelière de Lausanne shows that restaurants tend to expect their suppliers to provide sustainable solutions and tools for them (Demen Meier et al., 2013). In this perspective, branded food items are preferred to those produced by independent professionals. Indeed, because of the social pressure and of their own values, these companies implement processes to reduce their environmental footprint. For example, Malongo and Nestlé Professional provide their coffee suppliers with plants that require less water and pesticides while offering a better productivity (Malongo, 2012; Nestlé Professional, 2013a).

## Case studies of local procurement in restaurants

At a managerial level, several recommendations can be drawn from the experiences of restaurateurs who have implemented local procurement practices.

Regarding restaurant chains, USA chain Chipotle Mexican Grill shows that it is possible to combine local sourcing and financial success. Chipotle sources more than ten million pounds of locally grown products to ensure that each of its restaurants uses ingredients produced no further than 350 miles away. Transportation costs are thus reduced, and each restaurant communicates on the freshness and higher quality of its dishes (O'Reilly, 2012). However, due to this procurement method, Chipotle outlets do not benefit from economies of scale; this drives menu prices up. The company's success is all the more remarkable considering that Chipotle is operating within the highly competitive segment of fast food chains, where clients are especially price-sensitive. Thus, even in that segment, a qualitative differentiation is possible, and clients are ready to pay more for higher quality and freshness.

Regarding independent restaurants, a case study on The Pondicheri, an Indian restaurant located in Houston, USA, illustrates the challenges faced by restaurants aiming to buy more local products. The main difficulty is the absence of 'consistency in ingredient quality, pricing and viability of supply sources'; the managers confirm that 'it is difficult, if not impossible, to meet all the needs for its menu based solely on local producers' (Vilches and Cheng, 2012: 53). The authors' main recommendations are to use the corporate networks of local farms and a supplier specialised in local supplies, rather than establish direct relationships with the local farmers and food producers.

Finally, a French example shows that catering outlets focusing on local products can capitalise on their differentiation. The restaurant Kilucru indeed not only uses local food products, but also organises locally-themed events (aperitifs, art exhibitions, concerts). During these events, clients have the opportunity to discover tapas and dishes made only with locally sourced products (Lemestre, 2013).

## *Waste management in restaurants*

There are several ways for a restaurant to manage waste; they are influenced by legislation, managerial attitude and the manager's motivation. Restaurant waste is composed of food waste (organic material and used oils), packaging, and energy waste. Waste management falls into the environmental dimension of sustainable development.

Waste management can be highly profitable for restaurants. For example, Darden Restaurants (which owns restaurant brands such as Red Lobster, Olive Garden, Capital Grille and Longhorn Steakhouse) expects a recent improvement made to its supply chain to generate US$45 million of savings annually, notably because it reduces the amount of wasted food (O'Reilly, 2012). Waste management can thus be seen as a profitable field rather than as a costly constraint.

## Waste management laws

Several laws on waste management in food service outlets are already in place. For instance, in a majority of OCDE countries, directives and regulations that aim to reduce waste have been implemented or are being elaborated. They mainly concern the collection of food waste, which represents 24 per cent of restaurant waste and 'includes non-contaminated edibles, food scraps and waste oils' (Kubert, n.d.). For instance, Directive 2008/98/EC of the European Parliament (European Parliament and Council, 2008) stipulates that professionals are obligated to collect used oil. Moreover, some countries (France and Italy, for instance) are in the process of implementing new legal dispositions to collect non-contaminated edibles and food scraps (Eurogroup Consulting, 2012; Gianolio, 2012). New York City is currently testing this practice with voluntary restaurant chains like Chipotle (Rao, 2013).

## Actions taken by restaurants

Such obligations incite restaurants to implement a reverse logistics system. According to Steven (2004), a reverse logistics system is a management system for waste that stems from production, packaging and use of products. It consists in collecting and treating waste. A waste collecting company or professional often takes charge of the reuse or processing of the waste.

For restaurant chains, waste management is a crucial part of resource management and sustainable management. McDonald's excels in this domain: all its used oil is recycled, most of it becoming biodiesel for the company's trucks (Hagen, 2010). Another example of organic waste management comes from the Swedish fast food chain Max Burgers, which has reduced its food waste to less than 2 per cent (Max Burgers, n.d.).

Independent restaurants also have the possibility of exploiting or managing their food waste, notably by transforming it into compost. Thus, French restaurant Chantecler, located in the Negresco hotel in Nice, has set up a closed-loop supply chain. A closed-loop system is an integrated system which includes 'returns processes' (i.e., the waste is given 'back' to the producers); by implementing such a system, 'the manufacturer has the intent of capturing additional value and further integrating all supply-chain activities' (Guerrier-Buisine, 2013). As a result, every month, three tons of Chantecler's organic waste is transformed into compost, and then provided to the restaurant's food suppliers (Guide and Van Wassenhove, 2003).

Restaurants can also make a difference through the packaging they use and the responsibility of their suppliers. A company like McDonald's has implemented efficient processes in this domain; for instance, 91 per cent of their packaging is made of renewable raw material.

## Suppliers' actions for better waste management

Food suppliers have made efforts in waste management. For instance, Nestlé plans on implementing a closed-loop system in each of its factories before 2020. This has already been done in Switzerland and Germany, where waste is reused or transformed into energy through incineration (Boursier, 2013).

Thus, the whole food service supply chain is realising the importance of waste management. This represents an opportunity for new associations of professionals and suppliers. For instance, in Switzerland, the project United Against Waste brings together Nestlé Professional, Unilever Food Solutions, Compass, Hôtellerie Suisse, SV Group and many other companies and organisations. Its purpose is to identify the main improvements needed in the food service industry to reduce food waste and share best practices. The quantified objective of United Against Waste is to halve the amount of food wasted by 2020 (Nestlé Professional, 2013b).

## Energy waste management

Food waste management is not the only way for catering outlets to make savings while also preserving the environment. According to Horovitz (2008), the food service industry is the retail world's largest energy user: restaurants 'use almost five times more energy per square foot than any other type of commercial building'. In 2008, the average energy consumption of US restaurants amounted to 500,000kWh of electricity, 20,000thm of natural gas and 800,000 gallons of water. Kubert indicates that, in most restaurants, it is the cooking equipment which consumes the largest share of energy (35 per cent), followed by heating and cooling systems (28 per cent), dishwashing (18 per cent), lighting (13 per cent) and refrigeration (6 per cent). According to the United States Environmental Protection Agency, if 10 per cent of US restaurants substituted just one traditional light bulb with a compact fluorescent bulb, US$2.8 million would be saved (Horovitz, 2008).

Horovitz (2008) states that almost 80 per cent of the energy used by restaurants is wasted because of inefficient cooking equipment. The cost of this loss is estimated at US$8 billion each year for US restaurants. A study conducted in France by energy professionals (Fessard, 2013) highlights the savings hotels and restaurants could make by using more efficient equipment and installations: on average, hotels and restaurants could save 40 per cent of their energy bills, and implementing eco-friendly systems in the buildings would be paid off after only six years. Such figures explain restaurateurs' increasing interest in more efficient equipment.

A case presented by Du Jaiflin (2011) illustrates the global advantages of an efficient approach to energy consumption. For the French restaurant Le Bistro Marin (350 customers per day on average), a complete transformation of the kitchen led to €15,000 of savings in energy consumption per year. The replacement of cold rooms by refrigerators, the installation of induction hobs, and the automatic regulation and diffusion of energy amongst the various appliances all contributed to the reduction of the yearly energy bill by 20 per cent. Moreover, with the new, automatic ovens, baking processes could occur simultaneously and be programmed in advance. Not only did the resulting decrease in wasted products mean that food costs diminished, but, more importantly, staff costs were reduced. Finally, to optimise the use of the new equipment, the staff were trained and the management started better planning of the activities and the purchases. This shows that taking a step towards energy efficiency is an opportunity for a restaurant to improve its overall management.

## Ethical supply in restaurants

Ethical supply shows restaurateurs' willingness to improve the working conditions of local communities and to integrate ethical values into every stage of the supply chain. It does not take the same form in independent restaurants as in restaurant chains, as the impact these two types of outlets have on local communities are not measurable on the same scale.

Ethical sourcing means that 'a company at one stage of the supply chain . . . takes responsibility for the social and/or environmental performance at other stages of the chain' (Blowfield, 2003: 16). Primary producers are those most frequently helped in this way.

The United Nations declared that 2014 would be the International Year of Family Farming. As a consequence, several actions, communications and media coverage stressed the importance of local producer communities.

## International ethical sourcing

To comply with social requirements regarding ethics, restaurants have the option of using fair trade products to source foreign-produced items (e.g., fruit juice, coffee, tea). Fair trade is an alternative trade model to support small farmers and employees in developing countries so that they can build a stable future. Through a minimum price and long-term contracts, fair trade aims to help small producers overcome poverty and hunger. Well-known fair trade brands such as Max Havelaar are used by restaurants to highlight their commitment to this cause (Fairtrade Max Havelaar, n.d.).

Moreover, using fair trade products can be necessary to obtain a sustainable certification mark for a restaurant. In France, the certification Restaurant Durable ('Sustainable Restaurant') requires restaurants to use 'organic, local or fair trade products' (Bio-Marché. Info, 2012). In Nordic countries, the Nordic Ecolabel (also known as Nordic Swan) is a very well-known and renowned certification. Restaurants can obtain this certification under certain conditions; they must notably obtain a certain number of points which depend on the sustainability of their purchases and operational processes (waste management, energy efficiency). Using fair trade products like Max Havelaar, Rejäl or Rättvisemärkt helps to obtain this certification.

Catering chains also have the ability to directly impact small farmers' life conditions. For instance, in 2011, Starbucks won the Ethisphere Institute 'Most Ethical Company' award for the category 'Restaurant and Cafes' (Environmental Leader, 2011). The company supports tea, coffee and cocoa farmers' communities by improving their working conditions. More precisely, Starbucks 'protects the rights of workers and ensures safe, fair and humane working and living conditions. Moreover, compliance with minimum-wage requirements and prohibition of child and forced labour is mandatory' (Starbucks, 2012). Max Burgers is another example: to compensate for its carbon dioxide emissions, the company plants trees in Africa. This ensures a regular salary to the farmers who plant the trees, and their children attend school (Max Burgers, n.d.).

## Support of local farmers

Restaurant chains and independent restaurants also have a responsibility towards their suppliers: they have the ability to support local communities of farmers in their area through their supply choices. For instance, the restaurant chain Tender Greens provides fair conditions for its suppliers and adopts a 'win–win' approach in its relations with them. The prices it sets for its dishes allow profits for both the restaurant and the farmers (Tender Greens, n.d.).

Supporting nearby producers can also be a way to attract customers who want to support local communities. On its website, the restaurant the British Larder Suffolk even locates its suppliers on a map and explains which products they buy from each of them (British Larder Suffolk, n.d.). In Paris, several restaurants give small, local organic food producers the opportunity to sell their products directly to the clients. This programme was initiated by French food producer Xavier Guille in 2010 (Anastassion, 2010).

## Conclusion

This chapter illustrates the importance of sourcing and of the supply chain in sustainable practices. Whether an outlet is independent or chained, it can contribute to reducing pollution by using local products and improving the way it monitors its consumption of natural and energy resources. This chapter also highlights the financial advantages of these practices, such as making savings by monitoring food and energy consumption. Furthermore, as several case studies show, improvements oriented towards sustainable development positively influence outlet management, strengthening its efficiency.

Sustainable supply, sourcing and equipment also have indirect benefits. They can notably be marketing arguments, considering an increasing number of consumers are interested in the origins of their food. Such positive differentiation can therefore provide a competitive advantage.

The last part of the chapter illustrates the ethical responsibilities of restaurants. Again, both chained and independent outlets can actively implement ethical actions. The communities they support and help can be located abroad, for example in developing countries. But restaurants also have a responsibility towards their local suppliers, and some help create a sustainable and profitable local agri-food sector.

Whether their motivations are social, legal or linked to company values, food brands and major suppliers contribute to sustainable supply chains and to the improvement of practices. If they keep taking such initiatives, situations like documented cases of slavery in the seafood industry in Asia (Winn, 2012) will come to an end. Decisive steps have already been taken, but sustainable supply chain initiatives need to affect more actors and be more intensive.

# References

Anastassion, L. (2010) *Xavier Guille rapproche restaurateurs et producteurs bio de la région parisienne*, L'Hôtellerie Restauration, www.lhotellerie-restauration.fr/journal/restauration/2010-11/Xavier-Guille-rapproche-restaurateurs-et-producteurs-bio-de-la-region-parisienne.htm.

Bio-Marché.Info (2012) *Le label 'Restaurant Durable' est lancé*, www.bio-marche.info/web/Nouvelles_en_bref/Politique/rest-dur/356/283/0/13153.html.

Blowfield, M. (2003) 'Ethical supply chains in the cocoa, coffee and tea industries', *Greener Management International*, 43: 15–22.

Boursier (2013) *Nestlé: fini les déchets inutiles en usine en 2020 en Europe*, www.boursier.com/actions/actualites/news/nestle-fini-les-dechets-inutiles-en-usine-en-2020-en-europe-550711.html.

British Larder Suffolk (n.d.) *Our Cherished Suppliers*, www.britishlardersuffolk.co.uk/our-suppliers.

Chou, C.-J., Chen, K.-S. and Wang, Y.-Y. (2012) 'Green practices in the restaurant industry from an innovation adoption perspective: evidence from Taiwan', *International Journal of Hospitality Management*, 31(3): 703–711.

Clément, M.-C. (2010) *Du bio dans ma cantine!* Pause Santé, www.pausesante.fr/article-saveurs-216-du-bio-dans-ma-cantine.php.

Community Research and Development Information Service (n.d.) *Search: alimentation locale*, http://cordis.europa.eu/newsearch/index.cfm?page=simpleSearch.

Demen Meier, C., Siorak, N., Bonsch, S. and Cornuz, C. (2013). *Job Observatory in the F&B Industry: Purchasing Function*, Lausanne: Food & Beverage Industry Chair, Ecole hôtelière de Lausanne.

Du Jaiflin, J.-G. (2011) *Frima System Rational aide un restaurant à optimiser ses process*, L'Hôtellerie Restauration, Paris, France: Du Jaiflin.

Earth Markets (n.d.) *Short Food Chain*, www.earthmarkets.net/pagine/eng/pagina.lasso?-id_pg=2.

Elkington, J. (1998) *Cannibals with Forks: The Triple Bottom Line of 21st-Century Business*, Gabriola Island, BC: New Society Publishers.

Environmental Leader (2011) *Ford, Starbucks Among 'Most Ethical Companies'*, www.environmentalleader.com/2011/03/17/ford-starbucks-among-most-ethical-companies.

Eurogroup Consulting (2012) *Etude économique sur le secteur de la restauration Partie I/IV*, www.eurogroupconsulting.fr/IMG/pdf/Etude-Secteur-Restauration-ok.pdf.

Euromonitor International (2013) *Mapping The New World: Global Consumer Foodservice in 2013 and Beyond*, London, UK: Euromonitor.

European Commission (2000) *Marketing Local Products: Short and Long Distribution Channels*, Brussels, Belgium: European Commission, Agriculture and Rural Development.

European Parliament and Council (2008) *Directive 2008/98/EC of the European Parliament and of the Council of 19 November 2008 on Waste and Repealing Certain Directives*, http://eur-lex.europa.eu/LexUriServ/LexUriServ.do?uri=CELEX:32008L0098:en:NOT.

Fairtrade Max Havelaar (n.d.) *Fairtrade renforce les productrices et les producteurs*, www.maxhavelaar.ch/fr/fairtrade/fairtrade/was-ist-fairtrade.

Fessard, J.-L. (2013) *Efficacité énergétique: un enjeu majeur pour l'hôtellerie-restauration*, www.lhotellerie-restauration.fr/journal/gestion-marketing/2013-02/Efficacite-energetique-un-enjeu-majeur-pour-l-hotellerie-restauration.htm?fd=economies%20and%20d%27energies.

Gianolio, U. (2012) *La gestion des déchets organiques en Italie: le cas*, www.rencontres-organique.com/2012/res/conf-euro_ugianolio.pdf.

Guerrier-Buisine, V. (2013) *Le Negresco dans la course pour l'Écolabel européen*, L'Hôtellerie Restauration, www.lhotellerie-restauration.fr/journal/hotellerie/2013-11/Le-Negresco-dans-la-course-pour-lecolabel-europeen.htm?fd=compost.

Guide, V.R. and Van Wassenhove, L.N. (2003) *Business Aspects of Closed-Loop Supply Chains*, Pittsburgh, PA: Carnegie Mellon University Press.

Hagen, K. (2010) *What Does McDonald's Do with Its Used Cooking Oil?* Yahoo! Voices, http://voices.yahoo.com/what-does-mcdonalds-its-used-cooking-oil-6332394.html?cat=57.

Handfield, R.B. and Nichols, E.L. (1999) *Introduction to Supply Chain Management*, Upper Saddle River, NJ: Prentice-Hall.

Hauguel, V. (2013) *Metro veut devenir une vitrine pour les produits régionaux*, Novae, http://novae.ca/actualites/2013-05/metro-veut-devenir-une-vitrine-pour-les-produits-regionaux.

Horovitz, B. (2008) 'Can restaurants go green, earn green?', *USA Today*, 19 May, http://usatoday30.usatoday.com/money/industries/environment/2008-05-15-green-restaurants-eco-friendly_N.htm.

Huijgen, A. and Lentschner, K. (2013) *Metro, fournisseur des bistrots et des étoilés*, Le Figaro, www.lefigaro.fr/societes/2013/04/13/20005-20130413ARTFIG00311-metro-fournisseur-des-bistrots-et-des-etoiles.php.

Info Energie Rhône-Alpes (n.d.) *Scénarios d'évolution du prix de l'énergie et investissement*, www.infoenergie69.org/IMG/pdf/scenarios_d_e_volution_du_prix_de_l_e_nergie_et_investissement_dans_les_e_conomies.pdf.

Krause, D.R., Vachon, S. and Klassen, R.D. (2009) 'Special topic forum on sustainable supply chain management: introduction and reflections on the role of purchasing management', *Journal of Supply Chain Management*, 45(4): 18–25.

Kubert, C. (n.d.) *Going greener: Opportunities to Improve Your Restaurant Environmental Practices*, Chicago, IL: Environmental Law & Policy Center.

Leenders, M.R. and Fearon, H.E. (2008) 'Developing purchasing foundation,' *Journal of Supply Chain Management*, 44(2): 17–27.

Lemestre, G. (2013) *Kilucru: l'amoureux des produits locaux*, L'Hôtellerie Restauration, www.lhotellerie-restauration.fr/journal/restauration/2013-09/Kilucru-l-amoureux-des-produits-locaux.htm?fd=produits%20and%20locauxilches.

Malongo (2012) *Responsabilité Ethique d'Entreprises 2011*, Carros: Malongo.

Maloni, M.J. and Brown, M.E. (2006) 'Corporate social responsibility in the supply chain: an application in the food industry', *Journal of Business Ethics*, 68(1): 35–52.

Max Burgers (n.d.) *Annual Report 2011 – On Climate Impact and Initiatives*, www.maxburgers.com/Global/Press/MAX_klimatbokslut-2011-ENG-digital.pdf.

Mealey, L. (n.d.) *Ten Reasons Restaurants Should Buy Local Foods*, About.com, http://restaurants.about.com/od/menu/a/local_Foods.htm.

Ministère de l'agriculture, de l'agroalimentaire et de la forêt (2011) *Manger bio et local à la cantine de Bagneux*, http://alimentation.gouv.fr/cantine-produit-bio.

Nestlé Professional (2013a) *Initiative sectorielle contre le gaspillage des denrées alimentaires*, www.nestleprofessional.com/switzerland/fr/OurCompany/Publikationen/Pages/Pressemitteilung.aspx.

Nestlé Professional (2013b) *NESTLÉ soutient la recherche et l'amélioration du café*, www.nestleprofessional.com/france/fr/SiteArticles/Pages/Nestle_soutient_la_recherche.aspx.

O'Reilly, J. (2012) *Restaurant Logistics: Serving up the Perfect Meal*, Inbound Logistics, www.inbound-logistics.com/cms/article/restaurant-logistics-serving-up-the-perfect-meal.

Portier, M. (2013) Matières premières agricoles: 'Une hausse des prix et de la volatilité', *Cafeduforex.com* 4 November, http://www.cafeduforex.com/archive/article/matieres-premieres-agricoles-hausse-prix-volatilite#.

Rao, T. (2013) 'For restaurants, composting is a welcome but complex task', *The New York Times*, 20 June, www.nytimes.com/2013/06/20/dining/for-restaurants-composting-is-a-welcome-but-complex-task.html?pagewanted=1&_r=3&.

Starbucks (2012) *Starbucks Ethical Coffee Sourcing and Farmer Support*, http://globalassets.starbucks.com/assets/6e52b26a7602471dbff32c9e66e685e3.pdf.

Steven, M. (2004) 'Networks in reverse logistics', in H. Dyckhoff, R. Lackes and J. Reese, *Supply Chain Management and Reverse Logistics*, Berlin: Springer-Verlag, pp. 163–180.

Tender Greens (n.d.) www.tendergreens.com/community.

Vilches, K.A. and Cheng, L.-C. (2012). 'Procurement strategy in an entrepreneurial food company's supply chain: a case study of Pondicheri café', *International Journal of Business Strategy*, 12(4): 49–55.

Winn, P. (2012) *Did These Ex-Slaves Catch Your Lunch?* GlobalPost, www.globalpost.com/dispatch/news/regions/asia-pacific/thailand/120425/seafood-slavery-part-1.

World Commission on Environment and Development (1987) *Our Common Future*, Oxford: Oxford University Press.

Zhang, Z., Ye, Q., Law, R. and Li, Y. (2010) 'The impact of e-word-of-mouth on the online popularity of restaurants: a comparison of consumer reviews and editor reviews', *International Journal of Hospitality Management*, 4: 694–700.

# 25

# HOW SELF-SUFFICIENT CAN A RESTAURANT BE?

## Introducing the Foodzone model, a managerial tool

*Jaap Peter Nijboer, Peter R. Klosse and Jan Arend Schulp*

### Introduction

El Celler de Can Roca, Mugaritz and Arzak are illustrious names that represent the leading role of the Spanish regions Catalunya and País Vasco within the gastronomic world. These restaurants, all of them present in the top ten of the 2013 San Pellegrino list of the world's 50 best restaurants, follow the lead of El Bulli (William Reed Business Media Ltd., 2013). For a decade, the Catalan restaurant of Ferran Adrià dominated the culinary craft. Along with men like Harold McGee and Hervé This, Adrià brought science into the kitchen, and pioneered in what is nowadays popularly termed 'molecular gastronomy'.

One of Adrià's disciples is René Redzepi. This Danish chef with roots in Albania started Restaurant Noma in Copenhagen. Through preaching Nordic Cuisine, Redzepi has brought Noma to the top of the same San Pellegrino list. He took the first place for three years in a row (2010–2012) and moved to 2nd in the 2013 list. Seemingly in contrast with his master's complicated chemical processes, Redzepi added an extra dimension to his cuisine: he aims at being supplied only by producers within a radius of 50km. He stresses the importance of understanding seasonality, the region and the soil. 'I see a restaurant having some type of pact with nature', the chef argues (Phaidon Press, 2010). The relationship with surrounding nature is the essence, and with that he is one of the forerunners for the movement of locavores. However, the pact that Redzepi talks about goes further. Together with an expert he goes into the countryside where they pick their ingredients themselves: an example of culinary homesteading. It leads us in the direction of the concept of food self-sufficiency in restaurants. The romantic idea of serving self-grown products is the ultimate culinary practice of Jean-Jacques Rousseau's 'back to nature'.

Ideas on self-production are also strongly advocated by Michael Pollan in his books *In Defense of Food* (2009) and *Cooked* (2013). His reason for doing so is calling a halt to the industrialization of the food system, which – in his view – has all kinds of negative consequences.

The idea of running a food self-sufficient restaurant to a certain extent seems to gain popularity. It fits ideals such as sustainable entrepreneurship and reducing food miles. This chapter aims at providing the conditions for making this idea successful. It analyses the realism of the concept and it endeavours to provide a framework for a (future) restaurant-owner with ambitions towards self-sufficiency in food: to what extent can a self-sufficient restaurant become a success? Furthermore, we present the Foodzone model as a managerial tool to define to what extent a restaurant wants to source its products locally and to assess if the set goals are met.

## Self-sufficiency: defining the concept

A human being's instinct reaches out for survival. To maintain the bodily machine, food is indispensable. It is the main necessity. To provide the food need and other needs, an individual can receive help, but can also be self-sufficient. Self-sufficient is defined as 'providing for oneself' (Kruyskamp, 1976), 'being self-supporting' (Verhoeff-Schot and Cauberghe, 1977). 'Self-sufficiency' as a noun is directly linked to the term 'autarky'. Etymologically, the word 'autarky' was born in the Greek language, where *auto* means 'self' and *arkeoo* means 'being enough/sufficient' (Oxford English Dictionary, 2013). 'Autarky is self-sufficiency, both in a philosophical and psychological, and, especially, an economic sense; the aspiration of a state to be totally independent from foreign imports by providing in all its own needs, striving for a closed economy' (Kruyskamp, 1976).

The opposite of self-sufficiency is the phenomenon adhered to and developed by, amongst others, eighteenth/nineteenth-century economists Adam Smith and David Ricardo: *free trade*. It exists with specialization and interdependence. 'Rather than people trying to be self-sufficient and do everything themselves, it makes sense to specialise' (Sloman and Garratt, 2010: 428). Through trade, individuals receive help in the provision of their needs. As Valentinov (2008: 345) defines clearly, 'the basic difference between the concepts of *exchange* and *self-sufficiency* is found to be the extent to which individuals are relieved from producing the goods they consume'.

In the context of gastronomy, an extra dimension can be added. The intention to be fully self-sufficient implies being dependent on what the region provides year-round. Ultimately the restaurant must shut down if there are insufficient products to work with. Also it would imply that a restaurant in a moderate region could not use products from tropical or subtropical regions – no pineapples, cloves, nutmeg, cocoa, or coffee in restaurants around the 50th parallel. However self-sufficient, from a consumer and managerial point of view, a balance between self-sufficiency and free trade is required.

## Backward vertical integration

Just like every individual and every nation, restaurants have the choice to be self-sufficient or to exchange products: to trade. This is revealed in the way restaurants are supplied. These days, most restaurants purchase all of their goods at the wholesaler. However, several restaurants have started to produce their own food, at least to some extent. Complete food self-sufficiency in a restaurant is the opposite of getting totally supplied by the wholesaler. In between, two other situations are to be found. Closer to the wholesaler is the situation in which several regional producers collaborate in cooperation and deliver directly to more restaurants in the region. Closer to complete food self-sufficiency is the situation in which one producer directly supplies one specific restaurant.

The decision of a restaurant to aim at providing itself with its own food needs is a form of backward vertical integration. Instead of outsourcing the supply of food, the restaurant can choose to occupy the preceding links within the supply chain. This means it will operate in other activities than those related to its core business. Clearly, this requires other compet-ences, and additional costs need to be covered by the guests in the end (Slack et al., 2009). Food self-sufficiency in a restaurant is then defined as a 'restaurant providing for 100 in its own food needs'. Seeds and plants can be obtained from seed-houses and nurseries.

## Assessment of the feasibility of food self-sufficiency in restaurants

We will expand on the conditions, but also the impossibilities, of running a food self-sufficient restaurant. First we establish a set of preconditions; next we review the indispens-able product groups in the kitchen, one by one. The information is acquired from both literature and practice.

In literature, Thoreau (1972) and Nearing and Nearing (1989) describe their experiences with self-sufficient living. Nearing and Nearing's aim was for example 'to get a year's liveli-hood in return for half a year of bread labour' (Nearing and Nearing, 1989: 52). They worked only one-third of their time to maintain themselves. Thoreau's conclusion is similar: 'I found that by working about six weeks in a year, I could meet all the expenses of living' (1972: 59). In both accounts, context plays an important role. Nearing and Nearing demonstrated self-discipline and good planning. Thoreau could have been a good cynic, wanting, in the most literal sense, no more than he needed. Both experimental homesteads relied on what season, climate and soil provided them with. And both were successful. Nearing and Nearing (1989: 194) report that their 'idea of a subsistence homestead economy proved easy of realisation'. Thoreau (1972: 53) learned from his experience 'that it would cost incredibly little trouble to obtain one's necessary food'.

Clearly, a private household is not a commercial restaurant. To assess whether self-sufficiency could also be a success in the commercial setting of a restaurant, the experiences of Thoreau and Nearing were examined through five interviews with both restaurant owners and producers of indispensable products.

## *Preconditions*

Being a farmer is a profession, just as is being a chef. Plants and animals do not just grow by themselves. They need to be treated to maximize the output both in quantity and in quality. Successful agriculture requires knowledge and experience. Can it be expected that a cook should also be a gardener, a dairy farmer, a pig breeder, a wheat grower, etc.?

The land needs to be worked on. So, a team of farm-workers should be formed. Clearly, the acreage required to produce enough ingredients to obtain at least some degree of self-sufficiency is a function of the size of the restaurant (Chapter 12 in this volume by Jan Arend Schulp makes an effort in calculating the minimum size of land). Part of the work could be done by mentally and/or physically disabled people; a project with the municipality and other insti-tutes could be set up. But especially this category of workers needs leadership and guidance.

Third, one should take the seasons and the whims of the climate into consideration. Self-sufficiency requires taking risks and a flexible organization with a menu that can be adapted daily. Risks should be spread through diversity in products. Early and late cultivars should definitely be used. Mastering preservation techniques is indispensable to being able to use and eat ingredients outside of their growing season.

This brings us to the last of the preconditions: realism. Besides skills, capacity and an adaptive organization, this type of backward integration requires capacity in storage and money. And perhaps even a certain mentality: doing things the hard way.

## Vegetables, fruit and herbs

Of all ingredients to be used in the kitchen, growing your own vegetables, herbs and fruits is conceivably the 'easiest' to achieve. But even then you need the right conditions. The composition of the soil and the climate are factors to consider if you want to grow certain varieties. An interesting example is set by Alain Passard (restaurant l'Arpège, in Paris, three-star Michelin), whose restaurant specializes in vegetables. Much of what he needs he grows himself. He has three separate areas in production, each with a specific soil type that gives him the desired variety of fruits and vegetables. Interestingly, his farmlands are quite far apart. Furthest away is a piece of land close to the sea, across from Mont St Michel, about 350km from Paris. This illustrates that self-sufficiency is not necessarily the same as local and moreover it illustrates the trouble it may take to grow your own vegetables, fruits and herbs.

## Animal proteins and animal fats

To supply your own kitchen with eggs is not the hardest thing. However, dairy, including the (important) fatty compound butter, is a different matter. Milk is quite perishable and making dairy products (yoghurt, butter, cheese) requires a lot of skill, attention, special facilities and money.

Keeping cattle and pigs for their meat also costs time and care, but it should not be impossible. Besides meat, pigs could supply another fatty compound: lard. The butchering is a serious problem. A certified butcher should come by to kill an animal once in a while. Then, to make raising your own animals feasible, the kitchen should use the whole animal to create sufficient economic value out of a pig or cow. This means that literally each part of the animal should serve a culinary purpose. This is not new, but may have been somewhat forgotten. After all, our modern and organized food system has given us food safety and the opportunity to choose exactly the types of meat that we want to use. Culinary tradition has given wonderful techniques and products to the world that can make full use of all the meat that an animal can give. As stated before, self-sufficiency requires a certain mentality and new skills, like knowledge of preservation techniques.

## Fatty compounds

We have already dealt with two possible fatty compounds to use in the kitchen: butter and lard. It is clear that they are, to say the least, not ideal options. An alternative for a food self-sufficient restaurant would be walnut, sunflower or rapeseed oil. However, the number of plants or trees needed to yield the amount of oil needed in the kitchen is too large in this respect. Producing one's own oil does not seem feasible for a culinary homestead.

## Carbohydrates

Within the carbohydrates we evidently need to distinguish sugar and starch. Sugar in its well-known crystalline form is not really available for the truly self-sufficient. It is obtained from beets or cane and only after an intricate process. Honey and syrups are alternatives and of these, the syrups are easiest to make. However, they are not neutral in flavour and you need to make a sufficient quantity at the time that your fruit is at maximum ripeness.

As far as starch is concerned, we face similar challenges. There are many types of grains and they can be grown in many climates, but the composition of the grain is crucial in what can be done with it. You may not be able to bake the perfect bread.

## Salty and sour compounds

Producing your own salt is hardly possible. As an alternative, purified seawater could be used. However, for brining and curing meats and fish, extra salt is necessary, especially since we already have established that food preservation is indispensable in self-sufficiency.

Sour is also a crucial ingredient in preservation. It could be obtained by letting, for instance, wine turn into vinegar. But then again, you would need (local?) wine.

## So how self-sufficient can a restaurant be?

The above items make clear that self-sufficiency is largely a romantic, not very feasible concept. If at all, it is more like a hobby that only the most expensive restaurants can afford. Often they are blessed with a big staff of people that work for their experience and their curriculum vitae, not for a (big) salary.

Both the location and the season of a food self-sufficient restaurant will give it many limitations when it comes to the products it will be able to make use of. There must be some form of a table d'hôte menu that changes with what nature offers to limit the complications of à la carte choices. The kitchen needs enough creativity to come up with at least acceptable dishes.

Irwin (2005) forecasts the costs of ingredients will drop. On the other hand, capital and personnel costs will probably be higher. Self-sufficiency is likely to necessitate extra investments in land, treatments and people. Furthermore you need to calculate the inefficiency of doing your own harvesting, under- and overproduction. Normally you would only buy what you need with the desired quality. Considering the extra costs it is questionable if the restaurant will be able to realize a sufficient return.

Although it is unlikely that one single closed farm-restaurant will achieve full food self-sufficiency, Sloman and Garratt (2010) point out the advantage: autarchy means independence. Influencing the quality you need and doing whatever you want. We would like to add that growing your own ingredients gives identity and character to a restaurant. It creates involvement of staff clients.

An interesting option could be cooperation. It would lead to economies of scale. One large mixed farm or a group of farms could supply a number of (in that way food self-sufficient) restaurants. It would bring an interaction between supply and demand, which is likely to lead to a better coordination of restaurant needs and farmers' capacities. In addition, this farm could sell to private customers, and guests of the restaurants. Some of the obstacles remain, but there is a good chance that this alternative will prove feasible.

## How local do you want to be? Introducing the Foodzone model

As full food self-sufficiency is not realistic, any restaurant needs free trade. This leads to a different, yet related question: what do you need to buy and where does it come from? Self-sufficiency and locavorism are not the same, but they share the wish to be close to the source of the ingredients that are used. Buying from farmers and producers in your region fits sustainable practice and reducing food miles. It is the practical alternative to self-sufficiency. On the other hand, it is likely that not all products can be economically produced in a certain region in a sustainable way.

The Foodzone model was developed as a tool for the restaurant of the Hotel Management School Maastricht to help make buying decisions. It consists of five zones, ranging from close-by to the whole world. This tool enables chefs to set targets for the five zones to indicate what percentage of the total ingredients can be bought from every zone. The restaurant decides how local it wants to be. Once targets are set, they are used to control if the objectives are met. As such, the Foodzone model quantifies the objectives of the buying decisions.

Figure 25.1 shows the outcome for the Maastricht area in Holland and the choices of an individual restaurant. The model supposes that every restaurant makes its own analysis and

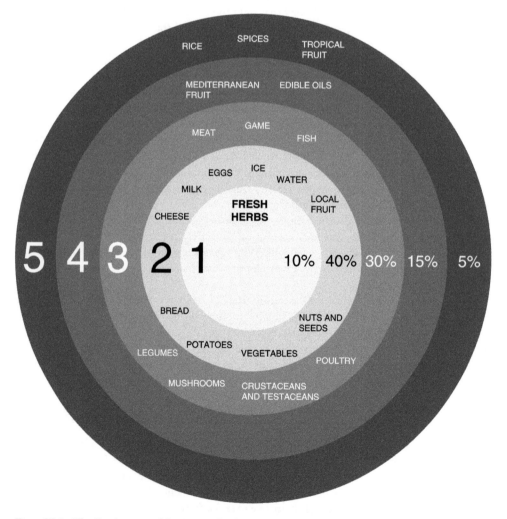

*Figure 25.1*  The Foodzone model outcome for the Maastricht area in Holland. © HMSM, Dr P. Klosse.

choices. The higher the percentage of the first two zones, the clearer the indication of the intentions of the restaurant of working locally, supporting local farmers and the region.

## Conclusion

Buying local and reducing food miles are popular themes in prolific restaurants, providing identity and character. Yet full food self-sufficiency must largely be regarded as romantic and hardly feasible. Regions cannot just produce everything, and nature is not very accountable. Restaurants that want to be close to producers need to be very flexible. Food costs may be lower, but cost of labour is likely to be higher. Furthermore, specific expertise and even investments are required. Moreover, there are ingredients that you may want to use because guests don't want to be without. Would a restaurant without coffee or tea in the Western world be a success? In practice every restaurant will need to find a balance on a scale ranging from self-sufficiency to free trade. The Foodzone model is a practical model that can be applied as a managerial tool. A chef or buyer for a restaurant can decide on what percentage of the total will be acquired from a certain zone around the restaurant. It leads to a set of targets that can be evaluated. The higher the percentage of products bought from zones closer to the restaurant, the more local the restaurant can be considered to be.

## References

Bakker, T. (1985) *Eten van eigen bodem*, Wageningen: Landbouwhogeschool.
Irwin, D. (2005) 'The welfare cost of autarky', *Review of International Economics*, 13(4): 631–645.
Kruyskamp, C. (1976) *Van Dale: Groot woordenboek der Nederlandse Taal*, Gravenhage: Martinus Nijhoff.
Nearing, H., and Nearing, S. (1989) *The Good Life: Helen and Scott Nearing's Sixty Years of Self-Sufficient Living*, New York: Schocken Books.
Oxford English Dictionary (2013) Oxford: Oxford University Press.
Phaidon Press (2010) *René Redzepi and the Story of Noma*, www.youtube.com/watch?v=ygTaJC5FeD4.
Pollan, M. (2009) *In Defense of Food: An Eater's Manifesto*, New York: Penguin.
Pollan, M. (2013) *Cooked: A Natural History of Transformation*, New York: Penguin.
Slack, N., Chambers, S. and Johnston, R. (2009) *Operations Management*, New York: Prentice-Hall.
Sloman, J. and Garratt, D. (2010) *Essentials of Economics*, Harlow: Pearson Education Limited.
Thoreau, D. (1972) *Walden*, London: Dent.
Valentinov, V. (2008) 'On the origin of rules: between exchange and self-sufficiency', *The Social Science Journal*, 45(2): 345–351.
Verhoeff-Schot, E. and Cauberghe, J. (1977) *Standaard Nieuw Engels-Nederlands Nederlands-Engels Woordenboek*, Antwerp: Scriptoria.
William Reed Business Media Ltd. (2013) *The World's 50 Best Restaurants*, www.theworlds50best.com.

# 26

# BUSINESS MODEL DEVELOPMENT FOR A SUSTAINABLE AND RESPONSIBLE RESTAURANT CONCEPT

## The dimensions and business rationales of CSR and sustainability

*Anders Justenlund*

> CSR is not about how you spend the money you make. It's about how you make the money you spend.
>
> *(McElhaney, 2007)*

### Introducing corporate social responsibility and sustainability

Many definitions and aspects of corporate social responsibility (CSR) and sustainability are used in both academic and industry contexts. Some definitions are more general and wide, while others only make sense in a specific context. For example, is there a difference in how the UN and the European Commission, as supranational institutions, define the terms CSR and sustainability and how the terms are interpreted by smaller and medium-sized enterprises? Further, are there differences in how businesses interpret sustainable and responsible practices within different industries? With an endless number of definitions and practices of CSR and sustainability principles, a common platform of understanding is needed in order to create sustainable innovation within a business context.

Alexander Dahlsrud (2006) defines five dimensions of CSR.

1.  The environmental dimension – refers to the natural environment.
2.  The social dimension – refers to the relationship between business and society.
3.  The economic dimension – refers to social-economic or financial aspects, including defining CSR in terms of business operations.
4.  The stakeholder dimension – refers to related stakeholders or stakeholder groups.
5.  The voluntariness dimension – refers to actions not prescribed by law.

Dahlsrud's five dimensions of CSR provide a wide general definition of the perspectives of social responsibility and sustainability. To be able to adapt the understanding of the dimensions into a more specific business context, it is relevant to look into the interrelatedness of the dimensions. In an industry context this could, for example, be how a restaurant would select only local producers/suppliers for its operations. When a restaurant chooses local producers this benefits the local economy/society (economic and social dimensions). When the transportation of commodities from producers to restaurant is shortened this would result in lower $CO_2$ emissions (environmental dimension). Developing local supply of commodities creates an interrelated connection between restaurant and producer where the latter will be a primary stakeholder in the restaurant operation (stakeholder dimension). A restaurant is not obliged to buy local produce; however, it could be a rational choice related to the core business propositions of a restaurant (voluntariness dimension).

Dahlsrud's five dimensions of CSR are, as mentioned, wide in their definitions, which leaves room for interpretation of what can be defined as responsible and sustainable practices. In the thought example of the interrelationship between restaurant and producer, an emphasis on local trade and the positive effect it has on limiting $CO_2$ emissions is made, due to limited need for transportation. However, this is only one perspective in relation to environmental sustainability. A restaurant also needs to focus on, for example, farming methods (ethical and sustainable), seasonality in relation to produce, fair trade, etc. What seems a responsible and sustainable practice is suddenly the opposite.

---

### Sustainable Restaurant Association

The Sustainable Restaurant Association (SRA) is a network of restaurants in the United Kingdom and Ireland dedicated to minimizing food waste and use of resources and at the same time increasing the level of food quality. The SRA defines a sustainable restaurant using three terms: sourcing, environment and society. Sourcing is based on a set of standards within environmentally positive farming, local and seasonal food, sustainable fish, ethical meat and dairy, and fair trade. Environment refers to water saving, workplace resources, supply chain, and waste management. The last category, society, refers to community engagement, treating people fairly, healthy eating, and responsible marketing. Altogether, this defines a holistic approach to a sustainable restaurant concept. To learn more, see www.thesra.org.

---

It can be a complex process to reorganize the conventional business practices of a restaurant and align the business practices with principles of CSR and sustainability, especially when these principles should make sense when related to the primary task of a restaurant, the provision of food and beverages. It is important to define the business rationale for CSR and sustainability within the context of a restaurant's business model, making sure that these principles are fully integrated into the restaurant business practices and not limited to an add-on philanthropic activity.

Zadek (2000) presents four categories to describe the business rationale for a company to implement CSR into business practices:

1. Defending reputation.
2. Justification of benefits over costs.

3.  Integration of CSR in broader business strategies.
4.  Relation to learning, innovation, and/or risk management.

These four categories are supplemented by Kurucz et al. (2008), who suggest four perspectives that define the business rationale for CSR:

1.  Reduction of costs and risks.
2.  The ability to gain a competitive advantage.
3.  Development of legitimacy and a positive reputation.
4.  Seeking win–win outcomes through synergistic value creation.

The eight business rationales for CSR contain three general, different approaches that a business can apply to its practice/behaviour: reactive, active and proactive/forward-thinking.

1.  Reaction: the business reacting to demands from the outside (e.g., from customers) – refers to the defence of business reputation.
2.  Action: the business engages in acting according to CSR/sustainability standards, defined by societal expectations (e.g., UN Global Compact, ISO-certification) – refers to the justification of benefits over costs, reduction of costs and risks, the ability to gain a competitive advantage, and development of legitimacy and a positive reputation.
3.  Proactive/forward-thinking: the business implements initiatives and defines a strategy where day-to-day business operations become a positive contributing factor, for the future sustainable development of society – refers to the integration of CSR into broader business strategies, learning, innovation, risk management, and seeking win–win outcomes through synergistic value creation.

The three approaches to apply aspects of CSR and sustainability in business practices are also an indicator of what kind of role social responsibility and sustainability plays, and to what extent this is integrated into the daily business operations and the business model of a restaurant.

The approaches range from a reactive approach where a company only takes action if it is required (or forced to do so) to a proactive approach where the way a company does well in relation to CSR and sustainability principles is fully integrated into normative business practices.

---

### Brasserie Storm

Crowne Plaza – CPH Towers in Ørestad, Copenhagen, has been recognized as one of the most sustainable hotels in the world. Every single aspect of the operation is defined by socially responsible and sustainable principles. The hotel's main restaurant, Brasserie Storm, is developed on the same concept as the hotel. The menu is based on local produce from an organic farm outside the city and follows seasonal changes. The brasserie has also established a herb garden on the rooftop of the hotel. Furthermore, all kitchen waste is collected in containers and transported to a local bioenergy plant and turned into electricity. The hotel and restaurant also participate in a recruitment programme where people who have difficulties entering the job market are trained and given a job at the hotel. To learn more, see www.cpcopenhagen.dk/en.

The business rationale is a summary of why restaurants should engage in CSR and the sustainability 'cause'. The rationale is defined on societal expectations of the restaurant industry and not the other way around. The question is then how restaurant businesses can shift from a normative focus on successful business performance measurements such as cost, revenue, stakeholder issues, key resources, staff performance, etc., to also include CSR and sustainability principles as key value propositions systematically implemented in the restaurant operations.

In order to understand the business rationale for CSR and sustainability better, restaurant business stakeholders should focus on the implementation of CSR principles within a conceptual understanding of the different aspects of a business model and the interrelationship between these aspects. This is in order to understand why and how CSR and sustainability principles can create value and support the development and sustainability of a restaurant business model that in the end can result in a successful business performance. It is important again to emphasize that the CSR perspective should be seen as an integrated part/block of the business model and not as an 'add-on' that can be delineated from the rest of the business model setup without any effect on the performance of the model.

Further, the understanding of CSR and sustainability principles should go beyond the person aspect within a business, meaning that the definition and execution of the social responsible and sustainability aspects should lie within the model structure and not be powered by managers' personal sets of values and interests (Hemingway and Maclagan, 2004).

Applying this understanding of CSR and sustainability principles within a business model setup might conflict with a traditional understanding of the core essence of business activities and what Osterwalder and Pigneur (2003) define as the culmination of a business model, the financial aspect. It is, however, assumed that applying an integrated understanding of CSR and sustainability principles to the business model should define the platform for financial income and not contradict it. Seeing CSR and sustainability as such, the perspective moves away from the field of venture philanthropy and social entrepreneurship (Dees et al.,

1998; Mair and Marti, 2004; Austin et al., 2006), which is based on the personal motivation of an entrepreneur to solve a given external social problem of a structural aspect within the business model ontology.

Going from a general to a more specific perspective, the rest of the chapter will focus on, how restaurant businesses can develop and implement CSR and sustainability principles into a business model setup. Through a conceptual understanding of a business model setup, combined with practical examples, the chapter will illustrate how a proactive approach to sustainability and CSR can develop the business practice for restaurant operations.

## The business model canvas

Osterwalder and Pigneur (2010) define a conceptual understanding of a business model, in what they refer to as the business model canvas. A business model is a description of the rationale on how a business creates, delivers, and captures value. Osterwalder and Pigneur define the business model canvas from nine 'building blocks', which are all interrelated with each other and together describe how a business basically operates.

The business model canvas creates a basic common understanding of a business model that can be used to create and develop new alternative strategies for a business operation. The keyword is innovation and the canvas works as a blueprint for a strategy that can be implemented through current organizational structures and operation processes/systems (Osterwalder and Pigneur, 2010). The nine building blocks are:

1. Customer segments
2. Value propositions
3. Channels
4. Customer relationships
5. Revenue streams
6. Key resources
7. Key activities
8. Key partnerships
9. Cost structures

All together the nine basic business model building blocks form the basis for the business model canvas.

### *Customer segments*

The customer segment building block is the most important block in any business model canvas. If a business does not have any profitable customers, operations will end within a short period of time. The profitable customer segment is equally important to the social responsible/sustainable business model as to a conventional business model. The way restaurant operations segments guests is no different from other businesses when they group restaurant guests into distinct segments with common needs, common behaviour or other specific needs the guests might have. Based on the business model, the restaurant needs to be aware of which segments to serve and which to ignore.

Applying principles of CSR and sustainability to the segmentation of guests will be a focus demand; will restaurant guests demand that the restaurant they dine at has engaged in CSR/ sustainability activities? Restaurant guests who have this demand make their choice based on ethical, environmental, and political motives. When a restaurant guest has these behavioural motives in their restaurant selection, it is based on a wish, for the guest, to affect (and address) issues of CSR/sustainability directly to the restaurant industry.

It is a tendency that individuals, based on well-informed choices, attempt to change industry practices – also defined as political consumption (Andersen and Tobiasen, 2001).

With engaged guests (political consumers) it is possible for the restaurant business to engage in a mutual relationship with them, to further develop the CSR and sustainable initiatives in operations. The guests become a resource for continuous sustainable innovation. Involved restaurant guests are willing to pay for different aspects of the service/product offered (including sustainable/ethical production).

## *Value propositions*

The value proposition block defines all the products and services that create value for a specific customer segment. The unique value proposition offered to restaurant guests should be the reason why they chose one restaurant over another. When a restaurant engages in CSR/sustainability in relation to day-to-day business operations this could be the underlying value proposition of the sustainable restaurant concept. The primary product of a restaurant will typically be the gastronomic experience. The dining experience will differ in relation to the restaurant concept and depends on the target segment (from Michelin-star rated restaurants to middle-ranged and low-budget/fast food restaurants). All restaurant concepts meet the expectations of different guest-segments; however this does not necessarily have an impact on the level of action taken on CSR/sustainability issues.

The most important perspective on value propositions and CSR/sustainability is the context and relatedness between the two. As mentioned earlier, there has to be a link between the core business activities and the CSR-approach the restaurant chooses to implement, to avoid that social responsible and sustainable activities become an 'add-on'/symbolic-concept rather than the way the restaurant performs its business. The task is to avoid any contradictions between the restaurant operations (or doings) and what a restaurant communicates to its guests. For example, it does not make sense that a restaurant promotes itself on environmental sustainability while it imports most of its supplies from far distances based on a cost-reduction strategy regarding availability of supply.

Further elements/principles that, among others, could be linked to the development of socially responsible and sustainable value propositions include newness, performance, customization, price, cost, accessibility, and/or convenience/usability (Osterwalder and Pigneur, 2010).

---

### Noma

Restaurant Noma in Copenhagen has been recognized as the best restaurant in the world for three consecutive years (2010–2012) and holds two Michelin stars. The unique value proposition of Restaurant Noma is to offer creative and innovative dishes based on local and primary produce and raw articles found in the Nordic regions. This includes items not considered edible by modern urbanized people. The Nordic food concept has challenged the Central and Southern European norm for high-end gastronomy. Noma is an abbreviation for the Danish words 'Nordisk mad' (Nordic food). To learn more, see www.noma.dk.

---

Photo Mikkel Heriba

## *Channels*

The channels block represents the link between a restaurant's value propositions and the customer segments. Activities imply communication, distribution, and sales and comprise a restaurant's interface with guests. It is the channels that help guests to evaluate the value propositions and thereby choose to take advantage of a restaurant's dining services. Essentially, it is about bringing the value propositions to the market.

When communicating the value propositions of a responsible/sustainable restaurant concept it is important to focus on the message that the business communicates. It is the message that defines the guests' expectations, and if a restaurant is not able to meet the expectations created by the communication of value propositions a mismatch will occur resulting in the risk that a restaurant will be accused of 'green washing'. A mismatch between expectation and experience will further result in a missed opportunity to strengthen restaurant–guest relationships.

The purchase decision is also implied in the channel between value propositions and guests segments. This includes: awareness, evaluation, purchase, delivery, and after-sales. If the guest is satisfied by the restaurant experience, this creates the opportunity to provide extra awareness about responsibility/sustainability issues paving the way for a guest visiting a restaurant a second and third time.

## Customer relationship

Channels focus on meeting the customer with a specific set of value propositions; however, the customer relationship is more about building a mutual relationship between restaurant and guest. This includes a focus on guest retention – the more we interact with our guests, the more we will understand the guests' needs and understanding of CSR/sustainable principles. If this relationship is well developed it can help a restaurant to develop the right CSR strategy related to the restaurant concept. By mutual relationship it is important to point out that a restaurant not only listens to the guest, but also positively challenges the guests' understanding of CSR and sustainability principles.

---

### Nose2tail

'Nature decides the menu' is the slogan of the sustainable diner, Nose2tail, based in Copenhagen, Denmark. The principles behind the restaurant concept are, as the name of the restaurant implies, that all parts of an animal should be put to use. All meat used at the restaurant comes from small or medium-sized organic farms. By using all parts of the animal, food waste is reduced to a minimum and at the same time costs decrease. By using untraditional cuts and offal, guests learn to appreciate all parts of the animal as a delicious meal. The inspiration for this food concept originates from Hugh Fearnley-Whittingstall and his River Cottage in Axminster, England. To learn more, see www.nose2tail.dk and www.rivercottage.net.

---

It is important for a restaurant to figure out what kind of relationship the business would like to establish with its guests, and even more important to evaluate the value of developing and maintaining this relationship, both in relation to financial costs/revenue and the link to positive continuous development and adjustments of value propositions. Guest relationships are directly maintained through the personal interaction between restaurant staff and guests, and more indirectly by interaction between restaurant and guests (and potential guests) via online communities such as Facebook, Instagram, Pinterest and Twitter. With well-established and continuous mutual communication between restaurant and 'online-guests', the potential for establishing a co-creation relationship grows. The practical outcome of a co-creation relationship is when, for example, guest reviews play a vital role for the development and adjustment of the restaurant concept or when guests have the possibility of making co-decisions on the restaurant menu, or which produce should be used in the kitchen. A beneficial and positive co-creation relationship is vital to make sure that the CSR/sustainable principles implemented in the restaurant concept make rational sense for the guests, and thereby the business model as a whole.

## Revenue streams

The revenue stream building block is naturally linked to how a restaurant generates income from the guest segments it targets. Revenue streams relate to how much the guests are willing to pay for the service provided for them. More important in relation to the issues of CSR and sustainability is the question of whether guests are willing to pay a premium to dine and drink more responsibly.

In Denmark it is common that a restaurant donates a percentage of the money earned from dining guests, based on the entire sale made or on 'add-on' purchases on a special menu. An example of the latter is the Tapas restaurant Pingvin in Aalborg, Denmark. All through December it was possible for guests to purchase a glass of Cava and thereby support the Red Cross organization. All income made was directly donated to the organization. A concept like this is philanthropic in its nature and in the end it is up to the guest if he/she is willing to support the Red Cross by making an active purchase. It is, however, not incorporated directly into the business model concept of the restaurant, and thereby, as mentioned, it is defined as an add-on activity to support a worthy cause.

To define CSR and sustainability principles as directly related to the core business activities, a restaurant should make its revenue simply by performing well in its daily operations related to the five dimensions of CSR with a positive outcome for the greater community/society – put simply, when a business is doing well it benefits the future development of society.

## Key resources

The key resources building block is a vital part of the business model. Key resources refers to what is needed to produce and offer the value propositions. Key resources can be divided into physical assets, intellect, human, and financial. In relation to a restaurant operation, physical assets play an important role. They refer, of course, to the quality of the produce used in the kitchen. Furthermore, it is important to have professional chefs to prepare the primary produce the right way, meaning that human and intellectual resources are important.

When it comes to a restaurant concept based on CSR/sustainability principles physical, intellectual, and human resources play an even more important role. Human resources are crucial in relation to arranging day to day operations and linking these to the guest segments that are willing to pay for the services and products – even more importantly, to maintain a restaurant's integrity towards the communicated CSR principles. Professional kitchen and restaurant staff are the guests' guarantee and reference that the food and drinks consumed are of the same quality as presented. It is implied that restaurant staff are important for the storytelling behind a restaurant's CSR and sustainability strategy.

## Key activities

The key activities block is directly linked to key resources and the engine of the restaurant business model. Key activities refers to the production, preparation, and cultivation of the primary produce in the kitchen providing restaurant guests with a superior-quality F&B-product, based on CSR and sustainability principles. This is also where, for example, head chefs come up with new, creative and innovative ways to prepare, for example, local produce that functions as a symbol of sustainability for the guest.

### Melsted Badehotel

The Danish seaside hotel, Melsted Badehotel on the island of Bornholm, is a valuable example of local produce connecting the dining experience with the history of the island. The hotel restaurant only uses local seasonal produce in all dishes. All produce used in the kitchen is from the island or caught in the surrounding waters. The use of local produce and raw sources from nature has created a unique connection between the kitchen and nature telling a unique story of the culture and nature of Bornholm. The interpretation of this is seen in the special dishes that are served. To learn more, see www.melstedbadehotel.dk/en.

## *Key partnerships*

The key partnerships block is important for the key activities and key resources of a restaurant concept. Key partnerships refers to the suppliers and partners that are vital for the business model. Getting the right suppliers in relation to a socially responsible and sustainable restaurant concept is a necessity. It is important that a restaurant can believe that primary produce is acquired according to responsible and sustainable principles (e.g., that heavy livestock have lived in proper conditions and that, for example, fruit and vegetables are organic). To reduce the risks a restaurant can choose only to use organically certified producers or to enter a mutual partnership on how production should be planned and what kind of products should be produced.

Basically restaurants should enter partnerships to maximize the positive effects of their business model and to reduce risks related to business activities.

## *Cost structure*

The last building block is costs; it refers to all the costs that are related to the operations of the restaurant business model. Development and delivery of value propositions, maintaining customer relationships, and making revenue are all activities that come with a cost. The costs are calculated after defining key resources, key activities, and key partnerships.

Restaurant business models can (as other businesses) be defined as either cost-driven or value-driven. If a restaurant is cost-driven it minimizes costs wherever possible. This could be on the quality of food produce, drinks, staff, service, facilities, etc. However, all these things are also related to the guests' willingness to pay a premium for the products and service at a restaurant. When it comes to a restaurant concept driven by CSR and sustainability principles, such an operation tends to be value-driven, which refers to less concern with costs and more focus on value creation. Premium value is in this case provided by a focus on the quality of the food and drinks consumed together with an awareness of the responsible and sustainable conditions these are produced in.

## Conclusion

There is no fixed recipe for how to set up a socially responsible and sustainable business model. The nine building blocks of Osterwalder and Pigneur's (2010) business model canvas is one way to construct an easily understandable business model and to understand how all parts of a business model are interrelated and interdependent on one another. When it comes to implementing CSR into the business model context there are no final answers to how this is done; however there are some guidelines that are worth following: to have an active or proactive CSR-strategy it is important that socially responsible and sustainable principles are brought into all parts of the day to day operations of a restaurant. The business model canvas helps to visualize and understand the importance of creating (and how to create) unique value propositions in a restaurant's key activities, resources, and partnerships and further how to market these value propositions through strong customer relationships, channels and clearly defined guest segments and revenue creation. It is important to emphasize that the right CSR-approach is equally based on a restaurant's operations and the external societal expectations. When there is an alignment between the internal and external perspectives, the CSR-driven business model has proven its success.

# References

Andersen, J.G. and Tobiasen, M. (2001) 'Politisk forbrug og Politiske forbrugere: Globalisering og Politik i Hverdagslivet', in *Magtudredningen*, Aarhus: Aarhus Universitetsforlag.

Austin, J., Stevenson, H. and Wei-Skillern, J. (2006) 'Social and commercial entrepreneurship: same, different, or both?', *Entrepreneurship Theory & Practice*, 30(1): 1–22.

Dahlsrud, A. (2006) 'How corporate social responsibility is defined: an analysis of 37 definitions', *Corporate Social Responsibility and Environmental Management*, 15: 1–13.

Dees, J.G., Haas, P. and Haas, M. (1998) *The Meaning of 'Social Entrepreneurship'*, Kauffman Center for Entrepreneurial Leadership and Graduate School of Business, Stanford University.

Hemingway, C.A. and Maclagan, P.W. (2004) 'Managers' personal values as drivers of corporate social responsibility', *Journal of Business Ethics*, 50: 33–44.

Kurucz, E., Colbert, B. and Wheeler, D. (2008) 'The business case for corporate social responsibility', in A. Crane, A. McWilliams, D. Matten, J. Moon and D. Siegel (eds.), *The Oxford Handbook of Corporate Social Responsibility*, Oxford: Oxford University Press, pp. 83–112.

Mair, J. and Marti, I. (2004) *Social Entrepreneurship Research: A Source of Explanation, Prediction, and Delight*, IESE Business School, University of Navarra, Revised paper WP. 546.

McElhaney, K. (2007) *Inaugural International CSR Conference*, www.ey.com/IE/en/About-us/Entrepreneurship/Entrepreneur-Of-The-Year/CSR-Conference (accessed 5 February 2014).

Osterwalder, A. and Pigneur, Y. (2003) *Towards Business and Information Systems Fit through a Business Model Ontology*, http://inforge.unil.ch/yp/Pub/03_sms.pdf (accessed 21 January 2015).

Osterwalder, A. and Pigneur, Y. (2010) *Business Model Generation – A Handbook for Visionaries, Game Changers, and Challengers*, New York: John Wiley & Sons Inc.

Zadek, S. (2000) *Doing Good and Doing Well: Making the Business Case for Corporate Citizenship*, Research Report 1282-00-RR, New York: The Conference Board.

# Suggested reading

Carroll, A.B. and Shabana, S.M. (2010) 'The business case or corporate social responsibility: a review of concepts, research and practice', *International Journal of Management Reviews*, 12(1): 85–105.

Haslam, C., Anderson, T., Tsitsianis, N. and Yin, Y.P. (2012) *Redefining Business Models: Strategies from a Financialized World*, Abingdon: Routledge.

Matten, D. and Moon, J. (2008) ' "Implicit" and "explicit" CSR: a conceptual framework for a comparative understanding of corporate social responsibility', *Academy of Management Review*, 33(2): 404–424.

Osterwalder, A., Pigneur, Y. and Tucci, C.L. (2005) 'Clarifying business models: origins, present, and future of the concept', *Communications of AIS*, 16: 1.

Weber, E. (2008) 'The business case for corporate social responsibility: a company-level measurement approach for CSR', *European Management Journal*, 26: 247–261.

# 27

# THE SUSTAINABLE RESTAURANT: DOES IT EXIST?

*Charles Barneby and Juline E. Mills*

## Introduction

"Sustainability" is undoubtedly one of the top ten buzz words of the past decade. Countries, companies, and environmentalists are continually developing mandates and strategic plans aimed at massive improvements to sustainability initiatives. From Switzerland, Luxembourg, and Australia currently ranked as the most sustainable countries in the world for environmental health and ecosystem vitality by Yale University 2014 Environmental Performance Index; the US president signing an executive order aimed at greening and making federal agencies more sustainable (White House, 2009); to Bank of America (2014), a foremost leader in the field, dedicating $70 billion over the next 16 years to becoming more sustainable and efficient. While positive examples abound on sustainable improvements by countries, Fortune 500 companies, and key environmentalists, flaws do exist that prevent wider advancement in the field. Perhaps the greatest harbinger of problems that can arise with becoming a sustainable company is the 2006 lawsuit in which the developer of a restaurant and luxury condominium project became embroiled in a countersuit with the general contractor for losses in state tax credits and the Leadership in Energy and Environmental Design (LEED) certification due to construction delays (McDill, 2009). In 2010, in *Gifford Fuel Saving vs. the US Green Building Council (USGBC) and LEED*, the plaintiff brought a class action lawsuit claiming that it was misled into thinking that its building would be more energy efficient after following the guidelines and becoming LEED certified. Gifford Fuel Savings found instead of energy efficiencies, more was being paid in utility fees and the building had in fact become less efficient (Roberts, 2010).

Sustainability is an issue debated in all fields of businesses, governmental organizations, and industries and can be defined from differing viewpoints. Clarity in understanding sustainability can often be difficult, since no unilateral definition of the term exists. A summary review of more than 60 related articles on the subject finds no clear-cut meaning of the term with each industry and its sub-sectors creating its own by borrowing aspects of a definition from various disciplines. At a minimum, Merriam-Webster Dictionary (2013) defines sustainable as being "able to be used without being completely used up or destroyed; a method of harvesting or using a resource so that resource is not depleted or permanently damaged." In governmental circles, sustainability is viewed as meeting present needs without compromising the ability of future generations to meet their own needs. In scientific circles, sustainability is explained as using the natural resources at a rate equal to or less than their renewal rate. Companies, on the other hand, talk about sustainability in terms of "corporate social responsibility" while nature protection organizations use the term "saving the planet" (Strategic Sustainability Consulting, 2008). Common definitions also include "improving the quality of human life while living within the carrying capacity of supporting eco-systems," and developing a sustainable society, "one that can persist over generations, one that is far-seeing enough, flexible enough, and wise enough, not to undermine either its physical or its social systems of support" (National Research Council, 2013; WECD, 1987).

## Restaurant sustainability, the early years

Sustainability in the restaurant setting takes on the meaning that all the food is self-sufficient. It follows the sustainable agriculture definition, "a way of raising food that is healthy for consumers and animals, does not harm the environment, is humane for workers, respects animals, provides a fair wage to the farmer, and supports and enhances rural communities" (Social Ecology, 2010; Sustainable Table, 2014). Many restaurant operators choose not to engage in sustainable business practices, perceiving that using more sustainable ingredients leads to higher ingredient costs. Restaurants embracing sustainable approaches have not always been welcomed in the industry with open arms. In a three-way lawsuit between *Odren vs. Chetcuti vs. Fisher Road Properties* (2001) the plaintiff, Odren, owners of a Subway franchise, sued Chetcuti for opening a vegetarian and raw food bar in the same mall citing unfair competition. Chetcuti in turn sued the landlord, Fisher Road Properties, for breach of contract and fraud. The parties eventually settled allowing Chetcuti to operate (*Vegetarian Times*, 2001) due in part to the adverse media attention brought to the Subway franchise and the overwhelming customer support for the smaller business. For most restaurants choosing to highlight sustainability, the primary focus has been on the "greening" aspects via menus promoting local and sustainable food options and showing commitment to reducing their carbon footprint with such phrases as "fair trade," "farm to table," "hand-picked by the chef," "small-batch," "locally grown organics," and beverages and soda made from "public water sources." Palmer (2009) and Rosenblum and Rowen (2010) note that "green-minded consumers" consider a restaurant's ecological positioning when making "where to dine" decisions. The National Restaurant Association (2014) contends that 64 percent of consumers are more likely to visit a food establishment serving locally produced food items. American consumers spent 25 percent of their food dollar dining out in 1955 as compared with a projected 47 percent in 2014 (National Restaurant Association, 2014). Restaurants use the sustainable aspects of their menu to attract niche customer groups. Henry (2014) reports on the opening in Vancouver of the world's first 100 percent Ocean Wise sushi restaurant. Ocean Wise is Canada's largest sustainability program with specific rules, limiting the effects of overfishing. Restaurants, called into question for unhealthy food products, have been able to gain traction by using sustainable food products on their menus. McDonald's in 2013 became the first national restaurant chain to serve Marine Stewardship Council (MSC) fish at all loca-tions in the United States (McDonald's, 2013). MSC certification identifies suppliers with practices that work to protect future fish supplies while providing high-quality seafood. Rosenblum and Rowen (2010), in a study of environmental sustainability in restaurant retail, note that restaurant organizations choose to develop related practices to reduce both cost and waste and to create a greener brand image, leading to greater customer loyalty.

For organization purposes, a restaurant is typically divided into three distinct areas of operation: the menu, the front-of-house, and the back-of-house, with the menu being the driving force that determines the overall functioning and seamless operation of the other two areas. Over time, the sustainable restaurant movement transitioned into updating and promoting parts of the front-of-house that adhere to specific greening standards including tablecloths, napkins, employee uniforms, and footwear. Continuing to act on consumer demand for more eco-friendly dining brands, restaurant operators moved into recyclable takeout packaging. American restaurant consumers generate 1.8 million tons of quick-serve food packaging, from hamburger wrappers and insulated cups to pizza boxes, and the vast majority ends up in landfills and raises constant concerns over potential carcinogenic effects from the chlorine and polystyrene found in Styrofoam containers (Oko, 2006). In 2013 the National Restaurant Association predicted that 62 percent of fine-dining and 57 percent of casual dining restaurateurs were planning on utilizing eco-friendly packaging.

Arguably, the kitchen diorama itself is the taproot of where all sustainability truly begins for a restaurant. In essence, the green kitchen culminates the "trinity" of a true sustainable restaurant. Without a green mantra, the spirit of restaurant sustainability is arguably lost and the kitchen is just another scullery with messy chemicals and abrasive surfaces with no hope of an environmentally friendly or economically conscious identity. Traditionally, the eco-friendly kitchen starts with energy-efficient equipment and recyclable materials, leading chefs to more sustainable cooking practices. The principle of "reduce, reuse, and recycle" could arguably be the starting roots of the sustainable kitchen with the industry overtime transitioning into energy-efficient product lines including low flow water conservation devices and biodegradable components for disposables (English, 2007). According to a National Restaurant Association study, 44 percent of surveyed consumers are likely to select a restaurant based on energy and water conservation practices (Palmer, 2009). The addition of potted plants to naturally purify the air in the kitchen workspace, and the inclusion of indoor gardens to cultivate herbs for cooking, benefits air quality and lowers carbon footprint due to no waste from the empty containers, since the herbs continue to grow (MacVean, 2010).

## Current standards in restaurant sustainability

Advocacy groups from grassroots to larger standardization organizations such as Green Seal, Eco Crown, and Dine Green have molded the shape of what a sustainable restaurant should look like and feature. The UK-based Sustainable Restaurant Association (2014) focuses on the social and environmental impact of foodservice operations. The SRA describes "three courses," society, environment, and sourcing, that offer up 14 tasty bites. The first course (society) examines community engagement, treating people fairly, healthy eating, and responsible marketing. The second course (environment) covers water saving, workplace resources, supply chain, waste management, and energy efficiency. The third and final course (sourcing) offers up environmentally positive farming, local and seasonal foods, sustainable fish, ethical meat and dairy, and fair trade products. The most prominent and longstanding organization in the United States is Dine Green, developed by the Green Restaurant Association, a certification system that rates the degree of sustainability on a point-based system across seven categories: water efficiency, waste reduction and recycling, sustainable furnishings and building materials, sustainable food, energy, disposables, and chemical and pollution reduction. A restaurant must achieve at least ten points in each category, except the sustainable furnishings and building materials, with an additional 40 points possible in each category. In addition, in order to be considered "green" a restaurant must accumulate a total of 100 points, meet the minimum points in each category, have a full-scale recycling program, be free of Styrofoam, practice yearly education, and communicate with the Certification

Board (Green Restaurant Association, 2014). To date, the Green Restaurant Association has certified 521 restaurants, of which nine are charters following the 13 energy efficiency, sustainable food service and sourcing, pollution prevention, and recycling procedures. Among these restaurants, 343 hold a two-star rating, meeting the minimum 100 points requirement; 150 hold a three-star rating, achieving the minimum 175 points; 17 hold a four-star rating, achieving at least 300 points; and two are four-star sustainably built. As sustainability is contemplated more and more by gastro-patrons and proprietors alike, the question arises not only as to "how" but "how much" does it cost to be truly green in all aspects? While 521 certified green restaurants may appear commendable, the answer becomes more apparent and hints at a dearth of progress in the field when one considers that there are more than 990,000 restaurant locations in the United States (National Restaurant Association, 2014).

Leading environmentalists have been advocating for years that foodservice organizations utilize more green methods with less of a footprint on the planet in food preparation and delivery. The average restaurant uses approximately 500,000 kilowatt hours of electricity, 20,000 therms of natural gas, and 800,000 gallons of water annually producing 490 tons of carbon dioxide (Horovitz, 2008), making the restaurant industry the largest energy user in the retail sector. Buzz words aimed at raising industry awareness range from "energy audits," "energy efficiency," "water conservation," to "smart kitchens, lighting, HVAC, and equipment." LEED Retail, a certification by the United States Green Building Council, has the largest stock in certifying sustainable buildings and kitchens; while Energy Star is the leader in equipment standards for the sustainable kitchen. There are many tricks and tools of the trade presently available that facilitate restaurants in the retrofitting, revamping, and redesigning of current kitchens to make them more sustainable. Energy efficiency requirements, hood designs, and water flow ratings are major components of these certifications. Precise calculations and related five-year savings on standard kitchen equipment such as walk-in freezers and coolers, under-counter refrigerators, broilers, convection ovens, and ice machines have simplified the complexities associated with energy efficiencies. The most sustainable kitchen equipment is considered to be the solar cooker, which is similar to the inversion cooker but is powered by solar energy and emits no pollution. Strong, lightweight, easy to clean and disinfect options such as bamboo and cork, FSC-certified woods, and rapidly renewable materials dominate the sustainable commercial kitchen market. Cost is an inhibiting factor when one considers that in 2010 only 38 US restaurants had received LEED certification, of which 40 percent were large chain organizations demonstrating corporate social responsibility (Canter, 2010). However, higher spending on more efficient and longer-lasting equipment also means lowering long-term costs and mitigating negative impacts on the environment, due to a decrease in the replacement and repair costs in the long-term.

## The flaws in measuring restaurant sustainability

The traditional concept of sustainable development, also known as the anthropogenic view, involves three dimensions – ecology, economy, and society often depicted in Venn diagram format (Wilderer et al., 2004). More recently, a bio-centric view of sustainability has been adopted, which states that society and economy exist as a subset of environment, and therefore the environment should be considered as the life basis for humans (Ott, 2003). In sum, it is an interconnected system in which no entity can truly be sustainable without considering its impact on all its related linkages. The restaurant industry faces its own unique set of challenges with achieving a true interconnected system of sustainable linkages.

It can be argued that the current approach to restaurant sustainability still resides primarily in the "go green" sphere and the adage of "contributing to an equitable and ecologically sustainable economy" (WECD, 1987) has not come to the business. Contributing to a sustainable economy requires consideration of larger factors often grouped into two broad categories—external and internal. In this regard, the restaurant industry would be far off the sustainability grid map as not many restaurants, if any, can say that they have considered such a holistic approach. External factors of business sustainability include a consideration of the economy, society, and the environment. What is the overall economic output of a restaurant as a measure of gross domestic product (GDP)? The National Restaurant Association (2014) projects that industry sales will equal 4 percent of GDP. Therefore, what percentage of this figure does an individual restaurant contribute? Correspondingly, what is the intensity of energy use per unit of GDP by the said restaurant? And what is the overall contribution of the restaurant to workforce development and subsequent unemployment rate reduction? It could be argued that GDP is difficult to measure for a country, much more so for an individual restaurant to measure the direct and indirect effects of its economic contribution. Proponents of this approach contend that, at a minimum, a sustainable restaurant should be able to measure its direct impact on the immediate local and regional economy to qualify as such.

Societal contributions for restaurants become even trickier when measures of poverty reduction, life expectancy, literacy rate, education, health, and crime reduction are considered. Of critical importance to sustainable restaurants would be poverty reduction, health, and life expectancy. The large majority of restaurants in the United States pay tipped wages, or may pay at or below the minimum wage. Restaurants are dominant contributors to poverty, with food stamp usage at double the rate of other industries. More than half of all tipped workers live below the poverty line (Jayaraman, 2013).

Health as a measure of sustainability examines contribution to the overall healthiness of the society. For the past three decades, American restaurants have struggled with portion size, resulting in many accusations of contributing to the current health crises of the American population. Restaurants, sustainable-minded or not, continue placing taste and convenience before nutritional value. Despite the displaying of caloric information, most menu items do not conform to daily caloric intake requirements. Two-thirds of the US adult population aged 20 and over are overweight or obese (Ogden et al., 2014) resulting in an estimated $208 billion in lost productivity (Go et al, 2013). The US Food and Drug Administration (FDA) in 2011 proposed regulations to ensure calorie labeling on menus by chain restaurants, retail food establishments, and vending machines with 20 or more locations. This does not impact the more than seven in ten restaurants that are single-unit operations (National Restaurant Association, 2014). Many consumers believe that restaurants have a social responsibility duty that includes providing nutritional information on food items that may be detrimental to their health or contrary to their beliefs (Mills and Thomas, 2008). In tandem with larger portion sizes comes waste. Restaurants produce an average of 275 pounds of waste a day (Gaylord, 2007), which translates to 25 percent of total food supply and 2 percent of total annual national energy consumption (Biocycle, 2010).

Chang and Lee (2008), in an examination of social sustainability in urban renewal, call for the inclusion of "satisfaction of welfare requirements," "conservation of resources and the surroundings," and the "creation of a harmonious living environment." In sum, many currently considered sustainable restaurants might not meet a societal accountability audit. The same is true for environmental considerations that examine measures of greenhouse gas emissions, water quality, air quality, and natural resource usage. Restaurants would need to obtain passing scores on each of these factors to be certified as sustainable.

Business sustainability internal factors also consist of three broad categories—building/facility, workplace procedures, and customer business interaction. The first, and previously discussed, building/facility is consistent with current sustainability standards and the use of the LEEDS and Energy Star principles. In terms of workplace procedures, sustainable restaurants would need to be able to measure and show, beyond the use of reusable and renewable materials, increases in employee productivity and cost efficiencies and savings. Even more difficult to define as a true measure of restaurant sustainability would be the generation of smart customer interactions, which the business is effectively communicating to customers using the "one voice/unify" principle. In this regard measures of customer satisfaction and contribution to the consumer's overall quality of life would apply. Internally, Genaidy et al. (2009) argue that ergonomics and its two approaches, micro and macro, is a key feature of business sustainability and is critically important to "optimizing the worker–work environment" by addressing issues of work safety, quality, and productivity. If this theory holds true, then the restaurant industry is even further away from achieving sustainability. One of the largest employment sectors in the United States with an estimated 13.5 million employees, the restaurant industry includes the largest group of injured workers suffering burns, lacerations, slips and falls, and lifting strains (National Restaurant Association, 2014). One-third of occupational burns, the leading cause of work-related injuries in the United States, occur in restaurants (Suzman et al., 2001).

Complicating the ability to adequately measure restaurant sustainability is the emergence of a relatively new interdisciplinary approach termed cultural sustainability, arguing that culture impacts sustainable development, and how natural and other resources are valued and utilized (Throsby, 2008). Restaurant sustainability one could argue should have a strong linkage to culture capital given that all food preparation is reliant on one or more cultures. Food culture capital as a factor in restaurant sustainability would perhaps be the most controversial and difficult to measure. Would restaurants that feature more authentic cultural dishes be rated more highly? Would the plethora of American-Chinese cuisine, catering to the American palate, be ranked lower than restaurants serving homeland Chinese offerings in the United States?

## The future of restaurant sustainability

The concept of sustainability is increasingly paramount to achieving climatic and economic stability and social harmony as natural resources are exhausted in order to meet our food, fuel, and housing needs. The restaurant industry is making advances in the field of sustainability but it has a long way to go to achieve sustainability that "meet[s] present needs without compromising the ability of future generations to meet their needs" (WECD, 1987). Researchers in the field need to focus on the development of an all-encompassing methodology and index that allows for all restaurants to be viewed and measured in a rigorous manner that indicates more dedication to this field. Fricker (1998) argues that researchers should not ask how to measure sustainability but rather how we measure up to sustainability. In essence how effectively and to what extent are sustainable restaurants contributing to the quality of life of the local community in which they reside? Given the global impact of the dining trade, isn't it time to consider a legal definition for "restaurant sustainability" that brings together the concepts and ideas from all related organizations with the aim of developing a relatively easy to apply tool that each restaurant can use to determine their current sustainability status and provide a thorough guide on how to achieve higher/stronger levels of sustainability?

# References

Bank of America (2014) *Guiding Our Corporate Social Responsibility Efforts*, http://about.bankofamerica.com/en-us/global-impact.html?articleId=OUR-COMMITMENT{id=eq57iVK46pU.

Biocycle (2010). *Biocycle Global Roundup 2011*, 51(12): 49.

Canter, L. (2010) *McDonald's, Starbucks & Arbys Among Chains for LEED*, www.fooddigital.com/sectors/hotels-and-restaurants/mcdonald-s-starbucks-arbys-among-chains-leed.

Chan, E. and Lee, G. (2008) "Critical factors for improving social sustainability in urban renewal projects," *Social Indicator Research*, 85: 243–256.

English, J. (2007) "10 easy steps for a more sustainable kitchen," *Star Chef Magazine*, August, www.starchefs.com/features/trends/sustainability.

Environmental Performance Index (2014) *Country Rankings*, http://epi.yale.edu/epi/country-rankings.

FDA (2011) *Food Labeling; Nutrition Labeling of Standard Menu Items in Restaurants and Similar Retail Food Establishments; Proposed Rule*, Federal Register 76(66), Washington, DC: FDA.

Fricker, A. (1998) "Measuring up to sustainability," *Futures*, 30(4): 367–375.

Gaylord, C. (2007) "Welcome to the low-waste diner," *Christian Science Monitor*, 99(240): 13–14.

Genaidy, A., Sequeira, R., Rinder, M., and Rehim, A. (2009) "Determinants of business sustainability: an ergonomics perspective," *Ergonomics*, 52(3): 273–301.

Go, A.S., Mozaffarian, D., Roger, V.L., Benjamin, E.J., Berry, J.D., Borden, W.B., Bravata, D.M., Dai, S., Ford, E.S., Fox, C.S., Franco, S., Fullerton, H.J., Gillespie, C., Hailpern, S.M., Heit, J.A., Howard, V.J., Huffman, M.D., Kissela, B.M., Kittner, S.J., Lackland, D.T., Lichtman, J.H., Lisabeth, L.D., Magid, D., Marcus, G.M., Marelli, A., Matchar, D.B., McGuire, D.K., Mohler, E.R., Moy, C.S., Mussolino, M.E., Nichol, G., Paynter, N.P., Schreiner, P.J., Sorlie, P.D., Stein, J., Turan, T.N., Virani, S.S., Wong, N.D., Woo, D., and Turner, M.B. (2012) *Heart Disease and Stroke Statistics—2013 Update: A Report from the American Heart Association*, http://circ.ahajournals.org/content/127/1/e6.

Green Restaurant Association (2014) *Certification Standards for All Food Service Operations*, http://dinegreen.com/restaurants/standards.asp.

Henry, M. (2014) "Just Sushi is the world's first Ocean Wise 100% sustainable sushi restaurant," *Star Magazine*, www.thestar.com/life/food_wine/2014/01/10/just_sushi_is_the_worlds_first_ocean_wise_100_sustainable_sushi_restaurant.html.

Horovitz, B. (2008) "Can restaurants go green, earn green?" *USA Today*, http://usatoday30.usatoday.com/money/industries/environment/2008-05-15-green-restaurants-eco-friendly_n.htm.

Jayaraman, S. (2013) "Raise base wages," *The New York Times*, www.nytimes.com/roomfordebate/2013/06/23/to-tip-or-not-to-tip/tips-or-not-raise-the-minimum-wage.

MacVean, M. (2010) "Restaurants get a little greener," *Los Angeles Times*, http://articles.latimes.com/2010/mar/09/food/la-fo-sustain-20100311.

McDill, S. (2009) "First LEED lawsuit has attorneys talking," *Mississippi Business Journal*, http://msbusiness.com/blog/2009/04/13/first-leed-lawsuit-has-attorneys-talking.

McDonald's (2013) *McDonald's USA First National Restaurant Chain to Serve MSC-Certified Sustainable Fish At All US Locations*, http://news.mcdonalds.com/US/releases/McDondald-s-USA-First-National-Restaurant-Chain-to.

Merriam-Webster Dictionary (2013) "Sustainable," www.merriam-webster.com.

Mills, J.E. and Thomas, L. (2008) "A confirmatory factor analysis approach to assessing customer expectations of restaurant menus," *Journal of Hospitality and Tourism Research*, 32(1): 62–88.

National Research Council (2013) *Sustainability for the Nation: Resource Connection and Governance Linkages*, Washington, DC: National Academies Press.

National Restaurant Association (2013) *Operators Eye More Sustainable Packaging*, www.restaurant.org/News-Research/News/Operators-eye-more-sustainable-packaging.

National Restaurant Association (2014) *2014 Restaurant Industry Pocket Fact Book*, www.restaurant.org/Downloads/PDFs/Newsresearch/research/Factbook2014_LetterSize.pdf.

Ogden, C.L., Carroll, M.D., Kit, B.K., and Flegal, K.M. (2014) "Prevalence of childhood and adult obesity in the United States, 2011–2012," *Journal of the American Medical Association*, 311(8): 806–814.

Oko, D. (2006) "The doggie bag dilemma," *Mother Jones*, 31(6): 84.

Ott, K. (2003) "The case for strong sustainability," in K. Ott and P. Thapa (eds.), *Greifswald's Environmental Ethics*, Greifswald: Steinbecker Verlag Ulrich Rose.

Palmer, D. (2009) "Value, convenience, health and environmental sustainability in demand amongst restaurant customers," *Australian Food News*, www.ausfoodnews.com.au/2009/01/05/value-convenience-health-and-environmental-sustainability-in-demand-amongst-restaurant-customers-in-2009.html.

Roberts, T. (2010) "USGBC, LEED targeted by class-action suit", *BuildingGreen.com*, www.buildinggreen.com/auth/article.cfm/2010/10/14/USGBC-LEED-Targeted-by-Class-Action-Suit/?redirsupercede=0&utm_source=BuildingGreen.com+Bulletin&utm_campaign=1f6c39f5b9-Breaking_Class_Action_Suit10_14_2010&utm_medium=email.

Rosenblum, P. and Rowen, R. (2010) *The Better-Run Restaurant: Environmental Sustainability In Restaurant Retail 2010*, National Retail Federation, www.nrf.com/modules.php?name−ews&op=viewlive&sp_id=995.

Social Ecology (2010) *Definition of Sustainable Agriculture*, www.sustainabletable.org.

Strategic Sustainability Consulting (2008) *Sustainable Growth Report*, Washington, DC: Strategic Sustainability Consulting.

Sustainable Restaurant Association (2014) *What Are Sustainable Restaurants?* www.thesra.org/about-us/what-is-sustainability.

Sustainable Table (2014) *Definition: Sustainable Agriculture*, www.sustainabletable.org/intro/whatis.

Suzman, M., Sobocinski, K., Himel, H., and Yurt, R. (2001) "Major burn injuries among restaurant workers in New York City: an underappreciated public health hazard," *Journal of Burn Care & Rehabilitation*, 22(6): 429–434.

Throsby, D. (2008) "Linking cultural and ecological sustainability," *International Journal of Diversity in Organizations, Communities and Nations*, 8(1): 15–20.

*Vegetarian Times* (2001) "Food fight," *Vegetarian Times*, 287: 18–20.

WECD (1987) *Our Common Future*, Oxford: Oxford University Press, www.un-documents.net/our-common-future.pdf.

White House (2009) *Federal Leadership in Environmental, Energy, and Economic Performance*, www.whitehouse.gov/assets/documents/2009fedleader_eo_rel.pdf.

Wilderer, P., Schroeder, E., and Kopp, H. (2004) *Global Sustainability: The Impact of Local Cultures*, http://onlinelibrary.wiley.com/doi/10.1002/3527604251.fmatter/pdf.

# PART 7

# Culinary tourism

Different cultures have different languages; food has its own language.

*The editors*

Food has become an essential element to discover cultures and understand the way of life in particular geographical areas. Components of culinary or food tourism include respect for cultures and traditions, authenticity and experience. This section discusses culinary tourism in its various facets and also as an opportunity to revitalize and diversify the tourism offer and promote local economic development.

Food can form part of the social, cultural, economic and environmental history of destinations and form a marketing 'hook' to attract consumers. Moreover, in sampling local cuisines, tourists engage in an experience which goes beyond 'observing'. **Martyn Pring, Sean Beer, Heather Hartwell and Jeffery Bray** explore the concept of 'local food', discussing market trends for locally grown or produced foods. Environmental and sustainability issues linked with local food are presented before the role of local food in building a destination's image is debated.

Sustainable food tourism is closely linked to the concept of *authenticity*. The identity of places, historical roots and the involvement of host communities are all integrated parts of an authentic experience. This is core to the 'unforgettable tourist experience'. **Sonia Ferrari and Monica Gilli** present some examples for sustainable food tourism in Italy, with particular reference to the authentic and experiential dimension.

Authenticity is linked to the identity of places but in the same lines of thought, food is often the expression of local identity. Tourists often define those foods as 'local specialities'. It is the case with the autumn-pear of the Nature Park Pöllau Valley in south-eastern Austria. Beyond the dedication of local growers, the *savoir-faire* of distillers, the autumn-pear acts as a unique marketing initiative known as 'the Savoury Region'. **Ulrike Pröbstl-Haider, Elisabeth Hochwarter and Josef Schrank** present the autumn-pear, the park and the initiative and discuss the consequences for the region and its tourism development.

Traditional Samoan cuisine is rooted in organic, healthy, self-sufficient and sustainable agricultural practices even if imported food has a great appeal for Samoans with detrimental consequences. **Tracy Berno** presents how tourism can be used as a conduit to rejuvenate traditional Samoan foods through a value chain approach, linking the growing number of organic producers in Samoa to the tourism industry. The Mea'ai Samoa Project, an initiative that aims to valorize Samoa's traditional foods, is presented as a case study.

Food provides sustenance and serves as a cultural domain that is often elaborated into complex systems of meaning and values. In the Sariayahin community (Quezon, Philippines), these meanings manifest through the people's manner of food preparation, regulation and consumption. **Shirley V. Guevarra and Corazon F. Gatchalian** discuss how the local food culture can be mirrored through 'iconic' local delicacies. Three delicacies are presented with their respective meanings within the community and the linkages to possible sustainable food tourism programmes.

Gastronomy can be seen and used as a catalyst for local and regional development; however, the sustainability aspects of gastronomic tourism have largely gone ignored. **Clare Carruthers, Amy Burns and Gary Elliott** first discuss the development of gastronomic tourism and its link with sustainability. The potential of sustainable gastronomic tourism is then presented through a case study of County Cork in the Republic of Ireland and recommendations for application to other destinations are considered.

Communities can preserve their distinctive cultural and natural heritage through responsible travel. Responsible travel initiatives in Crete, Greece, have increased in reaction to the growing global trend in cultural–culinary tourism and the economic crisis. However not all initiatives can be considered 'responsible'. **Nikki Rose**, as the founder of Crete's Culinary Sanctuaries, outlines the 15-year history of Crete's Culinary Sanctuaries' initiatives, a noted international model in responsible travel, and provides a set of recommendations to increase initiatives globally.

# 28

# LOCAL FOODS

## Marketing and the destination

*Martyn Pring, Sean Beer, Heather Hartwell and Jeffery Bray*

### Introduction

During the past 25 years across Europe there has been a marked renaissance in the consumption and production of quality, regionally denominated foods (Chambers et al., 2007). The production of regional foods has been backed by EU initiatives that have included origin-labelled product designations and the increase in market for local authentic products (Ilbery et al., 2010). However, within the food sector, large corporate organisations comprising agri-businesses, restaurant chains and retailers are dominant and represent an industry that is well-organised, politically powerful and driven by an array of lobbyists, lawyers and trade organisations. Over the past 150 years these companies have been responsible for an explosion in processed and mass-produced foods. In spite of this industrialisation of food production and supply, recent market trends suggest that local and traditional products, defined by specific geographic territories, occupy a food production and hence destination marketing niche that provide strong growth opportunities for local producers, retailers and the tourist destination as a whole (Brownell and Warner, 2009; Oddy and Atkins, 2009).

The debate regarding what is 'local' has occupied academics and industry for some time and is well covered in other chapters within this volume. However, for the purpose of destination marketing there are differences in construction between what is perceived as local and what is perceived as regional. As Gorton and Tregear (2008) observe, some overlap between concepts is clearly possible. The notion of local food and local food systems has gained much consumer and industry attention as an alternative to the global corporate model where producers and consumers are separated through a chain of processors/manufacturers and retailers. The locality of food is becoming increasingly important, influencing both marketing practice (e.g., adding value to brands) and policy (e.g., accreditation and other name-protection schemes) (Mirosa and Lawson, 2012). Even so, there is a clear distinction between 'local' and 'locality' foods (Ilbery and Maye, 2005). Local foods are produced, sold and consumed within a limited geographical area – usually being produced within a 30–50-mile radius of the point of retail – whereas 'locality' foods are identified as having been produced and processed in a particular place but often circulated more widely (Ilbery et al., 2006).

## Local food and sustainability

The primary underpinning for this book is the concept of sustainability and for the purpose of this chapter the authors will be considering sustainability from the perspective of the triple bottom line (TBL), or 'people, planet, profit'. This approach was used by the United Nations through the International Council for Local Environmental Initiatives (ICLEI) to develop standardisation towards public sector full cost accounting and is increasingly being adopted by the private sector as part of corporate and social responsibility. It was first proposed by John Elkington in 1994 (see Elkington, 1994 and 1998) and implies that sustainability is a holistic concept that involves conducting our lives today in a way that will benefit people in the future, socially, economically and environmentally.

One way in which interests and concerns with regard to the sustainability of food seem to have come together is within the idea of 'local food'. This movement (in terms of history and process) has been described by authors in books such as Ackerman-Leist (2013), Pinkerton and Hopkins (2009) and Small (2013) and in academic papers, such as Feagan (2007), Giovannucci et al. (2010), Pearson et al. (2011) and Wittman et al. (2012). Beer (2001) describes how originally human beings experienced short food supply chains, they ate what they hunted and gathered and the supply chains then gradually lengthened with the process of specialisation and aggregation. In the late twentieth century these extended globally, but began to be viewed with increasing scepticism by some people who sought a greater understanding of where their food came from, how it had been grown or produced and the environmental impact of both food production and the international transportation of ingredients. The concept and consciousness of 'food miles' describing the environmental impact of the transportation of food stuffs emerged around the turn of the century and led to a steadily growing band of consumers seeking out food that had been produced more locally and in sympathy with ideas of sustainability.

There is a widely held belief that food produced closer to the point of consumption is likely to be more sustainable and therefore preferable. From a profit perspective, the argument is that the consumption of locally produced food benefits those that produce it and those that consume it by reducing the complexity of the supply chain and the number of 'middlemen' thus providing a direct link 'to market'. This 'local' trade also results in a recycling of money within the local economy, giving rise to a multiplier effect; the financial benefit is passed on to other individuals and businesses within the local community. Where local supply is through structures such as farmers' markets there may well be 'knock-on' spending in other shops. Also, despite shortening the supply chain, there may be opportunities for other businesses to develop adding value in some way to local produce, enhancing business networks, reinforcing local jobs and maintaining local employment.

From a people perspective, local food is considered to be a valuable opportunity for consumers. There may well be a strengthening of community spirit and quality of life given the closer and less sterile interaction between people within the food supply chain. In addition, often the information available to the consumer is far richer, allowing for a more informed choice. From a planet perspective, shorter food chains will give rise to decreased food miles, thus reducing the carbon footprint and potentially increasing freshness of the food. Local produce is also often characterised by minimal packaging and clearer provenance information. Finally, local supply chains in addition provide an important outlet for small-scale farmers producing food that is organic or less intensively produced. Certainly there is a positive perception about the sustainability of local food, although this is open to challenge (see Chapter 5 in this volume).

## Local food marketing

The celebration of local foods is not just restricted to retail and hospitality; culinary interest may extend beyond the dining experience to understanding local farming practices, how foods are produced, distributed and preserved. Local foods, like any food category, are a multifaceted tourism product and can be considered an essential component of a destination's offering which may be consumed and experienced in a variety of ways. Table 28.1 identifies some key themes through which food can enhance and promote the destination experience.

Food producers can plan their business and their distribution strategies around a number of 'routes to market' dependent on their individual product offering, where they are located and the size and scale of the business. Across the Western world there has been a steady expansion of direct farm marketing with consumers purchasing from farmers through a variety of retail mechanisms. Growth in this 'direct' form of retailing has taken off because it provides a platform for producers and consumers to interact on a face-to-face basis and form a relationship. Such engagement lies at the heart of the enhanced experience of consuming local foods (Nosi and Zanni, 2004).

In the UK, farmers' markets have re-emerged and grown substantially, fuelled by consumer interest and in part due to the response of the UK government following the foot-and-mouth disease outbreak of 2001 (McEachern et al., 2010). At this time, measures to stimulate the rural economy were introduced and farm shops were supported as a means to sell produce directly to the consumer. Quality farm shops became particular examples of rural-based specialist independent retailing, selling a range of higher-margin local and regional food products of known provenance. Some developed their hospitality offer by combining tea rooms and restaurants as well as broadening their retail scope to include gift items and other products associated with a rural lifestyle (Sharples, 2003a). Increasingly, shopping at such establishments and farmers' markets is regarded as a leisure pursuit (Megicks et al., 2012) where farm shops have become integral features of garden centres and other out-of-town retail operations, acting as an additional consumer pull to the destination.

In the UK since the mid–1990s there has been a steady movement towards quality local and regional food products with consumers welcoming individuality and rejecting 'standardized, highly processed product lines' that constitute 'placeless and faceless' foods (Ricketts Hein et al., 2006). Local foods can form part of a destination's fabric, where consumers/tourists with little interest in food beyond basic nourishment can enjoy an engaging gastronomic experience and participate in food-related activities forming part of a 'things to do' agenda, for example sampling local beers and cider.

For groups of consumers with a high interest in food, eating out can become the key purpose of the holiday experience, with quality, seasonal local foods of known provenance a

*Table 28.1* Local foods and destination routes to experience

| Theme | Experience pathway |
| --- | --- |
| Hospitality and food service | Hotels, restaurants, gastro pubs, tea rooms/café shops and takeaways |
| Attractions and Events | Pick your own, food events and festivals, producer visits, food and wine trails, tourism attraction |
| Shopping (includes online and mail order) | Farmers' markets, farm gate sales, farm shops, delicatessens, holiday camp, caravan and campsite shops, local convenience stores and supermarkets |

Adapted from Jolliffe (2008) and Pearson et al. (2011)

significant influence when selecting restaurants to dine in. Tourists may be motivated by meals prepared with certain in-season, local ingredients, produce sourced from a particular location, being entertained in a particular way in attractive venues or the meal cooked by a celebrated chef (Sharples, 2003b). The power of the 'celebrity chef' restaurant(s) in particular destinations is noted as a major food tourism attractor (Henderson, 2011). People indulging in this form of dining experience may be referred to or known colloquially as 'foodies' (Barr and Levy, 1984), a term that has evolved in everyday language to encapsulate anyone who now has an interest in food (Deleuze, 2012). At the heart is a celebration of food and in much the same way as tourists collect souvenirs, foodies collect food experiences (Morgan et al., 2008).

## Destination marketing

For both academic and tourism professionals, food represents an emerging theme in destination marketing that is increasingly seen as a core element of a destination's product offering providing a degree of uniqueness and differentiation (Beer et al., 2012). Food tourism is also inextricably bound up with experience and can create an additional level of complexity for destinations to manage successfully. Local foods are a valid construction in food tourism and for many consumers participating in local food ways and consuming local and regional specialities are important parts of the tourist experience (Mak et al., 2012). Experiences at the destination level are complex affairs; they move along a continuum between positivity and negativity that over time may change, but fundamentally involve individuals interacting with people and places (Haven-Tang and Jones, 2010). Destinations that embrace a constantly evolving vista where a mix of the urban, rural and coastal landscape interlocks with a distinctive local food provision are becoming popular. Local foods form part of a bundle of attributes that, when acting collectively, create a 'specialised regional product' (Bessiere, 1998). They can be considered a resource that enhances the destination, but one requiring careful coordination. Combined they provide an attribute that may appeal to consumers delivering enjoyable, distinctive and memorable local food experiences within the destination (Hall and Mitchell, 2002; Novelli et al., 2006).

For such a positioning, destinations will require the coordination of many actors, representing a complex web of supply relationships that, when acting in tandem, will be capable of providing spontaneous but also carefully choreographed participation. This in turn will start to define a destination, its image and brand and provide a level of differentiation. The establishment of place-brands that tie in food, cuisine and tourism are powerful mechanisms for the destination and, where this is managed in a coordinated effort, represents the first stages of 'collaborative advantage' (Fyall et al., 2012; Hall, 2012) that contributes to an overall sustainable agenda. In addition, as a shared common resource, food and drink may also be utilised to create collaborative advantage with neighbouring destinations such as adjoining counties.

Increasingly, destination and tourism providers are adopting more strategic approaches and new forms of customer-oriented experience. Merely stage-managing experience in isolation has been considered an 'out of date' notion that reflects a product-orientated culture (Major and McLeay, 2012). To be mindful of consumers' desires to create their own experiential platform, providers of food tourism experiences need to craft their offer, recognising altruistic and hedonic components by building and adding to existing provision with an experience that may be considered to be indulgent and/or memorable. A chalkboard outside a restaurant simply highlighting seasonal and local foods does not deliver experience per se, it is one of a number of variables that can have a part to play but for customers to be attracted by local food they need to be engaged in a highly personal way (Gibbs and Ritchie, 2010; Lugosi and Walls, 2013). The simple pleasure of eating a freshly baked Cornish pasty on a headland overlooking the Atlantic Ocean may provide the perfect authentic setting; for the individual this may be an intensely personal encounter that defines a holiday.

The place local foods have within a destination is largely determined by how destinations are funded and managed and by the interests of key stakeholders. In the UK, tourism devolution has led to very specific and proactive approaches adopted by home country national tourism organisations. Over the past five years food tourism has been fully utilised and integrated with tourism strategies; local foods now form part of a culinary agenda promoting special characteristics of national and speciality dishes. Notwithstanding, the disbanding of regional tourism boards in 2010 has significantly altered both the tourism climate and where the private sector has had to accept a greater degree of responsibility but also influences and streamlines the way in which destinations work (Coles et al., 2012).

This has culminated in a form of 'patchwork' where no two destinations are the same even though a shared local food resource may be close at hand. While local foods are not identified as specific elements of national sustainable tourism, there remains a clear relationship at destination level where local foods can be linked to local sustainability development. At the national level, VisitEngland identifies sustainability as a key business tool to secure increasing numbers of customers who have an interest in authentic experiences. Local foods are thus connected to this and in England a range of experience dimensions are at play in destination marketing. Leading coastal resorts such as Bournemouth, Poole, Torbay and Plymouth demonstrate a strong hospitality theme with particular emphasis placed on eating out in 'Michelin' starred, celebrity chef and leading local chef personality restaurants. In addition, due to the proximity of the ocean, a seasonal seafood proposition is heavily promoted. In the large urban destinations of Bristol, Bath and Exeter, food tourism experiences are based on a variety of culinary themes coupled to a strong association with individual local delicacies such as the 'Bath Bun, Olivers and Chaps'.

Across the EU, a strong relationship can be observed between local foods and tourism. In countries such as France and Italy, food is engrained in national culture and in the fabric and images of the countries' individual regions and destinations. Authentic and interesting foods attract modern tourists – many of whom will be searching for new sensations and experiences (López-Guzmán and Sánchez-Cañizares, 2012). Given the maturity of the European tourism market and the competitive nature of destination marketing, it is hardly surprising that destinations are increasingly being drawn to the potential of food tourism. Interest in local cuisines is leading many of them to focus on food as a core tourism resource (Karim and Chi, 2010; Lin et al., 2011), and as such forms part of a sustainable agenda. Consumers are becoming more sophisticated in their demands of destinations. A trend, perhaps, is identifiable as destinations begin to explore and manage their tourism resources by constructing destination products with the ability to deliver distinctive and memorable encounters (Kim, 2014). Foodscapes are thus changing and becoming more localised as tourists increasingly expect true taste experiences based on provenance and knowledge of where food comes from. Quality locally grown, reared, produced and sourced foods, integrated into tailored hospitality and foodservice offers – together with appropriate local food and drink product, direct marketing and retailing – provide an effective platform for destination marketing. This in the longer term should build and reinforce destination competitiveness and sustainability. A summary of the key features associated with local foods and destination resource is presented at Figure 28.1.

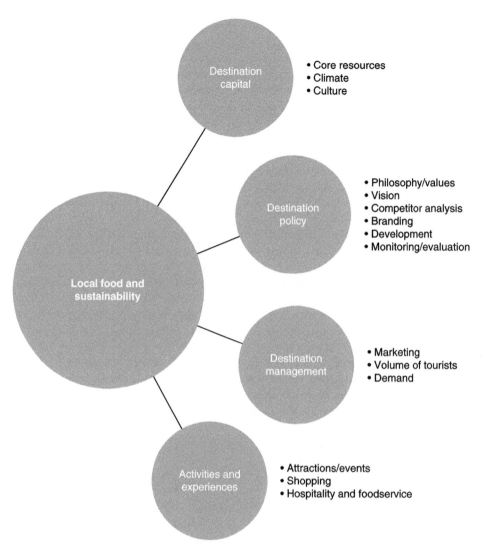

*Figure 28.1* The role of local food as a tourism destination resource. Adapted from Hartwell et al. (2012).

## Conclusion

A number of authors have considered the broader implications for gastronomic tourism, culinary tourism and food tourism. Some view these descriptions to be one and the same whilst others regard them as distinctly separate and catering for tourists from very different and specific market segments. Therefore, one of the most important issues to be faced by destinations in the future will be how this resource or attribute is best managed and how it fits within the context of destination marketing. Certainly, the challenges of the creation and nurturing of a clear and consistent 'food identity' and how local foods fit into these 'food tourism categories' will not disappear. Destinations and their stakeholders will have to evolve thinking and in particular the utilisation of local foods as a tool for destination marketing and branding. In this way too, 'people, planet and profit' merge into a win–win situation.

# References

Ackerman-Leist, P. (2013) *Rebuilding the Foodshed: How to Create Local, Sustainable, and Secure Food Systems (Community Resilience Guide)*, Vermont: Chelsea Green Publishing Company.

Arnould, E., Price, L. and Zinkhan, G. (2004) *Consumers*, 2nd edn, New York: McGraw-Hill/Irwin.

Barr, A. and Levy, P. (1984) *The Official Foodie Handbook*, London: Ebury Press.

Beer, C.L., Ottenbacher, M.C. and Harrington, R.J. (2012) 'Food tourism implementation in the Black Forest destination', *Journal of Culinary Science & Technology*, 10(2): 106–128.

Beer, S.C. (2001) 'Food and society', in J.F. Eastham, E. Sharples and S.D. Ball (eds.), *Food Supply Chain Management*, Oxford: Butterworth Heinemann, pp. 21–36.

Bessiere, J. (1998) 'Local development and heritage: traditional food and cuisine as tourist attractions in rural areas', *Sociologia Ruralis*, 38(1): 21–34.

Brownell, K.D. and Warner, K.E. (2009) 'The perils of ignoring history: big tobacco played dirty and millions died. How similar is big food?', *Milbank Quarterly*, 87(1): 259–294.

Chambers, S., Lobb, A., Bruce Traill, W., Butler, L. and Harvey, K. (2007) 'Local, national and imported foods: a qualitative study', *Appetite*, 49(1): 208–213.

Coles, T., Dinan, C. and Hutchison, F. (2012) 'May we live in less interesting times? Changing public sector support for tourism in England during the sovereign debt crisis', *Journal of Destination Marketing & Management*, 1(1/2): 4–7.

Deleuze, M. (2012) 'A new craze for food: why is Ireland turning into a foodie nation?', in *Dublin Gastronomy Symposium June 2012*, Dublin: Dublin Institute of Technology.

Elkington, J. (1994) 'Towards the sustainable corporation: win-win-win business strategies for sustainable development', *California Management Review*, 36(2): 90–100.

Elkington, J. (1998) *Cannibals with Forks: The Triple Bottom Line of 21st-Century Business*, Gabriola Island: New Society Publishers.

Feagan, R. (2007) 'The place of food: mapping out the "local" in local food systems', *Progress in Human Geography*, 31(1): 23–42.

Fyall, A., Wang, Y. and Garrod, B. (2012) 'Destination collaboration: a critical review of theoretical approaches to a multi-dimensional phenomenon', *Journal of Destination Marketing and Management*, 1(1–2): 10–26.

Gellynck, X., Kühne, B., Banterle, A., Carraresi, L. and Stranieri, S. (2012) 'Market orientation and marketing management of traditional food producers in the EU', *British Food Journal*, 114(4): 481–499.

Gibbs, D. and Ritchie, C. (2010) 'Theatre in restaurants: constructing the experience', in M. Morgan, P. Lugosi and J.R.B. Ritchie (eds.), *The Tourism and Leisure Experience: Consumer and Managerial Perspectives*, Bristol: Channel View Publications.

Giovannucci, D., Barham, E. and Pirog, R. (2010) 'Defining and marketing "local" foods: geographical indications for US products', *The Journal of World Intellectual Property*, 13(2): 94–120.

Gorton, M. and Tregear, A. (2008) 'Government support to regional food producers: an assessment of England's Regional Food Strategy', *Environment and Planning C: Government and Policy*, 26(6): 1047–1060.

Hall, C.M. (2012) 'Boosting food and tourism-related regional economic development', in *Food and the Tourism Experience: The OECD-Korea Workshop*, OECD Studies on Tourism, Paris: OECD Publishing.

Hall, M. and Mitchell, R. (2002) 'Tourism as a force for gastronomic globalization and localization', in A.-M. Hjalager and G. Richards (eds.), *Tourism and Gastronomy*, London: Routledge.

Hartwell, H., Hemingway, A., Fyall, A., Filimonau, V. and Wall, S. (2012) 'Tourism engaging with the public health agenda – can we promote "wellville" as a destination of choice?', *Public Health*, 126: 1072–1074.

Haven-Tang, C. and Jones, E. (2010) 'Delivering quality experiences for sustainable tourism development: harnessing a sense of place in Monmouthshire', in M. Morgan, P. Lugosi and J.R.B. Ritchie (eds.), *The Tourism and Leisure Experience: Consumer and Managerial Perspectives*, Bristol: Channel View Publications, pp. 163–181.

Henderson, J.C. (2011) 'Celebrity chefs: expanding empires', *British Food Journal*, 113(4–5): 613–624.

Holbrook, M.B. and Hirschman, E.C. (1982) 'The experiential aspects of consumption: consumer fantasies, feelings, and fun', *Journal of Consumer Research*, 9(2): 132–140.

Ilbery, B. and Maye, D. (2005) 'Food supply chains and sustainability: evidence from specialist food producers in the Scottish/English borders', *Land Use Policy*, 22(4): 331–344.

Ilbery, B., Watts, D., Simpson, S., Gilg, A. and Little, J. (2006) 'Mapping local foods: evidence from two English regions', *British Food Journal*, 108(3): 213–225.

Ilbery, B., Courtney, P., Kirwan, J. and Maye, D. (2010) 'Marketing concentration and geographical dispersion: a survey of organic farms in England and Wales', *British Food Journal*, 112(9): 962–975.

Jolliffe, L. (2008) 'Connecting farmers' markets and tourists in New Brunswick, Canada', in C.M. Hall and L. Sharples (eds.), *Food and Wine Festivals and Events Around the World*, Amsterdam: Elsevier/ Butterworth-Heinemann.

Karim, S.A. and Chi, C.G.-Q. (2010) 'Culinary tourism as a destination attraction: an empirical examination of destinations' food image', *Journal of Hospitality Marketing & Management*, 19(6): 531–555.

Kim, J.-H. (2014) 'The antecedents of memorable tourism experiences: the development of a scale to measure the destination attributes associated with memorable experiences', *Tourism Management*, 44: 34–45.

Lin, Y.-C., Pearson, T.E. and Cai, L.A. (2011) 'Food as a form of destination identity: a tourism destination brand perspective', *Tourism & Hospitality Research*, 11(1): 30–48.

López-Guzmán, T. and Sánchez-Cañizares, S. (2012) 'Culinary tourism in Córdoba (Spain)', *British Food Journal*, 114(2): 168–179.

Lugosi, P. and Walls, A.R. (2013) 'Researching destination experiences: themes, perspectives and challenges', *Journal of Destination Marketing & Management*, 2: 51–58.

Major, B. and McLeay, F. (2012) 'The UK "grey" market's holiday experience', in R. Sharpley and P.R. Stone (eds.), *Contemporary Tourist Experience Concepts and Consequences*, Abingdon: Routledge.

Mak, A.H.N., Lumbers, M. and Eves, A. (2012) 'Globalisation and food consumption in tourism', *Annals of Tourism Research*, 39(1): 171–196.

McEachern, M.G., Warnaby, G., Carrigan, M. and Szmigin, I. (2010) 'Thinking locally, acting locally? Conscious consumers and farmers' markets', *Journal of Marketing Management*, 26(5/6): 395–412.

Megicks, P., Memery, J. and Angell, R.J. (2012) 'Understanding local food shopping: unpacking the ethical dimension', *Journal of Marketing Management*, 28(3/4): 264–289.

Mirosa, M. and Lawson, R. (2012) 'Revealing the lifestyles of local food consumers', *British Food Journal*, 114(6): 816–825.

Morgan, M., Watson, P. and Hemmington, N. (2008) 'Drama in the dining room: theatrical perspectives on the foodservice encounter', *Journal of Foodservice*, 19(2): 111–118.

Nosi, C. and Zanni, L. (2004) 'Moving from "typical products" to "food-related services" – the Slow Food case as a new business paradigm', *British Food Journal*, 106(10/11): 779–792.

Novelli, M., Schmitz, B. and Spencer, T. (2006) 'Networks, clusters and innovation in tourism: a UK experience', *Tourism Management*, 27(6): 1141–1152.

Oddy, D. and Atkins, P. (2009) 'Introduction', in D. Oddy, P. Atkins and V. Amilien (eds.), *The Rise of Obesity in Europe: A Twentieth Century Food History*, Farnham, Surrey: Ashgate Publishing.

Pearson, D., Henryks, J., Trott, A., Jones, P., Parker, G., Dumaresq, D. and Dyball, R. (2011) 'Local food: understanding consumer motivations in innovative retail formats', *British Food Journal*, 113(6–7): 886–899.

Pinkerton, T. and Hopkins, R. (2009) *Local Food: How to Make it Happen in Your Community: How to Unleash a Food Revolution Where You Live*, Cambridge: Transition Books.

Ricketts Hein, J., Ilbery, B. and Kneafsey, M. (2006) 'Distribution of local food activity in England and Wales: an index of food relocalization', *Regional Studies*, 40(3): 289–301.

Sharples, L. (2003a) 'Food tourism in the peak district national park, England', in C.M. Hall, L. Sharples, R. Mitchell, N. Macionis and B. Cambourne (eds.), *Food Tourism Around the World: Development, Management and Markets*, Oxford: Butterworth-Heinemann.

Sharples, L. (2003b) 'The world of cookery-school holidays', in C.M. Hall, L. Sharples, R. Mitchell, N. Macionis and B. Cambourne (eds.), *Food Tourism Around the World: Development, Management and Markets*, Oxford: Butterworth-Heinemann.

Small, M. (2013) *Scotland's Local Food Revolution*, Argyll: Argyll Publishing.

Walls, A., Okumus, F., Wang, Y. and Kwun, D. J.-W. (2011) 'Understanding the consumer experience: an exploratory study of luxury hotels', *Journal of Hospitality Marketing & Management*, 20(2): 166–197.

Wittman, H., Beckie, M. and Hergesheimer, C. (2012) 'Linking local food systems and the social economy? Future roles for farmers' markets in Alberta and British Columbia', *Rural Sociology*, 77(1): 36–61.

# 29

# AUTHENTICITY AND EXPERIENCE IN SUSTAINABLE FOOD TOURISM

*Sonia Ferrari and Monica Gilli*

### Introduction[1]

The aim of this paper is to analyze the practices of sustainable food tourism in Italy. In recent years, food sustainability has found in tourism practice an important channel for promoting and developing itself (Everett and Aitchison, 2008; Sims, 2009). Also, in the past, food tourism was an established practice in Italy, but only in recent years have relations with sustainability been defined more clearly. This alliance between food and sustainability principles has given a different direction to food tourism.

As is well-known, sustainability affects many aspects of life and can be considered, at a macro level, as a different development pattern for society and, at a micro level, as a different way of life for individuals. Sustainability covers many aspects: at an institutional level it orients macroeconomic decisions (energy, agriculture, industry, etc.); at an individual level it is expressed in mobility and food choices and also in the environmental education of children.

An important field for developing a sustainable lifestyle is that of holidays, since they have become an indispensable part of the life of individuals, even in times of economic crisis. Holidays, in fact, are taking on a new role in postmodern society, and they do not mean just a moment of rest from work and escape from one's own social roles (Feifer, 1985). On the contrary, they often are opportunities to learn, increasing the wealth of every experience, and to exercise, strengthen, and better define our own values (Urry, 1990; Desforges, 2000; McCabe, 2005; Palmer, 1999, 2005). This means that a person who has a sustainable lifestyle rarely undertakes consumerist holidays exerting opposite values. In this sense, holidays have become an important viewpoint to understand sustainability.

We have chosen to present sustainable food tourism in Italy through two important directions of this practice: experiential tourism and authenticity (Prentice et al., 1998; MacCannell, 1973, 1976; Gottlieb, 1982; Pine and Gilmore, 1999; Quan and Wang, 2004). These are two fundamental dimensions to tourism, but they seem to be particularly suited to explaining the specific characteristics of tourism related to sustainable food.

The paper is organized as follows: the first two paragraphs are devoted to authenticity and experiential tourism in sustainable food tourism, trying to show the specificity of the Italian case through some examples. Conclusions will follow in presenting a unique overview of sustainable food tourism trends today.

## Authenticity in sustainable food tourism

Consumers, tourists included, are increasingly demanding authentic food (Beer, 2008), and the centrality of authenticity to sustainable food tourism seems obvious. In this section, starting from a perspective of sustainability, we try to elucidate what authenticity could mean in the tourism experience. We also consider some critical points possibly impinging on the implementation of sustainable food tourism in Italy.

Authenticity is one of the oldest and more basic subjects in the sociology of tourism. The theme was raised in tourism studies around the 1970s. At that time, a general devaluation of mass tourism was prevalent, considered as an experience in which individuals could hardly find opportunities of growth because of standardization and artificiality (Boorstin, 1964). MacCannell (1973, 1976), in some sense, reversed this position; he suggested that tourism might be considered as an institution functionally similar to pilgrimage in premodern society, and that modern tourism, and even mass tourism, is pervaded by the search for authenticity. Accordingly, the relations between tourists and local communities should be read in terms of authenticity, distinguishing, in the local community space, between "front regions" where authenticity is scarce and "back regions" characterized by a higher level of authenticity.

The interpretation of tourism as a quest for authenticity proposed by MacCannell has stimulated a wide scientific debate. Over the years, the notion of authenticity has been artic-ulated more precisely, and (at least) three different meanings of the term have emerged. The first, "objective" authenticity, evokes some kind of museum authenticity, the same used by the experts in determining whether an art object belongs to a particular period or another. The second meaning, "constructive"/"symbolic" authenticity, is based on the assumption that even the authentication process of an art object is a social process and, as such, is often socially constructed and reconstructed (Bruner, 1994). Finally, the meaning of "existential" authenticity starts from the observation that every search for authenticity is first of all an individual search, in which several levels of the individual's participation and commitment are involved (Hughes, 1995; Wang, 1999).

While several authors have considered each of these phenomena an autonomous experi-ence, others (Gilli, 2009) admit a possible confluence: authenticity may result from objective data, from a social confirmation, and, finally, from the experiential dimension of the subject. Anyway, the meaning of authenticity, and the way this notion can be used, continues to be debated in tourism literature. We think that this notion can be very useful in the analysis of certain types of tourism, such as cultural or historical tourism. Since, according to the literature (Richards, 2002; Scarpato, 2002; Beer, 2008; Sims, 2009; Chang et al., 2011), food tourism is but a part of cultural tourism, it seems correct to extend considerations of authen-ticity to food production and consumption. In this field, authenticity has increasingly acquired a strong economic relevance, and much energy (commercial, political, and intellectual) is spent on defining it: the national and international regulations in the direction of "local food," protected food, etc., are typical expressions of this interest (Beer, 2008).

Broadly speaking, while authenticity is often evoked as a concrete asset in tourist supply, there has been little attempt by the academic literature to read and analyze concrete tourist situations in terms of authenticity. In fact, it is impossible to apply a unique notion of authen-ticity to any tourist situation: the authenticity that is desirable for a museum is different from that which should be desirable for an archaeological site, or for a "historical" road, or for a folk festival, or, finally, for a food experience. The notion of authenticity should be reformulated from time to time as the characteristics of the tourism scenario change. In addition, authenti-city has not an absolute value, in the sense that it is not an all-or-nothing characteristic. Every tourist situation is a complex situation, and each constituent may be valued as more or less authentic (consider how many steps are covered by "food," from the crop or from the cowshed to the kitchen). Finally, the same tension existing between commercial stakeholders and local "philologists" about what authenticity should mean (Bruner, 1994), exists also about food authenticity (Beer, 2008). The philological perspective tries to get authenticity all along the line, notwithstanding the fact that some kinds of authenticity do not touch the tourists, or could even hurt them. The commercial perspective is oriented, on the contrary, to satisfying tourists, and the idea of authenticity is often influenced (sometimes, strongly mitigated) by this goal. Sustainable food tourism lives in this complex scenario. In the following pages we try to highlight—with particular reference to Italy—some critical points for the implementation of a sustainable food tourism.

As said above, food experience is not just "eating well," but is a complex cultural experience, in which all the steps of the production chain before the dinner-table are open, maybe only symbolically or through a narration, to the tourist: above all, the farming and food preparation activities (Richards, 2002; Scarpato, 2002; Beer, 2008; Sims, 2009; Chang et al., 2011). The sustainability of this kind of experience is guaranteed by the fact that at every step some basic conditions are authentic. The characteristics of authenticity that sustainable food tourism should have recall the three well-known dimensions of sustainability: environmental, socio-cultural and economic.

The environmental dimension emphasizes an optimal utilization of physical and natural resources that constitute a key element in tourism development, ensuring the maintenance of essential ecological processes and the conservation of the natural heritage and of biodiversity. This dimension is basic to sustainable food tourism, since the entire food chain depends directly on the presence of the above-mentioned environmental conditions. One should note that the attention paid to these conditions involves a sort of enlargement of the notion of landscape, and one could say that sustainable food tourists are particularly sensitive to the landscape, which is often perceived as an essential ingredient of their experience.

How can authenticity be part of this dimension? In our opinion it is important that biodiversity is really respected and can become an element of the landscape. In this way landscape appears as truly natural, and not as a scene designed for the tourists.

Landscape must be the expression of the rural economy that has molded it, even if the condition of being authentically rural might in part compete with the aesthetic dimension traditionally ascribed to every landscape. This does not mean that the landscape that can be appreciated by food tourists is the landscape as it was in the past: it should show the elements of modernity that the current rural economy entails. In this sense, authenticity in the food tourism scenario is easier to obtain compared to that of a historic site, divided between a hard search for philology and tourists' need-for-the-past (Bruner, 1994).

This direction of authenticity is not always clear to local communities. Castelrocchero (Piedmont), a small rural village that produces high-quality wine, decided in 2008 to develop local tourism. In many municipal debates previous to the creation of tourism initiatives the farmers were worried about having to hide tractors and agricultural machinery: they used to move around completely freely, and even to wash their tractors at the public fountains. The farmers had difficulty understanding that, in a rural environment, the tourists are not interested in seeing a country cleaned up as new, but a real country, where tractors are visible and, when dirty, they are so because they are used, and are washed in the main square still today as in the past. Similarly, in many places at the foot of the Italian Alps shepherds think that the passage of flocks of sheep and of herds of cows that go up and come down from the mountain pastures may disturb the tourists, while the opposite is true: the passage of sheep or cows is a guarantee, to the eyes of sustainable food tourists, that the meat and the cheese they eat are genuine, because they are local: and to be local is a *via regia* to authenticity (being local means also the openness to be looked over). One might add that, besides evidencing that the food is produced by a local economy, these passages of animals offer a view scarcely equaled in the everyday life of the Alpine community, and no "historical" re-enactment could match their beauty.

The socio-cultural dimension involves the respect of the socio-cultural identity of the host community, where "culture" means material, immaterial, and symbolic culture. In sustainable food tourism, this respect is crucial, since the entire culinary experience depends closely on the presence of these cultural traditions.

Here, how could authenticity be achieved? It seems important (to say it with a slogan) that the culinary "back region" and the culinary "front region" coincide, that is, that the food offered to the tourists is the same as that consumed by the locals in everyday life. This raises a problem that emerges in any form of ethnic tourism. Tourists are accustomed to the tastes offered by ethnic restaurants transplanted to the West, where food always has a "simplified register" (Ferguson, 1981) and extreme tastes are frequently mitigated. When they go abroad and eat local cuisine, they are unprepared for strong flavors (Cohen and Avieli, 2004). Even in Italy the recipes may sometimes be simplified or modified to match the tourists' taste more closely. A typical example is a traditional Piedmont recipe, "bagna caôda," consisting of cream, anchovies, and garlic. In some cases the true flavor of the recipe is renounced: the garlic is not used because it seems that some tourists don't like it.

The same thing happens to milk and butter, whose taste and nourishing content have been strongly mitigated by the food industry: hence the disappointment of some tourists before the wealth of the farm milk and of its derivatives. Another example of this difficulty in developing sustainable food is river fish. In a recent survey on the communities living on the banks of the river Po in northern Italy, it was found (Gilli, 2010, 2011) that, while some tourist development projects were focused on a re-proposal of the local cuisine (where river fish is one of the chief elements), many in-depth interviews with stakeholders indicated that the river fish flavor is not always appreciated by the people (especially children), who are used to lighter tastes. One could conclude that many people, especially those who live in urban settings and have few (if any) experiences of rural food, have an "anesthetized" palate, used to sweetened flavors and insensitive (or even worse) to strong flavors. In particular, the young generations have no taste or olfactory rural "memory" (here, one could mention the taste education of children carried out by the Slow Food movement, a movement for the protection and development of local food, born in Italy but now widespread in many parts of the world). Anyway, although no sustainable food project would neglect the actual taste of the tourist, one should always make room for a sort of re-education of the tourists toward an appreciation of strong and authentic flavors.

The economic dimension of sustainability consists in stimulating economic initiatives whose socio-economic benefits may be equitably distributed among all the stakeholders. The goal of a local development can hardly be pursued with the traditional instruments of government that follow the institutional political ways: much more useful would be a perspective of governance characterized by a bottom-up configuration, which enhances the role of local communities and a diffuse public–private partnership on a local basis. This kind of governance, in opposition to the hierarchical control model, is characterized by a greater degree of cooperation between local actors, public and private, within the mixed decision-making networks (Mayntz, 1999).

What could authenticity mean in this last dimension? It probably consists in fostering the direct access of the tourists to the local markets—the more local the better. Fostering a direct access to the small producers, to restaurants run directly, without any mediation by the major tour operators who like the big operators best; the opportunity to purchase food and wine in local stores or markets (finding the same products just eaten at a restaurant), or even to buy products (milk, cheese, vegetables, fruits) directly from the farmers and the ranchers, thus contributes to the economic maintenance of the local community. The slogan of "zero kilometer," already well-known in Italy, has grown stronger in recent years, as sustainability has become a cultural value, as evidenced by the widespread practice of GAS, the joint purchasing groups.

A typical example of how to achieve sustainable food tourism is farm tourism. In farm tourism visitors stay in the farmhouse and eat local products. At the same time they have the opportunity to observe many agricultural and animal breeding activities. This type of tourism is addressed both to children in school curricula, as well as to families. In our opinion this type of tourism—that, for a few years, has spread throughout Italy—respects the three dimensions mentioned above (environmental, socio-cultural, economic) of genuine sustainable food tourism. It takes place in a farmhouse nestled in a genuine rural environment conceived for farming and animal breeding, and not as a tourist scene. Here, all the elements of authenticity involved by the farm life are present, even those that tourists unaccustomed to the country might consider unpleasant. The farm life enables the tourists to understand the whole production chain behind the preparation of food, and allows them to eat authentic food. Finally, farm tourism takes place directly at the farm, without any mediation by economic operators: farmers make some profit from this activity, without neglecting their main agricultural activity.

## Experiential sustainable food tourism

Today consumers look for products and services that intrigue and stimulate them; they are interested in emotionally and mentally enriching goods that grant holistic, unique, and memorable consumption experiences (Fabris, 2002: 207; Schmitt, 1999; Holbrook and Hirschman, 1982: 132; Addis and Holbrook, 2001: 50). Besides, the increasing demand for entertainment and amusing experiences promotes development in the supply of global experiences, mixtures of activities that were previously offered separately, such as entertainment in restaurants, shopping during holidays, and shows in shopping centers (Fabris, 2002: 207; Ferrari, 2006).

As a consequence, during their holidays modern-day tourists seek new sensations, physically and emotionally enriching experiences. More and more visitors avoid mass holidays and standard tourist packages. In fact, they want to visit places that are different from those sought in the past; they are increasingly willing to grasp the more authentic aspects of a destination and, particularly, those that are linked with local history, traditions, and culture. They search for strong emotions, high involvement, and unusual situations, together with a desire to return to ancient sensations and to rediscover tastes and scents (MacCannell, 1973: 589).

Each tourist experience has two types of components, which may have different levels of importance. These components are: *peak experiences* (that are linked to out-and-out "tourist" resources, in stark contrast with everyday life) and *experiences of support* (including auxiliary and ancillary services, such as accommodation, food, etc., which are more easily assimilated to daily experiences, and represent an extension and, at times, an intensification).

As Uriely (2005) points out, in the past the tourist experience has been seen as separate from daily life, as a moment in stark contrast to the everyday, an "out-of-the-ordinary" experience (Urry, 1995: 132). In the social sciences (Moutinho, 1987; Swarbrooke and Horner, 1999) the tourist experience has been considered as a peak experience. In this approach, tourist attractions were not directly related to support services, such as accommodation and catering; they were exclusively related to resources that enable people to live unforgettable and unique experiences, not comparable to those of everyday life, that is to say peak experiences such as rafting, parachute jumping, etc.

Instead, today, visitors are more interested in knowing the everyday life of visited destinations (Richards, 2011). More and more people want to live simple, everyday experiences, and participate in common activities (such as walking, enjoying a simple meal) to reclaim the contemplative time, which seems to have disappeared (Harvey, 1990; Carù and Cova, 2003).

For this reason, perhaps a more correct, sustainable, and complete concept of "experience" has to run right through everyday life, rather than through the "amazing" (magical and fairytale) items and entertainment that in the past companies offered to attract tourists. As a consequence, tourist suppliers are highlighting the less visible component of their offer, the support experiences, which include multisensory stimuli, to rediscover daily, authentic, simple things and forgotten aspects of everyday life often overlooked. In this way a new form of cultural tourism, called "creative tourism," has evolved, which is designed to "provide the creative knowledge to be a local or engage in locally-based forms of creativity" (Richards, 2011). Therefore, the importance and attractiveness of the component of tourism that is closest to everyday experience and is dependent on the fulfillment of basic needs (services and supporting infrastructures) is rising (Quan and Wang, 2004).

Thanks to these changes in tourism, the importance of food and culinary tradition as a tourist resource is also rapidly growing, together with the value of attractions linked to food and wine. More engaging than the simple tasting of food is the active involvement of visitors in more participative and authentic experiences such as food festivals, traditional gastronomic events, gourmet and wine routes, farm holidays, theme and theatrical restaurants, tasting museums, visits to food production places, vineyards, and wineries, etc.

In Figure 29.1, the two types of experiences, peak and daily, are integrated into one, because they are seen as a collection of activities experienced during the holiday. The influence of the physical environment is strong, as is that of the social environment (made up of personnel, other clients, and local community). All these elements, shown in the figure, together constitute the environment in which the experience takes place (Prahalad and Ramaswamy, 2003; Mossberg, 2007). In addition, many organizations and destinations have conceived myths or stories to communicate and coordinate their offerings and created souvenirs related to these issues.

The involvement of residents as a component of tourist products can increase in a sustainable way the experiential value of the holiday, offering unique and unforgettable experiences to visitors (Prentice et al., 1998; Pine and Gilmore, 1999; Quan and Wang, 2004). In fact, the success of tourism is based on the goodwill of local residents and on their hospitality (Gursoy et al., 2002). Despite the fact that it has been overlooked in the literature, the role of residents is very important, because they help to determine both the quality of the tourism experience and the image of the destination. As for the first aspect, the host community is, in fact, one of the three interdependent elements that impact on the tourism experience (together with other tourists and the natural environment) (Wearing and Wearing, 2001). The host community is considered directly and indirectly part of the environmental setting (Jennings and Polovitz Nickerson, 2006: 116) and is a part of the destination's macro-environment (Kotler et al., 2003: 47).

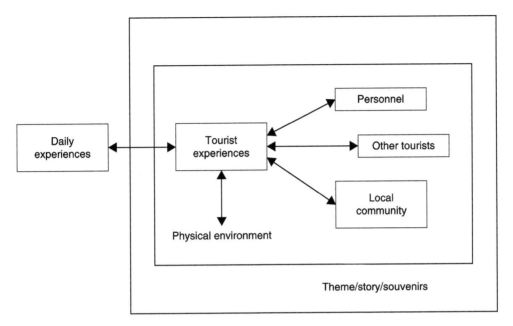

*Figure 29.1* Factors that influence consumers' experience in the tourism sector.

*Source:* Adapted from Mossberg (2007).

Local community also has an important role as a supplier of information to potential tourists (Arsal et al., 2010). In addition, residents see things from inside the destination, causing a strong emotional involvement in tourists who come into contact with them and a certain intimacy with a place (Trauer and Ryan, 2005), which increases the value of the tourism experience.

Additionally, good interaction between host community and tourists could be an effective instrument to improve residents' attitude towards tourism, showing it as a sustainable and non-invasive form of economic development and creating empathy between the two groups. In fact, as Wearing and Wearing (2001: 153) state: "the more the tourist commoditizes and inferiorizes the hosts' culture, the more the hosts regard the tourist with hostility." If, on the other hand, residents and tourists share a value system, then visitors behave acceptably for residents and they in turn view tourism favorably. If not, there will be intolerance and there will be no community support for possible tourism development. A positive attitude on the part of residents towards tourists therefore increases the levels of satisfaction, improving the capacity to welcome tourists and the experiential value of the tourist experience creating a favorable climate towards visitors (Harrill, 2004; Ritzner, 1996; Perdue et al., 1990).

In conclusion, the involvement of the host community in tourist offers is a prerequisite for the sustainability of tourism development. In fact, tourist attractions, if presented to visitors as representations of the spirit of the place, are more authentic and compatible with alternative and sustainable forms of tourism. They eventually act as connectors between tourists and residents.

Tourist resources based on local peculiarities, such as culinary traditions and typical agrofood production, may, therefore, become the strengths of tourist brands that represent core values of the community and at the same time points of convergence between the place's identity and the outward manifestations of local image and the way in which the community represents itself and the image used by tour operators to promote the destination. A very interesting case of an experiential food tourism product, which represents a good example of sustainability in tourism based on a form of experience offered to visitors with the involvement of residents, is Ceneromane (Roman Dinners). It is a community, born in 2012 in Rome, that has adopted an innovative and unconventional hospitality pattern, opening residents' homes to tourists and sharing a dinner with them. The offer has a cost, is by appointment and strictly reserved to Italian and foreign tourists. The clients are members of online communities and use the Internet to organize their holidays. They are of various ages and are mainly foreign tourists, looking for a personalized travel experience. For the reservation, they can choose the house, together with the menu and the date on the website of Ceneromane. Before joining the project, the hosts that are part of the community have to take an online course.

The network, which today comprises 40 homes in different districts of Rome, offers a home-restaurant service, allowing tourists to live a unique experience. It represents an opportunity for interaction, cultural exchange, and a way to improve the impact of tourism in social terms. Strengths of the offer are the comfort and the priceless feeling of being at home, together with the familiar atmosphere, the Roman traditional menus, and the use of local products. For guests, the dinners are good ways to better get to know the Roman way of life and to have unique experiences, thanks to the renowned hospitality of Italian people.

Every month Ceneromane organizes about 80–100 dinners; the offer is growing and in the future it could interest other cities (probably Torino, Milano, Firenze, Verona, Bari, Lecce, Palermo), as the organization is studying the possibility of expanding to other cities, and creating a national-level network. It represents a sustainable form of tourism, which allows the rediscovery of typical dishes and traditional cuisine, and preserves local food culture, also transmitting it to new targets.

## Conclusion

The aim of our work is to present some of the current experiences of sustainable food tourism in Italy through two key components of this type of tourism: authenticity and experience. In fact, tourists today want to have unique, engaging, and authentic experiences that have to be well-connected and closer to the everyday life and culture of the visited places. The selection of such experiences, which are moments of inner growth and self-actualization related to the "living or intangible culture" of destinations (Richards, 2011), is a form of sustainable tourism that is based on the interest in local culture and the co-production of the tourist experience by the tourist him/herself.

The tourists, more aware, sensitive and demanding, want to have unique and authentic experiences related to the culture of the places they visit. As a result, to be more and more competitive and sustainable, food and wine tourism has to focus on two elements that create value for visitors and competitive advantage for firms and destinations: authenticity and experience. These two aspects are linked to the postmodern approach to tourism, which focuses on the exploitation of tourist destinations that are little known and more distant from mass routes.

These elements make tourist products not only more competitive but also more sustainable. In fact, they are elements that encourage the involvement of residents, strengthening local culture and identity and, in some cases, becoming the basis for effective destination branding policies.

In this way, the development of tourism becomes a tool for discovering, rediscovering, and spreading local culture, and also a glue for social fabric, through which the self-esteem and pride of belonging of local people can grow. So tourism has not only an impact in terms of economic flow but also a more significant effect in social terms, becoming an element of cohesion and strengthening of local identity. It can play this role, enhancing food culture and local agricultural production and promoting the conservation of biodiversity, becoming an instrument to protect natural heritage and cultural traditional landscapes.

Our work has produced some specific results. With regard to the experiential dimension in sustainable food tourism, this does not seem to bring out particular problems. On the tour operators' side, they seem to have understood the importance of the active involvement of the tourist. Therefore, the objectives of the tourists and those of operators and local communities seem, to some extent, to coincide.

There is a difference of opinion about authenticity in sustainable food tourism. On the one hand, it may happen that local communities try to attract tourists by means of a rural land-scape that is a bit too bucolic and a cooking that is too sweetened, so as not to upset the tourist. On the other hand, it can also happen that the tourists themselves are not able to enjoy some authentic dishes, because of the softer and sweeter eating habits acquired in urban life.

It follows that a typical problem of authenticity in tourism comes to light: authenticity is a social construction, which must be continuously renegotiated among the various stake-holders. At the same time it may be useful to consider that sustainable food tourism has to be supported or that it should also have some sort of didactic function, which allows tourists with little authentic food experience to be able to distinguish authentic and not authentic food.

## Note

1   Monica Gilli is the author for the Introduction and 'Authenticity in sustainable food tourism'; Sonia Ferrari is the author for 'Experiential sustainable food tourism' and the Conclusion.

## References

Addis, M. and Holbrook, M.B. (2001) "On the conceptual link between mass customisation and experiential consumption: an explosion of subjectivity," *Journal of Consumer Behaviour*, 1(1): 50–66.

Arsal, I., Woosnam, K.M., and Baldwin, E.D. (2010) "Residents as travel destination information providers: an online community perspective," *Journal of Travel Research*, 49(4): 400–413.

Beer, S. (2008) "Authenticity and food experience—commercial and academic perspectives," *Journal of Food Service*, 19: 153–163.

Boorstin, D. (1964) *The Image: A Guide To Pseudo-events in America*, New York: Harper.

Bruner, E.M. (1994) "Abraham Lincoln as authentic reproduction: a critique of postmodernism," *American Anthropologist*, 96(2): 397–415.

Carù, A. and Cova, B. (2003) "Revisiting consumption experience: a more humble but complete view of the concept," *Marketing Theory*, 3(2): 259–278.

Chang, R.C.Y., Kivela, J., and Mak, A.H.N. (2011) "Attributes that influence the evaluation of travel dining experience: when East meets West," *Tourism Management*, 32: 307–316.

Cohen, E. and Avieli, N. (2004) "Food and tourism: attraction and impediment," *Annals of Tourism Research*, 31(4): 755–778.

Desforges, L. (2000) "Traveling the world: identity and travel biography," *Annals of Tourism Research*, 24(4): 926–945.

Everett, S. and Aitchison, C. (2008) "The role of food tourism in sustaining regional identity: a case study of Cornwall, south west England," *Journal of Sustainable Tourism*, 16(2): 150–167.

Fabris, G. (2002) *Il nuovo consumatore: verso il post-moderno*, Milan: Franco Angeli.

Feifer, M. (1985) *Going Places*, London: Macmillan.

Ferguson, C. (1981) " 'Foreign talk' as the name of a simplified register," *International Journal of the Sociology of Language*, 28: 9–18.

Ferrari, S. (2006) *Modelli gestionali per il turismo come esperienza. Emozioni e polisensorialità nel marketing delle imprese turistiche*, Padua: Cedam.

Gilli, M. (2009) *Autenticità e interpretazione nell'esperienza turistica*, Milan: Franco Angeli.

Gilli, M. (2010) *Dossier preliminare del Piano Socio Economico del Sistema delle Aree protette della fascia fluviale del Po tratto torinese e della Collina torinese: aspetti sociologici*, www.paesaggiopocollina.it/piano/dossier/dossier_20genn2011.pdf.

Gilli, M. (2011) "Lo sguardo dall'acqua: la crociera fluviale in Europa," in E. Marra and E. Ruspini (eds.), *Altri turismi crescono. Turismi outdoor e turismi urbani*, Milan: Franco Angeli, pp. 85–111.

Gottlieb, A. (1982) "American's vacations," *Annals of Tourism Research*, 9: 165–187.

Gursoy, D., Jurowski, C., and Uysal, M. (2002) "Resident attitudes: a structural modelling approach," *Annals of Tourism Research*, 29(1): 79–105.

Harrill, R. (2004) "Residents' attitudes toward tourism development: a literature review with implications for tourism planning," *Journal of Planning Literature*, 18(3): 251–266.

Harvey, D. (1990) *The Condition of Postmodernity*, Malden: Blackwell Publishing.

Holbrook, M.B. and Hirschman, E.C. (1982) "The experiential aspects of consumption: consumer fantasies, feelings, and fun," *Journal of Consumer Research*, 9: 132–140.

Hughes, G. (1995) "Authenticity in tourism," *Annals of Tourism Research*, 22(4): 781–803.

Jennings, G. and Polovitz Nickerson, N. (eds.) (2006) *Quality Tourism Experiences*, Oxford: Butterworth-Heinemann.

Kotler, P., Bowen, J., and Makens, J. (2003) *Marketing or Hospitality and Tourism*, 3rd edn., Englewood Cliffs, NJ: Prentice-Hall.

MacCannell, D. (1973) "Staged authenticity: arrangements of social space in tourist settings," *American Journal of Sociology*, 79: 589–603.

MacCannell, D. (1976) *The Tourist: a Theory of the Leisure Class*, New York: Schocken.

Mayntz, R. (1999) "La teoria della *governance*: sfide e prospettive," *Rivista italiana di scienza politica*, 1: 3–21.

McCabe, S. (2005) "Who is a tourist? A critical review," *Tourist Studies*, 5(1): 85–106.

Mossberg, L. (2007) "A marketing approach to the tourist experience," *Scandinavian Journal of Hospitality and Tourism*, 7(1): 59–74.

Moutinho, L. (1987) "Consumer behaviour in tourism," *European Journal of Marketing*, 21(10): 3–44.

Palmer, C. (1999) "Tourism and the symbols of identity," *Tourism Management*, 20(3): 313–321.

Palmer, C. (2005) "An ethnography of Englishness: experiencing identity through tourism," *Annals of Tourism Research*, 32(1): 7–27.

Perdue, R.R., Long, R.T., and Allen, L. (1990) "Resident support for tourism development," *Annals of Tourism Research*, 17(4): 586–599.

Pine, B. and Gilmore, J. (1999) *The Experience Economy: Work is Theatre and Every Business a Stage*, Boston: Harvard Business School Press.

Prahalad, C.K. and Ramaswamy, V. (2003) "The new frontier of experience innovation," *Sloan Management Review*, 44: 12–18.

Prentice, R.C., Witt, S.F., and Hamer, C. (1998) "Tourism as experience: the case of heritage parks," *Annals of Tourism Research*, 25(1): 1–24.

Quan, S. and Wang, N. (2004) "Towards a structural model of the tourist experience: an illustration from food experiences in tourism," *Tourism Management*, 25: 297–305.

Richards, G. (2002) "Gastronomy: an essential ingredient in tourism production and consumption?" in A.M.H. Hjalager and G. Richards (eds.), *Tourism and Gastronomy*, London: Routledge, pp. 3–20.

Richards, G. (2011) "Creativity and tourism: the state of the art," *Annals of Tourism Research*, 38: 1225–1253.

Richards, G. and Wilson, J. (eds.) (2007) *Tourism, Creativity and Development*, Oxford: Routledge.

Ritzner, G. (1996) *Sociological Theory*, 4th edn., New York: McGraw-Hill.

Scarpato, R. (2002) "Gastronomy as a tourist product: the perspective of gastronomy studies," in A.M. Hjalager and G. Richards (eds.), *Tourism and Gastronomy*, London: Routledge, pp. 51–70.

Schmitt, B. (1999) *Experiential Marketing*, New York: The Free Press.

Sims, R. (2009) "Food, place and authenticity: local food and the sustainable tourism experience," *Journal of Sustainable Tourism*, 17(3): 321–336.

Swarbrooke, J. and Horner, S. (1999) *Consumer Behaviour in Tourism*, Oxford: Butterworth-Heinemann.

Trauer, B. and Ryan, C. (2005) "Destination image, romance and place experience—an application of intimacy theory in tourism," *Tourism Management*, 26: 481–491.

Uriely, N. (2005) "The tourist experience: conceptual developments," *Annals of Tourism Research*, 32(1): 199–216.

Urry, J. (1990) *The Tourist Gaze*, London: Sage Publications.

Urry, J. (1995) *Consuming Places*, London: Routledge.

Wang, N. (1999) "Rethinking authenticity in tourism experience," *Annals of Tourism Research*, 26(2): 349–370.

Wearing, S. and Wearing, B. (2001) "Conceptualizing the selves of tourism," *Leisure Studies*, 20: 143–159.

# 30

# THE AUTUMN-PEAR

## A symbol for local identity, local specialities, biodiversity and collaborative park management, an Austrian case study

*Ulrike Pröbstl-Haider, Elisabeth Hochwarter and Josef Schrank*

### Introduction

This article focuses on a local speciality from the south-east of Austria – the autumn-pear. The case study is of interest because this traditional fruit tree has influenced not only the local identity in the past, but also the overall development of the region since the 1980s. The article will first describe the historical development of the autumn-pear, and will then analyse its recent development and success factors. The article is based on historical documents, empirical studies (Pröbstl and Schuster, 2011; Pröbstl-Haider and Schrank, 2013; Hochwarter, 2014) and regional information (Tourismusverband Naturpark Pöllauer Tal, 2013; Sommer and Höbaus, 2012; Weiß, 2013). Finally, the chapter will address the question of how recent societal trends and demand may influence the persistence and market opportunities of this local speciality, considering the food market, tourism development and its effect on the local quality of life.

### Location and history

The focus area is located in the eastern foothills of the Alps, behind the main alpine mountain range, around 150km south of Vienna and 55km north of Graz. It is characterised by small villages and farmland in rural and remote countryside. The autumn-pear was already mentioned in several early historical documents. In the eighteenth century, the brother of the Austrian emperor, Archduke Johann, wanted to improve the poor nutritional situation of the local population in Styria (Land Steiermark, 2014). One of the challenges was to increase the knowledge and distribution of all kinds of agricultural products. He fostered knowledge exchange and education and initiated exhibitions of agricultural products and methods. The tradition was also kept in Styria after his death. In an exhibition of suitable and attractive fruit trees in 1888, the autumn-pear was already listed and recommended. The high relevance of the autumn-pear for the region, and explicitly for the Pöllau valley, was described by a local chronicler in 1893. He mentions that hundreds of horse-drawn wagons in the Pöllau valley were typically filled with the autumn-pear, and that the pear served as an important source of income for the local population. The chronicler also refers to the widespread distribution of the

*Figure 30.1* The autumn-pear in the Pöllau valley in Austria.

autumn-pear and other local fruit products. He highlights that dried autumn-pear and other dried regional fruits were not only sold regionally, but were also sold in Vienna, and via Vienna also to German customers. He mentions several hundred centner (one centner is about 50kg) in this context. The Pöllau valley and the whole region offer excellent climatic conditions for growing fruit and even wine. These conditions are characterised by a low risk of frost days, a strong influence of warm winds ('Föhn') and the mild climate associated with the alpine foot-hills. This led to a very diverse landscape dominated by orchards, vineyards, small agricultural fields and forests. The autumn-pear is the most distinctive feature of this landscape. It is a large tree that can live to be over 100 years old (Wilfling and Möslinger, 2005: 30).

Unlike most known pears bred and used for food in Europe, the autumn-pear derives from the snow-pear (*Pyrus nivalis*). Therefore, it differs from most other pears in certain character-istics, such as the hairiness of the leaves. The autumn-pear is counted among the 'must'-pears, and ripens between the last week of September and the third week of October. As the historical sources already indicated, the pear is not traditionally used as the fruit itself, but is rather made into juice (called 'must') or is dried. The flavour is distinctly different from that of other pears and used in all juice products – schnapps, liqueurs, jams, ice creams, etc. – with an unmistakable aroma. Autumn-pears were traditionally planted as standard trees in so-called meadow orchard culture, either spread across meadows or in lines along paths.

Available historical documents indicate that the autumn-pear was once widespread in the east of Austria (in Burgenland, Styria and the south of Lower Austria), and enriched the diversity of fruit trees in those regions. The intensification of agriculture in the 1960s and

1970s led to a substantial loss of meadow orchards in many traditional fruit-growing areas. Economic reasons, a change of consumer behaviour and demand, and work and safety related issues were the decisive factors (Kornprobst, 1994; Lucke et al., 1992). Plantation orchards proved to be far more economical than traditional meadow orchards, and new varieties of fruit became more popular – especially ones that were also fit for direct consumption. The very large pear trees in meadow orchard culture required considerable maintenance, and harvesting the fruit could be dangerous. All of these factors led to a sharp decline in this exceptional pear, even in eastern Styria around the Pöllau valley. In the Pöllau valley itself, however, the 'old giants' were largely left standing. The reasons are not entirely clear. The locals say that people in this valley tend to be quite conservative and are not quick to follow new developments. Others say that the intensive use of this pear, going back centuries, has strengthened the valley population's affection for the pear's unique flavour. This was combined with a certain pride of being able to produce a local speciality – even if it was only for personal requirements. A detailed survey of the autumn-pear's occurrence (see Figure 30.2) revealed that only a few focus production areas are left from the original range.

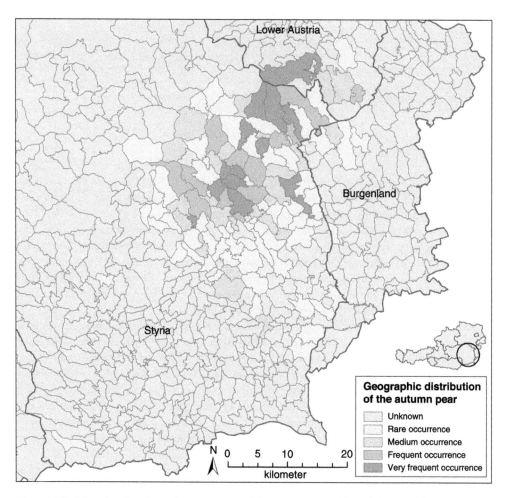

*Figure 30.2* Map showing the main occurrence of the autumn-pear (altered from Wilfling, 2009).

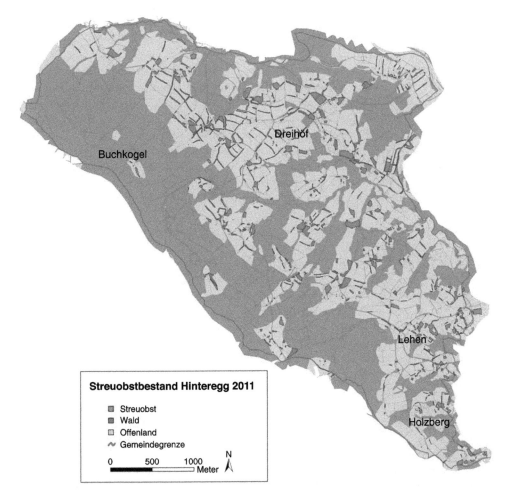

*Figure 30.3* Map of the small-scale landscape of one community in the nature park (Hinteregg). The areas with fruit trees in 2011 are highlighted in dark grey.

Figure 30.2 shows the province of Styria, parts of Burgenland and Lower Austria in eastern Austria. The different shades of grey indicate regions in which the autumn-pear occurs. The darker the colour, the more records of occurrence were indicated during the inventory initiated by the communities in the Pöllauer valley. Light grey indicates surveyed regions without any occurrence of autumn-pear.

Thanks to the widespread preservation of traditional land use and the distinctive autumn-pear trees in meadow orchard culture, a unique landscape, cultivated on a small scale and attractive in all seasons, was also preserved. Parts of this landscape have found legal protection as landscape conservation areas. This, in turn, allowed six municipalities of the Pöllau valley to apply for the status of a nature park, based on conservation law.

## The autumn-pear – a key for the development of a nature park

The purpose of a nature park is to maintain attractive landscapes, often of a cultivated nature, as unique features. Nature parks provide areas for recreation and regeneration, but also environmental education and nature-based tourism. Their protected status should ensure the maintenance of unique landscapes shaped by sustainable, often traditional land use and local culture (Pröbstl, 2004).

Nature parks ought to be developed by a bottom-up approach, and are typically based on local cooperative planning processes. Nature parks consist mainly of private land and/or communal land. They are only partly dominated by state-owned land. In a nature park, conservation work mostly focuses on species that are typical for traditionally cultivated landscapes and biotopes. These biotopes, such as dry meadows or open forests supported by traditional cattle grazing, are often characterised by a high level of species richness, but depend on traditional land use to maintain that biodiversity. Nature parks provide exemplary solutions for the continued maintenance of a more diverse cultural landscape, and should typically provide a model for land use even in the surrounding areas outside the nature park (Pröbstl, 2008).

Nature parks are the only category of protected area that targets recreation and tourism explicitly. Recreation and physical regeneration are supported by outstanding landscape beauty, and by the desired infrastructure and related facilities. Therefore, nature parks offer excellent conditions for nature-based tourism. Besides the income from recreation and nature-based tourism, a nature park also offers additional opportunities for regional development, based on sustainable forms of land use, specific local products and cultural traditions (Job et al., 2005). Many nature parks have now successfully developed local labels and brands promoting their traditional land-use and its contribution to species conservation. It is crucial, therefore, to consider the interests of agriculture, regional economic development and social aspects, and to combine them into one integrated framework.

In 1983, the province of Styria decided that the Pöllau valley would be awarded the status of nature park. At the time, the nature park comprised six municipalities with a total of approximately 8,500 inhabitants in a 122km² area. The reason for the park's designation was its outstanding scenic beauty, thanks to its diverse and small-scale agriculture made up of grassland, forests, numerous meadow orchards and crop land.

Styrian nature parks have always attached great importance to the conservation of the natural and scenic features providing their very basis. In the Pöllau Valley Nature Park, these are the old meadow orchards, extensively used grassland and small-scale landscape with hedgerows and unploughed strips between fields. The focus of conservation efforts is, therefore, 'conservation through use', and this applies in particular to the remaining meadow orchards. The attractive recreational landscape is made accessible to tourists and excursionists through family-friendly hiking trails, adventure playgrounds, bicycle routes and horse-riding trails. These attractions also contribute to the quality of life for the local people – as surveys in the population have shown (Pröbstl and Schuster, 2011). The nature park is also characterised by a comprehensive offering of educational programmes, for tourists and locals alike. These include guided excursions, themed trails, seminars, exhibitions and numerous other events. The so-called nature park schools also play an important role in Styria. Six of the eight schools in the Pöllau Valley Nature Park fulfil the special requirements to carry this title, and make active use of the nature park as a learning environment. Regarding the nature park's role in regional development, the focus lies on marketing the park as a 'Savoury Region' (GenussRegion) revolving around the autumn-pear. A cooperation of farming, tourism, trade and culture has led to the development of new products ranging from autumn-pear 'Leberkäse' (a type of meat loaf popular in Austria and southern Germany), to autumn-pear ice-cream, vinegar, juice, schnapps and chocolate, to the autumn-pear 'dirndl' (a traditional dress) and a regional cookbook. Thanks to these stimuli for the regional economy, to the socially and environmentally friendly level of tourism, and to the intelligent marketing of nature-park produce and specialities, the nature park is very highly regarded in the population (Pröbstl and Schuster, 2011).

The landscape character of the Pöllau Valley Nature Park (Figure 30.3), but also its touristic profile and economic stimuli in the region, depend strongly on the preservation of large areas of meadow orchards.

## The autumn-pear – a key to becoming a Savoury Region

In their effort to preserve and promote regional specialities, the Agrarmarkt Austria Marketing and the Austrian Ministry of Life developed the new registered trademark 'Savoury Region' (GenussRegion). The goal of the Savoury Regions is to draw consumer attention to the culinary specialities of different regions, the focus always being on regionally specific agricultural products. The products are meant to be associated directly with their respective regions and should have an intimate connection with their agricultural landscapes. Austria's many cultivated landscapes and their regionally specific products should establish the Savoury Regions as an unmistakable trademark, strengthening and contributing to the added value of rural areas (GRM, 2013a). The trademark should improve cooperation between agriculture, trade, gastronomy and tourism, and should target national and international guests alike

*Figure 30.4*   Marketing logo of the Savoury Region – Pöllau Autumn-Pear.

*Source:* GRM (2013a).

(GRM, 2013b). Development of the Savoury Regions should boost regional added value, create jobs and shorten transport distances (BMLFUW, 2010: 68).

The title of Savoury Region, awarded by the minister for agriculture, is bound to strict criteria. The region must be clearly defined geographically, and the regionally typical product must be of certified high quality. Furthermore, the product must be produced locally and must be used by at least five local gastronomic businesses. Proof of direct marketing of the typical product in the Savoury Region must also be provided (GRM, 2013c). Despite these strict terms, the programme has proven to be a great success. There are currently 113 Savoury Regions in Austria (Kastner, 2010).

The age-old tradition of the autumn-pear, the wide range of products made from it and the participation of businesses and gastronomic partners all provided the basis for the application of the Pöllau valley to become a Savoury Region. The Pöllau valley was awarded the title in 2006. Many already established products then needed to apply for participation and use of the logo. While this wasn't always a simple process for the producers of autumn-pear products, cooperation with gastronomic and trade businesses was easily implemented. Today, the Savoury Region logo can be found in all businesses, in menus and marketing material. The name and logo 'Pöllauer Hirschbirne' (Pöllauer Autumn-Pear) is now protected (Österreichisches Patentamt, 2012).

## Consequences for the region and its development

Considering the various titles the valley has been awarded, and its efforts to preserve this old variety of fruit tree, the question arises of whether this has had a positive effect for the region. Figure 30.5 shows the respective goals of the nature park and the Savoury Region. An area of overlap is visible at first glance, pertaining to regional development. Both titles are intended to have a positive effect on the economic development of the region, achieved by landscape preservation, recreation and environmental education on the one hand, and the promotion of

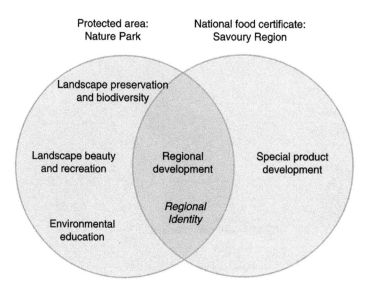

*Figure 30.5* Goals of nature park and Savoury Region. Promoting a regional identity (in italics) isn't an immediate goal, but a desired side-effect.

a special local product on the other hand. Further possible benefits from both titles can be expected for the promotion of a regional identity – even if this isn't one of the immediate goals.

## Economic benefits

The nature park and Savoury Region have had obvious economic benefits. These apply both to tourism and to the agrarian sector. The price of the autumn-pear, for example, has risen to twice that of other must-fruit varieties. Autumn-pear trees are once again being raised in nurseries and are commercially available. Many new autumn-pear products have been, and continue to be, developed and offered. Events and recreation infrastructure, such as the autumn-pear hiking trail, regularly attract guests to the region, and communicate the region and the products to the outside. Hochwarter (2014) summarises the various positive economic effects as follows:

• Increase of overnight stays.
• Increase of day-trippers, for example thanks to events such as the 'autumn-pear hiking day'.
• Increase in sales of local products through numerous sales partners in gastronomy and trade.
• Positive development of sales.
• Leverage effect for other regional products, such as honey.

The aim of the nature park and Savoury Region – to have a beneficial and stabilising effect on added value, employment and culture of the region – appears to have been achieved. Tourism has been of particular benefit, since it has led not only to direct added value, but also to indirect and induced effects amounting to between 1.4 and 1.8 times the direct added value. This effect is largely attributable to the nature park (Pröbstl-Haider, 2013).

## Social benefits

The social benefits were studied in two separate surveys, focusing on the effects of the nature park on the one hand, and on those of the Savoury Region on the other hand. For both surveys the data were collected in the six municipalities.

The questionnaire on the benefits of the Pöllau Valley Nature Park was addressed to the local population. and distributed via administration, local associations, in shops and other local servicing facilities (Pröbstl and Schuster, 2011). The following results are based on 125 questionnaires.

Overall, it seems that the nature park has greatly contributed to the perceived quality of life and regional identity. Responses to the question 'What defines the Pöllau Valley Nature Park?' covered the cultivated landscape and its unique features (small-scale landscape, valley floor, autumn-pear as a symbol for the region), but also the park's economic contribution to a 'gentle' form of tourism and to an especially high quality of the businesses associated with the nature park. The nature park also conveys a feeling of home and security. A lot of respondents believed that nature and landscape conservation is taken seriously in the region, and that the nature park is characterised by high biodiversity. At the same time, they emphasised that a 'beautiful environment' wasn't everything, and that the nature park also needed to contribute to sustainable development of the region. Many responses and personal comments made it clear that the nature park had increased the individual quality of life.

Responses to the question 'Does the nature park offer financial benefits?' illustrated clear differences between various groups. While the general population largely could not make out any financial benefits, self-employed people working commercially in the nature park had a very different opinion. The question 'What are the advantages of the Pöllau Valley Nature Park?' also brought out socio-cultural effects and connections to local politics. The nature park is seen as a kind of 'protective framework', particularly by the smaller municipalities. Respondents were under the impression that municipalities, but also touristic and commercial providers, have been cooperating better since the nature park's establishment – for the collective good of the whole population. This cooperation is seen as a strength, awarding the partners a stronger presence in their external communication. All respondents supported the concept of the nature park and would vote for its establishment again.

In a second survey, we asked all gastronomic and sales businesses as well as the local management (N:11) about the success and effects of the Savoury Region, and about the economic and social benefits it has had for the Pöllau valley. Overall, the labelling as a Savoury Region seems to be perceived mostly as very positive. It appears that the Savoury Region has had a predominantly positive effect on regional identity and tourism (see 'tourism development'; 'something special for our guests' in Figure 30.6). It has, however, had considerably less influence on the palette of products (number of regional specialities) and the regional culinary culture. The Savoury Region has had a moderate influence on social life, and even the effects on marketing have been of less relevance, from the perspective of business proprietors and sales outlets in the Pöllau valley. A comparison of data with another Savoury Region (Hochwarter, 2014) underlined this finding, because the autumn-pear in its many forms had already been perceived as a well-established product with clear market shares, and was therefore less likely to profit from the Savoury Region than other regions with less well-known local products.

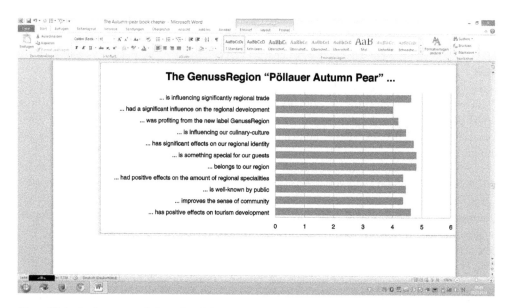

*Figure 30.6* Socio-economic benefits of the Savoury Region, rated from 1 = poor to 5 = high, by local enterprises and management (N:11).

## *Ecological benefits*

Taking stock of the natural environment also paints a predominantly positive picture, as a survey on the development of the nature park showed (Wilfling and Möslinger, 2005). Many of the traditionally species-rich habitats and many species are still preserved in the Pöllau valley. A closer look at the meadow orchards, however, highlights a need for action – as a census of fruit trees for one part of the Pöllau valley revealed (Schrank, 2012). Since fruit-production played a substantial role in the supply of food in the postwar period, a fruit tree census from 1947 exists for the community of Hinteregg, which can be compared to the current data. The comparison shows that the number of meadow orchard fruit trees in Hinteregg dropped by 52 per cent – more than half – in 64 years. Apple trees have decreased most, followed by pear trees. The recent census also revealed that the current total stock of fruit trees consists predominantly of overaged trees.

Due to the high age that autumn-pear trees can reach, today's profits are being made from trees planted by the parent and grandparent generation. Rejuvenation is clearly necessary, and the high market prices for the pear as well as the favourable sales and marketing possibilities will surely facilitate actions to this effect.

## Conclusion

The autumn-pear and its associated land use are the key elements of both the nature park and the Savoury Region. The described positive effects on regional development, quality of life and regional and cultural identity are supported by these two instruments, based on conservation law and the marketing of agricultural products. Comparing the influence of the two instruments, the nature park seems to be more important and effective. A nature park is explicitly designed for the protection of cultural elements and landscape aesthetics, as well as for the maintenance of cultural assets and a sustainable land-use. This focus, combined with a significant offer of environmental education and development of tourism, recreation and tourism-related products, leads to a high relevance of nature parks for nature-based tourism.

Besides these two instruments for the marketing and branding of rural areas (the nature park and the Savoury Region) there are also general societal trends supporting this local success story. Several authors highlight an increasing demand for rural and nature-based tourism (Bell et al., 2007; George et al., 2009; Pröbstl, 2010a, 2010b). Recent publications raise hope that this development could be supported by new societal trends (Bell et al., 2009; Pröbstl et al., 2010). One factor, at least in industrial societies, is demographic change, characterised by an increasing shift towards the elderly generation, which is typically much more attracted by nature and nature experiences. People of this older generation are now much more mobile than they have ever been before, and are interested in returning to their roots. They are also interested in a combination of wellness and nature-based offers. George et al. (2009) explain this desire for returning to one's roots as a possible effect of globalisation. The feeling of being lost in a globalised world is compensated by a retreat into one's own private sphere, the home and garden (so-called 'cocooning'), and awakens new demands in tourism for regional authenticity and environmentally sound offerings. Selecting a tourist destination in a rural area could also be motivated by a certain quest for the meaning of life, which might more likely be found while being active in nature, rather than in the triviality and strict functionality of modern urban life.

Parallel to this trend in tourism, Hochwarter (2014) highlights similar trends in the fields of food and consumerism. The past 20 years have been characterised by an increasing demand for exotic products and menus. Trend research now shows a significant shift back to focusing on local and regional products and traditional menus, at least in Austria and many alpine countries. In 2013, two of the main food store chains in Austria promoted themselves by highlighting that they offer truly regional products (Spar, 2013; Merkur, 2013). The amount of organic products and marketing of so-called 'forgotten' local specialities is also increasing. These trends, along with an emerging demand for especially healthy local products, may also contribute to the success story of the autumn-pear.

The article illustrates a successful combination of nature conservation, tourism, land use and tradition with the development of new products by different local groups. Overall, the nature park and the traditional pear variety contribute significantly to the development of the rural region, and work as catalysts for an emerging new regional identity. The results of a survey within the local population underline these findings. Challenges exist in maintaining the very extensive form of land-use and in rejuvenating the still dominant fruit trees and meadow orchards. But the autumn-pear has already achieved a high level of prominence. Due to the increased demand, it is now again available on the market and can even be planted in private gardens.

# References

Bell, S., Tyrväinen, L., Sievänen, T., Pröbstl, U. and Murray, S. (2007) 'Outdoor recreation and nature tourism: a European perspective', *Landscape Research*, 1(2).

Bell, S., Murray, S., Tyrväinen, L., Sievänen, T. and Pröbstl, U. (eds.) (2009) *European Forest Recreation and Tourism, A Handbook*, New York: Taylor & Francis.

BMLFUW (2010) *Lebensmittelbericht Österreich 2010*, www.lebensministerium.at/lebensmittel/lebensmittelbericht/lebensmittelbericht.html (accessed 23 October 2013).

George, E.W., Mair, H. and Reid, D.G. (2009) *Rural Tourism Development: Localism and Culture Change*, Bristol: Channel View Publications.

GRM (2013a) *Die Marke*, www.genuss-region.at/initiative/die-marke.html (accessed 12 September 2013).

GRM (2013b) *Vision und Mission*, www.genuss-region.at/initiative/vision-und-mission.html. (accessed 12 September 2013).

GRM (2013c) *Kriterien*, www.genuss-region.at/initiative/kriterien.html (accessed 12 September 2013).

Hochwarter, E. (2014) *Einfluss der 'GenussRegion Österreich' auf die regionale Entwicklung anhand der Beispiele 'Zickentaler Moorochsen' und 'Pöllauer Hirschbirne'*, Master's thesis, Institut of Landscape Development, Recreation and Conservation Planning, University of Life Sciences (BOKU), Vienna.

Job, H., Harrer, B., Metzler, D. and Hajizadeh-Alamdary, D. (2005) *Ökonomische Effekte von Großschutzgebieten*, Munich, Germany: Bundesamt für Naturschutz, BfN-Skipten 135, 111S.

Kastner, R. (2010) *GenussRegionen Marketing – Dreijahresbericht 2008–2010*, Vienna.

Kornprobst, M. (1994) *Landschaftspflegekonzept Bayern, Band II, 5, Lebensraumtyp Streuobst*, Munich: Hrsg., Bayerisches Staatsministerium für Landesentwicklung und Umweltfragen.

Merkur (2013) *Das Beste aus unseren Regionen*, www.merkurmarkt.at/Nachhaltigkeit/Regionalitaet/Regionalitaet/mm_Content.aspx (accessed 18 September 2013).

Land Steiermark (2014) *Erzherzog Johann*, www.steiermark.at/cms/beitrag/10000758/1947/ (accessed 3 April 2014).

Lucke, R., Silbereisen, R. and Herzberger, E. (1992) *Obstbäume in der Landschaft*, Stuttgart: Eugen Ulmer Verlag.

Österreichisches Patentamt (2012) Antrag auf Eintragung einer Ursprungsbezeichnung 'Pöllauer Hirschbirne – gU', www.patentamt.at/Media/Poellauer_Hirschbirne_Antrag.pdf. (accessed 16 October 2013).

Pröbstl, U. (2004) 'Nature parks as an instrument to protect mountainous regions: a comparison in Central Europe', in T. Ito and N. Tanaka (eds.), *Social Roles of Forests for Urban Population – Forest*

*Recreation, Landscape, Nature Conservation, Economic Evaluation and Urban Forestry*, Tsukuba: Japan Society of Forest Planning Press.

Pröbstl, U. (2008) 'The role of protected areas for rural tourism and regional development in Central Europe', in Y. Kumagai (ed.), *Proceedings Searching for Sustainable Tourism*, Japan: Akita.

Pröbstl, U. (2010a) 'Tourism development in peripheral regions and the role of protected areas', in H. Yi-Chung (ed.), *Proceedings of the Conference on Vision and Strategy for World's National Parks and Issues Confronting the Management of the World's National Parks*, Taiwan: Hualien.

Pröbstl, U. (2010b) 'Strategies for tourism development in peripheral areas in the Alpine area', in C.A. Brebbia and F.D. Pineda (eds.), *Sustainable Tourism IV*, Boston: WITpress.

Pröbstl, U. and Schuster, S. (2011) 'Naturpark Pöllauer Tal. Eine Bilanz nach 20 Jahren Entwicklung im ländlichen Raum', *Österreichische Schriftenreihe für Landschaft und Freiraum*, 18: 13–17.

Pröbstl, U., Elands, B., Wirth, V. and Bell, S. (2010) *Management of Recreation and Nature based Tourism in European Forests*, Heidelberg: Springer Science.

Pröbstl-Haider, U. (2013) 'Regionalwirtschaftliche Effekte von Naturparken, in *Verband der Naturparke Österreichs (VNÖ)*, Graz: Naturparke und nachhaltige Regionalentwicklung.

Pröbstl-Haider, U. and Schrank, J. (2013) 'Citizen Science als Beitrag zum Schutzgebietsmanagement? Eine konzeptionelle Untersuchung am Beispiel von Streuobstbeständen im Naturpark Pöllauer Tal', *Naturschutz und Landschaftsplanung: Zeitschrift für angewandte Ökologie*, 45/6: 165–170.

Sommer, E. and Höbaus, E. (2012) *Pöllauer Hirschbirne*, www.lebensministerium.at/lebensmittel/ tradlebensmittel/obst/poellauer_hirschbirn.html (accessed 23 October 2012).

Spar (2013) 'Wir sind Regionalkaiser!', *Mahlzeit!Magazin*, www.spar.at/de_AT/index/mahlzeit-magazin/Artikel/Regionales.html (accessed 18 September 2013).

Schrank, J. (2012) *Erfassung des Streuobstbestandes in Hinteregg*, Streuobstmonitoring durch Laien als Beitrag zum Naturschutz in Naturparken, Diplomarbeit am Institut für Landschaftsentwicklung, Erholungs- und Naturschutzplanung an der Universität für Bodenkultur Wien.

Tourismusverband Naturpark Pöllauer Tal (2013) *Pöllauer Hirschbirne*, www.naturpark-poellauertal.at/ de/essen-trinken/poellauer-hirschbirne (accessed 21 October 2013).

Weiß, W. (2013) *Pöllauer Hirschbirne. Kuratorium Kulinarisches Erbe Österreich und Lebensministerium*, www.genuss-region.at/pdfs/509fe932821b9.pdf. (accessed 15 October 2013).

Wilfling, A. (2009) *Die 'Pöllauer Hirschbirne' – wissenschaftliche Daten zu einer 'legendenumwobenen' Kulturpflanze*, Präsentation zum Forschungsprojekt im Auftrag der GRM GenussRegionen Marketing GmbH, Gleisdorf.

Wilfling, A. and Mösslinger, M. (eds.) (2005) *Biodiversität im Naturpark Pöllauer Tal. Wissenschaftliche Grundlagenforschung als Basis für künftiges Management*, Endbericht Band I/1 Untersuchungsgebiet und Lebensräume, Unveröffentlichter Projektbericht im Auftrag des Vereins Naturpark Pöllauer Tal. 420 S., Gleisdorf

# 31

# TOURISM, FOOD TRADITIONS AND SUPPORTING COMMUNITIES IN SAMOA

## The Mea'ai Project

*Tracy Berno*

## Introduction

Situated in the Polynesian triangle approximately halfway between New Zealand and Hawaii, Samoa is known for the rugged beauty of its rainforest-covered volcanic mountains and valleys leading down to spectacular tropical coastlines. People travel to Samoa – 124,677 international arrivals in 2013 (Samoa Bureau of Statistics, 2014) – to enjoy the diversity of natural sea- and land-based attractions and experience *fa'a Samoa* – the distinctive Samoan way of life. It is fair to say, however, that tourists do not travel to Samoa for the food. Indeed, Polynesian food in general has a less than favourable reputation. Victor Bergeron, who founded the Polynesian-themed Trader Vic's restaurant chain, once said in an interview, 'The real, native South Seas food is lousy. You can't eat it' (Reddinger, 2010: 208).

Samoa's tropical climate and fertile soils produce fresh agricultural ingredients that are healthy, nutritious and vitamin rich, and the in-shore coastal fishery teams up with marine-based proteins and nutritious sea vegetables. However Samoa's food culture is more commonly associated with quite the opposite. 'Turkey tails', mutton flaps and tinned meats have become almost synonymous with Samoan cuisine. Now it is towering mountains of super-sized tins of corn beef in local supermarkets that are the ubiquitous symbol of Samoan food (Koa Dunsford, 2010/2011; Oliver et al., 2013). So powerful is the appeal of this processed tinned meat that New Zealand-Samoan artist Michael Tuffery uses flattened corned beef tins as his medium, his sculptures symbolising the way this imported, high-fat food has undermined local fishing, cultivation and cooking skills in the Pacific (Te Ara, 2013). Perhaps Bergeron's disparaging comments were in reference to this more contemporary food culture in Polynesia. Questions need to be asked: how did Samoa's cuisine transition from its tradition of organic, healthy, self-sufficient and sustainable to that of a 'dumping ground' for poor quality, unhealthy imported products and processed foods, and what, if anything, can be done to address this? This chapter will consider whether tourism, the main driver of economic development in Samoa, can be used as a conduit to rejuvenate traditional Samoan foods.

## Food culture in Samoa

Although pre-colonial Samoan food was limited in choices by modern standards, the traditional subsistence-based cuisine was healthy, and rich in nutrients and vitamins. Staple foods such as root crops (taro, cassava, yams and kumara), coconut, fruits, vegetables (land and sea) and primarily fish-based protein were widely available throughout the seasons. Food preparation methods could be time consuming, for example the preparation of the *umu* (earth oven), but they were healthy methods and suitable to the products so readily available. Food insecurity was rare, and malnutrition generally only occurred as a result of drought, cyclones and/or plant diseases. Such was the case for thousands of years, only changing with the arrival of outsiders to the islands (Koa Dunsford, 2010/2011; Melby, 2011; Oliver et al., 2013).

Although many view the influx of unhealthy processed foods into Samoa as a contemporary phenomenon, it was nineteenth-century traders and missionaries who first introduced the Samoans to imported products, thus starting the transition away from traditional foods. Samoans took quickly to 'exotic' ingredients such as tinned meats and fish and flour. Not only were they quicker and easier to prepare, cook and store than traditional foods, Samoans acquired a taste for these processed ingredients and incorporated them into their diets alongside their more traditional fare. By the 1900s, widespread colonisation throughout the Pacific coupled with the military presence during the World Wars led to dramatic changes in the availability of new sources of imported foods in the Pacific. Globalisation and the integration of the Pacific into the world economy further exacerbated this by increasing the availability of yet more imported processed foods, as well as seeing the introduction of multinational food corporations, such as McDonald's (Melby, 2011; Oliver et al., 2013).

Trade liberalisation between Pacific island countries and developed countries soon saw nations such as Samoa become the 'dumping ground' for low-quality, high-fat products such as the ubiquitous mutton flaps and turkey tails (Legge et al., 2013; Oliver, 2013a). And in a country where healthy carbohydrates in the form of root crops and fruits are readily available, imported processed foods like sugar, rice, cabin biscuits, white bread, potatoes, breakfast cereals and instant noodles have emerged as the carbohydrates of choice (Melby, 2011; Oliver et al., 2013). As discussed by Egan et al. (2006), the broader social, economic and political issues associated with a decline in local food production/consumption and an increased consumption of imported foods are numerous, and can include cultural disruption. In Samoa, preference for imported goods has seen people selling locally grown agricultural products to use the revenue to purchase tinned and processed foods. This has been attributed in part to the social value placed on imported goods, with a suggestion that local foods are 'underappreciated and devalued. Local products are associated with a poorer lifestyle while imported goods are associated with economic success' (Schultz, FAO, quoted in Melby, 2011: 25). Recent research suggests that one third to one half of the Samoan diet comprises imported products (Melby, 2011). An outcome of this 'food colonisation' (Koa Dunsford, 2010/2011: 17) is that Samoans now present one of the highest rates of obesity and non-communicable diseases in the world (World Health Organization, 2013).

Not all contemporary Samoan food is based on imported products, however. Traditional staple foods continue to have an important role in the day-to-day life of Samoans. Despite the significant impacts of colonisation, trade liberalisation and influences of Western lifestyle on food habits, local ingredients and traditional cuisine are still highly regarded, not only as a means for sustenance but as the foundation for meaningful exchanges and expressions of culture (Oliver et al., 2013: 38). For example, Melby (2011: 21) found that most Samoans ate taro on a daily basis, and fresh fish, breadfruit, pork, yams and other local crops were consumed regularly. Traditional dishes are still a part of everyday Samoan life and can be found at all significant holidays and occasions, in the homes of Samoans and ready-prepared (a form of Samoan 'takeaways') in many of the country's markets and roadside stalls. Where you are unlikely to find traditional Samoan cuisine, however, is on the tables of the country's tourism industry (Berno, 2011; Oliver et al., 2013; Oliver, 2013a).

## Tourism and food culture

So what does tourism have to do with changes in traditional dietary patterns in Samoa? The answer to this is twofold. Food, cuisine and food traditions are among the most foundational elements of culture (Timothy and Ron, 2013: 275). As the prime minister of Samoa reflected: 'Food is the gateway into all cultures. For Samoa, our food expresses our intimate relationship with the land, the sea and our ancestors' (Malielegaoi, quoted in Oliver et al., 2013: 11). Tourism is significant as it can play an important role in creating demand for and reinforcing the importance of traditional foods as a cultural product (Berno, 2011; Gössling and Hall, 2013; Timothy and Ron, 2013; Oliver, 2013a; Melby, 2011). For an increasingly significant number of tourists, food is an integral part of their travel experience. They believe that experiencing a destination's food is essential to understanding its culture (Berno, 2011; Berno et al., 2014). Traditional foods as an element of the tourism experience can be a powerful means for sustaining and reinforcing both cultural identity and economic self-sufficiency (Egan et al., 2006). To fully appreciate the potential for tourism to help sustain food traditions, it is important first to understand the significance of tourism as a global phenomenon and its role as a key economic driver for the South Pacific region.

One of the most significant economic, social and cultural phenomena since the mid-1900s has been the growth of tourism. Over the past 60 years, international tourism has increased exponentially, growing from 25 million international tourist arrivals in 1950 to one billion by the end of 2012 (UNWTO, 2013). Along with this expansion of tourism has come a growing awareness of the need for tourism to be sustainable. This has led to an increasing interest in the use of local resources in tourism development, along with the idea that host communities should benefit as much as possible from tourism, particularly in the areas of social and economic opportunities.

It is safe (and rather obvious) to say that food is one of the most important areas of the tourism industry – all tourists eat as part of their tourist experience. It is estimated that 70 billion meals per year (more than 200 million meals per day) may be consumed in tourism (Gössling et al., 2011). Ironically, however, despite the now well-accepted need for sustainable tourism, it has only been relatively recently that attention has been paid to the relationship between food production systems, culinary traditions, tourist consumption and sustainability. These relationships, however, can be critical to sustainability (Berno et al., 2014). Research suggests that distinctive local cuisines can be important as both a tourism attraction, and a means of shaping the image of a destination (Gössling et al., 2011; Cohen and Avieli, 2004; Hall et al., 2003; du Rand and Heath, 2006). Additionally, research also suggests that local food experiences in tourism can contribute to sustainable development, support agricultural diversification and contribute to climate change mitigation by reducing the 'carbon footprint' through a decrease in imported products (Gössling et al, 2011; Clark and Chabrel, 2007; Evert and Aitchison, 2008; Knowd, 2006; Sims, 2009). Significantly, Timothy and Ron (2013) suggested that cuisine, as a part of cultural heritage, is an important marker of social identity. They argue that traditional gastronomy as part of the tourist experience can empower communities, supporting them to achieve their goals for sustainability, and help them cope with tourism and achieve its potential in more responsible ways. How this can be operationalised in countries such as those in the South Pacific, where traditional foods are not a salient component of the tourism product, warrants further consideration.

## Tourism and food in the South Pacific

In global terms, the countries of the South Pacific[1] account for less than 1 per cent of the world's international tourist arrivals, but this small number is enough for tourism to be the mainstay of the region's economy. For many small South Pacific island nations tourism is one of the only (if not *the* only) economic sectors with sustainable growth potential (SPTO, 2013). Samoa is one such country. Samoa is heavily reliant on tourism to drive its economy. Tourism plays a leading role in foreign exchange earnings, equivalent to 25 per cent of GDP, and almost 10 per cent of the national workforce is engaged in tourism-related employment (CIA, 2013; Small Business Enterprise Centre of Samoa, 2010).

Traditionally, tourism to the South Pacific has been built on the 'sun, sea, sand' image associated with larger-scale mass tourism. In the South Pacific, this form of tourism has often resulted in a high degree of economic leakage, much of which can be attributed to the importing of food products to support the industry (Berno, 2011). Recent research by Sofield (2011) found that 70 per cent of food in the tourism industry in Samoa was imported (and up to 90 per cent for some of the larger hotels), which represented approximately US$24 million per annum. Of this, about 30 per cent of the products could not be replaced with local substitutes. However, the other 70 per cent of imports (with a total market value of US$17 million) could potentially be grown locally. The impact of this import substitution is significant – it has been identified through a value chain analysis that potentially 8,000 of Samoa's 14,000 smallholder farmers could each earn an annual income of US$2,000 (only 21 per cent of the population is employed in the formal economy earning wages, with a minimum wage of US$1,750 per annum) (Sofield, 2011).

Further, the *Samoan Tourism Development Plan 2009–2013* indicates that the future of tourism in Samoa will be strategically focused on promoting and delivering a unique and distinct 'Samoan experience'. This vision for tourism in Samoa aspires for tourism to contribute significantly to the long-term economic, environmental, cultural and social development and sustainability of the country, with equitable distribution of benefits throughout all of Samoa. Underpinning this is the understanding that to achieve this vision, Samoa must differentiate itself as a destination through unique competitive advantages and value-added through a genuinely authentic and unique Samoan experience. Part of this experience is the food; as discussed above, the way local ingredients are combined, prepared and consumed forms an important element of a destination's cultural identity and cultural heritage (du Rand and Heath, 2006).

## Samoa: organics, food and tourism – creating the foundation for dynamic change

With all of the positive benefits of including more Samoan foods and local products in tourism, why are there not more local products on the tourists' plates in Samoa? It would be naive to suggest that there is a singular reason for the high level of imported products in the tourism industry, and there are in fact a range of factors that act as both barriers and facilitators to the uptake of local foods in tourism in the South Pacific (Berno, 2011). As discussed above, traditional Samoan foods are 'alive and well' in the homes of Samoans. However, over the past century in particular, there has been a rapid increase in the preference for and consumption of imported food products. Reflecting this, one significant factor in the high degree of imported foods in tourism is that for the most part in the South Pacific tourism industry traditional Pacific food culture has been side-lined in favour of Western-style menus. Some menus do offer 'Pacific food'. This cuisine, however, is often devoid of authentic Pacific content and is what has come to be expected as Pacific Island 'tourism food' at themed island-night events. It is more often than not a mere parody of traditional foods (Berno, 2011; Oliver, 2013a).

Rather than reinforcing the cultural integrity and heritage value of traditional Samoan foods, tourism has often had quite the opposite effect. As Pacific chef Robert Oliver (2013a: 16) stated in response to the absence of Pacific foods in the tourism industry: 'Consider the consequences of telling a whole region that their food isn't good enough. Food is core to who we are . . . it is what nurtures us, it is our culture and sense of self . . . it is us.' This does not have to be the case in tourism, however. As Timothy and Ron (2013) suggest, highlighting traditional foods in tourism can empower local communities, and despite the apparent pess-imistic situation in Samoa, an innovative initiative is indeed empowering communities through linking local organic agricultural production, Samoan food heritage and the tourism industry.

## Case study: the Mea'ai Samoa Project

Many rural settlements in Samoa have small, diminishing populations, are isolated and lack the attributes for tourism development; there are few economic opportunities other than agriculture in these rural areas. For many years, agriculture was the backbone of Samoa's economy. Since the early 1990s, however, the world markets for Samoa's main export crops have diminished. Organic agriculture, however, has the potential to provide opportunities for Samoa particularly through supplying the tourism industry. In addition to the economic development opportunities it presents, organic agriculture is relevant for Samoa through the promotion of self-reliance, food security and food sovereignty. Organic agriculture is not a new concept in Samoa. Current farming practices in many communities are still based on traditional systems utilising organic approaches that sustain environmental integrity. The production of agri-food products that can be certified, labelled and sold as organic produce that meets international standards serves to both reinforce traditional husbandry practices as well as provide an opportunity to supply high-value products for a proximate (tourism) market (Mapusua, 2009).

In many ways, Samoa is leading the South Pacific in terms of organic agriculture. A local non-governmental organisation, Women in Business Development Inc. (WIBDI), has been instrumental for organic farming in Samoa, creating a network of farmers and working with them to achieve organic certification. In 2001, five WIBDI farms gained organic certification from the National Association for Sustainable Agriculture, Australia. To date, WIBDI has assisted more than 700 farms to become certified. Currently, there are 35,000 hectares of organic land in Samoa, representing more than 10 per cent of its entire geography (Oliver, 2014). This level of organic certification is unique within the Pacific and is an attribute which can be exploited (Duncan and Gray, 2011).

The potential opportunities to use tourism as a means to reinforce traditional Samoan agricultural systems and Samoan food culture, increase and spread the benefits of tourism and contribute to rural social and economic development have been recognised in Samoa. In a unique public–private sector collaboration, the Samoa Tourism Authority (STA), WIBDI, government departments and the tourism industry identified the opportunity to contribute to and support sustainable rural livelihoods and food security by better capitalising on existing and future opportunities to create additional income through improving market access for organic cash crops in the tourism sector. It was recognised that this required a multi-sectoral approach that would build unique relationships between agricultural production and tourism policy, planning and promotion. In doing so, the approach would also address broader socio-economic development and specific sectoral needs as identified in the *Samoa Tourism Development Plan 2009–2013*, the *Strategy for the Development of Samoa 2008–2012*, the *Fruit and Vegetables Sector Strategy for Samoa* and the *Framework for Action on Food Security in the Pacific 2011–2015*.

## *Mea'ai Samoa*: can a cookbook empower a community?

Increasing the uptake of local products and traditional cuisine in tourism is not just a supply issue; just because it is grown does not mean anyone is going to buy it. Along with increasing the production of local agricultural products, demand also needs to be stimulated. The idea of increasing the use of local agricultural products in tourism is by no means a new concept. However, what is being suggested here is different from other 'farm-to-table'-type approaches as it identifies the need to produce high quality organic agricultural products as well as create a new tourism product (a distinctive Samoan cuisine as a cultural tourism product) to stimulate demand and create benefits at both ends of the value chain. It also seeks to use cuisine to reinforce cultural identity and economic self-sufficiency, as well as contribute to national health and well-being.

Based on stakeholder consultation with the Samoan organisations discussed above, one of the solutions suggested was the development of a book that would act as a development tool to highlight the traditional cuisine of Samoa (and its contemporary interpretations) and promote it as one of the tourism attributes. The vision was not that of 'just another pretty cookbook', rather, it was of a book that would take a value chain approach ('plantation-to-plate') built on a foundation of empirical research, sustainable agriculture and sustainable cuisine. In taking this approach, the book would become a template for agricultural and tourism-related economic development by stimulating demand for local products in the tourism industry, and would help promote healthier lifestyles by encouraging Samoans to return to their traditional foods. Furthermore, by presenting the local cuisine as an authentic, healthy and desirable part of the Samoan experience, it would instil a sense of pride and confidence in the cultural value of Samoan foods, helping to '[shake] off the last vestiges of colonialism' (Oliver, 2013b; Oliver et al., 2013) (see Figure 31.1). But would others share this vision for a cookbook that could empower communities and provide a path for improved national health and economic prosperity? The answer was 'yes'.

## Sharing and committing to the vision: using tourism as a tool for development . . . one meal at a time

In recognition of the opportunities that tourism presents for economic development in Samoa, the New Zealand government (through its international development programme) is making a significant contribution to the Samoan tourism sector over a five-year period through the Samoa Tourism Support Programme (STSP) with a total budget of NZ\$19.8 million (US\$16 million). The STSP is designed to complement the efforts of the Samoan government and the private sector to develop tourism as the leading economic sector for the

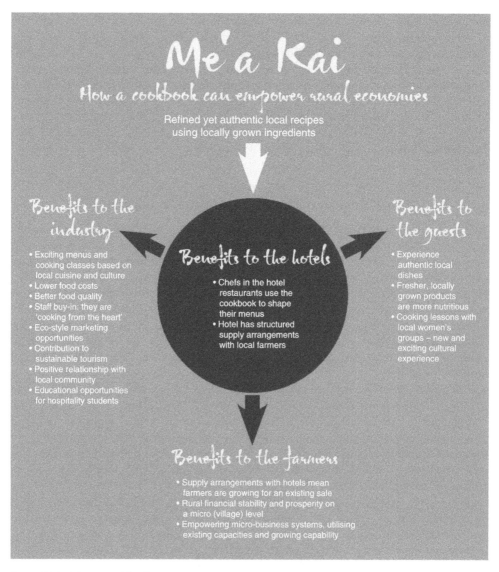

*Figure 31.1* How a cookbook can empower rural communities.
*Source:* Oliver et al. (2010: 476). Used with permission from Random House New Zealand.

country. A key aim of the funding is to produce co-benefits for agriculture through investment in public infrastructure that improves access to markets, and specific initiatives to increase demand for local products in the tourism industry (NZAP, 2011). At the recommendation of the Samoan stakeholders consulted, particularly the Samoa Tourism Authority, one of the initiatives funded under this programme was the Samoa Organic Cookbook Project – the development of a book highlighting locally grown and sourced organic products linking the tourism sector and the farmers to develop and promote Samoan cuisine through the 'plantation-to-plate' concept.

Just as the organic Samoan tourism cuisine cookbook was never conceptualised as 'just a cookbook', the way in which the book was developed reflected the shared goals of improved health, economic development and community empowerment. The book that resulted from the project, *Mea'ai Samoa: Recipes and Stories from the Heart of Polynesia*, was a collaborative effort between the cookbook team (two New Zealand consultants – a professional chef and an academic – and a Fijian photographer) and an in-country advisory committee comprising members of the Samoa Tourism Authority, WIBDI and the broader community. Extensive stakeholder consultation was undertaken in Samoa to inform the development of the book, which was written over a two-year period, and included conversations with experts in tropical organic husbandry, traditional healers (advice about health, nutrition and non-communicable diseases), farmers, tourism industry professionals and the people of Samoa themselves, who gifted the book team with their personal recipes and stories about the food and food culture of Samoa. A Samoan cultural advisor worked with the team throughout the entire project and provided a final cultural edit of the book to ensure its cultural validity.

The book was launched in November 2013 and, at the time of writing, anecdotal evidence suggested that it was having the desired effect. Even before the book went to press, WIBDI reported an increase in demand for organic dried bananas produced by some of their farmers. As their contribution to the cookbook, a restaurant, in Apia (the capital of Samoa) had developed a Samoan-style dessert using the bananas and added the dish to their menu. The dessert proved to be very popular and the restaurant placed two orders (totalling 5kg) with WIBDI for their dried organic bananas in a single week. The demand for this local dish was so high that WIBDI came close to running out of the bananas the following week. The chef of the restaurant continued to develop recipes for her establishment, and in response to having featured in a television production based on *Mea'ai Samoa* and its precursor publication *Me'a Kai: The Food and Flavours of the South Pacific* (Oliver et al., 2010) reported:

> Since finishing my time with Robert [chef and co-author of the book] . . . I am more inclined to take risks and experiment with local ingredients . . . There has definitely been a shift in my choice of ingredients when creating dishes at work . . . [I have been inspired] to look beyond food per se and really understand how my choices as a restaurateur could actually influence our economy here in Samoa . . . I have taken steps to support our local farmers by shopping mostly locally and introducing new dishes prepared with amazing Samoan organic produce. A new menu is in the works at the moment and I am very excited to showcase more Samoan produce especially to our overseas tourists.
>
> *(D. Rossi, quoted in Real Pasifik, 2013)*

Further anecdotal evidence (Oliver, 2013c.) indicated that additional tourism establishments were also adjusting their menus to highlight more traditional Samoan foods, with one re-working their menu based on the foods in *Mea'ai Samoa*, and another featuring a Samoan menu on Fridays. The Friday menu was as a direct result of the prime minister's speech at the launch of the book, in which he urged the tourism industry to incorporate traditional foods and local organic products into the menus (Netzler, 2013). Additionally, at the time of writing, the chef consultant who co-authored the book was in Samoa starting a pilot project with WIBDI, their organic farmers, and two hotels and two restaurants using *Mea'ai Samoa* as the foundation. There are further plans to establish a supply model that could be rolled out into other Pacific countries and other small island developing states (Oliver, 2013c).

# Conclusions

So can tourism be used as a conduit to rejuvenate traditional Samoan cuisine? Can a cookbook empower communities, contribute to sustainable food systems and reinforce cultural identity? In Samoa it appears that tourism can be a powerful tool for reinforcing the value of traditional foods and a book can be used as more than just a cookbook, it can also be used as a tool for development to help facilitate these outcomes. As chef and cookbook author Robert Oliver stated: 'In a small island state whose chief industry is tourism, the menus [in the tourism industry] are the business plan of the nation' (Oliver, 2014).

The sustainability of the benefits of the Mea'ai Project will be dependent on the ongoing commitment of the stakeholders, but initial indications are positive. Like most initiatives to support sustainable development, to operationalise the full value chain approach successfully, a broad range of stakeholders must continue to be involved. These include interests such as relevant government ministries, providers of tourism and hospitality education, chefs and/or hospitality management, the national tourism organisation, communities of interest (i.e., rural producers, non-governmental organisations, etc.) and others with interests in rural development, agricultural and/or tourism sectors. Implemented well, however, the value chain approach has the potential to sustain linkages between local agricultural producers, sustainable cuisine and the tourism industry, resulting in positive outcomes for a broad range of beneficiaries (Berno, 2011). *Mea'ai Samoa* used as a tool for sustainable development has the potential to drive increased use of local produce, raise the standards of Samoan cuisine in the tourism industry, reinforce pride in local foods and enhance the overall visitor experience, without a tin of corned beef in sight.

# Note

1  Members of the South Pacific Tourism Organisation (SPTO).

# References

Berno, T. (2011) 'Sustainability on a plate: linking agriculture and food in the Fiji Islands tourism industry', in R. Torres and J.H. Momsen (eds.), *Tourism and Agriculture: New Geographies of Consumption, Production and Rural Restructuring*, London: Routledge, pp. 87–103.
Berno, T., Devlin, N., Ezaki, A., Wilson, D. and Wolf, E. (2014) 'Sustainability in food and drink tourism', in E. Wolf (ed.), *Have Fork will Travel: A Practical Handbook for Food & Drink Tourism Professionals*, Portland: World Food Travel Association.
CIA (2013) *Samoa*, www.cia.gov/library/publications/the-world-factbook/geos/ws.html (accessed 29 November 2013).
Clark, G. and Chabrel, M. (2007) *Measuring Integrated Rural Tourism*, Department of Geography, Lancaster University, http://eprints.lancs.ac.uk/465/1/tvtg4.pdf (accessed 1 December 2013).
Cohen, E. and Avieli, N. (2004) 'Food in tourism: attraction and impediment', *Annals of Tourism Research*, 31(4): 755–778.
Duncan, S. and Gray, B. (2011) *The WIBDI Story: Technology, Tradition and Trade*, Dunedin: University of Otago.
du Rand, G. and Heath, E. (2006) 'Towards a framework for food tourism as an element of destination marketing', *Current Issues in Tourism*, 9(3): 206–234.
Egan, J.A., Burton, M.L. and Nero, K.L. (2006) 'Building lives with food: production, circulation and consumption of food in Yap', in R. Wilk (ed.), *Fast Food/Slow Food: The Cultural Economy of the Global Food System*, Lanham, MD: Altamira Press, pp. 31–47.
Evert, S. and Aitchison, C. (2008) 'The role of food tourism in sustaining regional identity: a case study of Cornwall, south west England', *Journal of Sustainable Tourism*, 16(2): 150–167.
Gössling, S. and Hall, C.M. (2013) 'Sustainable culinary systems: an introduction', in C.M. Hall and S. Gössling (eds.), *Sustainable Culinary Systems: Local Foods, Innovation, Tourism and Hospitality*, London: Routledge, pp. 3–44.

Gössling, S., Garrod, B., Aall, C., Hille, J. and Peeters, P. (2011) 'Food management in tourism: reducing tourism's carbon "foodprint" ', *Tourism Management*, 32: 534–543.

Hall, C.M., Sharples, L., Mitchell, R., Macionis, N. and Cambourne, B. (2003) *Food Tourism around the World: Development, Management and Markets*, Oxford: Butterworth-Heinemann.

Knowd, I. (2006) 'Tourism as a mechanism for farm survival', *Journal of Sustainable Tourism*, 14(1): 24–42.

Koa Dunsford, K. (2010/2011) 'Kaitiakitanga: protecting our oceans, islands and skies by inspiring a climate change of consciousness', *Dreadlocks: Islands, Oceans and Skies*, 6/7: 1–22.

Legge, D., Gleeson, D., Snowdon, W. and Thow, A.M. (2013) *Trade Agreements and Non-communicable Diseases in the Pacific Islands*, www.who.int/nmh/events/2013/trade_agreement.pdf (accessed 19 November 2013).

Mapusua, K. (2009) 'Organic agriculture in the Pacific region', in H. Willer and L. Kilcher (eds.), *The World of Organic Agriculture: Statistics and Emerging Trends 2009*, FIBL-IFOAM Report, Bonn: IFOAM/Frick, pp. 262–279.

Melby, D. (2011) *Gimme SAMOA That!: The Changing Diet in Samoa*, http://digitalcollections.sit.edu/cgi/viewcontent.cgi?article=2156&context=isp_collection (accessed 18 November 2013).

Netzler, J. (2013) *'Mea'ai Samoa' Cookbook Launched*, www.samoaobserver.ws/other/community/7858-meaai-samoa-cook-book-launched (accessed 1 December 2013).

NZAP (2011) *New Zealand–Samoa: Joint Commitment for Development*, www.aid.govt.nz/webfm_send/114 (accessed 18 November 2013).

Oliver, R. (2013a) 'The power of Pacific cuisine', *Spasifik*, 58: 14–18.

Oliver, R. (2013b) *Mea'ai Presentation*, presentation, University of Auckland, 6 November.

Oliver, R. (2013c) *Chef Consultant*, personal communication, 2 December.

Oliver, R. (2014) *Samoa: Small Nation, Big Story*, www.huffingtonpost.com/robert-oliver/samoa-small-nation-big-st_b_4909205.html (accessed 2 April 2014).

Oliver, R., Berno, T. and Ram, S. (2010) *Me'a Kai: The Food and Flavours of the South Pacific*, Auckland: Random House.

Oliver, R., Berno, T. and Ram, S. (2013) *Mea'ai Samoa: Recipes and Stories from the Heart of Polynesia*, Auckland: Random House.

Real Pasifik (2013) *Real Pasifik Chef: Dora Rossi Writes From Samoa*, http://realpasifik.com/real-pasifik-chef-dora-rossi-writes-from-samoa (accessed 19 November 2013).

Reddinger, A. (2010) 'Pineapple glaze and backyard luaus: Cold War cookbooks and the fiftieth state', in G. Barnhisel and C. Turner (eds.), *Pressing the Fight: Print, Propaganda, and the Cold War*, Boston: University of Massachusetts Press, pp. 193–208.

Samoa Bureau of Statistics (2014) *International Arrival Statistics February 2014*, www.sbs.gov.ws (accessed 2 April 2014).

Sims, R. (2009) 'Food place and authenticity: local food and the sustainable tourism experience', *Journal of Sustainable Tourism*, 17(3): 321–336.

Small Business Enterprise Centre of Samoa (2010) *Tourism Sector Profile*, Apia: Small Business Enterprise Centre of Samoa.

Sofield, T. (2011) *Tourism Value Chains for Poverty Alleviation*, seminar, Lincoln University, New Zealand, 28 March.

SPTO (2013) *Tourism and Sustainable Development in Pacific Islands. Sustainable Development Brief 15 April, 2013/SDWG*, www.forumsec.org/resources/uploads/attachments/documents/25-%20Tourism%20and%20Sustainable%20Development%20SDWG%20(18%20April%2013)%20FINAL.docx (accessed 19 November 2013).

Te Ara (2013) *Te Ara: The Encyclopedia of New Zealand*, www.teara.govt.nz/en/object/24262/corned-beef-tin-bull (accessed 19 November 2013).

Timothy, D.J. and Ron, A.S. (2013) 'Heritage and cuisines, regional identity and sustainable tourism', in C.M. Hall and S. Gössling (eds.), *Sustainable Culinary Systems: Local Foods, Innovation, Tourism and Hospitality*, London: Routledge, pp. 275–290.

UNWTO (2013) *1 Billion Tourists: 1 Billion Opportunities*, http://1billiontourists.unwto.org (accessed 19 November 2013).

World Health Organization (2013) *Towards Healthy Islands: Pacific Noncommunicable Disease Response*, www.wpro.who.int/southpacific/pic_meeting/2013/documents/PHMM_PIC10_3_NCD.pdf (accessed 19 November 2013).

# 32

# FOODWAYS OF LOWLAND SARIAYA

## Towards a sustainable food tourism

*Shirley V. Guevarra and Corazon F. Gatchalian*

### Introduction

Food tourism is one of the fastest growing areas of tourism. It is classified under cultural heritage tourism, which also includes the destination's history, gastronomy, values, beliefs, ideas, arts, traditional events and lifestyles, architecture, music, and festivals. Simms (2008) postulates that the concept of heritage finds significance from the fact that tourists value local foods, not only because of their perceived local character but also because of the "tradition" that they carry, having a long history of production in that particular destination. One of the selling points therefore of holiday foods is their ability to showcase the culture of the people in a destination—their hopes, aspirations, values, and beliefs. Food serves as an identity marker of the people of a certain destination, lending an authentic holiday experience.

This study specifically aims to: (a) describe the distinct performativities and values in the production and consumption of Sariaya's selected delicacies and beverage, making them central to its tradition; and b) harness the meanings and values derived from these foodways in the development of a sustainable food tourism.

Its arguments are grounded on Judith Goode's (1992) implicit notion of food as a folk tradition or folklore (foodlore or foodway). Goode posits that food does not only function as a means of survival but also as a cultural domain that is often elaborated into complex systems of meaning. More often than not, this complexity of meanings is manifested through the relationships that exist among the people or a group of people involved in food preparation, regulation, and consumption. These relationships feature social inclusion and exclusion, social status, and power/authority. It was noted, however, that the discourse on foodlore or foodway is more or less linked with the solidarity of a community, which was very evident among the locals of Sariaya. This validates Goode's theory that, "sharing certain special food communicates a positive identity and solidarity."

When this discourse is linked to the issue of sustainability, it is important to develop a sense of pride and ownership of these foodways/performativities among the local folks. Further, these should neither be commoditized, nor imposed on them but rather, allowed to be performed naturally.

## Folklore (folk tradition) in the context of food culture

Dan Ben-Amos (1984) defines folklore as an organic phenomenon, a body of knowledge, a mode of thought, or a kind of art. Thus, it is expected to exist with a structured group. In a social context, folklore exists as an artistic process or may be found in any communicative medium: musical, visual, kinetic, or dramatic. In sum, "folklore is artistic communication in small groups." Henry Glassie (1999) describes the center of folklore as a merger of individual creativity and social order, be it philosophical or political. He refers to it as a domain that upholds the right of man to construct a meaningful reality through artistic action. The author further posits that folklore stresses the interdependence and interplay of various areas: personal, social, aesthetic, ethical, cosmological, the beautiful, the good, and the true. He argues that practically, "folklore is the study of human creativity in its own context."

Culture is always associated with "traditions" that can be understood through folklore. Tradition is invented, reinvented and/or modified. There is a continuum and dialectic of invention/creation and modification of older ones. In the process of creation, the "small group" or the community invokes or creates a microcosm—a world—a worldview, a perspective, a prejudice, an interpretative framework. Part of this so-called microcosm is the normative. These are the things or behaviors that are accepted and not accepted as good, true, right, among others. In other words, the microcosm is very much involved in the group's judgmental capacity and/or ethical and aesthetical nature. Individual judgment is normally based on the group's norms. This microcosm marks the group's identity and individual identity as well. This creation, being a process, involves history. History involves human agents (actors), who in this study are the Sariayahins. It can therefore be deduced that in understanding food and culture, there is always an interplay of history, folklore (tradition), and human agencies.

Philippine folk cooking, which refers to the traditional domestic cuisine of the Filipinos, is historically hybrid (Lopez, 2006). Despite this hybridity, however, the archipelagic makeup of the Philippines—with 7,100 islands—gave rise to regional food identity that is given much weight by the Filipinos. Lopez attributes this to the fact that the "Philippines is a country where food is least nationalized" (Lopez, 2006: 362). Thus, the author considers Philippine cooking, in general, as non-existent. The arrival of Malays, Indonesians, Chinese, Americans, and Spanish has left a strong imprint on Philippine cooking. Spain apparently contributed 80 percent to the local dishes. Chinese cooking ranks second as shown by the adaptation and modification of the Chinese chow mein into pancit: bihon (rice noodle), canton (egg noodle), sotanghon (mung bean noodles), among others. Down south, Malay and Indonesian influences are very evident with the exclusion of pork in the region's menu. Spanish cooking can be seen from various carry-over recipes such as: arroz a la Valencia (Spanish cooking using Valencia rice). The Americans introduced hamburger, ice cream, pizza, and French fries.

What is interesting, however, is the fact that Philippine folk cookery is still strongly characterized by taboos, rituals, and value systems of the people. It is thus, a very good area to study.

## Anthropology of performance

The notion of performance has evolved from the usual stage performance. Performance in anthropology is known as performativity (performative element). Anthropologists and cultural theorists such as Victor Turner, Richard Schechner, Judith Butler, Clifford Geertz, and Michel Foucault regard culture as performative or possessing an element of performance.

This therefore explains their radical suggestion that understanding culture is to understand its performative complexities. Gender, for example, is performed and so are power, social status, and sexuality. Performance is a mimetic behavior. To imitate is to perform. What a performer imitates is action. In imitation, there is transference of action, performance being the product. In Levi-Strauss' (1973, in Layton, 2001) theory, this product is "cooked" (as opposed to raw food). The product is a mixture of symbols, thus regarded as a representation.

Performance also involves the communicative aspect of human interaction; it is socially co-related since there is an evaluative force in performance, there is an involvement of judgment, morally and aesthetically. Performance is intentional. It is always objective oriented, implicitly and explicitly. It aims "to transform." This performing power is exemplified by a cook reprimanding an assistant in the process, explicitly transforming the attitude towards his work. Performance therefore functions to affect human affairs—leaving individuals involved in a changed state. More importantly, performance is invented, planned, and contested (negotiated).

## Sustainable food tourism

Much has been written about sustainable tourism. Tao and Wall (2009: 138) mention the definition of the Brundtland Commission for sustainable development as one that meets the needs of the present without compromising that of the future. For Crococcis (1996), it involves sensitivity to the needs and aspirations of the host population. Altman and Finlayson (2003: 83) define sustainability as encompassing ecological, economic and cultural parameters—requiring a balance between commercial success, cultural integrity, and social cohesion. On the one hand, Getz (1991: 21) defines sustainability as "fostering and supporting conservation and ecologically responsible developments which do not deplete non-renewable resources and do not cause degradation of the environment." Simms (2008) tackled this in the context of recognizing the contribution of the major implications of food and drinks that are offered to tourists, in the economic, cultural, and environmental sustainability of tourism destination. She further argues in her paper that "local" food and drinks can improve the economic and environmental sustainability of both tourism and the rural host community through the encouragement of agricultural practices, in support of local commerce, and the creation of branding for the whole locality.

Given these various perspectives, it can be said that there are two major actors in the achievement of sustainability: the visitor and/or the visited. The former ensures sustainability whenever he patronizes the products of the destination and respects the physical/built and socio-cultural environments of the destination. The latter's role aims to provide the visitor with the products and services that would give him/her a total tourismic experience. It is important therefore that these factors are considered "in developing a viable food tourism program."

## Research methodology

Data gathering was conducted using several stages, the first of which was food mapping to determine the different food products that are peddled on sidewalks, in the marketplace, the *pasalubong* (items visitors buy as souvenirs or coming home presents) centers, and in the farms. It also aimed to determine the character of traditional Sariaya food and the apparent foreign or local influences. In general, food mapping was used to capture the foodscape of the locality.

The next stage included visits to informants' homes to get a feel of Sariayahins' hospitality. Central to these visits were the various meals and snack foods that were usually served to visitors. The local folks' food regulation, production, and consumption practices and their food habits/preferences and food patterns were also observed. The process was capped with product sampling on selected primary food products of Sariaya, which included *pinagong*, *minukmok*, and *lambanog*, and other secondary products. A result of cultural mapping is the profiling of Sariaya's major products that helped the researchers identify which of them best reflect the locality's culture.

To gain an insider's point of view, participant observation and interview sessions with selected locals were conducted. The group joined the celebration of Lent, the "Agawan" held during the Feast of San Isidro and the Feast of St Cristo de Burgos, the town's patron saint. Subsequent visits were also conducted to observe the daily lives of the people of Sariaya. Local "informants" were also regularly consulted for a detailed description of Sariaya's food culture. These included local cooks and a *lambanog* manufacturer. Preparation of fiesta food by a cook who is well known for his skill in cooking rice using a *kawa* (big frying pan made of cast iron, a version of a Chinese wok) was also observed. A focus group discussion was also conducted to validate the results of the interview and observation sessions.

Specifically, ethnography was used to identify the ways in which the Sariaya people construct meanings for themselves in their everyday lives (MacDonald et al., 2000). The focus of the study then was to analyze in detail interaction between individuals or within a group of people. This is where the participant observation technique became useful as it enabled the researchers to have first-hand information on the activities of the "subjects." Direct participations were done in the preparation and consumption of the three products that were identified as potential tourism products: *lambanog* (coconut wine) through *tagayan* (ritual of drinking), *nilupak* (crushed banana) through the ritual of *mukmukan* (production of nilupak), and *pinagong* (turtle bread).

More than the process, however, one of the key focal points of the study was the language used by the participants. In ethnomethodology, language is the fundamental resource or medium for micro-social interactions in order to capture the meaning of the interactions by the locals (MacDonald et al., 2000). Listening to conversations of the local informants provided additional data with special attention given to the peculiarity of Filipino terms or words that are used by the locality. An example is *"titimtiman ko lang po"* whose counterpart in the widely used version of the Filipino language is *"titikman ko lang po"* (I will just taste it). More than anything else, however, the shared understanding in the use of language by the participants gave more meaning to the study.

Data analysis used interpretive methodology in the surfacing of embedded meanings, themes, symbols, and values in the production and consumption of the three iconic products and other foods served every day and during town celebrations. Analysis of conversations with and among the locals also helped a lot in the analysis. The second phase of data collection involved visits to libraries and internet surfing to search for secondary sources of data. Secondary data included articles written about Sariaya by local historians, articles in souvenir programs of previous Sariaya town fiestas, journals, food culture and tourism books, and internet files on related topics.

## Discussion of findings

Sariaya is a lowland community in Quezon province that is located 126km southeast of Manila, well-known for its reputation as a haven for food *pasalubong* (souvenirs). It is a quaint town whose *poblacion* (town center) is dotted with grand Art Deco houses, some of which were declared heritage houses by the Philippine Historical Commission. These used to be the abode of coconut landlords, Sariaya being the site of coconut plantations during its glorious past in the early 1900s. Sariaya is also blessed with a beautiful landscape, the only town in Quezon province that is blessed on both sides, with a bay (Tayabas Bay) and the mystical Mt Banahaw, an extinct volcano that once spewed lava and ashes that fertilized the Sariaya lands. Just like most towns in the Philippines, Sariaya has a very rich culture that is deeply rooted in Catholicism. This rich culture can be gleaned from its three "iconic" product, namely *lambanog, pinagong*, and *minukmok*. Though believed to have originated from nearby provinces, these evolved into products that bear the locality's tradition and thus, are considered traditional Sariayahin food.

## Lambanog: magic of the spirit and words

*Lambanog* is a Sariayahin traditional alcoholic beverage made from fermented coconut. It is an indispensable fixture during birthdays, weddings, baptisms, festivals, and other social gatherings in the locality. The latter include the Agawan Festival or Bagakay Festival in May, the St Cristo fiesta in September, and even Holy Week, an occasion when drinking alcoholic beverages is prohibited. Today, *lambanog* has been reinvented to cater to foreign markets under the international pseudonym, Coco Vodka. This beverage is a combination of the Russian strong alcoholic beverage vodka (from fermented potato) and the main ingredient of the local wine, coconut. In Sariayahin folklore, *lambanog* is also considered by some as a spiritual drink, the spirituality being associated with Mt Banahaw, a sacred sanctuary for the folks in Quezon and other spiritual leaders and healers in the country. Many believe that the sacred waters of Mt Banahaw nourish the coconut trees in Sariaya. Mt Banahaw is a tourist attraction and is frequented especially during Holy Week due to its mystique.

Today, *tagayan ng lambanog* has adopted an alternative performance seemingly similar to the stereotypical *tagayan* of male members in most urban Philippine societies. In *tagayan*, participants assert certain aspects of their masculinity as they take issues and exchange ideas and personal stories during the drinking sessions. While the *tagayan* is regarded as a masculine domain, women in rural areas gather together to partake of lambanog. The latter is a social norm because women who join men during *tagayan* are labeled as *kiri* (easy girls) and are ostracized. During Holy Week, *lambanog* with *salabat* (ginger tea) keeps women awake while reading and/or chanting the *pasyon ni Kristo* (Passion of Christ), a ritual that is performed until the wee hours of the morning. The brew is also served as a substitute to chewing *nganga* (betel nut).

The *tanggero* (lead person in the drinking ritual) initiates the norms on how much alcohol or how many bottles must be consumed and how the lone glass moves. For example, will the glass move counterclockwise or clockwise? How high will the *tagay* (amount of *lambanog* in the glass) be? After the preliminaries, he will then officially declare the start of the ritual by proclaiming "*Na-ay po!*" (Here it is!). The members of the *umpukan* (group) are expected to reply "*pakinabangan po!*"—which literally means to share together or simply an acceptance of the invitation. The use of a single glass by the drinkers symbolizes fraternization (if the whole circle is composed of male members), trust, or *pakikisama* (cooperation) with one another. Usually, the person in authority or of higher status gets to drink first from the glass, thereby reflecting the deference by the participants to power and social status. In return, he is expected to act as the "leader" of the group. Linton (1936, in Layton, 1997) articulates that a person who is accorded a status is expected to act accordingly and be treated in a certain way during interaction. This practice can also be gleaned from the Subanons in Mindanao, the second biggest island in the Philippines. What is interesting in *tagayan* is the verbal jousting between two or more participants especially during conflict resolutions or negotiations. *Tagayan*, therefore, serves as a venue for colorful negotiations or management of conflicts. The fluidity in the discussion is fueled by the spirit of the *lambanog*, the drink being unusually high in alcohol. In the past, the resolving parties exchanged words by singing and dancing to the accompaniment of a guitar, a ritual that is occasionally performed in the outskirts of the town and during fiestas or before important guests of the local government in the poblacion.

Lastly, *tagayan* also served as a venue for romantic linguistic practice between a male and a female who are in an intimate relationship or in the courting stage. A female member not used to drinking but trapped into joining the *umpukan* (group), may be saved by a male member by exclaiming *"Sasakupin ko na lang po!"* (I'll take the drink for her). It can be said therefore that *tagayan* has played a very important role in the cultivation and nurture of relationships among the local folks. While it showcases solidarity/community, it also features class and gender divide.

### Nilupak and the (he)art of courting

*Nilupak*, commonly known as *minukmok* in Sariaya, is a sweet delicacy made from crushed *saba* (a banana variety) or *balinghoy/kamoteng kahoy* (cassava) mixed with milk, sugar, butter, and young coconut meat. It is formed into a cake (*laok*) then shaped in various forms: a plate, a bird, or a heart. Modern variants include the addition of ground peanuts or grated cheddar cheese for garnishing, the latter of foreign influence.

The ritual of producing *mukmuk*, called *mukmukan or pagmumukmok*, played various roles in the olden days. A Sariayahin remarked that, *"Ang mukmukan ay ang puso ng ligawan noong mga araw!"* (the *mukmukan* was the heart of courtship during the olden days!). It served as the young gentlemen's strategy of courting in the barrio. The young men interjected their hearts' intentions with the *pagbabayo* (pounding of the mixture) to win the hearts of their love interests or sweethearts who either give in to the sweet words or play hard-to-get (*pakipot*). The art of *panliligaw* (courtship) in the *mukmukan* was usually transformed into *biruan* (joking).

Today, *pagmumukmok* has been elevated and/or has been reinvented to serve as a forum for bigger socialization and recreational activities: during fiestas, welcoming of guest(s), a venue for *tête à tête* among local folks, where issues are discussed. It has remained, however, associated with *taga-linang* (those residing in the plains at the town's outskirts) and the mountains. An informant living at the foot of Mt Banahaw shared that *mukmukan* also serves as a venue for *tupadahan* (get together) among the people in the community. Each member in the whole neighborhood brings ingredients for the *minukmuk* and they convene in a designated spot, usually the house of a *barangay* (barrio) official. While performing the ritual, they commune by exchanging pleasantries and stories/anecdotes, discuss issues, update each other on gossip and happenings in the community. Adults and children alike happily partake of the finished product. Sometimes, the *mukmukan* and the drinking of *lambanog* or *tagayan* are held simultaneously, with women assisting younger male members in the *pagbabayo* (pounding using a big wooden mortar and pestle) and children playing games while most of the adult male members congregate for the *tagayan*. These activities may or may not be accompanied by singing and dancing. Needless to say, the *tupadahan* or mukmukan exemplifies the community's solidarity.

## *Pinagong: the ode of a sweet accident*

*Pinagong Sariaya* has remained one of the most popular snacks or *pasalubong* (gift from a trip) that travelers usually buy and bring from Sariaya to Manila or to the nearby Bicol region. It is a sweet bread shaped like a *pagong* (turtle), which owes its sweetness to carabao's milk and coconut oil. It is considered by the local folks as the cupcake or cheesecake of Sariaya, an ordinary *pangkape* (for coffee breaks) and *pambisita* (for visitors). While most people point to a certain Eusebio Pisigan of the nearby town of Lucban, as the one who accidentally formed the turtle-shaped product out of *pandesal* (popular breakfast bread), its production was given more importance in Sariaya and thus became Sariayahin. Its production is a masculine domain requiring skills (talent) and strength.

What is given more enthusiasm by the Sariayahins, however, is the manner of consuming *pinagong*. The locals go to the extent of teaching visitors the proper way of eating it—which is to dip it into black coffee, in the process lending sweetness and a creamy taste to the brew. One informant said that relatives who had been away for quite a time and had forgotten this traditional manner of consumption are reminded and/or "reprimanded." *Pinagong* is also served during special occasions like birthdays, *pabasa* (reading of the passion of Christ), and even during fiestas either as food for visitors or vended alongside *kakanins* (native cakes). Children usually mix it with spaghetti, which is an unusual combination. In general, the enthusiasm that the locals show for its preparation and consumption had truly made *pinagong* a distinct Sariaya product.

These delicacies prove that the local folks recognize their continuous engagements with other cultures. The dynamism of food regulation, production, and consumption in Sariaya lies in the colorful negotiations with other folk traditions. As Doreen Fernandez (2003: 61) explains, Filipino cuisine "is as dynamic as any live and growing phase of culture, has changed through history, absorbing influences, indigenizing, adjusting to new technology and tastes, and thus, evolving." The Sariayahins throughout their history absorbed outside influences either through acculturation or by simply assimilating these influences from other Quezon towns, from other southern Tagalog provinces, and from their past colonial masters.

In the process of historicizing the various influences in Sariaya's food culture, the folks have managed to engage in "creative" negotiations to modify these influences. The resulting products become a fusion of various tastes which were embraced as distinctly Sariayahin. Manufacturers of *pinagong* in Sariaya, for example, have lent a different taste that made it pleasantly different from and better than its predecessor, *Lucban pinagong*. Thus, it was successfully reinvented into what is now called *pinagong Sariaya*. This only proves that the process of borrowing food culture by local folks elicited a conscious and unconscious cultural reaction. Specifically, they made necessary adaptations in preparing or cooking a "foreign" product. They were not aware that, in the process, they were able to transform a product and made it their own. Through enculturation and by handing down these recipes from generation to generation (while continuously undergoing modification), the younger generations are able to learn the culture. Specifically, children are taught how to combine various ingredients and learn how to adopt the value of patience as Philippine cookery is generally sequential and involves slow cooking, making the whole process a whole patterned piece (Lopez, 2006).

Another product of the processes of adaptations and/or borrowings can be manifested in the semantic shifting of terms or names (like that of *nilupak* to *mukmuk*), ingredients (like in the *pinagong*), cooking processes, flavorings, and even social positions (Fernandez, 2003). An example is the *pancit habhab*, an equally popular noodle dish in Sariaya and other towns in the Quezon province due to its unique taste and manner of consumption. The noodles are placed and eaten directly from small squares of banana leaf. The Sariaya version of this product has deviated a little bit from the original, tangy and less spicy to a stronger taste profile. Lastly, the processes of acculturation and adaptation or borrowings also enrich local food terms or build the local food dictionary.

Sariaya's food culture therefore is a fusion of both local and foreign cuisine, thus, a hybrid. It is evolving and so is the Sariayahins' identity. This argument is based on Fenella Cannell's (1999) notion of cultural identity, which she argues to be dynamic and in constant flux. Her articulation was gleaned from her study of Bicol culture, a nearby province of Sariaya, which she described as "sitting oddly in anthropological discussions because its 'identity' seems guaranteed neither by its own claims to the possession of unchanging authenticity, nor by its involvement in political and cultural 'resistance' " (Cannell, 1999: 254).

In this sense, Cannell (1999) believes that ambiguities and ironies among others are essentials in the descriptive identity of a culture. As she points out, "ambiguity, irony and irresolution are also kinds of social fact, not to be explained away simply as a way-station en route to a higher degree of cultural certainty, any more than they are to be portrayed as the 'post-modernist' fragmentation of some cultural coherence." Most of the time, these irregularities, ironies, and ambiguities are manifested through the actors' continuous negotiations with several relationships and engagements such as other communities' traditions, religions, folklores, and individualities. These social facts are instrumental in the fluidity of a culture.

The economic condition and the geographical location are also considered material to these engagements. Thus, perhaps, a more crucial discourse in tracing "indigenuity" is the process of indigenization as culture is never static and not written in stone. It is always fluid and dynamic as pointed out by Fernandez (2003). Cannell (1999) believes that Philippine culture is always a process of negotiation. This study therefore suggests that the quest for the indigenous is also a quest for the folks' continuous engagements with different traditions. Perhaps these engagements can be used as references in understanding the meaningful worldviews of the Sariayahins on food and other cultural forms. During indigenization, Sariayahin folks do not claim the exclusivity of these foods as indigenous to Sariaya, but recognize the "importation" of these influences.

Most of the folks recognize their delicacies as products of evolutionary borrowings and adaptations of their food performances and non-exclusive indigenous food performers. In these processes, they embraced these delicacies as local items of pride. *Nilupak* is considered as one of the Sariayahin delicacies but folks believe that *nilupak* is predominantly a southern Tagalog delicacy and not necessarily belonging to Sariaya alone. *Pinagong* today is believed to be indigenous to Sariaya with commuters demanding *pinagong Sariaya* from bus vendors along the major highways to and from the neighboring towns. While the nearby Lucban town is the origin of *pinagong*, this delicacy was given a new character in Sariaya and thus, the bread has reinvented itself into a fully fledged Sariaya product. *Lambanog* traces its origin from nearby San Juan, Batangas, but became part of Sariayahin culture. These products evolved into iconic local foods, which were identified as having a big potential in developing Sariaya's food tourism program. Local food provides the tourists a sustainable tourism experience because of its appeal to the visitor as they quest for authenticity in the destination. The three iconic products, having been re-invented by the local folks to form part of Sariaya's food culture, are considered "traditional" and bearers or symbols of Sariayahin culture. They are actually being mistaken as authentic products of Sariaya.

## Towards a sustainable food tourism program

An equally important issue is discourse on harnessing Sariaya's foodways towards sustainable food tourism. This should be viewed in three ways: economic, environmental, and socio-cultural. Economic sustainability can be achieved from the use of raw materials that are planted/grown and cooked/manufactured in the locality, thereby benefiting the local farmers, fishermen, and producers. Local products should be prioritized over those coming from other places. Sariaya happens to be blessed by the bounty of the sea, mountain, and the plains. The latter explains why its patron saint is St Isidore (San Isidro de Labrador), the patron saint of farmers.

Environmental sustainability on the one hand, can be achieved when the methods of planting, growing, and harvesting/catching (fish) do not destroy the environment or nature. Sariaya should thus continue its program of preserving its natural resources such as the regulation of fishing activities and methods of catching fish and the planting of mangroves along rivers. Socio-cultural sustainability is dictated by the locals' preservation of their traditional or local rituals of food production and consumption of food. While food culture is evolving to match the needs of tourists, this should not be commodified. For as long as culture remains humane and functions towards the betterment of the lives of the people, it should not be tampered with. As much as possible, the rituals or performativities that accompany the production and consumption of food should be conducted in their natural form and natural setting. After all, the traditional element is what attracts the tourist who generally wants to see, smell, and taste the exotic, the natural and the unique.

## Concluding reflections and recommendations

It can be concluded therefore that the foodways of Sariaya are a product of a continuous inter-action between structure and the agency which is in line with the post-structuralist theory that Bourdieu, Foucault, Giddens, and Berger (Layton, 2001) advocate. While the Sariaya folks, who in this study represent the agency, were able to transform some of their products from their original form (which represents tradition/structure) to what they are now, these products still bear their basic character and/or the rituals that accompany their production and consumption. This seeming balance shows that the agency does not dominate the structure and vice versa, but rather they interact to arrive at an acceptable result that will benefit the end-users. This can be gleaned from the three iconic products which are results of the fusion of the indigenous Sariayahin and what are considered foreign tastes. Through the continuous modification of the latter, the locals were able to create products that were considered as local Sariaya products. In *lambanog*, they transformed the product into an inter-national brand but preserved the ritual of *tagayan*. In *mukmukan*, the use of cheddar cheese and/or peanuts was a departure from the product's usual flavor profile, the former being of Western origin. Also, its use as a venue for courtship is slowly fading. However, in this fast-paced world that is dominated by technology, the *tupadahan* remains as a communal activity for *mukmukan* among the local folks in the outskirts of Sariaya. In *pinagong*, the locals' success in creating a unique way of consuming it—at times, zealously imparting it to visitors and "enforcing" it on relatives—is a manifestation of modifying a consumption practice without necessarily creating a distinctly different product.

It can be said that in the process of indigenizing these influences, local values, meanings, and symbols were interwoven by the local folks into the regulation, production, and consumption of the products thereby breathing a new character into the product, which makes it truly

Sariayahin in nature. This explains their continuous engagements with their culture, their community, and their environment. Social inclusion and exclusion are some of the norms that characterize the regulation, production, and consumption of the local products especially the three "iconic" Sariaya products. It is, however, interesting that these norms are tempered by the negotiations that usually dominate the food performances. This also gives credence to the notion that food serves as a great democratizer of classes. Another common manifestation in Sariayahin food culture is a sense of social solidarity. The historical developments of these delicacies also point out a sense of community or *communitas* (Turner, 1969). Moreover, the value of patience and resilience can be seen in the production of *lambanog* and *minukmok*. The brewing of lambanog, for example, involves the tedious process of collecting the sap of the palm atop coconut trees using makeshift bamboo bridges that connect one tree to another. Patience is one of the values, alongside meanings and symbols, that reflect the people's world-views to the community. They shape the existence of individuals in accordance to his/her interaction with other people. The metaphors and meanings derived from this study are good reflections of the richness of Sariaya food culture. This food culture is an amalgam of the various influences from the town's colonizers and neighboring towns. These worldviews, the values, and the meanings that are embedded in the production and consumption of the three products and the town's other products should therefore be highlighted in Sariaya's food tourism program. Food as a means of expressing the region and its culture can be used as a way of differentiation for a destination in an increasingly competitive global marketplace (Hall et al., 2003). It creates branding that Sariaya achieved through its local products.

Lastly, the sustainability of Sariaya's food tourism should be measured in terms of economic, environmental, and socio-cultural factors. It should help the locality economically by using or promoting local raw materials. It is environmentally sound when it does not destroy the natural or physical well-being of the place. It is socio-culturally sustainable if it ensures the preservation and respect of the socio-cultural integrity of Sariaya's foodways.

Furthermore, capability-building seminars such as values-infusion programs and other technical programs, such as food safety, cost control, and marketing, should be conducted. These interventions will equip the locals with the technical knowhow on how to standardize the products without diluting their cultural character. Whether Sariaya's food products are iconic or not, these find significance in their role as cultural lenses through which tourists get a glimpse of the place and the people who prepared them (Simms, 2008). By buying these local foods, tourists can somehow easily connect with the local folks and the locality. This connection will also play a role in the tourists' place and memory-making. Simms (2008) validates this by saying that local foods play a role in the development of an integrated tourism program. This is because they symbolize the destination and its culture, "provide a moral feel-good factor associated with their consumption and enable visitors to experience a sense of connection to the destination—before and after their visit" as the author also articulates. This can be enhanced if tourists are allowed to immerse themselves in the culture of Sariaya by providing venues where they can naturally participate in these rituals. Another approach is through the conduct of storytelling sessions or allowing local folks to give oral narratives on the production and consumption of these local products. It can be said therefore that the above-mentioned Sariaya delicacies are not merely reduced to being *pasalubong* that tourists buy and bring to their families and friends but rather, they serve to evoke memories of their genuine food experience in Sariaya. This is definitely a sensory experience—seeing, feeling, smelling, and tasting the place. Lastly, for tourists to gain a strong sense of connection, observation tours should be interactive, in order to encourage them to participate in the events and, in the process, capture that "authentic feel" of the tourist destination. This lived experience validates Brass' (in Yeoman et al., 2007: 1128) take on the tourists' quest for "authenticity"—also their search for "non-material" and deeper experience.

A replication of this study to cover other regions or provinces is recommended. Lopez (2006) mentions that minimal studies are evident in the analysis of the patterns and meanings of Filipino consumption, thus, needing further research.

## Acknowledgements

This study, which aimed to develop a tourism program for Sariaya, is a centennial gift of the University of the Philippines (UP) in 2008 to help alleviate poverty in the municipality. True to its mandate as the lone National University in the Philippines and as a research university, UP funded a multi-disciplinary open grant to five UP colleges: Home Economics, Asian Institute of Tourism, Music, Architecture, and Human Kinetics. The authors would therefore like to thank the University, through the Office of the Vice Chancellor for Research and Development, for extending financial support to this project. Assistant professor Sir Anril Tiatco, the project's university research assistant and now a UP faculty member, is also sincerely acknowledged for his invaluable contribution in writing the initial reports from which this article was extracted and for documenting the various activities and materials needed for the project. The authors also thank the Sariaya Tourism Council and the local respondents, Sariaya Mayor and Mrs. Rosauro Masilang, Mikaela V. Guevarra, student assistant, Joy Quiambao, support staff, and Dr. Nanette Dungo for her comments.

## References

Altman, J. and Finlayson, J. (2003) "Aborigines, tourism and sustainable development," *The Journal of Tourism Studies*, 14(1): 78–91.

Ben-Amos, D. (2008) "Seven strands of tradition: varieties in its meaning in American folklore," *Journal of Folklore Research*, 21(2–3): 97–131.

Cannell, F. (1999) *Power and Intimacy in Lowland Christian Philippines*, Quezon City: Ateneo de Manila University Press.

Coccossis, H. (1996) "Tourism and sustainability, perspectives and implications," in G.H. Priestly, J. Edwards, and H. Coccossis (eds.), *Sustainable Tourism? European Experiences*, Wallingford: CAB International, pp. 1–21.

Fernandez, D. (2003) "Culture ingested: on the indigenization of Philippine food," *Gastronomica*, 3(1): 58–71.

Fernando, G. (1976) *The Culinary Culture of the Philippines*, Manila: Bancom Audio-Vision Corp.

Getz, D. (1991) *Festivals, Special Events, and Tourism*, New York: Van Nostrand Reinhold.

Glassie, H. (1999) *Material Culture*, Bloomington, IN: Indiana University Press.

Goode, J. (1992) "Food," in R. Bauman (ed.), *Folklore, Cultural Performances, and Popular Entertainments*, Oxford and New York: Oxford University Press.

Hall, C.M., Sharples, L., Mitchell, R., Macionis, N., and Cambourne, B. (2003) *Food Tourism Around the World*, Oxford: Butterworth-Heinemann.

Layton, R. (2001) *An Introduction to Theory in Anthropology*, Cambridge: Cambridge University Press.

Lopez, M. (2006) *A Handbook of Philippine Folklore*, Quezon City: University of the Philippine Press.

MacDonald, M., Harvey, L., and Hill, J. (2000) *Theories and Methods*, London: Hodder and Stoughton Educational.

Simms, R. (2008) "The role of food tourism in sustaining regional identity: a case study of Cornwall, south west England," *Journal of Sustainable Tourism*, 16(2): 150–167.

Tao, T. and Wall, J. (2009) "A livelihood approach to sustainability," *Asia Pacific Journal of Tourism Research*, 14(12): 137–152.

Turner, V. (1969) "Liminality and communistas," in *Ritual Process: Structure and Anti-Structure*, Chicago: Aldine Publishing.

Yeoman, I., Brass, D., and McMahon-Beattie, U. (2007) "Current issues in tourism: the authentic tourist," *Tourism Management*, 28(4): 1128–1138.

# 33

# GASTRONOMIC TOURISM

## Development, sustainability and applications – a case study of County Cork, Republic of Ireland

*Clare Carruthers, Amy Burns and Gary Elliott*

## Introduction

Food and gastronomy have a long-established link with tourism and have become a key factor in the development and promotion of tourism. Local cuisine defines a destination and is an integral aspect of local culture; it is often synonymous with the history and heritage of a place, identifying and distinguishing one destination from another nationally, regionally and, in some cases, locally. Intensified tourism competition often means that such localised identities become a powerful marketing tool as 'local culture is becoming an increasingly valuable source of new products and activities to attract and amuse tourists' (Vasileska and Reckoska, 2010: 1622). Hall and Mitchell (2005: 73) note that food and drink have, in fact, become 'a significant component in popular culture in the developed world', an 'important part of contemporary lifestyles' and hence an important part of tourism.

More recently, specific initiatives to draw together the two concepts of food and tourism are emerging at the local level, and these have a contribution to make towards strengthening the tourism product; sustaining local food production and enhancing the visitor experience, in particular in rural areas (Boyne et al., 2003). It is within this context that the authors propose gastronomic tourism on the island of Ireland as a viable option for sustainability in terms of economy, environment and society.

## Gastronomic tourism – definitions, development and growth

Gastronomy is particularly difficult to define, with many differences arising within the literature linking it to the art, science and culture of food, and has different traditions across the world. Culinary traditions represent an aspect of a region's gastronomy, and culinary tourism has been defined as 'the intentional, exploratory participation in the foodways of an other – participation including the consumption, preparation and presentation of a food item, cuisine, meal system, or eating style considered to belong to a culinary system not one's own' (Long, 2004: 21).

Also referred to as gastronomic, gourmet or cuisine tourism, it involves travelling to a region famous for a particular food/style, food/cuisine or wine or travelling to take food/ wine courses, festivals, events, educational trips/tours, trails and courses, etc. Specifically, gastronomic tourism, as opposed to culinary, gourmet or cuisine tourism, is 'typically related to interest in the broader dimension of wine and food and the cultures and landscapes that produce them' (Hall and Mitchell, 2005: 75). This is not an unimportant point when discussing the link specifically between food, tourism and sustainability, as inherently the culture and landscapes of food are vitally important aspects of such sustainability. Food tourism encompasses all the elements of gastronomic, culinary and gourmet tourism as defined by Hall and Mitchell (2001: 308) as 'visitation to primary and secondary food producers, food festivals, restaurants and specific locations for which food tasting and/or experiencing the attributes of specialist food production regions are the primary motivating factors for travel'.

Motivation for gastronomic tourism has tended to be in the background or a secondary factor of the tourist experience, but that is changing as decisions about where to travel based on food choices are becoming primary motivating factors (Hall and Mitchell, 2005), rather than secondary or tertiary, as noted by Mintel (2009: 1): 'Gastronomy is hot around the world.' Vasileska and Reckoska (2010: 1622) discuss the increasing focus of wine and food being central in travel decision making and being in fact 'the hallmark attraction of a number of destinations around the world'.

Factors fuelling this growth include the increased interest in food and the raised profile of food in the media. This is coupled with increased multiculturalism, increased immigration to the UK and North America and the free movement of people within Europe. Mintel (2009: 1–2) notes that, while there is a lack of empirical evidence in regard to the growth and development of this sector, and indeed the market profile of a gastronomic tourist, certainly 'anecdotal evidence suggests . . . that it is precisely because ethnic restaurants have proliferated in recent years that more and more people want to travel to the countries where the food originates, in order to sample it first-hand'.

## Consumer trends and the gastro-tourist

Consumer trends in relation to both food and tourism as separate concepts have changed radically. The growth in the short-break market and niche tourism offerings, wider opportunities for travel, wider travelled and more sophisticated consumers in terms of their tourism consumption habits and the seeking out of more specific types of tourism activity associated with culture, education, lifestyles and unique, enriching and memorable experiences are all contributory factors. These trends are coupled with increased interest in food issues and the raised profile of food in the media such as health and lifestyle, food safety and standards, demand for more organic food and less food waste, food provenance, food miles and rising food costs, all of which are raising concerns regarding the sustainability of local food and food-related industries, socially, economically and environmentally. Initiatives and responses to such issues include the rise in the focus on aspects such as local food and food production, artisan food producers, farm shops and the resurgence of the traditional farmers' market. Initiatives such as Eat Local and the Slow Food movement, once considered to be relatively marginal, are becoming increasingly more mainstream. As a result 'travellers are becoming ever more knowledgeable about food and they avidly follow gastronomic trends, seeking out new destinations, where they can sample authentic fare that is native to a particular country or region' (Mintel, 2009: 1).

This becomes a virtuous circle, as consumer concern for more locally produced, sourced and organic products then leads to increased demand and expenditure and hence helps sustain these local initiatives and contribute towards the economic sustainability of local food production, manufacturing and processing. Further, Boyne and Hall (2004) discuss the potential to be gained from the visiting friends and relatives (VFR) tourism market, in that, as a consequence, local people increase their spend on local produce as part of the hosting of friends and family. Indeed they note that this can 'assist the purpose and potential of prompting food and tourism as the basis for developing a rural brand' (Boyne and Hall, 2004: 82), yet du Rand et al. (2003) note that the link between food and destination marketing is something that has received very little attention in the extant literature.

While Mintel (2009) notes that detailed demographic details in this niche market are sparse, some general trends are apparent in the European market. These are that gastronomic tourists are thought to be professionals, at the peak of their careers, in the 30–50+ age group, that they are adventurous and cultural travellers, with a higher level of educational attainment and higher than average disposable incomes. They seek experiences beyond just enjoying food and wine, but that incorporate activities that are based on learning and active participation, etc. Mintel goes on to note that, in addition, the greying market is a major driver. Everett and Aitchison (2008) identified a similar profile in their study on food tourism in Cornwall. Here they identified typical food tourists as empty-nest, 50+, well-informed consumers with higher than average disposable incomes, prepared to spend on quality food produce and that, in particular, they were not the typical high-season tourists commonly associated with Cornwall.

This profile fits closely with that of the creative tourist, as proposed by Richards and Wilson (2007). Richards and Wilson (2007: 18) propose creative tourism as an extension/ alternative to cultural tourism that 'depends far more on the active involvement of tourists' and many tourism destinations are seeking these creative/experiential aspects of tourism as a more sustainable model, often with gastronomic tourism as an aspect. Richards suggests that future growth in cultural tourism is much more likely to be found in more specific niche offerings such as 'arts tourism, architectural tourism, festival tourism, opera tourism, gastronomic tourism and creative tourism' (Richards, 2003). Further, Croce and Perri (2010: 6) identify the common features of both cultural tourism and food and drink tourism, noting that holidays 'based around offering a gastronomic experience will necessarily include one or more components of cultural tourism'. As many tourism destinations are seeking these creative/experiential aspects of tourism as a more sustainable model, there is certainly further scope and opportunity for gastronomic tourism to offer just such a niche. Du Rand et al. (2003) also argue that as culture plays an increasingly important role in tourism, so too does food, as a key element of that culture.

There are also clearly links here to other tourism niches with similar market segment profiles, including rural tourism, slow tourism and agri-tourism, all of which are closely related to the underlying concepts of sustainability in food and gastronomic issues. For example, agri-tourism usually includes holidays on farms, which might include any aspects of the local food and produce and/or experiential learning, hence gastronomic tourism and agri-tourism are inextricably linked as the concept revolves around the lived experiences of agricultural communities and hence their food.

## Food, tourism, gastronomy and sustainability

Gastronomic tourism can benefit a destination in many ways. It can help position and market a destination for tourism, enhance tourism image and visitors' experiences, contribute towards place/destination branding, contribute towards the sustainable development of the local food industry and economy, provide the economic stimuli for primary food production, processing and manufacturing through tourist spend, stimulating demand from new market sectors and expanding existing markets through, for example, souvenir foods and developing new tastes. It can also help to diversify the tourism product and develop new market opportunities for food providers, for example local farmers, local food producers, etc. Indeed Hall and Sharples (2003) specifically note that new agricultural products and tourism have commonly been pursued as economic diversification models in rural economies in response to economic restructuring. Boyne and Hall (2004) discuss how local food produce not only strengthens the local tourism product, but also has the capacity to contribute towards stimulating demand and expanding the markets for local foodstuffs, through both local consumption and tourists then seeking out that produce upon returning home.

There are many examples of these gastronomic tourism opportunities that evidence growth in this market, such as Balti breaks in Birmingham (Hatch, 2006), gastronomic tours of London incorporating culinary skills (Savy Club, n.d.) and Ireland Gourmet Tours (Cellatours, n.d.). Culinary tours and trails are also a common feature of gastronomic tourism and a key element in rural and regional development strategies, such as that of the Isle of Arran taste trail in western Scotland. The trail initiated by the local enterprise agency, the Argyll and the Islands Enterprise Agency, aims to bring together food producers, suppliers, outlets, restaurants and retailers and establish closer links with tourism, promoting gastronomic tourism as a niche tourism product on the Island of Arran, the focus of which is very much on local produce, and encouraging back-linkages between farms and the point of sale (Boyne et al., 2002: 91).

Similarly the case of Cornwall, in the south-west of England, evidences the potential for gastronomic tourism to contribute towards sustainable development as well as bringing the tourism benefits associated with economy and society. With Rick Stein, Jamie Oliver and Paul Ainsworth championing the regional local fresh produce, in particular its seafood, Cornwall is firmly established on the gastronomic tourism map. However, there are significant environmental issues related to tourism in Cornwall, in particular associated with its intensely seasonal nature and associated congestion, which highlight the inherent tensions in the links between gastronomy, tourism and sustainability. When we consider the very nature of many of the initiatives and movements surrounding gastronomy, contemporary food issues and sustainability, for example the Slow Food movement and artisan food production, they are often the very antithesis of many aspects of tourism development, with their very essence being anti-commercialisation and commodification. The difficulties lie in managing the relationships between tourism development, food and sustainability.

In their study on Cornwall, however, Everett and Aitchison (2008: 157) found that local hospitality and tourism businesses in the area acknowledged that a reconnection with 'the tourist and the landscape via local food production networks could help reduce the negative environmental impact'. Further, they found that food tourism has the capacity to contribute towards increased visitor spend and extend the tourist season, hence contributing towards sustainable development, in particular in rural locations. Boyne et al. (2003: 134) discuss the reciprocal benefits, as 'local foodstuffs enhance and strengthen the tourism product while tourists and visitors provide a market for these products', underlining the clear link between food, tourism, gastronomy and sustainability. Indeed Boyne and Hall (2003) discuss the need to establish 'back linkages between the tourism and food-production sectors [which] can add value within an area's local economy'.

Further, du Rand et al (2003: 98) note that local food has the potential to contribute towards sustainability, authenticity and the economy in terms of destination development and marketing and that in fact food and drink offerings of a destination may be among 'its most important cultural expressions', in that cultural identity is often reflected in food experiences, ingredients and cooking methods. They argue that on this basis 'local and regional food is a feature that can add value to a destination . . . and may contribute to the sustainable competitiveness of a destination' (du Rand et al., 2003: 98). Everett and Aitchison (2008: 150) also identify the correlation between gastronomic tourism, regional identity, sustainability and social and cultural benefits, noting that food tourism has the capacity to assist in 'securing the "triple bottom line" ', hence not just contributing towards economic and social benefits to a region, but making a contribution towards achieving environmental sustainability also. Hall and Sharples (2003: 26), however, suggest that 'the development of strong local food identities and sustainable food systems have substantial potential to grow, with tourism playing a significant role'. This sentiment is also echoed by Croce and Perri (2010: 39) as they identify the links between gastronomic tourism and sustainable development, as gastronomic tourism has the capacity for 'maintaining and developing the environment, the economy, culture and society'. They go on to note that, in fact, compared with 'other types of tourism [which have] brought impoverishment, gastronomic tourism can reinforce the environment and the autonomy and identity of a region' (Croce and Perri, 2010: 39–40).

## The Cork model

County Cork is situated in the south-west corner of Ireland, a peripheral county; in particular, the less accessible West Cork stretches along the south-west coast and has traditionally been associated with agriculture, fishing and, more recently, tourism. With the rural economy of Ireland suffering significantly from the contraction of its traditional agricultural industries, 'farm diversification is one of the cornerstones of any rural development programme' (West Cork Development Partnership, n.d.). Within this context the Ireland Rural Development Programme 2007–2013, with a budget of €5.778 billion, identifies specific measures as contributing towards improving the competitiveness of agriculture, improving the environment and improving the quality of life in rural areas.

Among these measures are diversification into non-agricultural activities and the encouragement of tourism activities specifically. Such diversification might include provision of tourism facilities, developing niche tourism products – including speciality food provisions – and the development of farm shops selling home/locally grown produce, thus clearly illustrating the policy commitment towards rural diversification with a specific focus on tourism, food, gastronomy and sustainability (Department of Agriculture, Fisheries and Food, n.d.). This policy commitment is further evidenced by Teagasc, the Agriculture and Food Development Authority in Ireland, which aims to 'support science-based innovation in the agri-food sector and the broader bioeconomy that will underpin profitability, competitiveness and sustainability' (Teagasc, n.d.). To this end it supports a range of projects related to food, tourism and the rural economy. These include the development of rural tourism, artisan food production and organic farming.

At the local level, the West Cork Development Partnership (2003) identifies rural tourism as 'closely correlated with agricultural activity and . . . a valuable source of income' and, more specifically, specifies agri-tourism as a complementary activity to farming. Again here, the development of niche tourism, including speciality food provision, is specifically identified. In this context, from a national to a local policy level, gastronomic tourism in County Cork has further developed.

Cork has successfully branded its food and tourism product, building on the very traditional aspects of its local food production heritage, notably the English Market in Cork City, and further developing the more contemporary side of food through its associations as a renowned food tourism destination and initiatives such as the Kinsale Good Food Circle of Restaurants, Taste of Kinsale breaks, numerous food festivals such as the Kinsale Gourmet Festival, Baltimore Seafood Festival, Cork Food Week and the West Cork Food and Drink Festival, and further expansion into creative/educational/experiential food tourism with food schools such as the world famous Ballymaloe House and Cookery School.

To draw out a couple of examples further, the English Market in Cork City, established as a municipal market in 1788, is billed as the 'best covered market in the UK and Ireland' (English Market, n.d.) and the 'mother of all markets' (McKenna and McKenna, 2001: 98). The market underwent considerable refurbishment in the late 1990s and early part of the subsequent decade after a fire caused considerable damage in 1980. Traditionally the market housed the local fishmongers, butchers and vegetable stalls; however, recent years have seen significant growth in the more contemporary foodstuffs, led by the trends identified earlier in this chapter, where the market has become a place where 'tradition and innovation sit side by side' (McKenna and McKenna, 2001: 98) and is now also home to the Farmgate Restaurant, which sits above the covered market in the gallery, a new addition at the time of refurbishment. Also in resurgence and regrowth in Cork are country markets and farmers' markets, increasingly occupied again by alternative and artisanal producers who have 'reinvigorated the market by broadening the range and increasing the volume of produce' (Sage, 2003: 55).

This growth and development is also complemented by Ballymaloe House and Cookery School, further strengthening and developing the gastronomic tourism brand in Cork. Originally established in the 1940s as a small mushroom farm and apple orchard, expanding into the restaurant trade in the 1960s as one of the first ever country house restaurants in Ireland, Ballymaloe quickly established a reputation for its 'distinctive Irish culinary' experiences (Sage, 2003: 57), where produce was either grown on the farm itself or locally sourced. Ballymaloe has since expanded into a hotel and cookery school but, perhaps more importantly, Myrtle Allen, the founder of Ballymaloe, quickly gained a reputation as an ambassador and supporter of quality, locally grown Irish produce, both at home and overseas. This reputation has been furthered by subsequent generations and their rising media profiles, principally through television programmes and cookery books, presented and authored by both Darina and Rachel Allen (Sage, 2003). Indeed, such is the significance of Ballymaloe and its association with Cork that Sage (2003: 58) notes that it 'has consequently established a high profile and worldwide reputation [which has] proven an unassailable platform from which to broadcast an important message about the integrity of food'. Indeed the Slow Food movement in Ireland has its roots in Cork, when the first local convivium of the movement was established in 1998, led by Myrtle Allen and subsequently coordinated by Darina Allen.

Numerous other food-related initiatives have been established in Cork in recent years, including Taste Cork, the Fuchsia brand and Cork's Coastal Food Trails. Taste Cork is a brand that aims to develop linkages between food producers and marketers, and 'promote sustainable regional food production' (Taste Cork, n.d.) across the county. The Cork food brand has been further strengthened with the West Cork marketing initiative, the Fuchsia brand; developed by Failte Ireland, it brings together local tourism and food companies in a 'single regional identity'. Fuchsia Brands Ltd. has a membership of around 100 tourist and 40 food enterprises, the objective of which is to 'emphasise excellence and quality [reflecting] local characteristics, environmental quality and richness of the heritage, culture and landscape' (Fuchsia News, 1998, as cited in O'Reilly, 2001: 6).

The purpose of the initiative was to establish a brand that would indicate indigenous regional produce quality, promote the food product as a differentiating factor in the Cork tourism product portfolio and further develop marketing linkages between the various sectors of food, tourism and local craft. Indeed it is recognised that the 'linkages between the food and tourism industries create a synergy in the region, with high quality local food . . . becoming an integral part of visitors' quality experience' (Placebrand, n.d.). Further, artisan and organic food enterprises in Cork, and in particular West Cork, have proliferated in recent years into a network that includes organic farmers and growers, artisanal food producers and food markets (Sage, 2003). Indeed, West Cork is home to the largest 'concentration of rurally-based speciality food producers in Ireland' (Placebrand, n.d.). Further linkages to development and marketing of artisanal food production are exemplified by the accreditation of many of them as Fuchsia brands.

The Cork's Coastal Food Trails initiative, developed by Failte Ireland, promotes three food trails that incorporate a broad range of artisanal, organic, indigenous produce, including artisan food producers, cooperatives, wholefood and organic retailers, restaurants, cafés, pubs, breweries, markets, bakeries, farm shops, smokeries and cookery schools. The trails cover the geographic region of Cork, from Cork City to Youghal in the east of Cork and as far as Schull to the west. In the promotion of the trail there is a clear focus on developing and marketing sustainable gastronomic tourism across the whole county.

The gastronomic tourism product of Cork is further strengthened by the reputation of Kinsale as a high-quality food tourism resort. Situated on the south coast of Cork, Kinsale is a traditional fishing village and popular tourist resort and has established a reputation around its many eateries including bars, cafés and fine-dining restaurants, so much so that 12 fine-dining restaurants are marketed under the umbrella of Kinsale's Good Food Circle. The Circle organise a number of food-related events and offers throughout the year, such as Taste of Kinsale breaks and the Kinsale Gourmet Festival (Failte Ireland, n.d.). In addition, numerous other food-related initiatives are well-established in Kinsale that promote the sustainable development of indigenously grown and produced food, including the Community Supported Agriculture Project (a shared self-sufficiency initiative between the local community and local farmers) and Kinsale Green Growers (an enterprise that grows and sells vegetables to local households).

The Kinsale Gourmet Festival is also just one of a whole portfolio of food-related festivals that have been developed and marketed across the county of Cork in recent years. These include the Baltimore Seafood Festival, Cork Food Week, West Cork Food and Drink Festival, Mitchelstown Food Festival and Food Awards, Taste of West Cork, Cork Folk and Food Market, Belling West Cork Artisan Food Awards and the Christmas in Cobh Food Fair (Go Ireland, n.d.).

A final example is that of the Midleton Distillery, in south-east Cork, founded in 1825, and home to some of the major Irish whiskey brands including Jameson, Powers and Paddy. The original distillery was closed in 1975, making way for an ultra-modern facility and lay unused until its restoration in the 1980s. It is now home to the Jameson Experience tourist attraction, incorporating a tour of the original distillery building and its original kilns, pot stills, water wheel and warehouses. The restoration of the distillery as a tourist attraction makes a clear and established link between the gastronomic heritage of the county and tourism development. Indeed the town of Midleton and the distillery itself are identified as highlights in the aforementioned Cork's Coastal Food Trails. Along with the Midleton food market, an annual food and drink festival and a growing reputation for its food and drink establishments, Midleton also adds to the overall gastronomic reputation of the county.

Du Rand et al. (2003) recommend a number of strategies that can be utilised to contribute towards the optimisation of destination development and marketing around its food offering.

These include generating media coverage, funding to develop and exploit the food experience, promoting speciality restaurants, developing local food as a tourist attraction, branding locally produced foods, developing food festivals and events and developing a food route. When we examine the experience of Cork we can appreciate that many of these strategies contribute to this objective. In so doing, it is evident that Cork has developed and marketed its gastronomic tourism offering very successfully, creating a clear and established link between tourism, gastronomy and the sustainable development of its indigenous food production industry to create an enviable model of sustainable gastronomic tourism development.

## Conclusion

This case study of Cork is presented here as an 'investigation of a particular contemporary phenomenon within its real life context' (Robson, 2002: 178), and hence is not necessarily a suitable basis from which to make generalisations (Yin, 2009). However, Veal (2006) notes that the conclusions from cases can present general propositions and have validity in relation to theory and/or policy, which is the intention here.

There are clearly lessons to be drawn here around replication and suitability of the development of gastronomic tourism on the island of Ireland for regional destinations possessing similar competitive advantages. There are clearly established and growing links between tourism, rural tourism, food, agri-tourism and the agri-food sector, in particular as evidenced by the case of Cork. Numerous issues emerge in this case, including the diversification of the tourism product and the rural economy, increasing visitor spend, developing niche tourism, contributing towards sustainability of local food production and suppliers, developing and maintaining artisan and niche food production, extending the tourist season and creating back linkages between the food and tourism sectors. Not every destination has a Ballymaloe or an English Market, nor necessarily the extensive restaurant network of Kinsale. However, many possess advantages in relation to food, tourism and sustainability that may well be the seeds of the development of sustainable gastronomic tourism and the adoption of the Cork model, if not, at least, development and marketing of a destination towards such.

Ultimately there are still many underexplored issues surrounding food, tourism and sustainability in general and on the island of Ireland in particular and so the authors call for more empirical work in this area. Such investigations might include a closer examination of the relationship between local food initiatives and tourism, and the relationship between local food branding and its appeal to the tourist market. Investigation into the potential tensions between tourism development, gastronomy and sustainability is also desirable, given that managing the development of gastronomic tourism in the context of sustainability may well be, for many, a contentious debate. More case studies focusing on gastronomic tourism and sustainable development are also desirable, given the suitability of case study research to this topic, a growing body of which might help in in making comparisons and generalisations (Yin, 2009; Veal, 2006; Eisenhardt, 1989, 1991; Easterby-Smith et al., 2008) and identifying suitability for application and replication elsewhere.

## References

Boyne, S. and Hall, D. (2003) 'Managing food and tourism developments: issues for planning and opportunities to add value', in C.M. Hall, L. Sharples, R. Mitchell, N. Macionis and B. Cambourne (eds.), *Food Tourism Around the World*, Oxford: Elsevier, pp. 285–295.
Boyne, S. and Hall, D. (2004) 'Place promotion through food and tourism: rural branding and the role of websites', *Place Branding*, 1(1): 80–92.

Boyne, S., Williams, F. and Hall, D. (2002) 'On the trail of regional success: tourism, food production and the Isle of Arran Taste Trail', in A.M. Hjalager and G. Richards (eds.), *Tourism and Gastronomy*, Oxford: Routledge, pp. 91–114.

Boyne, S., Hall, D. and Williams, F. (2003) 'Policy, support and promotion for food related tourism initiatives: a marketing approach to regional development', in C.M. Hall (ed.), *Wine, Food and Tourism Marketing*, New Jersey: Haworth Hospitality Press, pp. 131–154.

Cellartours (n.d.) 'Ireland Gourmet Tours', www.cellartours.com/ireland/private-tours/luxury-gourmet.html (accessed 13 February 2013).

Croce, E. and Perri, G. (2010) *Food and Wine Tourism*, Wallingford: CABI.

Department of Agriculture, Fisheries and Food (n.d.) *Ireland Rural Development Programme, 2007–2013, Summary of Measures*, Dublin: Department of Agriculture, Fisheries and Food.

du Rand, G.E., Heath, E. and Alberts, N. (2003) 'The role of local and regional food in destination marketing: a South African situation analysis', in C.M. Hall (ed.), *Wine, Food and Tourism Marketing*, New Jersey: Haworth Hospitality Press, pp. 97–112.

Easterby-Smith, M., Thorpe, R. and Jackson, P.R. (2008) *Management Research*, 3rd edn, London: Sage.

Eisenhardt, K.M. (1989) 'Building theories from case study research', *Academy of Management Review*, 14(4): 532–550.

Eisenhardt, K.M. (1991) 'Better stories and better constructs: the case for rigour and comparative logic', *Academy of Management Review*, 16(3): 620–627.

English Market (n.d.) www.englishmarket.ie (accessed 10 December 2013).

Everett, S. and Aitchison, C. (2008) 'The role of food in sustaining regional identity: a case study of Cornwall, South West England', *Journal of Sustainable Tourism*, 16(2): 150–167.

Failte Ireland (n.d.) *Cork's Coastal Food Trails*, Dublin: Failte Ireland.

Go Ireland (n.d.) www.goireland.com (accessed 11 December 2013).

Hall, C.M. and Mitchell, R. (2001) 'Wine and food tourism', in N. Douglas, N. Douglas and R. Derrett (eds.), *Special Interest Tourism: Context and Cases*, Oxford: Wiley, pp. 307–309.

Hall, C.M. and Mitchell, R. (2005) 'Gastronomic tourism', in M. Novelli (ed.), *Niche Tourism*, Oxford: Butterworth-Heinemann, pp. 73–88.

Hall, C.M. and Sharples, L. (2003) 'The consumption of experiences or the experience of consumption? An introduction to the tourism of taste', in C.M. Hall, L. Sharples, R. Mitchell, N. Macionis and B. Cambourne, *Food Tourism Around the World: Development, Management and Markets*, Oxford: Routledge, pp. 2–24.

Hatch, D. (2006) 'Baltilicious in Brum's own spice triangle: Dinah Hatch takes a tour of the city's Sparkbrooks district, where the exotic flavours of Pakistan's culinary tradition are creating a Balti boom', *The Observer*, 19 February, p. 6.

Long, L.M. (2004) *Culinary Tourism*, Kentucky: University Press of Kentucky.

Mintel (2009) *Gastronomic Tourism – International*, London: Mintel Group Ltd.

McKenna, J. and McKenna, S. (2001) *The Bridgestone Food Lover's Guides to Ireland: The Shopper's Guide*, Durrus: Estragon Press.

O'Reilly, S. (2001) *Fuchsia Brands Ltd.: A Case Study of Networking Among the Food Producer Members*, Cork: University College Cork.

Placebrand (n.d.) *West Cork – A Place Apart, the Creation of the Fuchsia Brand*, Canada: Placebrand.

Richards, G. (2003) 'What is cultural tourism?', in E. den Hartigh and A. van Maaren (eds.), *Erfgoed voor Toerisme*, Stichting: National Contact Monumenten.

Richards, G. and Wilson, J. (2007) 'The creative turn in regeneration: creative spaces, spectacles and tourism in cities', in M.K. Smith (ed.), *Tourism, Culture and Regeneration*, Wallingford: Cabi, pp. 12–24.

Robson, C. (2002) *Real World Research*, 2nd edn, Oxford: Blackwell.

Sage, C. (2003) 'Social embeddedness and relations of regard: alternative "good food" networks in south-west Ireland', *Journal of Rural Studies*, 19: 47–60.

Savvy Club (n.d.) www.savvyclub.co.uk/page/Gastronomic-Tour-Experience-UK (accessed 13 February 2013).

Taste Cork (n.d.) www.tastecork.com (accessed 11 December 2013).

Teagasc (n.d.) www.teagasc.ie/topics/rural_dev (accessed 11 December 2013).

Tourism Ireland (n.d.) *Cork's Coastal Food Trails*, Dublin: Tourism Ireland.

Vasileska, A. and Reckoska, G. (2010) 'Culinary identity as important segment of tourist offer', *Tourism and Hospitality Management Conference Proceedings*, pp. 1622–1628.

Veal, A.J. (2006) *Research Methods for Leisure and Tourism: A Practical Guide*, 3rd edn, Essex: Prentice-Hall.

West Cork Development Partnership (n.d.) www.wcdp.ie/project-funding/tourism, West Cork Development Partnership (accessed 10 December 2013).

Yin, R.K. (2009) *Case Study Research: Design and Methods*, 4th edn, London: Sage.

# 34

# RESPONSIBLE TRAVEL AS A MEANS TO PRESERVE CULTURAL AND NATURAL HERITAGE

## Initiatives in Crete, Greece

*Nikki Rose*

## Introduction

Responsible travel covers a lot of ground today. There are interrelated categories—ecotourism, agritourism, geotourism, sustainable travel, ethical travel, green travel, alternative travel, etc. International research and more than 100 annual conferences focusing on this issue have produced suggestions and case studies generally referred to as "responsible travel" or "sustainable travel." To be considered a responsible travel practitioner or traveler, it is essential that people actively work to support and protect the communities in which they live, work, or visit.

Responsible travel is part of the solution to a growing number of global issues relating to social inequality, exploitation, cultural preservation, food safety, and environmental protection. Some of the factors that contribute to these issues are transportation, climate change, over-development, globalization, and depletion of cultural and natural resources.

Responsible travel is a fine theory, embraced the world over, yet the practice is challenging. While the number of responsible travel practitioners increases, the number of travelers partaking in such beneficial programs is approximately 7–10 percent (Becker, 2013; CREST, 2014). Many people say they prefer "real" or "ethical" travel experiences, yet there needs to be more outreach about the value, benefits, and fair wages offered to the communities providing these services (Adams, 2008).

According to the United Nations Environment Programme:

> Tourism is one of the world's largest industries and one of its fastest growing economic sectors. It has a multitude of impacts, both positive and negative, on people's lives and on the environment. Sustainable tourism development guidelines and management practices are applicable to all forms of tourism in all types of destinations, including mass tourism and the various niche tourism segments. Sustainability principles refer to the environmental, economic, and socio-cultural aspects of tourism development, and a suitable balance must be established between these three dimensions to guarantee its long-term sustainability.
>
> *(UNEP, 2014)*

Thus, sustainable tourism should:

1.  make optimal use of environmental resources that constitute a key element in tourism development, maintaining essential ecological processes and helping to conserve natural heritage and biodiversity;
2.  respect the socio-cultural authenticity of host communities, conserve their built and living cultural heritage and traditional values, and contribute to inter-cultural understanding and tolerance;
3.  ensure viable, long-term economic operations, providing socio-economic benefits to all stakeholders that are fairly distributed, including stable employment and income-earning opportunities and social services to host communities, and contributing to poverty alleviation.

This concept of linking visitors with culture, nature, and the environment in a harmonious way is not a new idea, but one that is now viewed on a global scale (Christ, 2008). Long-term, successful community involvement has preserved many popular rural tourist destinations such as the wine regions of Europe and the United States. Many rural communities have acted on instinct, rather than governmental directives, and usually with enough individual investment to achieve results, such as Napa Valley, California, and the Rhone Valley, France.

Even today, however, in the age of greater awareness of the impact tourism has on our communities and our planet, the majority of foreign visitors are accustomed to or expect familiar settings when they travel, which do not always resemble the landscape or lifestyle of their host country. This "package tour" pressure can lead to over-commercialization, while local communities relying on tourism attempt to maintain their own cultural heritage and a clean living environment. Over-commercialization can wipe out an entire community in a few "trendy" years, leaving a wasteland behind (Andriotis, 2008; Blangy, 2006; Briassoulis, 2003).

## General information about Crete, Greece

The isle of Crete, Greece is 8,336km² (6.3 percent of the total area of the Greek territory). It is located at the southern edge of the Aegean Sea, about 160km from the mainland. The length of the island is 256km. Its largest width is 57km and smallest width is 12km. The percentage of mountainous area is 49 percent. The population of Crete is 621,340, representing 5.76 percent of the population of the Greek territory (EL.STAT, 2010). The GDP of Crete amounted to €10.955 million (4.9 percent of the national GDP). Trade and tourism has the most important contribution to the added value of the products of Crete, with €4.589 million. The unemployment rate is about 23.7 percent.

Annually, Crete attracts about 2.8 million charter tourists during the season from April to October (HNTO, 2008). Because of the high level of tourism activity, there is a large proportion of seasonal working and self-employment. The island has remarkable natural, cultural and historical resources. The majority of tourists today are interested in seaside holidays, rather than cultural heritage (Andriotis, 2011).

## Responsible travel in practice: the case of Crete's culinary sanctuaries eco-agritourism network

Crete is blessed with a fascinating history spanning more than 4,000 years, natural beauty and an abundance of healthy food choices, both wild and cultivated. There is much to discover and enjoy. There is also much to protect. Beyond the seaside resorts and imposing limestone cliffs are people preserving their heritage (sustainable organic farmers, artisan bread bakers, cheese makers, beekeepers, chefs, and many others). They are maintaining what most of us have lost touch with—a connection between themselves, their community, and nature. Their knowledge of sustainable living practices is beneficial to the global community. Many people around the world are striving to "return to the land," while many people in rural Crete have never left the land. But modern society beckons and rural communities are often abandoned or developed.

The premise of the Mediterranean diet originated in Crete shortly after World War II, resulting in "The Seven Countries Study." The basic findings were that some people in Crete lived long, healthy lives because of what they ate (and did not eat) during those hard times. There was no laboratory food, chemical agriculture, or mass tourism yet. The only option was fresh and local food (Rose, 2000, 2007, 2011; Miller, 2008; Simopoulos and Robinson, 1999).

Crete's Culinary Sanctuaries (CCS) introduces visitors to residents like Yiorgos, who maintains his small family farm much like his ancestors, using sustainable organic methods. He refuses to buy food from outside sources and even collects salt from a rocky beach nearby. "The chicken I eat must first dine at my house," he says.

When we travel to foreign lands, it seems so natural to connect with residents outside of the tourism industry, to spend time in their villages and enjoy a leisurely meal together. CCS offers this opportunity. Before we eat bread, we meet farmers to see how grains are cultivated. Before we sample olive oil, we meet the farmers at their groves and factories. Before we sample cheese, we meet shepherds to discover how their flocks live—roaming the slopes and eating wild plants. Many of these plants are used in cooking and natural medicine, which we discover during hikes in the countryside and cooking demonstrations.

The renowned traditional healthy cuisine of Crete is not a phenomenon; it is a matter of respecting the land and the bounty it provides. Every great chef will tell you that they are only as good as their ingredients. The foundation of the Mediterranean diet concept is fresh, local, organic food and a clean environment. Both residents and visitors benefit from community-based preservation programs. Careful consideration and strong alliances are required to sustain these programs, with residents investing their time and money to share valuable knowledge. CCS celebrates Crete's heritage in an ethical and professional manner; our seminars offer visitors a rare opportunity to discover the heart of Crete and obtain information that can enrich their lives.

Tourism and agriculture are primary industries in Crete. The majority of tourism planners support generic services, such as large beach resorts and imported continental food. Most operations are of little benefit to local communities in terms of providing financial stability or protecting Crete's cultural and natural heritage. More than 70 percent of Crete's residents are still involved in agriculture—primarily olive oil and wine production on a part-time basis. Both industries compete for increasingly scarce natural resources, particularly fresh water in this drought-afflicted region. To help mitigate this competition for resources, CCS promotes the benefits of educational travel via the window of traditional food ways. As agriculture is an integral part of Crete's culture, our programs center on the work of organic farmers and interrelated preservation work to serve several purposes at once.

Industrial agriculture in Crete is composed of cooperatives, some of which represent hundreds of families cultivating a variety of produce on small plots of land. Slowly, some cooperatives and individuals are converting to organic production. Yet, they face challenges if their neighbors are growing conventionally and public entities are not supporting their work. An increasing number of specialized organic farmers are implementing projects, with most producers incorporating agritourism into their work to promote their products, share their knowledge, and generate supplemental income. But not all producers or stakeholders are collaborating with residents involved in interrelated preservation work or current responsible travel initiatives that can enhance the quality of agritourism and the quality of life for residents (Rose, 2014).

## Recommendations for implementing responsible travel in agricultural regions

The fact that a destination has excellent cuisine and nature reserves does not mean that communities are able to open up the area to visitors. Before residents invite tourists to their villages and farms, they need to consider how they will present and sustain their programs and protect their communities.

Since most of us are not farmers, we do not know what to expect from an agritourism experience. Agritourism is meant to support farmers and their communities. In the case of organic agriculture, it also helps to protect our environment. If done right, agritourism can make a difference as part of the bigger picture of preservation and responsible travel. Supplying the world with excellent food and wine is more challenging than we might ever know or appreciate, and organic farming is not a "nine to five" position, but a lifelong commitment. While it is a lovely notion for farmers or fishers to take the day off to entertain us, we are asking for a lot. The time they devote to sharing their knowledge with us is a rare privilege.

It is the responsible travel practitioner's job to develop valuable programs and create awareness of that value, which will be offered at a fair price. Preservation work is a partnership between providers and beneficiaries. Enjoying an action-packed series of cultural activities requires the participation of many local people. It must be financially rewarding, otherwise the arrangement is not mutually beneficial or ethical. Further, if eco-agritourism is not advantageous for communities, there is no incentive to provide these valuable services or expand organic production. Thus all beneficiaries—the public and private sectors, the media, and travelers—need to be aware of the value of these programs.

## Results: sharing the benefits of responsible travel

By tailoring small-group seminars in harmony with the seasons, cultural and environmental impacts, availability of residents, and interests of attendees, CCS has the advantage of flexibility. In consideration of our collective and individual projects, CCS seminars serve a dual purpose—to support local preservation work and share those benefits with visitors. We link organic farmers with other members of the community and foreign tourists through:

1. our educational programs;
2. staying in locally owned lodges and eco-lodges in small villages;
3. providing free training and referral services;
4. global promotion of projects;
5. sharing seminar revenues (in contrast with standard tourism practices).

Many travelers benefit from community-based preservation work. We stress that communities must benefit the most if we expect to enjoy such services, including excellent fresh, local, organic cuisine. CCS acts as a gateway for communities to expand or create their own programs.

There are established Women's Agricultural Cooperatives in Crete, producing and selling traditional products within their communities or beyond, depending on their resources and support for their work. There are also excellent home cooks, gardeners, and artisan producers who do not have the resources to join cooperatives or host visitors. CCS invites residents from varied backgrounds to participate in our programs. By collaborating with the community, eco-agritourism stretches beyond the boundaries of a single farm. Communities maintain their way of life as they choose, rather than altering it to suit an outsider's vision of foreign travel.

CCS is an internationally acclaimed responsible travel program. Our approach can be implemented anywhere in the world. We also organize workshops for colleagues and our success has encouraged others to follow our lead.

## Discussion: the need to promote responsible travel

As with all market trends, travel providers offering alternative forms of tourism in an unethical manner is damaging to authentic programs. This is referred to as "greenwashing" (Christ, 2008). Outreach is required on the part of advocacy groups and the media (Rose, 2007). The majority of travel agencies are not yet trained in ethical travel practices. It requires that they modify their business methods and form mutually beneficial partnerships with local communities. More travelers are asking agencies questions such as "How does your company contribute to the well-being of local people and their environment?"

While responsible travel options are increasing, practitioners are competing with volume discount travel and powerful public relations campaigns that overshadow their distinctive work. Mass media rarely covers small-scale programs because there is no apparent benefit to them. Discount deals cut in mega-travel cannot be cut in rural communities. Most media outlets expect free food and lodging, consultancy, and entertainment. Small-scale practitioners cannot afford this form of advertising, nor are they certain to benefit from it, as the coverage is rarely specific to their work and could be subjective.

The first step to launch a small-scale program is from the ground up in collaboration with other local businesses, advocacy groups and public agencies, if possible. With the rapid growth of responsible travel advocacy groups, entrepreneurs' participation in programs is increasing. Responsible travel is not a trend; it is a necessity.

## Conclusion

Responsible travel provides a wide range of benefits to communities and visitors (IRCT, 2014; UNEP, 2013). It provides an opportunity for entrepreneurs and travelers to be active participants in sustainable development programs. It requires direct collaboration with preservationists and tangible returns on their investments. Responsible travel can help preserve our world's sanctuaries and even reverse some damage caused by unsustainable development. It can build meaningful careers for future generations and protect the very reason why people visit countries like Greece—to discover her significant cultural legacy and natural beauty.

## References

Adams, B. (2008) *The New Agritourism: Hosting Community & Tourists on Your Farm*, California: New World Publishing.

Andriotis, K. (2008) "Integrated resort development: the case of Cavo Sidero, Crete," *Journal of Sustainable Tourism*, 16(4): 428–444.

Andriotis, K. (2011) "A comparative study of visitors to urban, coastal and rural areas – evidence from the Island of Crete," *European Journal of Tourism Research*, 4(2): 93–108.

Becker, E. (2013) *Overbooked: The Exploding Business of Travel and Tourism*, New York: Simon and Schuster.
Blangy, S. (2006) *Le Guide Des Destinations Indigènes*, Montpellier : Indigène Editions.
Briassoulis, H. (2003) "Crete: endowed by nature, privileged by geography, threatened by Tourism?" *Journal of Sustainable Tourism*, 11: 97–115.
Christ, C. (2008) Beyond the Edge, National Geographic Adventure Blog. Definitions of Green Travel, http://adventureblog.nationalgeographic.com/2008/11/11/defining-green-travel-terms.
CREST (2014) *The Case for Responsible Travel Trends and Statistics*, www.responsibletravel.org/resources/documents/reports/Crest_RTI_TrendStats_email1_4%20%282_Small%29.pdf.
EL.STAT (2010) Hellenic Statistical Authority.
HNTO (2008) *Statistics: Athens*, Hellenic National Tourism Organisation.
IRCT (2014) www.icrtourism.org/publications/journal/.
Miller, D. (2008) *The Jungle Effect: The Healthiest Diets from Around the World – Why They Work and How to Make Them Work for You*, New York: HarperCollins.
Rose, N. (2000) "What's the Mediterranean Diet?" *Stigmes Magazine*, www.cookingincrete.com/Articles-MedDiet.html.
Rose, N. (2007) http://ecoclub.com/news/093/interview2.html.
Rose, N. (2011) *Crete: The Roots of the Mediterranean Diet*, San Francisco: Blurb Books.
Rose, N. (2014) *Development Endangers Med Diet Foods*, http://destinationcenter.org/2014/02/development-endangers-med-diet-foods.
Simopoulos, A. and Robinson, J. (1999) *The Omega Diet: The Lifesaving Nutritional Program Based on the Diet of the Island of Crete*, New York: HarperCollins.
UNEP (2013) *Green Economy Report, Tourism Chapter*, www.unep.org/greeneconomy/Portals/88/GETReport/pdf/Chapitre%207%20Tourism.pdf.
UNEP (2014) *Definitions, Tourism*, www.unep.org/resourceefficiency/Business/SectoralActivities/Tourism/FactsandFiguresaboutTourism/Definitions/tabid/78773/Default.aspx.

## Additional resources

Bonn-Muller, E. (2010) "Interview: The Joy of Cretan Cooking," Archaeological Institute of America Magazine, www.archaeological.org/news/aianews/3303.
Center for Food Safety, www.centerforfoodsafety.org.
Center for Responsible Technology, www.responsibletechnology.org.
Environmental Working Group, www.ewg.orghttp://www.ewg.org.
Food Democracy Now! www.fooddemocracynow.org.
International Federation of Organic Agriculture Movements, www.ifoam.org.
Kyriakopoulos, V. (2007, 2010) *Lonely Planet Guidebook to Crete*, London, UK: Lonely Planet Publications.
National Geographic Center For Sustainable Destinations, Resources for Tourism Professionals, http://travel.nationalgeographic.com/travel/sustainable/professionals.html#general.
Rose, N. (2013) Lecture Series, National Hellenic Museum, Chicago, www.youtube.com/watch?v=pG_Pl8ou3i0.
United Nations, International Year of Biodiversity Success Stories, www.cbd.int/2010/stories.

# PART 8

# General issues/world food crisis

Those who eat too much or eat too little, who sleep too much or sleep too little, will not succeed in meditation. But those who are temperate in eating and sleeping, work and recreation, will come to the end of sorrow through meditation.

*Krishna quotes from* The Bhagavad Gita

Food purchasing decisions and food availability can no longer be considered without contemplation of a wide range of socio-political, environmental and human well-being factors. In the West, responsible consumers are faced with a vast array of ethical, health and planetary issues when filling their supermarket trolleys while more than a billion of the world's poorest see their ability to buy even the most meagre foodstuffs diminish.

The way many hospitality operators are trying to balance the huge environmental and social footprints the industry is leaving for future generations is described by **Nicolas Siorak, Christine Demen Meier, Stéphanie Bonsch Buri and Clémence Cornuz**. The role of governmental regulations is promoted as a decisive factor in the development of sustainable foodservice outlets. Regulations that favour sustainable development in the hospitality industry are presented. Best practices stemming from regulations that incentivize sustainability are emphasized and the efforts made by the media and government to make domestic consumers more aware of these issues are highlighted.

**Christina Ciambriello and Carolyn Dimitri** explain how current niche food production and distribution systems, such as fair trade, organic and local, attempt to mitigate some of the external costs embedded in the global food system. Yet they argue that such certifications and alternative systems only address individual aspects of global market failure. They present the foundation stones for a sustainable food system that references the external environmental and social costs of food production, distribution and consumption. Meeting the needs and expectations of all stakeholder groups (the ecosystem, humans, workers, businesses) is often a practical impediment to achieving a fully sustainable food system.

According to **Christine Demen Meier, Nicolas Siorak, Stéphanie Bonsch Buri and Clémence Cornuz**, the demand for healthier products by Western consumers is mainly derived from endemic factors in developed economies such as the prevalence of obesity, snacking and the massive increase in food allergies. This article describes how the desire for

377

better nutrition can be linked to the growth of the junk food industry that has fostered a drop in consumer confidence. The present tendency by some sectors of the food industry towards giving consumers more nutritional information on packaging is analysed from the point of view of the restaurateur.

# 35

# INTERNATIONAL AND NATIONAL REGULATIONS IN FAVOUR OF SUSTAINABLE OPERATIONS IN FOOD SERVICE

*Nicolas Siorak, Christine Demen Meier, Stéphanie Bonsch Buri and Clémence Cornuz*

## Introduction

Sustainable development is defined as development that meets present needs without compromising the ability of future generations to meet their own needs (WCED, 1987). Because of this new trend, the food service industry faces numerous challenging realities. It notably faces pressure regarding greenhouse gas emissions, landscape pollution and the use of natural resources. Moreover, there is a growing consumer demand for healthier products.

First, food production is considered responsible for up to 57 per cent of the total annual amount of greenhouse gas emissions. Among these, up to 15 per cent come from agricultural production; up to 18 per cent from deforestation; up to 20 per cent from transformation; up to 20 per cent from transport, packaging and distribution; and, finally, up to 4 per cent from waste (Réseau Action Climat France and Fondation Nicolas Hulot, 2010).

Second, the Food and Agriculture Organization stresses the major impact of the agro-industry, notably of livestock farming, on landscape pollution and the use of natural resources (FAO, 2006). Pesticide use and water consumption is regularly examined and criticised by both authorities and citizens. For instance, an increasing number of people are aware of the water footprint of meat (1,000 litres per steak) or the amount of cereal used for livestock feeding (70 per cent of world production) (FAO, 2006). Both consumers and food operators are thus increasingly expected to change their consumption and production habits, and are held more accountable for the way their behaviour and practices impact the environment.

Third, the number of food-related health concerns is growing (as one might expect, considering the ageing of the world population). Consumers are notably concerned about additives and chemicals used in the preparation of food products. In response, according to Laisney (2011), consumers can be tempted to regain control over their diet by consuming local or organic products.

These three challenges are typical of agriculture and of the whole food industry, and as such directly impact the food service industry. To address these concerns, the term 'regulation' is frequently used as a mantra by civil societies and leaders. Broadly speaking, 'regulation' refers to bringing stability to a system and correcting imbalance (Ghersi and Malassis, 2000; Boyer and Saillard, 1995). However, it is actually a polysemous term whose definition varies across countries. In North America, it refers mainly to public policies, i.e., laws, taxes and market constraints. In Europe, the term has a wider understanding, as it includes not only public policies but also all actions undertaken by citizens and the private sector to foster stable situations. In this regard, competition, businesses and prices are part of market regulation. Unions, NGOs and consumer associations can contribute to regulation as well. International institutions tend to go by the broader definition of the term, but still emphasise public policy. When public regulation is associated with regulations enacted by the private sector or by citizens, the European Union tends to use the concept of 'co-regulation'.

This chapter will discuss the regulatory elements impacting the Western food system as a whole,[1] and more specifically the food service industry, first at the international level and then at the national level. The focus is quite broad: while laws on certifications, organic products and pesticide use concern primarily the production part of the food system, they indirectly affect the food service industry by impacting product availability and prices.

## International regulation

Many concerns for sustainability in food service are global issues, and should be addressed as such. The notion of 'worldwide public goods' (which include the climate) is indeed gaining traction, and the future needs of the world population are likely to foster a strong international collaboration between actors. Furthermore, in most cases, actions taken by one country have an impact on the global situation.

### *Main global challenges*

There are financial and quantitative obstacles to the implementation of sustainable practices and behaviours. However, it is undoubtedly necessary to change current production, processing and consumption practices. This presents difficulties, notably in terms of finances, but operators also benefit from such changes.

### *Inaction is not an option*

Every economy, state and company has to implement sustainable processes. Facts and figures stress the limits of our current behaviours in the long term. The carbon footprint already indicates that humanity consumes 1.5 times the amount of natural resources produced by the planet each year (Ewing et al., 2010). If the whole world population adopted the standards of North American food consumption, five planet Earths would be necessary to supply enough resources.

### *Health issues*

Obesity will undoubtedly be considered an international pandemic before 2050. Current trends and projections show that, in 2050, 45 per cent of US citizens, 50 per cent of British citizens and 60 per cent of the European population will suffer from obesity (Bradt, 2010). National health systems and public regulators have already begun giving incentives for healthy eating behaviour (Le Figaro, 2013).

The demand for healthier food and more nutritional information will continue to increase. To meet this demand, food producers and providers – whatever country they operate in – will have to improve the nutritional quality of, and the information they provide on, their products.

## *Price as a limitation to sustainable practices*

Sustainable products are in general 30 per cent more expensive than traditional products (Centre d'études et de prospective, 2012). At the same time, the food industry (including food service) is characterised by a strong competition and, on average, low profit margin rates. Thus, bridging the gap between 'traditional' and sustainable product prices is an obligation.

One of the identified causes for this price difference is the fragmentation and atomicity of sustainable food producers (Fessard, 2010). Indeed, organic or local farms are often too small for economies of scale to be possible. In addition, reducing the use of pesticides and water is costly for farmers, because it entails using more expensive materials, more labour-intensive production methods, and having higher losses.

For food service operators, especially restaurants, reducing the amount of salt, fat or sugar requires using more expensive substitutes. Moreover, since there is no specific and well-identified sustainable industry, it is costly to look for sustainable suppliers. Finally, calculating the carbon footprint or ecological impact of products can be unbearably expensive (Oqali, 2012).

The current world population (7.2 billion) will have increased to more than 9.6 billion in 2050 (UN DESA, 2013; UN, 2013). As a consequence, the increasing demand for food and the insufficient agricultural production will lead to a rise in food prices. This increase will be an opportunity for operators, as sustainable products will become more competitive (Schieb, 1999).

## *Benefits of market regulation*

A growing demand and rising prices will have prompted a concentration of food operators worldwide by 2050 (FAO, n.d.a), which will make it easier for state regulators, consumer groups and NGOs to influence and monitor sustainable practices. It will also benefit operators, as it will induce an increase in productivity and economies of scale, notably for sustainable producers.

Moreover, market and economic constraints motivate a better use of food products, and a good calibration of menus and dishes is a competitive advantage in food service outlets. It indeed represents a big opportunity for improvement, as 40 per cent of the food is currently wasted (Gustavsson, 2011).

## *International institutions*

Sustainability being a global issue, the legitimacy of international institutions should help them address it as such. In practice, international institutions mainly produce recommendations and foster discussions with key players of the food industry. The actions listed below illustrate this point.

## *The United Nations and the Zero Hunger Challenge*

In June 2012, UN Secretary-General Ban Ki-moon launched the Zero Hunger Challenge, inviting all nations to be ambitious as they work for a future where no one goes hungry.

The Challenge of Zero Hunger means:

- 100% access to adequate food all year round.
- Zero stunted children under 2 years, no more malnutrition in pregnancy and early childhood.
- All food systems are sustainable.
- 100% growth in smallholder productivity and income, particularly for women.
- Zero loss or waste of food, including responsible consumption.

*(UN, n.d.)*

### *Food and Agriculture Organization and the World Food Day*

The FAO is deeply involved in the progress towards more sustainable food systems. It produces regular reports highlighting the main challenges our societies face or will soon face regarding food quantity and quality, as well as the risks faced by both developed and developing countries regarding food supply. It also provides a collaborative platform facilitating discussion and aims to raise key players' and citizens' awareness of sustainability issues.

FAO also celebrates the World Food Day on October 16, the day on which the organisation was founded in 1945.

The objectives of World Food Day are to:

- encourage attention to agricultural food production and to stimulate national, bilateral, multilateral and non-governmental efforts to this end;
- encourage economic and technical cooperation among developing countries;
- encourage the participation of rural people, particularly women and the least priv-ileged categories, in decisions and activities influencing their living conditions;
- heighten public awareness of the problem of hunger in the world;
- promote the transfer of technologies to the developing world; and
- strengthen international and national solidarity in the struggle against hunger, malnutrition and poverty and draw attention to achievements in food and agricultural development.

*(FAO, n.d.b)*

## The FAO, the World Health Organization and the Codex Alimentarius

Although the FAO and the WHO focus on contributing to knowledge, fostering discussions and raising awareness, they also try to regulate food-related activities in a more direct way. For example, the Codex Alimentarius shows that they have an influence on national legislations.

> The Codex Alimentarius Commission, established by FAO and WHO in 1963, develops harmonized international food standards, guidelines and codes of practice to protect the health of the consumers and ensure fair practices in the food trade. The Commission also promotes coordination of all food standards work undertaken by international governmental and non-governmental organizations.
>
> While being recommendations for voluntary application by members, Codex standards serve in many cases as a basis for national legislation. They apply to several areas linked to sustainability in the food industry, such as organic products, use of water, and certifications.
>
> *(Codex Alimentarius, n.d.)*

## United Nations Conference on Trade and Development

UNCTAD is the UN body responsible for dealing with development issues, particularly international trade, which is the main driver of development. It has the same objective and methods as other UN institutions: studying issues, sharing information, providing expertise and facilitating collaboration between international governments.

In 2013, UNCTAD published a *Trade and Environment Review* report on sustainable agri-culture whose title stood out amongst the usually very traditional and formal documents of UN bodies: 'Wake up before it's too late: Make agriculture truly sustainable now for food security in a changing climate.' The attention international organisations pay to this topic and the sense of urgency conveyed by this title demonstrate the importance of sustainable food systems and the implication of public agencies in related regulation (UNCTAD, 2013).

## The European Union

The European Union differs from the institutions mentioned above due to its political and democratic nature. It is not a global institution, but its regulations have to be implemented in its 28 member states, notably because of its directives.

It also adopts strategies which will then be translated into resolutions and legislations, such as the Europe 2020 Strategy and the Roadmap to a Resource-Efficient Europe. Besides, as explained below, the EU also tackles unhealthy food and helps European states produce effective regulation on health matters.

> The Europe 2020 Strategy calls for an increase in resource efficiency to: '. . . find new ways to reduce inputs, minimise waste, improve management of resource stocks, change consumption patterns, optimise production processes, management and business methods, and improve logistics.'
>
> The Roadmap to a Resource-Efficient Europe follows up on this, and stresses that our natural resource base is being eroded by growing global demand, highlighting the food sector as priority area for taking action and calling for: '. . . incentives for healthier and more sustainable production and consumption of food and to halve the disposal of edible food waste in the EU by 2020.'
>
> The Roadmap states that the Commission will assess how best to limit waste throughout the food supply chain, and consider ways to lower the environmental impact of food production and consumption patterns, via a Communication on Sustainable Food, in 2013.
>
> *(European Commission, 2013b)*

## International companies

Sustainable reports of food supply companies show that their objectives are well defined. For instance, Unilever Food Solutions (the food service branch of Unilever) aims to halve its carbon footprint (Unilever Food Solutions, n.d.). Nestlé Professional has implemented specific plans for products such as cocoa and coffee in order to monitor and improve the company's ecological impact (Nestlé Professional, n.d.). As for Danone, it favours local communities by buying locally produced milk in every country it operates in (Danone, 2011).

The clear definition of suppliers' sustainable actions is linked with their certifications. A concentration of certifications has begun since the end of the 2000s. A certification like 'Ensemble' has organic and fair trade specifications, while 'Alter Eco' includes 'AB' and 'Max Havelaar', as well as the carbon footprint of products.

## International associations and organisations

Like certifications, professional and consumer associations and NGOs have an increasingly worldwide scope. Associations such as Greenpeace launch worldwide campaigns all the more easily now that they rely primarily on social networks to mobilise people. The 2010 campaign against the use of palm oil by food processing companies illustrates this well: initially intended for the UK, Germany, China and Indonesia, it was eventually broadcast internationally on YouTube, getting several million views from all over the world.

On the business side, global professional associations encourage the adoption of greener practices in the hospitality industry. For instance, the International Hotel and Restaurant Association (IHRA) promotes an efficient use of natural and agro resources among its members. It recommends not only measuring the resources used, but also managing and reducing energy consumption and intermediate consumption costs. IHRA also reminds its members of the usefulness of such measures in terms of reports, communication to clients, and operational profitability.

# National regulations

Legislation provides guidance, helping users know which practices are allowed and which are forbidden. International legislation on sustainable food and food service industries is difficult to implement. On a national scale, on the other hand, governments have the authority and the means to implement appropriate laws. Thus, national regulations tend to be more coercive than international ones, even though sustainability-related laws are 'soft laws' – meaning that they are indirect, influencing behaviour rather than establishing obligations. At the micro and mezzo economic levels, operators are incited to self-regulate for competitive reasons and to comply with pressure from consumers.

As a consequence, green certifications are becoming more common in the food service industry. They facilitate the transition towards more sustainable practices and help companies show their commitment in a way that inspires trust. Finally, because there is a concentration of the suppliers' market, food suppliers are increasingly responsible for the market regulation of sustainability.

## *State regulation*

National legislation is not created unilaterally by governments, but shaped by pressure groups, actions and lobbying. Because these laws are the result of discussions between the actors, they are more easily implemented and applied than international laws.

## *Soft legislation*

At the moment, sustainable development is a 'soft law': words such as 'guidelines', 'best practices' and 'sustainable report' have become common in state communication. For example, in France, Article 48 of the *Loi Grenelle I* sets an objective for school restaurant purchasers: 20 per cent of products should be organic. This goal is manageable, as buyers can adapt this quota to their own constraints: they can choose products according to their means and to the contracts with their suppliers. In reality, though, this law mostly encourages companies to make an effort: there is no sanction for institutions who order less than 20 per cent of organic products (Ministère de l'agriculture, de l'agroalimentaire et de la forêt, 2011).

In some countries, publicly traded companies must publish sustainability reports every year. This obligation can be considered a 'soft law', as it stimulates transparency and actions from companies, but does not define these actions. This is the case for French companies since 2001, when the Nouvelles Régulations Economiques (New Economic Regulations) was adopted by the French National Assembly. It will soon be an obligation across Europe (European Commission, 2013a).

## *Hard legislation*

Some aspects of sustainability in food service operations are more demanding, and can therefore be considered 'hard laws'. Food safety is already one of the main constraints for restaurants; norms, legislations and controls are very strict. Moreover, across countries, public health officers increasingly demand recommendations and incentives to prevent and fight obesity and diabetes, two big challenges for modern societies. They tend to be translated into innovative tax instruments.

Allergenic products are already targeted by regulators. However, in most countries, further information on the amount of fat, sugar or number of calories contained in a meal might have to be indicated on menus and products in the near future. Public documents such as *Dietary Guidelines for Americans* could become the basis for a new set of regulations (US Department of Agriculture and Health and Human Services, 2010). In Europe, dietary guidelines have the same objective (European Food Safety Authority, 2010). Such laws would affect food supply chains and restaurant practices: if this type of information had to be provided for every food item or dish served in a restaurant, consumers' and food suppliers' behaviour would be greatly impacted (European Food Safety Authority, 2010).

Finally, sustainable actions can be gradually improved by tax policies. The tax on sugary drinks adopted in France in 2012 (the *taxe soda*, €0.02 per soda can) illustrates how directly and strongly regulation might influence consumers' and restaurants' purchases in the future (Le Sucre, 2012). Similarly, in 2011, Denmark instituted a fat tax of €2.3 per kilogram of saturated fat (Pasanau, 2011). Moreover, as of 2016, according to the decree on the sorting and collecting of bio-waste, French restaurants providing more than 250 meals per day will have to either implement a method of sorting waste in perspective of agricultural exploitation, or pay a tax (EuroGroup Consulting, 2012). Such tax incentives will undoubtedly be extended to a wider range of products or ingredients.

## Restaurant initiatives

The studies conducted by the Food & Beverage Industry Chair of EHL in Europe (Demen Meier et al., 2013a) and Shanghai (Demen Meier et al., 2013b) show that independent restaurants expect their suppliers to provide them with solutions ensuring safer, more sustainable dishes. This means that they encourage suppliers to implement sustainable practices.

Implementing sustainable processes gives restaurants two kinds of advantages. The first one is internal; the second one is linked to the environment. Likewise, two kinds of green standards are used by restaurants: external (certifications) and internal (labels).

## Sustainability and profits

For restaurants, the first and immediate advantage of implementing sustainable practices is a better use of intermediate consumption. Restaurants indeed tend to use energy and water more efficiently when they start implementing sustainable processes. Their use of food and beverages is then monitored to reduce waste and increase profitability. The calibration of dishes is a competitive advantage, not only because it means using fewer products, but also because laws regarding the recycling of organic waste are currently being implemented in some countries, such as France.

The second advantage lies in the business environment. For institutional catering companies such as API, sustainability is a way to get closer to suppliers and to improve processes and relationships (API, 2012). Facing the same difficulties (lack of organic products, high prices of sustainable items, etc.) is indeed a way for restaurateurs and suppliers to know each other better. Moreover, the demand for catering in public institutions requires ecological measures from suppliers: if companies like Sodexho, API or Compass want to obtain public procurement contracts, they have to prove that they are sustainability-oriented (Fessard, 2010). Implementing sustainable practices is therefore compatible with commercial and financial successes.

Customer demand for more information and sustainability in food service is increasing. To meet this demand, restaurants have to prove their commitment. Information on menus will therefore continue to become more exhaustive and precise, with indications notably on the origins of the products, seasonality and health. Some restaurants even offer '100 per cent local dishes'. Such initiatives can be an element of differentiation and justify higher prices.

## Certifications and labels

Obtaining a certification mark entails becoming part of an association whose members have specific constraints. The number of sustainable certifications for restaurants is progressing, and so is the number of restaurants using them (cf. Green Globe Label, Green Restaurant or Chefs Collaborative in the United States). For instance, in the UK, the Sustainable Restaurant Association got 100 per cent new members between 2012 and 2013; it now has more than 1,000 active members with diverse backgrounds in food service operations (SRA, 2012).

There is also a qualitative evolution: some institutional restaurants implement sustainable certifications and join forces with other businesses to improve them. The certification mark 'Restauration Durable', used in educational institutions in France, is a good illustration: launched in June 2012, there are now 49 campuses in France that have implemented these standards.

Internal labels are used to inform clients and to adapt sustainability constraints to the specific constraints of the operation. For instance, at Buffalo Grill restaurants, a feather signals healthier dishes (*'produits plume'*).

## Market regulation

Food suppliers are strongly responsible for market regulation (Demen Meier et al., 2013a). Three crucial facts about sustainable food supply should be stressed: the endurance of sustainable processes; a web of initiatives from various organisations and businesses, which allows a better definition of positive actions; and the concentration of food operators.

## Continuing and improved processes

The first important characteristic of sustainable food supply is the enduring nature of an economy oriented towards sustainability. The 2012 Green Business Survey shows that sustainable business practices are expected by consumers, even in a struggling economy (Cohen, 2012). Since the beginning of the latest financial crisis, in 2008, sustainability has been less covered by the media, notably in the food processing and food service industries. Furthermore, for businesses, the priority has been the preservation of margins, sometimes even mere survival. However, there remain sustainable processes in companies, even though related budgets have in general not increased.

The economic crisis did not lead to CSR-related legislations being challenged. Consequently, food suppliers' ecological constraints have not been reduced, motivating suppliers to improve their productivity. To do so, measures to reduce intermediate consumption of natural resources and energy have continuously been implemented.

## A web of initiatives

Food service companies regularly take initiatives that favour sustainable development. For instance, Burger King has opened two 'green restaurants' in Germany; thanks to state-of-the-art technology and solar and wind power, these outlets reduce energy costs by 45 per cent and $CO_2$ emissions by more than 120 metric tons every year (Burger King, n.d.; GreenBiz, 2010). It should be noted that Germany is a country where consumers have very high expectations regarding sustainable development; it is no coincidence that the first ecological certification for organically produced food, Demeter, was created there in 1928 (Diver, 1999).

Several declarations from business leaders in the food processing sector and the food service industry illustrate an interesting phenomenon: the convergence of private sustainable initiatives that were taken independently. Contract specifications regarding food are notably increasingly common among food operators, with suppliers respecting the sustainable standards set by purchasers. Time is indubitably an ally to the convergence of good practices, as it is increasingly probable for operators to encounter clients, distributors or suppliers requesting or providing sustainable process and information.

## Concentration of operators

Sustainable product prices are currently decreasing due to market concentration. Migros, Auchan, Carrefour and Metro, for example, are able to provide sustainable products at cheaper prices than before thanks to the economies of scale made by their suppliers. Companies such as Aldi and Lidl also contribute to the structuration of integrated sustainable chains through the volume of their purchases and the quality criteria and certifications they emphasise. These criteria include the development of sustainable fishing and fair trade, for example.

## Conclusion

Regulation favouring sustainability in food service depends on numerous factors, and it is difficult to study it without taking into consideration its position within the food system. Arguably, implementing regulations that contribute to increasing the quantity and lowering the prices of sustainable products appears to be the main issue. In that perspective, international institutions raise awareness of sustainability challenges in the food industry and help governments implement effective legislation and incentives. The global influence of business companies and consumer groups is getting stronger, as are their responsibilities and accountability. They contribute not only to private regulation, but also to the media and the general public's awareness of sustainability. Moreover, private actors compete with the state and civil society to make current laws appear sufficient. This competition eventually encourages a faster implementation of sustainable practices.

Finally, there is market regulation in the food service sector, where suppliers need to accommodate a growing number of sustainable requirements. A convergence of initiatives should eventually contribute to a better definition of sustainable practices and to their adoption by a majority of actors within the food system, notably the food service sector.

## Note

1 A food system is the way food production and consumption are organised in a society, from the farm to the fork and including the food service market (Malassis, 1997).

# References

API (2012) *Rapport Développement Durable*, www.api-restauration.com/services/rapport-devdur.aspx (accessed 31 August 2013).

Boyer, R. and Saillard, Y. (1995) *Théorie de la régulation, l'état des savoirs*, Paris: La Découverte.

Bradt, S. (2010) 'Obesity rate will reach at least 42%', *Harvard Gazette*, 4 November, http://news.harvard.edu/gazette/story/2010/11/obesity-rate-will-reach-at-least-42 (accessed 23 January 2015).

Burger King (n.d.) *Wir über uns*, www.burgerking.de/company/ueber-uns (accessed 15 December 2013).

Centre d'études et de prospective (2012) *Document de travail n°5, l'alimentation en France*, Paris: Centre d'études et de prospective.

Codex Alimentarius (n.d.) *About Codex*, www.codexalimentarius.org/about-codex/en (accessed 11 December 2013).

Cohen, S. (2012) 'SCA Tork's 2012 Green Business Survey: "green" and "sustainable" the new norm', *FSR*, August, www.fsrmagazine.com/kitchen-sink/sca-tork-s-2012-green-business-survey-green-and-sustainable-new-norm (accessed 23 January 2015).

Danone (2011) *Sécuriser l'accès à ses matières premières*, http://danone11.danone.com/fr/6-enjeux/04-securiser-l-acces-a-ses-matieres-premieres (accessed 31 August 2013).

Demen Meier, C., Siorak, N., Bonsch, S. and Cornuz, C. (2013a) *Job Observatory in the F&B Industry: Purchasing Function*, Lausanne: Food & Beverage Industry Chair, Ecole hôtelière de Lausanne.

Demen Meier, C., Siorak, N., Bonsch, S. and Cornuz, C. (2013b) *Job Observatory in the F&B Industry: Purchasing Function in Shanghai*, Lausanne: Food & Beverage Industry Chair, Ecole hôtelière de Lausanne.

Diver, S. (1999) *Biodynamic Farming & Compost Preparation*, https://attra.ncat.org/attra-pub/summaries/summary.php?pub=290 (accessed 12 December 2013).

EuroGroup Consulting (2012) *Etude économique sur le secteur de la restauration Partie I/IV*, Puteaux: EuroGroup Consulting.

European Commission (2013a) *Proposition de Directive du Parlement Européen et du Conseil*, http://eur-lex.europa.eu/LexUriServ/LexUriServ.do?uri=COM:2013:0207:FIN:FR:PDF (accessed 31 August 2013).

European Commission (2013b) *Sustainable Food*, http://ec.europa.eu/environment/eussd/food.htm (accessed 16 December 2013).

European Food Safety Authority (2010) *EFSA Sets European Dietary Reference Values for Nutrient Intakes*, www.efsa.europa.eu/en/press/news/nda100326.htm (accessed 31 August 2013).

Ewing, B., Goldfinger, S., Oursler, A., Reed, A., Moore, D. and Wackernagel, M. (2009) *The Ecological Footprint Atlas 2009*, Oakland: Global Footprint Network.

Ewing, B., Goldfinger, S., Oursler, A., Reed, A., Moore, D. and Wackernagel, M. (2010) *The Ecological Footprint Atlas 2010*, Oakland: Global Footprint Network.

Fabrégat, S. (2013) *OGM: en 2012, les surfaces cultivées ont progressé de 6% dans le monde*, www.actu-environnement.com/ae/news/cultures-ogm-2012-isaaa-18080.php4 (accessed 31 August 2013).

FAO (n.d.a) *About World Food Day*, www.fao.org/getinvolved/worldfoodday/about/en (accessed 11 December 2013).

FAO (n.d.b) *Comment nourrir le monde en 2050*, www.fao.org/wsfs/forum2050/wsfs-forum/fr (accessed 31 August 2013).

FAO (2006) *Livestock's Long Shadow: Environmental Issues and Options*, Rome: FAO.

Fessard, J.-L. (2010) *Pour s'approvisionner durable: quelques idées clés*, www.lhotellerie-restauration.fr/journal/gestion-marketing/2010-07/Pour-s-Approvisionner-Durable-quelques-idees-cles.htm (accessed 31 August 2013).

Ghersi, G. and Malassis, L. (2000) 'Les cinquante premières années de la sfer. Quel avenir pour l'économie rurale?', *Economie rurale*, 255–256.

GreenBiz (2010) *New Burger King Restaurant Powered By Wind and Solar Energy*, www.greenbiz.com/news/2010/06/16/new-burger-king-restaurant-powered-by-wind-solar-energy (accessed 15 December 2013).

Gustavsson, J., Cederberg, C., Sonesson, U., van Otterdijk, R. and Meybeck, A. (2011) *Global Food Losses and Food Waste: Extent, Causes and Prevention*, Rome: Food and Agriculture Organization.

Info'OGM (2013) *Quels sont les OGM autorisés (culture et importation) dans l'UE?* www.infogm.org/spip.php?article3438 (accessed 31 August 2013).

Laisney, C. (2011) 'L'évolution de l'alimentation en France. Tendances émergentes et ruptures possibles', *Futuribles*, 372.

Le Figaro (2013) *Un quartier de Londres veut mettre les obèses à l'amende*, http://sante.lefigaro.fr/actualite/2013/01/03/19655-quartier-londres-veut-mettre-obeses-lamende (accessed 31 August 2013).

Le Sucre (2012) *Taxe soda*, www.lesucre.com/fr/article/alimentation-sante/taxe-soda (accessed 31 August 2013).

Malassis, L. (1997) *Les trois âges de l'alimentaire: essai sur une histoire sociale de l'alimentation et de l'agriculture*, Paris: Cujas.

Ministère de l'agriculture, de l'agroalimentaire et de la forêt (2011) *Manger bio et local à la cantine de Bagneux*, http://alimentation.gouv.fr: http://alimentation.gouv.fr/cantine-produit-bio (accessed 31 August 2013).

Nestlé Professional (n.d.) *Responsabilité sociale*, www.nestleprofessional.com/france/fr/OurCompany/Notre_responsabilite/Pages/Responsabilite_sociale.aspx (accessed 31 August 2013).

Oqali (2012) *Evaluation de l'impact potentiel des chartes d'engagements volontaires de progrès nutritionnel sur les apports en nutriments de la population française*, Paris: Observatoire de la qualité de l'alimentation.

Pasanau, J. (2011) 'La France interdit le ketchup, l'angleterre taxe les obèses: jusqu'où ira-t-on?', *Le Plus*, 10 October, http://leplus.nouvelobs.com/contribution/201224-la-france-interdit-le-ketchup-l-angleterre-taxe-les-obeses-jusqu-ou-ira-t-on.html (accessed 23 January 2015).

Réseau Action Climat France and Fondation Nicolas Hulot (2010) *Agriculture et gaz à effet de serre: état des lieux et perspectives*, www.rac-f.org/Agriculture-et-gaz-a-effet-de,1836 (accessed 23 January 2015).

Savadori, L., Rumiati, R. and Bonini, N. (1998) 'Expertise and regional differences in risk perception: the case of Italy', *Swiss Journal of Psychology*, 57: 101–113.

Schieb, P.-A. (1999) 'Nourrir la planète de demain', *L'Observateur de l'OCDE*, 217–218.

SRA (2012) *Sustainable Restaurant Association Report*, www.thesra.org/wp-content/uploads/2012/01/SRA-Annual-Report-smaller-file1.pdf (accessed 31 August 2013).

UN (n.d.) *Zero Hunger Challenge: The Challenge*, www.un.org/en/zerohunger/challenge.shtml (accessed 11 December 2013).

UN (2013) *World Population Projected to Reach 9.6 Billion by 2050 – UN Report*, www.un.org/apps/news/story.asp?NewsID=45165#.UiXev395cp9 (accessed 31 August 2013).

UN DESA (2013) *World Population Prospects: The 2012 Revision*, http://esa.un.org/wpp/index.htm (accessed 31 August 2013).

UNCTAD (2013) *Trade and Environment Review 2013 – Wake up Before it is Too Late: Make Agriculture Truly Sustainable Now for Food Security in a Changing Climate*, United Nations Conference on Trade and Environment.

Unilever Food Solutions (n.d.) *Engagement Durable*, www.unileverfoodsolutions.fr/Sustainable_living/des_rgles_scolaire_equilibre (accessed 31 August 2013).

US Department of Agriculture and Health and Human Services (2010). *Dietary Guidelines for Americans 2010*, Washington, DC: US Departments of Agriculture and Health and Human Services.

WCED (1987) *Our Common Future*, Oxford: Oxford University Press.

# 36

# THE POLITICAL AND ECONOMIC REALITIES OF FOOD SYSTEM SUSTAINABILITY

*Christina Ciambriello and Carolyn Dimitri*

## Introduction

Food is necessary for sustaining human life. Yet the system that produces and distributes our food has many elements that contribute to food system unsustainability. These factors, known as externalities, are associated with the various stages of food production, distribution, and consumption, and impose social costs on the ecosystem and human health. Starting from the farm, social costs incurred depend on the farming system adopted: the act of producing food necessarily disrupts the ecosystem, but a link between specific farming practices and ecosystem health is well documented (Jackson, 2002; Tilman et al., 2002; Reganold et al., 2011). Humans are similarly vulnerable, as human health depends on the quality and quantity of food consumed. Obesity, diabetes, and other diet-related diseases are increasing around the world, even as disparities in access to food vary by socioeconomic status (WHO and FAO, 1990; Walker et al., 2010). In the US, food system workers are particularly prone to food insecurity, partially due to low incomes. Farm laborers receive low wages and work in poor conditions, lacking the power to negotiate a better circumstance because they are often undocumented (Martin, 2012). A large share of food system workers, or those who work in restaurants and supermarkets, earn incomes below the poverty level and rely on federal nutrition benefits (Allen and Sachs, 2013; Food Chain Workers Alliance, 2013).

While there are many possible forms a sustainable food system could take, we work from the assumption that, at its core, a sustainable food system considers the health of the ecosystem and of humans, as well as admits that, in a market economy, individuals (farmers and workers) need to earn a living. Lastly, agreeing with the UN Special Rapporteur on the right to food, a sustainable food system ensures that all humans meet this basic need (UN General Assembly, 2010). While it is impossible to suggest definitive solutions to this wicked problem, it is our intention to provide a guiding principle that can be applied at points along the entire food supply chain to aid in identifying strategies to move towards a more sustainable and resilient system. A key element of sustainability is the consideration of the intertemporal implications of today's choices on resource availability for future generations (Solow, 1991).

One vision of an idealized food system, which we attempt to incorporate in this analysis, adheres to the zero-waste principle, from soil and seed all the way through to post-consumption: refuse what you do not need, reduce what you do need, reuse what you consume, recycle what you cannot refuse, reduce or reuse, and rot (compost) the rest. Applying the logic of this principle to each point along the supply chain illuminates some possible best practices for sustainability. The basic assumption of this maxim implies constant movement, connection, and regeneration between the layers and across the entire system—emphasizing that nothing functions in isolation. This is a critical point when considering the many disparate parts that form the complex global food supply chain, posing a challenge to the partial equilibrium approach to economics which does not acknowledge the broader implications for the economy as a whole (Ayres and Kneese, 1969).

This discussion does not discount the benefits society has received from our current global food system, which includes an abundant, affordable food supply that is largely divorced from the seasons. A line from a 1955 US Department of Agriculture (USDA) presentation, aptly named "More and better foods from today's paycheck," conveys the sense of accomplishment in the food system: "An hour of your labor will now buy more food—and better food—for your family than ever before. Farmers, food processors, manufacturers, and distributors helped to make this possible using science and innovation to increase efficiency and improve their service to consumers." Yet these accomplishments are not costless, and have profound implications for the future of the agro-ecosystem and the ability to produce food for future generations.

While identifying shortcomings in the food system is easy, defining and embracing sustainable alternatives is not a simple task. There are practical impediments to achieving a fully sustainable food system in a market economy, particularly given that the current system is the product of market forces. Policy intervention might be beneficial along the supply chain, to promote sustainable practices within a nation. Yet, from a global perspective, policy is unlikely to address food system sustainability: there is no authority able to legislate on a global scale, and coordinated actions of nations have been largely unsuccessful (for example, a global accord on climate change has yet to be attained). Given the importance of the issue, we suggest that individual action along with national level policies should be addressed simultaneously. Note that the bias of our paper is towards developed countries, which is not intended to discount the importance of food system issues in developing countries.

## The global food system

The structure, productivity, and market integration of the food and agriculture sector changed significantly over the last century, particularly in the post-World War II period. During the mid-twentieth century, technological developments altered farming systems, by replacing human labor with machines, such as tractors and combines, and chemical inputs, such as pesticides and fertilizers. The use of tractors and other costly farm implements is only cost-effective for relatively large farms, and thus their adoption encouraged farm sizes to increase over the century. The widespread availability of and reliance on chemical inputs such as fossil-fuel-derived fertilizers, herbicides, and pesticides, in turn, made it possible for farmers to manage many of the risks of farming and increase productivity, plus reduced the need for farm labor (Dimitri et al., 2005). Beyond the farm, to processing and marketing, firms have captured economies of scale by employing larger meat packing plants, slaughter facilities, and processing plants for other manufactured foods, which operate at lower average costs. Vertical integration along the supply chains has further streamlined the production and distribution of foods, reducing procurement costs, again contributing to a consolidated and coordinated food production and marketing system (Calvin et al., 2001).

The rising influence of consumers has also affected food markets, the result of rising household disposable income and increased scarcity of time. The combination of rising affluence and the feeling of being stretched for time has encouraged consumer demand for convenient foods, such as processed and pre-packed foods, fresh-cut produce, and out-of-season foods (Dimitri et al., 2005). In the US, for example, year-round consumption of lettuce, tomatoes, strawberries, and other fresh foods is common (Dimitri et al., 2003). Demand for imported produce from Mexico, Peru, Chile, and other countries has contributed to increased global-ization of agricultural markets.

The changes described above generally apply to agri-business in the US and Western Europe, but developing and transitioning countries have also undergone significant changes in the past decades—shifting from domestically oriented, state-controlled systems to globally integrated food supply chains controlled by private interests with increasingly vertically integ-rated supply chains (Swinnen and Maertens, 2006). While social benefits have resulted from these increased efficiencies—primarily in delivering low-prices to consumers—it is necessary, however, to question the social costs that accrue from continued expansion of firm size.

The increased production and consumption of the last century comes with a range of opportunities and risks as we progress into the twenty-first century. A major challenge is satisfying the nutritional needs of steadily increasing global populations—the looming ques-tion of 9 billion by 2050—using less available land, water, and energy while addressing the threats posed by climate change and escalating energy (oil) costs (*The Economist*, 2010). As the UN Millennium Ecosystem Assessment Synthesis report pointed out, "humans have changed ecosystems more rapidly and extensively than in any comparable period of time in human history, largely to meet rapidly growing demands for food, fresh water, timber, fiber, and fuel" (Kirschenmann, 2010). The pervasive conversation regarding the question of feeding the 2 million plus expected to be welcomed into the global population in the next 37 years, emphasizes increased production and yields—a continuation of the status quo agribusiness model (Godfrey et al., 2010; Clay, 2011).

The technological advances of the last century were based on the supply and use of non-renewable energy, which has led to natural resource depletion and environmental degradation: inefficient use of limited water supplies (irrigation) and extensive damage to soil health and erosion; run-off of agricultural chemicals into the water supply; greenhouse gas and carbon emissions from intensive livestock production; loss of genetic and biodiversity through GM patenting and monoculture production; and severely damaged seafood ecologies. Worldwide consumption of meat is increasing, at a rate higher than those for other foods, especially in coun-tries where household incomes are rising (Trostle, 2008). These forces create additional pressures on our global food system, making sustainability more important yet more difficult to attain.

We believe, agreeing with others, that the conversation needs to shift to think about investments in ecological methods of agriculture that consider local food security, especially for small-scale farmers in developing countries (De Schutter, 2013; Holt-Giménez et al., 2012). Furthermore, with the abundance of low-priced calories produced around the world, the millennium marked the first time that the overweight equaled the number of under-nourished worldwide. A "nutrition transition" has occurred in which developing countries face both obesity and hunger concurrently (Stix, 2007). About 1 billion people are hungry, while more than 2 billion are overweight, suggesting that the global food system is somehow failing to meet the world's basic dietary needs.

## Tensions in the global food system

Forming an understanding of the interconnectedness of the layers and identify externalities in the global food supply chain (Figure 36.1) relies on a "systems" purview that examines the

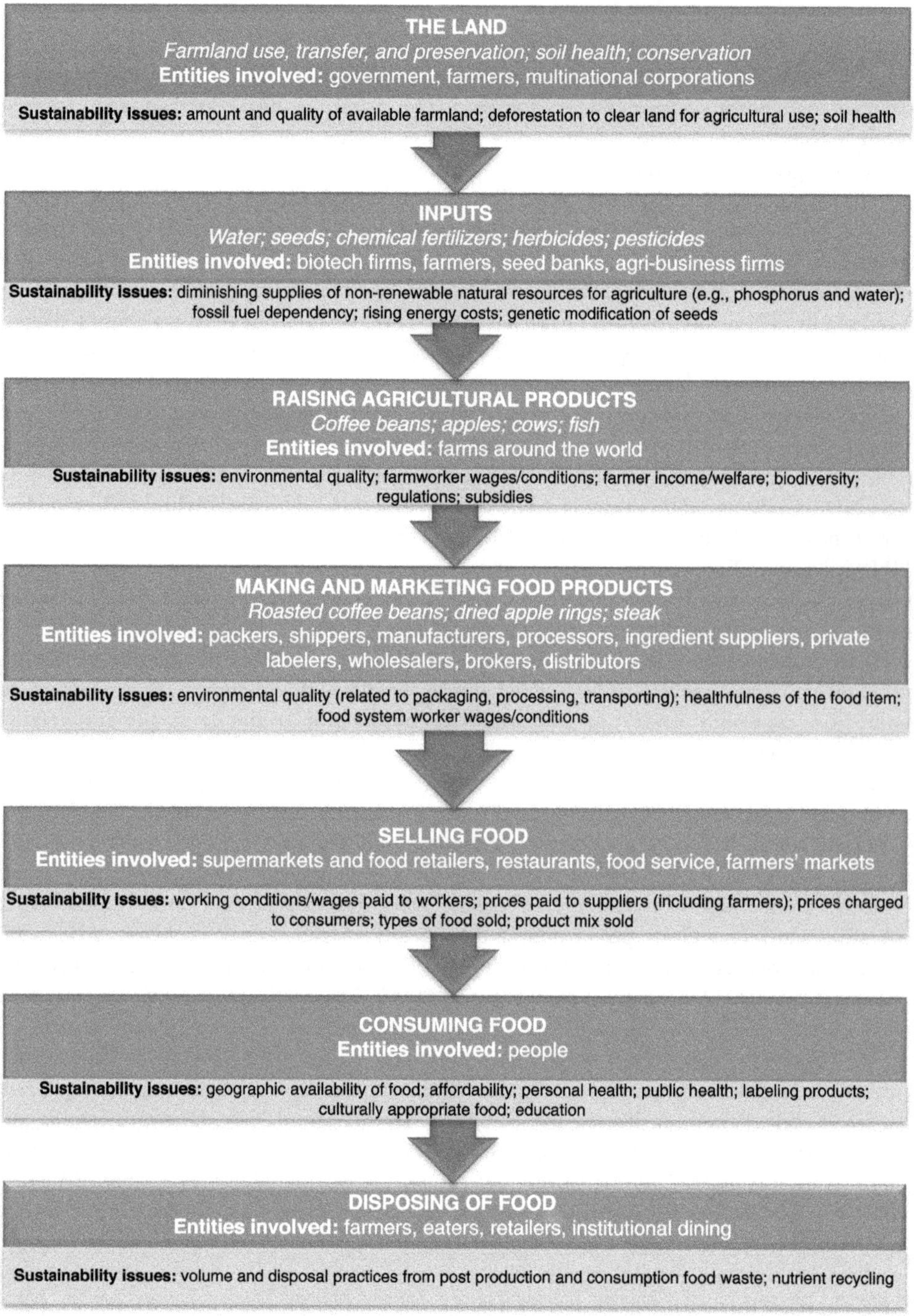


*Figure 36.1* The global food supply chain.

*Source:* the authors.

complex whole from related parts. The "food system" denotes the flow of inputs and food products over the segments in the supply chain: landowners, input suppliers/users, farms and farmers (producers), food industry firms that make and market food (midstream: wholesale/ logistics and processing; downstream: retailers), consumers, and all those that dispose of food products along the way (Reardon and Timmer, 2012). It is not sufficient, however, to merely grasp the flow along the supply chain—it is also vital to understand the interconnectedness of the food system, public health, and economics in relation to the social and political context. A supply chain approach differs in that the focus is on the function performed, not the economic agents or firms that perform it; competition occurs in the form of supply chains competing for consumer food dollars, rather than individual firms competing with each other (Boehlje, 1999).

Tensions among the various agents along the supply chain are present, since increasing the well-being of one agent may necessarily cause another's to decline. More specifically, a conflict exists between human rights and the mission of corporations. On the one hand, the basic premise of the right to food is that people should be able to produce or purchase adequate food. Further, the role of government is to develop policies, such as social safety nets and wages that support the individual's ability to access his or her basic right to food (De Schutter, 2013). On the other hand, profit maximization is the main objective of the firms involved in producing and distributing food, and such firms are not pursuing the public health or social goals of ensuring optimal (or even adequate) human diet and nutrition. In fact, consumer choices are influenced by a few multinational food companies who, through the products they choose to sell, have encouraged a shift away from traditional diets to highly processed foods (Stuckler and Nestle, 2012). This is not to say that corporations are evil, but that their basic mission is to earn profits, which may not be compatible with the pursuit of social goals. Furthermore, firm governance structure impacts the ability of firms to incorporate non-economic objectives into profit maximization, and in many cases the profit maximization goal reduces the pursuit of social goals leading potentially to greenwashing (Woolverton and Dimitri, 2010). In the end, unless governments intervene through policies and regulations, the market is likely to be dominated by corporate interests rather than human rights.

In an increasingly global marketplace, the policies of the nations involved in producing or consuming agricultural commodities are interdependent. (Note this essentially includes all nations.) In particular, the domestic agricultural policies of developed nations have implications, both positive and detrimental, for the agricultural sectors in other countries. Most developed countries offer farmers subsidies or other forms of support, many of which distort market prices and consequently alter the relative competitiveness of agriculture production across the globe. Trade policy and non-tariff barriers are also key components of the global food supply chain. As an example, the low cost of corn production in the US has implications for Mexican corn farmers, who are unable to compete in terms of price, and the no-tariff proscription in the North American Free Trade Agreement provides little buffer for Mexican farmers. At the same time, the low prices of US feed corn have proven beneficial for the growing livestock sector in Mexico (Zahniser and Coyle, 2004). Relative prices of agricultural products affect immigration and migration patterns when farmers cannot earn a profit from selling their crop and there are no available non-agricultural jobs. Similarly, tax policies in one country can affect grain prices, triggering unrest globally—tax incentives to increase corn cultivation for biofuel production in the US could alter global grain production and, subsequently, prices. US corn farmers benefit from higher prices, but consumers, particularly those who are food insecure, suffer as their food choices change in response to higher prices (Trostle, 2008).

Given the concerns detailed above, it is obvious that a clear path forward is not visible: for each set of winners, there are losers. Through global trade, agricultural sectors of different countries are not independent, with the consequence that domestic policy in each country produces a group of winners and losers, spread around the globe. These inherent tensions make it difficult to sustainably produce, consume, and distribute. Sustainability depends on the ability of farmers and consumers to respectively continue to produce and eat food without impairing the ability of future generations to produce food. A first step forward is identifying some of the externalities that have been created as the current system developed, using the lens of the supply chain.

# The land

Food and biofuel production is the primary use of land in the twenty-first century. According to the United Nations Food and Agriculture Organization (FAO), croplands cover 1.53 billion hectares and pasturelands cover another 3.38 billion hectares of all available land worldwide. The largest proportion of prime agricultural land currently in cultivation is in Central America and the Caribbean (42 percent), followed by Western and Central Europe (38 percent) and then North America (FAO, 2011). The global land area available to produce food has grown only slightly over the past 50 years and in light of the rising global population, the agricultural land available per person to grow food declined from 1.30 to 0.72 hectares in the period 1967–2007 (Foresight, 2011). Furthermore, agricultural land is under increasing pressure from competition for other uses including development, urbanization, biofuel production, conservation, and recreational uses (Leaver, 2011). Changing land use contributes to nearly 15 percent of our carbon emissions, primarily the burning of tropical rainforests to clear land for food and biofuel crops.

Agricultural land is also under pressure to increase the amount of food produced, in response to population growth. Increasing productivity on land currently in agricultural use may be possible, but unless the productivity increases come through ecologically based farming methods, there is a risk of completely depleting the soil's reproductive capacity. Because nature is dynamic and every regional ecosystem is unique, proper management can only be extended by local managers who understand local conditions and systems. Thus ensuring a healthy global agri-environment is possible only when the local ecosystems are healthy (Kirschenmann, 2010). Organic farming systems are the most effective at promoting ecosystem health, yet there is debate as to whether the yield gap between organic and large-scale conventional growing methods can be closed (Reganold et al., 2011; Badgley et al., 2007; Seufert et al., 2012). While incremental changes in farming practices, such as two-year crop rotations or precision agriculture, are improvements over conventional production methods, experts have called for transformative changes to the food system, such as pasture-raised livestock and organic farming systems (Reganold et al., 2011). In the absence of a shift to ecological farming methods, however, few gains will be realized in terms of the environmental and social externalities of surface and groundwater pollution, poor soil health and erosion, biodiversity, ecosystem services, as well as loss of agricultural employment due to mechanization. Further, we argue that sustainability of a food system suggests that the question should not be a consideration of the tradeoffs between current yields and ecosystem health, but instead should consider both the current yields and future potential yields, in other words, the productive capacity of the ecosystem over time.

Understanding governance structures and matching land-use systems with the abilities and willingness of land managers, local environmental conditions, and the demand for ecosystem services is important in achieving sustainable land management (Verburg et al., 2013). Land use and land-use changes have important economic and environmental implications for commodity production and trade, open space, soil and water conservation, air quality, and greenhouse gas concentrations in the atmosphere. These factors have become increasingly important as large swaths of land—primarily in the Global South and Sub-Saharan Africa—have been subject to massive land acquisitions (commonly referred to as "land grabs") by large foreign multinational companies and governments. Farm real estate is the major asset on the farm balance sheet. Because of this, changes in agricultural land values are a critical barometer of farm health and the financial well-being of agricultural producers. These changes also have implications for a range of policy issues, including agricultural competitiveness, industry structure, conservation programs, farmland protection, and property taxes. In addition to being the largest single investment in a farmer's portfolio, farm real estate is the principal source of collateral for farm loans (ERS, 2014).

Applying the zero-waste principle, a more sustainable land tenure system might be achieved by optimizing food production in those areas best suited for more intensified ecological farming and shifting production away from biofuel production, which does nothing to further the food security agenda. Furthermore, the possible contribution of local solutions to regional and global food needs can be investigated by testing a "complete-diet model" to better understand how diet influences the demand for agricultural land (Peters et al., 2007). Reducing consumers' demand for meat and dairy and focusing on waste in the production process would greatly affect the carrying capacity of current agricultural land. Growing traditional species, rather than the few specialized varieties marketed by large seed companies, would also make it possible for production to be locally resilient. Overall, social welfare might benefit from a change in the direction of the flow of farming knowledge: rather than moving from the agribusiness firms in the developed nations to farmers in the developing world, traditional farmers can share knowledge about region-specific agro-ecological farming practices with farmers in the developed world.

## Purchased inputs

Sustainability in terms of on-farm inputs—water, seeds, fertilizers, pesticides—is determined primarily by how efficiently the production site manages the application of these materials, especially nitrogen and phosphorus, the two main elements necessary to control plant growth (most commonly applied in the form of chemical fertilizers, but also applied by organic and agro-ecologic farmers in the form of manure and compost) (Tilman et al., 2002; Pimentel et al., 2005). Diminishing global ground and freshwater as well as phosphate ore—a finite resource from which phosphorus is extracted to produce phosphorus—also poses severe threats to continued agricultural production (Cordell et al., 2009). Mis/over application of these elements can lead to leaching into groundwater supplies and runoff into waterways, creating nonpoint source water pollution, including algae blooms (Ribaudo et al., 1999). Heavy reliance on fossil-fuel derived energy, in particular for synthesis of nitrogen fertilizer, is also a critical issue challenging sustainability as well (Neff et al., 2011).

The Green Revolution in the post-World War II period paved the way for an agricultural model reliant on heavy chemical inputs. The "big six" chemical and seed companies—Monsanto, BASF, Bayer, Dow, DuPont, and Syngenta—now have oligarchic control on inputs into the food system at the expense of consumers, farmers, and smaller seed companies (with more heirloom and diverse varieties available for planting and saving). According to the Pesticide Action Network (2011), Monsanto alone controls 23 percent of the world's seed market, and Bayer controls 20 percent of the global pesticide market. The privatized, patented control of seeds places farmers in a vulnerable position, with higher costs and limited choice, as well as challenging traditional seed saving and recycling practices. Furthermore, an increasingly limited, genetically modified seed stock, along with chemical use, presents real threats to agro-biodiversity and overall food security (Thrupp, 2000). Promise can be seen in the growth in farmer seed exchanges, yet interdisciplinary research and policy support are needed to improve the ability of such farmer-led movements to preserve agro-biodiversity (Thomas et al., 2011).

The private, commercial use of "common property" resources—air, streams, lakes, and the ocean—for production inputs and the abuse of the assimilative capacity of the environment to "dispose of" or dilute wastes and residuals are the major externalities in this part of the food system (Ayres and Kneese, 1969). In order to achieve a more sustainable system, the material substance remains of these inputs must be controlled with improved soil management to curb soil erosion, which leads to the leaching of chemicals into waterways; maximized recycling and composting of on-farm organic matter and manures; and more judicious application of fertilizers and pesticides (Pretty, 2008). While organic farming methods typically result in less soil erosion, higher soil quality, and higher levels of biodiversity, the environment would benefit from conventional farmers' adoption of organic practices, such as using cover crops during the off-season and biodiversity to reduce use of chemicals (Pimentel et al., 2005). That said, the escalating costs of inputs may provide an incentive to shift towards an ecologically based nutrient recycling.

## Raising agricultural products

The current global agribusiness model predicated on the availability of cheap oil and available land—both nearing an exhausted supply—and based on industrial principles of specialization, consolidation, and concentration, faces daunting challenges in light of severe environmental threats and escalating energy costs. While this system has, to its credit, produced remarkable yields and plenty of low-cost food for consumers (especially meat produced in concentrated animal feeding operations, CAFO), the mounting ecological damage from this agricultural system (e.g., loss of habitats for biodiversity, pesticides leading to pollinator population decimation, nutrient runoff forming "dead zones" in the Gulf of Mexico, nitrate contamination of well water from leaching of fertilizers and animal wastes, malodors originating from CAFOs) is well documented (Conway and Pretty, 1991). This is not to mention the deleterious effects of the low-priced calories on human health, nor does it consider lack of food access by low-income consumers (Walker et al., 2010). Additionally, the value chain model favors processors, distributors, and retailers, leaving producers vulnerable to contract farming arrangements and with little access to markets (especially in developing countries).

Current niche food production and distribution systems, such as fair trade and organic, attempt to mitigate some of the social and environmental costs embedded in the food system, but these certifications and alternative systems only address one aspect of the market failure: for example, fair trade attempts to increase the standard of living of certain farmers, while organic addresses ecosystem health. Further, even in the current environment of concern about food and the environment, these certifications and systems garner only a small share of the market, and thus have limited impact on the overall sustainability of the food system (Dimitri and Oberholtzer, 2009). The challenge is to develop cost-effective, low-input systems that can be adapted and easily transferred globally, especially to developing countries, and that will provide farmers with incentives to shift from current practices.

One proposed alternative is an agro-ecological system of production. Although agriculture is inherently an unnatural activity imposed by humans on the environment, necessarily disrupting the environment, an agro-ecological model comes closer to mimicking the functioning of natural ecosystems (Lichtenberg, 2004; Altieri and Nichols, 2012). An agro-ecological system adapted to local conditions and fitting the cycle and ecological balances in nature depends less on fossil fuel forms of energy. As mentioned above, inputs would be reduced by reuse, recycling, and efficient management of materials; the quality of land improved, and resources conserved; the physical and mental health of the humans involved in food production respected (farmers and farmworkers); crops and animals integrated into the farm; and biodiversity privileged and resilience promoted in extreme weather events. Agriculturalists are now recognizing that resilience is at least as important to food security as maximum production levels. An agro-ecosystem also acknowledges the contribution of ecosystem services—soil formation and structure, soil fertility, nutrient cycling and provision of water, carbon sequestration, biological pest control, among others—and can aid in developing markets and proper valuation of these services (Swinton et al., 2007).

Furthermore, in order to achieve more sustainable methods of production, farmers and farm workers need economic sustainability. After all, aren't the people who produce, tend, and harvest our food entitled to earn a living from doing so? The economic problems faced by farmers and farm workers differ, but are equally concerning from a sustainability perspective. Historically, farmers have struggled to earn a profit on crops produced on the farm, and farm bankruptcies in the United States were widespread in the 1920s through the 1930s and again during the 1980s (Stam and Dixon, 2004). Farms located on the rural/urban fringe, for example, are dependent on high prices for long-term viability (Batie, 2003; Heimlich, 1989). Medium-sized farmers, called the agriculture of the middle, are poorly served by the current structure of the agricultural sector, and are unable to sell their output in the existing channels. The creation of regional food hubs linking production and processing would mitigate some of the current externalities and bolster market access for smaller and medium sized producers (Stevenson et al., 2011). Others suggest that small farms are technologically inefficient, and unlikely to survive in the current competitive farming environment (Paul et al., 2004).

Farm workers face a different set of problems, but similarly struggle for economic stability. As one of the most maligned groups of workers, farm workers face potentially hazardous working conditions with pesticide application, handling heavy machinery, and long hours in variable weather with few health and safety regulations, or access to benefits. In 2001, more than half (53 percent) of the farm workers in the US were unauthorized workers. During the same time period, 30 percent of farm workers had income below the poverty line, and larger families were more likely to be living in poverty (US Department of Labor, 2005). Farm workers with undocumented status are not eligible for federal safety net programs, such as Medicaid or federal nutrition benefits, and those who are injured on the job are not eligible for unemployment insurance. Yet, not all crops are easily mechanized, in particular fresh fruits and vegetables, and their harvest is reliant on workers. The farmers who hire the workers face competition, mostly from imported products, for their output; if farmers paid the hired workers higher wages, they would need to sell their output for higher prices than those paid for imported substitute products. In this case, the villain isn't the farmer who pays hired workers low wages, but the competition inherent in the global food system which drives the prices of agricultural products (and consequently the wages paid to workers) to low levels.

While increasing fresh fruit and vegetable production is high on the agenda of those interested in food system reform in the US, to accommodate this increase more farm workers would need to be employed to harvest the specialized crops requiring manual attention. Thus, increasing the production of specialty crops would create an additional burden for farm workers and the farmers who rely on them, particularly in the context of the global market forces.

## Making and marketing food products

The food manufacturing and processing industries transform raw livestock and agricultural commodities (e.g., corn, rice, wheat, beef, pork, chicken, apples, peanuts) into foodstuffs for intermediate or final consumption. The global food industry is characterized by many types of food manufacturing firms operating with different market orientations—some produce only for regional or local markets, while others service national or global supply chains. While this leg of the supply chain is the most obscured from consumers, food processing and distribution is a critical part and demands a large market share of the food system. It is through processing that most value is "added" to food, increasing profit margins. The firms in the industry invest heavily in technology and increased automation and production enhancements have allowed companies to increase output while relying on fewer employees, which makes it possible for firms to capture economies of scale through large levels of production. The largest global food-manufacturing firms are Nestlé, Cargill, Kraft Foods, and Unilever, and they are multinational corporations with a presence around the globe.

Rising commodity prices and speculation on commodities futures markets worldwide have had a great impact on the industry, with key inputs experiencing price fluctuations. In the global food procurement landscape, food commodity buyers face a series of risks: inadequate supply; seasonality; perishability and quality; and potential volatility in commodity markets (Jones et al., 2007). In select industries, such as broilers, processors try to reduce their risks of price volatility and product quality by writing contracts with their suppliers, where the contracts specify quality and size requirements, and include best farmer, best practice methods, delivery dates, and the mechanism for price determination (Martinez, 1999). Higher energy costs, as well as volatility in costs, are also a source of risk among manufacturers in the food industry who are increasingly looking for ways to conserve energy in manufacturing processes to reduce costs. Many are increasing their recycling efforts and redesigning packaging to lessen the impact on the environment. For example, the plastic gallon milk packaging was redesigned for Walmart and Costco in 2008; the new shape reduced the cost of shipping and eliminated the need for delivery via reusable milk crates (Rosenbloom, 2008). These efforts, while commendable, are prompted by profit maximization, not concern about the environment, meaning that such firms will only engage in activities that enhance the environment if they are cost-reducing or profit-enhancing. While the mutual gains for corporate profits and the environment are not problematic per se, it is not clear if such gains are sizable enough to have an impact on food system sustainability.

The healthfulness of the food items being produced in this system is of question—most are heavily processed with additives and are short on nutrition and high in calories, fats, and sugars—and the aggressive marketing techniques prey on consumer choice. Further, studies have found that BPA and other packaging materials disrupt the endocrine system, and that 90 percent of the US population have detectable levels of BPA in their urine (Rudel et al., 2011). The President's Cancer Panel suggests that an individual can reduce his/her cancer risk by eliminating all drinks packaged in plastic containing BPA (Reuben, 2010). Overall, the healthfulness of processed food, including the human health cost of its packaging, is questionable. Adding to the human health costs are environmental costs, where waste is created when food packaging is produced, resources are used in shipping the packaged food, and garbage is created when the consumer uses the product (Marsh and Bugusu, 2007). In the zero-waste model, packaged food has few redeeming qualities.

Furthermore, the marketing of less-healthful food products to children and adults on television, radio, internet, product packaging, and through apps and e-games holds considerable power over consumer food consumption choices. In fact, the way food is marketed is commonly identified as one of the main contributors to the global obesity epidemic, although the food industry's response to this accusation is that individuals need to take responsibility for their own diets (Nestle and Nesheim, 2012; Brownell et al., 2010).

Kirschenmann reflects on creating healthy agro-ecosystems, "when agricultural products become valued more as market commodities to be sold to the highest bidder rather than as food to nourish us . . . then the agro ecosystem becomes more of a drain than a contribution to the life support system" (Kirschenmann and Falk, 2010: 51). True sustainability in this manufacturing stage of the food system requires consideration of the environmental quality issues associated with the packaging, processing, and shipping of all of these products across the globe with a mind to shortening the supply chains and reducing the distances traveled.

## Selling food

Over the past several decades, the structure of the grocery industry has changed significantly with food retailers consolidating through mergers and acquisitions in response to competitive forces due to a rise in "supercenters" and specialty retailers (Kaufman, 2000). Concurrently, alternative food outlets, such as farmers' markets, community-supported agriculture (part shares in a farm paid in advance of the growing season), cooperatives, and other sources of fresh local produce have proliferated in more affluent communities. However, there is a problem of availability and access to fresh fruits and vegetables for those in less affluent communities (Ver Ploeg et al., 2009). Large swaths of the global population lack access to nutritious, affordable, and high quality food that is culturally appropriate (Pinstrup-Andersen et al., 2001). The current food system is synchronously delivering under- and overnutrition, with 1 billion people hungry and 2 billion people overweight globally. Not only do these access issues affect public health, without fresh-food retailers these communities miss out on possible economic gains through the presence of such stores. Furthermore, as with most of the other points along the global food supply chain, employees in the retail food sectors (including restaurants and institutional dining settings) face low wages and poor working conditions (Schlosser, 2002).

The zero-waste maxim would dictate a reduction of unhealthful options available at grocery retail outlets as well as overall reductions in the cost of healthful food options. However, as the global food system is designed to focus on profit maximization, not the delivery of optimal diets for sustained health, there are major challenges to reorienting the system without political will and agribusiness cooperation.

## Consuming food

The confluence of rising populations and the shift in consumption patterns (especially increased net consumption) places considerable onus on consumers, especially those in Western countries, to make educated and informed food choices. Grain-fed animal products are extremely inefficient convertors of calories and resources—nearly half the water used in the US goes towards meat production and it takes 11 times as much fossil fuel to produce the equivalent plant-based calories. If the land and grain used for meat production was diverted to humans for consumption, global food production would increase by some two billion tons and available food calories would increase by 49 percent (Gunders, 2012). As "food citizens," consumers have the power of their food dollars to leverage and influence appropriate changes in our food system. A move towards more healthful choices can be difficult, however, as modern-day consumers are not only faced with a barrage of marketing and advertising swaying their consumption habits, but also face issues of "time scarcity," or the feeling of not having sufficient time to cook and shop. As Jabs and Devine (2006) write, time scarcity "has been implicated in changes in food consumption patterns such as a decrease in food prepara-tion at home, an increase in the consumption of fast foods, a decrease in family meals, and an increase in the consumption of convenience or ready-prepared foods." Furthermore, dispar-ities between food production policies and suggested dietary guidelines that call for increased consumption of foods that many people do not have access to call attention to the vested interests of industrial food companies over dietary guidelines.

The development of a social "ecological conscience" would facilitate the development of a more sustainable food system (Kirschenmann, 2010). Similarly, an appreciation for the system, and the people involved, that produces the food we eat would make it easier for those affluent enough to pay a higher price for the food consumed. Studies by behavioral econom-ists have shown that the more consumers are aware of the impact of their consumption, the greater the probability is that they can drive the market in alignment with social and envir-onmental concerns (Sebastiani et al., 2011). As an example, when considering the demand for food produced in an alternative food production and distribution system that is more sustain-able (e.g., organic, or fair trade), consumer preferences for these products can be influenced by perceptions of fairness and distribution of benefits across the food supply chain (Toler et al., 2009). Along with an overall reduction in consumption of calories as well as consumer waste, education to raise awareness on food systems issues will be the greatest challenge to sustainability in this sector.

## Disposing of food

According to the United Nations Environment Programme, one third of the food produced by the global agricultural system is being lost or wasted (UNEP, 2011). This may be one of the most pervasive threats across the entire supply chain and poses a serious challenge to the planet's ability to reduce hunger and meet the food needs of the expanding global population. The largest portion of food waste is on the consumer level, primarily on account of food spoilage, perceived blemishes, and cooking too much food. Significant losses also occur at the production level—especially with the tight quality requirements of contract farming—as well as post-harvest handling and storage losses (especially true in developing countries that lack infrastructure). The issue of food waste is one of the least discussed externalities of the food system.

A move towards sustainability might be achieved with raised awareness about food waste standards at each point in the system. Both consumers and farmers can contribute to waste reduction. Consumers can waste less food by shopping for less food in each grocery outing, knowing when food goes bad, not discarding food that is cosmetically unattractive, and cooking only the amount of food they need. On-farm recycling includes using discards for compost, ultimately used for fertilizer, or for energy production, such as that created by anaerobic digesters.

## Concluding thoughts

Incorporating sustainability in the food system is essential for the future of humanity, as several facts are indisputable: the global population is growing; food production necessarily disrupts the ecosystem; obesity is no longer confined to the developed world; and future generations will need to eat as well. Clearly, more food for human consumption will need to be produced on roughly the same amount of land. Also indisputable is that previous generations realized significant gains through technological advances in the form of farm inputs, machines, and seed technologies. The innovations made it possible for farming to occur, with fewer farmers producing food. Seasons no longer determine our diets, and summer berries and cool-weather crops are available year round in the developed world.

Despite their remarkable contributions, these accomplishments did not solve the world's problems regarding food: hunger still exists, and not all human beings have consistent access to food. And for those with access, the food available may not be health promoting. Farming remains a risky business, forcing governments in the developed world to use policy to protect their farm sectors. As they do so, these same policies spill over into the farming sectors of countries in the developed world, harming those farmers. Farm workers receive little protection, as they labor in the fields for low wages. Many, but not all, farmers struggle to earn a profit, including the traditional (and perhaps subsistence) farmers in the developing world.

At the same time, new problems have emerged: obesity is rising, even in countries that still experience undernutrition, and the food supply is dominated by processed, costly food, marketed by multinational food companies. Waste of food and resources is rife along the food supply chain. The agri-environment is polluted from intensive production methods and chemical inputs. Our bodies may be undernourished from the kinds of foods consumed, we are likely to be obese or overweight, and our bodies are quite likely polluted with the chemicals from food packaging.

Multiple factors would need to change in order to shift the current food system to one that could be considered sustainable. The current condition of the food system is largely the result of decisions made by the private sector. For example, the types of food that are available in the supermarket, how it is produced, and how it is packaged are the result of corporate behavior. Thus, we believe it is unlikely that the free market will provide sufficient incentives to improve human health and reduce environmental damage. Science-based policies that protect human health would be an excellent starting point, but we argue that caution is important: food companies have been able to exploit science to market processed food enhanced with vitamins and other nutrients. Government regulations in the form of labeling requirements have not fundamentally altered the spectrum of food products available in the market. Additionally, past farm policy played a role in creating the current food system: in tandem with technological advances, policies encouraged farms to grow larger and to engage in monocropping practices.

Good starting points for reform, through the lens of the zero-waste model, are those with multiple externalities. An obvious choice is packaged and processed foods. Not only are the contents of these packages (generally) unhealthy for the consumer, but the packaging creates garbage and subjects humans to avoidable health risks. The production of dairy and meat products through confinement systems is another choice: the widespread use of antibiotics in livestock and dairy production creates a public health risk through antibiotic resistance; the manure lagoons pollute water bodies; animal welfare is compromised; and dairy, cattle, and broiler farmers have little bargaining power relative to the large processors who buy their products.

Policies, such as taxes on companies and their products, or payments into a human or animal health care fund, could actively discourage the production and consumption of processed and packaged foods. The dollar amounts would have to be large, so that behavior responds. Some will argue that taxes and fees would impede consumer choice, but we argue that the social costs of the food system are so large and well hidden, preventing consumers from considering the individual components: it is not feasible for a consumer to know whether the farmer who raised the food earned a profit, if the workers were fairly paid and treated well, if the food is healthy, if the workers in the food system were fairly paid, if the packaging is recyclable, if the plastic in the bottle containing a beverage is going to harm their endocrine system. And, even if consumers had the capacity to analyze each step, this consumer is likely too busy to even cook dinner, never mind think through all of these steps. In such cases, where the process is so complex and opaque, and the social costs so great, it is the responsibility of the government to protect the consumer through regulation. Yet stakeholder interests can prevent, and have repeatedly prevented, such policies from being implemented. Our hope is that growing interest in the food system will provide impetus for success in the future.

From the perspective of a domestic food sector, government policy can be helpful in protecting the health of the local environment and the public. Yet, in the global economy, the agricultural sectors of different countries are linked through trade; government policy will provide benefits to its citizens (including the land contained in its borders), but such policies are likely to inflict harm on the countries that are their trading partners. There is no entity with the power to impose fairness on the global food system. Thus, a sustainable global food system, while critically important, is likely out of reach for the time being, and perhaps engaging in civil discourse would be a tremendous first step.

# References

Allen, P. and Sachs, C. (2013) "Women and food chains: the gendered politics of food," in P.A. Williams Forson and C. Counihan (eds.), *Taking Food Public: Redefining Foodways in a Changing World*, Oxford: Routledge.

Altieri, M.A. and Nicholls, C.I. (2012) "Agroecology scaling up for food sovereignty and resiliency," *Sustainable Agriculture Reviews*, 11: 1–29.

Ayres, R. and Kneese, A. (1969) "Production, consumption, and externalities," *The American Economic Review*, 59(3): 282–297.

Badgley, C., Moghtader, J., Quintero, E., Zakem, E., Chappell, M., Aviles-Vazquez, K., Samulon, A., and Perfecto, I. (2007) "Organic agriculture and the global food supply," *Renewable Agriculture and Food Systems*, 22(2): 86–108.

Batie, S.S. (2003) "The multifunctional attributes of Northeastern agriculture: a research agenda," *Agricultural and Resource Economics Review*, 32(1): 1–8.

Boehlje, M. (1999) "Structural changes in the agricultural industries: how do we measure, analyze and understand them?" *American Journal of Agricultural Economics*, 81(5): 1028–1041.

Brownell, K.D., Kersh, R., Ludwig, D.S., Post, R.C., Puhl, R.M., Schwartz, M.B., and Willett, W.C. (2010) "Personal responsibility and obesity: a constructive approach to a controversial issue," *Health Affairs*, 29(3): 379–387.

Calvin, L., Cook, R.L., Denbaly, M., Dimitri, C., Glaser, L., Handy, C., Jekanowski, M., Kaufman, P., Krissoff, B., Thompson, G., and Thornsbury, S. (2001) *US Fresh Fruit and Vegetable Marketing: Emerging Trade Practices, Trends, and Issues*, Washington, DC: US Department of Agriculture, Economic Research Service.

Clay, J. (2011) "Freeze the footprint of food," *Nature*, 475(7356): 287–289.

Conway, G.R. and Pretty, J.N. (1991) *Unwelcome Harvest: Agriculture and Pollution*, London: Earthscan.

Cordell, D., Drangert, J.O., and White, S. (2009) "The story of phosphorus: global food security and food for thought," *Global Environmental Change*, 19(2): 292–305.

De Schutter, O. (2013) *Assessing a Decade of Right to Food Progress*, report to the UN General Assembly, 25 October.

Dimitri, C. and Oberholtzer, L. (2009) *Marketing US Organic Foods: Recent Trends From Farms to Consumers*, Washington, DC: US Department of Agriculture.

Dimitri, C., Tegene, A., and Kaufman, P.R. (2003) *US Fresh Produce Markets: Marketing Channels, Trade Practices, and Retail Pricing Behavior*, Washington, DC: US Department of Agriculture, Economic Research Service.

Dimitri, C., Effland, A., and Conklin, N. (2005) *The Twentieth Century Transformation of Agriculture and Farm Policy*, www.ers.usda.gov/publications/eib3/eib3.htm.

*The Economist* (2010) "Fields of tears," *The Economist*, December 6, www.economist.com/node/17722932.

ERS (2014) Land Use, Land Value & Tenure: Overview, www.ers.usda.gov/topics/farm-economy/land-use,-land-value-tenure.aspx.

FAO (2011) *The State of the World's Land and Water Resources for Food and Agriculture: Managing Systems at Risk*, Rome: FAO Natural Resources Management and Environment Division.

Food Chain Workers Alliance (2013) *The Hands that Feed Us: Challenges and Opportunities for Workers Along the Food Chain*, www.uusc.org/handsreport.

Foresight (2011) *The Future of Food and Farming: Final Project Report*, London: Government Office for Science.

Godfray, H.C.J., Beddington, J.R., Crute, I.R., Haddad, L., Lawrence, D., Muir, J.F., Pretty, J., Robinson, S., Thomas, S.M., and Toulmin, C. (2010) "Food security: the challenge of feeding 9 billion people," *Science* 327(5967): 812–818.

Gunders, D. (2012) *Wasted: How America is Losing up to 40 Percent of its Food From Farm to Fork to Landfill*, Natural Resources Defense Council Issue Paper.

Heimlich, R.E. (1989) "Metropolitan agriculture: farming in the city's shadow," *Journal of the American Planning Association*, 55(4): 457–466.

Holt-Giménez, E., Shattuck, A., Altieri, M., Herren, H., and Gliessman, S. (2012) "We already grow enough food for 10 billion people . . . and still can't end hunger," *Journal of Sustainable Agriculture*, 36(6): 595–598.

Jabs, J. and Devine, C. (2006) "Time scarcity and food choices: an overview," *Appetite*, 47(2): 196–204.

Jackson, W. (2002) "Natural systems agriculture: a truly radical alternative," *Agriculture, Ecosystems & Environment*, 88(2): 111–117.

Jones, K., Raper, K.C., Whipple, J.M., Mollenkopf, D., and Peterson, H.C. (2007) "Commodity-procurement strategies of food companies: a case study," *Journal of Food Distribution Research*, 38(3): 37.

Kaufman, P. (2000) "Grocery retailers demonstrate urge to merge," *Food Review – Washington DC*, 23(2): 29–34.

Kirschenmann, F. (2010) "Alternative agriculture in an energy- and resource-depleting future," *Renewable Agriculture and Food Systems*, 25(2): 85.

Kirschenmann, F. and Falk, C. (2010) *Cultivating an Ecological Conscience*, Lexington, KY: University Press of Kentucky.

Leaver, J.D. (2011) "Global food supply: a challenge for sustainable agriculture," *Nutrition Bulletin*, 36(4): 416–421.

Lichtenberg, E. (2004) "Some hard truths about agriculture and the environment," *Agricultural and Resource Economics Review*, 33(1): 138–147.

Marsh, K. and Bugusu, B. (2007) "Food packaging—roles, materials, and environmental issues," *Journal of Food Science*, 72(3): R39–R55.

Martin, P. (2012) "Immigration and farm labor: what next?" *Choices*, 27(1), www.choicesmagazine.org/choices-magazine/policy-issues/immigration-and-farm-labor-what-next.

Martinez, S.W. (1999) *Vertical Coordination in the Pork and Broiler Industries: Implications for Pork and Chicken Products*, Washington, DC: US Department of Agriculture, Economic Research Service.

Neff, R.A., Parker, C.L., Kirschenmann, F.L., Tinch, J., and Lawrence, R.S. (2011) "Peak oil, food systems, and public health," *American Journal of Public Health*, 101(9): 1587–1597.

Nestle, M. and Nesheim, M. (2012) *Why Calories Count*, Berkeley: University of California Press.

Paul, C., Nehring, R., Banker, D., and Somwaru, A. (2004) "Scale economies and efficiency in US agriculture: are traditional farms history?" *Journal of Productivity Analysis*, 22(3): 185–205.

Pesticide Action Network (2011) *Agrochemical TNCs Target of Upcoming Permanent People's Tribunal*, www.agricorporateaccountability.net/en/post/media-resources/26.

Peters, C., Wilkins, J., and Fick, G. (2007) "Testing a complete-diet model for estimating the land resource requirements of food consumption and agricultural carrying capacity: the New York State example," *Renewable Agriculture and Food Systems*, 22(2): 145–153.

Pimentel, D., Hepperly, P., Hanson, J., Douds, D., and Seidel, R. (2005) "Environmental, energetic, and economic comparisons of organic and conventional farming systems," *BioScience*, 55(7): 573–582.

Pinstrup-Andersen, P., Pandya-Lorch, R., and Rosegrant, M.W. (2001) *Global Food Security: The Unfinished Agenda*, Washington: IFPRI.

Pretty, J. (2008) "Agricultural sustainability: concepts, principles and evidence," *Philosophical Transactions of the Royal Society B: Biological Sciences*, 363(1491): 447–465.

Reardon, T. and Timmer, C. (2012) "The economics of the food system revolution," *Annual Review of Resource Economics*, 4(1): 225–264.

Reganold, J.P., Jackson-Smith, D., Batie, S.S., Harwood, R.R., Kornegay, J.L., Bucks, D., Flora, C.B., Hanson, J.C., Jury, W.A., Meyer, D., Schumacher, A., Sehmsdorf, H., Shennan, C., Thrupp, L.A., and Willis, P. (2011) "Transforming US agriculture," *Science*, 332(6030): 670–671.

Reuben, S.H. (2010) *Reducing Environmental Cancer Risk: What We Can Do Now: President's Cancer Panel 2008–2009 Annual Report*, Bethesda, MD: President's Cancer Panel.

Ribaudo, M., Horan, R.D., and Smith, M.E. (1999) *Economics of Water Quality Protection From Nonpoint Sources: Theory and Practice*, Washington, DC: US Department of Agriculture, Economic Research Service.

Rosenbloom, S. (2008) "Solution, or mess? A milk jug for a green Earth," *New York Times*, June 30, www.nytimes.com/2008/06/30/business/30milk.html?_r=0.

Rudel, R.A., Gray, J.M., Engel, C.L., Rawsthorne, T.W., Dodson, R.E., Ackerman, J.M., Rizzo, J., Nudelman, J.L., and Green Brody, J. (2011) "Food packaging and bisphenol A and bis (2-ethyhexyl) phthalate exposure: findings from a dietary intervention," *Environmental Health Perspectives*, 119(7): 914–920.

Schlosser, E. (2001) *Fast Food Nation: The Dark Side of the All-American Meal*, New York: Houghton Mifflin Harcourt.

Sebastiani, R., Montagnini, F., and Dalli, D. (2012) "Ethical consumption and new business models in the food industry: evidence from the Eataly case," *Journal of Business Ethics*, 114(3): 473–488.

Seufert, V., Ramankutty, N., and Foley, J. (2012) "Comparing the yields of organic and conventional agriculture," *Nature*, 485(7397): 229–232.

Solow, R.M. (1991) *Sustainability: An Economist's Perspective*, Eighteenth J. Seward Johnson Lecture to the Marine Policy Center, Woods Hole Oceanographic Institution, Woods Hole, MA.

Stam, J.M. and Dixon, B.L. (2004) *Farmer Bankruptcies and Farm Exits in the United States, 1899–2002*, Washington, DC: US Department of Agriculture, Economic Research Service.

Stevenson, G.W., Clancy, K., King, R., Lev, L., Ostrom, M., and Smith, S. (2011) "Midscale food value chains: an introduction," *Journal of Agriculture, Food Systems, and Community Development*, 1(4): 27–34.

Stix, G. (2007) "A question of sustenance," *Scientific American*, 297(3): 54–58.

Stuckler, D. and Nestle, M. (2012) "Big food, food systems, and global health," *PLoS Medicine*, 9(6): 1001242.

Swinnen, J. and Maertens, M. (2006) *Globalization, Privatization, and Vertical Coordination in Food Value Chains in Developing and Transitioning Countries*, paper presented at International Association of Agricultural Economists Conference, Gold Coast, Australia, 12–18 August.

Swinton, S., Lupi, F., Robertson, G., and Hamilton, S. (2007) "Ecosystem services and agriculture: cultivating agricultural ecosystems for diverse benefits," *Ecological Economics*, 64(2): 245–252.

Thomas, M., Dawson, J.C., Goldringer, I., and Bonneuil, C. (2011) "Seed exchanges, a key to analyze crop diversity dynamics in farmer-led on-farm conservation," *Genetic Resources and Crop Evolution*, 58(3): 321–338.

Thrupp, L.A. (2000) "Linking agricultural biodiversity and food security: the valuable role of agrobio-diversity for sustainable agriculture," *International Affairs*, 76(2): 283–297.

Tilman, D., Cassman, K.G., Matson, P.A., Naylor, R., and Polasky, S. (2002) "Agricultural sustainability and intensive production practices," *Nature*, 418(6898): 671–677.

Toler, S., Briggeman, B., Lusk, J., and Adams, D. (2009) "Fairness, farmers markets, and local production," *American Journal of Agricultural Economics*, 91(5): 1272–1278.

Trostle, R. (2008) *Global Agricultural Supply and Demand: Factors Contributing to the Recent Increase in Food Commodity Prices*, Washington, DC: US Department of Agriculture, Economic Research Service.

UN General Assembly (2010) *Report of the Special Rapporteur on the Right to Food*, www.srfood.org.

UNEP (2011) *Food Waste Facts*, www.unep.org/wed/quickfacts.

US Department of Labor (2005) *Findings from the National Agricultural Workers Survey (NAWS) 2001–2002*, Research Report Number 9, www.doleta.gov/agworker/report9/toc.cfm.

Ver Ploeg, M., Breneman, V., Farrigan, T., Hamrick, K., Hopkins, D., Kaufman, P., and Tuckermanty, E. (2009) *Access to Affordable and Nutritious Food: Measuring and Understanding Food Deserts and Their Consequences*, report to Congress, Washington, DC: US Department of Agriculture, Economic Research Service.

Verburg, P.H., Mertz, O., Erb, K.H., Haberl, H., and Wu, W. (2013) "Land system change and food security: towards multi-scale land system solutions," *Current Opinion in Environmental Sustainability*, 5(5): 494–502.

Walker, R.E., Keane, C.R., and Burke, J.G. (2010) "Disparities and access to healthy food in the United States: a review of food deserts literature," *Health & Place*, 16(5): 876–884.

WHO and FAO (1990) *Diet, Nutrition and the Prevention of Chronic Diseases*, No. 797, Technical Report Series.

Woolverton, A. and Dimitri, C. (2010) "Green marketing: are environmental and social objectives compatible with profit maximization?" *Renewable Agriculture and Food Systems*, 25(2): 90.

Zahniser, S. and Coyle, W.T. (2004) *US–Mexico Corn Trade During the NAFTA Era: New Twists to an Old Story*, Washington, DC: US Department of Agriculture, Economic Research Service.

# 37

# CUSTOMER EXPECTATIONS REGARDING ORGANIC AND HEALTHY FOOD

*Christine Demen Meier, Nicolas Siorak,*
*Stéphanie Bonsch Buri and Clémence Cornuz*

## Introduction

Consumers' interest in organic products and healthier items is one of the major trends in the restaurant industry. It is not as recent a preoccupation as one might think: the first certification for organically produced food, Demeter, was created in 1928 in Germany. The Demeter standards of biodynamic agriculture are based on the theories developed by Rudolf Steiner in a series of conferences in 1924. Demeter International still exists and is considered by some as the highest grade of organic agriculture (Weleda, 2012).

From the beginning of the organic movement, organic production has been associated with different methods and standards. Thus, defining 'organic products' is necessary. Organic products are grown under strict control. More precisely, 'organic vegetables and particularly farm animals are raised without the use of drugs, hormones, or synthetic chemicals, and are not subjected to ionising radiations to improve shelf life. The animal feed must be grown without pesticides, herbicides or inorganic fertilizers' (organic lifestyle choices). In many countries, there are certification programs that producers must follow. As for biodynamic products, they include not only organic standards, but also agronomic guidelines, greenhouse management, structural components, livestock guidelines and post-harvest handling and processing procedures (Delmas et al., 2006).

The value of the global organic products market has been growing continuously; in 2011, it reached a value of €45 billion. This trend seems independent of the financial context, as market value has increased by 25 per cent since the beginning of the 2008 economic crisis (Soil Association, 2013).

The market of organic product consumers is essentially located in Europe and the USA. Together, they represent 90 per cent of world sales, and their demand is increasing – even though organic consumption declined in the United Kingdom in 2011 (Soil Association, 2013).

Giving a precise definition of 'healthy food' is more difficult, as no nomenclature or certification exists. Nevertheless, it is possible to have a general idea of the main types of healthy products and of the evolution of the demand for this kind of food. According to *Dietary Guidelines for Americans* (US Departments of Agriculture and Health and Human Services, 2010), a healthy regime favours the consumption of fruits, vegetables, whole grains, and fat-free or low-fat milk and milk products. Lean meats, poultry, fish, beans, eggs and nuts will also be preferred to aliments containing high percentages of saturated or trans fat, cholesterol, salt and sugar.

It is difficult to evaluate the healthy food market, but some studies on food and food service trends stress its growing importance. For instance, a study done for the Sirha World Cuisine Summit in 2013 (L'Hôtellerie Restauration, 2013) shows that, out of four trends concerning food service, three feature health and wellness recommendations. Moreover, in 2011, data collected by Euromonitor (Euromonitor International, 2011) demonstrate the resistance of the health and wellness market. Indeed, between 2008 and 2009, in the United States, the value of 'better for you' products (e.g., reduced fat) increased by 5 per cent, or US$7 billion. As for 'naturally healthy' products (those containing whole grains, for example), their value also increased by 5 per cent in the same period, reaching US$10 billion.

Organic products and healthy items are increasingly requested by customers. It is therefore both legitimate and important to inquire whether this trend might become a norm and to examine how the food service market is adapting to this new shift. To do so, this chapter will first examine the motivations and profiles of customers who order organic products and the different strategies restaurants adopt to comply with this demand. The second part of the chapter will focus on the profiles of healthy food consumers and seek to explain how restaurants take part in the healthy food trend.

## Organic products: which consumer for which restaurant?

### Consumer behaviours and motivations

#### Differences and similarities between countries

According to Laisney (2011), the main trends in sustainability and food service are the consumption of organic food and the consumption of local products. However, there are differences between national organic food markets.

In France, the organic product market is experiencing a steady and strong growth. In 2011, its value was twice that of 2005. Its global value nevertheless remains moderate (2 per cent of market share). In Europe, the value of the organic food market was €19.6 billion in 2010. It continued growing during the financial crisis: the value of the market was €18 billion in 2009 (Reisch et al., 2013).

Considering how frequently organic products are consumed, one can argue that they are becoming more common. For instance, in France, 46 per cent of consumers eat organic products at least once a month (Mercier et al., 2013). Moreover, because of new legislations it is now obligatory for school restaurants in some places (France and some Italian cities, for example) to use organic items (Ministère de l'agriculture, de l'agroalimentaire et de la forêt, 2011; Clément, 2010).

The price of organic products is the main element hindering their consumption, and also makes them likely to be impacted by economic downturns. Agence BIO (Mercier et al., 2013) states that they are 30–40 per cent more expensive than traditional products. On the other hand, according to Reisch et al. (2013), the price difference varies between 10 per cent and 50 per cent, depending on the product, the season and the retailer. It should be noted that prices vary between countries (even in Europe) and types of products.

There are also differences between countries regarding the consumption of organic products. In France, consumers allocate 1.4 per cent of their food budget to such products. In

Germany, Austria, Denmark and even the UK, the consumption of organic food represents more than 4 per cent of people's total food budget (Soil Association, 2013).

Consumers' organic food purchases do not systematically follow the evolution of the economic situation. For instance, some organic food markets have not been affected by the economic crisis of 2008: the growth rate stayed the same in the French and Italian markets (Research Institute of Organic Agriculture, 2010). However, in the USA, the growth of the organic market was only 2 per cent in 2009, whereas it was in the double digits between 2004 and 2008 (Euromonitor International, 2011). In the UK, this growth was even negative in 2011, with a decline of 3.7 per cent (Soil Association, 2013).

Thus, while price is the main limitation to organic consumption, organic consumers' price sensitivity differs between countries.

## *Consumer profiles and attitudes*

Because values guide people's behaviour and actions, consumers' motivations to buy organic food have already been widely studied. Knowledge and beliefs (e.g., that organic products are 'better for the environment, taste better, healthier . . .') play an important role (Thøgersen, 2009). Consumers tend to value organic products primarily for their health and safety added value, and then for their environmental friendliness and the possibility of consuming fewer industrially produced products. Aertsens et al. (2009) highlight three key values: security, hedonism and universalism. The literature confirms the importance of these values for organic consumption.

Consumers of organic products are mainly motivated by health and food safety (Harper and Makatouni, 2002). Previous studies have shown that consumers' anxieties about food components are determining for the consumption of organic food. Indeed, additives such as hormones, pesticides or antibiotics, which are excluded from organic products, explain consumers' increasing reluctance to buy traditional products. As Verhoef (2005) points out, fear influences the behaviour of meat consumers when they have to select traditional or organic products.

People who value hedonism are more likely to purchase organic products: psychological studies suggest that there is a bias in the way organic certification marks are perceived, with customers thinking that organic products are healthier and contain more nutritional elements than traditional products (Wan-chen Lee et al., 2013). Similarly, regarding beverages, Olsen et al. (2012) demonstrate that hedonistic people are more inclined to buy organic wines rather than traditional wines.

Universalism is another value which makes consumers more inclined to buy organic products. Aertsens et al. (2009) define universalism as a value expressing tolerance for and understanding, appreciation and protection of the welfare of all people and for nature. They state that consumers endorsing this value can be expected to have a greater propensity to buy organic products. According to Harper and Makatouni (2002), sensitivity to ethical issues is an important motivation as well, as concern for animal welfare, the environment and ethical trade encourage organic consumption.

## *Future consumers of organic products*

Anticipating consumer behaviour towards organic products must be done carefully. While the attitude of young people can provide indications, there are still strong debates on the concrete added value of organic products.

After conducting a study on a North American campus, Dahm et al. (2010) stressed the high awareness and positive attitude of campus students towards organic products. They value them and support them by purchasing them, and would consume more if their availability increased. Another study carried out by Jang et al. (2011) focusing on generation Y (i.e., people born between 1980 and the end of the 1990s) gave similar results, even outlining two clusters of students favourable to sustainable consumption, including consumption of organic products. Together, they represent more than 60 per cent of the campus students. This generation is thought to be decisive for food production because of the purchasing power and influence on producers these students will soon have. Besides, they will transmit their values to the next generation; considering that they developed their awareness of sustainable issues on their own, the next generation might be even more favourable to organic food.

There are also, however, issues that could hinder the development of organic markets. First, there is still an intense debate on the actual added value of organic products compared to traditional products. Some scientific studies suggest that eating organic products has almost no benefit and conclude that organic consumers spend more money pointlessly (Mercola, 2012). Even advocates of organic food acknowledge that these doubts might explain the decrease in organic consumption in the UK (Gray, 2010). A second problem regarding organic products is their unsustainable nature. Indeed, while they do have a positive impact on soils and water because their production requires no (or fewer) pesticides than traditional products, they are not local products. Actually, the majority of European organic products are imported (Euromonitor International, 2011). Thus, in terms of carbon footprint, organic products cannot be considered sustainable.

## Diversity of organic product implementation in restaurants

Organic products are being implemented in food service outlets in different ways. To better control restaurant managers' initiatives, some governments monitor organic certification marks in restaurants. For instance, since November 2011, the French legislation defines what kind of certification marks restaurants can use in their communication to clients, depending on the extent to which they use organic products. Three stages of organic product usage are defined: use of organic items, elaboration of a 100 per cent organic dish or menu, and using exclusively organic food.

## Organic ingredients or dishes

The first and easiest possibility for restaurant managers who want to implement organic products in their menu is to select a few organic items according to product availability and prices, and to include them in one or several dishes. This option is increasingly popular; it is communicated to clients by a certification mark identifying the organic products on the menu. Any restaurant can adopt this practice: independent or chained, high-end or fast food, traditional or ethnic, etc. A decrease in prices and a better availability of organic products are supposed to encourage these actions. For example, in France, the organic wine market is experiencing a double-digit growth (Agrapresse Hebdo, 2013), and the prices of these wines are getting closer to traditional wine prices (Brugvin, 2013).

Another option for restaurants is to elaborate a full organic dish or menu. This entails more constraints and requires purchasers and kitchen chefs to think differently, as the purchaser and the kitchen chef must elaborate a concept around the organic products.

411

## Fully organic restaurants

For food service operators, the highest level of commitment to and involvement in the organic food trend is to use only organic products. This kind of specialisation is less common: out of the 166,000 restaurants located in France, Agence BIO (Mercier et al., 2013) references 146 'fully organic' outlets; in Paris, there are only six (Couturier, 2013).

This kind of specialisation is often linked to other types of businesses. For instance, in France, the gardening shop chain Botanic is implementing fully organic restaurants in its outlets. The goal is to have more practical infrastructures and to make the time customers spend in the shops more agreeable. Likewise, a trend in European hotels is to offer both a spa and an organic restaurant: in terms of marketing, adding an organic restaurant is beneficial for them. Even the Estonian tourism department promotes hotels featuring both a spa and a fully organic restaurant (Visitestonia.com, n.d.).

## Influence of main restaurant companies

As mentioned above, some major chained restaurants add organic products to their offer. For instance, McDonald's provides organic fruit juices and dairy products. But companies that handle catering in public institutions (Sodexho, API, Compass, etc.) also need to show that they are sustainability-oriented to get public procurement contracts (Fessard, 2010). Hence, in France, Sodexo has long-term contracts with producers to help them manage a conversion to organic products. This is a way to orient the suppliers' market towards sustainability. This practice is currently applied in Brest, Nimes and the Rhône-Alpes region.

For major businesses, purchasing organic products is a way to get closer to their suppliers and to improve processes and relationships (API, 2012). Facing the same difficulties as them (lack of organic products, price issues on these items, etc.) is indeed a way to get to know them better.

Fast food restaurants, notably chained ones, have a big influence on the organic food market. In France, for instance, more than 8,000 fast food restaurants feature organic products in their offer. It is a way for them to offset the negative perception consumers have of the unhealthiness of their products. These big restaurant and catering businesses thus decisively influence the improvement of the organic food industry. By ensuring a high volume of demand and long-term contracts, they help organic producers grow and benefit from economies of scale and thus reduce the prices of their products.

Both key players and smaller operators should be prompted to keep on serving organic products, whatever form their commitment takes. Indeed, according to Euromonitor International (2013), in most major European markets, emphasising the high quality of the products offered in a restaurant (notably the fact that they are organic) is a way to increase the average ticket of clients, even in fast food outlets.

## Limits

Several factors can limit the diffusion of organic products in the F&B industry: the fact that independent restaurateurs are less interested in implementing them, differences in sustainable initiatives between countries, and restaurant managers focusing on other categories of products.

According to a study on restaurant purchases in Europe conducted by the F&B Chair of Ecole Hôtelière de Lausanne (Demen Meier et al., 2013b), when restaurant managers and purchasers select suppliers, organic products are not a priority. This is especially the case in independent restaurants, which represent 70 per cent of the food service market value in Europe. Rather, restaurateurs often favour local producers and long-term relationships with their suppliers. Moreover, restaurant purchasers' perception can lead them to reduce the amount of certified organic products used in restaurants, for example if they believe that their suppliers provide products of the same, or even higher, quality than organic producers.

In addition, restaurateurs favour different types of sustainable initiatives depending on the country in which they operate. The latest study of the F&B Chair, which focuses on restaurant managers and kitchen chefs (Demen Meier et al., 2013a), highlights such differences between French and Spanish restaurants. In France, sustainability is often associated with local products and, to a lesser extent, organic products. In Spain, on the other hand, restaurants are more likely to use technology to monitor their consumption of energy and natural resources.

Finally, restaurant managers have understood that the origin of a product is generally more important for customers than its organic nature. Indeed, for 90 per cent of French consumers, having the opportunity to buy local and seasonal products is crucial (Ipsos Public Affairs, 2009). This reflects consumers' pursuit for more authenticity, traceability and knowledge about products. Restaurant managers could therefore be reluctant to use organic products because, for the moment, most of them are imported.

## Healthy food: between a trend and a global norm

Healthy products are less clearly defined than organic products. They are notably linked to fat, salt and sugar content. Gluten-free, anti-allergenic or whole-grain products are included in this category, which is growing strongly. Two major demographic evolutions sustain this growth: ageing and obesity.

To meet the demand, restaurants offer a greater choice of products and communicate on the measures they implement to provide better food. Each restaurant is encouraged to better inform customers, either by legal pressure or simply to meet customers' expectations regarding transparency. In doing so, they allow clients to enjoy eating out again despite allergies or health problems such as diabetes, obesity or high cholesterol. These actions can be included in a larger trend illustrated by the 'slow food' movement and its development, especially in Europe.

### *Drivers of an expanding trend*

#### *Regular and particularly strong growth*

Agriculture and Agri-Food Canada (2011) defines the main categories of the health and wellness market.

The main component of this market is the 'naturally healthy' segment; it represents 38.5 per cent of market share. It concerns 'little or no processed food, which retains basically all its original state and is consumed for its natural health benefits, such as vitamins and nutrients in their natural state (fibre, calcium, etc.)'.

The second segment of the market, which concerns 'enriched and functional' food and beverage products, has 30.5 per cent of market share. The products in question are items to which healthy ingredients have been added. These products should have a specific physiological function and/or be enhanced with added ingredients not normally found in the

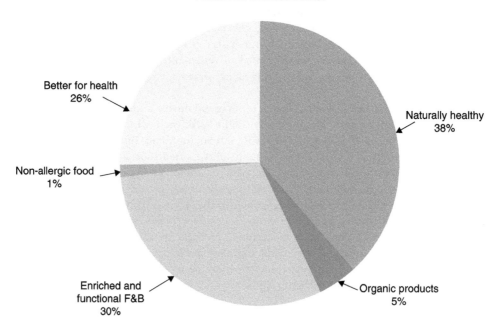

Health and wellness market

product, thus providing additional health benefits. They can be enriched with antioxidants or with organisms like probiotics, for example.

The third category, 'better for health' (25.5 per cent of market share), concerns products containing lower amounts of lipids, sugar or salt. The fourth category is organic products, which is defined above. Its market share is 4.7 per cent. The last category is non-allergenic food (gluten-, lactose- and peanut-free products, for example), which represents only 1.3 per cent of the health and wellness market.

Research conducted by Euromonitor International (2013) provides the following data on the sales value (in US dollars) of the health and wellness market in four areas of the world:

- North America: 170 billion in 2010, 205 billion expected in 2015.
- Western Europe: 165 billion in 2010, 180 billion expected in 2015.
- Asia-Pacific: 130 billion in 2010, 185 billion expected in 2015.
- South America: 55 billion in 2010, 80 billion expected in 2015.

According to data published by Euromonitor International (2011) on the USA health and wellness market, non-allergenic food was the most dynamic segment between 2008 and 2009: its annual growth was 8 per cent. During that period, the 'better for you' and 'naturally healthy products' had a similar annual growth: 5.1 per cent for the former, 4.8 per cent for the latter. 'Enriched and functional' products and organic items had slower annual growth rates (2 per cent).

## Consumer expectations and needs

Several factors explain the vitality of the demand for healthy food products. While motivations are mainly psychological when it comes to organic products, for healthy diets, they are sociological, demographical and physiological.

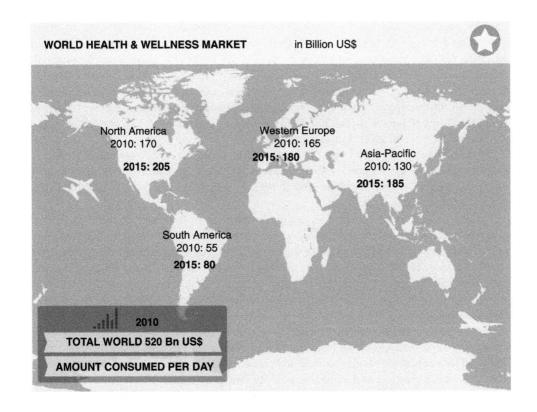

At a sociological level, obesity is clearly becoming pandemic. According to forecasts, the situation will worsen. The World Health Organization (WHO) defines being overweight as having a body mass index (BMI)[1] equal or superior to 25, while obesity is defined as a BMI equal or superior to 30. The figures of WHO (2013) regarding obesity and overweight are alarming:

- The worldwide number of people suffering from obesity has doubled since 1980.
- In 2008, 35 per cent of adults were overweight and 11 per cent were obese.
- 1.4 billion adults (aged 20 or over) are overweight. This includes more than 200 million obese males and 300 million obese women.
- More than 40 million children under the age of five suffer from excess weight.

The two major markets for health and wellness products, the USA and Europe, have a high prevalence of obesity, and the situation is unlikely to improve. In the USA, 68.8 per cent of adults were overweight in 2012, and 35.7 per cent were obese (Food Research and Action Center, n.d.). The obesity rate is predicted to reach 42 per cent in 2030 (Centers for Disease Control and Prevention, 2013). In Europe, according to estimates for 2012, more than 35 per cent of men and women were overweight, and roughly 20 per cent of women and 16 per cent of men were obese. According to the latest available data, approximately 35 per cent of all adults in the EU are overweight, and approximately 17 per cent are classified as obese. On average, these figures continue to rise across Europe (OECD, 2012).

At a demographical level, there is a clear ageing of the population in most OECD countries. In the upcoming decades, the population of these countries will continue to age, and the 80+ population will reach an unprecedented proportion. In Europe, 16 per cent of the population was aged 65 or over in 2008. In thirty years, almost all major European regions will have the same proportion of elderly people (26 per cent); only in Southern Europe will this proportion be slightly higher (27 per cent) (French National Institute for Demographic Studies, 2013). In the USA, people aged 45–64 represent more than a quarter of the population (81.5 million people). This is the segment of the population that has increased the most since 2000 (over 30 per cent). The rate of 65+ people will increase from 13 per cent to 21 per cent between 2010 and 2050 (Hayutin et al., 2010).

These two factors directly impact food consumption: ageing and a growing awareness of excess weight and obesity incite consumers to adopt healthier diets (Euromonitor International, 2011). Moreover, governmental and fiscal policies influence this shift to healthier diets (Le Sucre, 2012; Pasanau, 2011).

A third factor leads to an increase in the consumption of healthier products. Thanks to progress in the scientific study of allergies and genetic factors, diets tend to become more individualised. Food allergies and intolerance are now part of the constraints that characterise the food sector. Labels help consumers avoid potentially harmful items, and products are created to meet people's specific needs. Some of these products are increasingly frequently consumed by people who are not sure that they have food intolerance, but find that it improves their well-being.

Finally, science helps consumers adapt their diet to their physiological needs. Genome sequencing allows individuals to be aware of illnesses for which they are potentially at risk. They can thus anticipate health problems and choose products adapted to their specific needs. This will probably be one of the major changes in food consumption. Companies are already investing intensely in this domain; Nestlé has notably created the Nestlé Institute of Health Sciences at the Swiss Federal Institute of Technology in Lausanne (EPFL), investing more than €400 million for the next ten years in this research centre. This shows the importance of such research for food companies.

## Implementation of healthier products in restaurants

In Western Europe, quality is both a requirement and a potential sales driver. There are several ways for restaurants to meet the demand for quality food products.

A study of the National Public Health Institute of Quebec (Institut national de santé publique du Québec, 2009) references initiatives taken by 26 restaurants to implement healthier meals in North America and Europe.

As shown in Table 37.1, restaurants encourage the consumption of healthy food mainly by guiding the customers' choices towards better products. Even restaurant chains like McDonald's communicate on their '400 calories meals'. Being aware of the calories contained in products and improving the purchasing process are therefore necessary. Finally, the eight initiatives related to staff training show that that is an important dimension of healthier practices.

Offering better options to customers is a goal shared by numerous restaurants, both chained and independent. For example, the German chain Vapiano offers whole-wheat pasta in all its restaurants. In Paris, the independent restaurant De Sères indicates how many calories each dish contains. Finally, in Sweden, the fast food chain Max features low GI and gluten-free menus.

*Table 37.1* Ways Quebec restaurateurs implement healthy practices

| *Ways restaurateurs implement healthy practices, in descending order of importance* | *Number of initiatives* |
|---|---|
| Symbol on the menu | 21 |
| Nutritional criteria | 20 |
| *Total fat, saturated fat, salt, sugar, added fat, cholesterol, calories, fibre, protein, trans fat* | |
| Internal promotion | 17 |
| *Symbol on the menu, flyer, sticker on the window, leaflet, poster* | |
| Ingredients and dishes | 15 |
| *Fresh vegetables and fruits, healthy preparation and cooking methods, size of the portions, low-fat milk, whole-wheat products, healthy meal for children, lean meats, low-fat substitutes, balanced proportion of food groups* | |
| Directory of restaurants implementing healthy practices | 13 |
| External promotion | 12 |
| Healthy preparation methods | 6 |
| Menu analysis | 5 |
| Training for waiters | 4 |
| Training for chefs and kitchen staff | 4 |
| Healthy preparation manual | 4 |
| Healthy menu for children | 3 |
| Nutritional analysis | 3 |
| Advice from a nutritionist or dietician | 3 |
| Award for restaurants implementing healthy practices | 2 |
| Nutritional information available for clients only upon request | 2 |
| Certification | 1 |
| Table of nutritive values | 1 |
| Sample of modified (healthier) dishes offered to clients | 1 |
| Discount coupons for healthy dishes | 1 |
| Helpline giving advice for restaurant managers and chefs who want to reduce the fat content of dishes | 1 |
| Elaboration and sharing of healthy recipes by kitchen chefs | 1 |
| Price policy encouraging customers to choose healthy dishes | 1 |

*Source:* translated and adapted from Institut national de santé publique du Québec (2009).

## An environment favourable to healthier practices

Institutions, local governments and businesses are prompting a shift towards healthier restaurant menus. In some areas like New York, fast food restaurant chains must indicate the number of calories for each dish. According to a study conducted at Yale University, this information leads to a 14 per cent decrease in the calories consumed by customers (Dumanovsky et al., 2011). Numerous smartphone applications enable people to evaluate how many calories their dishes contain, which is an additional motivation for restaurant managers and kitchen chefs.

Associations also contribute to healthier diets. Some associations advocating healthier restaurant practices communicate best practices to their members and to customers. These associations can be professional, like the Quebec Restaurant Association, or public, like Sortir Sans Gluten, which lists gluten-free restaurants across Europe. Finally, several programmes – for example the European programme FOOD (Fighting Obesity through

Offer and Demand) – provide tools that help and encourage restaurants to improve the nutritional balance of their menus.

## *Slow Food: a taste for healthier, greener meals*

Slow Food is a powerful association created in 1986 in Italy by 'activists' who 'aim to defend regional traditions, good food, gastronomic pleasure and a slow pace of life' (Slow Food, n.d.). Slow Food is now a major worldwide association with members in 160 countries. Its founder, Carlo Petrini, was one of the '50 people able to save the planet' listed by *The Guardian* in 2008 (*The Guardian*, 5 January 2008). The association organises annual or biennial events on all five continents. In 2004, Slow Food founded a University of Gastronomic Sciences in Italy, close to the Slow Food headquarters. In 2009, the association launched the International Presidia Project in order to facilitate the involvement of restaurants in its sustainable and gastronomic objectives. More than 300 chefs working in Europe and North Africa have already been involved in the project, which is considered effective in the catering industry, as it relies on the experience and communications of practised and renowned chefs. The latter's role consists in explaining the interest of this project to other catering professionals, as well as how they deal with price and purchasing constraints caused by the implementation of practices related to healthy food. Finally, the recommendations on the association's website are both clear and very practical for kitchen chefs. For example, they explain how to design an improved menu and give advice on creativity, seasonality and food cost management.

The success of this association proves several elements. First, there is a social demand for new food practices and new consumption behaviours. Second, people are interested in food-related information and education. Third, alternative food systems are possible. Finally, food service operators, notably chefs, are willing to take initiatives to train operators and improve practices. The success of Slow Food is all the more remarkable given that this association promotes products that are at once healthy, organic and local, developing a vision of food with a high sustainable value.

## Conclusion

Several conclusions can be drawn from this presentation of the main issues linked to organic and healthy products and to their impact on the food service industry. First, organic products are increasingly important to restaurant operators. However, this importance remains moderate: the trend is far from becoming a norm. It is rather easy for restaurant managers or chefs to select a few organic items, but specialized restaurants implementing a 100 per cent organic offer remain uncommon. As long as the debate on their added value has not been settled and they are not produced locally, organic products will not be widely used in professional kitchens.

On the contrary, health and wellness food products are likely to become a norm, if only because they will be offered as alternatives in every restaurant. Not only do sociological and demographical factors favour this trend, but science and technology also enable increasingly more individualised diets. Finally, thanks to associations like Slow Food, healthier practices and a sustainability vision are highlighted and promoted through wide-ranging communication, education and training, and by involving professionals.

## Note

1  BMI = (mass (kg)/(height (m))$^2$.

# References

Aertsens, J., Verbeke, W., Mondelaers, K., and Van Huylenbroeck, G. (2009) 'Personal determinants of organic food consumption: a review', *British Food Journal*, 111(10): 1140–1167.

Agrapresse Hebdo (2013) 'Le marché du vin bio en croissance de 15% en France en 2012', *Agrapresse Hebdo*, 13 November.

Agriculture and Agri-Food Canada (2011) *Tendances canadiennes et mondiales du marché des aliments de santé et de mieux-être – Octobre 2011*, Canada: Agriculture and Agri-Food Canada.

API (2012) *Rapport Développement Durable*, www.api-restauration.com/services/rapport-devdur.aspx (accessed 31 August 2013).

Brugvin, E. (2013) *Stabilisation des prix sur le marché du vin bio*, www.pleinchamp.com/viticulture/actualites/stabilisation-des-prix-sur-le-marche-du-vin-bio (accessed 16 December 2013).

Centers for Disease Control and Prevention (2013) *The State of Aging and Health in America 2013*, Atlanta, GA: Centers for Disease Control and Prevention, US Department of Health and Human Services.

Clément, M.-C. (2010) *Du bio dans ma cantine!* www.pausesante.fr/article-saveurs-216-du-bio-dans-ma-cantine.php (accessed 15 December 2013).

Couturier, E. (2013) *Manger bio au restaurant, c'est possible?* www.consoglobe.com/bio-trouve-place-en-restauration-cg (accessed 17 December 2013).

Dahm, M.J., Samonte, A.V., and Shows, A.R. (2010) 'Organic foods: do eco-friendly attitudes predict eco-friendly behaviors?', *Journal of American College Health*, 58(3): 195–202.

Delmas, M.A., Doctori Blass, V., and Shuster, K. (2006) *Ceago Vinegarden: How Green is Your Wine?* Donald Bren School of Environmental Science and Management Program on Governance for Sustainable Development, UC Santa Barbara.

Demen Meier, C., Siorak, N., Bonsch, S., and Cornuz, C. (2013a) *Job Observatory in the F&B Industry: Kitchen Chef and Restaurant Manager in France and Spain*, Lausanne: Food & Beverage Industry Chair, Ecole hôtelière de Lausanne.

Demen Meier, C., Siorak, N., Bonsch, S., and Cornuz, C. (2013b) *Job Observatory in the F&B Industry: Purchasing Function*, Lausanne: Food & Beverage Industry Chair, Ecole hôtelière de Lausanne.

Demen Meier, C., Siorak, N., Bonsch, S., and Cornuz, C. (2013c) *Job Observatory in the F&B Industry: Purchasing Function in Shanghai*, Lausanne: Food & Beverage Industry Chair, Ecole hôtelière de Lausanne.

Dumanovsky, T., Huang, C.Y., Nonas, C.A., Matte, T.D., Bassett, M.T., and Silver, L.D. (2011) 'Changes in energy content of lunchtime purchases from fast food restaurants after introduction of calorie labelling: cross sectional customer surveys', *British Medical Journal*, 343(d4464).

Euromonitor International (2011) *Navigating the Health and Quality Nexus in Consumer Foodservice*, London, UK: Euromonitor International.

Euromonitor International (2013) *Mapping The New World: Global Consumer Foodservice in 2013 and Beyond*, London, UK: Euromonitor International.

Fessard, J.-L. (2010) *Pour s'approvisionner durable: quelques idées clés*, www.lhotellerie-restauration.fr/journal/gestion-marketing/2010-07/Pour-s-Approvisionner-Durable-quelques-idees-cles.htm (accessed 31 August 2013).

Food Research and Action Center (n.d.) *Overweight and Obesity in the US*, http://frac.org/initiatives/hunger-and-obesity/obesity-in-the-us (accessed 11 December 2013).

French National Institute for Demographic Studies (2013) *Le vieillissement démographique en Europe*, www.ined.fr/fr/ressources_documentation/focus_sur/vieillissement_demographique_europe (accessed 10 December 2013).

Gray, L. (2010) 'Organic sales fall as consumers tighten their belts', *The Telegraph*, 13 April, www.telegraph.co.uk/earth/earthnews/7582361/Organic-sales-fall-as-consumers-tighten-their-belts.html.

*The Guardian* (2008) '50 people who could save the planet', *The Guardian*, 5 January.

Harper, G.C. and Makatouni, A. (2002) 'Consumer perception of organic food production and farm animal welfare', *British Food Journal*, 104(3–5): 287–299.

Hayutin, M.A., Dietz, M., and Mitchell, L. (2010) *New Realities of an Older America: Challenges, Changes and Questions*, Stanford: Stanford Center on Longevity.

Institut national de santé publique du Québec (2009) *Analyse sommaire d'initiatives favorables à l'amélioration de l'environnement alimentaire des restaurants*, Quebec: Institut national de santé publique du Québec.

Ipsos Public Affairs (2009) *L'Observatoire de la qualité des aliments: un nouvel état des lieux des attentes des consommateurs – Troisième vague*, www.profrance.org/ressources/pages/Presentation_agriconfiance. pdf (accessed 27 March 2014).

Jang, Y.J., Kim, W.G., and Bonn, M.A. (2011) 'Generation Y consumers' selection attributes and behavioral intentions concerning green restaurants', *International Journal of Hospitality Management*, 30(4): 803–811.

Laisney, C. (2011) 'L'évolution de l'alimentation en France. Tendances émergentes et ruptures possibles', *Futuribles*, 372): 5–23.

Le Sucre (2012) *Taxe Soda*, www.lesucre.com/fr/article/alimentation-sante/taxe-soda (accessed 31 August 2013).

L'Hôtellerie Restauration (2013) *Sirha World Cuisine Summit pour anticiper le futur de l'alimentation*, www.lhotellerie-restauration.fr/journal/restauration/2013-01/Sirha-World-Cuisine-Summit-pour-anticiper-le-futur-de-l-alimentation.htm (accessed 15 December 2013).

Mercier, E., Fléchet, D., Lacarce, E., Le-Douarin, S., Moreau, C., and Rison, N. (2013) *Chiffres Clés 2013*, Montreuil-sous-Bois, France: Agence BIO, Agence française pour le développement et la promotion de l'agriculture biologique.

Mercola, J. (2012) *Organic Foods are Safer and Healthier than Conventional . . . True or False?* http://articles.mercola.com/sites/articles/archive/2012/09/17/organic-vs-conventional-food.aspx (accessed 10 December 2013).

Ministère de l'agriculture, de l'agroalimentaire et de la forêt (2011) *Manger bio et local à la cantine de Bagneux*, http://alimentation.gouv.fr/cantine-produit-bio (accessed 31 August 2013).

OECD (2012) *Health at a Glance: Europe 2012*, http://dx.doi.org/10.1787/9789264183896-en (accessed 27 March 2014).

Olsen, J., Thach, L., and Hemphill, L. (2012) 'The impact of environmental protection and hedonistic values on organic wine purchases in the US', *International Journal of Wine Business Research*, 24(1): 47–67.

Pasanau, J. (2011) 'La France interdit le ketchup, l'angleterre taxe les obèses: jusqu'où ira-t-on?', *Le Plus*, 10 October, http://leplus.nouvelobs.com/contribution/201224-la-france-interdit-le-ketchup-l-angleterre-taxe-les-obeses-jusqu-ou-ira-t-on.html (accessed 23 January 2015).

Reisch, L., Eberle, U., and Lorek, S. (2013) 'Sustainable food consumption: an overview of contemporary issues and policies', *Sustainability: Science, Practice, & Policy*, 9(2): 7–25.

Research Institute of Organic Agriculture (2010) *Country Report About Organic Agriculture in Italy*, www.organic-europe.net/country-info-italy-report.html (accessed 15 December 2013).

Slow Food (n.d.) *Our History*, www.slowfood.com/international/7/history (accessed 18 December 2013).

Soil Association (2013) *Organic Market Report 2013*, Bristol, UK: Soil Association.

Thøgersen, J. (2009) 'Consumer decision-making with regard to organic food products', in T. de Noronha Vaz, P., Nijkamp, and J.-L. Rastoin, *Traditional Food Production and Rural Sustainable Development: A European Challenge*, Farnham: Ashgate, pp. 173–192.

US Departments of Agriculture and Health and Human Services (2010) *Dietary Guidelines for Americans 2010*, Washington, DC: US Departments of Agriculture and Health and Human Services.

Verhoef, P.C. (2005) 'Explaining purchases of organic meat by Dutch consumers', *European Review of Agricultural Economics*, 32(2): 245–267.

Visitestonia.com (n.d.) *Healthy and Versatile Food*, www.visitestonia.com/en/things-to-see-and-do-in-estonia/holidaying-for-health-pampering-body-and-soul/healthy-and-versatile-food (accessed 12 December 2013).

Wan-chen Lee, J., Shimizu, M., Kniffin, K.M., and Brian, W. (2013) 'You taste what you see: do organic labels bias taste perceptions?', *Food Quality and Preference*, 29(1): 33–39.

Weleda (2012) *Our Standards*, www.weleda.co.uk/about-weleda/our-standards/stry/subcategorytitle04#bad (accessed 16 December 2013).

World Health Organization (2013) *Obesity and Overweight*, www.who.int/mediacentre/factsheets/fs311/en (accessed 10 December 2013).

# INDEX

For Product Safety Concerns and Information please contact our EU
representative  GPSR@taylorandfrancis.com
Taylor & Francis Verlag GmbH, Kaufingerstraße 24, 80331 München, Germany